Tobias Haller, Samuel Weissman

Disenchanted Modernities

Action Anthropology
Aktionsethnologie

Volume/Band 3

LIT

Tobias Haller, Samuel Weissman

Disenchanted Modernities
Mega-Infrastructure Projects,
Socio-Ecological Changes and Local Responses

LIT

Cover pictures: Flurina Werthmüller; Bettina Wyler

Printed with support of the Faculty of Humanities, University of Bern, Switzerland.

This book is printed on acid-free paper.

Bibliographic information published by the Deutsche Nationalbibliothek
The Deutsche Nationalbibliothek lists this publication in the Deutsche Nationalbibliografie; detailed bibliographic data are available on the Internet at http://dnb.dnb.de.

ISBN 978-3-643-80378-8 (pb)
ISBN 978-3-643-85378-3 (PDF)

A catalogue record for this book is available from the British Library.

© LIT VERLAG GmbH & Co. KG Wien,
Zweigniederlassung Zürich 2024
Flössergasse 10
CH-8001 Zürich
Tel. +41 (0) 76-632 84 35
E-Mail: zuerich@lit-verlag.ch   https://www.lit-verlag.ch
Distribution:
In the UK: Global Book Marketing, e-mail: mo@centralbooks.com
In Germany: LIT Verlag Fresnostr. 2, D-48159 Münster
Tel. +49 (0) 2 51-620 32 22, Fax +49 (0) 2 51-922 60 99, e-mail: vertrieb@lit-verlag.de

Table of contents

Introducing Disenchanted Modernities: Towards an institutional and political ecology analysis of MIPs from an anthropology perspective 1

Tobias Haller (Institute of Social Anthropology), Christoph Oberlack (Centre for Development and Environment; CDE) and Samuel Weissman (Institute of Social Anthropology) University of Bern, Switzerland

Imposing the New Silk Road in a Contested Nation: The China-Pakistan Economic Corridor, Balochistan Province 21

Yuri Forster, Institute of Social Anthropology, University of Bern, Switzerland

On the Margins of the Belt and Road. Commons Grabbing and Environmental Degradation on the Tibetan Plateau 52

Tenzin Dawa Kongpo, independant researcher; Stephy-Mathew Moozhiyil, Institute of Social Anthropology, University of Bern, Switzerland

The Disenchantment of Mining and its Politics Machine: a Cautionary Tale from Mongolia 80

Troy Sternberg, School of Geography, University of Oxford, UK

From Enchantment of Development to Disenchantment of Water Grabbing: Delhi-Mumbai Industrial Corridor 106

Marco Grogg, Institute of Social Anthropology, University of Bern, Switzerland

Smart Cities, Smart Land Grabbing and Legal Pluralism: An MIP Case
from Gujarat, India 130

Oliver Stettler, Institute of Social Anthropology, University of Bern, Switzerland

Unfulfilled Promises and Impacts of a Green Energy Enchantment: The
Benban Solar Park in Egypt 147

Anja Furger, Social and Cultural Anthropology, University of Lucerne, Switzerland

Manoeuvring Enchantment of Mega-Infrastructure Projects in Northern
Kenya: LAPSSET and the Crude Oil in Turkana County 179

Benard Musembi Kilaka, School of Global Studies, University of Gothenburg, Sweden; Elisabeth Schubiger, Anthropology & Sociology Department of the Graduate Institute of International and Development Studies, Geneva, Switzerland

Fishing in Troubled Waters: the Impacts of LAPSSET on the Local
Fisheries in Lamu, Kenya 208

Flurina Werthmüller, Institute for Social Anthropology, University of Bern, Switzerland

"Whose Growth, Whose Loss?" The 'Southern Agricultural Growth
Corridor of Tanzania' (SAGCOT) and Impacts on Smallholders in Iringa
District. 230

Sandro Fiechter, Felix Gallauer Alves de Souza, Désirée Gmür and Belinda Bösch, Institute of Social Anthropology, University of Bern, Switzerland

'Dam(n)ing the Kunene River? Namibian Dam Resistance across Space
and Time' 255

Richard Meissner, Department of Political Sciences, University of South Africa, Pretoria, South Africa; Jeroen Warner, Department of Social Sciences, Wageningen University, Netherlands

Small Project – Big Disaster: Large-Scale Problems within the
Small-Scale Hydropower Project 'San José del Tambo' in Ecuador 280

Hannah Plüss, Institute of Social Anthropology, University of Bern, Switzerland

From Enchanted Alienation to Transformative Responses: Agro-industrial MIPs and Local Reactions towards Reproduction of Life in Bolivia 306

Aymara Llanque, Leuphana University, Lüneburg, Germany, and Universidad Mayor de San Simón, AGRUCO Cochabamba, Bolivia; Marta Irene Mamani, Fundación Tierra, Bolivia; Johanna Jacobi, Institute of Agricultural Sciences, ETH Zurich, Switzerland

When the Black Snake Crosses Sacred Land: The Dakota Access Pipeline and the Ontology of Protest in North Dakota, USA 338

Anna Katharina Vokinger, Institute of Social Anthropology, University of Bern, Switzerland

Fighting against Windmills: Contested Knowledge, Resilience Grabbing and the Feeling of History repeating itself in Storheia, Norway 367

Bettina Wyler, Institute of Social Anthropology, University of Bern, Switzerland

Pipelines, Flows and Roots: Power Struggles Over the Trans Adriatic Pipeline in Southern Italy 399

Antonio Maria Pusceddu, Centro em Rede de Investigação em Antropologia, Iscte – Instituto Universitário de Lisboa, Portugal

Walk to Resist: Contesting a Large-Scale Road Project in the City of Biel, Switzerland 428

Lucien Schönenberg, Institute of Social Anthropology, University of Bern, Switzerland

From Enchantment to Disenchantment and the New Participatory Politics of Infrastructure Development: A Conclusive Comparison 449

Tobias Haller and Samuel Weissman, Institute of Social Anthropology, University of Bern, Switzerland

Alphabetical list of Biographies 479

Introducing Disenchanted Modernities:
Towards an institutional and political ecology analysis of MIPs from an anthropology perspective

Tobias Haller (Institute of Social Anthropology), Christoph Oberlack (Centre for Development and Environment; CDE) and Samuel Weissman (Institute of Social Anthropology) University of Bern, Switzerland

Introduction and rationale of the book

Mega-Infrastructure Projects (MIPs) represent a central element of globalised development today. Ports, railways, highways, and airports increase the mobility of people and goods. Wires, satellites and server centres increase digital connectivity. Pipelines and transmission lines enable energy connectivity. Large hydropower, wind farms and solar parks contribute to global climate change mitigation and energy security. Diversification of local manufacturing capacities strengthens the resilience of global supply chains. This becomes evident in several major global initiatives that aim to create thousands of MIPs worldwide. They include the Chinese-driven 'Belt and Road Initiative' (BRI), the EU-driven 'Global Gateway Initiative' and the US-driven 'Build Back Better World Initiative'. Many other MIP investments are being planned, interlinked and built, pushed by states and companies as well as local elites.

MIPs are investment projects in infrastructure that are large-scale in terms of financial volume and/or geographical extension in the areas they cover. They are complex ventures that incorporate significant national and/or international capital and a large number of stakeholders (*Flyvbjerg 2017*). Often planning and implementation is done by states and companies across many years of development and building.

Many MIPs are subject to competing discourses. On the one hand, proponents often argue for development opportunities and benefits in terms of mobility, climate change mitigation, energy security, health or digitalisation (e.g. Dimitriou et al. 2015). Many states have set up major investments in infrastructure as part of their economic recovery measures from the Covid-19 pandemic. On the other hand, critical perspectives emphasise the adverse social and environmental impacts that MIPs can have (e.g. Foggin et al. 2021). Many MIPs involve the displacement of local land users through direct expropriation or indirect dynamics such as increase of local land prices. MIPs have environmental impacts such as increased pollution and CO_2 emissions or loss of cultural landscapes and biodiversity (Li et al. 2021). They can trigger increased urbanisation with indirect implications for land use change and climate change (Ascensão et al. 2018). Greater connectivity can come with the expansion of capital interests that drive greater extraction of resources and wage-dependent labour (Thame 2021). Even though Environmental Impact Assessments (EIAs) typically require the participation of local populations in MIP planning, the promise of true participation remains unfulfilled, when planners of MIPs leave less room for heterogeneous local actors to shape the way MIPs are implemented (Harvey and Knox 2012, Rassmussen and Lund 2018). As the theoretical literature discussion below will show, in most cases, in the local heterogeneous action arenas we see so-called 'anti-politics machines' (Ferguson 1994) in operation, when it comes to co-shaping how MIPs are to be established. This means that only the positive aspects of MIP development are highlighted, hiding the large power asymmetries between governments and investors on the one side and heterogeneous local actor groups on the other side. Often also, the processes that precede the in situ infrastructural development can be uncertain and imbedded in complex negotiations between major stakeholders, such as governments, investors, and companies. This can lead to political agendas that are hidden from the local context but nevertheless affect them to a high degree. As we will come to learn throughout the 16 case studies, however, there are examples where local actors are well aware of the unfulfilled promises and where they empower themselves through various means in order to participate in, or gain access to, a political process, thereby enabling what we will call a 'politics machine'. Therefore, this book will aim to provide insight into the often-neglected perspectives and strategies of local actors who are confronted with such anti-politics machines, changing institutional settings due to shifting power relations and environmental justice concerns. The difficulties that they face are, however, numerous, as we will discuss in the following.

Another issue is that MIPs are increasingly justified with reference to the 17 Sustainable Development Goals (SDGs) of the UN Agenda 2030. For example, MIPs are legitimised based on arguments that they would contribute to partnerships between public and private actors (SDG 17), affordable and clean energy (SDG 7), economic growth (SDG 8), industry and infrastructure (SDG 9) or climate action (SDG 13). In this perspective, MIPs are seen as part of green development pathways, e.g. based on large-scale solar, wind and biofuel projects (Coenen et al. 2021). Thereby, referring to the SDGs, proponents conceive of MIPs as a promise of new frontiers for sustainable development worldwide. By contrast, a critical sustainability perspective argues that this justification through SDGs entails a danger of the misuse of Agenda 2030 for a new wave of global land and commons grabbing (Haller et al. 2020, Larsen, Haller and Kothari 2022), because the rush for MIPs features some of the most important risk factors for land and commons grabbing, including the significant size of MIPs, the associated displacement of local land users and procedural limitations in project governance and planning (ibid., Oberlack et al. 2016, Nanhthavong et al. 2021). Critical scholars see MIPs as instruments of capital accumulation and new options for geo-strategic dominance (e.g. Baev and Overland 2010, Thame 2021). When MIP planning is framed in technical, non-political terms, and lacks understanding of on-the-ground impacts as well as procedures for meaningful stakeholder participation, MIP planning resembles 'anti-politics machines' (Ferguson 1994) that are hiding rather than dealing with power-asymmetries and capital interest by green development discourses (Larsen et al. 2022). While the positive discourse can be used to provide legitimacy for MIPs focusing on material gains and physical interconnectivity for all, the critical discourse looks at who the decision-makers are on the MIPs and the way these decisions are structured and implemented. This also includes the question of who are the winners and the losers of the MIPs and what drives local reactions to the MIPs.

Despite many of the critiques, little has been discussed on how local groups in some cases show that they have successfully implemented their viewpoints into discussions. They have also not only achieved acknowledgement of their predicament but been able to include their own wishes and strategies to be integrated into the implementation plans of MIPs. Or they have even reversed or halted decisions made by the project planning organisations. Therefore, the present book aims to discuss the complex relations between MIPs and sustainable development. To this end, the 16 case study chapters covering examples from Asia, Africa, Americas and Europe, shed light on the economic, social, and ecological promises and challenges of MIPs as well as responses by local groups. MIPs affect and are affected by sustainable development in multiple ways. Therefore, the book mobilises four selected theoretical angles to reflect on those relations. These angles are (a) the new frontier approach, (b) anti-politics and desire machines, (c) new institutional political ecology and (d) environmental justice. These approaches were selected because they conceive the relations of MIPs and sustainable development from contrasting angles, and their interplay allows for a deeper understanding of the promises, limitations and conditions of MIP contributions to sustainable development at local to global scales.

Theoretical outline

Since the debate on the Belt and Road Initiative (BRI) of China there has been a focus on the way that mega-infrastructure projects are affecting rural populations in the global South and North as a new wave of development. This is of interest as some of the dynamics may resemble land-grabbing processes, in which a new form of expansion has been discussed since 2008. Capital investments in land mainly in the global South (Nolte et al. 2016, Lay et al. 2021) were seen by critical observers as a new neo-colonial expansion as well as commons and land grabbing, discursively also known as 'large-scale land acquisition' or 'dispossession by elites' (Borras et al. 2011, Haller et al. 2020, Gerber and Haller 2021). These investments led and still lead to many challenging impacts and are far from the win-win-win development solutions they were presented and implemented as in the first place in response to the financial, food and fuel crisis of 2008/09 (Cotula et al. 2014, Giger et al. 2019, Lay et al. 2021, Oberlack et al. 2021). Irrespective of this critical debate, the BRI, Global Gateway, Build Back Better World and other drivers of MIPs may have triggered investments in large-scale infrastructure projects. With more than 1,500 projects above 25 million EUR identified as part of the BRI alone (MERICS 2022), this global rush for infrastructure projects may be of a greater magnitude regarding size and technological change than the "global land rush" after 2008 (Cotula et al. 2014). New infrastructures are emerging or planned on a possibly much larger scale than the previous capitalist enclosure via expansion. A major issue in the unfolding MIP rush is connectivity between countries and continents. What we also see is a new form of legitimacy production that claims positive impacts of MIPs on SDGs, including their principle of "leaving no one behind" (Fukuda-Parr 2019). This claim includes new hopes of bringing connectivity and speed from which also marginal people stand to profit. However, given the lessons of the land and commons grab debate and the adverse social and ecological impacts of previous MIPs, the likelihood that this so-called enchantment through MIPs will not only lead to new disappointments but also come with new expropriation processes is very high.

In this book, we draw on four analytical approaches to discuss the interactions between MIPs and sustainable development: new frontiers; anti-politics, desiring machines and enchantment; new institutional political ecology; and environmental justice.

The New Frontier Approach

In the first approach it is argued that what we have been experiencing in recent years is the extension of frontier spaces in the form of a capitalist expansion (see Rasmussen and Lund 2018). New Mega-Infrastructures can be seen as examples of changing local contexts and processes of territorialisation as new territories are entered into this expansion. According to the new frontier theorists, this leads to a transformation of old resource rights, de-contextualisation of resource contexts, territorialisation and commodification. A further step in this logic are land- and green-grabbing processes, as the capitalist expansion tries to incorporate new territories that are mainly used for extraction and to a certain degree for production. At the same time, such areas also come to be of interest for commodified conservation business actors and companies. In this context, we see that new frontier-making comes with ideas of pioneering development and – as we will argue later on – also using frameworks of not just modernity but also sustainable development.

However, we criticise the new frontier approach as being too top-down in its analysis. It does not really focus on local-level dynamics or how this change influences local power relations and how also local states and economic elites gain bargaining power in these contexts. While the new frontier theorists claim that such contexts are also characterised by processes of exclusion and of transformation of property rights constellations, the approach does not explain how these processes manifest themselves. In addition, we argue that the "new frontier" is not so new, as its actors capitalise on institutional transformations of previous colonial settings. Thus, the new frontier is not just a wave breaking on an untouched pristine area but rather is having an impact on transformations that took place earlier on. This includes power relations between actors, discursive appropriation and degradation of local land and land-related common-pool resources, as well as the selection of institutions within an increasingly institutional diversity ('institution shopping') (Haller 2019a). What especially needs to be looked at more closely is that there is not just a new frontier that is sweeping across vast areas like a hurricane but rather that externally driven changes of value of certain elements of a landscape (i.e. land and/or land-related resources and territories) are triggering specific interests and aspirations of more powerful actors, who then try to harness the new opportunities in changing local contexts. Therefore, the question is not so much what constitutes a new frontier, but for whom and how it does so.

Anti-Politics, Desiring Machines and Enchantment

Therefore, in order to explain local processes and link these with external economic and political dynamics, we need further approaches that analyse the legitimacy production framework of these processes, which are linked with these new aspirations that interrelate with the discourse of development: Ferguson's Anti-Politics Machine (1994). An anti-politics machine arises if development is framed in technical and bureaucratic terms without politicising the past and current power asymmetries. Thereby, anti-politics machines operate by hiding such asymmetries and enable further exploitation. Furthermore, they serve the extension of a technocratic state apparatus linked to international actors. It is also an approach that highlights how, in the name of development, powerful external and local actors are enabled to access land and resources. As an extension of Ferguson's approach, de Vries (2007) proposes what he calls a 'Desiring Machine' in the context of MIPs. By this, legitimations create additional desires by MIP proponents (De Vries 2007). This leads to the question of how local people cope with these anti-politics and desiring machines, because the latter is also often linked to companies promising Corporate Social Responsibility (CSR) schemes (see Dolan and Rajak eds. 2018, Gerber and Haller 2021). Harvey and Knox (2012) propose the term 'enchantments of infrastructure'. They argue that the hiding of power asymmetries and the production of desires leads to the production of 'magic ideas' related to speed, mobility, access to new areas and new hopes. But this feeling is also ambiguous as such changes might also lead to instability and insecurity. Interfering with such ambiguities are what we call processes of "docking stations": If a project is under way, new and old infrastructure desires can dock to the large-scale project and also attract or help to find funding (e.g. green economy and climate change measures). This means that a new set of actors and also specific local actors might be enabled to use enchantment synergy or enabling effects due to the docking options. The impact of such options is often limited to the most powerful actors.

Anti-politics and desiring machines can turn into disenchantments, while targeted areas may see increasing conflicts when adverse impacts are experienced and lead to politicisation over longer time periods. This might happen after desires and aspirations have vanished and costs for local actors as well as losses of resources have accumulated. These costs include evictions, loss of the common property rights over land and land-related common-pool resources (water, pasture, fisheries, forests, wildlife, non-timber forest products). Such processes might lead to a loss of resilience (Gerber and Haller 2021, Haller 2022). But such an approach would also need to anticipate that we need a differentiated view on all actors and their diverse aspirations, positions, and power relations (Müller-Mahn et al. 2021).

The New Institutional Political Ecology (NIPE) approach

However, what is lacking in these approaches is what the frontier approach had proposed but was unable to differentiate: It is the question of how and by whom MIPs are proposed and initiated in the external planning and financing arenas. It is in this context that new technologies or new green demands, as well as new legal arrangements, are negotiated for which a combined new institutional and political ecology approach (NIPE) could be of help (Haller 2019a). In this approach based on the work of the US anthropologist Jean Ensminger (1992), investments in MIPs can be discussed that are driven by external actors (initiating and following the economic-legal environment, demographic changes and technological change) and thus impact the relative prices of goods and services (see the issue on changes of value of resources and territories). This impacts the bargaining power of actors in a local arena, their way of selecting and transforming institutions (rules, regulations laws, values, norms etc.), the shaping of local organisations and the ways to legitimise the selection of institutions and forms of organisation through the ideology of modernity, narratives of underdevelopment and discourses of development. This process then leads to specific forms of distribution of costs and gains and to local behaviour towards these changes.

In the context of MIPs, the outcomes of structural adjustments and neoliberalism since the 1980s have reduced state capacities and shifted the economic orientations to the promotion of export. These changes are now interlinked with colonial legal legacies such as the transformation of local common property to state property, which are now further changed either into de facto open access (failed state) or transformed into private property driven by neoliberalism (see Haller 2019b). This goes along with new forms of inward and outward migration of people in territories now labelled as either open access or private property, and the use of new technology such as MIPs is leading to a new valuation of localities as well as goods and services: Land and land-related common-pool resources previously held as common property face a change in value (relative prices). Therefore, there is not just a new instant frontier happening before the expansion process, but this expansion is also falling on local pre-colonial, colonial and post-colonial power and institutional constellations, and on territories which are not pristine nature but cultural landscape ecosystems (see Ellen 1982, Fairhead and Leach 1996, Haller 2019b). These constellations are then affected by the new value of land that is no longer in the legal local forms of mostly common property and shared, but now transferred into privatised goods and fragmented sections of territories (large-scale plantations of monoculture, mining, conservation areas etc.). For local contexts this means that this new valuing of land as soil for agro-industries or space for infrastructure can no longer serve as cultural landscapes for a multipurpose use (see Haller 2019b). It also means for the internal action arena of local actors that the bargaining power of local actors/groups (elites and external actors have more power) is transformed by external actors (states and companies) in collaboration with local elites and not with communal users. This happens because local elites as well as powerful outsiders attracted by the shifting – often increased – value of land and resources can select new institutions (i.e. from common to state and private property and other legal plural institutions) and perform what can be called institution shopping: the selection of institutions can be legitimised by ideologies of modernity and progress, narratives of underdevelopment and idle land and enchantments of (green) development, with discourses of sustainability, functioning as green anti-politics machines in different forms.

However, the approach does not rest with this analysis and the hypothesis that commons grabbing on a large scale is happening now via MIPs. It argues that the realisation of the disenchantment and undermining of livelihoods also lead to the undermining or also grabbing of local resilience strategies (Haller, Käser and Ngutu eds. 2020). However, what is still lacking in this analysis, as in the previous approaches, is the analysis of power relations. We thus propose to link the new institutionalism framework with the analysis of power on all levels as per Ensminger's framework (1992) of institutional change (external variables, relative prices, internal variables and outcomes) based on three approaches of power from the political ecology: a political economy notion of power, informed by a Marxist approach (structuralist power); a post-structuralist and constructivist power analysis informed by Foucault; and a feminist approach looking at patriarchal power constellations and the question of whose ontology has more power than other ontologies and why (see Descola 2013, in Haller 2019a,b). In the last level of analysis of power, it is argued that local ontologies on the world and the ecosystems (such as animism and totemism) have much less power than capitalist, naturalist ontologies, which focus on the separation and capitalisation of humans and their environment, which, in order to exert power, exploit the environment, local inhabitants and especially women (see Haller 2019a). Figure 1 brings these elements together by using Ensminger's New Institutionalism Model from social anthropology on institutional change as a basis, while including the three different forms of power analysis taken from political ecology and applying these on all the levels of the model. In this way, the blind spots on how power dynamics impact actors' relations between the external relative price-induced processes and the internal mechanism of interaction can be studied.

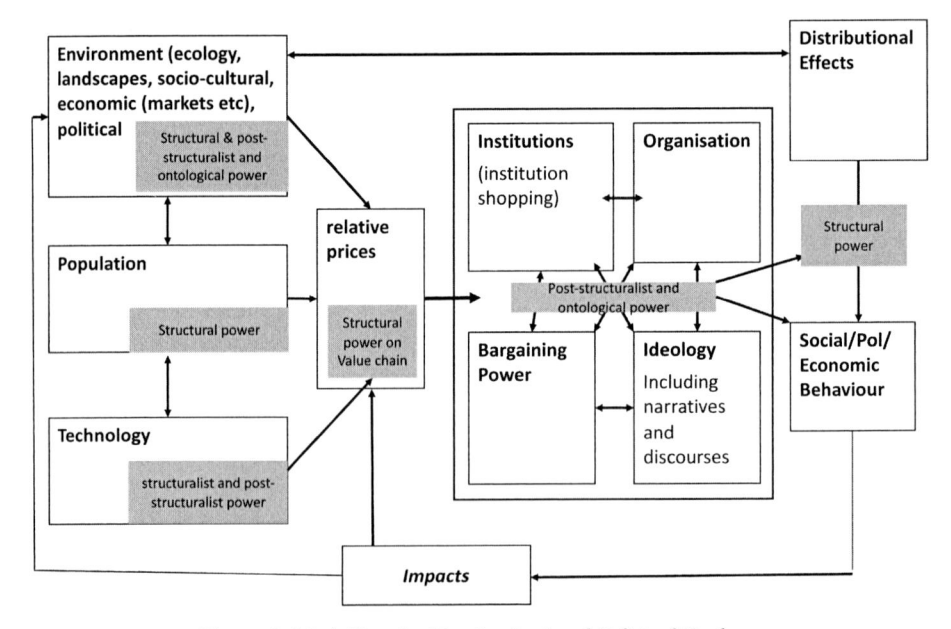

Figure 1: Modelling the New Institutional Political Ecology
(Source: based on Ensminger 1992, adapted and extended by T. Haller 2019a)

Finally, we argue that we are not faced with the 'tragedy of the grabbed commons' at even larger levels, as previous land rush processes might be presented (see Dell'Angelo et al. 2018). Rather, we also experience local responses to these anti-politics machines of enchantment of MIPs and strategic options and agency from below, which we would describe as 'dramas' and not just prescribed 'tragedies'. The outcomes of these dramas depend on local bargaining power constellations, ontologies, and ideological resources of legitimacy. These present themselves differently depending on their timeline and impacts as well as the processes of disenchantments to which local people respond.

Environmental justice

Referring to the issue of drama, it becomes evident that moral and ethical issues are also importantly at stake and have not really been debated in the previous theoretical reflections on MIPs. As we showed before, MIPs typically generate negatively and positively perceived impacts not just on land tenure and livelihoods but also simultaneously related to environmental issues, for example as proposed by the sustainable development goals (SDGs). As MIPs implemented by governments and investors transform land tenure systems in their targeted area, the use of land and land-related natural resources are some of the key components in such dynamics. These dynamics are often externally framed and implemented, for example by the UN, without incorporating moral and ethical debates, while the SDGs themselves could be used as proxies for pros and cons. For example, a special economic zone project may expropriate land from hundreds of smallholder farmers, thereby aggravating their risks of poverty and hunger (SDGs 1,2), increasing precarious health situations (SDG 3), and triggering adverse impacts on biodiversity (SDG 15), while exacerbating inequality within the targeted region (SDG 10). These adverse effects of the project may occur through a public-private partnership mobilising significant financial resources for a developing country (SDG 17), pursuing economic growth and job generation (SDG 8) through industrialisation and infrastructures (SDG 9). The beneficiaries of these changes may be project developers, companies finding an attractive production site in the special economic zone, as well as often more powerful elite households who find the new job opportunities attractive. The losers from these changes may be the land users who are displaced, community members who face greater environmental impacts, and poorer community members who may be disproportionally affected by local price inflation (Farole and Akinci 2011).

These distributive inequalities that arise from MIPs may be partly rooted in inequalities in the governance of land and natural resources in the targeted region. The decision-making procedures at local to national and international scales in the target region may give particular voice and influence to proponents of the MIPs, with comparatively less voice and influence for the stakeholders who are facing adverse impacts. Thus, environmental justice asks the question of not just who has the power to drive these developments, who is able to profit or who has to pay the costs, but how this relates to issues of justice. The concept of environmental justice offers a three-dimensional perspective to assess justice in accessing, using or protecting land and the natural environment (Fraser 2009, Schlosberg 2019). The dimensions are distributional, procedural, and recognition justice. Unequal distribution of benefits and costs is often rooted in unequal opportunities to participate in decision-making procedures (e.g. bargaining power, alliances, oligopolistic market structure). Such procedural injustice is, in turn, often linked to the power to ignore the claims and rights of particular groups (Martin et al. 2016). This echoes the NIPE approach and the power definitions from political ecology approaches, by disentangling the power asymmetries and interactions between differently perceived kinds of injustices and how these are defined, are operating and being reproduced. The clear majority of environmental justice research on MIPs has focused on the injustices and conflicts triggered by MIPs, as can be seen, for example, in the EJ Atlas that documents thousands of struggles for environmental justice, including and beyond MIPs (Temper et al. 2015). Schlossberg also includes the element of ontologies in the environmental justice issue, as MIPs might also violate the relationship between humans and non-humans and a sense of belonging to the environment affected by MIPs (Schlossberg 2009), as well as discussing the NIPE approach. However, all sides have notions of what they see as being morally and ethically environmentally just, and that it is also a question of bargaining power: It is about who has the most ontological power to define that his view of justice and moral ethical considerations shall be hegemonic (see Haller 2019a). We will explore in this book the hypothesis that environmental justice may be a necessary condition to strengthen the positive effects of infrastructure projects on SDGs, while limiting their adverse effects.

In summary, as we deal with each case study, we will be asking in what way have MIPs been shown to affect the local context. Through the theoretical frameworks presented above, each case will be analysed in order to show to what extent enchantments, anti-politics machines and shifting power relations have changed a local action arena. Out of the critique, we will then try to determine what other mechanisms are developed by local actors who are or become disenchanted, such as political action leading to a reversal of anti-politics into politics machines, and what the drivers might be that enable true or partially successful participation. One important aspect in analysing these traits in each case study is the way in which we have structured the chapters. Therefore, in the following, we first present an overview of this structure, how each chapter was built using an outline that all authors followed. Secondly, we will present the structure of how the chapters were arranged in this book to give an overview, including short summaries of each chapter.

Structure of the book chapters

The original contents grew out of a seminar and workshop lead by Tobias Haller at the Institute of Social Anthropology, University of Bern in 2019, whereby students of social anthropology and geography were tasked with critically engaging with MIPs through working on chosen cases in their essays. These essays resulted in the first topical engagement with placing MIPs in the aforementioned theoretical framework. Over the course of the last two years, the editing team then built and gathered the contents for this book, whereby some of the students from the workshop, as well as international scholars dealing in MIP research, were asked to contribute.

Outline of the book

In order to structure the contents, a special framework for the various chapters was established, where critical questions could be dealt with in a similar manner. This means that the individual contributions follow a predetermined outline, as was first worked out in the workshop, and then adjusted to allow for the variety of cases being presented in this edited volume. This outline has the benefit of asking the same questions and discussing the same aspects throughout the variety of cases presented, enabling similarities and differences to come to the forefront. Therefore, we will first describe this structural outline, whereby we hope to give the reader a sense of the overall orientation of the chapters in the book.

All the chapters have an *introduction* in which the case study is situated and contextualised in the debate over Mega-Infrastructure Projects. In *Part 1*, the *historical, environmental, ethnographic and political context* is given, including local history and the current context (pre-, colonial and post-colonial), geography and ecosystem/cultural landscape features of the case, as well as information on the local population and resource use (ethnographic data, institutional setting/property rights/commons). Finally, there is information on the national economy and legal framework. In *Part 2, the respective MIP* is presented, including a) *a description of the project* and its history and drivers as well as information on the companies, b) *environmental and social impacts,* followed by c) *local and NGO strategies* and d) *state and company strategy.* In the *conclusions* section, the perspectives and strategies of the local and NGO context vs. the state and company context are compared (see graphs) and related to theoretical frameworks of enchantment, frontier theory, anti-politics machines, commons debate and the new institutional political ecology, where applicable.

Of course, as will become apparent in some cases, certain parts within the chapters will vary according to the contextual arrangements. These are often very localised cases within widely complex social, economic and political landscapes that have very different histories. However, we have found that most, if not all, cases were comparable within the theoretical aspects, even if on the surface they would not appear so.

The goal is hereby not to list the pros and cons of a project, but to discuss them from the various viewpoints that can surround such pros and cons in the eyes of the stakeholders, which already are part of a highly asymmetric power constellation that has to be placed in its historical context.

Therefore, over the course of the next few hundred pages, the reader is invited to read about the 16 case studies from around the world (see Table 1). We have arranged the chapters based on geographical proximity and structured them along continental divisions, whereby we have covered examples from at least four continents, from Asia over Africa, the Americas and Europe (see Table 1). The chapters were arranged according to geographical regions within the same continents, spanning sixteen regions in total across the four continents of Asia, Africa, the Americas, and Europe.

Table 1: Overview of case studies

Asia
– Pakistan/Balochistan (Belt & Road Initiative: port and road)
– Tibet Initiative (Belt & Road Initiative: road and dams)
– Asia/Mongolia (OK Tedi Mining)
– India Mumbai (Delhi–Mumbai Corridor)
– India Dholera (DMIC Dholera Special Investment Region – Smart City)

Africa
– Egypt (Benaben Solar Park)
– Kenya (LAPSSET, Lamu Port)
– Kenya (LAPSSET, Turkana Oil)
– Tanzania (SAGCOT)
– Namibia (hydro-power dams)

Americas
– Bolivia (Agrarian MIPs for soy production)
– Ecuador (River dam projects)
– USA (Black Rock Pipeline)

Europe:
– Norway (Storheia Wind Park)
– Italy (Oil Pipeline Project Bari)
– Switzerland (Highway access road, Biel)

In the Asian part we will discuss five cases, covering extensions of the Belt and Road initiative in Pakistan and Tibet, a mine in Mongolia, as well as two cases of the Delhi-Mumbai industrial corridor in India. In the African section, the cases will cover a solar park in Egypt, two cases within the LAPSSET in Kenya, a case from the SAGCOT large-scale agro-investments in Tanzania, and hydro-dams in Namibia. The third section includes cases from the Americas, discussing an agricultural growth corridor in Bolivia, a smaller-scale river dam project in Ecuador, and a pipeline project in the USA. Lastly, we discuss present cases from Europe, with examples of a wind park in Norway, a pipeline project in Italy and finally a highway extension project in Switzerland.

Asian case studies

The first chapter, 'Imposing the New Silk Road in a Contested Nation: The China–Pakistan Economic Corridor, Balochistan Province' by *Juri Forster* introduces the reader to Asia and a case from the Silk Road, a very particular and interesting part of the Belt and Road Initiative (BRI) taking place in Balochistan, to this day a contested province in Pakistan, on the border with China. Seen as the flagship of the BRI, investments as well as developments of the China-Pakistan Economic Corridor, or CPEC, carry high expectations for both nations. This case is a good example as an introduction to this book, as it shows the vastly different views of the two nations who welcome this MIP and a local context that resists and opposes the changes taking place.

Following one region bordering China is then another in the chapter entitled: 'On the Margins of the Belt and Road. Commons Grabbing and Environmental Degradation on the Tibetan Plateau'. It's authors, *Tenzin Dawa Kongpo and Stephy-Mathew Moozhiyil,* focus on the infrastructure-development-extractivism nexus of the Belt and Road Initiative on the Tibetan Plateau and the resulting processes of marginalisation. The current forms of implementation undermine land use by pastoralists who depend on commons and related institutions of shared management. Moreover, environmental conservation projects running parallel to the Belt and Road Initiative are further leading to land enclosure and diminishing access to land, forcing people into resettlement projects and to abandon their traditional forms of pastoralist subsistence. Pastoralist knowledge about the institutions of commons and resource use would provide a key to fight land degradation and to a sustainable future; however, it is largely ignored in the dominant development discourse.

The third chapter 'The Disenchantment of Mining and its Politics Machine: A Cautionary Tale from Mongolia' written by *Troy Sternberg* then deviates somewhat from the BRI and comes to investigate the role of the Oyu Tolgoi megamine in Mongolia's Gobi Desert. For years, conflict over water and pasture has defined community-mine relations. A complaint by local herders to an international lender (the IFC, World Bank) started a lengthy mediation process. This led to a successful resolution and settlement between the community, the mine and the local government.

The next chapter by *Marco Grogg* then moves to India under the heading 'From Enchantment of Development to Disenchantment of Water Grabbing: the Delhi–Mumbai Industrial Corridor in Rajasthan, India'. The Delhi–Mumbai Industrial Corridor (DMIC) is one of the largest infrastructure projects in the world and promises economic growth and progress for India. However, the example of the Khushkhera-Bhiwadi-Neemrana investment region in the state of Rajasthan shows that not everyone benefits from this project. Water scarcity that has increased, a lack of compensation for the expropriated, the open question of who benefits from the newly created jobs and the loss of common pool resources are additional aspects that are highlighted in connection with this project.

Staying with the DMIC, the last case from Asia is written by *Oliver Stettler* and entitled 'Smart Cities, Smart Land Grabbing and Legal Pluralism: An MIP Case from Gujarat, India'. The paper focuses on the Dholera Special Investment Region and deals with the conflicts of interest between private and state actors, illustrated by the mega-infrastructure project of the Dholera Special Investment Region on the Delhi–Mumbai Industrial corridor. The conflict over land tenure is at the centre of the analysis, with small farmers and pastoralists in a legal dispute with the state of Gujarat to defend their interests against private entrepreneurs.

African Case Studies

The first chapter of the African case studies, called 'Unfulfilled Promises and Impacts of a Green Energy Enchantment: The Benban Solar Park in Egypt', by *Anja Furger,* describes a case of green energy production in a mega-infrastructure project in a marginal area of the country. Based on her MA fieldwork, Furger analyses its impacts on the environment and society. Moreover, this article examines the workings of the anti-politics machine, as development promises in arid lands are not being fulfilled by government and investors because the local people are perceived as weak and backward. However, the chapter also shows local communities' counter-strategies and frustration with these grabbing processes, as well as the powerful actors' counter-reactions to push for strategies legitimising green energy production.

Chapters two and three on the African continent then both deal with the LAPS-SET (Lamu Port-South Sudan-Ethiopia Transport Corridor) in Kenya. First, the chapter 'Maneuvering Enchantment of MIPs: LAPSSET corridor and Project Oil Kenya in Turkana County' by *Benard Musembi Kilaka and Elisabeth Schubiger* seeks to present an account of two interrelated 'enchanting' infrastructural initiatives in Turkana County, namely the LAPSSET corridor and Project Oil Kenya. Illustrating the local pastoralists' hopes and anxieties generated by the variety of opportunities and risks of the MIP, the authors show how regular disruptions of oil operations through protests and resistance strengthened the bargaining power of local actors. Protests and community agitation have strengthened various local stakeholders despite the enormous commercial and political power of multinational companies and the (national) government. The disenchanted and emancipated community forced a realignment of relations, which is demonstrated by acquiescence to some of the community demands. Secondly, the chapter 'Fishing in Troubled Waters: the impacts of LAPSSET on the local fisheries in Lamu, Kenya' by *Flurina Werthmüller* then deals with the Port Lamu Infrastructure project of LAPPSET on the Kenyan coast. Since the beginning of the construction of a new mega-port in Lamu, the initially positive expectations of the local people have turned into disappointment and worries. This article aims to answer questions about what the construction of the port in Lamu means for the local fishing community, how it is be responded to and what the impacts of the new developments are on local economic, environmental, and social conditions.

South of Kenya, the next case deals with an agricultural MIP in Tanzania. In 'Whose Growth, Whose Loss? The 'Southern Agricultural Growth Corridor of Tanzania' (SAGCOT) and Impacts on Smallholders in Iringa District', *Sandro Fiechter, Felix Gallauer Alves de Souza, Désirée Gmür and Belinda Bösch* deal with questions of land rights and access to resources that are historically central factors and remain at the origin of many conflicts in Tanzanian society today. The case study shows how large-scale agricultural projects and their related development narratives obscure the historical struggles of smallholders.

Lastly, the final chapter from Africa, 'Dam(n)ing the Kunene River? Namibian Dam Resistance across Space and Time' by *Richard Meissner and Jeroen Warner*, describes and explains the role and involvement of interest groups in the planned Epupa and Baynes hydro-power dams on the Kunene River. For decades Namibia has been planning a series of hydro-power projects on the lower Kunene, which has seen resistance from indigenous and transnational interest groups. The advocacy against the planned dams indicates that the meanings of "public" and "good" are not stable and coherent concepts when such dams are proposed in the interest of the "public good".

American Case Studies

Across the Atlantic, we will discuss three studies from the Americas: In the first, *Hannah Pluss* presents a context in South America. In 'Small Project – Big Disaster: Large-Scale Problems within the Small-Scale Hydropower Project 'San José del Tambo' in Ecuador' she outlines an untypical case in the context of MIPs as she shows the negative impacts of a small hydroelectric power plant in rural Ecuador, which resemble the findings of the other MIPs in this volume in spite of its smaller size. Problems of infrastructure projects therefore may not be only about scale – as the literature around mega-dams suggests – but about structural problems of initial enchantment giving way to disenchantment due to poor construction, non-governance and entrenched power hierarchies impeding an inclusive and peaceful approach to the construction of infrastructure in Latin America and beyond.

A second case from South America then introduces an additional example of an agricultural growth corridor as an MIP presented by *Aymara Llanque Marta Irene Mamani and Johanna Jacobi*: Their chapter entitled 'From Enchanted Alienation to Transformative Responses: Agro-industrial MIPs and Local Reactions towards Reproduction of Life in Bolivia' analyses agro-extractivism as a mega-infrastructure in the Bolivian lowlands. Based on the concept of the alienation and enchantment of the private sector in alliance with government bodies and key actors, such as local communities, the authors interpret the phenomena associated with extractive policies in extensive agriculture as an anti-political machine. Special emphasis is placed on power relations, and legal pluralism, where actors increase options for selecting among multiplicities of institutions ('institution shopping') and offer different responses; some of them are examples that put an emphasis on policies of care work ('reproduction of life'), as a kind of resistance to the ongoing capitalist economy that creates conditions of vulnerability.

The last case in the Americas then deals with a pipeline in the USA. In 'When the Black Snake Crosses Sacred Land: The Dakota Access Pipeline and the Ontology of Protests in North Dakota, USA' *Anna Katharina Vokinger* shows how multiple groups with different motivations protest with the same goal: halting the pipeline. While the consequences are different for all, history has not changed much: Indigenous groups continue to be displaced for economic gain and their land rights are disregarded. At the same time, it becomes visible how one's position is either supported by various arguments that can be considered as 'institution shopping' or making use of 'enchantment'.

European Case Studies

Finally, the last section of cases deals with Europe. A case from green energy production in Norway by *Bettina Wyler* starts this final part. In her paper entitled 'Fighting against Windmills: Contested Knowledge, Resilience Grabbing and the Feeling of History repeating itself in Storheia, Norway' she draws on her own ethnographic fieldwork, showing that the Storheia wind farm threatens the continuation of reindeer husbandry by local South Saami herders. Furthermore, the case illustrates how the herders draw on an indigeneity discourse and put the wind farm in a historical perspective to resist it, while authorities and politicians use a powerful discourse on green energy and depoliticise their respective responsibility to legitimise the construction.

The next chapter, 'Pipelines, Flows and Roots: Power Struggles over the Trans-Adriatic Pipeline in Southern Italy' by *Antonio Maria Pusceddu*, then examines the contentious construction of a transnational natural gas infrastructure from the standpoint of its final destination in Italy. Situating the case study in the broader energy politics of the Italian state and the EU, the chapter highlights the contradictions of European energy policies that aim at the "decarbonisation" of the economy, while at the same time supporting the long-term construction of new energy mega-infrastructures for fossil fuel transport.

The final case relates to a larger MIP starting in the 1960s in Switzerland and shows the most advanced local reaction to MIPs: *Lucien Schönenberg* illustrates in 'Walk to Resist: Contesting a Large-Scale Road Project in the City of Biel, Switzerland' a successful resistance movement against a planned highway project. The chapter shows how the creative resistance method of raising awareness via a 'city walk' made it possible to experience the effects of a road project beyond imagination and to produce a counter-discourse. This led to the highway project being stopped and thus resisted the enchantment of infrastructure, speed and modernity.

Concluding comments

While working on this book has given all the participants new insights and ways of thinking about MIPs, it has also stirred up many new questions. Many of these have been raised due to the comparison of the different cases, which are themselves each unique but still show on a more abstract level how differently MIPs are perceived by state and investors and a heterogeneous local community with regard to enchantment and disenchantment. The concluding chapter shows that in most of the cases local groups are not much enchanted but develop a rather disenchanted view of MIPs, while even for those few enchanted groups a feeling of frustration among the majority takes place after long-term experience with MIPs. It also illustrates who has the power to devise the rules of the game in planning, building and implementing the rules of use and governance of MIPs, which are again based often on a colonial or historical asymmetric power relationship. This is also why institutional change observed historically – most importantly, legal tenure changes from common property to state and private property – is so important for the analysis. And, last but not least, there is the range of local responses towards the negatively perceived impacts of MIPs. These are ranging from the 'weapons of the weak' low level of not greatly recognised resistance, to what we call the change from anti-politics to politics machines, and finally to local innovative institution-building from below regarding how infrastructure in a global-local ('glocal') world should look. The NIPE analysis used for these cases helps to address how actors interact based on structural levels of interaction in relation to the power dynamics (structural, post-structural and ontological) between the external/international and internal dynamics. It also helps to explain the range of outcomes of who profits and who is perceived to pay the costs in the final distributional process. While local actors also would like to see basic infrastructure such as roads, it matters if they have the bargaining power or not regarding the decision process on where the road is built, how it is built and who finally can use it. The critical discourse many local groups in the case study areas have does not show local disinterest or simple rejection of infrastructure per se. It is rather about the way in which infrastructure is planned and implemented and how promises of development are perceived as not being for the benefit of many of the local actors. What then makes such perceptions even more negative is the view that MIPs finally bring with them the loss of their basic access to resources local people need for their livelihoods. However, it is interesting to see also how local creative responses in some of the cases show that MIPs are not always a tragedy but rather a drama of the grabbed commons. However, if these grabbing outcomes continue, they have critical negative impacts on the resilience of local groups.

References

Ascensão, Fernando, Fahrig, Lenore, Clevenger, Anthony P., Corlett, Richard T., Jaeger, Jochen A., Laurance, William F. and Henrique, M. Pereira 2018: Environmental challenges for the Belt and Road Initiative. Nature Sustainability, 1(5), 206-209.

Baev, Pavel K., & Øverland, Indra 2010: The South Stream versus Nabucco pipeline race: geopolitical and economic (ir) rationales and political stakes in mega-projects. International Affairs, 86(5), 1075-1090.

Borras Jr, Saturnino M., Hall, Ruth, Scoones, Iain, White, Ben and Wolford, Wendy 2011: Towards a better understanding of global land grabbing: an editorial introduction. The Journal of Peasant Studies, 38(2), 209-216.

Coenen, Johanna, Bager, Simon, Meyfroidt, Patrick, Newig, Jens and Challies, Edward 2021: Environmental Governance of China's belt and road initiative. Environmental Policy and Governance, 31(1), 3-17.

Cotula, Lorenzo, Oya, Carlos, Codjoe, Emmanuel A., Eid, Abdurehman, Kakraba-Ampeh, Mark, Keeley, J. and Rizzo, Matteo 2014: Testing claims about large land deals in Africa: Findings from a multi-country study. Journal of Development Studies, 50(7), 903-925.

Dell'Angelo, Jampel, D'Odorico, Paolo, Rulli, Maria C. and Marchand, Phillippe 2017: The tragedy of the grabbed commons: coercion and dispossession in the global land rush. World Development, 92, 1-12.

DeVries, Pieter 2007: Don't Compromise Your Desire for Development! A Lacanian/Deleuzian Rethinking of the Anti-Politics Machine. Third World Quarterly, 28(1), 25–43. https://doi.org/10.1080/01436590601081765.

Dimitriou, Dimitrios J., Mourmouris, John C., and Sartzetaki, Marias F. 2015: Economic Impact Assessment of Mega Infrastructure Pipeline Projects. Applied Economics, 47(40), 4310–22.

Descola, Philippe 2013: Beyond nature and culture. University of Chicago Press.

Dolan, Catherine and Rajak, Dinah (eds) 2016: The Anthropology of Corporate Social Responsibility. New York, NY Oxford: Berghahn.

Ellen, Roy 1982: Environment, subsistence and system. The ecology of small-scale social formations. Cambridge. Cambridge University Press.

Ensminger, Jean 1992: Making a market. The institutional transformations of an African society. CUP: Cambridge.
Farole, Thomas and Akinci, Gokhan (eds.) 2011: Special economic zones: progress, emerging challenges, and future directions. World Bank Publications.
Ferguson, James 1994: The Anti-Politics Machine: Development, Depoliticization, and Bureaucratic Power in Lesotho. Minneapolis, London: University of Minnesota Press.
Fairhead, James and Leach, Melissa 1996: Misreading the African landscape: society and ecology in a forest-savanna mosaic (Vol. 90). Cambridge University Press.
Flyvbjerg, Bent 2017: The Oxford Handbook of Megaproject Management. Oxford University Press. p. 2. ISBN 978-0198732242
Foggin, J. Mark, Lechner, Alex M., Emslie-Smith, Matthew, Hughes, Alice C., Sternberg, Troy and Dossani, Rafiq 2021: Belt and Road Initiative in Central Asia: Anticipating socioecological challenges from large-scale infrastructure in a global biodiversity hotspot. Conservation Letters, 14(6), e12819.
Fraser, Nancy 2009: Scales of justice: Reimagining political space in a globalizing world. Columbia University Press, New York.
Fukuda-Parr, Sakiko 2019: Keeping out extreme inequality from the SDG Agenda–the politics of indicators. Global Policy, 10, 61-69.
Gerber, Jean-David and Haller, Tobias 2021: The drama of the grabbed commons: antipolitics machine and local responses. The Journal of Peasant Studies, 48(6), 1304-1327, DOI: 10.1080/03066150.2020.1758673
Giger, Markus, Nolte, Kerstin, Anseeuw, Ward, Breu, Thomas, Messerli, Peter, Oberlack, Christoph and Haller, Tobias 2019: Impacts of large-scale land acquisitions on common-pool resources: evidence from the land matrix, in: Haller, T., Breu, T., de Moor, T., Rohr, C., Znoj, H. (eds.) The Commons in a Glocal World: Global Connections and Local Responses. London: Routledge. pp. 257-279.
Haller, Tobias et al. (eds.) 2007: Fossil Resources, Indigenous Peoples and Oil Companies. Lit-Publishers, Hamburg, London.
Haller, Tobias, Ngutu, Maria and Käser, Fabian 2020: Does Commons Grabbing Lead to Resilience Grabbing? The Anti-Politics Machine of Neo-Liberal Agrarian Development and Local Responses. Special issue LAND https://www.mdpi.com/journal/land/special_issues/landgrabbing; now published as a book.
Haller, Tobias 2019a: Towards a new institutional political ecology: how to marry external effects, institutional change and the role of power and ideology in commons studies, in: Haller, T., Breu, T., de Moor, T., Rohr, C., Znoj, H. (eds.) The Commons in a Glocal World: Global Connections and Local Responses. London: Routledge. pp. 90-120.
Haller, Tobias 2019b: The Different Meanings of Land in the Age of Neoliberalism: Theoretical Reflections on Commons and Resilience Grabbing from a Social Anthropological Perspective. Land, 8(7), 104. https://doi.org/10.3390/land8070104
Harvey, Penny and Knox, Hannah 2012: The Enchantments of Infrastructures. Mobilities, 7(4), 521-536.
Larsen, Peter Bille, Haller, Tobias and Kothari, Ashish 2022: Sanctioning Disciplined Grabs (SDGs): From SDGs as Green Anti-Politics Machine to Radical Alternatives?. Geoforum, 131, 20-26.
Lay, Jann, Anseeuw, Ward, Eckert, Sandra, Flachsbarth, Insa, Kubitza, Christoph, Nolte, Kerstin and Giger, Markus 2021: Taking stock of the global land rush. Analytical report III. Land Matrix.

Li, Yuanli, Xiang, Pengcheng, You, Kariui, Guo, Jin, Liu, Zhaowen and Ren, Hong Ren 2021: Identifying the key risk factors of mega infrastructure projects from an extended sustainable development perspective. International Journal of Environmental Research and Public Health, 18(14), 7515.

Martin, Adrian, Coolsaet, Bendan, Corbera, Esteve, Dawson, Neil. M., Fraser, James A., Lehmann, Rodriguez, and Iokine, Ina 2016: Justice and conservation: The need to incorporate recognition. Biological Conservation, 197, 254-261.

MERICS 2022: Mapping the Belt and Road initiative: this is where we stand. URL: https://merics.org/en/tracker/mapping-belt-and-road-initiative-where-we-stand [06.06.2022)

Müller-Mahn, Detlef, Mkutu, Kennedy and Kioko, Eric 2021: Megaprojects—mega failures? The politics of aspiration and the transformation of rural Kenya. The European Journal of Development Research, 33(4), 1069-1090.

Nanhthavong, Vong, Oberlack, Christoph, Hett, Cornelia, Messerli, Peter and Epprecht, Michael 2021: Pathways to human well-being in the context of land acquisitions in Lao PDR. Global Environmental Change, 68, 102252.

Niederberger, Thomas, Haller, Tobias, Gambon, Helen, Kobi, Madlen, and Wenk, Irina (eds.) 2016: The Open Cut. Mining, Transnational Corporations and Local Populations. Lit: Hamburg.

Nolte, Kerstin, Chamberlain, Wytske and Giger, Markus 2016: International land deals for agriculture: Fresh insights from the land matrix: analytical report II (p. 68). Bern Open Publishing.

Oberlack, Christoph, Tejada, Laura, Messerli, Peter, Rist, Stefan and Giger, Markus 2016: Sustainable livelihoods in the global land rush? Archetypes of livelihood vulnerability and sustainability potentials. Global Environmental Change, 41, 153-171.

Oberlack, Christoph, Giger, Markus, Anseeuw, Ward, Adelle, Camilla, Bourblanc, Magalie, Burnod, Pierrine ... and Messerli, Peter 2021: Why do large-scale agricultural investments induce different socio-economic, food security, and environmental impacts? Evidence from Kenya, Madagascar, and Mozambique. Ecology and Society, 26(4), 18.

Rasmussen, Mattias Borg and Lund, Christian 2018: Frontier Spaces: Territorialization and Resource Control. Policy Briefs (Copenhagen Centre for Development Research), 1, 1-3.

Schlosberg, David 2019: Disruption, community and resilience governance: environmental justice in the Anthropocene in: Haller, T., Breu, T., de Moor, T., Rohr, C., Znoj, H. (eds.) The Commons in a Glocal World: Global Connections and Local Responses. London: Routledge. pp. 72-89.

Temper, Leah, Del Bene, Daniela and Martinez-Alier, Joan 2015: Mapping the frontiers and front lines of global environmental justice: the EJ Atlas. Journal of Political Ecology, 22(1), 255-278.

Thame, Charlie. 2021: The economic corridors paradigm as extractivism: Four theses for a historical materialist framework. Review of International Studies, 47(4), 549-569.

Imposing the New Silk Road in a Contested Nation: The China-Pakistan Economic Corridor, Balochistan Province

Yuri Forster, Institute of Social Anthropology, University of Bern, Switzerland

Introduction

In late 2013, China unveiled its plan for the Belt and Road Initiative (BRI). It's an open framework that includes many different aspects of cooperation, such as better road connectivity, railways, energy projects, special economic zones, building ports and also better security cooperation[1]. It contains two main routes to connect China to the Middle East, Africa and finally Europe – one route overland, and one route by sea, the new 21st Century Maritime Silk Road[2]. The China-Pakistan Economic Corridor, or CPEC, is the flagship for the new Chinese vision of the BRI (Shah 2018: 379). The various Stakeholders in CPEC have deployed at least USD 62 billion[3] for a quick realization of this vision. This incredible amount of resources indicates the importance given to this ambitious undertaking by both China and Pakistan. The Pakistani province of Balochistan is home to the first completed element of CPEC, Gwadar Port. Therefore, the story of CPEC in Balochistan offers valuable insight into the many different ramifications of a mega-infrastructure project and is a fertile ground for academic research. The two core questions of this chapter are about the history of, and the driving forces behind, this project, and how it is affecting the local population and the environment of Balochistan.

Alleged benefits of the project are tirelessly advocated by both Chinese and Pakistani officials, who are saying that the benefits of CPEC will be transferred to the local Pakistani communities (Kanwal et al. 2019: 1). Promises of a better standard of living, a better income, millions of new jobs, business promotion and opportunity, and a better quality of education are some of the main talking points from the official sides (2019: 8–9). This 'enchantment' (Harvey and

---

[1] Akins 2017: 8–9; Kondapalli 2012: 174–184; Shah 2018: 379–380; Summers 2016: 1636–1637
[2] Arase 2015: 30; Casarini 2016: 96-98; Shah 2018: 378
[3] Casarini 2016: 100; Kanwal et al. 2019: 2; Small 2017: 80

Knox: 2012) around positive development seems to be following the narrative of mega-infrastructure projects. The BRI and CPEC are framed as inclusive win-win projects (Arase 2015: 30), but how the local population will profit and how the benefits will be shared inside Pakistan largely remains in the dark. Whether, on the local level, the promises made will remain true or if a 'disenchantment' will take place is a big question mark, as is the issue of whether this mega-infrastructure project is an anti-politics machine (Ferguson: 1990) or rather becomes a politics machine fuelling local resistance.

Big global economic players like the United States and China are competing for access to resources and to open up new markets, pushing their political and economic 'frontiers' (Rasmussen and Lund: 2018B). Although both countries are employing different strategies, they both eventually want to facilitate flows of capital and products. The US is following the principle of the free market while China is employing the strategy of cooperation through the bilateral development of political and economic ties, local infrastructure and transport networks (Summers 2016: 1635–1638). The Pakistani government welcomes China's plans warm-heartedly, but internal ethnic and political divisions are compromising a peaceful implementation of CPEC, especially in Balochistan. Local resistance to CPEC is strong and expressed in many different forms. Meanwhile, the national government forcefully tries to implement its strategy for the region. The country's political and religious history strongly influences and exacerbates this internal conflict.

This chapter first explores the multifaceted background of the BRI and CPEC, respectively, through an analysis of available academic research and through information gathered in media articles and social media. Secondly, it will try to shine some light on the historical factors of CPEC, the driving forces behind it, the social and environmental impacts, and finally the strategies employed by the different actors.

Part 1: Historical, environmental, ethnographic and political context

History and current context

The State of Pakistan was formed on August 14th, 1947 after its bloody partition from British India and the decolonization of southern Asia. High tensions, at some points open conflict, with India persist until the present day and are a defining part of Pakistan's political landscape. Even though Pakistan was to be a democratic state it has experienced long periods of military and military-backed rule (Jaffrelot 2004: 1–2; Talbot in Long et al. 2015: 1).

This might be due to the fact that Pakistan inherited the more economically and politically underdeveloped areas of British India at the time of partition. Ian Talbot (in Long et al. 2015: 1) names this 'democratic deficit', along with the massive dislocation of the Muslim population of British India, as reasons for Pakistan's struggle to consolidate a democratic system. Under British rule, the five provinces of Pakistan (Punjab, the North-West Frontier Province (NWFP), Balochistan, Sindh and East Bengal) received very different degrees of attention and development. The eastern Punjab province of Pakistan was the biggest beneficiary of British development and this is still felt today regarding economic and political dominance in modern Pakistan (2015: 24). The British developed a vast irrigation system in Punjab that led to a big take-off in agriculture, shortly followed by road and railway construction, town development and the beginning of a mechanical industry (Jaffrelot 2004: 153–154). Other provinces such as Sindh and Balochistan did not do as well due to the fact that their physical conditions were less favourable for economic development in the eyes of the British, the provinces were autonomous political units under indirect rule and the local population was far more resistant to foreign rule (Jaffrelot 2004: 154–156; Akins 2017: 5).

In the early years of Pakistan, Western foreign aid, mostly from the USA, the IMF and the World Bank, was a crucial factor in the development of a national economy, but it stagnated after the country slipped more and more into political isolation and away from democracy. Extremist movements and fundamentalism saw a rise. Violence, inefficiency and corruption pervaded the regimes of Bhutto and later Nawaz Sharif and it took until 2002 for democratic institutions (albeit under strong military influence) to be restored (Jaffrelot 2004: 163–186).

After September 11, 2001, Pakistan ceased to support the Taliban and joined the USA in the fight against Al-Qaeda. This led to the return of foreign investment. However, the agriculture sector remained underdeveloped and continued to perform poorly. Paying more attention to the army for so many years due to the constant threat or fear of India had its price, meaning that there was only a little funding available for infrastructure development, education or health services. The government only started to emphasize the development of rural infrastructure in its 2004–5 budget, but a growing gap between urban elites and rural masses and the many federal financial handicaps hindered such plans notably (2004: 186–189).

Despite being members of opposing security blocks during the Cold War, Pakistan has a special place in Chinese foreign policy. Both countries came together from the late 1950s and built what is now called an 'all-weather' friendship. The mutual antipathy towards India gave a solid common ground for the two neighbouring countries since China saw India as a proxy for Western expansionism and hegemonism. For China, Pakistan is a low-cost secondary deterrent to India's rise, and China in return is a high-value guarantor of security against India (Kondapalli 2012: 174; Akins 2017: 11).

Srikanth Kondapalli (2012: 174–175), Professor of East Asian Studies at Jawaharlal Nehru University in New Delhi, India, names six major objectives for Chinese policies towards Pakistan:
– security and stability of its north-western peripheries
– counterterrorism/insurgency efforts
– nuclear stability
– balance of power in the region
– economic development of remote regions
– seizing initiatives that are favourable to the rise of China

Kondapalli (2012: 174–175) argues further that fulfilling these six objectives is at the root of Chinese policies towards Pakistan and other neighbouring countries, and ensuring its 'all-weather' relations with Pakistan is a key element in ensuring a long-term and comprehensive presence of China in the region. The disintegration of the Soviet Union in the late 1980s, the formation of independent states in Central Asia in the early 1990s and also the spread of religious extremism have all brought new challenges to the peaceful development of China. It fears that 'spillover' effects will jeopardize its frontier stability and internal security and also that major Western countries will take advantage of the turmoil in the area to erode China's influence. Although China is aware of the long-term instability of Pakistan, it has over the years proposed a series of measures to overcome these problems. The six objectives mentioned above aim to establish proactive relations with regional states, bettering political communication with regional actors, to further military cooperation by engaging in bilateral/multilateral counterterrorism exercises and developing economic ties with key regional states. The cooperation of the two states further includes nuclear cooperation, both military and civil (2012: 174–179).

Kondapalli states that both China and Pakistan are in fear of internal separatist movements (2012: 174–182) and mentions militant attacks on Chinese citizens at Gwadar Port in May 2003 to exemplify his claims. The attacks killed three Chinese engineers and injured nine. The Pakistani government blamed Baloch separatists for the incident but Chinese authorities suspected Uyghur separatists to be responsible. This, according to Kondapalli, led to an intensified cooperation between the two states to overcome these security issues. China started to enhance the capacity of the Pakistani military to counter extremism and terrorism, and also various joint counterterrorism exercises by both Pakistani and Chinese military were undertaken (ibid.).

Generally, housing conditions and the overall economic situation of many people have improved in Pakistan since independence, but this material progress has largely bypassed the sparsely populated region of Balochistan. With the political and material changes also came social transformations. The Pakistani culture – a term somewhat insufficient to describe the vast cultural landscape of this country – has been changing at a fast pace. New values and norms are supplanting traditional rules, and many conventional practices are assuming new meanings and purpose (Qadeer 2006: 146–147).

Geography and ecosystem/cultural landscape

Pakistan covers an area of 881,912 km² and is inhabited by roughly 216.5 million people. This makes it the 36th largest and the fifth-most populated country on the planet[4]. Within Pakistan, Balochistan is the largest province in terms of area (347,190 km²) but has the smallest population (about 12.3 million in 2017[5]) (Qadeer 2006: 5). The sparsely populated province of Balochistan on the border with Iran and Afghanistan is a very resource-rich area. It is a land of extremes – an arid region with a few semi-permanent rivers cutting through the vast deserts and mountains. The ash-yellow colours of the deserts and the iron-grey hillsides and mountains have been described as a veritable moonscape and are sharply contrasted by the bright green of the river basins and some oases that are supplied by subterranean channels from nearby mountains. Most villages are dotted along these green twines that wind through the dusty landscape and have the same colour as the valley, because the houses are built with the stones and clay from the desert soil (Fabietti 2011: 1, 11; Akins 2017: 4).

Fig 1: Oases and villages of the Kech river valley, Balochistan. Source: Jaffrelot, C. (Ed.). (2004). A History of Pakistan and its Origins. Anthem Press.

---

[4] http://worldpopulationreview.com/countries/pakistan-population/
[5] http://www.pakinformation.com/population/balochistan.html

The province has been a historic gateway to India through central and western Asia and its geostrategic position and strong martial traditions are the basis of its political and cultural role in the Pakistani state (Qadeer 2006: 5). Since antiquity, Balochistan has been a transit area between the Arabic West and the Asian regions of the East, a kind of corridor that has now become a new frontier due to the conflicting strategic interests of Pakistan itself, China, the United States and other Western allies, as well as other actors. Control over the passage from central Asia to the Arabian Sea was, and still is, in the interest of all the regional actors (Fabietti 2011: 3–5). Ugo E.M. Fabietti (2011: 5) described Balochistan as a land immensely rich in resources yet poor and thinly populated. Far removed from the logic and reproduction of capitalism, this "frontier" area, as he calls it, "was looking for a way of confronting as best it could the diktats of globalization" – a place that "might be described as where tradition and modernity, the forces of the global market and those of tribal life came together; where different types of logic and a variety of 'cultures' interacted to harbinger the social forms of a large part of the globe at the turn of the 21st century". This echoes what Rasmussen and Lund (2018B) write about frontier spaces but not only includes geostrategic but also economic interests as discussed in the New Institutional Political Ecology approach as the value of the area is increasing with the proposed infrastructure projects. This leads to changes in power constellations of actors and institutional transformations, which are being legitimized by state actors using development discourses.

Local population and resource use

At the heart of Pakistani society lies the village. In Balochistan, however, the tribe has remained the most important social structure with small villages of around 300–400 people at its heart (Qadeer 2006: 112–118). There are regional differences, though. The north of Balochistan is home to large nomadic tribes, but further south there is no large-scale nomadism. Small groups of shepherds live a seasonal life and the majority of the people are settled farmers living in highly stratified communities in terms of social, political and economic characteristics (Fabietti 2011: 1, 11; Akins 2017: 4). On the coastline of the Arabian Sea, the rural population is dominated by Baloch fishermen (Akins 2017: 8).

Historically, the Baloch population is viewed as a fierce tribal society, ruled by customary laws and as a home to distinct subcultures (Qadeer 2006: 5). A Baloch tribe has historically comprised a cluster of lineage groups (clans), not necessarily of the same ancestry, collectively owning land and water resources under common property institutions regulating access to these resources. A tribe is quite stratified, headed by *sardars* (rulers), with free tribesmen forming the cultivator/herdsmen class in the middle, and menial workers called *hizmatkar* (dependent) constituting the base. Tribesmen have inheritable rights to pieces of land and water share for use and profit, but they also have an obligation to pay tribute to the *sardars* (2006: 112–118).

The complicated irrigation systems of the oases are symbolic for the identically complicated rules for sharing the water among owners or tenants: how it is inherited, sold and bought is highly complex and not easily comprehensible to outsiders. It is important to mention that agricultural property was often not calculated in terms of land surface, but in 'quantity of water' (Fabietti 2011: 31–33). Within Balochistan, regional differences exist in tribal land tenures because of the many different tribes, such as Afghan and Makrani tribes, who differ from the Baloch. The historic land entitlements confer private rights for use and profit, but not for the sale of tribal land. The custom of *vesh* (redistribution), whereby a tribe periodically redistributes lands to its component clans, and from thereon down to families and individuals to ensure fair distribution of good- and poor-quality lands, was the main basis of this tenurial system. In the settled districts, this traditional tribal common property tenure with institutions of distribution of land evolved into a landlord-tenant system and a peasant economy. The British then later laid the foundations of landlordism by conferring individual proprietary and tenancy rights. Although economic conditions improved under British rule, an overwhelming majority of the rural population still lived at subsistence levels without health and educational facilities at the time of independence. Even after 50 years of Pakistani independence, two-thirds of the rural population was still illiterate. Balochistan stands out in this as lagging even further behind in terms of both urban and rural illiteracy and widespread poverty[6] (Qadeer 2006: 112–118).

The symbiotic relationship between the *sardars* and public officials formed the new power structure of the traditional village and has continued to dominate even after Pakistan's independence. Although repression of the people was less common, the mixed power structure remained exploitative and the poor remained powerless and dependent (2006: 144–145).

Social interactions in Balochistan were historically based on a social code known as *Balochiat*, the "way of the Baloch", which is centred around the two core values of *izzat* and *malmastu*. *Izzat* (meaning 'honour' and 'respectability') is the core value in all the provincial cultures, but in Balochistan in particular it stands above all else. The interpretation of what is considered honourable or dishonourable still remains subject to regional differences and the particular perspective of cultural change. *Malmasta* expresses the emphasis on hospitality and protection according to defined expectations (Akins 2017: 4; Qadeer 2006: 146–147).

While until the late 19th century the political climate of Balochistan was still principally influenced by rivalries among chieftains of various villages, the on-

---

[6] A 2016 report by Pakistan's Ministry of Planning, Development and Reform found that 71% of Balochistan's total population still lives in multidimensional poverty, compared to 31% in Punjab and 43% in Sindh (Akins 2017: 10).

Fig 2: A Baloch village. Source: Jaffrelot, C. (Ed.). (2004). A History of Pakistan and its Origins. Anthem Press.

going political restlessness and the resulting instability of the region after independence translated for the most part into manifestations of local nationalism and opposition to the central Pakistani government (Fabietti 2011: 18). Although stratification is deeply rooted in Baloch society and until today has played a major role in the reproduction of social relations, the hierarchic features are often far less important in the context of an extra-local dimension. To be able to claim their autonomy from the Pakistani state, the Balochi people think in the national context of themselves as a single homogeneous group that has to reduce to the minimum every form of differentiation within. On a symbolic level, despite in reality being deeply divided, the Baloch people share a common history, identity and a unitary tradition (2011: 104–105).

Balochistan has always suffered from chronic neglect, underdevelopment and a lack of political representation in the modern Pakistani nation state. Over the past 60 years, this has led to five different rebellions and has further ignited the nationalist tendencies and the desire for independence from Pakistan (Akins 2017: 3). Balochistan's integration into Pakistan was rocky from the beginning. Under the indirect rule of the British, the four princely states of the region existed as autonomous political units, and because of that, at the time of partition, the rulers of these princely states were given the choice regarding which new state they would join or if they wanted to be independent. Three of the four Baloch princely states agreed to join Pakistan, but the ruler of the fourth, the Khan of Kalat, initially wanted to establish an independent state. After lengthy negotiations and pressure from Pakistan, he finally decided to join the new state on the promise of maintaining internal autonomy. Many of his own people did disagree with his decision and saw the new state as a vehicle for Punjabi domination of Balochistan. The Khan's own brother led the first Baloch revolt in 1948. He was defeated after two years. Further tensions and revolts followed through several decades and the call for Baloch independence never really ended (2017: 5–7).

The Balochi do not see themselves as Pakistani and sense a strong alienation from the state. In an interview with BBC Hindi, Baloch activist Mazdak Baloch stated:

"We are not Pakistani. We are not of any concern for Pakistan. We are Pakistan's colony. [...] There is no education, there are no jobs. A common Balochi can find only a menial job. Islamabad has appointed Pakistani Muslims in all important positions in Balochistan. Its army has created a mess in the entire region. The economic resources of our land are plundered. Pakistan has opened the doors for Chinese companies for mining coal reserves and other natural resources" (2017: 7).

Ian Talbot (in Long et al. 2015: 3-8) states that the military's interventions in politics were often justified by saying that the army was the only institution that actually worked, but the military rule has in turn also perpetuated the weak political institutionalization of Pakistan. Ethnic, linguistic and regional forces have been reinforced through the colonial recruitment policies that draw personnel mostly from the Punjabis (approx. 75%). In contrast, Baluchistan and Sindh together only make up about 5% of army personnel. Talbot further argues that this makes the national army look like an occupying force when it is deployed to settle regional unrest because army-backed governments tend to view demands for autonomy in smaller provinces as 'law and order' issues rather than legitimate demands that should be resolved through political compromise. This, and the fact that the army is clearly Punjab dominated, also shows that ethnic allegiances play a crucial role in Pakistan's politics. Although there are several parties in the political landscape, Pakistan's parties, except for the PPP (Pakistan People Party) and the PML-N (Pakistan Muslim League-Nawaz), lack the ability to move beyond regional and sectional appeals (2015: 3–8).

This might be an additional explanatory factor for the struggle to institutionalize democratic institutions. Ian Talbot and Abdur Rehman Shah agree that sectarian violence, insurgencies, and terrorism also remain a big challenge for Pakistan (Long et al. 2016: 8–9; Shah 2018: 379–380). Only 2% of its GDP has been allocated to education over a sustained period, and administrative incapacity, which gave rise to corruption, led to a situation where even these limited resources were poorly utilized and allocated. High adult illiteracy, neglected youth regional and gender disparities, and unconnected systems of public, private and religious schools are just some of the effects of these policies (Talbot 2012: 228–230).

National economy and legal framework

The traditional village economy has fundamentally changed in post-independence Pakistan. Economic transactions, which were traditionally made through *seypi* (customary and obligatory barter of goods and services), have been monetized, giving way to cash transactions and pricing mechanisms and social relations of production have evolved from interlocking obligations to contractual dealings. Villages ceased to be self-sufficient and started to produce cash crops, goods and services for national and international markets. These capitalist trends even touched the rather remote tribal communities of Balochistan, even though feudal and peasant relations survived in modified forms (Qadeer 2006: 121).

Pakistan originally had good prospects for agriculture in its western provinces but almost no industry after its partition from India. After partition, Pakistan received Western foreign aid to develop a national economy. But extremist movements, a growing presence of fundamentalists and violence as a normal occurrence made economic development rather difficult. Many foreign investors left the country or did not dare to enter this explosive territory (Jaffrelot 2004: 163–186).

This changed after September 11, 2001 when Pakistan ceased to support the Taliban and joined the United States in their fight against Al-Qaeda. Pakistan then again started to receive foreign investment. However, the agriculture sector remained underdeveloped and continued to perform poorly. A very fast-growing population (dating back only 70 years, the Pakistani population was around 37.54 million people, compared to roughly 216.5 million nowadays[7]) also increased the pressure on the most vital resource of Pakistan's economy: water. Per capita availability of water dropped steadily, and the national transport system was very inefficient and costly (2004: 186–189).

The management of water resources is the most pressing issue in the region. Climate change has deteriorated the surface and groundwater balance, and droughts have become a permanent feature in the region. The groundwater table is depleting rapidly, threatening the fragile environment. Such changes also have a great influence on regional socio-economic dynamics (Farooqui and Aftab 2018: 5; Talbot 2012: 20–22; Wu et al. 2019: 484, 492–493). This highlights the importance of the common properties, especially water in this case.

Harrison Akins and Srikanth Kondapalli (Akins 2017: 8–9; Kondapalli 2012: 174–184) explain that despite being a rather small partner in terms of trade, Pakistan still has a special place in the Chinese calculus. It is one of the few countries that has a free trade agreement (FTA) with China. China has also continuously expanded its investment in the construction, transport and other related economic

---

[7] http://worldpopulationreview.com/countries/pakistan-population/

sectors in Pakistan, probably to counterbalance US influence in the region. Infrastructure projects and cooperation in other areas like mining and transport saw a significant increase in recent years. In the seventies, China played a vital part in the upgrade of the Karakoram Highway, which connects northern Pakistan to western China, and is involved in the construction of various dam projects as well. Another Chinese-backed major infrastructure project is Gwadar Port in Balochistan, which has been called a landmark in the bilateral relations. All these infrastructure projects, along with the proposed PRC military base in Gwadar Port, point to the strategic objectives of China to put military and political pressure on India, to limit US influence in the region and to monitor directly the activity of 'Uyghur separatists' inside Pakistan. Finally, Pakistan's economic integration with China provides the opportunity for both countries to gain access to regional markets (Akins 2017: 8–9; Kondapalli 2012: 174–184).

Pakistan's legal system also plays an important role regarding infrastructure projects. Pakistan is a member party of the International Covenant on Civil and Political Rights (ICCPR), and by ratifying it, it has made a commitment to respect, protect and fulfil the obligations of that treaty. The treaty, in particular, includes the rights to life, freedom of opinion and expression, freedom of thought, conscience and religion or belief, as well as personal integrity, equality before the law, freedom from discrimination, the right to a fair trial and prohibition of arbitrary detention. Pakistan's blasphemy laws violate these international legal obligations and enable prosecutions on the basis of unfounded accusations by complainants (Amnesty International 2016: 14).

In January 2015, Parliament authorized the establishment of military courts to try civilians accused of 'terrorism motivated by religion or sectarianism'. These courts imposed the death penalty on hundreds of individuals in secret trials and in violation of international standards. Accusations of 'anti-state' or 'anti-Islam' activities and 'blasphemy', which are often incited by sections of local media, have led to tough restrictions on freedom of expression and association. Many accused of such 'crimes' were tried under anti-terrorism laws or under sharia laws, without being subject to parliamentary oversight. This resulted in a lack of accountability and violations of human rights (Amnesty International 2017A: 5–10).

These legal premises can deeply influence how the nation state handles opposition to proposed infrastructure projects and are testimony to an existing legal pluralism.

Part 2: China-Pakistan Economic Corridor (CPEC)

After several decades of remarkable constant economic growth, the Chinese government now faces challenges to keep this trend up. Domestic industrial overcapacity is threatening the political legitimacy of China's Communist Party since the promise of sustained economic growth is what mostly has been keeping them in power. Some think of the changes in Chinese policy from the 'peaceful rise, peaceful development and scientific development' under Hu Jintao to China's outwards-directed policy under Xi Jinping as a way to leverage nationalism, with slogans such as the 'Chinese dream', and China's overseas achievements to stabilize the fragile domestic situation (Shah 2018: 379; Shen 2015: 2).

To achieve its new dream, whatever the motivation might be, China's leadership is abandoning the traditional approach of lying low and concentrating on building its domestic economy and is trending towards a more proactive stance (Casarini 2016: 96–98). The 'Belt and Road' or 'One Belt, One Road', or more commonly the BRI, is an expression of this new attitude. As of January 2020, the Chinese government had signed 200 cooperation documents with 138 countries and 30 international organizations, according to the Belt and Road Forum[8]. How this new Chinese attitude will affect its neighbouring countries and the local communities and environment is still to be studied and evaluated since many of the projects under the BRI framework have still not been realized. The 'Chinese dream' gives new hope to developing countries and also strong incentives to follow the initiative, but there is not a lot of research available on the resulting impacts for local communities in the receiving countries. This article focuses on the 'flagship of the BRI' (Shah 2018: 379), the China-Pakistan Economic Corridor (CPEC) and how this project is affecting the Pakistani province of Balochistan.

Description of the project, its history and its drivers

The Chinese Belt and Road initiative was unveiled by President Xi Jinping in late 2013 and he uses the term 'community of common destiny' or 'community of shared fate' to express his vision of China's future role in the region. Beijing's intention is to build a new Eurasian land bridge and to develop six economic corridors: China-Mongolia-Russia; China-Central Asia-Northern Europe; China-Central Asia-West Asia; China-Pakistan; Bangladesh-China-India-Myanmar; and the China-Indochina peninsula. Aside from the land routes, the 21st century Maritime Silk Road, which was also introduced in late 2013, is planned to complement these overland trade routes and to form a network of ports and other coastal infrastructure connecting China to its periphery and to the rest of the world. In all, the BRI will connect 65 countries, which together form one-third of the global economic output, 40% of global trade and 62% of the world population (Arase 2015: 30; Casarini 2016: 96–98; Shah 2018: 378).

The emphasis on 'going out' by increasing foreign direct investment, exporting labour and establishing economic cooperation projects mirrors the geographical focus of the BRI initiative: it could help China and participating countries to open new markets for their goods, and the investments in infrastructure and

---

[8] Coenen et al. 2020

connectivity will further enhance the ability of capital flows to grow. This is essentially a state-led spatial fix that China seems to be pursuing since its export-oriented economy is more and more threatened by domestic industrial overcapacity (Shah 2018: 379–380; Summers 2016: 1636–1637).

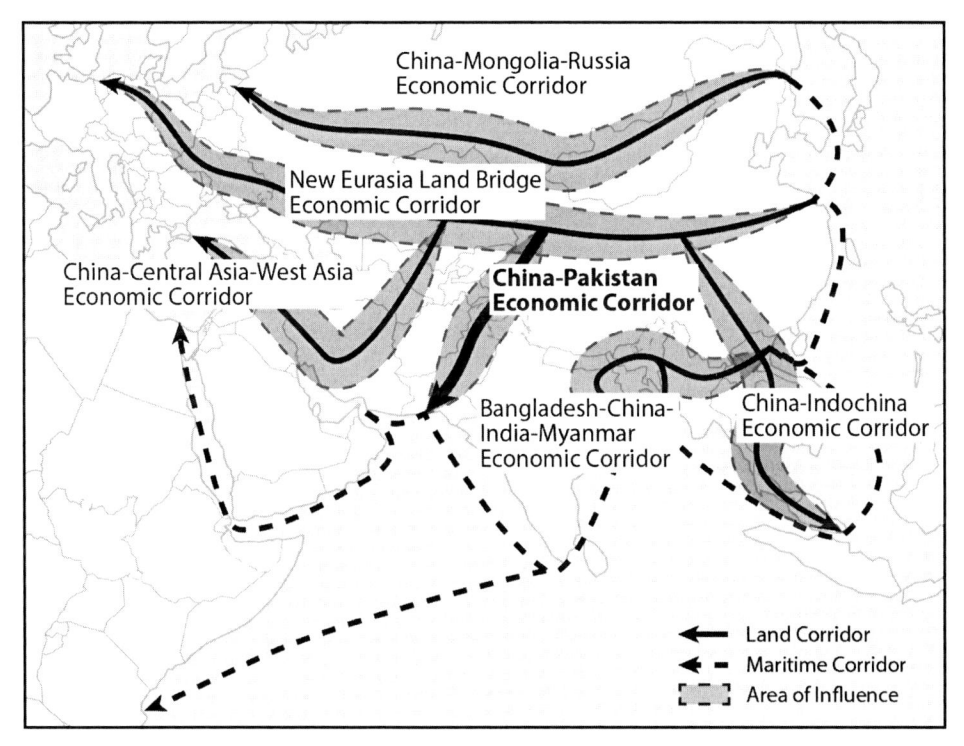

Map 1: Belt and Road Initiative BRI. Source: Map compilation and design by Manuel L. K. Abebe (2021), CDE, University of Bern, Bern, Switzerland.

The attempt at a revival of the ancient Silk Road is not a new concept. Various countries had and still have their own concepts, ideas, programmes and strategies, but due to the instability in Central Asia in recent decades these concepts have been hard, if not impossible, to realize. China and Pakistan jointly made the first major effort by building the Karakorum Highway in the seventies. After the Cold War, two different concepts for the revival of the Silk Road emerged and were pushed forward: the Chinese-backed concept, which ultimately resulted in the present vision of the BRI, and the Western-backed concept, led by the USA and supported by its European and Asian allies. This concept is today known as the 'New Silk Road Initiative', or NSRI (Rahman 2013: 132).

In 1999, the US Congress passed the 'Silk Road Strategy Act', which provided broad-based assistance for combating drug trafficking, border security and the development of free-market economies in Central Asia (2013: 133). China's approach to regional integration centres on policy-led trade facilitation, which features the improvement of trade connectivity by building more efficient transportation linkages, providing more trade and investment finance, streamlining trade and investment approvals, and multiplying human exchange opportunities. This approach does not require the negotiation of a multilateral trade liberalization agreement, but rather builds on bilateral cooperation between China and its neighbours. In contrast, the Western approach focuses on economic liberalization. Multilateral treaties remove legal and institutional barriers to trade and investment and create legally binding rules, standards and dispute resolution mechanisms to create a free open space for private sector activity. It is left to the free market to provide physical infrastructure or to channel trade in any particular direction (Arase 2015: 32–33).

The NSRI has been widely promoted by the USA and its allies. In July 2011, the then Secretary of State Hillary Clinton shared her vision of a New Silk Road in the Indian city of Chennai: "[…] Let's work together to create a new Silk Road. Not a single thoroughfare like its namesake, but an international web and network of economic and transit connections. That means building more rail lines, highways, energy infrastructure, like the proposed pipeline to run from Turkmenistan, through Afghanistan, through Pakistan into India" (Clinton 2011, cited in Rahman 2013: 134).

Notable here is the course of the intended Silk Road. Western and Chinese interests alike want to have an economic route through Pakistan, highlighting the strategic location of the country at the heart of the colliding interests of global powers. Afghanistan seems to be at the heart of US-led activities to gain control of the region.

New markets are needed to satisfy the international hunger for economic growth and the BRI seems to be Beijing's answer. Economic interdependence, cooperation and development, so China's notion, will bring peace and stability and China's continuing growth will enhance the security of any country linked to it. Its great power identity definitely makes them consider traditional security and geopolitical interests as well (Arase 2015: 39–40).

David Arase (2015: 30) mentions Xi Jinping's framework for future cooperation with China's neighbours:

– *The use of China's advantages in economy, trade, technology and finance to build "win-win" cooperation with its neighbours;*
– *Construction of the two Silk Roads;*
– *The use of trade and investment to create a new kind of regional economic integration;*
– *An Asian Infrastructure Investment Bank, internationalization of the Chinese currency and regional financial stability;*
– *The development of Chinese border areas as gateways to neighbouring countries;*

– A new concept of security, based on mutual trust, reciprocity, equality and co-ordination through enhanced cooperation mechanisms;
– Public diplomacy and people-to-people exchanges including tourism, technology, education and provincial-level cooperation.

Despite being quite promising for China's neighbours, the Chinese development model is not free from self-centred motivations, economic predominance, cultural or systemic clashes, and economic and environmental issues (Shah 2018: 379, 381). China's diplomatic practice might give some insight into the challenges for the participating countries:

China's Central Administration often favours bilateral negotiations and is always committed to its core interests. Those include the preservation of absolute power in the hands of the Chinese Communist Party and the state apparatus; the sovereignty and territorial integrity of the Chinese state; and the continuing stability and development of China's economy. It reserves the right to use any means at its disposal if anyone challenges these core interests. The fact that China does not turn to international tribunals to resolve sovereignty disputes but rather insists on direct bilateral negotiations might indicate that smaller countries could have a difficult stand in negotiations (Arase 2015: 32–35).

The China-Pakistan Economic Corridor (CPEC) was first announced during Xi Jinping's state visit to Islamabad in April 2015 and is China's largest overseas investment project to date. It consists of extensive investments in Pakistan's transport, telecommunications and energy infrastructure, which will eventually link the port of Gwadar in Pakistan's province Balochistan to the city of Kashgar in China's Xinjiang province (Casarini 2016: 100). It parallels the existing Karakorum Highway, which today connects China, through Pakistan, to the Arabian Sea (Arase 2015: 39). The estimated value of the project was USD46 billion in 2015, later rising to USD51 billion in 2016 and finally increasing to USD62 billion in 2017 (Casarini 2016: 100; Kanwal et al. 2019: 2; Small 2017: 80). CPEC is also considered the 'flagship project' of the BRI and is being marked as an ideal model of intergovernmental coordination and regional integration. Around USD35 billion of the total budget is planned for energy projects such as solar, coal, wind, hydro and wind energy, which will add an additional 10,400 megawatts of energy into Pakistan's power grid and end the chronic power shortages that cost Pakistan around 2% of its annual gross domestic product. Roughly USD15 billion are to be invested in infrastructure projects, special economic zones and mass transit schemes (Ali et al. 2018: 48; Shah 2018: 379–380).

The election of the Pakistan Muslim League-Nawaz party in 2013 was a good fit for China's BRI plans since it was also in favour of large-scale infrastructure projects and was prone to fix the ongoing energy crisis. The close security and political relationship between the two states also means that Pakistan has a unique level of comfort with the strategic factors that underpin the BRI: for instance, ports like Gwadar that can serve both commercial and military purposes, as well as a

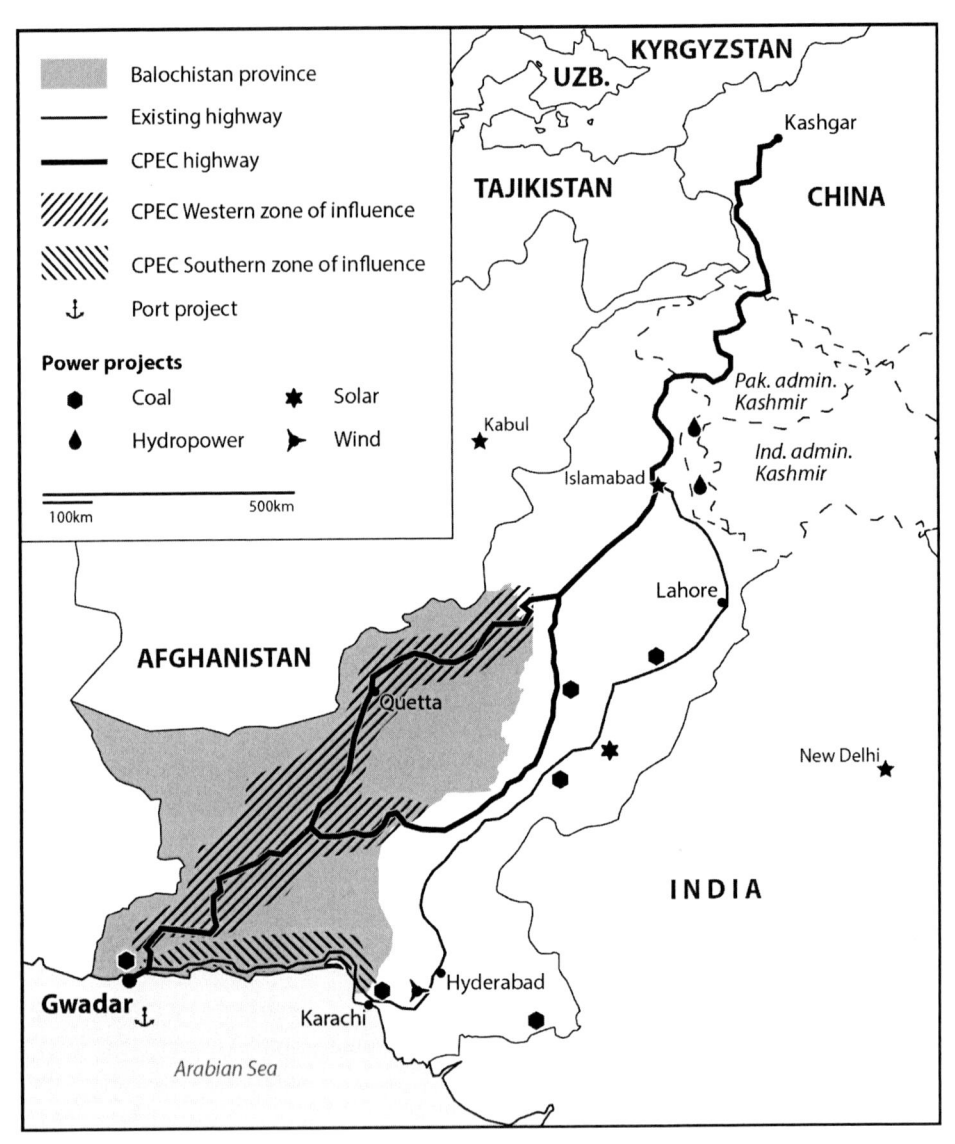

Map 2: CPEC route from Gwadar to Kashgar. Source: Map compilation and design by Manuel L. K. Abebe (2021), CDE, University of Bern, Bern, Switzerland. Geodata: OpenStreetMap contributors

rare willingness to provide Chinese firms with privileged access to its economy (Small 2017: 82).

Alleged benefits are tirelessly advocated by both Chinese and Pakistani officials, who say that the benefits of CPEC will be transferred to the local Pakistani communities (Kanwal et al. 2019: 1). Promises of a better standard of living, a better income, millions of new jobs, business promotion and opportunity, a better quality of education and better connectivity for the rural communities to the big cities are some of the main talking points from the official sides (2019: 8–9). This all sounds very good and beneficial for the local population, but how sure can they be that this is not only a marketing strategy but actually the plan of the two governments? And since Pakistan's population is already heavily divided along ethnic lines, who is meant by the 'local population'? The project is framed as an inclusive win-win project (Arase 2015: 30) between the two governments, but how the actual population will profit and how the benefits will be shared inside Pakistan largely remains in the dark.

Financial risks, security threats and local unhappiness with the project should not be ignored. Rushed agreements and a lack of transparency seem to be inherent with the financing of the project: even the governor of Pakistan's central bank stated that he did not have a clear overview of the financing (Shah 2018: 383–384; Small 2017: 81).

Environmental and social impacts

The Balochistan province in Pakistan covers 45% of the nation's territory but is only home to 6% of the total population. It is the least educated, least connected and most deprived province, thus CPEC could actually help Balochistan to mitigate its current status quo[9]. So, why is it that many of the Baloch people are strongly opposed to the project?

For many of them, China, as well as the Punjab-dominated state of Pakistan, are seen as an occupying force trying to plunder their resource-rich province[10]. The Baloch people are proud of their traditions, culture and the natural environment and are very well aware of their natural resources (Farooqui and Aftab 2018: 4–5). They see CPEC not as development but rather as an industrialized and politically charged exploitation of their land and people. Their struggle for independence from Pakistan dates back decades, but in the face of CPEC, it comes to light once again. Tranag Baluch, a contributor for Balochwarna News, writes:

"We [the Baloch people] are well educated; we can differentiate between exploitation and development. China and Pakistan must not worry about the future of Balochistan because we know our welfare and we will not allow occupiers to decide about our faith and future"[11].

CPEC has revived or even exacerbated the internal ethnic divisions between the Pakistani provinces. The three major ethnicities of Pakistan, besides the dominant Punjabis, that is, Pashtuns, Sindhis and Baloch, have long had strong resentments

---

[9] https://www.business-standard.com/article/international/balochistan-the-biggest-hindrance-to-china-s-cpec-ambitions-117082100302_1.html
[10] https://unpo.org/article/19988
[11] http://balochwarna.com/2018/05/13/cpec-a-death-warrant-for-the-baloch-nation/

that Punjabis have annexed the national resources and power to their sole advantage. The fact that the Punjab-based Pakistan Muslim League-Nawaz party is controlling the central government has also led to accusations of disproportional priority given to the Punjab province (Shah 2018: 382–383).

The Baloch fear that not only will CPEC not bring them the promised benefits but that their province will be handed over to foreign interests and that they might soon be a minority in their own territory due to increased immigration related to CPEC (Kanwal et al. 2019: 9; Small 2017: 8). This old and strong resentment towards foreign powers trying to influence Baloch affairs historically gave rise to Baloch nationalistic and violent separatist movements.

*Fig 3: Gwadar Port. Source: Pakistan-China Institute. The CPEC Portal:
‹http://www.cpecinfo.com/gwadar-port-city›_accessed on 28.11.2019*

Since CPEC is not yet completed, it is impossible to make statements about the long-term impacts on the local population or the environment, but some examples of already finished projects might give some valuable insights into how a mega-infrastructure project is impacting and changing the Baloch province.

A lot of Chinese investment is centred around Gwadar Port. Its construction was one of the first projects that was realized under CPEC and the aim was to create a modern trade and tourist hub in the image of Shenzhen or Dubai. Gwadar also has significant strategic importance due to its naturally deep warm-water port and geographic proximity to the Middle East (Akins 2017: 8). While construction has gone ahead, Baloch fishermen, who historically inhabited the region and used the port area for fishing, have been barred from the port and have been told to do something else to earn a livelihood[12]. These fishermen will not, for the most part, be able to carry out their livelihood as fishermen and will not be able to be a part of economic activities in the new port due to their lack of education and

---

[12] https://www.business-standard.com/article/international/balochistan-the-biggest-hindrance-to-china-s-cpec-ambitions-117082100302_1.html

skills[13]. This will result in a loss of access to their former common property and livelihood, and may greatly affect the traditional common property institutions of these people.

Their story is not unique: according to Balochwarna News, schools, colleges and the university are being closed and turned into Frontier Corps checkpoints, people are often being forced to migrate and Baloch people are therefore under high psychological strain[14]. Often these actions are either being denied altogether or justified by labelling the Baloch as anti-CPEC insurgents or even terrorists. A curfew was imposed along the routes of CPEC to show the world that there is peace, but for Javed Mengal, a Baloch political activist, Balochistan is in a 'state of war' against its perceived occupiers[15]. These human rights violations were even called a systematic genocide by Abdul Nawaz Bugti, a representative of the Baloch Republican Party (BRP), at the Human Rights Council in Geneva, and he requested a UN Special Rapporteur for Pakistan. He stated: "Mass graves are being found in Balochistan, which is clear evidence of Pakistani war crimes." According to Bugti, people are being killed or abducted by military forces, and the targeted population is generally the educated elite, such as political activists, teachers, students, lawyers and intellectuals[16].

Chinese workers have been targeted by extremists, and in some instances this resulted in violent and deadly attacks on the foreign CPEC workers. China and Pakistan reacted with a heavy securitization of the construction sites of CPEC and it has become one of the top priorities of the national security agendas (Shah 2018: 382–383). Although CPEC might have the potential to enhance the standard of living in the region and to remove poverty from society, the implementation of CPEC in Balochistan does not seem to offer much hope for the local communities. Mir Suleiman Ahmedzal, Khan of Kalat, said to ANI:

"CPEC has no developmental value whatsoever and is simply one 'occupier' taking the help of another 'occupier' in plundering the region, which is rich in natural resources. We are not going to enjoy anything, nor are we going to benefit from it. We are not even being asked as it is our land"[17].

Beside atrocities committed in the wake of the CPEC mega-infrastructure project, there is the dimension of what might come after the project's completion. In Pakistan, skilled labourers constitute only 6% of the entire labour force, and in Balochistan, the situation is even worse (Farooqui and Aftab 2018: 9). So, since Balochistan already has very few highly educated people – who could actually fill positions around CPEC projects – there is the potential danger that new jobs and

---
[13] https://balochistantimes.com/cpec-a-game-changer-or-a-disaster/
[14] https://balochwarna.com/2018/05/13/cpec-a-death-warrant-for-the-baloch-nation/
[15] https://unpo.org/article/19988
[16] https://unpo.org/article/19988; Amnesty International (2014); Amnesty International (2017C)
[17] https://unpo.org/article/19988

opportunities coming along with CPEC could disproportionately benefit Chinese workers or professionals from other origins instead of the local Baloch population.

The propagated idea of CPEC was that this project should be jointly built through consultation to meet the interests of all, but in reality, the deals of CPEC are signed between Chinese stakeholders and a small circle of Pakistani government officials, without proper feedback from other institutions, not even the provincial government. Because of this practice, the Chinese side was able to procure deals that are more favourable to them, and critical questions about the transparency and methodology of such arrangements remain unanswered. Also, financial incentives disproportionately favour Chinese contractors through tax breaks or exemptions, which in turn puts the local investors at a big disadvantage. As an example of such implications, one could project that energy produced by projects under the CPEC might be too expensive to be afforded by local consumers, which strongly contradicts the propagated benefits for the local communitie. (Shah 2018: 379, 383–384).

As for how CPEC is, or will be, influencing the social structure of Balochistan's tribal society, there is almost no research available. With new transport infrastructure and new mining activities, both of which CPEC is bringing, several forms of land- or rather commons-grabbing processes are highly likely to take place, though. This not just in agricultural but pastoral land as well. The access to land and, even more vitally, the access to water will likely be removed or restricted while compensations and options for jobs are not in sight. Also, the environment will definitely be impacted by a project of this size. Balochistan has huge deposits of dimension stones like limestone, granite, marble, sandstone and onyx, which are rarely available in the northern parts of Pakistan and even in western China. Also, metallic and non-metallic minerals like gold, copper, iron, chromium, barium, magnesium, aluminium and many more are widely available in the region. Many of them are already being mined, and most of them are being exported to China through the port of Karachi for further refining and processing. The same applies to raw materials for cement production and to chromium. Chromium is an essential ingredient for the production of steel and Balochistan has the second-largest deposit in the world. The raw materials are also exported to China through Karachi at a very low cost, and the processed ore (ferrochrome) is then imported back at a very high cost (Farooqui and Aftab 2018: 10–12).

Environmental conservation has developed significantly in China over the past 20 years, pointing towards a new understanding that inclusive biodiversity conservation is of great importance and value (Foggin 2018: 1). In his research, J. Marc Foggin (2018: 1) suggests that lessons learnt in China are also being implemented in BRI partner countries in Central Asia, but there is no evidence, to the best knowledge of the author of this chapter, that suggests that this will be the case under CPEC.

It rather seems that with CPEC, economic development will take precedence over biodiversity and environmental protection. The project is likely to cause heavy pollution, degradation, fragmentation and habitat loss. These factors could eventually lead to the extinction of various endangered species in the region. Endangered mammals like the Himalayan brown bear, the Indian wolf, the Indian leopard and the snow leopard – to name just a few – and also birds such as the peregrine falcon and the cheer pheasant could be victims of the advancing CPEC (Nabi et al. 2017: 3003–3004).

Local and NGO strategies

The province of Balochistan has seen high levels of investment because of CPEC, mainly in Gwadar Port and its surrounding infrastructure, but a lot of local people are still living in multidimensional poverty. According to Harrison Akins (2017: 10), questions about the allocation of funds and political motives behind CPEC occupy the minds of the Baloch people and old fears of exploitation have led to many of them taking a hard stance against the project in their province. The alleged benefits of the project – promises of a better standard of living, a better income, millions of new jobs, business promotion and opportunity, and a better quality of education (Kanwal et al. 2019: 8–9) – seem to remain an attempt to enchant the local population and external actors in order to gather support for the project.

Majid Sohrabi, mayor of Gwadar in 2005, expressed his concerns quite clearly: "Gwadar is supposed to be a city for the future, but every day these people are crying about water and basic health facilities. If the government can build a port, why can't they build a new school?" Not only do the port, five-star resorts and new shopping centres appear to be more important to the developers than building basic infrastructures like water and food supply, but land acquisitions have also led to the displacement of many local communities, reinforcing the 'disenchantment' of the locals and further confirming that land grabbing is taking place.

A local Baloch fisherman commented on the displacement: "They enter our homes and turn us out, settling others from far away. If someone breaks into your home and throws you out, and you scream your powerless scream, can you be blamed?" (as cited in Akins 2017: 10).

Resistance against these practices grew over the years and many different actors have emerged in the fight against the perceived invaders of Balochistan. This resistance is also a representation of the disenchantment of the Baloch people in regard to CPEC. One way to respond was armed resistance. Since 2007, when construction on Gwadar Port began, terrorist attacks within Balochistan have seen a steady increase, from 35 attacks in 2007 to 483 attacks in 2015. Most of these attacks targeted infrastructure projects and Chinese workers around Gwadar, and most of them were ascribed to the 'Balochistan Liberation Army'. As a result, the national government also increased its military presence in the region, allocating 15,000 military personnel to the protection of Chinese workers and the infrastructure around CPEC. Even China increased its military presence in the region (2017: 10).

Nationalistic rhetoric and anti-foreign sentiments are not a new phenomenon in Balochistan, but in combination with violent armed resistance, it is now explicitly canalized against CPEC infrastructure projects and the growing influence of China and Chinese companies.

Fig 4: Members of the Baloch Liberation Army. Source: telesur US News (July 2019): US Labels Anti-Pakistan Baloch Army a 'Terrorist' Organization ‹https://www.telesurenglish.net/news/US-Labels-Anti-Pakistan-Baloch-Army-a-Terrorist-Organization-20190703-0012.html›_accessed on 29.11.2019

Other forms of resistance can be found as well. Twitter seems to be an important tool for circulating 'independent' information and for organizing collective action against CPEC. Local Baloch fishermen who are worried about their future and who are in fear of displacement demonstrated against the port construction in Gwadar. Faiz Baluch, a Baloch freedom activist, wrote on Twitter about the demonstrations:

"hundreds of local #Baloch fishermen out on streets of #Gwadar protesting against the #Pakistan and #China's imperialistic projects, which causing economic genocide of Baloch people in Gwadar. #CPEC is only beneficial for Punjab and China & death and destruction for #Balochistan"[18].

---
[18] https://twitter.com/Faiz_Baluch/status/1078292234452287489

The local resistance to CPEC, i.e. in Balochistan, also poses considerable risks to the successful implementation of the project since internal ethnic divisions between the provinces are likely to be exacerbated rather than resolved through CPEC (Small 2017: 86). In response to a bomb attack on a Sufi shrine in Balochistan in November 2016 that killed 52 and wounded 106, the then Minister of Planning, Development and Reforms Ahsan Iqbal stated that protestors against CPEC would be charged under Pakistan's anti-terrorism laws (Akins 2017: 11), which shows that institution shopping is being done. This legal practice resulted in disturbing actions against the local population of the region and has led many NGOs to accuse Pakistan of various human rights violations. This is a clear indication that both sides are positioned in a field of legal pluralism and that they are using whatever power they have to push their respective agendas. Both the nation state and the resisting forces seem to be 'institution shopping'. Amnesty International and other organizations like the Human Rights Council of Balochistan and the Baloch Human Rights Organization all share their concerns over the human rights situation in Pakistan, and in Balochistan in particular. So-called 'enforced disappearances' have become a regular practice of the nation state. Political activists are being targeted and their families as well. Over the past several years, hundreds, possibly even thousands, of cases have taken place. A UN fact-finding team's 2013 report indicated that 14,000 individuals were missing and that the bodies of around 1,000 persons had been discovered, often marked by torture, mutilation or riddled with bullet holes. The Amnesty International Commission on Inquiry on Enforced Disappearances received nearly 300 cases of alleged enforced disappearances from August to October 2017. Victims are at considerable risk of torture and other ill treatment and even death. There seems to be a climate of impunity and authorities are not sufficiently dedicated to investigating cases of enforced disappearances and holding perpetrators accountable (Akins 2017: 7; Amnesty International 2017C).

State and company strategies

China's interests in Pakistan are still heavily debated. One version of analysis holds that there is a strategic interest in gaining a land bridge to the Indian Ocean, with CPEC functioning as a transit route for goods and energy to flow between Xinjiang and Gwadar Port, thus reducing China's vulnerability to maritime choke points. This is debatable because the topography of the land route between China and the Arabian Sea is a huge challenge for a good transit route (Small 2017: 83). Although the existing Karakoram Highway was improved – with China's help – in the seventies (Rahman 2013: 132), the land route is regularly closed by landslides and also the costs of transporting energy by land via pipelines or other means are very expensive. The most reliable and economically efficient trade route will probably still be by sea (Small 2017: 83–84). Because the focus of the project lies on energy projects and internal infrastructure connections it is more likely that the two countries are envisaging broader-based industrial cooperation through special economic zones and other ventures. Although the term 'corridor' is evocative, CPEC is probably more accurately described as an investment package (2017: 84). Another argument can be made for strategic goals. Through CPEC, Pakistan's dependence on China will definitely increase and give China even more leverage over Pakistan. Although this might be a plausible argument, it is at odds with the historic relationship between the two states. Pakistan is already highly accommodating to Chinese preferences and, if necessary, China has already been able to forcefully exercise its leverage (2017: 85). A more striking explanation for China's strategic reasons for CPEC might be in relation to a broader security scheme of the region. In bolstering Pakistan's capabilities, China is creating an economically thriving partner who can fulfil the roles as a balancer in South Asia and security partner in and beyond the region. While China is stabilizing its western periphery through mitigating conflict risks and addressing militant threats, Pakistan can be a counterbalance to India and Western interests (2017: 85–86). Another reason for the big commitment of China in Pakistan might be the desire that CPEC as the 'flagship' of the BRI can demonstrate that the broader scheme can succeed and that being a friend of China brings clear economic benefits to participating countries. This line of argument suggests that CPEC, as an example of successful development through infrastructure, is being used by China to enchant other countries and actors in the BRI framework and that CPEC is in itself an anti-politics machine.

Inside Pakistan, tensions between Baloch nationalists and the Pakistani military led to various violent outbreaks resulting not only in enforced disappearances but also in extrajudicial killings. Military operations led to a great loss of civilian lives and have forced thousands of villagers to migrate to safer places. In some cases, security forces have burnt entire villages, forcing systematic migration of the indigenous Baloch people, indicating clearly that even systematic land grabbing is occurring. It remains very difficult for NGOs to obtain reliable data for Balochistan because of the inaccessibility of the region. Foreign journalists are given little, if any, access to Balochistan and local media often censor themselves in fear of retribution. Also, the Internet has been suspended in most parts of Balochistan, which makes the monitoring of the situation on the ground very difficult for human rights organizations[19]. This might be interpreted as an effort of the anti-politics machine to enchant external eyes and ears.

The government's recent actions are increasingly concerning because they restrict the space for human rights defenders and NGOs. In 2015, a new policy for the regulation and registration of international NGOs was introduced. All international NGOs had to reapply for registration, and although a 60-day period

---

[19] Human Rights Council of Balochistan & Baloch Human Rights Organization (2018)

for the processing of applications was stipulated, many NGOs have been waiting for months for a result. While applications are pending, international NGOs are barred from working, and even if they were approved there is the fear that they would only be allowed to work in specified fields and locations in Pakistan after 'consultations with relevant federal and provincial authorities'. Many Organizations fear that work on human rights advocacy might be curtailed in certain regions of the country as a result. Balochistan is especially at risk of being a victim of such practices (Amnesty International 2017B: 6).

In regard to foreign companies, most of them being Chinese, Pakistan is still perceived as a difficult, unfamiliar and insecure location. Although the Pakistani government is welcoming and tries hard to assure foreign investors and companies that they will be protected, it seems that operating under constant armed guard is not seen as reassuring. High potential returns and healthy financing from state development banks hardly change that (Small 2017: 83).

Conclusion

Globalization is changing the fundamental structures of our political, social and economic realities and the world seems to become smaller through increasing connectivity and cooperation between nation states. National territory is often not enough anymore to satisfy the needs of consumers and investors, so new solutions to this phenomenon are surfacing around the globe. Capitalism is expanding and thus implies the contest over the definition and control of resources (Rasmussen and Lund 2018B: 388). Many national states are trying to push their 'frontiers'. Mega-infrastructure projects like the BRI (and CPEC) can be seen as such an attempt to push one's development and need for cooperation even further. Projects of this size have considerable impacts on almost every aspect of life in the area where this development takes place, thus naturally such projects ignite expectations and desires in the minds of the people in its reach. CPEC was introduced eight years ago. It is a highly ambitious project under the BRI framework of the Chinese government and was welcomed warm-heartedly by the Pakistani government and the process of implementation started almost immediately. In the case of CPEC, this 'frontier' entered a difficult territory. The historic, religious, political, social and economic context of Pakistan and its province Balochistan is very complex and poses a strong challenge for the implementation of such a project.

Historically, Balochistan has always been a frontier space where local and global interests collide. Not only its geographic position but also its vast natural resources are of great strategic value to big global actors like the United States and China. Both have a vested interest in 'territorializing' this section of the earth. Since Balochistan is rich in resources, CPEC brings about a change in the perceived value of the area. Because of better access to strategic resources the prior mostly neglected region suddenly becomes very interesting for many actors. This brings into motion what Ferguson (1990) calls an 'anti-politics machine', which ultimately results in a situation where the local population and the existing systems of resource control are being overlooked and replaced, giving way to land and commons grabbing. Economically, Pakistan is a rather small partner of China, but the political and military cooperation of the two countries is at a very high level. Evidence suggests that Pakistan has a high level of comfort in accommodating Chinese preferences (Small 2017: 85) and that the Chinese government is trying to gain, or rather make, an important ally in Pakistan against the outside pressure from mainly the United States and its local ally India. In bolstering Pakistan's capabilities, China is trying to create an economically thriving partner that can fulfil the roles of a balancer in South Asia and security partner in and beyond the region (2017: 85–86). This research suggests that CPEC itself can actually be seen as an anti-politics machine deployed by the Chinese government, aimed at enchanting the Pakistani government and the local population as well as external eyes and ears. The United States has attempted similar development efforts in the region for a long time, but in this case, there is a tendency for Pakistan to be more comfortable in aligning itself with China rather than with the United States (Kondapalli 2012: 174–182). While there is no evidence that the national government is resisting this process in any way, the local population in Balochistan does not seem to fall for the attempts at enchanting them with promises and elicited desires. This is probably due to its long and troublesome history of dealing with the nation state.

Pakistan is a centralized nation state but at the same time scarred by internal divisions and conflicts. Because of its colonial history, the Punjab province is highly dominant in national affairs, which leaves a province like Balochistan – which constitutes almost half of the country's territory – at a great disadvantage. Balochistan has been a neglected province from the very beginning of the nation's history. Its people, although equally internally diverse and divided, generally feel a strong alienation towards the nation state and are united in strong opposition to CPEC. Five violent revolts since Pakistan's independence illustrate how the Baloch feel about foreign influence and dominance. This can be seen as a possible explanation for their disenchantment towards China's and Pakistan's anti-politics machine. CPEC is perceived as a foreign occupation and a plan for exploitation by the Punjab-dominated national government, and now China as well. There is even the fear that because of CPEC and its ramifications, the Baloch people will soon be a minority in their own land. Reported incidents of land and commons grabbing suggest that this fear is justified.

The official actors from both China's and Pakistan's government are exclusively highlighting the positive prospects linked to CPEC, clearly showing the attempt at enchantment. It is framed as a 'win-win' project for anybody involved (Arase 2015: 30). Promises of a better standard of living, a better income, millions of new jobs, business promotion and opportunity, and a better quality of education, are some of the main talking points from the official sides (Kanwal et al. 2019: 8–9). This enchanting narrative appeals to the natural desire to better one's living situation, but nevertheless, new economic opportunities through CPEC are likely to bypass the Baloch communities. The lack of education and skills required to fill positions around the modern set-up of CPEC projects poses an almost insurmountable hindrance for the local population of Balochistan to participate in and profit from the proposed development. As regards the environment, research suggests that China has advanced notably in the field of environmental protection, but still, massive negative effects can be expected from CPEC's realization (Foggin 2018: 1; Nabi et al. 2017: 3003–3004).

Reasonable questions and concerns about who will actually profit from CPEC are only vaguely, if at all, answered by the involved actors, and there is no evidence that the different affected local communities were included in a consultative process during the planning of CPEC. Although China propagates an inclusive process, it rather appears that this deal was negotiated in a very small elite circle of politicians and economists. The Chinese and Pakistani governments both badly want CPEC to be a success and are pushing for its swift implementation. This at times results in extreme measures. So-called 'insurgents' or opponents of the project are being dealt with by any means at the disposal of the nation state. Opposing forces to CPEC are officially viewed as insurgents or terrorists and the national government of Pakistan handles their pleas accordingly – with the endorsement and support of China. Various NGOs have mentioned deep concerns about the practices of the Pakistani government. They mention cases of civilians being tried by military courts and Islamic laws against blasphemy being utilized to suppress critical voices. This clearly illustrates the legal pluralism in the region and is intimately linked to the shift in value of the region due to CPEC. New power relations have emerged due to new circumstances generated by CPEC and are being legitimized by the different actors through development discourses on the one hand and mostly human rights and land-grabbing discourses on the other. Accusations of forced migration and human rights violations at the hand of the national government are high in number and only deepen the concern over cruel practices against the Baloch population. Land grabbing is taking place along the route of CPEC, but commons are also affected as the example of Baloch fishermen illustrates.

This research suggests that instead of lifting up its provinces, the nation state of Pakistan seems to rather invest in the securitization of its assets in the Baloch region to protect its own interests. So far, it appears that Pakistan's internal ethnic and economic divisions between the provinces are more likely to be exacerbated rather than resolved through CPEC. Eight years into the realization of CPEC, it is still difficult to make conclusive statements about who will eventually be able to profit from this project. It seems, though, despite heavy resistance, that the expansion of China's and the Pakistani national government's 'frontier', through its enchanting anti-politics machine CPEC, will not be halted in Balochistan. The Baloch people ultimately are the ones who suffer the consequences.

Property and access rights are changing due to the new increase in value of the region. This leads to land grabbing and commons grabbing, which can explain their violent resistance (Haller 2019; Haller et al. 2020). The anti-politics machine does not seem to work on the local level: the Baloch people resist the enchantment and try to strengthen their own bargaining power by deploying discourses of human rights violations and land grabbing. This research suggests that these circumstances do eventually lead to a situation where the local population is exposed to forms of resilience grabbing (Haller et al. 2020). The loss of their land and the access to commons, paired with the oppressive tactics of the nation state, leaves these communities weakened and often desperate. On the local level, the anti-politics machine seems to become a politics machine. The nation state seems to only deploy the discourse of development towards external eyes and ears since it is clearly aware that the Baloch people are not likely to be enchanted by infrastructure projects like CPEC.

References

Published books and articles

Amnesty International (2014). Amnesty International Public Statement (5 February 2014). *Pakistan: Mass graves a stark reminder of violations implicating the state in Balochistan* ‹https://www.amnesty.org/download/Documents/8000/asa330012014en.pdf› last accessed on 29.11.2019

Amnesty International (2016). *"As good as dead": The impact of the blasphemy laws in Pakistan* ‹https://www.amnesty.org/download/Documents/ASA3351362016ENGLISH.PDF› last accessed on 25.11.2019

Amnesty International (2017A). Amnesty International submission for the UN universal periodic review, 28th session of the UPR working group (November 2017). *Pakistan: Widespread Human Rights violations continue* ‹https://www.amnesty.org/download/Documents/ASA3365132017ENGLISH.PDF› last accessed on 28.11.2019

Amnesty International (2017B). Submission to the United Nations Committee on economic, social and cultural rights, 61st session (May-June 2017). *Pakistan* ‹https://www.amnesty.org/download/Documents/ASA3361002017ENGLISH.PDF› last accessed on 24.11.2019

Amnesty International (2017C). *"… Pakistan: End enforced disappearances now"* ‹https://www.amnesty.org/en/latest/research/2017/11/pakistan-end-enforced-disappearances-now/› last accessed on 14.11.2019

Akins, H. (2017). *China in Balochistan: CPEC and the Shifting Security Landscape of Pakistan.* Policy Brief. Tennessee, USA: Howard H. Baker Jr. Center for Public Policy.

Ali, A., Shang, J., & Saif, U. (2018). *Socio-economic impact of CPEC on agricultural productivity of Pakistan: A principal component analysis.* International Journal of Food and Agricultural Economics (IJFAEC), 6(1128-2019-549), 47-57.

Arase, D. (2015). *China's two silk roads initiative: What it means for Southeast Asia.* Southeast Asian Affairs, 2015(1), 25-45.

Casarini, N. (2016). *When all roads lead to Beijing. Assessing China's New Silk Road and its implications for Europe.* The International Spectator, 51(4), 95-108.

Coenen, J., Bager, S., Meyfroidt, P., Newig, J., & Challies, E. (2020). *Environmental governance of China's Belt and Road Initiative.* Environmental Policy and Governance, 31(1), 3-17.

De Vries, P. (2007). *Don't compromise your desire for development! A Lacanian/Deleuzian rethinking of the anti-politics machine.* Third World Quarterly, 28(1), 25-43.

Fabietti, U. (2011). *Ethnography at the Frontier. Space, Memory and Society in Southern Baluchistan.* Zurich: Peter Lang.

Farooqui, M. A., & Aftab, S. M. (2018, September). *China–Pakistan Economic Corridor; Prospects and Challenges for Balochistan, Pakistan.* In IOP Conference Series: Materials Science and Engineering, 414(1), p. 012046). IOP Publishing.

Ferguson, James (1990). *The Anti-Politics Machine: "Development," Depoliticization and Bureaucratic Power in Lesotho.* Cambridge: Cambridge University Press

Foggin, J. M. (2018). *Environmental conservation in the Tibetan Plateau region: Lessons for China's Belt and Road Initiative in the mountains of Central Asia.* Land, 7(2), 52.

Haines, C. (2012). *Nation, Territory, and Globalization in Pakistan: Traversing the Margins.* Routledge.

Haller, Tobias (2019). Towards a new institutional political ecology: how to marry external effects, institutional change and the role of power and ideology in commons studies. In: Haller, Tobias; Breu, Thomas; De Moor, Tine; Rohr, Christian; Znoj, Heinzpeter (Hg.) *The Commons in a Glocal World: Global Connections and Local Responses. Earthscan Studies in Natural Resource Management.* London: Routledge.

Haller, T., Käser, F., & Ngutu, M. (2020). *Does Commons grabbing lead to resilience grabbing? The anti-politics machine of neo-liberal agrarian development and local responses.* Land 2020, 9(7), 220.

Harvey, P., & Knox, H. (2012). *The enchantments of infrastructure.* Mobilities, 7(4), 521-536.

Human Rights Council of Balochistan & Baloch Human Rights Organization (2018) *Balochistan: The State of Human Rights 2018* ‹https://secureservercdn.net/160.153.138.163/mhz.7b9.myftpupload.com/wp-content/uploads/2019/05/annual-report-2018-final-2.pdf› last accessed 19.11.2019

Jaffrelot, C. (Ed.). (2004). *A History of Pakistan and its Origins.* Anthem Press.

Kanwal, S., Chong, R., & Pitafi, A. H. (2019). *China–Pakistan economic corridor projects development in Pakistan: Local citizens benefits perspective.* Journal of Public Affairs, 19(1), e1888.

Kondapalli, S. (2012). *Testing China's Rise: China–Pakistan relations. Pakistan's Stability Paradox (pp. 174-189).* London: Routledge.

Lau, M. (2005). *The Role of Islam in the Legal System of Pakistan.* Brill Nijhoff.

Long, R. D., Singh, G., Samad, Y., & Talbot, I. (Eds.). (2015). *State and Nation-building in Pakistan: Beyond Islam and Security.* Routledge.

Nabi, G., Khan, S., Ahmad, S., Khan, A., & Siddique, R. (2017). *China–Pakistan Economic Corridor (CPEC): an alarming threat to the biodiversity of Northern Pakistan.* Biodiversity and Conservation, 26(12), 3003-3004.

Qadeer, M. (2006). *Pakistan-social and Cultural Transformations in a Muslim Nation.* Routledge.

Rahman, K. (2013). *New Silk Road Initiative and Pak-China Relations.* Policy Perspectives, 131-145.

Ramay, S. A. (2016). *China Pakistan economic corridor: A Chinese dream being materialized through Pakistan.* Sustainable Development Policy Institute. http://hdl.handle.net/11540/6694.

Rasmussen, M. B., & Lund, C. (2018A). *Frontier spaces: Territorialization and resource control.* Policy Briefs (Copenhagen Centre for Development Research), 2018(01).

Rasmussen, M. B., & Lund, C. (2018B). *Reconfiguring frontier spaces: The territorialization of resource control.* World Development, 101, 388-399.

Shah, A. R. (2018). *How does China–Pakistan economic corridor show the limitations of China's 'One Belt One Road' model.* Asia & the Pacific Policy Studies, 5(2), 378-385.

Shen, S. X. H. (2015). *New Silk Road project.* East Asia, 32(1), 1-5.

Small, A. (2017). *First movement: Pakistan and the Belt and Road initiative.* Asia Policy, 24(1), 80-87.

Sternberg, T., Ahearn, A., & McConnell, F. (2017). *Central Asian 'characteristics' on China's new Silk Road: The role of landscape and the politics of infrastructure.* Land, 6(3), 55.

Summers, T. (2016). China's *'New Silk Roads': Sub-national regions and networks of global political economy.* Third World Quarterly, 37(9), 1628-1643.

Talbot, I. (2012). *Pakistan: A New History.* Hurst.

Unrepresented Nations & Peoples Organization (March 2017). *Balochistan: An Insight into the CPEC and its Consequences for the Baloch* ‹https://unpo.org/article/19988› last accessed on 28.11.2019

Wu, S., Liu, L., Liu, Y., Gao, J., Dai, E., Feng, A., & Wang, W. (2019*) . The Belt and Road: Geographical pattern and regional risks.* Journal of Geographical Sciences, 29(4), 483-495.

Media and social media sources

Baluch, F. (2018): Twitter post (December 27, 2018) ‹https://twitter.com/Faiz_Baluch/status/1078292234452287489› last accessed on 28.11.2019

Baluch, T. (2018): Balochwarna News (May 2018). *CPEC: A death warrant for the Baloch nation* ‹http://balochwarna.com/2018/05/13/cpec-a-death-warrant-for-the-baloch-nation/› last accessed on 26.11.2019

BBC News Asia (May 2019*) . Pakistan attack: Gunmen storm five-star hotel in Balochistan* ‹https://www.bbc.com/news/world-asia-48238759› last accessed on 27.11.2019

Business Standard (August 2017). *Balochistan: The biggest hindrance to China's CPEC ambitions* ‹https://www.business-standard.com/article/international/balochistan-the-biggest-hindrance-to-china-s-cpec-ambitions-117082100302_1.html› last accessed on 27.11.2019

Dashti N. (2017): Balochistan Times (May 2017). *CPEC: the Baloch Perspective* ‹http://balochistantimes.com/cpec-baloch-perspective/› last accessed on 27.11.2019

Fatah, T. (2019): Twitter post (May 20, 2019) ‹https://twitter.com/TarekFatah/status/1130
    415660058775553› last accessed on 28.11.2019
Kulmeer, A. (2017): Balochistan Times (December 2017). *CPEC: A game changer or a
    disaster?* ‹https://balochistantimes.com/cpec-a-game-changer-or-a-disaster/› last accessed on 28.11.2019
Pakistan Population (2019). ‹http://worldpopulationreview.com/countries/pakistan/› last
    accessed on 22.11.2019
Population of Balochistan Census 2017 (2017). ‹http://www.pakinformation.com/population/balochistan.html› last accessed on 25.11.2019
Population of Cities in Pakistan (2019). ‹http://worldpopulationreview.com/countries/pakistan-population/cities/› last accessed on 23.11.2019

On the Margins of the Belt and Road.
Commons Grabbing and Environmental Degradation on the Tibetan Plateau

Tenzin Dawa Kongpo, independant researcher; Stephy-Mathew Moozhiyil, Institute of Social Anthropology, University of Bern, Switzerland

Introduction

The Belt and Road Initiative (BRI) is an infrastructure project officially launched by the People's Republic of China under Xi Jinping in 2013. It comprises two ambitious projects. On land, the *Silk Road Economic Belt* envisions new infrastructures in the form of roads, railways, industrial estates and special economic zones stretching across Central Asia to Europe. On water, the *21st Century Maritime Silk Road* focuses on maritime trade routes, deep-water ports, and special development zones throughout the South China Sea and the Indian Ocean. To reach these ambitious goals, China is mobilizing enormous financial resources through powerful policy banks and dedicated financial infrastructures (Rippa, Murton and Rest 2020: 85).

The BRI has to be interpreted as a project aimed at externalizing China's overproduction and overaccumulation as well as related crisis tendencies (Sum 2019: 528). It is therefore mainly a geo-economic project, which is at the same time intertwined with geopolitical aspects and challenges (Jessop and Sum 2018: 476). In recent years, large-scale infrastructure development has also been implemented on the Tibetan Plateau. The reconstruction of historical trade routes and the reopening of border crossings throughout the region have resulted in new overland connections, which are significantly transforming political-economic systems and sociocultural relations for the population of Tibet (Murton 2016: 328). At the same time, the Chinese central government is implementing the construction of hydropower projects, the upgrading of road networks, the expansion of trade and border facilities, and is surveying the possibilities for new infrastructural megaprojects, such as the trans-Himalayan railway and international transmission lines. The largest recent infrastructure project in Tibet is the extension of the railway network between Chengdu (Sichuan) and Lhasa, as well as from Lhasa to the Nepalese border.

As it has become nearly impossible for researchers to do fieldwork in Tibet in recent years due to current political developments[20], new ethnographic insights about local contexts are almost non-existent. Therefore, this chapter also relies on NGO reports and mainly addresses larger 'trends', discourses and conflict lines that emerge in the context of the BRI on the Tibetan Plateau. These are related to the mutually reinforcing nexus between infrastructure and mining, of which the extension of the railway network is part, dam and hydropower projects as well as related resettlement projects, especially of pastoralist nomads. These projects are accompanied by discourses and related measures of sustainable development and environmental conservation. However, due to processes of commons grabbing they result in land use conflicts and diminishing territories for pastoralism, as well as in resettlement projects and precarity of existence for pastoralist nomads, and, moreover, to the environmental degradation of grasslands. The BRI generally remains highly contested and is bound to further exacerbate both environmental and social conflicts on the Tibetan Plateau and to reproduce underlying contradictions and crisis tendencies emanating from GDP-oriented growth.

Part 1: Historical, environmental, ethnographic and political context

History and current context

Since its incorporation by the People's Republic of China in 1951, Tibet has become an area of development and economic reform for the central government in Beijing. While the government under Mao Zedong until 1978 focused on implementing processes of collectivization as well as centralization of land use and agriculture, the Chinese Economic Reform from the 1980s under Deng Xiaoping initiated policies of decollectivization of land as well as regional development strategies. In 1999, the Chinese government proclaimed the 'Open up the West' or 'Going West' strategy with the aim of addressing uneven development and regional inequalities between eastern China and the western provinces (Yeh and Wharton 2016: 287, 297). The main agenda of the Going West strategy was the construction of large-scale infrastructure such as gas pipelines, electricity transfer projects and the South-North Water transfer project, as well as the Qinghai-Tibet Railway (Yeh and Wharton 2016: 290). While one effect of the Going West strategy has been an increase in resource extraction, the programme has been implemented in minority areas, particularly in Xinjiang and the Tibet Autonomous Region with the goals of consolidating state integration, social stability, national security and unity including through Han-Chinese in-migration to minority ar-

---

[20] Email correspondence with Prof. Dr Emily T. Yeh and Ariell Ahearn Ligham in August 2019.

eas (Yeh and Wharton 2016: 290). Additionally, resettlement and sedentarization projects for pastoralist nomads within policies of 'Constructing a Socialist Countryside', 'Ecological Migration' and 'Comfortable Housing Project' have been implemented since the mid-1990s and within the Going West strategy, leading to mass relocations on the Tibetan Plateau (Mills and May 2018: 3). Discourses of development for the western provinces and related practices of the Chinese government are therefore part of a longer and continual process.

In July 2010 a 'new round' of the Going West programme was announced by central authorities with the aim of turning western China into a "bridgehead" for the rest of Asia and on which the BRI builds (Summers 2016 in: Yeh and Wharton 2016: 291). Infrastructure projects from the Going West strategy, such as the Qinghai-Tibet Railway, are now being extended beyond China's borders under the BRI label (Yeh and Wharton 2016: 291). Hoering suggests that the BRI 'is a collective name for a conglomerate of already existing, planned or even just envisioned projects for which the Chinese government is still seeking partners' (2018: 19). The project has important technological and financial as well as clear infrastructural, commercial and commodity chain aspects (Jessop and Sum 2018: 475). At the same time, it is also a cybernetic project including telecommunication, fibre optics and cybersecurity (ibid.: 476).

Contrary to predominant Western interpretations, Tim Summers (2016: 1638) argues, while not denying the relevance of geopolitics, that the BRI is primarily a 'spatial fix' to (temporarily) resolve the inner crisis tendencies of capitalist development by means of geographical expansion and spatial restructuring (see Harvey 2001: 24–25), rather than a geopolitical manoeuvre. Zhang (2017: 317) observes an overproduction tendency and excess capacity of the Chinese economy since the mid-1990s. While China's economic development has lowered poverty levels, it has also sharply increased social inequalities (Panitch and Gindin 2013: 153). Household consumption has dropped from a share of 50% of GDP in the early 1980s to 36% in 2007 (compared to 70% in the United States), with purchasing power stagnating on a low level (ibid.: 153, 155). This implies that China's economic growth is mainly export driven, thereby explaining the importance of extending its connectivity through infrastructure projects and investments to reach new markets and to ensure the supply of raw material as well as labour. However, the expansion potential of the Chinese economy has become restricted due to the weakening of significant export markets and trade conflicts, especially with the United States. At the same time, wages in the main industrial areas along the Chinese east coast are rising due to years of labour disputes; together with massive overcapacities, profitability and growth rates in heavy industries are declining (Hoering 2018: 27–28). Therefore, the BRI, which brings together China's westward and outward strategies, whereby Tibet is situated at the crossroads of these strategies (Yeh and Wharton 2016: 291; 310), is a central part of an internal (temporary) crisis solution to overaccumulation tendencies by combining the restructuring of production conditions with new geographical spaces for manoeuvre and accumulation for Chinese corporations (Hoering 2018: 32; Sum 2019: 528; 533).

As a connection of joint efforts of the state and representatives of Chinese capital, this form of crisis solution is at the same time transfigured as a contribution to the development of participating regions and countries, but also as a crisis solution for the global capitalist system (Hoering 2018: 32). The official narrative of the Chinese government conveys a harmonious and romantic picture of the project drawing from the legacy of the ancient Silk Road leading to prosperity, economic growth and stability through the provision of infrastructure and connectivity for the international community with proactive state support from China (Hoering 2018: 20). In the context of the ongoing global economic stagnation since 2007/2008, the Chinese government suggests a new inclusive development and globalization paradigm, which seems to offer an alternative to Western development discourses and previous neoliberal globalization models (Hoering 2018: 20), underlining a win-win outcome for all partners (Jessop and Sum 2018: 477). Additionally, the BRI is linked with the justification that it would address global challenges such as climate change and contribute to global ecological security (Jessop and Sum 2018: 477). Official plans state the necessity of combining sustainable development with ecological protection, which includes the creation of biodiversity conservation and environmental restauration areas (Bixler et al. 2015: 174; Foggin 2018: 7; Zheng 2017). Moreover, protected areas are introduced by the Chinese government as a means to achieve the *UN Sustainability Goals* and the linked *Paris Agreement* to limit global warming (Foggin 2018: 8; Ministry of Foreign Affairs of the People's Republic of China 2016a, 2016b). The BRI, therefore, has also been summarized by the Chinese government under the slogan of a '[g]reen, healthy, intelligent and peaceful Silk Road' (State Information Center 2017).

While these are, according to Harvey and Knox (2012: 524), processes of 'enchantment', which are a constitutive part of development projects, and while the new financial institutions created with the BRI do indeed offer an alternative to the dependence on the International Monetary Fund and the World Bank, there are at the same time disenchanting developments of the BRI, which the Tibetan case foregrounds. Contrary to win-win discourses, political economic approaches underline that the true costs of mega-projects are in general externalized and mainly borne by local populations (Rogers and Wilmsen 2020: 260). Moreover, mega-infrastructure projects are constitutively linked with the aim of increasing extraction of natural resources for a mode of production determined by economic growth (Hildyard and Sol 2017: 18). This tendency in turn reinforces potential land use conflicts with local populations.

Mega-infrastructure projects and ideas of development are therefore a conflicting field. This aspect is often veiled by processes of depoliticization by reducing them to dimensions of implementation and technical matters without considering conflicts of interest, related political processes and contexts of power relations causing the problems, which 'development' actually aims to overcome (e.g. poverty) (Ziai 2016: 109-110) and therewith leading to what Ferguson (1990: 256) calls an anti-politics machine. With regard to Tibet, conflicts are centred on the question of pastoral forms of living and production in the context of infrastructure projects, which reinforce extractivism as well as dam construction projects and related programmes of resettlement and land enclosure. The latter two are also part of environmental conservation programmes running parallel to infrastructure and extraction projects.

Geography, ecosystem, cultural landscape and resource use on the Tibetan Plateau

Grasslands account for about 42% of China's territory. They are mainly located in the five key pastoralist provinces of Inner Mongolia, the Tibet Autonomous Region (TAR), Qinghai, Xinjiang and Gansu. This area is inhabited by 161.5 million people, who herd the largest population of sheep and goats and the fourth-largest concentration of cattle in the world (Williams 1996; Liu 2010 in Yeh 2015: 1175). Part of it is the Tibetan Plateau, which comprises the Tibetan Autonomous Region, the Province of Qinghai and parts of Gansu and Sichuan as well as the southern part of Xinjiang. The traditional Tibetan denomination of the regions divides the Tibetan Plateau into three parts, namely Ü-Tsang, Amdo and Kham.

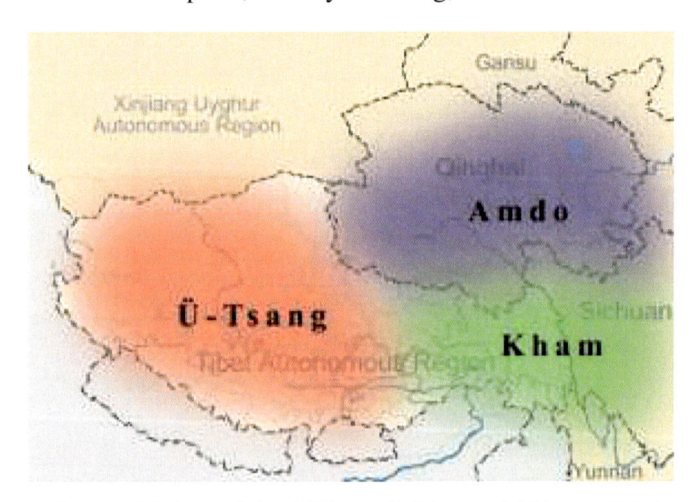

Map 1: Tibetan Plateau with the traditional Tibetan divisions and Chinese administrative regions. Source: Wikivoyage ‹https://en.wikivoyage.org/wiki/Old_Tibetan_provinces#/media/File:Tibet_provinces.png›_accessed on 31.10.2021

It spreads over a distance of 3,000 km from east to west and 1,500 km from north to south, with an estimated 1.6 million square kilometres of grasslands. A third of the population on the Tibetan Plateau, i.e. over two million, are pastoralists and agro-pastoralists, who herd around 12 million yaks and 30 million sheep and goats (Kernan 2013: 3; Næss 2013: 124). The large majority of the population are Tibetan and speak different regional varieties of the language. Kazakh and Mongolian nomads are a minority mainly living in the Province of Qinghai.

As the altitude in most parts of the Tibetan Plateau is above 3,500 m and therefore too cold for crop cultivation, pastoralist nomadism, i.e. animal husbandry, has been a predominant form of production and subsistence among the population for over 5,000 years (Foggin 2018: 9; Næss 2013: 124; Bates and Lees 1977 in Tan 2018: 2; Miller 1999: 16). Mobility is a key feature of nomadic subsistence on Tibetan rangelands and centred around the movement of livestock to different pastures and the search for favourable forage conditions while taking into consideration factors such as past use, snowfall and rainfall, growth stages of the grass and the conditions of the herd (Miller 1999: 17). While the specific migration patterns on the Tibetan Plateau are diverse, there are generally seasonal migration patterns between summer pastures (often located at higher altitudes) and winter pastures with a winter base (located at lower altitudes) and frequent smaller moves within these two areas (Joshi et al. 2020: 2; Yeh and Gaerrang 2011). While herding and livestock are traditionally organized on the household level, rangeland is held in common apart from some areas in central Tibet, where pastures were owned by monasteries rather than by tribal or kinship groups (Yudannima 2017: 273; Yeh and Gaerrang 2011). Pasture use and the movement of animals are organized along rules and commonly determined cycles of rotation, which take into account herd size as well as a fair access to good and bad pastures (Yudannima 2017: 275; Næss 2013: 128; Tan 2018: 27). In sum, pastoralism on the Tibetan Plateau is practised by means of shared access and resources, which are part of the commons and related forms of institutions and governance systems.

As well as seasonal migration to urban areas, diversification of labour, of livestock (yak and goats grazing on different plants and therefore maximizing rangeland vegetation use) and of products, mainly milk products and textiles from animal hair and to a lesser extent meat, are part of the survival strategy of Tibetan pastoralist nomadism. These products are exchanged against staples from agricultural production at lower altitudes or industrially manufactured goods such as canvas. Tibetan nomadic pastoralism is therefore constitutively linked to other forms of production. While trade and commodification, for instance of yak meat, goat wool or of the caterpillar fungus used in traditional medicine and traded for $31,000 per kg (as of 2018), are on the rise, there are at the same time countering actions of incarnate lamas and monks for vegetarianism and conservationism and an increased community censure of large-scale caterpillar fungus harvesting. Despite social change, religious and cultural aspects of normativity among Tibetan nomadic pastoralists persist, related to Buddhism, as expressed in the Tibetan term *drelwa*, foregrounding a mutual relationship of care and nurturing with other beings and nature, implying a relation with animals beyond the value of a commodity (Miller 1999: 18; Næss 2013: 125; Tan 2018: 5, 10, 25, 38–9, 143, 169).

Overall, mobility and diversification strategies that characterize the practices of nomadic pastoralism on the Tibetan Plateau permit the adaption to, and survival in, the extreme environmental conditions in the considered area (Tan 2018: 174, Naess 2013: 123). With its capacity to adapt to the environment by means of mobility and diversification, pastoralism is one of the most sustainable food production systems (Foggin 2018: 22). Moreover, Tibetan pastoralist nomadism forms an integral part of the ecology of the high grasslands. For instance, a type of sedge accounting for most of the grasslands cannot propagate without the specific grazing techniques of yaks (Tan 2018: 175). However, the constitutive aspects of mobility and shared access of pastoralist nomads to grasslands in western China have become a contentious issue in the context of governmentality and development as well as modernization and environmental conservation projects of the Chinese government.

National economy and legal frameworks: politics of development and processes of commons grabbing on the Tibetan Plateau since 1950

Under Chinese rule, the flexibility of access and use of pastures as well as mobility have been restricted. The corresponding reforms are related to discourses problematizing pastoralism as a form of life and production. These are especially the so-called 'tragedy of the commons' discourses (see Hardin 1968), which affirm the supposed unsustainability of pastoralism and the management of common-pool resources, linked to a discourse of 'backwardness' and inefficiency of pastoralism (Bum 2018: 522–523; Tan 2018: 49). This has led to the targeting of pastoralist nomadism since the People's Republic of China rule in Tibet in the 1950s.

While in a first step, the ownership of herds was transferred from household units to cooperatives and also the distribution of pastoral products collectivized under Maoist development projects from 1958 onwards (Tan 2018: 47; Yeh and Gaerrang 2011), livestock, in a second step, was decollectivized with the Household Responsibility System in the 1980s leading to a return to the household as the basic unit of production while pasture remained common property. It led to a system similar to traditional common property arrangements before collectivization in the 1950s (Yeh 2015: 1175). After the introduction of the Grassland Law in 1985, however, rangeland use rights also began to be reallocated to households with the argument that individual household tenure based on land leasing from the Chinese government is a necessary condition for sustainable rangeland management and increased production (Banks 2001 in Næss 2013: 128, Williams 1996 in Næss 2013: 128). The law was implemented in the eastern parts of the Tibetan Plateau in the 1990s and in the 2000s in the Tibetan Autonomous Region province.

This development has to be situated in the context of the Chinese Economic Reform initiated by Deng Xiaoping since 1978, and especially the 'Southern Tour' Reforms of 1992 adapting a neoliberal rationalizing discourse with the aim of an economic liberalization, which also included processes of decollectivization of land tenure by introducing fences with the aim of achieving individual accountability for a more sustainable use of pastures and the promotion of commercial lifestock production (Yeh and Gaerrang 2011: 165; Miller 2000: 104).

The *Going West* development strategy announced in 1999 led to the modification of the Grassland Law in 2002, addressing the problem of increased pasture degradation across China by means of restricting the access for nomadic pastoralists and resettlement projects. It is based on the erroneous but dominant view that nomadic pastoralism leads to degradation of pastures through irrational management and overgrazing beyond carrying capacity (Yeh, Samberg, Gaerrang, Volkmar and Harris 2017: 323). This has led to the introduction of fences and access bans as well as ecological resettlement projects, for instance in Sanjiangyuan, the watershed area of major Asian rivers in Qinghai, where pastoralists have been resettled from the mid-2000s onwards and a natural resource conservation area has been created (Bauer and Nyima 2010: 27–28; Dell'Angelo 2013; Bixler et al. 2015: 173). Moreover, in 2009 a complementary policy addressing pastoralist nomadism with the *Nomad Settlement project* was introduced with the aim of transforming nomadic pastoralism to intensive agriculture and ranching to achieve an increased output from animal husbandry (Tan 2018: 48).

Altogether, the implementation of the new policies with efforts to sedentarize pastoralist nomads and to intensify their production base through fencing, grazing limitations, resettlement and sedentarization have led, contrary to policy expectations, to intensified grassland degradation and more concentrated trampling and grazing because of the reduction of flexible mobility as well as the diminished capacity of pastoralist nomads to sustain livelihoods. This is caused by the infringement of the principle in pastoralist nomadism of minimizing the risk of disease or loss and maximizing scarce resources by means of diversification and mobility due to the reduction of customary access to common-pool resources with the establishment of nature reserves and conservation enclosures (Yeh, Samberg, Gaerrang, Volkmar and Harris 2017. 324; Tan 2018: 2, 48; Yeh 2015: 1173–4; Li, Fassnacht, Storch and Bürgi 2017: 2199).

Those developments can be compared to research from Sub-Saharan Africa, where nomadic pastoralists are confronted with policies introducing a transformation towards commercial ranching by means of demarcation of land, fencing and breed improvement in the context of the persisting myth of overgrazing, overstocking and land degradation by pastoralist nomads as well as projects of wildlife conservation and biodiversity on pastoralist land (Sullivan and Homewood 2003: 36–38; Haller 2020;). This linear development conception favours a transition away from small-scale and subsistence production towards capital-intensive investment and entrepreneurship-oriented large-scale agricultural production or industrial labour and is generalized by the expertise of international organizations as the World Bank (2008: 29). However, the related frameworks neglect the environmental and socio-economic rationalities of small-scale and subsistence production. While this results in people being separated from land, constituting their main means of subsistence, investors tend to externalize social and ecological problems such as questions of compensation, and meaningful poverty reduction and the transition to alternative forms of subsistence as they are not their main concern (Bauer and Nyima 2010; Li 2011: 281, 283).

Those processes of land grabbing, defined according to the International Land Coalition ILC as intransparent large-scale land acquisitions or concessions; violating human rights; not seeking free, prior or informed consent; disregarding social, economic and environmental impacts; or not based on democratic planning and participation (ILC 2011), are bound to rise in the context of infrastructure extension with the BRI and related development as well as resource extractivism projects. This often implies processes of 'commons grabbing' since systems of common property resources and institutions become disrupted, which also affects pastoralists, who depend on mobility and access to different pastures (Dell'Angelo, D'Odorico, Rulli and Marchand 2017: 2; 9), as is also the case on the Tibetan Plateau. Moreover, those processes are frequently legitimized by means of environmental agendas such as biodiversity and conservation. Affected communities come to be defined against nature as they are portrayed as environmentally destructive, backward and disordered and needing reconstruction to conform with modernist visions of sustainable development, which legitimizes processes of 'green grabbing' (Fairhead, Leach and Scoones 2012: 237–238; Adams 2004). This also constitutes a significant dimension of development projects and related land-grabbing processes on the Tibetan Plateau.

Furthermore, those policies and their implementation miss the point that land degradation in general is, according to Blaikie and Brookfield, to be set in context with processes of social marginalization. When land users are excluded from territories and hence marginalized due to environmental conservation or commercial exploitation such as infrastructure and mining, they are forced to use more marginal land. This land depletes at a faster rate and will be used by more people and livestock due to the exclusion from alternative territories. Therefore, land degradation will be additionally fuelled, and the economic viability of pastoralism or cultivation undermined. In sum, land degradation is both a result and cause of social marginalization (Blaikie and Brookfield 1994: 23). The loss of access to common-pool resources and the undermining of common property institutions generally lead to diminished livelihood options. Commons grabbing should therefore also be considered as 'resilience grabbing' as people lose a wide array of resources, which are not replaced within development projects and reduce the adaptive capacity within socio-ecological systems (Haller 2019: 2; 17–18; Gerber and Haller 2020: 17).

The following overview of BRI-related infrastructure and development projects on the Tibetan Plateau will serve to give more insights into discourses and conflicts with regard to commons and green grabbing as well as resettlement projects and forms of resistance.

Part 2: The belt and road initiative on the Tibetan Plateau

The BRI on the Tibetan Plateau and its impact cannot be reduced to a single specific project. Rather, it is characterized by a multitude of projects that reinforce the nexus between (sustainable) development discourses, infrastructure projects and resource extractivism.

Qinghai-Tibet Railway and the extension of the railway network on the Tibetan Plateau

After the occupation of Tibet by the People's Republic of China in 1950/51, a railway line to Tibet was planned for supplying the People's Liberation Army and Chinese settlers. In 1958, the construction of the first part of the line from Xining to Golmud was launched. Natural disasters and famines put the construction on hold. In 1979, the Xining-Golmud line was mainly completed by prisoners and initially only served to supply the Chinese army. It was not until 1984 that the Xining-Golmud line was opened for general rail traffic. The extension of the railway line from Golmud to Lhasa, known as the Qinghai-Tibet Railway, was only initiated in 2001 (Adler 2008: 9). The first train operated in 2006. As the world's highest railway, over 80% of the Qinghai-Tibet section is over 4,000 m above sea level. Passenger train services are available to Lhasa from several major cities in China, such as Beijing, with a journey time of 48 hours, or Shanghai and Guangzhou (Su and Wall 2009: 651). China's Ministry of Commerce and the China Railway Construction Corporation are currently extending the Qinghai-Tibet Railway across the Tibetan Plateau from Lhasa and Shigatse to Kyirong (30 km from the Nepalese border) between 2020 and 2022. A second major railway from Chengdu to Lhasa, the 'Sichuan-Tibet Railway', has been under construction since 2014/15 (The People's Government of Sichuan Province 2020). At the same time, China plans to extend the railway to bordering India, Nepal and Bhutan and aims to integrate Tibet into those new networks (ICT 2014).

Dam & hydro projects

With its sources of many of Asia's important rivers and river systems as well as its glaciers, Tibet is often called the "third pole of the world" or the "water tower"

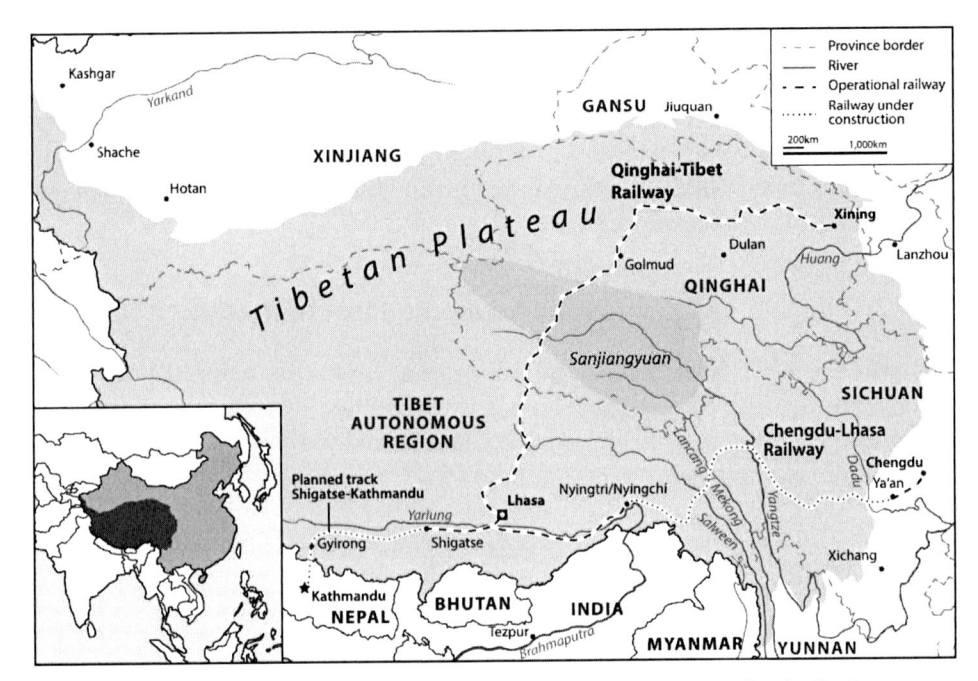

Map 2: The Tibetan Plateau with constructed and planned railway networks, the Sanjiangyuan conservation area and major rivers. Source: Map compilation and design by Manuel L. K. Abebe (2021), CDE, University of Bern, Bern, Switzerland. Geodata: GADM, Zhang et al. (2014)

(Yao et al. 2020). It has a fundamental significance to the environment of China, Asia and the world due to its downstream influence on approximately 40% of the world's population (Yu et al. 2012: 1979) and holds the largest store of fresh water outside the Arctic, providing water for one fifth of the global population, and it is a critical resource for the world's ten most densely populated nations surrounding it (Yao et al. 2020; Australia Tibet Council 2015: 8; ICT 2019: 3; Buckley 2015). However, the construction of mega-dams and bottling water directly from Tibet's glaciers are a high political priority for the Chinese authorities (ICT 2015a: 35).

Half of all the dams in the world are already on Chinese territory (Tilt 2015: xi). A major goal of China's Five-Year Plan (2016–2020) is to increase the number of hydropower dams on all major Tibetan rivers (ICT 2015a: 30) with the intention to integrate Tibet into the national grid to provide electricity for the urbanized east and locally; the electricity generated will also be used for mining and mineral processing (ICT 2015a: 29). A cascade of five large dams is planned for both the Salween, which still flows freely, and the Brahmaputra, where one dam has already been operational since 2015 (Buckley 2015). The Five-Year Plan of 2021–2025 suggests the implementation of the construction of new dams in the lower reaches of the Yarlung/Brahmaputra, close to the Indian border in the Nyingtri area (Stanway and Pullin/Reuters 2021; Modak 2020).

There are also hydro projects to divert water from Tibet's rivers for use in mines, factories and other industries. At the eastern edge of Tibet, canals from south to north diverting water from the Yangtze to the Yellow River, which would traverse the restive Tibetan prefectures of Ngaba/Aba, where the current wave of self-immolations began in 2009, and Kardze/Ganzi in Sichuan province are being built, with a third in the planning stage (ICT 2015a: 33). Moreover, plans call for the diversion of water from the Brahmaputra, the Salween and the Mekong, raising fears of a water war in Asia, especially from India (Arora and Goshal/Reuters 2020).

Mining in Tibet

Part of the 13th Five-Year Plan is the sourcing of raw materials needed for China's growth from Tibet rather than from imports. The ore deposits on the Tibetan Plateau are diverse, ranging from metals such as gold, copper, chromite, iron, aluminium, zinc, boron, lead and lithium to deposits of crude oil, asbestos, natural gas and coal (Del Bene and Gyaltsen 2015). Many of the large-scale mining sites are situated in the watersheds of Asia's major rivers (ICT 2015a: 58). The most detrimental form of mining for people's livelihoods is alluvial gold mining, which is generally small scale and unregulated. It is often practised with the use of cyanide or mercury (Nyima and Yeh 2016: 166). Copper and chromite are the other two main minerals on the Tibetan Plateau, which are also extracted on an industrial scale (ibid.). Apart from gold, which has become an important means of storing wealth among China's new rich (Lafitte 2013), Tibet's minerals do not have a large weight from a total supply perspective (Nyima and Yeh 2016: 167). Nevertheless, large-scale mining on the Tibetan Plateau is made profitable by means of concessional rate financing and state investment in infrastructure, especially with the extension of the railway network in Tibet, which has also been declared as part of the BRI (Nyima and Yeh 2016: 167; Del Bene and Gyaltsen 2015). The resulting extension of mining areas has led to a decrease in available land for nomadic pastoralists (Del Bene and Gyaltsen 2015).

Resettlement programmes and ecological conservation areas

Resettlement projects have been implemented in Tibet since the 1990s within the framework of poverty reduction, economic development, environmental protection strategies, ecology migration policy and sustainable development (Yeh and Wharton 2016; Bum 2018; Ptackova 2011). Since 2000, more than two million Tibetans have already been relocated or sedentarized (Mills and May 2018: 3). According to Human Rights Watch, the policies in Tibetan areas serve as a template for the resettlement of ethnic minority communities in other parts of the country, including Inner Mongolia and Xinjiang (2013: 4).

Figure 1: Mining in the Gyama Valley situated approx. 70 km east of Lhasa. Source: Tibetan Review ‹https://www.tibetanreview.net/china-expanding-controversial-mining-site-near-lhasa/›_accessed on 31.10.21

Figure 2: A nomadic resettlement village in Yulshul prefecture (Qinghai Province). Source: Tibetan Review ‹https://www.tibetanreview.net/wp-content/uploads/2017/10/ Tibetan-Nomad-Homes.jpg›_accessed on 31.10.2021

The Sanjiangyuan area is a current example of resettlement projects for pastoralist nomads legitimized by environmental conservation (Woo/Reuters 2019). The Sanjiangyuan area covering 363,000 km^2 in Qinghai, an important area for pastoralist nomadism, was formally established as a conservation area at the beginning of the 2000s within the Going West strategy and linked environmental sustainability plans (Bixler et al. 2015: 171, 174). It led to the sedentarization of pastoralist nomads from 2005 onwards as they are considered to be a stressor for the ecology and responsible for the degradation of the grasslands in this area, where the headwaters of the Yellow, the Yangtse and the Mekong rivers are located (Dell'Angelo 2013; Foggin 2018: 9). However, research from Lehnert et al. (2016) foregrounds that climate change and not overstocking is responsible for the degradation of grasslands on the Tibetan Plateau. Meanwhile, the Sanjiangyuan area was declared as the first pilot national park with effect from 2020 (Foggin 2018: 7). Moreover, as of 2018, roughly two thirds of the Tibetan Plateau are considered to be 'National Key Ecological Function areas', either for water source conservation or for biodiversity maintenance (ibid.: 8). It remains to be seen how the extension of those new policies and projects for environmental conservation will affect pastoralist nomadism on the Tibetan Plateau beyond the Sanjiangyuan area.

Environmental and social impacts of the development-infrastructure-extractivism Nexus

With regard to resettlement projects, although government subsidies and material provisions are provided, the socio-economic transformation in terms of integration into new means of livelihoods and the time and resources that are necessary to appropriate new labour skills for an urban labour market are not taken into consideration (e.g. Gyal 2015; Sodnamkyid and Sułek 2017; Nyima and Yeh 2016: 164). This problem is further accentuated as former Tibetan pastoralist nomads face discrimination from ethnic majority groups in the resettlement areas in daily life as well as in recruiting processes and on the labour market in general (e.g. Gyal 2015: 252, 256; Ptackova 2012; Bum 2018). Overall, it leaves them more dependent on subsidies and with reduced standards of living, working and health conditions (Nyima and Yeh 2016: 164). Tashi and Foggin (2012: 149) summarize the challenges from cultural matters– the technical issues of particular concern include the irrigation system (water pumping stations), loss of quality farmland topsoil, inappropriate house design, poor extension service or acquisition of new information, and loss of traditional agricultural knowledge – to inadequate levels of contentment in resettled areas. As families often have to cover follow-up costs resulting from resettlement, they are also more likely to be driven into debt (Fischer 2015). Notwithstanding, the incentive to resettle is also set by a reduction or withdrawal of health and educational services in rural areas. Fischer (2012) observes a correlation between the geographic spread of the Tibetan protests, including incidents of self-immolation, and resettlement projects. Moreover, the implementation of enclosure policies has been widened as tools for broader national development projects in infrastructure and the control of areas for mineral extraction, although they are legitimized by the argument of environmental protection (Bauer and Nyima 2010: 27–28). While the Grassland Law fencing policy leaves a degree of agency and negotiation with local officers regarding the implementation on the local level, ecological resettlement has led to more intense forms of social dislocation and exacerbation of the vulnerability of Tibetan livelihoods (Nyima and Yeh 2016: 165), throwing into relief at the same time the dimension of resilience grabbing.

However, it is mining that causes the gravest environmental problems for Tibetans, as Nyima and Yeh argue (2016: 166). Conflicts are related to environmental pollution of pastures and water bodies by heavy metals, which also causes the death of livestock and is a potential threat to downstream water quality, as well as land alienation or access bans and broken promises for compensation and restoration (Nyima and Yeh 2016: 167; Del Bene and Gyaltsen 2015; ICT 2015a: 58). The infrastructure projects under the BRI are bound to extend related conflicts over land use. Moreover, mining is dependent on hydroelectric plants and dams (Del Bene and Gyaltsen 2015), which are an additional source of land use conflict. While reducing the availability of land and river ecosystems, Chinese environmentalists, as well as scientists such as Wang Weiluo from the University of Dortmund, raise their concerns about the safety of populations due to the construction of dams in high mountain and earthquake-prone areas (ICT 2015a: 32). Furthermore, mining was extended in 2013 to parts of the Sanjiangyuan nature conservation area (Del Bene and Gyaltsen 2015), throwing into relief the difficulty of combining BRI development aims with environmental conservation.

In sum, there is a continuity of marginalization of nomadic pastoral forms of subsistence in the context of the BRI development-infrastructure-extractivism nexus and related discourses of environmental conservationism, reinforcing tendencies of commons grabbing.

Local people's and NGO strategies

Voices against the extension of the railway network

Already with the construction of the Qinghai-Tibet Railway doubts about the benefit for the local rural population have been raised amid fears of 'colonization' from the Tibetan government in exile (DIIR 2007) and 'sinicization' by means of 'civilization' and development projects (Adler 2008: 10) as well as distortions created by the industrial and urban orientation of the infrastructure project for a majority of the population that still lives in rural areas depending on subsistence production (Holcombe 2002 in ICT 2002). According to the Free Tibet Campaign, the local population is often unfavourable toward railway construction due to social and environmental impacts (2007), which include the fuelling of exploitation of natural resources by means of railway infrastructure extended under the BRI (Chaudhury 2019).

Protest movements against dam, hydro & mining projects

There is also strong sympathy and activism in NGOs among many Chinese for the preservation of the Tibetan Plateau, despite the dangers of such support. For instance, the famous author Zhang Yihe asked in a message on social media: "Why must we also build dams on rivers, including the Yarlung Tsangpo? Why don't we leave something for the next generation?" The television director Zhang Ronggui wrote that he was opposed to the development of heavy industry and mineral resources in Tibet and hoped that the government would leave a blue sky, clean water and white clouds for the next generation (ICT 2015a: 37). Despite the violent dispersion and repression of protest on a local level on the Tibetan Plateau (Buckley 2015), resistance movements against mining were frequently reported, at least until 2016. They are directed against mining near villages, close to water bodies, sacred mountains or on nomadic grasslands whereby the aspect of the sacredness of nature is often foregrounded by the movements, which are often also supported by religious leaders (Del Bene and Gyaltsen 2015).

Moreover, 'water grabbing' in Tibet has also led to protest movements in Tibet and in Dartsedo, Kardze (Kham). More than 100 Tibetans from five villages joined together in May 2016 in a peaceful protest against a Chinese mining company to prevent further environmental destruction, notwithstanding the danger of brutal suppression, imprisonment and torture (Tibet Initiative Germany 2017b). According to Buckley, campaigns by Chinese environmentalists have stopped some dam projects, however the pro-dam lobby, backed by Chinese consortiums, is powerful. He explains that there are alternatives of solar and wind power, but China has not significantly deployed them in Tibet (ICT 2015a: 33).

In general, reports of protest movements against mining and dam projects have sharply decreased since 2016 (web research as of January 2021), leaving open the question of whether this is due to an unlikely halt in new projects or rather to more intensive measures to block the flow of information. According to Gamble's research between 2017 and 2019, local protests against dams have been muted by means of existing systems of political repression, censorship, surveillance and militarization (2019: 46). Therefore, the network of Tibetan NGOs has become important in raising international awareness of ongoing conflicts on the Tibetan Plateau.

Critical opinions on resettlement programmes in civil society

An increasing number of Chinese researchers and rangeland experts have become critical of government sedentarization policies, arguing that these programmes have caused overgrazing and degradation (ICT 2015a: 46). Tibetans from both farming and herding communities interviewed by Human Rights Watch between 2005 and 2012 reported a host of common disadvantages associated with relocation in the context of the New Socialist Villages policy. Yet, the Chinese government has consistently rejected all criticisms and expressions of concerns and labelled them as politically motivated (Human Rights Watch 2013: 8). Human Rights Watch (2013: 20) also reports that some Tibetans have also welcomed aspects of the housing policies and benefited from them; nevertheless, many are con-

Figure 3: Tibetans in Sangchu (Chinese: Xiahe County) opposing the mining on Gong-Ngon La Ri in 2016, a mountain sacred to the local community. Source: freetibet.org ‹https://freetibet.org/news-media/na/300-tibetans-stage-mining-protest-eastern-tibet›_accessed on 31.10.2021

cerned about their ability to maintain their livelihood in the long run. The majority of Tibetan nomads consider themselves targets of policies they are powerless to oppose or affect.

State and corporate strategy

Extension of the railway network in Tibet

The *China Internet Information Center* (CIIC 2006), which shares the official view of the Chinese government, promised sustainable economic development, increased revenues from tourism, access to mineral resources and the introduction of modern civilization to Tibet with the Qinghai-Tibet railway. Moreover, the ongoing construction of the Sichuan-Tibet Railway is proclaimed as a means of 'catalysing' the economic and social development of western China and of achieving national unity and solidarity by Xi Jinping (The People's Government of Sichuan Province 2020).

Dam & hydro projects as 'water conservation' projects

Major state-owned enterprises that rely on the support of the political regime are involved in the construction of dams in Tibet. These projects are carried out in the name of 'water conservation' projects. They are presented in the state media and to the Tibetan people with the political objective of "uniting the people" and allegiance to the Communist Party (ICT 2015a: 36). Jiao Yong, deputy head of China's Ministry of Water Resources, explained in 2015 that China planned to build many "water conservation" projects, with about half of them in western regions, also including water diversion for urban water supply for areas in eastern China, "in an attempt to promote urbanization". He further added that it "will help expand China's domestic demand and support economic growth" (Heying 2015).

Mining and violent suppression of protests

Infrastructure development in the context of Chinese state capitalism will fuel industrial-scale mining on the Tibetan Plateau in the coming years (Nyima and Yeh 2016: 167). This development foregrounds the aforementioned nexus between infrastructure development and extractivism, which will increase the importance of the Tibetan Plateau as a supplier of industrial raw materials and also accentuate conflicts related to the use of land and resources as well as related forms of living. The relation between mining companies and the Chinese state are tight according to local assessments as central or provincial governmental officials are also investors (Del Bene and Gyaltsen 2015). If attempts to diffuse resistance with arguments foregrounding that the mining projects are part of developing local communities fail, bribery and division of local communities are used as a strategy before violent suppression (Del Bene and Gyaltsen 2015).

Sustainable development, environmental conservation and resettlement programmes:

According to Rogers and Wilmsen (2020: 266), resettlement in China is shaped by Party supervision, campaign-style programmes, a constricted civil society and powerful discourses perpetuated by state-owned media. In recent years, the dimension of 'ecological resettlement' with the introduction of national parks and conservation areas to mitigate climate change and ecological degradation has become more prominent (ICT 2015a: 24). Furthermore, the PRC has established with the National Research Centre on Resettlement an institution to gather theories, models and strategies on resettlement promoting 'best practice', which also contributes to the normalization of resettlement (Rogers and Wilmsen 2020: 265). The extent to which these norms and practices are implemented by Chinese networks including with regard to the BRI is yet to be documented (Rogers and Wilmsen 2020: 266).

Nevertheless, Foggin observes a shift by the Chinese government since the mid-2010s in the context of the environmental conservation and national park system in Sanjiangyuan to include the social dimension of environmental protection and collaborative models of conservation with the inclusion of local stakeholders and forms of community co-management for a more efficient outcome (2018: 7, 17–18). While Foggin considers those approaches as a model for the BRI and the inclusion of the aims of sustainable community-oriented development and environmental conservation (2018: 17), Bixler et al. highlight that the rules guiding participation in the Sanjiangyuan environmental conservation programme have not resulted in any transfer of relevant decision-making powers to local actors. Tibetan nomads, with the exclusion of women, can participate in village assemblies. However, they have no representation above village government levels of decision-making where relevant policies and regulations with regard to access to land are decided (Bixler et al. 2015: 174, 176). Moreover, Bixler et al. consider those forms of participation "passive at best", with opportunities for powerful actors to continue overriding local actors' interests and to constrain their decision-making spaces (2015: 176, 177). If the described framework and power relations are not altered, the extension of national parks and environmental conservation as well as related development projects are set to lead to a continuation of green grabbing and commons grabbing along the BRI.

Conclusion

Seemingly located on the margins of the Belt and Road Initiative, the Tibetan Plateau is, however, a crucial area for this mega-infrastructure project. In 2016, China's deputy director general of the Department of External Security Affairs, Liu Yongfeng, called Tibet the gateway to South Asia during a talk on the BRI (Chaudhury 2019). Although available information about local contexts on the Tibetan Plateau has become very scarce, it can be concluded from a broader view that the related projects, development and conservation discourses as well as their forms of implementation are bound to exacerbate land use conflicts and processes of social marginalization as well as environmental degradation.

In the last two decades, environmental conservationists and sustainable development discourses, which are often part of the legitimizing structure of infrastructure and development projects, have accentuated the problematization of pastoralist nomadism as an inefficient and unsustainable form of production and life, which would fragilize or even degrade the environment. Fencing and enclosure movements have successively also been introduced to exclude nomadic pastoralists and other land users from territories for environmental conservation. Those movements are often linked to resettlement projects to urban areas, where resettled people live in precarious socio-economic conditions, and face difficulties and a lack of support in adapting to the conditions of the labour market of urban areas, which is aggravated by discrimination. Fencing and land enclosure has therefore become a means of distribution of access to land, including access bans and land alienation. Moreover, mining activities, fuelled by infrastructure projects of the Belt and Road Initiative and its extension of the railway network, have led to processes of commons grabbing. They reduce the availability of land for herding and subsistence and have become a major source of land use conflict on the Tibetan Plateau. Meanwhile, grassland degradation on the Tibetan Plateau has intensified.

Contrary to the assumption of a 'tragedy of the commons', environmental and land degradation has to be seen in a context of global heating and social marginalization in processes of land alienation, which result in more people and livestock using less and unfavourable land. The policies of development, including environmental conservation and discourses of environmental sustainability, have become a new technology of government, within which resettlement is used to shape the conduct of marginalized farmers and herders (Rogers and Wilmsen 2020: 262). These development and modernization projects, which are legitimized by discourses of a green economy or environmental conservation, and which also underline a supposed unsustainability of pastoralist nomadism, can be considered part of an anti-politics machine (see Ferguson 1990). The discourses of inclusiveness of the BRI withhold underlying processes of marginalization and exclusion and related power relations. They veil the fact that environmental and land degradation as well as poverty are the consequences of land-grabbing processes caused by the development-infrastructure-mining nexus as well as related resettlement and environmental conservation projects (green grabbing), which result in processes of commons grabbing and resilience grabbing undermining the subsistence of pastoralist nomads. The related conflicts of interest are depoliticized with a corresponding win-win narrative.

Meanwhile, there are warnings by scientists of an "ecosystem shift" due to climate change and human activities such as mega-infrastructure projects pushing the fragile ecosystems on the world's largest and highest plateau to the brink (ICT 2016; Xu and Grumbine 2014). This shift implies that Tibet will no longer be able to provide key environmental goods such as water supply for China and South(-East) Asia and carbon storage, and that areas of grasslands, alpine meadows, wetlands and permafrost, essential to the biodiversity of the Tibetan Plateau, will disappear within the next 35 years. Many Chinese economists and analysts have also criticized the current form of infrastructural, GDP-oriented growth and pointed out that it is potentially dangerous, unsustainable and could damage local resources and the environment beyond the Tibetan Plateau foregrounding that it is imposed in a top-down manner from Beijing, regardless of local ecological knowledge and livelihoods as well as corresponding needs (ICT 2015a: 25; Dell'Angelo 2013: 327, 329).

The ecological limits in the form of environmental degradation illustrate that crisis tendencies and contradictions of the capitalist mode of production are externalized into other spheres in the form of a spatial and temporal fix. This may well offer a temporary solution; however, the underlying contradictions continue to be reproduced on a larger scale. Resource extraction is the other side of the coin of a resource-intense economy and also the other side of a 'green economy', which is dependent on precious metals for its high-tech products (Brand 2012: 31), thus potentially reinforcing the infrastructure-extractivism nexus. China's plans to externalize its overcapacity by rearticulating socio-spatial organizations, infrastructure development, financing mechanisms and security measures intensify contradictions and conflicts of interest, extending also to an international level (Sum 2019: 546). With the restrictions for Tibetans in China on forming political and social movements, the organizations of Tibetans in exile have become important actors of visible resistance by building pressure and alliances as part of an international civil society movement foregrounding the externalized social and environmental costs. There are at the same time Chinese NGOs that sympathize with Tibetans against the reinforcement of infrastructure and related extractivism as well as resettlement projects. Outside China, debt-levered infrastructural expropriations, as in the case of Sri Lanka's Hambantota port or Pakistan's Gwadar port, not only trigger local resistance but accentuate geopolitical and geo-economic countertendencies, especially from the United States, India and Japan, over the struggle for resources, markets and geostrategic infrastructure (Sum 2019: 545–546). Due to its different components and contradictions, the BRI is therefore a "hypercomplex" project with no guarantee of success and which requires constant experimentation and repair work (Jessop and Sum 2018: 447).

At the same time, the Chinese government attempts to counter these insecurities by means of a consolidation of a governance configuration around security (Sum 2019: 546). The development of information and communication technologies and digitalization, i.e. the cybernetic component of the BRI, also known as the "Digital Silk Road" (Shen 2018), can be employed as a means of surveillance, control and repression of populations in the context of a securitization discourse, which is also employed in resettlement projects (Rogers and Wilmsen 2020: 266). The resettlement projects especially aim to bring labour closer to centres of industrial production and the consolidation of farmland for industrialized agriculture following resettlement, which might be seen as part of a broader project to 'optimize' the use of space (Rogers and Wilmsen 2020: 267–268). However, the contradictions and limits of the accompanying discourses, be they modernization, development, poverty reduction or sustainability and environmental conservationism, have already become evident.

Politics of development are structurally linked to economic and political interests and to an imperial logic (see Escobar 1995). This is also the case for OECD countries (Schiffauer 2020: 8). While aspects of enchantment and affective engagement promising a better future and living conditions are constitutive for projects of mobility and transnationalism (Harvey and Knox 2012: 534), they "also engender the opposite: immobility, entrapment, confinement, incarceration" (Navaro-Yashin 2003). Those aspects have to be considered as integral parts of current globalization processes (Harvey and Knox 2012: 534).

If the challenges of environmental degradation and forms of sustainable production and use of resources are to be addressed meaningfully, it is essential to include pastoralist knowledge in the context of the Tibetan Plateau. This pastoralist knowledge about geophysical and socio-economic conditions, as well as about forms of governance of the commons, should in general not be understood as traditionalist but as a source of information for sustainable forms of production and resilience in the context of climate change and geopolitical challenges (Haller et al. 2016: 411). This would imply that democratic forms of decision-making should be introduced and extended to all stakeholders to conserve commonly managed land in order to enable sustainable forms of production and resource use. Yet, as Brand argues, it is not enough to create adequate governance and democratization mechanisms to avoid resource conflicts, to reduce greenhouse gas emissions or to stop the erosion of biodiversity in order to deal with questions of wealth and social justice, environmental degradation and poverty. The underlying drivers of unsustainable capitalist production and consumption patterns need to be transcended and linked with democracy to include decisions about forms of production and consumption, forms of mobility and communication, housing and cities, agriculture and food, and about overall development paths (Brand 2012: 32). Those challenges are not limited to the People's Republic of China and need to be addressed on a global level.

Glossary

BRI	Belt and Road Initiative
ILC	International Land Coalition
PRC	People's Republic of China

References

Adams, Bill 2004: Against Extinction: The Story of Conservation. London: Routledge.

Adler, Ulrike 2008: Einfluss des Baus der Eisenbahnlinie nach Lhasa auf Tibet und seine Tourismusentwicklung. Sozialwissenschaftlicher Fachinformationsdienst soFid, Freizeit – Sport – Tourismus 2: 9-17.

Bauer, Kenneth and Yonten Nyima 2010: Laws and regulations impacting the enclosure movement on the Tibetan Plateau in China. Himalaya 30: 23-38.

Bixler, Patrick R., Jampel Dell'Angelo, Orleans Mfune, Hassan Roba 2015: The political ecology of participatory conservation: Institutions and discourse. Journal of Political Ecology 22 (1): 164-182.

Blaikie, Piers and Harold Brookfield 1994: Land Degradation and Society. London/New York: Routledge.

Brand, Ulrich 2012: Green Economy – the next oxymoron? No lessons learned from failures of implementing sustainable development. GAIA 21 (1): 28-32.

Bum, Tsering 2018: Translating ecological migration policy: A conjectural analysis of Tibetan pastoralist resettlement in China. Critical Asian Studies 50 (4): 518-536.

Cheng, Guodong, Sun, Zhiming and Fujun Niu 2008: Application of the roadbed cooling approach in Qinghai–Tibet railway engineering. Cold Regions Science and Technology, 53(3): 241-258.

Dell'Angelo, Jampel 2013: The sedentarization of Tibetan nomads. Conservation or coercion? In: Hali Healy, Joan Martínez-Alier, Leah Temper, Mariana Walter and Julien-François Gerber: Ecological Economics from the Ground up. London and New York: Routledge, 309-322.

Dell'Angelo, Jampel, Paolo D'Odorico, Maria Cristina Rulli, Philippe Marchand 2017: The tragedy of the grabbed commons: Coercion and dispossession in the global land rush. World Development 92: 1-12.

Du, Fachun 2006: Grain for green and poverty alleviation: The policy and practice of ecological migration in China. Horizons – Policy Research Initiative 9 (2): 45–48.

Escobar, Arturo 1995: Encountering Development. The Making and Unmaking of the Third World. Princeton: Princeton University Press.

Fairhead, James, Melissa Leach and Ian Scoones 2012: Green grabbing. A new appropriation of nature? Journal of Peasant Studies 39 (2): 237-261.

Ferguson, James 1990: The Anti-politics Machine. "Development," Depoliticization, and Bureaucratic Power in Lesotho. Cambridge: Cambridge University Press.

Fischer, Andrew 2015: Subsidizing Tibet: An interprovincial comparison of Western China up to the end of the Hu-Wen administration. The China Quarterly, 221: 1-20.

Foggin, J. Marc 2018: Environmental conservation in the Tibetan Plateau region. Lessons from China's Belt and Road Initiative in the mountains of Central Asia. Land 7 (52): 1-34.

Fratkin, Elliot 1997: Pastoralism: Governance and development issues. Annual Review of Anthropology 26: 235-261.

Gamble, Ruth 2019: How dams climb mountains: China and India's state-making hydropower contest in the Eastern-Himalaya watershed. Thesis Eleven 150 (1): 42-67.

Gerber, Jean-David and Tobias Haller 2020: The drama of the grabbed commons. Anti-politics machines and local responses. Journal of Peasant Studies 48 (6): 1304-1327.

Gyal, Hautse 2015: The politics of standardising and subordinating subjects. The Nomadic Settlement Project in Tibetan areas of Amdo. Nomadic Peoples 19: 241-260.

Haller, Tobias 2020: Institution shopping and resilience grabbing: Changing scapes and grabbing pastoral commons in African floodplain wetlands. Conservation and Society 18 (3): 252-267.

Haller, Tobias 2019: The different meanings of land in the age of neoliberalism: Theoretical reflections on commons and resilience grabbing from a social anthropological perspective. Land 104 (8): 1-22.

Haller, Tobias, Han Van Dijk, Michael Bollig, Clemens Greiner, Nikolaus Schareika and Christina Gabbert 2016: Conflicts, security and marginalisation: Institutional change of the pastoral commons in a 'glocal' world. Revue scientifique et technique 35 (2): 405-416.

Hardin, Garrett 1968: The tragedy of the commons. Science 162: 1243-1248.

Harvey, David 2001: Globalization and the "spatial fix". Geographische Revue 2: 23-30.

Harvey, Penny and Hannah Knox 2012: The enchantments of infrastructure. Mobilities 7 (4): 521-536.

Hildyard, Nicholas and Xavier Sol 2017: How Infrastructure is Changing the World. A Critical Introduction to Infrastructure Mega-Corridors. Brussels: Counter Balance.

Hoering, Uwe (2018): China's Long March 2.0. The Belt and Road Initiative as a Development Model. Hamburg: VSA.

International Land Coalition (ILC) 2011: Tirana Declaration. Rome: ILC.

Jessop, Bob and Ngai-Ling Sum 2018: Geopolitics: Putting geopolitics in its place in cultural political economy. Environment and Planning A. Economy and Space 50 (2): 474-478.

Joshi, Srijana, Lily Shrestha, Neha Bisht, Ning Wu, Muhammad Ismail, Tashi Dorji, Gauri Dangol and Ruijun Long 2020: Ethnic and Cultural Diversity amongst Yak Herding Communities in the Asian Highlands. Sustainability 12 (957): 1-25.

Kernan, Mark 2013: The displacement of Tibetan nomads, international law and the loss of global indigenous culture. Global Policy: 1-12.

Lafitte, Gabriel 2013: Spoiling Tibet: China and Resource Nationalism on the Roof of the World. London: Zed Books.

Lehnert, Lukas, Karsten Wesche, Katja Trachte, Christoph Reudenbach and Jörg Bendix 2016: Climate variability rather than overstocking causes recent large scale cover changes of Tibetan pastures. Scientific Reports 6: 24367.

Li, Li, Fabian E. Fassnacht, Ilse Storch, Matthias Bürgi 2017: Land-use regime shift triggered the recent degradation of alpine pastures in Nyanpo Yutse of the eastern Qinghai-Tibetan Plateau. Landscape Ecology 32: 2187-2203.

Li, Tania Murray 2011: Centering labor in the land grab debate. Journal of Peasant Studies 38 (2): 281-298.

Miller, Daniel J. 2000: Tough times for Tibetan nomads in Western China: Snowstorms, setting down, fences and the demise of traditional nomadic pastoralism. Nomadic Peoples 4 (1), 83-109.

Miller, Daniel J. 1999: Nomads of the Tibetan Plateau rangeland in Western China. Part two: Pastoral production practices. Rangelands 21 (1): 16-19.

Mills, Martin and Samantha May 2018: Mass relocation and nomad settlement on the Tibetan Plateau. Working Paper. Aberdeen: Scottish Centre for Himalayan Research.

Murton, Galen (2016): Trans-Himalayan transformations: Building roads, making markets, and cultivating consumption between Nepal and Chinese Tibet. In: Zhou, Yong-ming (ed.): Roadology: Roads, Space and Culture, Chongqing: Chongqing University Press, 328-340.

Næss, Marius Warg 2013: Climate change, risk management and the end of nomadic pastoralism. International Journal of Sustainable Development & World Ecology 20 (2): 123-133.

Navaro-Yashin, Yael 2003: 'Life is dead here': sensing the political in 'no man's land'. Anthropological Theory 3 (1): 107-125.

Nyima, Yonten and Emily T. Yeh 2016: Environmental issues and conflict in Tibet. In: Ben Hillman and Gray Tuttle (ed.): Ethnic Conflict and Protest in Tibet and Xinjiang. Unrest in China's West. New York: Columbia University Press, 151-178.

Panitch, Leo and Sam Gindin 2013: The integration of China into global capitalism. International Critical Thought, 3 (2): 146-158.

Ptackova, Jarmila 2012: Implementation of resettlement programmes amongst pastoralist communities in Eastern Tibet. In: Kreutzmann Hermann (ed.): Pastoral Practices in High Asia. Advances in Asian Human-Environmental Research. Springer: Dordrecht, 217-234.

Ptackova, Jarmila 2011: Sedentarisation of Tibetan nomads in China: Implementation of the Nomadic settlement project in the Tibetan Amdo area; Qinghai and Sichuan Provinces. Pastoralism: Research, Policy and Practice 1 (4): 1-11.

Rippa, Alessandro, Galen Murton and Matthäus Rest (2020): Building Highland Asia in the 21st Century. Verge: Studies in Global Asias 6 (2): 83-111.

Rogers, Sarah and Brooke Wilmsen 2020: Towards a critical geography of development. Progress in Human Geography 44 (2): 256-275.

Schiffauer, Leonie 2020: Eigennütziger Geber oder Retter in der Not? Chinas Entwicklungspolitik im Kontext der neuen Seidenstrasse. Berlin: Rosa-Luxemburg-Stiftung.

Shen, Hong 2018: Building a digital Silk Road? Situating the Internet in China's Belt and Road Initiative. International Journal of Communication 12: 2683-2701.

Sodnamkyid and Emilia Roza Sułek 2017: 'Everything costs money': Livelihood and economics in the new resettled village of Sogrima, Golok (Qinghai Province). Nomadic Peoples 21: 136-151.

Su, Ming Ming and Geoffrey Wall 2009: The Qinghai–Tibet Railway and Tibet tourism: Travelers' perspectives. Tourism Management 30 (5): 650-657.

Sullivan, Sian and Kathrin Homewood 2003: On non-equilibrium and nomadism: Knowledge, diversity and global modernity in drylands (and beyond). Centre for the Study of Globalisation and Regionalisation (CSGR). Working Paper No. 122/03. Coventry: University of Warwick.

Sum, Ngai-Ling 2019: The intertwined geopolitics and geoeconomics of hopes/fears: China's triple economic bubbles and the 'One Belt One Road' imaginary. Territory, Politics, Governance 7 (4): 528-552.

Summers, Tim 2016: China's 'New Silk Roads': Sub-national regions and networks of global political economy. Third World Quarterly 37 (9): 1628-1643.

Tan, Gillian G. 2018: Pastures of Change. Contemporary Adaptions and Transformations of Nomadic Pastoralists of Eastern Tibet. Cham: Springer.

Tashi, Gongbo and Marc Foggin 2012: Resettlement as development and progress? Eight years on: Review of emerging social and development impacts of an 'ecological resettlement' project in Tibet autonomous region, China. Nomadic Peoples 16 (1): 134-151

Tilt, Bryan 2015: Dams and Development in China. The Moral Economy of Water and Power. New York and Chichester: Columbia University Press.
Tsering Shakya 2012: Self-immolation, the changing language of protest in Tibet. Revue d'Etudes Tibétaines 25: 19–39.
World Bank 2008: World Development Report: Agriculture for Development. Washington DC: World Bank.
Xu, Jianchu and Edward B. Grumbine 2014: Building ecosystem resilience for climate change adaptation in the Asian highlands. Wiley Interdisciplinary Reviews: Climate Change 5 (6): 709-718.
Yao, Tandong, Lonnie Thompson, Deliang Chen, Yinsheng Zhang, Ninglian Wang, Lin Zhao, Tao Che, Baiqing Xu, Guangjian Wu, Fan Zhang, Qiuhong Tang, Walter Immerzeel, Tobias Bolch, Francesca Pellicciotti, Xin Li, Wei Yang, Jing Gao and Weicai Wang 2020: Third Pole climate warming and cyroshpere system changes. World Meteorological Organization Bulletin 69 (1): 38-44.
Yeh, Emily T. 2015: The politics of conservation in contemporary China. Journal of Peasant Studies 40 (6): 1165-1188.
Yeh, Emily 2013: Taming Tibet. Ithaca: Cornell University Press.
Yeh, Emily T. and Gaerrang 2011: Tibetan pastoralism in neoliberalising China. Continuity and change in Gouli. Area 43 (2): 165-172.
Yeh, Emily T. and Charlene Makley 2019: Urbanization, education, and the politics of space on the Tibetan Plateau. Critical Asian Studies, 51 (1): 1–11.
Yeh, Emily T., Leah H. Samberg, Gaerrang, Emily Volkmar and Richard B. Harris 2017: Pastoralist decision making on the Tibetan Plateau. Human Ecology 45: 333-343.
Yeh, Emily T. and Elizabeth Wharton 2016: Going West and going out: Discourses, migrants, and models in Chinese development. Eurasian Geography and Economics 57 (3): 286-315.
Yu, Chengqun, Yangjian Zhang, Claus Holzapfel, Rong Zeng, Xianzhou Zhang and Jingsheng Wang, 2012 : Environmental and ecological challenges faced by a developing Tibet. Environmental Science & Technology 46 (4): 1979-1980.
Yudannima, Yonten Nyima 2017: Rangeland use rights privatisation based on the tragedy of the commons: A case study from Tibet. Conservation and Society 15 (3): 270-279.
Zhang, Xin 2017: Chinese Capitalism and the Maritime Silk Road: A world-systems perspective. Geopolitics, 22 (2): 310-331.
Ziai, Aram 2016: Entwicklungstheorie nach der Post-Development Kritik. Plädoyer für eine Wissenssoziologie der Entwicklungstheorie und die Abschaffung des Entwicklungsbegriffs, in: Ziai, Aram. Im Westen nichts Neues? Stand und Perspektiven der Entwicklungstheorie, Baden-Baden: Nomos, 97-119.

Online sources and reports

Arora, Nehra and Devjyot Ghoshal/Reuters 2020: India plans dam on Brahmaputra to offset Chinese construction upstream. *Reuters* (1 December 2020). ⟨https://www.reuters.com/article/india-china-hydropower-idUSKBN28B4RB⟩
Australia Tibet Council 2015: Why Tibet lies at the heart of the great development challenges of the Asian century. ⟨https://drive.google.com/file/d/0B2EiDTMH9jx8d0lyZzVUby1iV00/view?resourcekey=0-Fn8x-Ubt9XXOerOxdSbGAA⟩

Buckley, Michael 2015: The price of damming Tibet's water. The New York Times (31 March 2015). ⟨http://www.nytimes.com/2015/03/31/opinion/the-price-of-damming-tibets-rivers.html⟩

Buckley, Michael 2014: Saving the Salween. ⟨http://www.meltdownintibet.com/f_river_salween.htm⟩

Chaudhury, Dipanjan R. 2019: BRI's impact on Tibet require far wider scrutiny. *The Economic Times* (2 Mai 2019) ⟨https://economictimes.indiatimes.com/news/international/world-news/bris-impact-on-tibet-require-far-wider-scrutiny/articleshow/69143542.cms?utm_source=contentofinterest&utm_medium=text&utm_campaign=cppst⟩

China Internet Information Center CIIC 2006: Sechs vorhersehbare Auswirkungen der Qinghai-Tibet-Eisenbahn auf Tibet. ⟨http://german.china.org.cn/german/245290.htm⟩

Del Bene, Daniela and Tempa Zamlha Gyaltsen 2015: Socio-environmental conflicts in Tibet, Environmental Justice Organizations, Liabilities and Trade (EJOLT). ⟨http://www.ejolt.org/wordpress/wp-content/uploads/2015/09/Tibet.pdf⟩

DIIR 2007: Tibet: A Human Development and Environment Report, 2007. Dharamshala: Department of Information & International Relations. ⟨https://tibet.net//wp-content/uploads/2011/08/TibetAHumanDevelopmentAndEnviromentReport.pdf⟩

Fischer, Andrew M. 2012: The geopolitics of politico-religious protest in Eastern Tibet. Hot spots, fieldsights. society for cultural anthropology. ⟨https://culanth.org/fieldsights/the-geopolitics-of-politico-religious-protest-in-eastern-tibet⟩

Free Tibet Campaign 2007: Chinas neue Bahn trägt zur Plünderung Tibets bei. ⟨http://www.igfm-muenchen.de/tibet/ftc/2007/Eisenbahn_Bodenschaetze.html⟩

Heying, Chen 2015: 27 water conservation projects planned, half in western regions. *Global Times* (1 April 2015). ⟨http://www.globaltimes.cn/content/914887.shtml⟩

Human Rights Watch 2013: "They say we should be grateful": Mass rehousing and relocation programs in Tibetan areas of China. ⟨https://www.ecoi.net/en/file/local/1229771/1476_1372338871_tibet0613webwcover-0.pdf⟩

International Campaign for Tibet ICT 2019: Damming Tibet's rivers: New threats to Tibetan area under UNESCO protection. ⟨https://savetibet.org/damming-tibets-rivers-new-threats-to-tibetan-area-under-unesco-protection/⟩

International Campaign for Tibet ICT 2016: Plans for second railway across Tibet confirmed: likely to have even greater impact. ⟨https://savetibet.org/plans-for-second-railway-across-tibet-confirmed-likely-to-have-even-greater-impact/⟩

International Campaign for Tibet ICT 2015a: Blue gold from the highest plateau: Tibet's water and global climate change. A report by the International Campaign for Tibet. ⟨https://www.savetibet.org/wp-content/uploads/2015/12/ICT-Water-Report-2015.pdf⟩

International Campaign for Tibet ICT 2015b: Major policy meeting on Tibet in buildup to sensitive anniversary. ⟨http://www.savetibet.org/major-policy-meeting-on-tibet-in-buildup-to-sensitive-anniversary/⟩

International Campaign for Tibet ICT 2014: New strategic rail network to Tibet's borders endangers environment, raises regional security concerns (Updated). ⟨https://savetibet.org/new-strategic-rail-network-to-tibets-borders-endangers-environment-raises-regional-security-concerns/⟩

International Campaign for Tibet ICT 2003: Crossing the line: China's railway to Lhasa, Tibet. International Campaign for Tibet. ⟨https://savetibet.org/crossing-the-line-chinas-railway-to-lhasa-tibet/⟩

International Campaign for Tibet ICT 2002: An NGO's view on development in Tibet. ⟨https://savetibet.org/an-ngos-view-on-development-in-tibet/⟩

Lafitte, Gabriel 2015: Pitching Tibet, in a new key. ⟨http://rukor.org/pitching-tibet-in-a-new-key/⟩

Ministry of Foreign Affairs of the People's Republic of China 2016a: China's Position Paper on the Implementation of the 2030 Agenda for Sustainable Development. ⟨https://www.fmprc.gov.cn/mfa_eng/wjdt_665385/2649_665393/t1357701.shtml⟩

Modak, Sayanangshu 2020: Spotlight on planet's largest hydropower project by China on Yarlung/Brahmaputra. New Delhi: Observer Research Foundation. ⟨https://www.orfonline.org/expert-speak/spotlight-on-planets-largest-hydropower-project-by-china-on-yarlungbrahmaputra/⟩

SNWTP Construction Committee Office (2015) "中国环境报：陕南持续发力清水永续北送" (China environment report: Southern Shaanxi continues to generate sustainable fresh water to be delivered north). ⟨http://www.nsbd.gov.cn/zx/mtgz/201512/t20151201_406204.html⟩

Stanway. David and Richard Pullin 2021: Tibet official urges China to start construction on Brahmaputra dam within one year. Reuters (8 March 2021). ⟨https://www.reuters.com/article/us-china-hydropower-tibet-idUSKBN2B00GU⟩

State Information Center 2017: Belt and Road Portal. ⟨https://eng.yidaiyilu.gov.cn⟩

The People's Government of Sichuan Province 2020: Xi Jinping Makes Important Instructions on the Construction of Sichuan-Tibet Railway (10 November 2020). ⟨https://www.sc.gov.cn/10462/10758/10760/10765/2020/11/10/bae25b59d467444d9421a373ae12e4c7.shtml⟩

Tibet Initiative Germany 2017a: Tibets Nomaden. ⟨https://www.tibet-initiative.de/informieren/themen/umwelt/tibets-nomaden/⟩

Tibet Initiative Germany 2017b: Tibets Flüsse im Würgegriff der Dämme. ⟨https://www.tibet-initiative.de/informieren/themen/umwelt/tibets-fluesse-im-wuergegriff-der-daemme/⟩

Tibet Third Pole ⟨https://tibet3rdpole.org/⟩

Woo, Ryan 2019: As China forges ecological future, Tibetans relinquish nomadic past. Reuters (26 September 2019). ⟨https://www.reuters.com/article/us-china-environment-resettlement-tibeta-idUSKBN1WB0C5⟩

Zheng, Jinran 2017: First National Park Receiving Strong Legal and Financial Support. China Daily (3 March 2017). ⟨http://english.gov.cn/news/top_news/2017/03/09/content_281475589549379.htm⟩

⟨All online sources were accessed for the last time in October 2021⟩

The Disenchantment of Mining and its Politics Machine: a Cautionary Tale from Mongolia

Troy Sternberg, School of Geography, University of Oxford, UK

Introduction

Mega-infrastructure, nomadic herders and a new democracy create unusual dynamics in the world's 3rd largest desert. At once the sparsest-populated country as well as home to $1.3 trillion in mineral resources, Mongolia is a unique context to study how forces intersect in the search for wealth and development. Where pastoralists once watered animals at a sacred spring a massive cooper and gold mine has displaced herders, disrupted tradition and spearheaded the nation's drive to a resource-based economy (Jackson 2015). Positive impacts (taxes, jobs) are mingled with negative implications (degradation, disputes, displacement) as the country attempts to reconcile extraction with social adaptation and stability. After twenty years of development the Oyu Tolgoi mega-mine remains a contentious process affecting elections, investment and social cohesion (Myadar and Jackson 2019).

Our case study of Oyu Tolgoi (OT) is in the Khan Bogd district of vast, mineral rich South Gobi Province. The mine exemplifies mega-infrastructure in its political, physical, and economic impact and dimensions (Flyvbjerg 2014). This includes its $12 billion cost, 80 km^2 land take, its dominance of national debate and centrality in several election cycles. It examines how mega-infrastructure can impact livelihoods, lead to local conflict and present opportunities for positive engagement between residents, mines and government. Here the herding community was assisted by NGOs to file a complaint with an international lender. This led to a novel collaborative process between herders, the company and the government that was able to resolve community problems and present a model for future mineral investment. Examining the context and process offers insight into contemporary mega-infrastructure engagement with host communities.

This chapter emerges from years of research and engagement in Mongolia. Visiting twice or more every year since 2011 framed the context, knowledge and long-term perspective to investigate the role of mega-infrastructure in the country. Starting with a first visit to Khan Bogd and meeting with officials in 2011 through extensive fieldwork in 2016-2017, work has provided the opportunity to note the development and evolution of the mine, its presentation and practice, community and national perceptions, governance challenges and the eventual resolution of disputes in 2019. Research based in the Mongolian Academy of Sciences Institute of Geography and the National University provided close contact and engagement with academics and stakeholders and access to government officials. Importantly, being embedded in national organisations enabled access to much material, including reports, research, 'grey literature' and government documents. Intensive research from 2015-2017 gave access to OT mining staff, the local community and NGOs that enabled broad-based evaluation and analysis of the mega-project.

Part 1: Historical, environmental, ethnographic and political context

History and current context

Rather than the more commonly written about facets of European colonialism, Mongolian mining infrastructure evolved from the Soviet, thus Russian, colonial legacy. Previously part of the Qing Dynasty, the then Outer Mongolia nominally gained self-rule as turmoil affected China in the early 20th century. Supported by Russia, the country claimed independence yet by 1924 was a *de facto* Soviet satellite state (Fernandez-Gimenez 1999). This saw imposition of Leninist and Stalinist reforms and policies, purges, collectivisation and conversion to the Cyrillic alphabet. Rationing was imposed and livestock systems regulated whilst health and education were improved. The fraught transition reflected Mongolia's independent nature, Buddhist history and role as a buffer state between the USSR and China. The sparse population focused on herding with COMECON nations being the designated export market for meat and animal products. Isolated for most of the 20th century, Mongolia was a remote land known for resource potential rather than exploitation. (Rossabi 2005).

In fact, mega-infrastructure is not new to Mongolia. During the communist era the Soviet Union created the Erdenet Copper Mine in 1974 (Ganbold and Ali 2017). Co-owned by the two states, the mine is viewed as a successful long-term enterprise with the resultant company town now the country's third largest city. The mine is regarded positively as it has contributed significant tax revenue for >50 years. Over decades mine management has not been contentious and the process showed the country's ability to work with foreign partners. Developed by the then all-powerful USSR, there was no need for debate or discussion about the mine. Terms were set, leadership arranged, and exports sent to the Soviet Union and its satellite states. The contemporary narrative is that mining has been beneficial for the country and thus that mining can be a path to development (Batchuluun and Lin 2010).

With the end of the Soviet Union Mongolia became a rare democracy in the region and is now rated one of the 'freest' countries in Asia (Freedom House

2019). With independence came the collapse of Soviet subsidies and markets, a great increase in poverty and systemic breakdown in economic and development terms. The international community supported the nascent state with western advice and funding due to geo-political interest in the country. Perhaps most importantly, in the 1990s this support was crucial in maintaining the heating system in Ulaan Baatar, the world's coldest capital city (World Bank 2001). Impoverished city residents relocated to the countryside, with herding again providing subsistence for up to half of the population. Mongolia embraced socio-economic reform and adroitly adopted a friendly 'third nation' policy stressing engagement with its superpower neighbours, the US, EU, Japan, South Korea etc. With time the egalitarian socialist approach fractured into growing social divisions, expanding bureaucracy and increasing corruption learnt from neighbours (Hojer 2019).

The conundrum was how to match the country's new democratic and social aspirations with economic realities. Industrialisation was a non-starter because China was far ahead and could undercut the tiny Mongolian market. Remoteness made imports costly and exports difficult. Russia was resource-rich yet had limited markets in neighbouring Siberia. China was becoming an economic powerhouse with a strong demand for resources and could provide technical expertise and ready investment. The challenge was identifying exploitable mineral resources and developing external partners, contracts and licenses to realise mining potential in a successful manner. The Erdenet copper mine was a positive example and Russia a natural partner. However, whilst Russia retained political interest in Mongolia, particularly to monitor China's growing influence in the country, its economic interaction focused on delivering energy (80% of Mongolia's oil) rather than on-the-ground investment (Goodson and Addleton 2020).

However, there are fundamental contradictions between mining and herding practices in perceptions of land, water use and relations to culture and tradition. Herding provides a livelihood for 30% of the national population; in South Gobi province pastoralism is challenged by limited precipitation (about 120 mm annually), high climate variability, sparse vegetation and a lack of surface water. Mongolian beliefs revere nature and find solace in the steppe and blue sky; in the same landscape large-scale mining operations seek to maximise profit within legal parameters. For example, Mongolian customary beliefs unite above-ground and below-ground processes. Thus if extraction disturbs the earth, there may also be corresponding ramifications for the environment, such as less vegetation or drought as a result of mining. The divergent interests lead to disputes between mining and herders, with mining companies pursuing legalistic justifications. The Oyu Tolgoi mega-mine exemplifies the tensions in communities when large-scale resource extraction commences (Jackson 2015).

Since 2009, when a landmark agreement was reached enabling the development of Oyu Tolgoi (OT), mining has been the economic centre of the country. Mining makes up more than 80% of exports with OT said to provide a third of national tax revenue (Dagys et al. 2020). As a top-down process, local communities are recipients rather than instigators of change. By 2017 the number of mining licenses in Mongolia was around 3000 (Ganbold and Ali 2017). These exports go to China and are thus dependent on good relations. In 2017 when the Dalai Lama visited Mongolia a blockade was put on mineral exports from Mongolia by China. When government spending, based on over-optimistic projected mining revenue, was unsustainable, the country, while opting for either additional loans from China or a $5.5 billion bailout from the IMF (International Monetary Fund), chose the latter. Some license deals are said to be off the books. Bureaucracy is inefficient and has become rent-seeking. The legal system is not robust and thus does not provide an alternate method of complaint or control. Whilst civil society often tries to resort to the courts to redress mining problems, this has not proved to be an effective method.

Contextualising Oyu Tolgoi Mine in the debate over mega-infrastructure projects

The Mega-Mine

The country optimistically encouraged international investment as a balance to its mighty neighbours. Speculation of great mineral wealth, once a Soviet secret, attracted attention and in the South Gobi was identified one of the world's largest copper and gold mines known as Oyu Tolgoi (Turquoise Hill), named after the colour of samples found in the soil. Discovered in 1957 by Soviet geologists, it was licensed to BHP Corporation in the 1990s, then sold for $5 million to Ivanhoe Mines (Canada) in 1997. As Ivanhoe began developing the Oyu Tolgoi mega-mine its president Robert Friedland stated the company 'had found an ATM machine in the desert' (Mines and Communities, 2006). In 2009 Rio Tinto Corporation (part owned by China's Chinalco) became the majority owner in what is now a $12 billion mega-mine (Sternberg et al., 2019). Imagine the herders' surprise as the 8 x 10-kilometre behemoth rose out of the desert.

As a country with a small population and developing economy, the Mongolian government has limited income sources. One of the enchantments of mega-infrastructure was the potential for mineral taxes that can be controlled and monitored. Previous experience with the Erdenet mine showed the potential of mining as a national revenue stream. However, the increasingly complex process for developing Oyu Tolgoi involved lengthy re-negotiations and fluctuating commodity prices. As public disenchantment set in and visible benefits did not materialise, resource nationalism amplified and the OT mine remained controversial.

Key stakeholders – State and Companies

Ivanhoe Mines, a Canadian company, was aware of both the challenges and potential outsize rewards were possible in developing nations. Key to the equation was proximity to Chinese markets, appetite for risk and willingness to engage on local terms, the last two factors enough to distance major corporations from competition. Mongolia had little experience in negotiating with foreign mining investors. To Ivanhoe this provided an opportunity to profit from the information and strategic gap. OT was the company's apex – a bold gesture in search of outsized returns. Potentially bigger than anything it had done before, it was a gamble that came good when Rio Tinto was attracted to invest first in the OT subsidiary, then taking 50.1% interest in Ivanhoe itself.

Rio Tinto was a much different corporate force. Valued at $70 billion at the time of purchase, it had both the technical expertise and economic resources to finance the billions needed to bring surface and underground mining operations into production. Rio Tinto also had much experience developing mining in remote and chaotic locations. As a major member of ICMM (International Council on Metals and Mining) it ascribed to industry best practices (sic). Rio Tinto had a history of addressing Corporate Social Responsibility and awareness of potential business and reputational risk if local conditions were not managed; this was particularly important for investor confidence. Thus greater acknowledgment of environmental impacts, such as the diverted Bor Ovoo Spring and pursuing a basic level of social license to operate, distinguished Rio Tinto from the Ivanhoe era. It was this change in direction that enabled effective community interaction at the Khan Bogd mine site. Throughout the 2010s Rio Tinto was interested in producing return on investment and undertaking a $5 billion underground expansion. To do this government approval was needed through election cycles. It was time for OT to address the details involved in public processes.

Interestingly, the Mongolian state is a one-third owner of the Oyu Tolgoi mine. However politically savvy this may once have seemed, the economic reality is the state pays for its investment out of its portion of royalties. Thus the perceived cash bonanza of ownership is a chimera. In fact, the first royalty payment is not expected until 2035 (Bauer and Namkhaijantsan 2019)! Tax revenue is received but national enrichment has not followed. Perhaps because of this investment obligation the central government has not been a participant in the OT dispute. On paper, as one-third owner, the state would appear to have significant input into how matters are resolved. In the state's absence the local government is burdened with the contradictory roles of embodying the state, monitoring the mine's environmental and social performance and representing citizen concerns. Comprised of elected locals, the roles of officials are untrained, baptised by fire and often changed in the four-year election cycle. Concern and knowledge are strong as are reports of favouritism, corruption and incompetence (Jackson 2018). It is unfair, even illogical, for a rural Gobi community to go head-to-head against an international mega-mine. As the International Finance Corporation's complaint process began the national government chose to not participate; only with progress and a clear need for engaged governance was the state represented locally.

Geography and ecosystem/cultural landscape

Landlocked, remote and seemingly lost in time, Mongolian herders convert sparse vegetation in the world's coldest desert into an environmentally sustainable livelihood (Sternberg et al. 2015). Sharing the 2.3 million km^2 Gobi Desert with northern China, the southern half of Mongolia has few surface water sources (springs) in a vast region that may have as little as 50 mm of precipitation annually. Livestock raising is only possible through wells built during the Soviet era, by international agencies, the government or occasionally by herders themselves. Much of southern Mongolia has a shallow water table so water may be accessible as little as 2 metres below the surface (Sternberg 2012). These shallow groundwater aquifers are essential to pastoral livelihoods but do not have the volume needed for industrial mining. For this deep aquifers or water transfer schemes are needed. Low precipitation equates to limited vegetation; thus, mobility has been key to Mongolian pastoralism. In order to access adequate pasture and fodder for animals, frequent movements of herds and campsites has been a staple of herding. Migration requires dispersed watering points; thus, each well and water source is essential (Sternberg 2012).

The second climatic concern is cold temperatures (to -40°C). Known as dzud, these conditions occur when snow or ice prevent livestock from grazing and accessing fodder (Sternberg 2018). Without external sources animals literally starve and freeze to death. Part of the challenge is building up animal weight gain and strength through summer and fall migrations. Again, this depends on access to water sources. An environmental corollary is drought, compelling in the desert as slight variations in precipitation disproportionally affect vegetation and biomass. Herding is an ecologically balanced system where natural factors define the number of animals that the land can reasonably support. Thus, changes in climate, human decision-making, economics and government policy affect the viability of customary livelihoods. As elsewhere, mega-infrastructure can significantly disrupt pastoral viability (Sternberg and Chatty 2016).

Environmentally-driven pastoralism has been based on traditional ecological knowledge, mobility and communal land tenure. Herders use < 10 litres a day of water per person with a series of wells the water source for humans and livestock. Formerly a subsistence livelihood, herding struggles to succeed in a modern socio-economic system. In contrast, the Oyu Tolgoi Mine has an 80 km^2 land footprint, is licensed to use 870,000 litres of water per second and has billions of dollars in financing from international lenders and the World Bank's International Finance Corporation (Mining Global 2015; CAO 2017).

Though nomadic pastoralism is key to Mongolian cultural identity, in fact herding has changed greatly in recent decades (Fig 1). The two major national holidays – Naadam in the summer and Tsaagan Sar New Year's festivities – are based on pastoral practices and seasons. Forbidden during Soviet times, these multi-day celebrations of herding skills and traditions are embraced as much in the cities as in the countryside. As Mongolia transitions to high-rise internet lifestyles in the capital and herders continue to move their *gers* (yurts) to the city outskirts, the concept and mythicization of pastoralism continues. Presidential candidates film advertisements riding horses through the snow, politicians stress rural knowledge and connections in custom and dress. But power, money and advancement remain in the capital. Mineral licensing and deal making is now the provenance of the elite with Members of Parliament the new aristocracy in the country. The perception of Mongolia as a herding nation continues yet bureaucratic and political corruption distorts interests and decisions – Transparency International (2019) ranks the country 93rd globally. Arranging mining endeavours is lucrative, especially with Chinese businesses, as western ethics, already a low standard in mining, are a minor concern. The national government interacts with mining at a distance; adequate laws are in place, yet not adequately enforced. The ensuing erosion of public trust in government drives volatile elections with the party in opposition likely to resort to resource nationalism – especially renegotiation of foreign (not Chinese) contracts – as a vote getter (Myadar and Jackson 2019).

Fig 1: Typical herder ger, Khan Bogd, Mongolia. Source: author

Local population and resource use

The vast country (1.56 million km^2) stretches the equivalent of the distance from London to Moscow and Amsterdam to Rome. Yet it is home to 3 million people. This contributes to the notion that there is plenty of space, that mining just spoils a tiny part. Perhaps it is then surprising that herders can be found even in the heart of the Gobi Desert. The conflict is over what companies perceive as empty land that herders claim as seasonal pasture. From another lens, this exemplifies customary land use patterns coming up against current economic conceptions of efficient land use. A herder, even a group of herders, has little power against notions of the corporation or the state. Pastoralism operates in an open land system where land is held communally unless assigned differently by the government. In theory herders have access to undeveloped land which is a key mechanism for pastoralists to deal with uncertain environmental conditions (Meesters and Behagel 2017). Thus, extractive licenses, granted by the national government, can displace herder access. The knowledge and extent of a license is difficult for a herder to ascertain. The mine asserts it has a right to land; the herder lacks ability or resources to verify claims. Often the local government is similarly uncertain. Customary pastoral practices can modify and muddle along until confronting the greater power of the profit-driven mining company. Mines often construe the license to include local water sources and seek to prevent herders using a water point regardless of prior access or practice (Fig 2). Herders may be late to grasp their secondary role in the mine development process.

Fig 2: Herder discussing role of water and mining in Khan Bogd. Source: J Mayaud

Another issue is that pastures excluded in a mine license area reduce available pasture. Herders compete for access and what effectively become migration corridors. Recognised winter camps assign a location that are often considered to confer *de facto* private land rights of 700m^2 for herders, often inferred to extended to a 2 to 3-kilometre radius. Similarly, herders claim the nearest well as part of their winter camp. If family members obtain conjoining camp rights they may aver the right to block migration through their area. The legality and effectiveness depend on the local government – they often let this happen although it is not the intent of the law.

The situation for elected local governments reflects their home in the community, limited training for the tasks at hand, susceptibility to mining interests, pressure from the national government and the need to answer to residents. This creates competing interests, local power struggles, corruption and opaque structures. Kinship networks, party affiliation and connections to external elites become important determinants of opportunities. Companies have greater wealth and knowledge, policing is limited, environment monitoring minimal and most often tax revenue goes to the central government. The public may express anger at the government yet remediation and amelioration are beyond citizens' reach or ability (Meesters and Behagel 2017).

The town dwellers and herders are a late beneficiary of mining. By its nature mining involves land take, pasture fragmentation, degradation, high water consumption and often ensuing contamination. For townspeople this may be seen through rapid changes, in-migration in search of work and schooling and new businesses; for herders, infrastructure can disturb or disrupt their livelihoods. Companies stress they have a license issued in the capital. Responsible parties are elusive and seldom on site; often they act with impunity or may be protected by powerful sources in the capital. When land becomes off-limits to a herder, they have few effective remedies and may not have access to information to legitimise a complaint. The compression of pasture space then entails intra-herder conflict based on registered winter camps and traditional herding practices that affect mobility and water access. As the economic system has changed in Mongolia the number of livestock has increased to meet livelihood expenses – *e.g.* education, health, transport and debt. Divisions are many, including those between herders and local government, between different districts, mining operations and amongst other herders. The pastoralists attempt to cope as few other livelihoods are available. Jobs at mines are promised more often than delivered. Climate change contributes to environmental uncertainty that affects pastoralism. As herding viability fluctuates, children, especially daughters, are encouraged to get educated for better job opportunities. By this progression, the future generations of herders are lost to modern lifestyles (Kingsley 2017).

Working with Mongolian researchers, trainers, NGOs and Khan Bogd herders and residents and participating in community development workshops organised by the World Bank placed this research in the community context (Fig 3). Extensive fieldwork and time in the district enabled a localised perspective and familiarity with key figures, points of conflict and events. Meetings, > 50 interviews, environmental assessments, participation in cultural and social events in temperatures from -25°C to +35°C and living in the district provided a great range of conditions and in-depth experience of mega-project dynamics in the Gobi Desert. In addition, interviews in the capital, access to expansive published material and data, interdisciplinary discussions and personal encounters framed the investigation.

Fig 3: Senior citizens answering questions about the impact of Oyu Tolgoi mine, Khan Bogd. Source: A. Ahearn

National economy and legal framework

Mining has become the driver of the national economy with mineral products now accounting for 90% of exports and 80% of foreign direct investments (Dagys et al. 2020). As the state's primary source of tax revenue extractive industries are significant in policy and governance. Exports increased >50% from 2015 to 2019 with 92% going to China (Workman 2020). Whilst herding and pastoral economic activity is vital to 30% of the populations (Campbell and Hatcher 2019), related products (cashmere, wool, meat) are less than 5% of exports. With a GDP of US$ 13.8 billion income per person is $3800 per year, yet this masks inequality and a high poverty rate of 28% (World Bank 2020). This is evident throughout the countryside and in large urban *ger* (round tent home) districts comprised of internal migrants. Rural workers, artisanal miners and town dwellers are part of the high informal/vulnerable employment rate of 78% that includes the variable and environment-dependent livelihoods of pastoralists. In positive resource cycles the economy booms (6.1% growth rate in 2019, yet can shrink when mineral prices fall. The country needed a $5.5 billion IMF bailout in 2017.

Land rights are unusual in Mongolia in that the 1992 constitution states that land is held communally and belongs to the citizens of the country. Over time limited property rights for households and businesses have been established. The mineral licensing process conveys rights to the owner though the nature of the claims are at times contested. In 2012 the Strategic Entities Foreign Investment Law gave the government the rights over major 'strategic' mining resources beyond existing law (Ahlers et al. 2020). There is public support for a greater domestic ownership role and less foreign involvement (implied: Chinese investment) in mining, yet corruption and abuse of power are common in parliament and amongst government officials (Ganbold and Ali 2017). This speaks to a lack of state institutional capacity at national and local levels. Whilst large-scale mining claims legal rights, artisanal mining in the country does not convey similar legal status. The regulatory structure advantages large-scale mining over all other land uses (Campbell and Hatcher 2019).

Part 2: The Mega-Infrastructure Project

As Flyvbjerg (2014) identifies, cost, size, political importance and economic implications of Oyu Tolgoi (OT) define the mine as a representative mega-infrastructure project. Situated in Khan Bogd district, the mine is located in vast, mineral rich South Gobi Province (Map 1). For example, the Gurvantes district alone has 27 major mining projects licensed with several in operation. Neighbouring Tsogt Ovoo district has one of the world's largest coking coal mines that is owned by the government. The community challenges, rather than being resolved, are being repeated in each mining locale. Reasons rest with governance, enforcement of policy, exploitative business approaches and a lack of local power or recourse to decisions and actions instigated from afar. The engagement and resolution of community and environmental issues marks OT as a significant achievement.

Description of the project

Our mega-infrastructure case study, the Oyu Tolgoi (OT) mine has significant deposits of copper and gold as well as silver and molybdenum. Its economic potential has reconfigured Mongolia's self-conception to that of a prime mining nation. This has affected a series of elections, become emblematic of the challenges of mega-projects in developing states and taken away the country's relative innocence and optimism of when it was perceived as a pastoral nation. Though much mining now exists, the scale and international dynamic of the mine has made it a lightning rod for national attention and the focus of social and civil society debate.

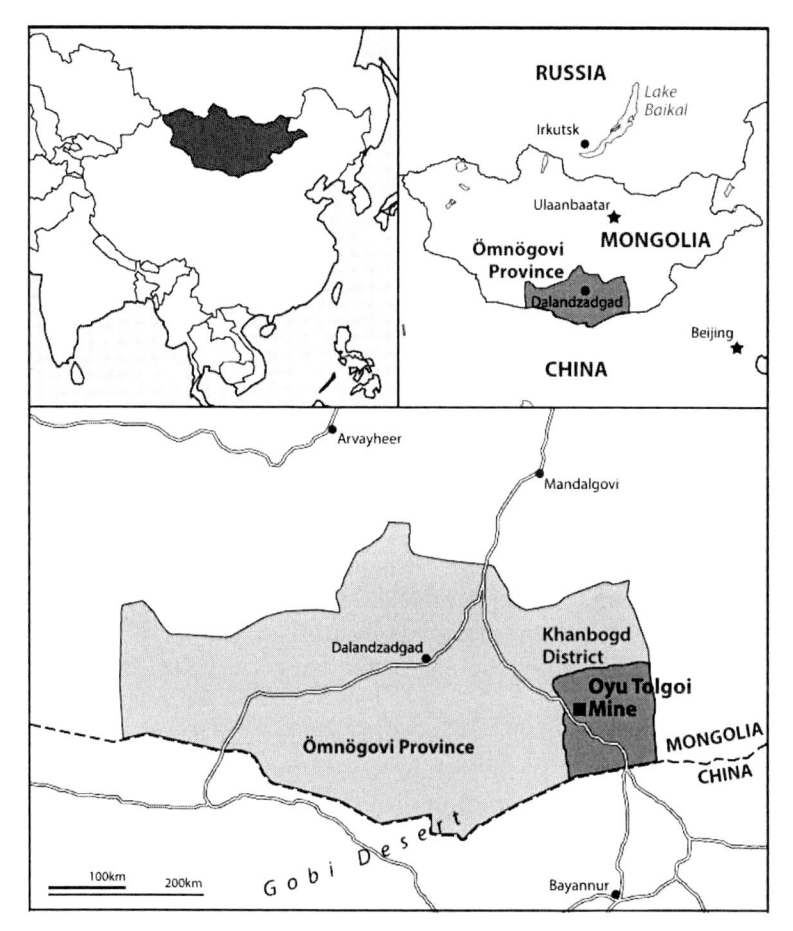

Map 1: The area of the mine in Mongolia. Source: Map compilation and design by Manuel L. K. Abebe (2021), CDE, University of Bern, Bern, Switzerland. Geodata: OpenStreetMap contributors

The promulgated idea of 'foreignness' has become emblematic and has seen the mine coruscated as failing to attain highest standards though in fact it may outperform other major mines in the country (Sternberg et al. 2019). Renegotiation of the OT contract has become an election trope that affects international participation but has not troubled regional investment of Russian or Chinese origin. At an investment of $12 billion, the success of Rio Tinto as a company and Mongolia's reputation as a mining nation may be at stake.

The developer of OT, Ivanhoe Mines, effectively realised the project's potential in order to sell the mine to a major corporation. From this framework its approach to community engagement, compensation and resettlement was driven by expediency rather than long term involvement and effectiveness. At the time of OT project initiation in 2003 only artisanal (individual) mining had taken place in the region with individuals selling ore at the Chinese border. The community had no experience with large scale mining, ensuing government prevarication, notions of community negotiation and development. When Ivanhoe's community relation team met with local herders, clever words and official pressure were enough to get herders to sign away rights for a few animals and sheds and resettle from a 10-kilometre exclusion zone from the mine license area. What was not recognised is that the only surface water in the district, Bor Ovoo Spring, and neighbouring pasture within the mine license area were no longer accessible. The exclusion zone, previously claimed for use by two hundred herder families, was off-limits as was the water therein. Herders complained to the local government, the government met with the mine, development continued apace. Herders, proudly independent, redoubled efforts. What went unremarked is that whilst the mega-mine grew, social practices and markers of success were also changing in Mongolia's market economy. For example, herding once done by horse or camel had been replaced by motorcycles and often vehicles, especially used Japanese SUVs (sport utility vehicles). This changed focus, introduced debt and pressured pastoral livelihoods. With time and talk, negative pasture elements were attributed to the mine whilst social changes were not considered related. The combination of perceived mining impact, alleged poor treatment of herders by Ivanhoe and weak decision-making processes created blame and toxic interaction between the mine and community (Sternberg et al. 2022).

When Rio Tinto came to direct operations at the mine the fresh approach ameliorated conditions somewhat. In 2011 a second round of compensation was initiated; community development efforts increased and make-work jobs were created for a member from each of 89 affected families. Over several years the host district, Khan Bogd, grew to about 5000 residents and livestock numbers doubled. Resultant pasture impacts were attributed to the mine, as were a perceived lack of development, area disputes, in-migration and similarly introduced factors. This included a coal transport road from another mine, a failed railroad project that blocked pasture routes and electrical lines from China (Fig 4). A breaking point was the herders' weakness vis a vis the corporation's and local government's ineffectiveness or indifference to their plight. The unique story pivot commenced in 2012 when a local herder NGO, with much direction from a national NGO, filed a complaint with the International Finance Corporation (IFC) alleging that their loan guarantee did not follow the bank's own guidelines to ensure fair treatment of the local community. Once the case was accepted by the IFC a lengthy joint fact finding and community engagement process began.

Environmental and Social Impacts

As the mega-mine slowly transitioned from a speculative hole in the desert to a vast open pit mine and then to include a large underground expansion, environmental impact assessments (EIA) were conducted and more recently social im-

Fig 4: 20 kilometre line of trucks outside mine, going to the Chinese border. Source: J Mayaud

pact assessments (SIA) were undertaken. The initial EIA in 2004 was over 600 pages; it was 'unlikely that the herders would or could understand the assessment' (Meesters and Behagel 2017, p 278). The EIA suggested there were some minor impacts that could be mitigated. Less concern was given to SIA as these appeared later in the project, particularly as issues of compensation had continued to grow. Ivanhoe followed protocols – perhaps they were not as thorough as would be desirable, reflecting the country's lack of experience in regulating mining. The assessments were hard to access locally and beyond a herder's or official's ability or interest to comprehend or challenge. They were not important to government oversight, but a requirement needed for international funding and financing. To address and resolve environmental and social issues required effort and involvement, factors that improved once Rio Tinto was involved.

Herder families in Khan Bogd district have lived in the region for generations. Unlike several other contentious global mine sites, the community is homogeneous rather than having ethnic, religious or social differences. During the Soviet era there was little inequality, with access to food and goods often rationed. Much changed after the shift to democracy and a market economy, including wealth divides, livelihoods, sedentarisation, out-migration to the capital and a transition to modern lifestyles. Women are well-represented in the work force, including in professional occupations, and in higher education. The mega-mine has drawn migrants from other regions of the country in a quest for jobs; these people may have tangential connections (a relative) but can be resented by locals. Town residents had often been herders or belonged to herding families, leading to shared social values and identity. Whilst a herder-centric outlook dominated, local government officials and mine employees developed nuanced perspectives that encompassed new realities. It was common for different perspectives within a family as a member may work at the mine whilst others remained herders. As part of local compensation many herders had part-time 'make' work (often picking up rubbish) paid for by the mine. For local government, a large employer, the mine contributed significantly to the district through development (roads, water, buildings) and jobs that stimulated the economy. Oyu Tolgoi became central to community perceptions and well-being.

For mobile pastoralists the environment is critical as it is the basis of herding practice; these conditions are exacerbated in Khan Bogd's desert landscape. The low precipitation and sparse vegetation make mobility a key coping strategy. Any conditions that affect pasture are disruptive, whether climatic or human-induced. Thus, both the reality of the mine land take and the perceived disruption of herding practices upset the community (Sternberg et al. 2022). The mine perspective was that the license area took a tiny part of a vast country out of herding production and provided significant tax revenue. To herders each manipulated or lost water source, fence or road interrupted their livelihood (Fig 5). The mine was slow to acknowledge these points. In fact, Oyu Tolgoi, particularly since 2009, has higher levels of corporate social responsibility in comparison to other mines in the country, including the state-owned Tavan Tolgoi mega coal mine 140 kilometres to the north.

Local and NGO strategies

In Mongolia's vibrant civil society NGOs were free to address issues of local and national scale. In a country where thousands of organisations existed the clear message of the NGO OT Watch – to monitor and promote domestic rights at Oyu Tolgoi – proved to be a lasting strategy. Run by the English-speaking daughter of a former Mongolian diplomat, OT Watch was able to tap into international NGO fora and experience to draw intermittent attention to conditions at OT. Part of its efforts in Khan Bogd was to encourage formation of local NGOs to contest the mine. From such efforts developed the Gobi Soil NGO run by herders. It was this group that filed the IFC complaint. Gobi Soils provided the face and the immediate context of the complaint; it was OT Watch that was able to write, frame and submit the complaint in English. As the grievance process progressed OT Watch was joined by San Francisco-based Accountability Counsel in advancing the herders' case. The knowledge differentials saw the herders, rather obviously, texting or calling OT Watch for advice during mediation meetings. NGO participation was essential to the dispute resolution process at OT in 2019.

The local community presented a range of perspectives from herders, townspeople and those who worked at the mines. The debate was dominated by herders

*Fig 5: Camel crossing sign reflecting how OT's road to the border disrupts herding practices.
Source: B Batbuyan*

who believed the mine negatively impacted their traditional livelihoods. This was driven by herder displacement from the 8km x 10km Mine License Area, degradation and loss of pasture and inadequate compensation for resettlement, the disappearance of Bor Ovoo Spring and perceived lost water sources and lost economic benefit (Fig 6). The town dwellers felt less direct effect from the mine. They came to appreciate that local development could be paid by the mine. This started with improvements to electricity and water systems, then paved roads, a park and a community centre. Later came a hospital, new school and most desired, a 37km paved road from the town to the mine. Another group were residents who worked at the mine. Most were labourers – drivers, cafeteria workers, construction crews as well as clerical staff. With a job their status and economic roles were enhanced; they were supportive of the mine yet were embedded in the herding culture.

A shared community conviction was to try to get more personal and development benefit from the mine. In fact, many conceived the mine in a role more suitable to the government, with responsibility for funding all development and providing leadership. The strategy was to complain to the mine through site visits, local government meetings, threats of boycotts and blocking roads and any media outlets, particularly at the national level. All ills were attributed to the mine. This met with small concessions but no resolution. Any word of success quickly spread

Fig 6: Author with local herders attaching a dust trap outside Oyu Tolgoi mine. Source: B. Batbuyan

through the community and others tried similar tactics. Herders complained about animal deaths, loss of water and no mine jobs. In the town, swollen by an influx of opportunistic outsiders, people demanded more jobs. The local government argued for more financial support for operations and development. Only when OT Watch engaged with the local community did new ideas of lawsuits and international greviance procedures become viable opportunities. Only when the International Finance Corporation agreed to investigate the herder complaint did new schemes and strategies for dispute resolution become possible.

State and company strategy

Simultaneously, the advent of the mine had social repercussions (CAO 2017). This was evident in who derived benefits, who was perceived as a politician, who were the job recipients or suppliers and who were seen as opportunistic migrants. Most residents lacked direct contact with the mine; this isolation from the largest development in the region encouraged resentment and speculation. The intermediary group, those that had been resettled or received compensation in 2004 and 2011 (including payment, job, education benefit), were recognised and thus vocal in any complaint or process that may increase their benefit. The dispute over the mine was waged nationally in the press, through politics and with international agencies through the lens that the mine was taking advantage of the country and not fulfilling its responsibility. It was an easy sell, steeped in decades of the poor record of mining companies in developing nations. The mine brought electricity from China, provided water and paved roads in the district town, graded dirt roads; the wells provided or maintained were viewed as not adequate and self-serving. The community reached the point where there was no satisfying their wishes, desires and expectation; each new effort resulted in more demands. What was occasioned by the mine vis a vis socio-economic change was not differentiated by the herders. In fact, the community had once been known for small scale artisanal mining and as experienced traders with China. Bringing water diversion, environmental impact, indigeneity, tradition and fragmentation to their argument were newly-mastered terms provided by experienced NGOs able to link with international agencies. Both the community and local government gradually ascribed to the hopeful view that OT should and could provide infrastructure and support (roads, electricity, jobs, abattoirs, local development) that is typically the provenance and role of the government. The government's inability to deliver a modicum of progress only enlarged OT as a target of disillusionment. Striking was that the central government, though one-third owner of the mine, was absent from the discussion.

Yet something unusual happened on the way to development (the company and government narrative) and exploitation (the herder, NGO and broad social perspective). Years of misunderstanding, community hostility and conflict gave way to discussion and dispute resolution acclaimed as 'Herders take on mega-mine and win' (Accountability Counsel 2017). Whilst this glosses over twenty years of difficulty, it stresses a contemporary agreement between the herder community and the mine to resolve ongoing quarrels on resettlement, compensation and community development. A Tri-Partite Council (TPC) process was the outcome of years of facilitated engagement between the herders, local government and mine staff. Now presented as 'best practice', the TPC is promoted internationally by the mine owner Rio Tinto and featured by the International Council on Metals and Mining (ICMM) as a positive example to its members (CAO 2017). Examining the context and process offers insight into contemporary mega-infrastructure engagement with host communities. Now respected, the TPC process shows that begrudging agreement can be reached between disparate actors for (hoped for) community benefit.

A profound shift following the IFC's investigation of the herder complaint slowly lessened and defused the animosity toward OT in Khan Bogd. The complaint investigation meant the mine must engage with the community as part of the IFC's internal review of their provision of a $1 billion loan guarantee. The process was comprised of the herders, mine staff and the local government was known as the Tri-Partite Council (TPC) and was strongly supported by the community. Three processes followed over time; a skilled facilitator was engaged to oversee joint fact-finding efforts and dispute resolution, the herders greatly improved their knowledge, skills and ability to negotiate and the mine, through efforts of its Mongolian employees, became sufficiently trusted to be partners to the agreed resolution. In community eyes the lengthy process recognised the complaint's validity, the risk of environmental damage and poor previous treatment of institutionally weak herders. More explicitly, herders were able to express anger and sadness at changes and some credence was given to herder's customary knowledge and land use patterns. Most importantly, a complaint and re-evaluation process was established whereby residents who felt they deserved benefit or compensation could present a case for evaluation to a government-herder-mine staff review committee. Corollary issues that arose, such as government land tenure regulations, were important yet beyond the scope of the complaint resolution.

On one level Khan Bogd is an homogenous herding community. Yet amongst the residents some personages were considered more powerful (i.e. from a large clan), with better access (linked to the NGO, mine or government) or in a favourable location (close to the mine). Thus herders far away from the mine, or without a connection to a TPC member or government employee, may have felt disadvantaged in the benefit process. Personal and political party rivalries developed. Whilst gender or age were less of a factor, kin or work networks could affect perceptions of fairness in the TPC process.

In 2019 a formal community development agreement (Sternberg et al. 2019) was signed to much fanfare and media attention between the community, the OT mine and the local government (Guardian 2019). The community felt their efforts had been recognised and were resolved successfully with the agreement with Oyu Tolgoi. Contention then shifted to who could apply and would receive the new compensation available. Whilst hyperbolic, the 'community that took on the mega-mine and won' was the tenor of the day.

Discussion

The case study presents a vital process that is very important as Mongolia is inexorably drawn into a mining-driven future. First, the OT-Khan Bogd case establishes the validity of mining impact and displacement in the country. Secondly, it gives agency to communities to affect mining outcomes locally. Through training (World Bank), guidance (NGOs) and personal effort herders greatly increased their capacity, skills, knowledge and confidence. This included technical (computers, data, report reading), social (feeling equal to others, orderly debate, herder pride) and strategic (clear goals and a path to achievement). Thirdly, it provides an example of engagement to the myriad of other Mongolian towns and districts encountering an explosion of mining. Fourthly, the agreement provides a standard at which foreign companies can operate. This is essential as issues of engagement, transparency and legality affects the industry in Mongolia. Often foreign investment comes without clear standards, complaint procedures, adequate environment protection or local participation. In fact, the term 'foreign' now signifies western (plus Japanese, Korean & Indian) firms claiming to follow standards such as promulgated by the IFC and ICMM (ICMM 2012). The predominance and practices of China, a source of ready capital and import demand, is now the *de facto* national model and learned by Mongolian companies. Here the OT agreement does not reach. Thus, it will be from experience and education that citizens and civil society continue to pursue rights and recognition through protest and legal means. Rural violence (seen in Sukhbaatar Aimag), policy disagreement expressed by border closures (China and Russia), resource nationalism (Peoples Party, Democratic Alliance) and political instability in Mongolia can be traced to mining development. Against this background the herder-OT agreement provides the lone example of positive dispute resolution in the country.

Mongolia's open democracy and dynamic civil society enabled a positive case study, one of the few in the greater region. Future challenges to mega-project mediation and dispute resolution are well known as government and Chinese investment interests intermingle. The case is particularly illustrative for other low- and middle-income developing nations that look to resource extraction as a way to develop. Here, international mechanisms were able to address mega-mining problems where domestic and government efforts and initiatives (or lack thereof) were unable to address and resolve basic social, economic and environmental problems. In a bleak situation where money, elites and power assert right and might, the OT mine is the rarest example of community driven processes leading to dispute resolution. In 2019 local residents in Kyrgyzstan were able to close a BRI mine through violence and fire. In Myanmar armed ethnic rebellions were able to cancel or at least postpone a $3 billion dam. In Tajikistan a land swap with China was presented by the government as resolving a border dispute whilst being regarded as a trade to enable Chinese mining. These fraught scenarios reflect the image of mega-infrastructure projects amongst populations as sites of contention and conflict without resolution. In this scenario investors as well as host countries face institutional risk of domestic discontent, protest and malfeasance. In Mongolia this was able to be resolved by dialogue and engagement; in Kyrgyzstan by protest and violence (Palz 2019). How will conditions in Tajikistan evolve? What will transpire in the inevitable next conflict in Mongolia when a foreign company and international lender, with the attendant methods of engagement and complaint, are absent and such mediation is unavailable? The OT agreement should be appreciated and acknowledged as a satisfactory accord rather than panacea for community mega-infrastructure challenges. For this to truly occur requires that citizens and communities are given a seat the negotiation table from the start. Mongolians across the country are well-connected through social media and know about the TPC process. They are able to discuss matters reasonably with their local representatives and can stress issues important to their lives. Now aware of the premise of Social License to Operate, communities are able to engage with mines to ensure local benefit from licensing through exploration and extraction phases. This needs official support and, most challenging, buy-in from companies to resolve disputes before conflict occurs.

Mega-projects share size and impact; with examination each unravels differently. Three points of the Oyu Tolgoi case are important to acknowledge. The project was set up to be sold rather than developed with a long-term perspective. This meant initial decisions were made for cost and profit motives to attract a buyer, rather than to embed in the community. This contributed to limited engagement with the community and nominal interest in the environment. For example, as a desert site water and vegetation were minimal; the search for deep aquifers resulted in concerns about herder water and pasture were not satisfactorily addressed (Fig 7). Second, without NGO participation the case would not have been resolved. This is a key benefit an open society gives to its citizens. Third, the state had conflicting roles as both owner (national) and overseer of the mine (local). The national government abrogated its role as state steward to be a silent investment partner. In this abandonment the local government oversight, training and monitoring was not effective to meet citizen demands. Only the initiation of the external IFC process enabled a dispute resolution agenda and outcome in Khan Bogd.

Fig 7: Author at deep aquifer water pumping station, Oyu Tolgoi mine. Source: B. Batbuyan

Conclusion

Mongolians already had Harvey and Knox's (2012) enchantment of 'speed' as the flat, hard Gobi surface was easily travelled by horse, motorcycle or vehicle. They also had political freedom and were vocal in its expression. What remained was pursuit of economic opportunity. After the brutal but cosseted state system of the Soviet era in the last century citizens held little hope or expectation for government action. Two forms of disenchantment emerged – that the mine was not responsive to herder perceptions of their deserved financial rewards, and that the government at all levels did not actively support their fight against the mine. Pastoralists stumbled upon a third way – civil society able to use legitimate processes to advocate for their rights. The evolution of the complaint procedure enabled the community to move beyond feeling like a maligned party to a dynamic group achieving justified benefits and redress. Whilst the original desire – closing the mine – was not possible, the residents became imbued with a sense of agency in their relationship with the mine.

In fact, Oyu Tolgoi could be said to reflect the anti-'anti-politics' machine where government at all levels willingly ceded power to the mine (Ferguson 1990). The national government, as one-third owner, avoided engagement with the community and is content to be a silent partner. The local officials view/perceive/hope the mega-mine will perform the role of the state in creating new infrastructure, jobs and opportunity. The scale of the project dwarfs all else in the country; it charms the residents with thoughts of money and development (Harvey and Knox 2012). The community chases the mine, not the government, for services and the district council chases the mine, not the central government, for funding. A certain restraint by the company manages a balance between roles of external interloper and benevolent organisation, their actions done to meet legal agreements rather than to assuage the community. The skills to monitor and engage the company are limited, a modicum of equivalence is not attainable. The people got the paved road and gained political experience that has been converted to participation in party politics. Much of the community transition over the last twenty years was driven by social and cultural change (internet, vehicles, climate impact on livestock, lure of the city) rather that the mine. But if the mine might be convinced to pay, the herders will present a claim.

Here the embedding of the mega-mine rather than pastoral exigencies led to concentration of pasture use. As the mine diverted a stream (part underground) and ended access to a rare surface water spring in the desert, herders were able to state with probable cause that the mine may have marginalised their livelihoods. The perception of company liability induced several pastoralists to move near the mine license area in hopes of developing a future financial claim. The predictable outcome was overgrazing, contestation amongst herders and an unwillingness of officials to resolve the issues. Where once herders drew water from a spring and migrated across the rangeland, they now clustered in the alienated space to join a queue of claimants. In the Mongolian sense of time, the fact the mine and fence were well established before their arrival was immaterial. It was a change in the economic organisation (the mine) rather than domestic institutional factors that reordered dryland use (Haller et al. 2016). Unspoken, there is a vast, secretive Qatari Wildlife Reserve of similar size east of the district town run by the military that is not part of local debate. A reasonable interpretation is that it is less the loss of commons that bothers locals but the ability to engage, resist and benefit that differentiates the mine from the reserve.

Mongolia's herders, desert, lack of water and nascent democracy make a volatile site for one of the world's largest copper and gold mines. Set in the barren Gobi, the dynamics of an international investor, vocal citizens and ineffective government made a challenging home for a $12 billion mega-project. That such a project continues shows the drive for tax revenue, the problems borne of inexperience, disillusion when benefits and dreams do not materialise as expected and the long-term view and patience that sees a fraught situation come to a modicum of resolution and fruition. At the Oyu Tolgoi mega-mine an internationally driven dispute resolution process has provided a veneer of legitimacy, recognition of social and environmental mining implications and greater social license for the investor Rio Tinto. Now that differences are resolved to wide acclaim it is bittersweet to learn that a collapsing sediment structure threatens the mine's underground expansion and with it the nation's fragile economic tax base. The $1 to 2 billion needed to remediate ground conditions has drawn international investor criticism and call for abandonment. Such an outcome would exemplify the vagaries of mega-infrastructure investment and serve as a warning for nations seeking development based on resource extraction alone.

Glossary

COMECON	Council for Mutual Economic Assistance
EIA	Environmental Impact Assessments
ICMM	International Council on Metals and Mining)
IMF	International Monetary Fund
SIA	Social impact assessments
TPC	Tri-Partite Council

References

Batchuluun, Amrita and Lin, Joung 2010: An analysis of mining sector economics in Mongolia. Global Journal of Business Research 4(4), 81–93.

Campbell, Bonnie and Hatcher, Pascale 2019: Neoliberal reform, contestation and relations of power in mining: Observations from Guinea and Mongolia. The Extractive Industries and Society, 6(3), 642–653.

Dagys, Kadirbyek, Heijman, Wim, Dries, Liesbeth and Agipar, Bakyei 2020: The mining sector boom in Mongolia: did it cause the Dutch disease? Post-Communist Economies, 32(5), 607–642.

Dong, Baomin, Zhang, Yu and Song, Huasheng 2019: Corruption as a natural resource curse: Evidence from the Chinese coal mining. China Economic Review, 57, 101314.

Ferguson, James 1990: The anti-politics machine. the anthropology of the state: a reader, Cambridge University Press, 270–86.

Ganbold, Misheelt and Ali, Saleem 2017: The peril and promise of resource nationalism: A case analysis of Mongolia's mining development. Resources Policy, 53, 1–11.

Fernández-Giménez, Maria 1999: Sustaining the steppes: a geographical history of pastoral land use in Mongolia. Geographical Review, 89(3), 315–342.

Flyvbjerg, Bent 2014: What you should know about megaprojects and why: An overview. Project Management Journal, 45(2), 6–19.

Haller, T, Van Dijk, Han, Bollig, Michael, Greiner, Clemens, Schareika, Nickolaus and Gabbert, Christina 2016: Conflicts, security and marginalobiasisation: institutional change of the pastoral commons in a 'glocal' world. Rev. Sci. Tech, 35, 405–416.

Harvey, Penny and Knox, Hannah 2012: The enchantments of infrastructure. Mobilities, 7(4), 521–536.

Højer, Lars 2019: Patriots, Pensioners and Ordinary Mongolians: Deregulation and Conspiracy in Mongolia. Ethnos, 1-22.

Jackson, S 2015: Dusty roads and disconnections: perceptions of dust from unpaved mining roads in Mongolia's south Gobi province, Geoforum, 66, 94–105.

Jackson, S 2018: Abstracting water to extract minerals in Mongolia's South Gobi Province. Water Alternatives, 11(2), 336.

Mayaud, Jerome and Sternberg, Troy 2018: Map of Mongolia. Published in Sternberg, T et al 2022. Herd It in the Gobi: Deserting Pastoralism?. Land. 11(6), p. 799.

Meesters, Marieke and Behagel, Jelle 2017: The Social Licence to Operate: Ambiguities and the neutralization of harm in Mongolia. Resources Policy, 53, 274–282.

Myadar, Orhon and Jackson, Sara 2019: Contradictions of populism and resource extraction: Examining the intersection of resource nationalism and accumulation by dispossession in Mongolia. Annals of the American Association of Geographers, 109(2), 361–370.

Rossabi, Morris 2005: Modern Mongolia: from khans to commissars to capitalists. Oakland: University of California Press.

Sternberg, Troy 2012: Piospheres and pastoralists: vegetation and degradation in steppe grasslands. Human Ecology, 40(6), 811–820.

Sternberg, Troy, Rueff, Henri and Middleton, Nick 2015: Contraction of the Gobi desert, 2000–2012. Remote Sensing, 7(2), 1346–1358.

Sternberg, Troy and Chatty, Dawn 2016: Marginality, climate and resources in pastoral rangelands: Oman and Mongolia. Rangelands, 38(3), 145–151.

Sternberg, Troy 2018: Investigating the presumed causal links between drought and dzud in Mongolia. Natural Hazards, 92(1), 27–43.
Sternberg, Troy, Ahearn, Ariell and McConnell, Fiona 2019: From conflict to a community development agreement: A South Gobi solution. Community Development Journal, 55, 44–44.
Sternberg, Troy, Mayaud, Jerome and Ahearn, Ariell 2022: Herd It in the Gobi: Deserting Pastoralism?. Land. 11(6), p. 799.

Online Reports

Accountability Counsel 2017: Mongolian Herders Secure Historic Agreement with Oyu Tolgoi Mine, Government to Protect Herds, Health and Livelihoods ⟨www.accountabilitycounsel.org/2017/06/mongolian-herders-secure-historicagreement-with-oyu-tolgoi-mine-government-to-protect-herds-health-and-livelihoods/⟩ Accessed on 12.01.2019.
Ahlers, Rodante, Kiezebrink, Vincent, Dugersuren, Sukhgerel 2020: Undermining Mongolia: Corporate hold over development trajectory. ⟨www.somo.nl/wp-content/uploads/2020/02/Undermining-Mongolia-EN.pdf⟩ Accessed on 12.09.2020.
Bauer, Andrew, Namkhaijantsan, Dorjdari 2019: Wild growth, an assessment of Erdenes Mongol. Natural Resource Governance Institute. ⟨resourcegovernance.org/sites/default/files/documents/wild-growth-an-assessment-of-erdenes-mongol-full-report.pdf⟩ Accessed on 12.02.2020.
Compliance Advisor Ombudsman (CAO) 2017: Multi-disciplinary team and independent expert panel joint fact finding. ⟨www.cao-ombudsman.org/documents/MDTIEPFINALREPORTENG.pdf⟩ Accessed 28.11.2019.
Goodson, Jeff, Addleton, Jonathan 2020: How Great Power Competition Is Changing the Geopolitics of Mongolia. Stratfor Worldview ⟨worldview.stratfor.com/article/how-great-power-competition-changing-geopolitics-mongolia-china-russia-united-states⟩ Accessed on 12.09.2020
Guardian 2019 'An example to all': the Mongolian herders who took on a corporate behemoth – and won. ⟨https://www.theguardian.com/global-development/2019/apr/08/mongolian-herders-corporate-behemoth⟩ Accessed on 20.4.2019.
Freedom House 2019: Freedom in the World 2019 ⟨https://freedomhouse.org/report/freedom-world/2019/mongolia⟩ Accessed on 30.01.2019
Kingsley, Patrick 2017: Nomads no more: why Mongolian herders are moving to the city. ⟨theguardian.com/world/2017/jan/05/mongolian-herders-moving-to-city-climate-change⟩ Accessed on 20.04.2019.
International Council on Mining & Metals 2012: Community development toolkit ⟨www.icmm.com/en-gb/publications/mining-and-communities/community-development-toolkit⟩ Accessed on 12.01.2019
MAC (Mines and Communities) 2006: Robert Friedland ⟨www.minesandcommunities.org/article.php?a=7459⟩ Accessed on 12.03.2019.
Mining Global 2015: Rio Tinto secures $4 billion financing deal for Oyu Tolgoi copper mine ⟨https://www.miningglobal.com/operations/rio-tinto-secures-4-billion-financing-deal-oyu-tolgoi-copper-mine⟩ Accessed on 12.03.2019.
Palz, Catherine 2019: Tensions flair at Kyrgyz gold mine. Diplomat. ⟨https://thediplomat.com/2019/08/tensions-flare-at-kyrgyz-gold-mine/⟩ Accessed on 12.02.2019.

Transparency International 2019: Global Corruption Index 2018. www.transparency.org/cpi2018. Accessed 12.12.2019.

World Bank 2001: Mongolia: Energy Efficiency in the Electricity and District Heating Sectors. Energy Sector Management Assistance Programme (ESMAP); no. ESM 247 / 01. Washington, D.C. ‹www.openknowledge.worldbank.org/handle/10986/20288› Accessed on 12.02.2020.

World Bank 2020: Mongolia ‹data.worldbank.org/country/mongolia?view=chart› Accessed on 12.02.2020.

From Enchantment of Development to Disenchantment of Water Grabbing: Delhi-Mumbai Industrial Corridor

Marco Grogg, Institute of Social Anthropology, University of Bern, Switzerland

Introduction

According to the McKinsey report (Khosla and Soni 2012: 15), India is facing a massive urbanization, from 340 million to an estimated 590 million people, until the year 2030. Therefore, a proposed mega project, called the Delhi-Mumbai Industrial Corridor (DMIC), will be a solution approach to this structural change (Khosla and Soni 2012: 15). The process of rapid industrialization in India has already led to a large displacement of people. Between 2001 and 2011 the number of farmers in India declined by about nine million people.[1] The DMIC will also have an impact on the environment. It will affect mankind's most important resource: water. India comprises about one-sixth of the world's population and farms 20% of the world's livestock, but it holds only 4% of the world's freshwater resources (Kumar, Singh and Sharma 2005: 796). The use of groundwater has risen by roughly 500% in the last 50 years in India. This causes a lot of problems, since India is highly dependent on groundwater (Stratton Sayre and Taraz 2018: 85). Therefore, India will be facing various challenges due to the DMIC project.

For the purpose of understanding the DMIC's effects on local populations, as well as local environments, this article focuses on a small part of the DMIC: the Kushkhera-Bhiwadi-Neemrana investment region (KBNIR) in the Alwar district of the state of Rajasthan. The focus of this study will mainly lie on the acquisition of land and the compensation payment by the state government. This is due to the fact that the project is still in its first phase. The environmental impacts, especially the availability of water, are another issue this article will focus on. To examine this matter, research has been done on the actual availability and quality of water in the project area. Furthermore, an attempt has been made to describe the socio-economic constellation of the region and the livelihoods in order to see how the project could affect the local people. For this purpose, various scientific articles related to the DMIC and Rajasthan were examined, while additional infor-

---

[1] Jha, Praveen 03.09.2014: "Social Resistance and the Land Question in Contemporary India". ⟨https://www.cetri.be/Social-Resistance-and-the-Land⟩ accessed on 31.01.2021.

mation regarding the project was gathered through government communications and official reports by various stakeholders, as well as NGO reports and newspaper articles.

The transformation that the project will bring about will have profound effects. It is hoped for development and economic upturn. However, social and ecological effects can also be identified, which will have a negative impact on certain groups. The article shows that the problems of water supply in the region cannot be solved by the project. Furthermore, there are problems in connection with land expropriation, especially when it comes to compensation. It is also questionable what will become of those who have sold their land for development in the future and how the spatial transformation will affect the local population and pastoral groups.

Part 1: Historical, environmental, ethnographic and political context

Historical context

There are still remnants from India's colonial past that are of central importance today. Besides the democratic system, which was modelled on the English majoritarian system, legal remnants and India's post-colonial economic development are of central importance for this study. The Land Acquisition Act from 1894 was, and still is, a central instrument of the state, which allows it to acquire land for public purposes (Levien 2012: 944).

After gaining independence in 1947, the Indian state under Nehru's leadership followed a course of economic restriction. The therein entailed withdrawal from world trade is due to two factors. On the one hand, India was short on resources after independence, which is due to the overseas war economy of the British during the World War. On the other hand, a renewed dependence on international powers was to be prevented. The Indian economy should therefore produce for itself in the future. The main focus was on heavy industry. Planning instruments were used in a targeted manner and the scope for private enterprise was limited (Schoettli 2009: 75f.). In the 1990s, neoliberal reforms were introduced in India and the country joined the world market. As a result, industrial and economic development has now been increasingly privatized and opened for private capital. This led to an increase in land acquisitions whereby rural areas increasingly became the target of such land acquisitions (Levien 2012: 944f.).

The environment of Alwar district

The Alwar district lies in the north-eastern part of Rajasthan and is about 100 km from India's capital New Delhi. The district has 12 subdivisions, which cover an area of 8,382 square kilometres. To the north and north-east it is bordered by the Gurgaon district of the state of Haryana and the Bharatpur district of Rajasthan. In the south-west and the south the district is bounded by Rajasthan's subdivisions Sawai Madhopur and Jaipur. Topographically, the district is shaped by the Aravalli Hills, which run from east to west and cover an area of 19% of the district's total area (Mishra and Sharma 1986: 16). In terms of climate, it lies in the arid and semi-arid zone, with an average annual rainfall for Alwar city of 724 mm. However, there are differences in the degree of aridity within the district and also significant fluctuations in precipitation from year to year (Tomozawa 2015: 17).

The agricultural sector is the biggest employer in the Alwar district and therefore an important economic factor. The total geographical area is 782,897 ha, of which about 509,107 ha are cultivated land.[2] In 2015, the district counted their livestock capacity at 1,662,517 animals (buffaloes, cows, pigs and coats) (Government of India, Ministry of MSME 2016: 8).

In the proposed investment region around Neemrana the climate is mainly semi-arid. The monsoon time in this region is very short but it is responsible for 90% of the average rainfall. The average rainfall between 1989 and 2009 distributes around 570 mm over 27 days per year. The whole region, therefore, almost exclusively depends on groundwater. The only surface resource for water is the Sahibi river. Due to the construction of several dams, the river is now more concentrated in certain areas and covers less land surface area. The groundwater in the Tehsils Behror and Mandawar is overexploited. This is mainly because of the characteristics of the soil, which is not able to store the water well (Kuiper Compagnons 2014: A-2-3f.).

In the region where an airport is proposed as part of the DMIC, the climate can also be described as semi-arid. Groundwater is the only source of water within a radius of 10 km around the project area (Delhi-Mumbai Industrial Corridor Development Corporation 2018: 0.4f.).

The people and their livelihoods

The Alwar district counted 3,671,999 people in the census year 2011. Of these, 3,017,711 settled in rural areas, which means that only about 18% of the population lived in urban areas.

The two projects, the airport near Bhiwadi and Knowledge City near Neemrana, will affect 56 villages and settlements according to the estimates of the Environmental Impact Assessment and the Master Plan. More than 80% of the people affected work in the farming sector (Delhi-Mumbai Industrial Corridor Development Corporation 2018: 0.4f., 4.56; Kuiper Compagnons 2014: A-2-9 – A-2-17).[3]

As can be gathered from demographic data on the Alwar district, agriculture and animal husbandry are the main drivers of the economy in Behror and

---

[2] Indian Council of Agricultural Research Homepage: ⟨http://alwar1.kvk2.in/district-profile.html⟩ accessed on 31.01.2021.

[3] These are the official page marks of the environmental impact assessment and the final master plan.

Mandawar. Not only men but especially women and girls have a very important role in the agricultural sector. While men tend to produce goods for the market, women and girls are responsible for providing their home with food and gathering common-pool resources such as water and firewood. They take care of the work that must be done on the farm.[4]

As can also be gathered from demographic data on the Alwar district, there is also a share of scheduled tribes. Scheduled tribes is the official designation for the many ethnic groups in India.[5] These groups include the Bawaria, which used to be a nomadic hunting community. Due to the tightening of the hunting laws and the expanding cities and villages, their lifestyle changed. In the 2000s, the main activity of the Bawaria was the so-called 'chowkidari', the protection of agricultural areas from crop-raiding animals. In their main job they are dependent on the farmers who hire them for this job. It is very important that they can carry out this activity, since the chowkidari is only seasonal and their other sources of income are less profitable. In the off-season they often provide a 'mating service' for female buffaloes by travelling around with a strong and healthy male. Because of their activity, the Bawaria are widely spread and do not live in larger communities, and, as shown, they are very dependent on farmers who are in need of their services (Dutt 2004: 262–265). Additionally, many rural inhabitants are dependent on common-pool resources, such as pastures and forests. These are especially pastoral nomads and scheduled tribes, as well as the Bawaria.[6]

Resources and their use

The most important and at the same time most scarce resource in the district is water. There are only two rivers in the Alwar district providing surface water supply. Therefore, most of the water is gained from groundwater extraction. In the rural areas and in the agricultural sector this is mainly done by using wells. In India, water as a common-pool resource is an open good, in state property, which means every citizen who has access to it can consume as much as they want (OECD 2018: 44). Therefore, a well-functioning water management is an important condition for the economy and people's lives. In 2014, in the proposed

---

[4] DownToEarth 25.04.2018: "Climate Change is Destroying Women's Lives in Alwar". ⟨https://www.downtoearth.org.in/blog/climate-change-is-destroying-women-s-lives-in-alwar--60306⟩ accessed on 31.01.2021.

[5] Scheduled tribes is the constitutional definition of the indigenous people, who often describe themselves as Adivasi. However, the state and discourse in India reject the term "indigenous people" (Das, Kapoor, Hall et al. 2014: 2).

[6] Birhmaan, Vikas 2014: 'Sacred Forests and Rainwater Harvesting in Rajasthan, India'. ⟨http://ecotippingpoints.org/our-stories/indepth/india-rajasthan-rainwater-harvest-restoration-groundwater-johad.html#krapavis⟩ accessed on 31.01.2021.
Bathla and Singh 06.10.2019: 'The Delhi-Mumbai Expressway Is a Short-Cut to Socio-Ecological Disaster'. ⟨https://thewire.in/environment/delhi-mumbai-expressway-nitin-gadkari-bharatmala-nhai⟩ accessed on 31.01.2021.

knowledge city area, 90% of the water was required for agricultural purposes. The annual use for irrigation was estimated to be around 39 MCM (million cubic metres). According to the master plan the proposed demand for water in 2041 for this region will be 380 MLD (million litres per day) or 141.14 MCM per year. It can be understood from the projection that agriculture has a very high water consumption and that industrialisation may make the water consumption more efficient. However, until 2041 the ground water usage is expected to rise in the KBN region (Kuiper Compagnons 2014: 6-20). The overuse of groundwater supplies ensures that the groundwater level continues to fall. Smaller farms are particularly affected by this, as they cannot raise enough money to invest in bigger pumps or deeper wells. On the other hand, larger companies whose machines and wells reach deep enough benefit above all others. The surplus is then sold to the farmers who have water shortages. This creates disincentives that further aggravate the problem, and the reserves are now further used up for profitable purposes (Sharma and Sharma 2006: 40).

Since the agricultural sector is the main employer in the district, land for crops and animals is an important resource for the income and the employment of many people. As also mentioned, farming land is an important resource for the self-sufficiency of many families. This resource is becoming scarcer due to land acquisition, growing cities and industries. Furthermore, the availability of water also has an influence on it. In the future, it will be more difficult for smaller farmers to farm their land cost-effectively. Beside private land use, there are also common pastures in common property of local communities, which are mainly used by nomadic pastoralists and managed in an ecological way.[7]

Another common-pool resource in Alwar District is the so-called 'orans'. These are forested hills, which are sacred. The respective oran is named after the local deity. They provide grazing land and water, which are used by the surrounding villages and pastoral nomads. They are also considered to be places of spirituality, which are visited for prayers, celebrations and discussions and which unite the communities religiously, culturally and socially. In the case of health problems, the blessing of the local deity is requested. The orans have been collectively managed by the local villagers as well as the pastoral communities. Dams and wells were built to store the water from the monsoon period, allowing the vegetation to recover quickly and meeting the demand for water, and therefore local groups have established a cultural landscape based on common property institutions to govern water and to deal with water shortages.

Before India's independence most of the forest land was used and managed by the community itself. Since independence the state centralization has in some cases removed decision-making from community hands. Furthermore, local values have been discounted by national development agendas. As a result, many

---

[7] Ibid.

sacred forests have been destroyed or damaged by development projects while many others have been included in government-managed areas, state forests and other national land classifications. These factors, along with increasing population, and erosion of traditional culture, values and norms put enormous stress on orans. All of this culminated in the abandonment of traditional practices of oran conservation and management. Participation of the local villagers in the management of forest and in holding livestock has been decreased. However, the livestock sector in Rajasthan still accounts for 19% and there are many who depend on the orans.[8]

Legal and economic framework

There are several agencies from the government of Rajasthan involved in the process of the DMIC. Their legitimization is given by several acts (Kuiper Compagnons 2014: 9–13). However, in this part the focus lies on the several laws and acts referring to the acquisition of land.

As already seen, parts of today's legal framework for land acquisition in India are a relic of the colonial era. The Land Acquisition Act (LAA) of 1894 remained the chief instrument for expropriating land from private persons until 2014 (Levien 2018: 46). The so-called principle of 'eminent domain' allowed the central government or the state government to acquire private land for public purposes (Sampat 2013: 41f.). Its key feature was a broad definition of the public purposes, which also included the expropriation and distribution of land to private companies. The acquired land had to be compensated for its market value but not for its future purpose. Therefore, farming land was compensated as such and not as developed land (Levien 2018: 46). In 2009, several key features of the LAA (Amendment) Bill and the Resettlement & Rehabilitation Bill were introduced and influenced the power of the eminent domain. As a result, scheduled tribes, for example, also had the right to a fair compensation. Therewith, the new Bills act as a guarantee for fair compensation for people, who have almost no proprietary rights over land.[9]

The 'Right to Fair Compensation and Transparency in Land Acquisition, Rehabilitation and Resettlement Bill' (RTFCTLARR), introduced in 2013, replaced the LAA from 1894 and tried to define the public purpose. Thereby, the state or central government can expropriate land for (a) its own use, (b) for public-private partnerships where the land remains in the hand of the government, and (c) for private companies. Projects that serve the public purpose are: strategic

---

[8] Birhmaan, Vikas 2014: 'Sacred Forests and Rainwater Harvesting in Rajasthan, India'. ⟨http://ecotippingpoints.org/our-stories/indepth/india-rajasthan-rainwater-harvest-restoration-groundwater-johad.html#krapavis⟩ accessed on 31.01.2021.

[9] Ritimo 14.05.2018: 'Dispossession and Resistance in India and Mexico. Land Acquisition and State Policy in India'. ⟨https://www.ritimo.org/Land-Acquisition-and-State-Policy-in-India⟩ accessed on 31.01.2021.

defence-related projects, and infrastructure projects, which are defined by the government of India as agricultural projects, mines, industrial corridors, national investment and manufacturing zones, transportation infrastructure, sanitary, healthcare, etc. Although there is now a definition of public purpose, it does not really affect the power of the eminent domain. It only makes it more transparent (Sampat 2013: 44).

Furthermore, the process of land acquisition presumes a Social Impact Assessment survey, the intent for the acquisition must be clarified and there must be a declaration of the time for the compensation. For the owners, the compensation of the expropriated land shall be four times the market value in the case of rural areas and twice in the case of urban land. For the intended use by private companies or PPP projects, a consent of 80% and 70% (PPP) of the displaced people is needed for land acquisition (Jenkins 2013: 595, 596). The later provisions really affected the principle of eminent domain, but the new bill did not last for long.

In March 2015, the Lok Shaba, the first chamber of the Indian parliament, passed a law that replaced the Land Acquisition Act from 2013. The new RTFCTLARR Act was introduced by the Minister for Rural Development Birender Singh.[10] The new act exempts projects for defence, rural development, affordable housing, industrial corridors and for infrastructure from the provisions in Chapters II and III of the RTFCTLARR from 2013 (RTFCTLARR (Amendment) Bill 2015: 2). Projects within these five categories no longer need an 80% or 70% consent and do not require a Social Impact Assessment survey (PRS Legislative Research 2015: 1) Therefore, under the pretext of the public purpose, the government is able to expropriate private land for several types of projects. This also includes irrigated land, which was not permitted to be acquired under the old RTFCTLARR.[11]

---

[10] PRS Legislative Research Homepage: ⟨http://www.prsindia.org/billtrack/the-right-to-fair-compensation-and-transparency-in-land-acquisition-rehabilitation-and-resettlement-amendment-bill-2015-3649⟩ accessed on 31.01.2021.

[11] Jain, Sreenivasan: 'Why an Acquisition Off the Delhi-Jaipur Highway Challenges Assumptions of the New Land Bill'. NDTV 15.03.2015. ⟨https://www.ndtv.com/india-news/an-acquisition-off-the-delhi-jaipur-highway-challenges-assumptions-of-the-new-land-bill-746714⟩ accessed on 31.01.2021.

Part 2: The Mega-Infrastructure Project

The Delhi-Mumbai industrial corridor

The DMIC is an industrial development and infrastructure programme that connects the cities of New Delhi and Mumbai. The corridor has an estimated length of nearly 1500 km, which leads through six states. Within this mega-infrastructure project 24 regions are identified, wherein smart cities, international airports, power plants, transit systems, industries and logistical hubs will be created. These investment regions and industrial areas will spread across the backbone of the project, the 'Western Dedicated Freight Corridor'. This freight corridor is a transport line, consisting of railways and highways.[12] The corridor will function as a fast transit system from the inland to the ocean ports in the west and embed the inland more into the global market. The estimated costs of the DMIC are about 90 to 100 billion US dollars. To meet these costs, the DMIC is projected to be handled as a public-private partnership, which means that the government of India is acquiring the land and developing it. When a basic infrastructure is set, the land will be sold to investors for further development or economic use. The budget for the first phase of the project is 10 billion US dollars. The rest should be provided by private investors.[13] Japan is the biggest foreign shareholder of the project so far (Annual Report 2017–2018: 39). The economic relationship between these two countries is growing. This is due to the perceived rising threat of China's economic growth to the Asian continent and because of the cheap labour forces and the strong economic growth in India. Furthermore, India has a growing purchase power, which makes the country attractive for Japanese exports.[14] For the development of the DMIC a special purpose vehicle has been built: the Delhi-Mumbai Industrial Corridor Development Corporation Ltd. With 49%, the government of India is the biggest shareholder of this corporation. These 49% of the shares are distributed among the six involved state governments (total 24%) and the central government (25%) (Memorandum of Understanding 2009). Therewith, India's central government and constituent state governments hold the biggest stake of the corporation, followed by the Bank of Japan with 26%; 24% are held by public institutions (Annual Report 2017–2018: 39f.).

---

[12] DMICDC Homepage: 'The Projects Influence Area'. ⟨https://dmicdc.com/DMIC-projects/project-influence-area⟩ accessed on 31.01.2021.
[13] CauseBecause 07.03.2016: "Delhi-Mumbai Industrial Corridor. Development Dilemmas". ⟨https://causebecause.com/delhi-mumbai-industrial-corridor-development-dilemmas/4495⟩ accessed on 31.01.2021.
[14] Timmons, Heather: "As Japan and India Forge Economic Ties, a Counterweight to China Is Seen". The New York Times 21.08.2007. ⟨https://www.nytimes.com/2007/08/21/business/worldbusiness/21rupee.html⟩ accessed on 31.01.2021.

Khuskhera-Bhiwadi-Neemrana investment region

The Khuskhera-Bhiwadi-Neermana Investment Region will be located roughly 110 km south of the national capital New Delhi, in the Alwar district of the state of Rajasthan. There, the whole investment region will cover 165 km². Within this area, a knowledge city, a centre of education with schools, universities and IT companies, surrounded by industries, residential areas and high-tech agriculture will be built near Neemrana. The city will be linked with the proposed new airport at Bhiwadi, which will have an estimated size of 24 km². The airport in turn will be used for cargo, as well as for public transport. Together, the airport, the knowledge city and the road connection comprise the early bird project in this region (Delhi-Mumbai Industrial Corridor Project: 54–57). These three projects of the KBNIR should be completed by 2021.

By 2031 the natural expansion of the knowledge city will be finalised. And in 2041 the high-tech agricultural sector and the industry will be set up (Kuiper Compagnons 2014: 5-3). The whole KBNIR adheres to the aspect of sustainability. According to the final master plan this means that the use of water should be optimised and firms should have solar panels on their roofs (Kuiper Compagnons 2014: 2-1). The knowledge city at Neemrana and the airport near Bhiwadi will be connected by a highway passing through Khushkhera. Khushkhera already has an industrial area of nearly 1,000 acres.[16] Under RIICO (Rajasthan State Industrial Development & Investment Corporation Limited) this area is to be further enlarged. However, this will not happen under the DMIC. The DMIC project will only link Khushkhera with the two other projects of the KBNIR.

There are 17 different state governmental agencies or companies involved in the process. There is an agency for urban development, one for power installation, one for water management, one for road building, etc. Therefore, there are many different actors from the state governmental side of Rajasthan (Kuiper Compagnons 2014: 9-13, 9-18). Kuiper Compagnons, a company from the Netherlands, is the consultant for the KBNIR and the editor of the master plan. The government of Rajasthan is responsible for the acquisition of land, while the governmental enterprise RIICO is responsible for the acquisition and the development of industrial areas.[17] In its entirety, the KBNIR is characterized as a National Investment & Manufacturing Zone. They are equally regulated and controlled as Special Economic Zones, they just differ in size. This means that the industries,

---

[15] Map 1 shows the 165 square kilometres investment region at Neemrana. Figure 2 shows Neemrana, Khuskhera and Bhiwadi Airport, which will be linked with a new highway. The black line is the Dedicated Freight Corridor.

[16] Official Site of Alwar: ⟨https://alwar.rajasthan.gov.in/content/raj/alwar/en/business/infrastructure.html#⟩ accessed on 31.01.2021.

[17] PDCOR Ltd. Online Homepage: ⟨https://www.pdcor.com/industry.htm⟩ accessed on 31.01.2021.

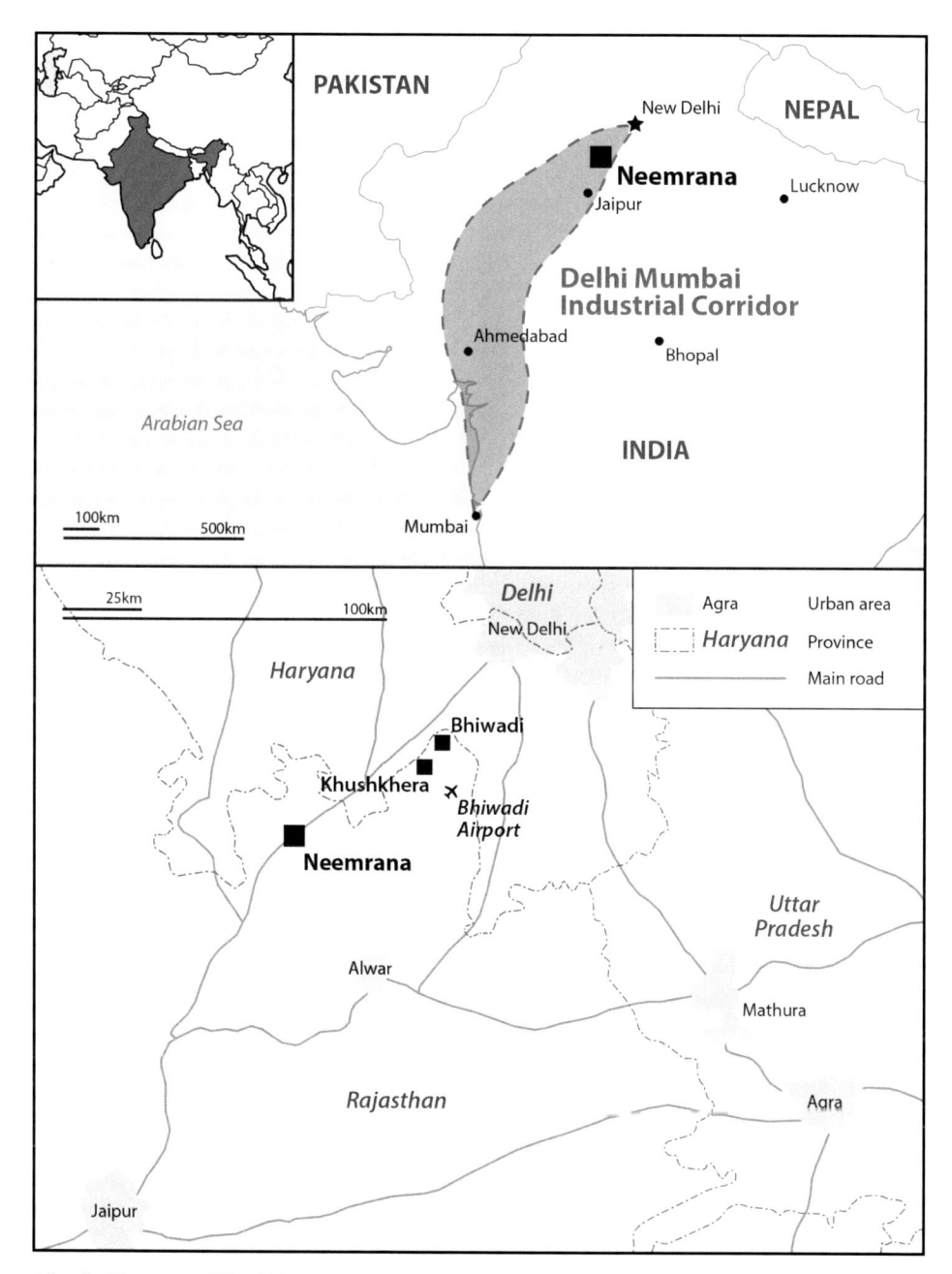

Map 1: Neemrana, Khushkhera, Bhiwadi Airport. Source: Map compilation and design by Manuel L. K. Abebe (2021), CDE, University of Bern, Bern, Switzerland.[15]

who will settle down in this region, will have benefits in their taxation and regulation (Malayalam, Kannada et al. 2019: 1f.).

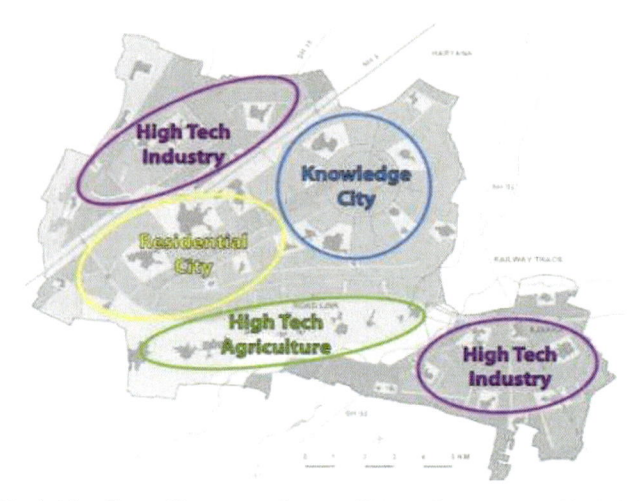

Fig 1: The City at Neemrana. Source: Kuiper Compagnons 2014: 2-5.

The site for the development of the KBNIR includes 42 villages. As per the Census 2001 of Alwar District, the combined population of villages falling under KBNIR comprised 68,041 people (Kuiper Compagnons 2014: 3-1). There should be no relocation of any population and jobs are expected to be created for the farmers by integrating them into the high-tech agricultural sector of the city. Key to the new city is that existing villages may not be wholly or partially destroyed in order to make way for new development. The existing villages will be embedded within the new developments and be retained and regenerated to become vital and vibrant elements in the new urban and rural structures (Kuiper Compagnons 2014: 2-2, 2-3). For the proposed airport at Bhiwadi, 14 villages will be directly or indirectly affected due to the process of land acquisition (Delhi-Mumbai Industrial Corridor Development Corporation 2018: 0.4).

Environmental and social impacts

As described earlier, in Rajasthan and in the Alwar district, the groundwater fulfils a high proportion of the drinking water requirements. The quality and quantity of the groundwater is critical for drinking and agricultural purposes. The rising cities of Rajasthan are facing the problem of the shrinking quality of the groundwater for different reasons, such as urbanization, the use of pesticides in agriculture, inappropriate water management, bad sanitation and the various industrial activities (Goyal, Tiwari and Sakar 2017: 657).

When we compare these images with the planned knowledge city with its industry and high-tech agriculture, we can see that the industry will be set up in the red zones (b), where the water quality is already very poor. The agricultural part and the residential area will be set up in the green area (b). The future quality of the groundwater in this area greatly depends on the use of pesticides and the

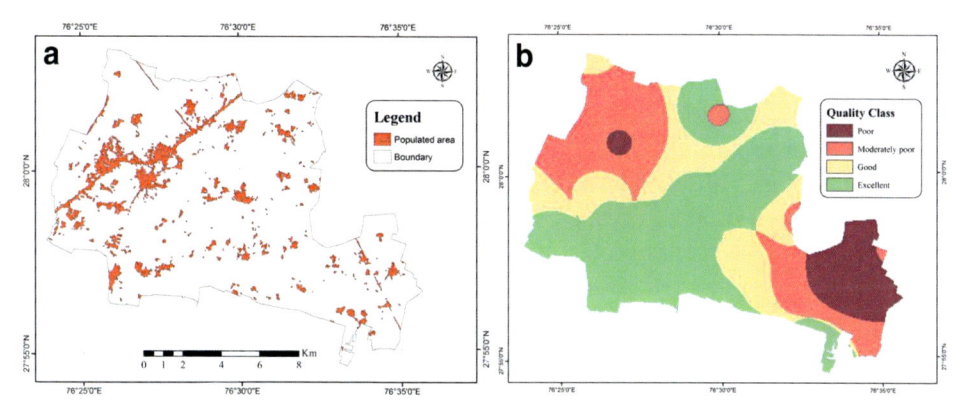

Fig 2: Distribution of the population compared to the quality of the groundwater. Source: Goyal, Tiwari and Sakar 2017: 658

waste management. If groundwater contamination in this area progresses, potable water could no longer be provided in the region. As things stand, 65.88% of the groundwater is hydrochemically good enough for drinking purposes (Goyal, Tiwari and Sakar 2017: 1). Furthermore, it is to be questioned how the industry will affect the groundwater and how the water demand and supply will be managed. The estimated demand for water in the whole KBN region (165 km^2) is estimated at around 380 million litres per day (Kuiper Compagnons 2014: 6-20). According to the groundwater resources assessment of 2017, the regions of Mandawar, Behror and Neemrana have already overexploited this capacity (GWRA 2017: 133). Therefore, in addition to the shrinking quality of groundwater for drinking purposes, the demand for groundwater will rise. According to the final development plan, the overdraft rate for groundwater is estimated to rise (Kuiper Compagnons 2014: 6-20), which means that the divergence between the pumped water and the natural refill is estimated to widen further.[18] If there is no clear management in the future, the overexploitation of the water will increase. As an alternative, it is proposed to use external resources: for example, the River Chambal. In this regard, a feasibility study is being done. But is taking water from a river that is hundreds of miles away a solution? How does this cut the supply of others? The possible issues seem apparent. There are many different solutions and approaches; there is, however, no fixed plan on how the water supply can be guaranteed (Kuiper Compagnons 2014: 6-20, 6-23).

The environmental impacts described above also have an impact on the people. The quality of groundwater as an important common-pool resource has an influence on the health of the population, as well as on the animals. Furthermore, the proposed KBN region will demand a much higher amount of groundwater, especially for farmers around the proposed investment region. As we have seen, the

---

[18] Water Education Foundation: ‹https://www.watereducation.org/aquapedia/overdraft› accessed on 31.01.2021.

agricultural sector needs a high amount of water and if there is no guarantee for it, peasant work will be more risk-bound. This in turn leads to another issue: the distribution of the resources. Sampat (2017: 43) shows that the private use of infrastructure in and around Special Economic Zones doesn't serve all. Therefore, the infrastructure, as well as the resources, such as water and electrical power, have mainly been used by private companies.

Another example of conflicts over water is found at Lewari village in Alwar District, due to industrialization. The groundwater there is used extensively by manufacturing industries. Sixteen pumps serve industry there, reducing groundwater supplies for the rest of the population. Every year, many farmers must invest in new pumps, which can penetrate deeper into the earth. In Lewari, the industrial consumption of water created a conflict over water between agriculture, industry and residential areas.[19] Furthermore, many farmers are concerned that the construction of the corridor's road will interrupt the groundwater supply for their fields.[20] As already seen, water shortages have built a new market, where bigger landholders sell their surpluses of water to other farmers. It can therefore be assumed that conflicts over water are already present in India and that they will spread and intensify.

The compensation payment and the resettlement are further factors that influence people's lives. Although the first phase of the project, the acquisition of land, is not finished yet, the next paragraph will address how the compensation payment produces problems in some cases. The announcement of the acquisition of land for the DMIC in 137 villages in the Alwar district was in 2012. The affected people had no information about the proposed acquisition of the land, and they also had no opportunity to participate, because back in 2012 no consent for land acquisition was required.[21] These figures are not consistent with those of the final development plan and the airport's environmental impact assessment. Therefore, the land acquisition for the DMIC affects many more villages in the Alwar district.

As previously mentioned, the new RTFCTLARR Act replaced the act from 2013. As we have seen, this new law paved the way for the infrastructure project in certain ways. Furthermore, the new bill also affects the compensation payments that the expropriated farmers will receive. The factors for the value of the compensations were changed by the several state governments in different ways. In

---

[19] Bhaduri, Amita: 'Alwar Homes, Farms and Factories Fight for Water'. India Water Portal 07.06.2018. ⟨https://www.indiawaterportal.org/articles/alwar-homes-farms-and-factories-fight-water⟩ accessed on 31.01.2021.

[20] Bathla and Singh 06.10.2019: 'The Delhi-Mumbai Expressway Is a Short-Cut to Socio-Ecological Disaster'. ⟨https://thewire.in/environment/delhi-mumbai-expressway-nitin-gadkari-bharatmala-nhai⟩ accessed on 31.01.2021.

[21] Jain, Sreenivasan: 'Why an Acquisition Off the Delhi-Jaipur Highway Challenges Assumptions of the New Land Bill'. NDTV 15.03.2015. ⟨https://www.ndtv.com/india-news/an-acquisition-off-the-delhi-jaipur-highway-challenges-assumptions-of-the-new-land-bill-746714⟩ accessed on 31.01.2021.

three states the compensation value for rural land has been halved.[22] One of these affected farmers is Sunil Chauhan, whose land was acquired in 2015. In January 2016, the government bought around 993 hectares of land from Sunil and other farmers. This implies that the government had already decided to take the land from Sunil Chauhan in 2015 but they did not buy it until the new bill was implemented. 'The value of the land now is about 30–35 lakh per bigha (281,155 $/ 1.13ha $\approx$ 24.90 $/m^2) while I was getting more than double that amount as per the compensation formula (implemented after the new Land Acquisition Act 2013),' said Sunil. 'The government rules did not allow them [the farmers] to either sell the land or mortgage it to meet emergencies such as marriage in a family or some medical emergencies. Today, the land prices have fallen by more than 50% as compared to the compensation amount that was being offered by the state government at that time,' said Shayam Singh Chauhan, the former sarpanch, the spokesman of the village of Gugalkota. This move has affected roughly 500 farmers.[23] The delay in compensation payment affected many farmers in the Alwar district. In 2012, the first acquisitions were made. But it was not until 2015 that the government of Rajasthan was able to declare the compensation payments. In these three years the farmers were not permitted to sell or mortgage it, as described above. Because of that, a few could not react to emergencies, marriages were delayed and many of the farmers took credits from moneylenders.[24]

As we have seen, most of the workers in the agricultural sector in the affected areas around Neemrana are women. So, if there is no proper compensation and no possibility of purchasing or getting new land for agriculture, they will be affected the most. Since they hardly own property, they are very dependent on the men and the compensation payments they receive. Since women are also less involved in decision-making, their voice is less heard by the competent authorities. In addition to a higher participation of men in terms of land acquisition and compensations, it also requires the involvement of women in the discussion. But it seems that both are not guaranteed. Furthermore, a television report by NDTV showed that only the landowners are getting compensation. Farmers in this video were complaining that agricultural labourers would receive nothing.[25]

---

[22] Wahi, Namita: 'How Central and State Governments Have Diluted the Historic Land Legislation of 2013'. The Economic Times 14.04.2018. ⟨https://economictimes.indiatimes.com/news/politics-and-nation/how-central-and-state-governments-have-diluted-the-historic-land-legislation-of2013/articleshow/63764378.cms?from=mdr⟩ accessed on 31.01.2021.

[23] Ahuja, Manoj: 'Move to De-acquire Land for DMIC Projects Hits Alwar Farmers Hard'. The Hindustan Times 16.02.2018. ⟨https://www.hindustantimes.com/jaipur/move-to-de-acquire-land-for-dmic-project-hits-alwar-farmers/story-XTnT0LyHYqNrYApDuCHuiP.html⟩ accessed on 31.01.2021.

[24] Tripathy, Srikanta: 'DMIC Derails in Rajasthan, Farmers Too Hit Hard'. The Times of India 07.05.2017. ⟨https://timesofindia.indiatimes.com/city/jaipur/dmic-derails-in-raj-farmers-too-hit-hard/articleshow/58556408.cms⟩ accessed on 31.01.2021.

[25] Jain, Sreenivasan: "Why an Acquisition Off the Delhi-Jaipur Highway Challenges Assump-

As the development plan for the KBNIR mentioned, there will be no relocation but instead an integration of the affected farmers into the new city by giving them jobs in the high-tech agricultural zone. But the estimated number of workers needed in this sector in 2040 is only 3,800 (Kuiper Compagnons 2014: A-3-3). Therefore, only a small fraction of the affected people is estimated to work in the proposed agricultural sector. This raises the question as to whether the local population also has access to the new jobs in the city. The farmers of Shahjahanpur interviewed by NDTV see this critically. In their village, 25 young men had technical training, but no one has found work in the surrounding industries. They were allegedly told: 'You are locals; we cannot take you.'[26]

Another group affected by the project are nomadic pastoralists like the Bawaria. As has been shown, their activities are extremely dependent on the farmers, and the influences that the DMIC has in Alwar on the farmers will also have an impact on the livelihood of the Bawaria. Due to the decline in the number of farms, there will be a falling demand for their main activity: the chowkidari. Furthermore, growing industries, cities and streets, such as the Dedicated Freight Corridor, impair the mobility of such nomadic groups and thus their way of life. According to Aman Singh and Nitin Bathla,[27] there are many tribal communities that were affected due to the construction of the 100 m-wide road of the corridor. For pastoral nomads in particular, the corridor represents an almost insurmountable barrier that cuts them off from common-pool resources, such as grazing pastures. This leads to a lack of mobility and access options to local common property as well as to commons grabbing. This could lead to an overuse of certain pastures, because mobility and pasture areas themselves are reduced, which will lead to a longer duration of use of the pastures and to an overstocking. Furthermore, the project passes through many orans, which are places of spirituality and culture, and important water reservoirs and pastures, used by pastoral communities and locals.

Another influence of the DMIC project in the Alwar district is rising prices, especially in real estate. In Neemrana and Bhiwadi, the prices are going up very fast. As a result, the rising prices might lead to a gentrification in Bhiwadi and the proposed city at Neemrana. Michael Levien took note of exciting changes in his field research in a village in Rajasthan next to which a Special Economic Zone was created. Due to the rising housing prices, many people who owned land entered the real estate market and became land brokers. This changed the social structure of

---

tions of the New Land Bill". NDTV 15.03.2015. ⟨https://www.ndtv.com/india-news/an-acquisition-off-the-delhi-jaipur-highway-challenges-assumptions-of-the-new-land-bill-746714⟩ accessed on 31.01.2021.
[26] Ibid.
[27] Bathla and Singh 06.10.2019: 'The Delhi-Mumbai Expressway Is a Short-Cut to Socio-Ecological Disaster'. ⟨https://thewire.in/environment/delhi-mumbai-expressway-nitin-gadkari-bharatmala-nhai⟩ accessed on 31.01.2021.

the village. Financial inequalities became apparent and social interactions among villagers decreased (Levien 2018: 240f.).

Government and investors' strategies

The official websites of the DMIC and the project in Rajasthan give only a small insight into the undertaking. However, it is advertised that the project makes economic and ecological sense and that the rural areas of Rajasthan are therefore to be developed by it.[28]

The new RTFCTLARR bill, which was enacted in 2015, was a strategy to deregulate the process around the DMIC. Because of the Lok Sabha elections in 2014, the BJP (Bharatiya Janata Party) of Prime Minister Modi received the majority in the first chamber of the parliament and so they had the majority to pass the new bill.[29] As explained in the previous chapter, in Gugalkota the government most certainly waited until the enactment of the new RTFCTLARR bill before they de-acquired the land there. The prices have fallen by about 50% since then, therefore the government of Rajasthan and the government company RIICO now have lower costs and can sell the final developed land to private investors at lower prices. RIICO makes large profits with the acquiring and selling of land to investors. Michael Levien (Levien 2018: 50) called the governmental company a broker for land when they acquired, developed and sold land after the implementation of the Special Economic Zone Act in India. This speaks to an act of 'institution shopping' on the part of the government. It can therefore choose between the different sets of rules and use them to its own advantage, such as to devaluate land regarding compensations and sell land again to private investors for higher prices, all of these actions legitimated by different formal laws to be selected by state and government actors in power.

Another example is the acquisition of land near Shahjahanpur, where RIICO bought land from farmers and resold it instantly to investors at a much higher price. In addition to that, a former NDTV research showed that around 50% of the land from five state governments, including Rajasthan's government, was vacant and undeveloped.[30] This indicates that there seems to be quite a lot of land owned by the state governments that could be used for the DMIC. The question then arises as to what the governments intend to do with this land and why it is not used for such projects. Is the land in an unfavourable position for the DMIC? Or is it perhaps about forcing a structural change? In other words, is it possible

---

[28] Ibid.
[29] Elections. In: ‹http://www.elections.in/parliamentary-constituencies/2014-election-results.html› accessed on 31.01.2021.
[30] Jain, Sreenivasan: "Why an Acquisition Off the Delhi-Jaipur Highway Challenges Assumptions of the New Land Bill". NDTV 15.03.2015. ‹https://www.ndtv.com/india-news/an-acquisition-off-the-delhi-jaipur-highway-challenges-assumptions-of-the-new-land-bill-746714› accessed on 31.01.2021.

the land for the rural population, which works mainly in the agricultural sector, is being redistributed in order to create space for cities and industry, and thus forcing people to give up their previous lifestyles and to participate in this change?

Without having a distinctive answer to this question, the delays in compensation payments also have a negative impact on the KBNIR. Since the respective state governments must look to their private investors for the respective projects, they are in competition with each other. Although Rajasthan has attractive prices in this regard, it runs the risk of delaying projects as land acquisition is sluggish. The Times of India[31] accuses the government in Rajasthan of unwillingness and incompetence. Necessary funds could have long been claimed from the central government in order to pay off the compensation. Thus, land would finally be in their possession, enabling them to pursue the projects. Another possibility would be to give land in the developed zones to the farmers as a form of compensation. Since not much has happened in this regard, it could come to an extensive delay of the project.[32]

No specific strategies regarding private investors could be found. The reason for that may be that the whole DMIC project is still in its first phase, which means it is all about acquiring land and developing it. It may therefore be assumed that when the basic infrastructure is guaranteed, the land will be sold to private investors for further development or for economic use.

Strategies and resistance by locals (local and NGO strategies)

When the acquisition of land started in 2012 there were a few protests from farmers against it. But there were also farmers who were willing to give up their land after the RTFCTLARR bill of 2013, because of the proposed high amount of compensation. Another explanation as to why many farmers were willing to give up their land is that the supply of water had decreased.[33] As described above, some local people near Special Economic Zones tried themselves as land brokers, and here this may also be the case. They see investment opportunities in such projects and therefore sell their land to invest it within the DMIC. They hope to make a profit on the basis of the promises carried by the project and were thereby enchanted (Harvey and Knox 2012). However, later on it became clear that contrary to this view a disenchantment process for local communities took place because of the loss of their commons and the lack of adequate compensations. Therefore,

---

[31] Tripathy, Srikanta: 'DMIC Derails in Rajasthan, Farmers Too Hit Hard'. The Times of India 07.05.2017. ⟨https://timesofindia.indiatimes.com/city/jaipur/dmic-derails-in-raj-farmers-too-hit-hard/articleshow/58556408.cms⟩ accessed on 31.01.2021.

[32] Ibid.

[33] Ahuja, Manoj: 'Move to De-acquire Land for DMIC Projects Hits Alwar Farmers Hard'. The Hindustan Times 16.02.2018. ⟨https://www.hindustantimes.com/jaipur/move-to-de-acquire-land-for-dmic-project-hits-alwar-farmers/story-XTnT0LyHYqNrYApDuCHuiP.html⟩ accessed on 31.01.2021.

the megaproject, which is framed as a possibility for development and economic upswing, is rather an anti-politics machine. However, it is not perceived as such by some of the local population, who see behind the anti-politics and have no trust in the government and its promises of development. In addition, it might be a politics machine instead as there are people who mistrust it and are not willing to give up their land and their livelihood.

As described in the chapter before, many farmers whose lands have been acquired were waiting a long time or are still waiting for their compensation payment and they cannot sell or mortgage their land. As a reaction, a few farmers from Bhiwadi and Neemrana have gone to Rajasthan's government seat in Jaipur and demanded their compensations, immediately and in payments of cash.[34] The whole population of Gugalkota, whose 500 farmers were affected by the acquisition of land after the implementation of the new RTFCTLARR bill, boycotted the Lok Shaba by-elections as a protest against the government.[35]

Protests and resistances also appeared in the industries in Alwar. Several factories went on strike in 2014. The workers demanded better working conditions and better wages in the face of the economic upswing. They also demanded recognition of their labour unions. The protests were fiercely opposed by the state. Near Bhiwadi around 150 workers were injured, and 22 were arrested. At the Shriram Piston factory in the Alwar district 1,200 workers were attacked by 2,000 policemen and 100 bouncers. Akash Bhattacharya says that such violent protests have become routine for the DMIC project (Bhattacharya 2014: 15).

While no NGO activities related specifically to the KBNIR could be found, there are some regarding the whole DMIC. Several NGOs, such as the National Alliance for Farmer/People Movement, All India Coordination Committee of Farmers, Bhartiya Kisan Union and Shetkari Sangathan, were present before the joint committee of the parliament. They were demanding the reimplementation of the clause for a Social Impact Survey and the need for a consent. Furthermore, there should be no acquisition of single or multi-cropped land by the government for infrastructure projects. Fair compensations were demanded, which doesn't necessarily mean cash compensations. They demanded land for land, a house for a house and the compensation of employment loss. The National Alliance for People Movement demanded a clear definition of the public purpose, because it fears several projects will be built in the name of economic development, which will not serve the public purpose. The representatives of the NGOs

---

[34] Tripathy, Srikanta: 'DMIC Derails in Rajasthan, Farmers Too Hit Hard'. The Times of India 07.05.2017. ⟨https://timesofindia.indiatimes.com/city/jaipur/dmic-derails-in-raj-farmers-too-hit-hard/articleshow/58556408.cms⟩ accessed on 31.01.2021.

[35] Ahuja, Manoj: 'Move to De-acquire Land for DMIC Projects Hits Alwar Farmers Hard'. The Hindustan Times 16.02.2018. ⟨https://www.hindustantimes.com/jaipur/move-to-de-acquire-land-for-dmic-project-hits-alwar-farmers/story-XTnT0LyHYqNrYApDuCHuiP.html⟩ accessed on 31.01.2021.

and the farmers were condemning the government for moving back in time. In their opinion, today's framework for land acquisition reminds them more of the act of 1894.[36]

The KRAPAVIS organization held discussions with affected people and tries to describe the importance of the orans through its work. In connection with the creation of the road of the corridor, they point out that, in addition to the ecological consequences, common lands are also being privatized, thus endangering the lifestyle of those who depend on them.[37]

Conclusion

As previously described, India will inevitably be facing a massive urbanization and the DMIC will be a solution to issues that arise during this process. However, the building of better infrastructure and new cities has a reinforcing influence. In particular, the prospects of new jobs will encourage many to move into the new urban areas. Therefore, there will be a high demand on real estate and living space, which in turn will lead to rising prices in the market. As we have seen, the prices in Neemrana and Bhiwadi are already high. The proposed city at Neemrana is facing the problem of gentrification if there is not enough provision of affordable housing. There will be a transformation of the landscape in India. The urban areas will grow, whereas the rural areas will shrink. Despite reacting to demographic transformations and development, the DMIC will guarantee the high economic growth in India. With an extensive industrialization and the provision of infrastructure this goal will be achieved. This will also lead to a massive structural change in the labour market. In the example of the KBNIR we can see which part of the Indian society loses the most: farmers, who are mainly affected due to the acquisition of land and loss of access to essential resources, such as pastures, forests and water. As has been shown, the availability and the quality of water resources for drinking purposes will shrink. Therefore, the enchanting promises of new development and economic growth will be at the expense of the agricultural sector, which is still the biggest employer in India. Additionally, one of the biggest challenges for India is the structural change and compensating for those who are at a loss due to this change. It seems to be expected that either the farmers will be well integrated into the new labour market or they will get fairly compensated for their loss. However, as is made apparent, the compensation payments are already problematic. It becomes evident in this struggle that not all those affected by the change will

---

[36] The Economic Times 15.06.2015: 'Land Bill. NGO's, Farmer Organisations Hit Out at Government'. ⟨https://m.economictimes.com/news/politics-and-nation/land-bill-ngos-farmer-organisations-hit-out-at-government/articleshow/47679048.cms⟩ accessed on 31.01.2021.

[37] Bathla and Singh 06.10.2019: 'The Delhi-Mumbai Expressway Is a Short-Cut to Socio-Ecological Disaster'. ⟨https://thewire.in/environment/delhi-mumbai-expressway-nitin-gadkari-bharatmala-nhai⟩ accessed on 31.01.2021.

be 'enchanted' as intended and resistance has already begun from those that in a sense have been 'disenchanted'.

As we have seen, the 500 farmers at Gugalkota are facing problems due to the land acquisition. The value of their compensations has fallen by almost 50% since the implementation of the new RTFCTLARR bill. Furthermore, because of the new bill there is no longer any need for a consent of 70% for PPP projects. Therewith, the political participation of the farmers is not given. This is particularly affecting women, since they are the main workers in the agricultural sector but have fewer opportunities to participate than men. As shown, there were protests against the process of land acquisition. But there were also farmers who willingly give or sell their land to the government, because they see an opportunity in the DMIC.

The DMIC construction in Alwar extends existing industries and infrastructure and transforms natural resources such as fields, pastures and hills. So, on the one hand, a spatial transformation is taking place. New boundaries, in the sense of Rassmusen and Lund (2018: 390), are being drawn. Private property has been taken over by the state for development and will be resold to private investors in the future. On the other hand, a non-spatial shift of boundaries is taking place. This can be seen in new legal and institutional frameworks, such as the new legislation on expropriation of land from 2015, but also at the societal level. The new borders make access to common-pool resources of pastoral nomads in the region more difficult. Characteristic of the emergence of these "new borders" is that they are also accompanied by resistance. There have been protests against the expropriation of land and compensation payments. Strikes were held in several factories demanding the recognition of trade unions. The 'New Frontier' along the DMIC is thus not only physical, but also political and legal, in the form of privatization and liberalization (Rassmusen and Lund 2018: 390).

The case study indicates that the expansion of the new frontier leads to concrete changes but also to local reactions and perceptions. It becomes evident that the enchantment and the anti-politics of the infrastructure development does not hold on the local level. Local farmers do not buy into the enchantment of development but clearly see that the process leads to commons grabbing and the undermining of their existence. This also becomes evident as the government and investors create and use multiple institutions (institution shopping), which eliminates the need for a Social Impact Assessment and to pay very low compensations for land (not even for the loss of water, pasture and forestry) while at the same time shaping and selecting government legal institutions in order to profit from the project financially by manipulating land prices. This also means that we have a case that offers empirical material to go analytically beyond the new frontier approach. It shows how government and investor actors use their bargaining power to shape and legitimize legally the institutions used. However, local people seem to understand the grabbing nature of their commons and this could lead also to local reactions in the sense of a politics machine after understating the grabbing and legitimizing process. It remains to be seen to what type of local strategies this disenchantment will lead.

Glossary

DMIC	Delhi-Mumbai Industrial Corridor
EIA	Environmental Impact Assessment
GSDP	Gross Domestic Product
HUDCO	Housing and Urban Development Corporation Limited
IIFCL	India Infrastructure Finance Company Limited
KBNIR	Khuskhera-Bhiwadi-Neemrana Investment Region
LAA	Land Acquisition Act 1894
LIC	Life Insurance Company of India
MCM	Million Cubic Metres (Liquid)
MLD	Million Litres per Day
PPP	Public-Private Partnership
RIICO	Rajasthan State Industrial Development and Investment Corporation
RTFCTLARR	Right to Fair Compensation and Transparency in Land Acquisition, Rehabilitation and Resettlement Bill
SEZ	Special Economic Zone
SNBUC	Shahjahanpur-Neemrana-Behror Complex

References

Bhattacharya, Akash 2014: The Battles against Modi. What an Industrial Strike Teaches Us. Economic and Political Weekly 49 (23): 15-18.
Das, Maitreyi Bordia, Hall, Gillette, Kapoor, Soumya, et al. 2014: Indigenous Peoples, Poverty and Development. India: The Scheduled Tribes.
Dutt, Bahar 2004: Livelihood Strategies of a Nomadic Hunting Community of Eastern Rajasthan. Nomadic Peoples, New Series 8 (2): 260-273.
Harvey, Penny and Knox, Hannah 2012: The Enchantments of Infrastructure. Mobilities 7 (4): 521-536.
Jenkins, Rob 2013: Land, Rights and Reform in India. Pacific Affairs 86 (3): 591-612.
Khosla, Romi and Soni, Vikram 2012 : Delhi-Mumbai Corridor. A Water Disaster in the Making? Economic and Political Weekly 47 (10): 15-17.
Kumar, Rakesh, Singh, R. D. and Sharma, K. D. 2005: Water resources of India. Current Science 5 (89): 794-811.
Levien, Michael 2012: The Land Question. Special Economic Zones and the Political Economy of Dispossession in India. The Journal of Peasant Studies 39 (3-4): 933-969.
Levien, Michael 2018: Dispossession Without Development. Land Grabs in Neo-liberal India. New York.

Malayalam, Kannada et al. 2019: Difference Between NIMZs and SEZs: Establishment of National Investment & Manufacturing Zones.
Mishra, S. M., Sharma, Kushal, Organisational Requirements of Village and Small Scale Industries, Delhi 1986.
Rasmussen, Mattias Borg, Lund, Christian 2018: Reconfiguring Frontier Spaces: The territorialization of resource control. World Development 101: 388-399.
Sampat, Preeti 2013: Limits to Absolute Power. Eminent Domain and the Right to Land in India. Economic and Political Weekly 48 (19): 40-52.
Schoettli, Urs 2009: Indien. Profil einer neuen Grossmacht. Zürich.
Sharma, Purushottam, Sharma R.C. 2006: Factors Determining Farmers Decision for Buying Irrigation Water. Study of Groundwater Markets in Rajasthan. Agricultural Economics Research Review 19: 39-56.
Stratton Sayre, Susan and Taraz, Vis 2019: Groundwater Depletion in India. Social Losses from Costly Well Deepening. Journal of Environmental Economics and Management 93: 85-100.
Tomozawa, Kazuo 2015: The Frontier of the Expanding Industrial Agglomeration in the National Capital Region of Dehli. Industrial Development in Alwar District, Rajasthan, especially focusing on the Japanese-Exclusive Industrial Estate of Neemrana. Journal of Urban and Regional Studies on Contemporary India 2 (1): 13-25.

Online reports

Delhi Mumbai Industrial Corridor Development Corporation 2018: Development of Greenfield International Airport at Bhiwadi, Rajasthan. Environmental Impact Assessment. From ‹http://environmentclearance.nic.in/writereaddata/EIA/12122018HARZWXO4EIAReport.pdf› Accessed on 31.01.2021.
Directorate of Census Operations Rajasthan 2011: District Census Handbook Alwar (9). From ‹https://censusindia.gov.in/2011census/dchb/0806_PART_B_DCHB_ALWAR.pdf› Accessed on 31.01.2021.
DMICDC, 10th Annual Report, 2017-2018. From ‹http://dmicdc.com/downloads/annual-report-of-DMICDC› Accessed on 31.01.2021.
Government of India, Ministry of MSME, Brief Industrial Profile of Alwar District 2015-16, Jaipur 2016. From ‹https://msme.gov.in/sites/default/files/MEME%20ANNUAL%20REPORT%202015-16%20FNG.pdf› Accessed on 31.01.2021.
Kuiper Compagnons 2014: Final Development Plan SNB/KBNIR, 2014. From ‹https://industries.rajasthan.gov.in/content/dam/industries/dmic/pdf/KBNIR/201408 04%20Final%20DP%20report%20August%202014.pdf› Accessed on 31.01.2021.
Memorandum of Understanding 2009: Between Government of Rajasthan and Delhi-Mumbai Industrial Corridor Development Corporation. From ‹http://www.industries.rajasthan.gov.in/content/dam/industries/dmic/pdf/MOU/DMIC_MOU_sw.pdf› Accessed on 31.01.2021.
OECD/ICRIER 2018: Agricultural Policies in India. OECD Food and Agricultural Reviews, Paris. From ‹http://www.oecd.org/officialdocuments/publicdisplaydocumentpdf/?cote=TAD/CA(2018)4/FINAL&docLanguage=En› Accessed on 31.01.2021.
PRS Legislative Research 2015: Comparison of the LARR Act 2013 with the LARR (Amendment) Bill 2015, New Delhi. From ‹https://www.prsindia.org/sites/default/fil

es/bill_files/Land_Acquisition_Act_2013_and_Bill_as_passed_by_Lok_Sabha_0.pdf⟩ Accessed on 31.01.2021.

PRS Legislative Research 10.07.2019: Rajasthan Budget Analysis 2019-2010. From ⟨https://www.prsindia.org/sites/default/files/budget_files/State%20Budget%20Analysis%20-%20Rajasthan%202019-20%20English%20v2.pdf⟩ Accessed on 31.01.2021.

The Land Acquisition, Rehabilitation and Resettlement Bill, 2011. From ⟨http://164.100.24.219/BillsTexts/LSBillTexts/asintroduced/land%20acquisition%2077%20of%202011.pdf⟩ Accessed on 31.01.2021.

The Right to Fair Compensation and Transperacy in Land Acquisition, Rehabilitation and Resettlement (Amendment) Bill, 2015. From ⟨https://dolr.gov.in/sites/default/files/RFCTLARR%20Act%20%28Amendment%29%20Bill%2C%202015%20as%20passed%20in%20Lok%20Sabha%20%28English%29_0.pdf⟩ Accessed on 31.01.2021.

Ahuja, Manoj: 'Move to De-acquire Land for DMIC Projects Hits Alwar Farmers Hard'. The Hindustan Times 16.02.2018. ⟨https://www.hindustantimes.com/jaipur/move-to-de-acquire-land-for-dmic-project-hits-alwar-farmers/story-XTnT0LyHYqNrYApDuCHuiP.html⟩ Accessed on 31.01.2021.

Bathla, Nitin, Singh, Aman 06.10.2019: 'The Delhi-Mumbai Expressway Is a Short-Cut to Socio-Ecological Disaster'. ⟨https://thewire.in/environment/delhi-mumbai-expressway-nitin-gadkari-bharatmala-nhai⟩ Accessed on 31.01.2021.

Bhaduri, Amita: 'Alwar Homes, Farms and Factories Fight for Water'. India Water Portal 07.06.2018. ⟨https://www.indiawaterportal.org/articles/alwar-homes-farms-and-factories-fight-water⟩ Accessed on 31.01.2021.

Birhmaan, Vikas 2014: 'Sacred Forests and Rainwater Harvesting in Rajasthan, India'. ⟨http://ecotippingpoints.org/our-stories/indepth/india-rajasthan-rainwater-harvest-restoration-groundwater-johad.html#krapavis⟩ Accessed on 31.01.2021.

CauseBecause 07.03.2016: 'Delhi-Mumbai Industrial Corridor. Development Dilemmas'. ⟨https://causebecause.com/delhi-mumbai-industrial-corridor-development-dilemmas/4495⟩ Accessed on 31.01.2021.

DMICDC Homepage: 'The Projects Influence Area'. ⟨https://dmicdc.com/DMIC-projects/project-influence-area⟩ Accessed on 31.01.2021.

DownToEarth 25.04.2018: 'Climate Change is Destroying Women's Lives in Alwar'. ⟨https://www.downtoearth.org.in/blog/climate-change-is-destroying-women-s-lives-in-alwar--60306⟩ Accessed on 31.01.2021.

Elections. in: ⟨http://www.elections.in/parliamentary-constituencies/2014-election-results.html⟩ Accessed on 31.01.2021.

Indian Council of Agricultural Research Homepage: ⟨http://alwar1.kvk2.in/district-profile.html⟩ Accessed on 31.01.2021.

Jain, Sreenivasan: 'Why an Acquisition Off the Delhi–Jaipur Highway Challenges Assumptions of the New Land Bill'. NDTV 15.03.2015. ⟨https://www.ndtv.com/india-news/an-acquisition-off-the-delhi-jaipur-highway-challenges-assumptions-of-the-new-land-bill-746714⟩ Accessed on 31.01.2021.

Jha, Praveen 03.09.2014: 'Social Resistance and the Land Question in Contemporary India'. ⟨https://www.cetri.be/Social-Resistance-and-the-Land⟩ Accessed on 31.01.2021.

Offical Site of Alwar: ⟨https://alwar.rajasthan.gov.in/content/raj/alwar/en/business/infrastructure.html#⟩ Accessed on 31.01.2021.

PDCOR Ltd. Online Homepage: ‹https://www.pdcor.com/industry.htm› Accessed on 31.01.2021.

PRS Legislative Research Homepage: ‹http://www.prsindia.org/billtrack/the-right-to-fair-compensation-and-transparency-in-land-acquisition-rehabilitation-and-resettlement-amendment-bill-2015-3649› Accessed on 31.01.2021.

Ritimo 14.05.2018: 'Dispossession and Resistance in India and Mexico. Land Acquisition and State Policy in India'. ‹https://www.ritimo.org/Land-Acquisition-and-State-Policy-in-India› Accessed on 31.01.2021.

Timmons, Heather: 'As Japan and India Forge Economic Ties, a Counterweight to China Is Seen'. The New York Times 21.08.2007. ‹https://www.nytimes.com/2007/08/21/business/worldbusiness/21rupee.html› Accessed on 31.01.2021.

Tripathy, Srikanta: 'DMIC Derails in Rajasthan, Farmers Too Hit Hard'. The Times of India 07.05.2017. ‹https://timesofindia.indiatimes.com/city/jaipur/dmic-derails-in-raj-farmers-too-hit-hard/articleshow/58556408.cms› Accessed on 31.01.2021.

The Economic Times 15.06.2015: 'Land Bill. NGO's, Farmer Organisations Hit Out at Government'. ‹https://m.economictimes.com/news/politics-and-nation/land-bill-ngos-farmer-organisations-hit-out-at-government/articleshow/47679048.cms› Accessed on 31.01.2021.

Wahi, Namita: 'How Central and State Governments Have Diluted the Historic Land Legislation of 2013'. The Economic Times 14.04.2018. ‹https://economictimes.indiatimes.com/news/politics-and-nation/how-central-and-state-governments-have-diluted-the-historic-land-legislation-of2013/articleshow/63764378.cms?from=mdr› Accessed on 31.01.2021.

Water Education Foundation: ‹https://www.watereducation.org/aquapedia/overdraft› Accessed on 31.01.2021.

Smart Cities, Smart Land Grabbing and Legal Pluralism: An MIP Case from Gujarat, India

Oliver Stettler, Institute of Social Anthropology, University of Bern, Switzerland

Introduction

'A completely new Singapore created in the heart of Gujarat' – Amitabh Kant, CEO of the DMICDC (National Alliance of People's Movements (NAPM)).

The Dholera Special Investment Region (DSIR) is planned to be the first smart city[1] along the Delhi Mumbai Industrial Corridor (DMIC). The region comprises 22 villages in Gujarat and the project will be implemented in three steps, each over the course of ten years (SENES Consultants India Pvt. Ltd. 2013: E-1/E-7). By shifting from a rural, agricultural area to a smart city, the government hopes to achieve economic prosperity. As McKinsey's report (Sankhe 2010: 8/9) 'India's urban awakening: Building inclusive cities, sustaining economic growth' predicts, the GDP will be five times higher and about 590 million people will live in India's cities by 2030. The report highlights the urgency of rethinking urban life and the structure of cities. This leads to my first point of interest about the DSIR: what is the goal of such a huge infrastructure project? Is it all about economic growth, attracting foreign capital and urbanization or is it intended to enhance social equality and establish ecologically sustainable solutions?

The Environmental Impact Assessment (SENES Consultants India Pvt. Ltd. 2013: 57) states that the suitability for the project in Dholera is mainly due to its great proportion of government-owned land, which is especially important at the outset for providing basic infrastructure. Nevertheless, the government is forced to obtain additional land from private actors, mainly farmers, in order to establish the DSIR. Sampat and Sunny (2016: 3/4) point out that the government is using questionable methods to acquire the land, by using various laws. As a result of these findings I will focus on the impacts of the legal status.

---

[1] A smart city in India includes core infrastructure elements such as ensured electricity supply and waste water treatment, as well as 'smart city features' such as good public transportation and lots of parks or green spaces (GoI MoUD 2015: 5–7).

One important aspect is the strategies that affected people use to cope with the project. How are the local communities going to integrate themselves in this new environment where the ways of making a livelihood are completely different from before? And how does the government promote the DSIR and the language used to talk about the DSIR to different parties.

Finally, the DSIR leads to a huge transformation of the landscape. Its government-led transformation into an investment region influences the ecosystems and the natural conditions. The State of Gujarat is an arid to semi-arid region where surface water is the only water available, and therefore it is dependent on rainfall or water from rivers and canals. But while farmers have now been waiting for canal water for years, the Dholera Special Investment Region Development Authority (DSIRDA) is optimistic about water availability (SENES Consultants India Pvt. Ltd. 2013: 73). My goal is to investigate how the ecology is planned to be integrated in this process of transformation and what impacts it will have.

This article is a literary analysis on the circumstances surrounding the mega-infrastructure project DSIR. It is based on primary research from other scientists, researchers and NGOs, as well as on secondary research. In particular, the research of Preeti Sampat (2015), 'Policy Report No. 13 Dholera Smart City: Urban Infrastructure or Rentier Growth?', was very helpful, as she conducted research surrounding the DSIR in the field. Additionally, I studied reports, plans, legal documents and policies, websites and other documents from the government or company side. This provided me with a lot of basic information. Furthermore, I conducted a semi-structured interview with a farmers' rights activist, which offered me insights into the activists' perspectives and strategies. These sources of evidence allow me to describe the broad aspects of the case, while information about the current status of the project requires future ethnographic research.

Part 1: Historical, environmental, ethnographic and political context

History and current context

Following India's economic opening in 1991, competition between the states arose to attract foreign investments and capital. In the following years Gujarat proved its potential with a steady growth rate, achieved through economic incentives like tax reliefs and deregulation of the labour market (Tommaso 2012). The Dholera Special Investment Region was introduced in 2009 when the Gujarat Special Investment Region (SIR) Act was enabled. It is mostly due to the work of the former Chief Minister of Gujarat and the current Prime Minister of India, Narendra Modi. With his politics of 'minimum government and maximum governance' he contributed to the high development indices of Gujarat. Datta (2015: 17) identified three key strategies for achieving this: 'first, an active lobbying for investment; second, the speed in their issuance clearances for capital projects; and finally, reducing what is seen by the corporate sector as "political interference" (or social resistance) to development projects'.

Along with the Act, two authorities were established. The Gujarat Infrastructure Development Board (GIDB) is the apex authority and a regional development authority (RDA) for each SIR was implemented. The DSIRDA has the responsibility of planning and development, while the GIDB mainly makes regulations, gives approvals and so on. Additionally, an SPV (special purpose vehicle) called Dholera Industrial City Development Limited (DICDL) has been created between the central government (DMICDC Trust) and the state government (DSIRDA) of Gujarat to implement the project (DSIRDA). The Dholera SIR Act includes the Gujarat Town Planning and Urban Development Act (GTPUDA), which has been used for urban expansion of existing cities, but now has been widened to cover 'greenfields' as well (Sampat 2015: 1–3). Furthermore, it enhances public-private partnerships with its new land pooling mechanism and the empowerment of the government to declare Investment Regions or Industrial Areas and designate them as Special Investment Regions (DSIRDA). In 2010, the global consultancy firm Halcrow presented the development plan for Dholera SIR (Datta 2015). Then, in 2013, global infrastructure giant AECOM was awarded a 30 million dollar and a five-year extendable contract for full programme management services in Dholera (Sampat 2015: 1–3). By this time the development plan had been sanctioned and rendered operational. The next steps were 1. the preparation and 2. sanctioning of the Town Planning Schemes (TPS); this included the process of land pooling (Infinity Infra 2018). However, in Dholera there has been no land acquisition since 2009[2]. From the TPS onwards it requires an Environmental Impact Assessment, which includes public hearings, an Environmental Clearance and an Engineering Design before the works may begin.

Dey and Grappi (2015: 153–156) argue that postcolonial urbanism in recent years has been accompanied by a shift from economic zones towards a corridor economy. The DMIC is a perfect example, as its aim is to connect major existing industrial and economic hubs and create new ones along the way. Ever since the liberalization of the Indian economy in the 1990s and the passing of the Special Economic Zone Act in 2005, this process has been accelerating (Dey and Grappi 2015: 153–156). Since smart cities are built through SEZs, they serve mainly to bring in foreign direct investment rather than provide housing (Varghese 2016). The government of India states in its 2007 'Concept Paper: Delhi-Mumbai Industrial Corridor' that the corridor model goes a step further than economic zones, as it includes the state through nodal agencies for the project's implementation (Dey and Grappi 2015: 154–156).

---

[2] Interview with the author, August 2019

Geographical description

The DSIR covers an area of approximately 920 km² and is comprised of 19 villages in Dhandhuka Taluka and three villages in Barwal Taluka[3], totalling 22 villages in the Ahmedabad District of Gujarat. The area is located 100 km south of Ahmedabad and 130 km from Gandhinagar and is adjacent to the sea, off the Gulf of Khambhat (in the Arabian Sea). It is described strategically as a very good place in terms of connectivity, proximity to other cities and existing infrastructure. Today most of the land is dominated by agriculture (47.46%), of which 39.97% is declared as fallow land and the remaining 7.49% as cropland, followed by salt-affected land with or without vegetation cover and salt encrustation (23.16%). The rest consists of mudflat land, mangroves, and land with dense or open herbaceous cover (SENES Consultants India Pvt. Ltd. 2103: E-4).

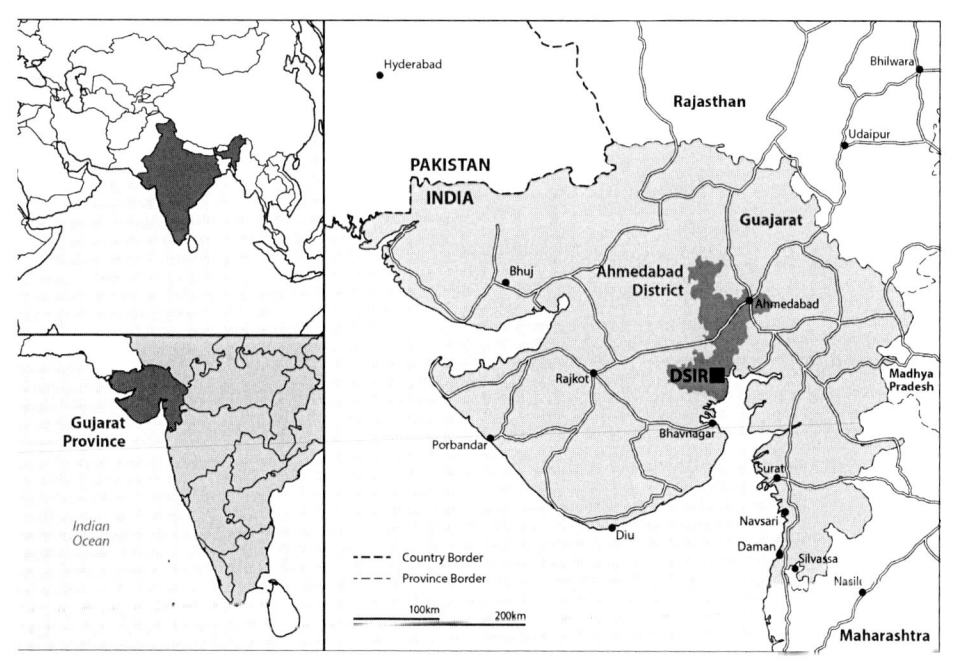

Map 1: Location Map of DSIR. Source: Map compilation and design by Manuel L. K. Abebe (2021), CDE, University of Bern, Bern, Switzerland. Geodata: GADM

The availability of water is the most critical resource for industrial or urban development along the DMIC. It will require two-thirds of the total water from rivers

---
[3] Since the GPAct 1993 (Gujarat Panchayat Act) there has been a three-tier system in Gujarat. In hierarchical order: a village panchayat is subordinated to the taluka panchayat and district panchayat, the taluka panchayat is subordinated to the district panchayat and all panchayats are subordinated to the state government and the development commissioner (Bhatt and Shah 2000). Taluka can be translated as "township" and panchayat as "council".

and the rest from already stressed and polluted groundwater aquifers (Khosla and Soni 2012: 16). This is especially true for the Dholera SIR since it is a semi-arid region with rainfall only during the monsoon months (mainly June, July, August and September) and no groundwater availability[4]. As much as an estimated 947 million litres per day (MLD) of fresh water will be required to meet demand by 2030 (DSIRDA 2012: 4). Also, it is currently lacking a canal system, even though the canals from the Sardar Sarovar dam across the Narmada dam are expected to be finished soon. Farmers claim that once water for irrigation is available there will be no need for further development (Times of India 2016). Another problem is the high salinity of the soil and therefore of the water, making it unsuitable for consumption (SENES Consultants India Pvt. Ltd. 2013: 73).

Adjacent to, or even within, the Dholera SIR are the Velavadar National Park and an eco-sensitive coastal zone. And due to the low altitude paired with the rise of the sea level, this region is losing at least 1 cm of its coastline to the sea each day (Datta 2015: 27). This leads to migration from wildlife out of the national park where conflicts between the communities and the wildlife arise. It is not only a threat to the animals and vice versa, but to the flora as well, especially the mangroves, which in turn are helpful in flood mitigation. The Velavadar Black Buck Sanctuary is famous for being one of the few blackbuck habitats on the subcontinent and is therefore especially important for the biodiversity. It hosts wolves and the lesser known florican and is considered to be one of the biggest harrier roosting grounds in the world (SENES Consultants India Pvt. Ltd. 2013: 156).

The quality of natural resources rises from the coastal to the outer zone and so does the wealth of the people, mostly because the fertility of the soil rises accordingly. While the soil is too salty for agriculture near the coastline, it turns into dry grassland in the transitional zone where pastoralists live with their cattle, and finally in the outer zone the quality is good enough to grow crops (SENES Consultants India Pvt. Ltd. 2013: 130–134). From the farmers' perspective, if there were more water available for irrigation the soil could even bear two or more yields a year[2].

Local population and their livelihoods

In the 22 villages of the Dholera SIR there were 6,532 households with a total population of 37,713, as per the 2001 census. Of these, 61.8% are from the Koli Patel caste, followed by Darbar (10.6%), Devipujak (5.7%), Vankar (5.2%) and Bharvad (3.8%) (SENES Consultants India Pvt. Ltd. 2013: 127). The Koli Patel are an indigenous fishing community and therefore about 88.2% of the population live near the coast (Sampat 2015: 27). Since the 2001 census does not include caste or tribal divisions, it does not represent the actual number of people living in this area

---

[4] Interview with the author, August 2019

(Salpeteur et al. 2017). The Rabari or Raika, a semi-nomadic pastoralist group in Gujarat and Rajasthan consisting of around 500'000-600'000 people (estimated in 1999), need to be considered. To maintain their nomadic lifestyle, it is important to have access to different areas to travel through or graze their livestock. In Gujarat, the lands are classified in three different ways: state lands, common lands and private lands. State lands are administered by different government bodies or sometimes by local authorities, which are village councils (panchayat). Common lands consist of common pastures (oran) or sacred groves (gauchar). Only members of the community are free to access these lands. Private lands belong to individuals or small groups and are mostly farms (Salpeteur et al. 2017).

The possibilities for making a livelihood vary from the coastal zone to the outer Dholera SIR. While fishing is only possible close to the shore, it is nearly impossible to grow crops there. Generally, most of the people work in natural resource-based occupations such as agriculture, fishery, livestock, charcoal farming, forest products, salt work, etc. With 62% of the working population in the agricultural sector, it is the predominant occupation, followed by labour work, mainly with diamonds (SENES Consultants India Pvt. Ltd. 2013: 131–133).

As rainfed agriculture is one of the main occupations in this region and it is only possible during the few months of monsoon, a lot of people, who do not possess land of their own, rely on work in a bigger city or village during the dry season. The farmer families who own the land, however, are mostly self-sustaining. In winter they change their crops from cotton or wheat to gram and cumin, which are less water intensive[5].

Legal and economic environment

The Dholera Special Investment Region is a project along the Delhi-Mumbai-Industrial-Corridor (DMIC). The DMIC is being implemented by the Delhi-Mumbai-Industrial-Corridor-Development-Corporation Limited (DMICDC), a special purpose vehicle (SPV), and as an apex authority (= the highest and central authority) headed by the Finance Minister for Commerce & Industry, Deputy Chairman, Planning Commission and other concerned Central Ministers and Chief Ministers as members. The shares are held as follows: 49% by the government of India represented through the Department of Industrial Policy & Promotion, Ministry of Commerce & Industry, 26% by the Japan Bank for International Cooperation, 19.9% by the Housing and Urban Development Corporation Limited, 4.1% by the India Infrastructure Finance Company Limited and 1.0% by the Life Insurance Corporation of India. This means that 51% of the shares are held by private institutes and companies and 49% are in the hands of the state (DMICDC.com 24.08.19).

---

[5] Interview with the author, August 2019

To establish the DSIR it was necessary to enact the Gujarat Special Investment Region Act 2009 by the Gujarat Infrastructure Development Board (GIDB) as a legal framework. The GIDB functions as the apex authority. Further, an SPV named Dholera Industrial City Development Limited (DICDL) was founded by the Government of Gujarat through the Dholera Special Investment Region Development Authority (DSIRDA) and by the government of India through the DMICDC. The DICDL stakes are shared with 51% for the DSIRDA and 49% for the DMICDC (DSIRDA). So, the DICDL is the executing agency, the DSIRDA is the governing agency of the DSIR and the GIDB oversees regulatory management.

The SIR Act's biggest benefit in terms of empowerment for the authorities lies in its ability to bypass India's Land Acquisition Act 1894. Additionally, it does not take the 2013 revision of the Land Acquisition Act (Right to Fair Compensation and Transparency in Land Acquisition and Rehabilitation and Resettlement Act, RTFCTLARRA) into account (Sampat and Sunny 2016: 1–4). Another point is that the SIR Act enables the authorities to declare the area as a Special Economic Zone (SEZ). The whole DMIC project is planned to be implemented through SEZs and the Land Acquisition Act 1894. SEZs are areas in which the regulatory regime for areas such as trade, investment, labour, and social and environmental protection is different from the rest of the country, as they are managed by development commissioners (Dey and Grappi 2015: 155–156).

According to India's Land Acquisition Act of 1894, 'land needed for public purpose' can be acquired by the state, but only certain types of land are specified as 'land needed for public purpose'. These are educational institutions, housing and health or slum clearance. The SIR Act, however, falls under the Gujarat Town Planning and Urban Development Act (GTPUDA) 1976 in which town planning, infrastructure and industrial projects are also deemed to be 'land needed for public purpose'. Therefore, it enables the GIDB to declare investment regions or industrial areas and designate them as Special Investment Zones (SIZs), without the need for consent (Datta 2015: 24/25). This process excludes the participation of the people and, according to Ferguson (1994), it is an anti-politics mechanism. Also, it includes now 'greenfield' or new cities instituted through public-private partnerships (PPPs) (Sampat 2015: 2–5).

Additionally, the GTPS 1976 enables land pooling, a mechanism by which no 'acquisition' or 'transfer of land' arises and therefore no need for fair compensation, unlike in the Land Acquisition Act 1894 or RTFCTLARRA, applies. However, the landowners are to be paid out for 50% of their land at market price and the rest will be returned as 'developed' land. In addition, a job in the project is promised for each family. But the original owners will have to pay a betterment charge deducted from the compensation award for half the land (Sampat 2015). Based on this legal pluralism, government officials and investment companies are able to select legal settings (institution shopping) that are favourable and most profitable for their interests, depending on opportunities that come along (Haller 2020). Via this mechanism, local communal land can be grabbed at low costs by the government, while still arguing that this process is legal and fair. This is a process that echoes what Ferguson meant by development as an anti-politics machine, hiding power asymmetries and the legalized grabbing process by also using the discourse that this investment will bring employment and a betterment.

When the DSIR has been built, or at least partially, the DICDL will focus on the following industries: defence, manufacturing, heavy engineering, auto and auto ancillaries, pharma and bio tech, electronics and agro and food processing (no farming considered)[6]. In 2016, the Government of Gujarat adopted a new 'Aerospace and Defence Policy' through the Department of Industries and Mines. This document indicates that India has the third-largest armed forces and eighth-highest defence expenditure in the world, with 60% of its defence needs being imports. Given that the defence industry is very capital intensive, the Government of India wants to set up its own defence industry in India, and in so doing gain access to the value chain (GoG 2016: 2–3). Gujarat, unlike other states in India, provides multiple benefits, such as having the DSIR, many large contiguous land parcels, an accessible port sector, an already thriving auto and engineering industry and a high number of excellent technical educational institutes (DICDL). Additionally, the DSIR is very well connected to the adjacent states and will, once built, provide overall eminent infrastructure, including an airport.

Part 2: The Mega-Infrastructure Project

Dholera smart city

The Dholera Special Investment Region is going to be not only the flagship for the government's 'Smart Cities Mission' but also the first smart city and industrial hub along the Delhi Mumbai Industrial Corridor. This corridor is an extension to the Golden Quadrilateral highway project linking the four major metros of Delhi/NCR, Bombay/Mumbai, Calcutta/Kolkata and Madras/Chennai. It is a mega-infrastructure project estimated at an investment flow of US$90 billion with financial and technical aid from Japan, stretching over 1,483 km long and 300 km wide from Delhi to Mumbai (Varghese 2016: 1862/1863).

The Dholera Special Investment Region is also known as Dholera Smart City. A major distinction from other smart city concepts in India is the fact that the DSIR is a greenfield smart city unlike other brownfield cities. While brownfield cities are adapting existing cities to fit into a smart city concept, greenfield cities are new cities built on agricultural, forest or other types of land (Infinity Infra 2018). The Smart Cities Mission was set up by Prime Minister Narendra Modi

---

[6] DICDL: What is Dholera SIR?, [online] https://dicdl.in/about-us/ [18.08.2019]

in 2015, through the Ministry of Urban Development. In its 'Mission Statement & Guidelines' it acknowledges that there is no universally accepted definition of a smart city, especially in an international frame. Nonetheless, it provides some definitional guidelines for approaching the Smart Cities Mission, with the following all being key infrastructure elements in a smart city: core infrastructure elements as well as 'Smart City Features'; an adequate water supply; guaranteed electricity supply; sanitation, including solid waste management; efficient urban mobility and public transport; affordable housing, especially for the poor; robust IT connectivity and digitalization; good governance, especially e-governance and citizen participation; sustainable environment; safety and security of citizens, particularly women, children and the elderly; and health and education. 'Smart City Features' would include approaches such as: good public transportation; lots of open spaces, i.e. parks and playgrounds; overall sustainability; applying smart solutions in different areas like traffic and governance; and giving the city its own identity (GoI MoUD 2015: 5–7).

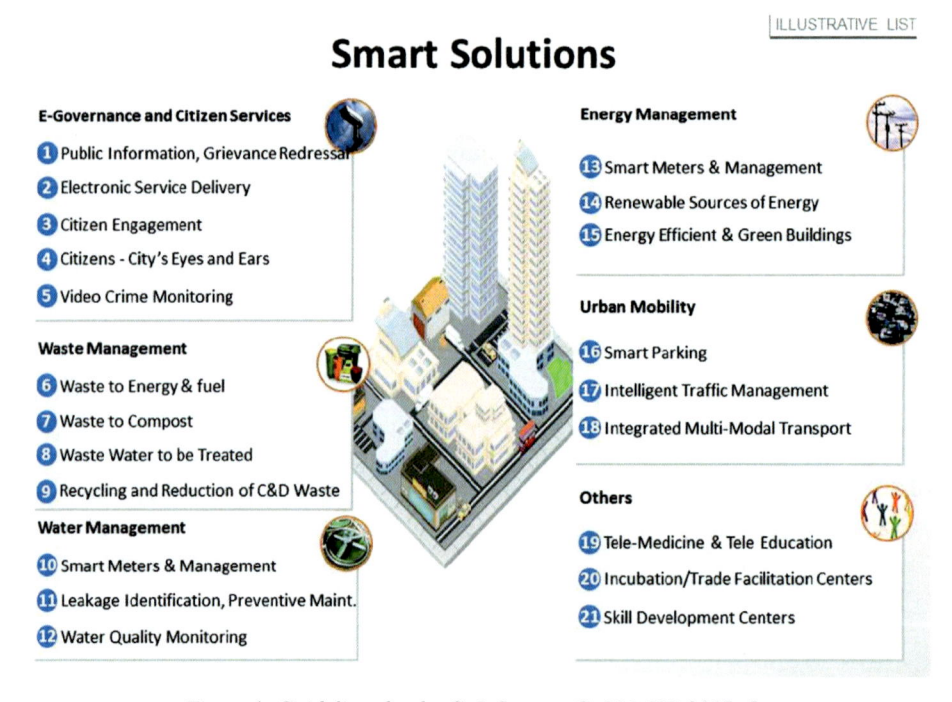

Figure 1: Guidelines by the GoI. Source: GoI MoUD 2015: 5

In order to develop the DSIR, huge transformations in terms of land use are inevitable. The biggest changes will be the transformation of agricultural land into industry hubs. For the spatial planning of the DSIR, the Draft Development Plan, provided by the DSIRDA, exemplifies key principles of the new city, of which the most notable are: the creation of a compact city with good public transportation and accessibility by walking; the integration of land uses and a sophisticated traffic system for industrial, residential and city traffic; and the integration and protection of existing villages, eco-sensitive zones and better agricultural land (DSIRDA 2012: 13–32).

For each of the three building phases there is/will be a town planning scheme as a main guideline. Phase 1 will comprise about 34%, phase 2 roughly 36% and phase 3 about 30% of the land. The development of the DSIR will start near Ambli Village on the north side, with the already existing State Highway (SH – 6), and then continue southwards along the highway (DSIRDA 2012: 4).

Environmental and social impacts

The biggest impact on the environment is expected to be increased depletion of water sources. As noted, the Special Investment Region has only monsoon rain and severely stressed groundwater aquifers (Khosla and Soni 2012: 16). In addition to the very limited availability of water, water has high salinity, as there is no sweet groundwater (DSIRDA 2012: 134). When the constructions begin, the demand for sweet water will rise again. As it is not clear when exactly what will be built, the canals of Sardar Sarvor dam across Narmada may be completed by that time to meet the need for water. Nonetheless, once the industry has been developed, water will be needed in even larger quantities. During the operation phase, there is the danger that the quality of the groundwater may deteriorate if the domestic sewage and industrial water generation are not treated properly or are discharged on open ground. To avoid the accumulation of storm water during a monsoon a drainage system may be needed in certain places and the construction of borrow areas for roads shall not take place near villages, as they can act as stagnant pools for mosquito breeding (DSIRDA 2012: 134/135).

Even though the DSIR area does not overlap with the Velavadar National Park, it will have an impact on it due to its proximity. As there is technically no loss of habitats for the blackbuck, road kills and floods are the main threat. Therefore, the development of the DSIR will include flood mitigation for the Velavadar National Park as well and the trunk-level infrastructure will plan for wildlife crossings. The Coastal Regulation Zone is another eco-sensitive zone adjacent to the DSIR. Until today no development is planned in the Coastal Regulation Zone, except for renewable energy projects, tourism resorts and some linear utilities such as pipelines. But no beach resort or hotels are allowed in ecologically sensitive areas such as marine parks, mangroves, coral reefs, breeding and spawning grounds of fish or wildlife habitats. But the proposed Kalpasar project, currently being reviewed for its environmental clearance, will have a huge impact on big parts of the Coastal Regulation Zone, transforming a prior saline/brackish environment into a freshwater one, leaving no doubt in long-term changes of the zone. Additionally, the Coastal Regulation Zone is highly vulnerable to illegal sourcing of natural material required for DSIR development (SENES Consultants India Pvt. Ltd. 2013: 289).

Despite these likely negative impacts along these two eco-sensitive zones on fauna and flora, most of the land used for the DSIR is covered only sparsely with vegetation, apart from commercial crops, and domesticated mammals. It is possible that after construction there will be more trees and shrubs in the DSIR as it is labelled a green and sustainable smart city with many parks and open spaces (DSIRDA 2012: 135).

In terms of air quality and potential greenhouse gas emissions, the impact of the development of the DSIR is uncertain. While the level of suspended particulate matter (SPM) and respirable suspended particulate matter (RSPM) may rise due to dust generation, fugitive emissions from vehicles, construction equipment and machinery during construction, it is supposed, will cease once it is finished. The quality of the air is linked with potential impacts on the climate. But because India currently has no greenhouse gas emission target agreements at international or national level, the Draft Development Plan and the Environmental Impact Assessment are lacking a proper evaluation of climate impacts (DSIRDA 2012: 132).

Although the government claims in the Draft Development Plan (DSIRDA 2012: 4) that no displacement or resettlement for any local inhabitant will happen, the rezoning according to the new city's development plan implies that the original agricultural plots can no longer be retained by owners and that they have to be relocated. The most vulnerable group relative to the land pooling are the farmers, as they own the biggest plots of land in the region. Additionally, most people/farmers are not able to wait years for their 'developed' and rezoned plots and are therefore forced to search for new options to make a livelihood (Sampat 2015: 37/38). Another issue is that some farmers do not own the titles to their land and are thus especially vulnerable; this goes back to the date of decolonialization[7].

Village settlements, even though they are protected by a buffer zone, will change, so it will no longer be possible to continue the old rural settlement in the same form (Sampat 2015: 37). The privatization of all the land plots makes it impossible for it to be used as common land. The employment opportunities will now focus on manufacturing and other jobs outside the agrarian sector, thus the people need to gain a set of new skills in order to adapt to the new working environment (Sampat 2015: 23). The Draft Development Plan claims that the inhabitants of the villages will be provided with training programmes and support to enable them to participate fully in the new development (DSIRDA 2012: 5).

The establishment of a six-lane highway and a metro rail between Ahmedabad and Dholera will provide good connectivity (DSIDRA), along with civic amenities and services like hospitals, schools, disposal of waste and provisions

---

[7] Interview with the author, August 2019

for drainage. Indeed, the DSIR is promoted as having 'world-class' infrastructure (SENES Consultants India Pvt. Ltd. 2013: 36). Aecom predicts the creation of approximately 800,000 job opportunities by 2050; by this time the city should be able to support a population of two million people (Aecom)[8].

Local and NGO strategies

A member of the NGO Khedut Samaj and a farmers' rights activist explains that a referendum is the only effective legal way to achieve some betterments. It was possible for the Khedut Samaj to gather enough signatures through a petition to launch a referendum in 2009 and challenge the land acquisition in the high court of Gujarat successfully. Therefore, since 2009 no land has been transferred from private parties to the state authorities. It was not easy to launch the referendum because a lot of the people did not even know that their land was to be taken away from them, or they had been fearful of opposing the government. Therefore, a great deal of work had to be put into informing the people about their rights and the project, thus disenchanting the smart city as it is stated by the government (Harvey and Knox 2012). After the petition was written, again it was examined by the local farmers before the signatures were collected[9]. Along with a short general description of the project, the petition points out the irreparable damage to the ecosystem and the loss of livelihood the DSIR will bring. Additionally, it raises the question of whether development like educational institutions, quality health care and improved infrastructure is not entitled to the people in any case, even without the DSIR (Dholera SIR Petition 2015).

With the successful stopping of land acquisition, a first step of resistance has been achieved. But still the project is being implemented on government-owned land plots. The resistance from the locals is now in the form of protest marches and information campaigns. The Khedut Samaj and other NGOs that are organizing the protest marches are making their way through the villages. This is very important to gain the sympathy and trust of the locals and to inform them properly, as a lot of them are illiterates. Information campaigns can be diverse: they range from spreading flyers to big festival-like meetings. The meetings are very important for networking with other communities and sharing knowledge, especially about specific topics such as regulatory frameworks.

Despite not being able to decide whether a project such as the DSIR is going to happen, the local population is allowed, at least partially, to co-determine how it will be implemented. In order to guarantee this, a public hearing must be held prior to the Environmental Impact Assessment, which had to be held prior to the start of the project. Public hearings are an efficient way for the local community

---

[8] Aecom Dholera Special Investment Region, [online] https://aecom.com/projects/dholera-special-investment-region/ [05.10.2020]
[9] Interview with the author, August 2019

to participate, because the objections need to be considered. For the DSIR a public hearing was held on January 3, 2014, organized by Gujarat Pollution Control Board, which was attended by 2,000 villagers who were unanimously against acquisition. The Analysis of the Environmental Public Hearing Report shows that most of the questions have remained unanswered (EPH report 2014).

State and company strategies

The McKinsey report (Sankhe et al. 2010) predicts a huge population growth in the coming decades and an accelerating migration from rural areas into urban areas. Thus, a rapid nationwide urbanization seems inevitable. Additionally, it says, in order to keep the GDP growth rates constantly high, a change in the economy is needed. This could be best achieved with a shift from the agricultural to the industrial sector. The government is using these predictions to create acceptance for the project in broad publicity. Another important aspect about creating acceptability is the way in which the project is talked about. For Dholera, the discourse is all about sustainability and development in the context of a smart city, which promises the creation of job opportunities, adequate housing and overall good infrastructure. It is promoted as being an economically and socially balanced world-class city along the DMIC (SENES Consultants India Pvt. Ltd. DSIRDA 2012). The enchantment of modernity and development in the case of Dholera smart city disguises the problematic implementation as well as the unequal opportunities to participate (Harvey and Knox 2012).

The DMICDC – a private company in which 51% of the stakes are held by private companies – is technically under the government's power, as it has four government directors on its board and a government nominee as a CEO (NAPM)[10]. This makes it a private company with the powers of the state. It mainly enables the company to obtain building permits easily. And given that a lot of the media in India are under the government's ruling, it seems quite simple to promote the project nationwide and give the feeling of an urgent need for such projects. On the other hand, the authorities are also able to set up definitions as they please. In relation to land acquisition, a classification of the plots is required, and the government tends to categorize a lot of land as 'unproductive' or 'barren land', which does not clearly represent its actual use and value (Sampat 2015: 33/34). Additionally, in some cases outdated maps have been used[11].

The narratives used by DSIR proponents to convince residents are as important as the sharing of information (NAPM). In the case of Dholera, the local inhabitants were not informed in advance about the project. The state authorities took

---

[10] The National Alliance for People Movements is an Indian NGO: 'Struggle Against Injustice and Discrimination, Assertion of Rights and Reconstruction Towards Sustainablity and Self-reliance' https://napm-india.org/ideology/

[11] Interview with the author, August 2019

consent and participation for granted (Varghese 2016: 1864). Afterwards only specific information was published step by step to the locals, leaving out crucial parts about compensation and land acquisition. Further, the DSIRDA actively tries to establish incentives in the form of rents in regard to compensation, in order to convince landholders to participate. Levien argues that compensation models in Special Economic Zones (SEZs) all around India are market-based. This will 'individualize the people's relation to the projects and thereby fracture their interests' (Levien 2013: 25). Another report by the NAPM shows that in 2011, even before any public hearing was held, the government tried to sell all its 'government land' to private companies.

A key tool for the implementation of the DSIR is a legal framework. This was achieved through the DSIR Act 2009. As mentioned in Section 2.4, the DSIR Act falls under the GTPUDA 1976 and thereby functions as an anti-politics mechanism, undermining the capacity of the people to politically interact in this process. The government is able to acquire land without the need for prior consent. The GTPUDA does not foresee 'forcible acquisition' or 'transfer of ownership', thus the case for compensation for loss of land only arises for the proportion of the land deducted for basic infrastructure provisions (Sampat and Sunny 2016: 3/4).

A fundamental strategy for the government to increase the economic value of such projects is the public-private partnership (PPP) model. For the DMIC the government was able to share risks and costs, as described above, mainly with the Japan Bank for International Cooperation and with the Housing and Urban Development Corporation. Also, the initial funds from the government, which are taxpayers' money, are only for basic 'infrastructure' built on government-owned land (NAPM). Then they can plan further profitable investments, and consider selling now 'developed land' at high prices (Sampat 2015: 40–45). The PPP model also offers a lot of options to attract companies and investments. Incentives for industrial development described in the EIA include, among others: interest subsidies, assistance for technology upgradation, market promotion and development by setting up for trade and conventional centres. And as it is an SEZ, the government can set up its own tax regulations and other terms of trade (SENES Consultants India Pvt. Ltd. 2013: 75/76).

Conclusion

Probably the most controversial and problematic topic in India and for the DSIR is land acquisition and resettlement. For the DSIR, a legal framework for obtaining land was enabled: the DSIR Act 2009. Since the DSIR Act 2009 is based on the GTPUDA 1976, the government is able to declare given areas as Special Economic Zones. The land needed for SEZs is classified as land for industrial development, which the GTPUDA 1976 declares as 'land for public purpose' and therefore can be acquired by the government without the need for a prior consent between the landowners and the government. This plurality of institution allows the government to take the land via land pooling, based on the institution shopping of the SEZ regulations (Haller 2020). This reduces the costs, as land pooling is a mechanism in which there is no need for fair compensation since no 'acquisition' or 'transfer of land' occurs (Datta 2015: 24/25, Sampat 2015: 4–7).

The Government of Gujarat is still talking about voluntary transfers of land. But the local community was able to successfully disenchant the DSIR. They realized the threat of land grabbing and pooling and handed in a referendum in 2009 to stop land acquisition and uphold the status quo. In addition, there are great concerns about the availability of water for irrigation.

While the project proponents are optimistic about the outcome, the promised development the DSIR will bring has yet to be proven. It can be assumed that it will bring a development to the economy by establishing good connectivity and by setting up an industry. Most of the local people are expected to benefit the least from the DSIR. Farmers, for example, are threatened the most to lose their land, as they own the biggest land parcels and rely on their land to earn a living. The Rabari pastoralists will face even bigger obstacles in their mobility.

In order to identify discrepancies between the promises of DSIR proponents and actual economic, social and environmental impacts, special attention needs to be paid to the Environmental Impact Assessment and the public hearing coming with it. As the EIA solely presents consent among all parties, other news reports of the public hearing on January 3, 2014 show no consent at all and even fisticuffs between pro-SIR supporters and locals (Times of India 2014). All farmers have been unanimously against the project (NAPM).

Glossary

BRI	Belt and Road Initiative
CPEC	China-Pakistan Economic Corridor
DICDL	Dholera Industrial City Development Limited
DIPP	Department of Industrial Policy & Promotion
DMIC	Delhi-Mumbai Industrial Corridor
DMICDC	Delhi-Mumbai-Industrial-Corridor Development Corporation
DSIR	Dholera Special Investment Region
DSIRDA	Dholera Special Investment Region Development Authority
EIA	Environmental Impact Assessment
GIDB	Gujarat Infrastructure Development Board
GTPUDA	Gujarat Town Planning & Urban Development Act 1976
NAPM	National Alliance of People's Movements
RDA	Regional Development Authority
SPV	Special Purpose Vehicle

References

Bhatt P. Mahesh and Ramesh M. Shah 2000: *Gujarat state finance commission: Implications of recommendations, Economic and Political Weekly*, Vol. 35, No. 24, 2003-2005

Datta, Ayona 2015: New urban utopias of postcolonial India: 'Entrepreneurial urbanization' in Dholera smart city, Gujarat, *Dialogues in Human Geography*, Vol.5 No.1. 3-22. ISSN 2043-8206, «https://doi.org/10.1177/204382061456574»_accessed on 05.08.2019

Datta, Ayona 2018: The digital turn in postcolonial urbanism: Smart citizenship in the making of India's 100 smart cities, in *Transaction of the Institute of British Geographers*. Vol. 00, 1-15, DOI: 10.1111/tran.12225

Datta, Ayona 2019: Postcolonial urban futures: Imagining and governing India's smart urban age, *EPD: Society and Space*, Vol. 37 No. 3), 393-410 DOI: 10.1177/02637758 18800721

Dey, Ishita and Giorgio Grappi 2015: Beyond zoning: India's Corridor of "Development" and new Frontiers of Capital, *The South Atlantic Quarterly*, 114, 1, Duke University Press DOI 10.1215/00382876-2831345

Dholera Special Investment Region Development Authority (DSIRDA) 2012: Final Development Plan

Ferguson, James (1994: *The anti-politics machine: "development," depoliticization, and bureaucratic power in Lesotho*. Minneapolis, MN: University of Minnesota Press

Government of Gujarat (GoG) Industries and Mines Department of Gujarat 2016: Aerospace and Defence Policy 2016

Government of India (GoI) Ministry of Urban Development (MoUD) 2015: Smart Cities Mission Statements & Guidelines

Haldar, Sayantan 2018: Mapping substance in India's counter-strategies to China's Emergent Belt and Road Initiative, *India Journal of Asian Affairs*, Vol. 31, No. 1 /2, P. 75-90 «https://www.jstor.org/stable/10.2307/26608824» accessed on 12.08.2019

Haller, Tobias 2020: Institution shopping and resilience grabbing: changing scapes and grabbing pastoral commons in Africa floodplain wetlands, *Conservation and Society*, Vol. 18 No. 3, 252-267

Harvey, Penny and Hannah Knox 2012: The enchantments of infrastructure, *Mobilities*, Vol. 7 No. 4, 521-536, CRESC, The University of Manchester, Manchester, UK

Kaura, Vinay 2016: Indian–Japan relations and Asia's emerging geopolitics, *Indian Journal of Asian Affairs*, Vol 29 No. 1 /2, 17-38 «https://www.jstor.org/stable/44123127» accessed on 03.09.2019

Khosla, Romi and Vikram Soni 2012: A water disaster in the making? *Economic and Political Weekly*, Vol. 47, No. 10, 15-17 https://www.jstor.org/stable/41419924

Levien, J. Michael 2013: *Regimes of dispossession: Special economic zones and the political economy of land in India*, University of California, Berkley

National Alliance of People's Movements (NAPM) (Year unknown) : *Delhi–Mumbai industrial corridor: A hype-busting analysis* «https://file.ejatlas.org/docs/2483/DMIC _Report_I_Rishit.pdf» accessed on 05.08.2019

Salpeteur M., Madella M., Patel H. R. and V. Reyes-García 2017: Adaptation, access to resources and mobility: from contemporary pastoral systems to ancient societies, *Nomadic Peoples*, Vol. 21, No. 2, Special Issue: Ancient Pastoralisms pp. 191-213

Sampat, Preeti 2015: Policy Report No. 13 Dholera smart city: Urban infrastructure or rentier growth?, The *Hindu Centre for Politics and Public Policy*

Sampat, Preeti 2017: Dholera the emperor's new city, *Economic & Political Weekly*, Vol. L1, No. 17, 59-67

Sampat, Preeti and Simi Sunny 2016: *Dholera and the myth of voluntary land pooling*, Socio-Legal Review, Vol. 12 No. 2, 1-17

Sankhe S., Vittal I.,Dobbs R., Mohan A., Gulati A., Ablett J., Gupta S., Kim A., Paul S., Sanghvi A. and Gurpreet S. 2010: *India's urban awakening: Building inclusive cities, sustaining economic growth*, McKinsey Global Institute, India, Delhi

SENES Consultants India Pvt. Ltd. 2013: Draft environmental impact assessment of Dholera Special Investment Region (DSIR) In Gujarat, New Delhi

Tommaso Bobbio 2012: Making Gujarat vibrant: Hindutva, development and the rise of subnationalism in India, *Third World Quarterly*, Vol. 33, No. 4, 657-672

Varghese, Paul 2016: *Exploring Other Concepts of Smart-Cities within the Urbanising Indian Context*, in Proccedia Technology (4) p. 1858-1867

Internet references

Aecom: Dholera Special Investment Region «https://aecom.com/projects/dholera-special-investment-region/» accessed 05.10.2020

Cohen, Boyd 2014: The Smartest Cities in the World «https://www.fastcompany.com/3038765/the-smartest-cities-in-the-world» accessed on 18.09.2019

DICDL: What is Dholera SIR? «https://dicdl.in/about-us/» accessed on 18.08.2019

DSIRDA: About us «http://dholerasir.com/about-us/» accessed on 22.08.2019

Infinity Infra 2018: Dholera SIR: Brief hstory of development & investment ||Dholera Smart City Dholera SIR «https://www.youtube.com/watch?v=6qtLr6yU6bQ&t=135s» accessed on 25.08.2019

Sampat, Preeti 2015: Why Dholera's Farmers Are Resisting Giving Up Their Land For A Shining, Smart City, «https://thewire.in/agriculture/why-dholeras-farmers-are-resisting-giving-up-their-land-for-a-shining-smart-city» accessed on 20.09.2019

Times of India 2014: Sparky fly at Dholera SIR public hearing, «https://timesofindia.indiatimes.com/city/ahmedabad/Sparks-fly-at-Dholera-SIR-public-hearing/articleshow/28356129.cms» accessed on 15.07.2019

Times of India 2016: Bhal farmers want Dholera SIR scrapped, «https://timesofindia.indiatimes.com/city/rajkot/Bhal-farmers-want-Dholera-SIR-scrapped/articleshow/51972640.cms» accessed on 28.08.2019]

Other references

Dholera SIR Petition 2015: Cancel Dholera SIR (Special Investment Region), save villagers and organic agriculture

EPH report 2014: Analysis of the EPH Report

Unfulfilled Promises and Impacts of a Green Energy Enchantment: The Benban Solar Park in Egypt

Anja Furger, Social and Cultural Anthropology, University of Lucerne, Switzerland

Introduction

In 2017, 92% of Egypt's energy was produced through thermal power and only 8% through renewable energy resources (Arab Republic of Egypt, Ministry of Electricity and Renewable Energy, Egyptian Electricity Holding Company (EEHC) 2017: 21ff). Egypt's growing population, its economic increase, the aging of the infrastructure and the inadequate generation and transmission of energy have caused several blackouts recently (ESIA 2017: 1). Hence, it is necessary for Egypt to exploit the great potential of its renewable energy '[...] in order to meet the increasing demand, diversify the national energy mix and improve the environmental and climate footprint of the power sector [...]' (Strategic Environmental and Social Assessment (SESA) 2016: 1).

Benban Solar Park is one already visible result of Egypt's new orientation in its energy policy. Named after the closest village, Benban, Benban Solar Park had become the largest[1] solar park in the world by the end of 2019 and is said to provide 1.5 gigawatts of clean energy per year to Egypt's electricity grid[2] (ESIA 2017: 28; IFC 2019: 81). The mega-infrastructure project will undoubtedly affect its surroundings in some way due to its immense extension. Therefore, this article aims to provide an analysis of the possible and already existing effects that this mega-infrastructure project has on the environment and the local society.

Not only the Egyptian government but also the local population of the village of Benban have high hopes for this mega-infrastructure project. As this case study will show, the promises made by different involved actors are even higher and,

---

[1] Benban Solar Park has become the largest solar park in the world in terms of power generation capacity (1.5 gigawatts) and area coverage (36.7 km^2) since its completion in October 2019, according to several sources, including ESIA 2017, SESA 2016, IFC 2019 and various newspaper reports.

[2] Benban Solar Park produces 1.5 and not the estimated 1.8 gigawatts since only 32 plots (out of 40) have been used for energy production as per October 2019 (correspondence with the FMC, 03.02.2020).

unfortunately, often not kept. The case also illustrates how the local community struggles with the label of being too backward to be worth involving in important decision-making and hiring processes. Therefore, this article will examine the local communities' counterstrategies to these labelling processes but also present strategies of other involved actors, such as the Egyptian state and international investors.

Fig 1: Benban Solar Park in Aswan Governorate, Egypt. Source: ib vogt GmbH: https://www.ibvogt.com/home/building-benban.html

The first project of Benban Solar Park was constructed in January 2017 and the entire solar park was finalized in October 2019[3]. Hardly any scientific literature can be found about the project because it is so recent. To date, no studies have been conducted except one assessment about potential environmental and social impacts demanded by international investors and the government of Egypt. The assessment was conducted between 2014 and 2015 and its results have been recorded in the Social and Environmental Strategic Assessment (SESA) report and the Environmental and Social Impact Assessment (ESIA) report. Both reports, as well as the data available on the Internet listed below, formed a crucial information source for this article:
– Online articles and reports prepared by the international investors (the European Bank for Development and Reconstruction (EBDR) and the International Finance Corporation (IFC)) and by the developers (the solar power companies such as ib vogt GmbH (Germany), ACWA Power (Saudi Arabia), etc.)
– Online articles, reports and newsletters
– Various documents and information available on the homepage of Benban Solar Park (benban.org[4]) such as newsletters, minutes of meetings, guidelines (working conditions, health and safety, code of conduct, etc.), management plans (sewage, traffic, wastewater, dust and air emissions, etc.).

---

[3] Kenning, Tom 2018: ib vogt Breaks Ground on 166.5MW Solar Project in Benban, Egypt. PV Tech. ‹https://www.pv-tech.org/news/ib-vogt-breaks-ground-on-166.5mw-solar-project-in-benban-egypt› accessed on 10.01.2020.

[4] It is necessary to say that the website is maintained by the Facility Management Company (the FMC) and therefore all data were uploaded by the FMC.

This above-mentioned data source is completed and supplemented by experiences and insights gained during my field visit, which took place from July 6th to July 11th 2019 and was made possible by two environmental and social managers from ib vogt GmbH. This journey to Aswan was part of the data collection process for my bachelor thesis[5]. Basic ideas and considerations in this article are based on my bachelor thesis, which also addressed Benban Solar Park. Mainly, I gained data through participant observation or informal interviews and conversations, which I conducted during the day or during a meeting with three women working as community liaison officers (CLOs) for the Facility Management Company (FMC) at the project site (with one woman coming from the village of Benban and the other two from Aswan). I received further data through a regular e-mail exchange with the environmental and social managers and the CLOs.

Part 1: History and Current Context

Before this chapter focuses on a few historical key points relevant for the region in which the project site is located, the following information box (Box 1: Key Points of Egypt's History) aims to provide a short overview of the country's recent history, starting with the colonial period after British occupation:

Box 1: Key Points of Egypt's History

1882–1922	British Occupation and Protectorate
1869	Inauguration of the Suez Canal
1902	Old Aswan Dam
1922	Independence of Egypt
1922–1952	Kingdom of Egypt
1952	Coup d'etat / 23 July Revolution
1952–1970	President Nasser
1970	Aswan High Dam
1970–1981	President Sadat
1981–2011	President Mubarak
2011	Egypt Uprising (Arab Spring)
2011–2012	President Morsi
2012–2013	Military Rule
2013–2014	President Mansour
2014–	President Al-Sisi

Upper and Lower Egypt, where Benban Solar Park is located, were separate political entities in predynastic times. According to tradition, it was Menes who unified

---
[5] Furger, Anja 2020: Benban Solar Park. Impacts, Promises and the Anti-Politics Machine.

Egypt in a single monarchy around 3100 BCE and that union gave him the royal title 'King of Upper and Lower Egypt'[6] (Manley 1996: 14). Today, thousands of years after Egypt's unification, it seems that there still exists a great rift between Lower and Upper Egypt. This rift might be shown, among other things, by the stereotypes that especially northern Egyptians associate with the so-called 'Sa'id' (meaning 'upland' in English). People from Upper Egypt are named Sa'idis and are said to own a Sa'id identity and culture (Nielsen 2006; Miller 2004). Further explanations on this subject and what role it plays in the context of Benban Solar Park will be given at a later stage.

In ancient times, Aswan was the ancient city of Swen-ett, which stood on the Nile's eastern bank right below the first cataract. Swen-ett was the southern frontier of pharaonic Egypt and thus it was considered that Egypt begins at Swen-ett. Today's city of Aswan became an important place for the trade with the centre of Africa since many great caravan routes leading to Sudan and Nubia, an ancient region in north-eastern Africa, had their starting point in Aswan (Kamil 1993: 4). The local quarries of the city, a few of which still operate today, provided granite for several ancient Egyptian monuments throughout the country[7] (SESA 2016: 79). Since then, Egypt has experienced several changes in governance: from the conquering by Alexander the Great through the Arab rule in the Middle Ages up to the British occupation in 1882 (Etheredge 2011; Al-Sayyid Marsot 2007). It was not until 1922 that Egypt gained independence. After the 'coup d'état' in 1952, President Nasser and his regime governed Egypt until his assassination in 1970 (Al-Sayyid Marsot 2007: 125ff). In 1970, the new Aswan High Dam (AHD) was built 17 km south of Aswan City after the Old Aswan Dam (or Aswan Low Dam) had already been built in 1902 on the Nile (Derr 2019: 45ff). The AHD holds back 132 km^3 of water in Lake Nasser (called Lake Nubia in Sudan) and generates 2.1 gigawatts of energy per year, approximately 30% more than Benban Solar Park (1.5 gigawatts)[8] (Negm et al. 2019: 5ff). The AHD not only enables the control of flooding and thus saves the destruction of villages and infrastructures in Upper Egypt, but also partly satisfies the demand for renewable energy (8% of all Egyptian energy demand in 2017), ensures regular water supply for irrigated land and improves the navigation of the river (Mohamed 2019: 55ff). Benbannis, which the inhabitants of Benban are also called, associate the AHD with economic

---

[6] The Editors of Encyclopaedia Britannica 2010: Lower Egypt. Geographical Division, Egypt. Encyclopaedia Britannica. ⟨https://www.britannica.com/place/Lower-Egypt⟩ accessed on 07.12.2019.
[7] Ibid.
[8] NASA Earth Observatory 2015: Aswan High Dam. NASA Earth Observatory homepage. ⟨https://earthobservatory.nasa.gov/images/85992/aswan-high-dam⟩ accessed on 04.12.2019.

prosperity and hope that Benban Solar Park initiates another economic boom[9] (UNESCO 2005: 3; Etheredge 2011: 37).

Geography and Ecosystem

Benban Solar Park is situated close to the village of Benban (13 km), which lies in the Governorate of Aswan, 40 km north of the same-named capital city (Map 1). Aswan Governorate is, compared to the other existing 27 governorates in Egypt, the hottest, driest and southernmost governorate (SESA 2016: 65; Adaption Fund Board 2012: 17). Moreover, Egypt can be separated into Upper, Middle and Lower Egypt, whereas Aswan Governorate constitutes the region of Upper Egypt together with four other governorates (Assiut, Sohag, Qena and Luxor) (Adaption Fund Board 2012: 4). The area of Aswan Governorate covers 62,726 km^2, approximately 6% of the entire country. Moreover, it is home to 1.6% of Egypt's population (1,501,000 people in 2017), of whom approximately 58% live in rural areas (SESA 2016: 64; CAPMAS 2018: 4ff). Egypt is considered a sun belt country since it is part of the great desert belt and therefore receives between nine and 11 hours of sunshine per day and 2,000 to 3,000 kWh/m^2/year[10] of direct solar radiation – more than double compared to Switzerland, where the annual radiation varies between 1,050 and 1,550 kWh/m^2, depending on the location[11]. The fertile land in Egypt, covering only approximately 3% of Egypt's entire land, can be found along the main source of water, namely the River Nile (Zahran and Willis 2009: 1). Benban Solar Park is situated in the so-called Western Desert of Egypt. This desert is also known as the Libyan part of the Sahara, stretching from the River Nile westward to Libya. The Western Desert, and hence also the project site of Benban Solar Park, belongs to the hyper-arid provinces and therefore to one of the most arid regions on earth[12]. This aridity results from the absence of high elevations, which may attract orographic rain, and the long distance away from seas (2009: 13). A narrow belt of cisterns and wells along the Mediterranean Sea and some springs at the foot of Gebel Uweinat (situated in the south-west on the borders with Libya and Sudan), which are fed by occasional rains, are the only water source in the Western Desert. Except for a few oases, the land in between is

---

[9] Farag, Mohamed 2018: Energy Projects in Benban Save Youth from Unemployment, Poverty. Daily News Egypt (22nd November). ⟨https://ww.dailynewssegypt.com/2018/11/22/solar-energy-projects-in-benban-save-youth-from-unemployment-poverty/⟩ accessed on 06.10.2019.

[10] Bissada Dina 2019: Egypt Country Commercial Guide. Egypt – Renewable Energy. Export.gov. ⟨https://www.export.gov/article?id=Egypt-Renewable-Energy⟩ accessed on 02.10.2019.

[11] Solarprofis 2015: Scheint in der Schweiz genug Sonne für Solarenergie? Die Solarprofis. ⟨https://www.solarprofis.ch/kampagne/scheint-in-der-schweiz-genug-sonne-fuer-solarenergie/⟩ accessed on 17.01.2020.

[12] Hyper-arid provinces are characterized by very hot summers (the average temperature of the hottest month is higher than 30 °C) and mild winters (the average temperature of the coldest month lies between 10 ° and 20 °C) (Zahran and Willis 2009: 6ff).

almost waterless (2009: 14). The ground of the project site, comprised of coloured sandstone and shale beds, is very flat and often covered with a thin layer of gravel and yellow sand (ESIA 2017: 91ff; Zahran and Willis 2009: 6ff). The closest water source to Benban Solar Park is thus the Nile, around 15 km eastward, and the nearest oasis is located 60 km east of Aswan and called Kurkur (2009: 89).

Local Population and Resource Use

Local Community

The closest village to the project site is Benban, which is made up of three subvillages, called Benban Qebly (29% of Benban's population), Benban Bahary (36%) and El Raqaba (35%), totalling around 26,000 inhabitants in total (cf. Map 1) (SESA 2016: 72). The village of Mansouria (also El Mansorya or El Mansouraya) is sometimes considered to be a fourth subvillage due to its short distance to, and close relationship with, Benban, even though it is actually an independent village located north of Benban[13] (cf. Map 1).

Egypt was under Arab rule until 1250, and in the 11th century a large number of tribesmen settled in Upper Egypt to further stimulate Arabization (Etheredge 2011: 102). This Arab descendance can still be found in the village of Benban, where it is said that ethnic groups with historical ties to the Arabian Peninsula settled there some 1,000 years ago (SESA 2016: 69). The majority of the Benbannis belong to these ethnic groups and a very small proportion are Nubians. Furthermore, almost all Benban inhabitants are Muslim, while about 3% are Christian (Copt) (SESA 2016: 70)[14]. The largest ethnic groups in the village of Benban are called 'El Ababda' and 'El Ansar' (SESA 2016: 69). Unfortunately, not much is known about the Ansar. Nevertheless, it is said that the Ansar (Engl. the helpers) were the people from Medina who helped Prophet Muhammad to travel from Mecca to their hometown of Medina. The term 'Ansar' is also applied to the descendants and followers of Prophet Muhammad (Al-Mahdi). The Ansar can primarily be found in central and western Sudan[15]. On the other hand, much more information can be found about the Ababda.

The Ababda lived as nomadic pastoralists in the Eastern Desert and in the region between Aswan and Qena (approximately 100 km north of Luxor), where they took care of herds of goats, camels and sheep (Etheredge 2011). Nowadays, only a small number still live in the aforementioned desert regions and the majority have settled along the River Nile and around the cities of Idfu and Daraw

---

[13] Correspondence with the FMC, 08.10.2019.
[14] Correspondence with the FMC, 06.08.2019.
[15] The Editors of Encyclopaedia Britannica 2016: Mahdist. Encyclopaedia Britannica. ‹https://www.britannica.com/topic/Mahdists› accessed on 07.10.2019.
Lastprophet.info 2010: Ansar (The Helpers). Last Prophet.info. ‹http://www.lastprophet.info/ansar-the-helpers› accessed on 07.10.2019.

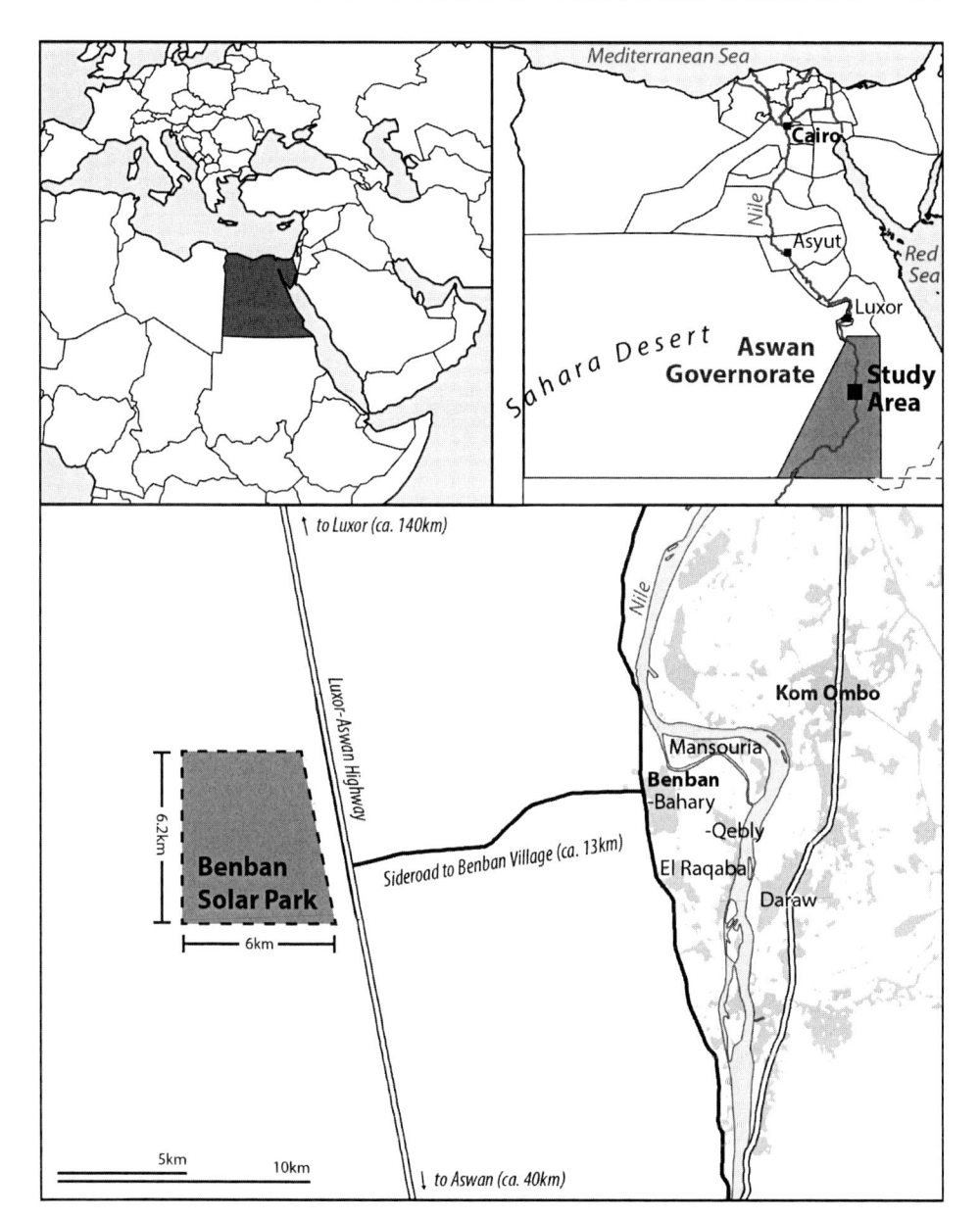

Map 1: Location of Benban Solar Park in the Governorate Aswan, Egypt. Source: Map compilation and design by Manuel L. K. Abebe (2021), CDE, University of Bern, Bern, Switzerland. Geodata: OpenStreetMap contributors, GADM, Corbane et al. (2018)

(Hopkins and Saad 2004: 216). Moreover, it is known that the Ababda belong to the ethnic group of the Beja, who are Arab Bedouins (nomadic people speaking

Arabic[16]). Arab Bedouins, and hence perhaps also the Ababda, own a tribal social organization, and conceive of having a common ancestor and being united by blood (Etheredge 2011). Although the majority of the Ababda have adjusted their way of life and are sedentary or semi-nomadic today, this change had, according to Hopkins and Saad (2004: 216), no significant impact on their social structure: '[...] even today little indicates that the tribe has assimilated or that the social fabric has been disrupted, as there is an astounding continuity in the social organization, in settlement patterns, and in the tribal history [...]'. Hence, social structures still exist today and play a crucial role in the daily life of the Ababda communities. Nielsen (2006: 128) agrees with Hopkins and Saad's assumption and says that what they call 'tribalism' has been, and is, central to social organization in the Upper Egyptian region. Moreover, according to the FMC, such 'tribal' elements can also be found in the village of Benban[17]. Another point to mention is the role that 'tribalism' plays in the stereotypes of the Sa'id community (Nielsen 2006: 28). Northern Egyptians often associate Upper Egyptians with being stubborn, backward and subject to a clan system with violent feuds and autocratic elders (Nielsen 2006: 28; Miller 2004: 1). In sum, it can be said that there exists a popular image that Upper Egyptians are backward. This labelling process plays an important role in the context of Benban Solar Park, as will be elaborated later.

Resource Use

No data are available on the actual management of, and access to, resources in Benban. Neither the SESA nor the ESIA report provides information on this issue. Nevertheless, I assume that at the time the Ababda lived as nomadic pastoralists, the pastures were managed as commons (Etheredge 2011). Hence the community probably owned a social institution that administered the common-pool resources. Since, according to Hopkins and Saad (2004: 216), the nomads became more sedentary, an institutional change may already have taken place. However, too little ethnographic knowledge is available on the reasons why this was happening.

Economy and Legal Framework

Economic Situation

Aswan has experienced economic prosperity since the building of the High Dam in Aswan in 1970 and holds a leading position in the tourism sector (UNESCO 2005: 3; Etheredge 2011). The annual number of tourists visiting Aswan increased from approximately 300,000 in 1997 to one million in 2010 (Mohamed 2019: 67). On the other hand, Aswan Governorate has a very high poverty rate and very limited economic opportunities. The European Bank for Reconstruction and Devel-

---

[16] The Editors of Encyclopaedia Britannica 2019: Bedouin People. Encyclopaedia Britannica. ‹https://www.britannica.com/topic/Bedouin› accessed on 06.07.2019.
[17] Correspondence with the FMC, 06.08.2019.

opment (EBRD) states that over 50% of the people in the region of Aswan are below the poverty line[18]. Furthermore, in 2010, 923 of the 1,000 poorest villages were found in Upper Egypt (UNDP 2010: 22). Similar conditions seem to prevail in the village of Benban, as it is written in a report in *Daily News Egypt*: '[...] poverty and neglect still shadows the village which is drowning in sewage [...]' and '[...] the village suffers from severe poverty and deterioration in health, education and sanitation services [...]'[19]. With one of the only viable economic sectors being agriculture, most of the Benbannis are engaged in agricultural activities, such as farming, trading agricultural products and raising cows. A small percentage of the inhabitants work in a brick factory, in a factory for drying tomatoes (in wintertime only), as merchants or as governmental employees (SESA 2016: 84ff)[20]. The unemployment rate amounts to 40% and is three times higher than the national average (12.5%) (CAPMAS 2018: 56; SESA 2016: 81).

Property Rights

The land of Benban Solar Park is non-demarcated desert land and hence, under Egyptian law, owned by the government of Egypt and administered by the Governorate of Aswan[21]. To provide land for Benban Solar Park, land ownership has been transferred from the Governorate of Aswan to the New and Renewable Energy Agency (NREA) (SESA 2016: 129; AFDB (n.y.): 3). Under Egyptian law, this transfer of ownership, also known as 'allocation', is a method for granting ownership rights to investors in certain ownership properties[22]. Since the land of the project site was already state-owned land, Law no. 10/1990 on 'Property Expropriation for Public Benefit' was not consulted (ESIA 2017: 55). These ownership structures are important for the compensation question too: '[...] the land of the project is not private property, it is government property, so there is no reason for compensation'[23]. Accordingly, as the community of Benban does not own the land of Benban Solar Park by Egyptian law, they are not legally entitled to any form of compensation. However, customary land rights also seem to play an important role in the legal context of Benban Solar Park, besides the already mentioned formal aspects. The FMC explained the informal land rights as follows:

---

[18] Zgheib, Nibal 2017: EBRD Approves US$ 500 Million for Private Renewable Projects in Egypt. ⟨https://www.ebrd.com/news/2017/ebrd-approves-us-500-million-for-private-renewable-projects-in-egypt.html⟩ accessed on 24.01.2020.

[19] Farag, Mohamed 2018: Energy Projects in Benban Save Youth from Unemployment, Poverty. *Daily News Egypt* (22nd November). ⟨https://ww.dailynewssegypt.com/2018/11/22/solar-energy-projects-in-benban-save-youth-from-unemployment-poverty/⟩ accessed on 25.08.2019.

[20] Correspondence with the FMC, 08.10.2019.

[21] Correspondence with the FMC, 06.08.2019.

[22] Taha, Ehab and Salma Basset 2015: Property Laws and Regulations in Egypt. Al Tamimi & Co. ⟨https://www.tamimi.com/law-update-articles/property-laws-and-regulations-in-egypt/⟩ accessed on 30.11.2019.

[23] Correspondence with the FMC, 06.08.2019.

officially, the Egyptian government owns the land, but culturally, the land belongs to the community of Benban. Every village owns a specific part of the surrounding land so that their future generations have enough space for living[24]. Hence, the land is '[...] given to the project in the shape of usufructuary right[25] for 25 years'[26]. In sum, the Benbannis have received no direct monetary compensation for the land of the project site, since this piece of land was already owned by the Egyptian government, according to Egyptian law. However, the Lenders and Developers have introduced a CSR programme[27] for the village of Benban since they are very much aware of the great importance that customary land rights have in this region.

Part 2: The Mega-Infrastructure Project

Bent Flyvbjerg (2014: 3) defines mega projects as '[...] large-scale, complex ventures that typically cost a billion dollars or more, take many years to develop and build, involve multiple public and private stakeholders, are transformational, and impact millions of people'. The following paragraphs use these characteristics of a mega project to thoroughly describe Benban Solar Park. The focus is on the multiple actors and the contracting as well as on the international investment.

Actors and Contracting

One prominent characteristic of mega projects is the great number of public and private players involved. As the same applies to Benban Solar Park, the following information box (Box 2: Key Actors) will help in providing a quick overview:

Benban Developers' Association (BDA)
The BDA was established by 'the Developers' (the solar power companies) to represent their interests and to facilitate communication between the different players (AFDB (n.y.): 9). Moreover, the BDA, and therefore all the Developers, are in charge of the implementation of the CSR programme.

Box 2: Key Actors

---

[24] Field notes by the author, 06–11.07.2019.
[25] The usufruct right is a right '[...] to use a property owned by another person for a specific period of time and on terms agreed between the parties. A person who holds a usufruct right over another person's property has all the rights granted by law to the owner, except for the right to sell or transfer the ownership of such property' (Taha, Ehab and Salma Basset 2015: Property Laws and Regulations in Egypt. Al Tamimi & Co. ⟨https://www.tamimi.com/law-update-articles/property-laws-and-regulations-in-egypt/⟩ accessed on 30.11.2019).
[26] Correspondence with the FMC, 06.08.2019.
[27] Moreover, the inclusion of a CSR programme was a mandatory part of the Environmental and Social Impact Assessment and the Social Impact Assessment, respectively (ESIA 2017: 202).

Egyptian Electricity Holding Company (EEHC)
The EEHC is in charge of producing, transmitting and distributing electricity with high efficiency at affordable prices. Therefore, the EEHC is a very important player in Egypt's electricity market (SESA 2016: 38).

Egyptian Electricity Transmission Company (EETC)
The EETC connects Benban Solar Park with the already existing high-voltage network, builds the control centre and four new substations. The EETC is a transmission system operator, owned by the Egyptian state, who buys the electricity generated by the project and offers a price guarantee for 25 years.

European Bank for Reconstruction and Development (EBRD) (Lender)
The EBRD is a development bank owned by 69 countries as well as by the European Union and the European Investment Bank. Their aim is to promote entrepreneurial and private initiative. The EBRD has financed 16 solar plants at Benban Solar Park under their US $500 million framework for renewable energy in Egypt. Financial support for this framework has been provided by several countries, including Australia, China, France and Germany.

Facility Management Consultant (FMC)
The management of the facilities is provided by the Egyptian company Hassan Allam Services. They are responsible for 'the logistical, environmental, security, and health & safety aspects of the Project, as well as the relations with neighbouring communities'

ib vogt GmbH (Developer)
ib vogt GmbH is a German company specialized in solar project development. They provide '[…] the entire downstream section of the solar value chain – from PV component selection and solar financing to project development and operational management'. ib vogt GmbH, together with Infinity Solar (an Egyptian renewable energy developer) under the Special Purpose Vehicle (SPV) 'Infinity Solar Energy S.A.E.', completed the first project in Benban.

International Finance Corporation (IFC) (Lender)
The IFC is the private investment arm of the World Bank and a member of the World Bank Group, which is the largest global development institution with a focus on the private sector in developing countries. The IFC, together with a pool of other Lenders provided a considerable loan for 14 solar plants at the Benban project site.

Box 2: Key Actors

> **Local Community**
> The village of Benban is the closest village to the project site and has three subvillages (Benban Qebly, Benban Bahary and El Raqaba). The village of Mansouria (also known as El Mansorya or El Mansouraya) is an independent village located north of Benban (cf. Map 1). However, because of the short distance and the close relationship between the two villages, Mansouria is considered to be a kind of a fourth subvillage (e-mail correspondence with the FMC). Terms such as 'community', 'local community' and 'Benbannis' used in this article refer to people living in the three subvillages of Benban and Mansouria, unless otherwise stated.
>
> **New and Renewable Energy Agency (NREA)**
> The NREA is one out of six agencies under the Ministry of Electricity and Renewable Energy (MoERE). MoERE is responsible for the generation, transmission and distribution of energy and electricity in Egypt and in charge of the development of Egypt's renewable energy sector. Since the NREA is the actual owner of the project, it is also responsible for the construction of roads and other needed infrastructure, for distributing the licences for construction and operation, and for transferring land plots to the different Developers and Lenders (SESA 2016: 8).
>
> **Multilateral Investment and Guarantee Agency (MIGA)**
> MIGA, also a member of the World Bank Group, wants to reduce poverty and support economic growth in developing countries through promoting foreign direct investment. MIGA provides risk insurance to some private Lenders and investors involved in Benban Solar Park.

Box 2: Key Actors

Some 37.2 km² of land, equivalent to approximately 5,200 football fields, has been allocated by the New and Renewable Energy Agency (NREA) under the Ministry of Electricity and Renewable Energy (MoERE). The entire area, 6.2 km in length and 6 km in width, has been separated into 40 plots (between 0.3 km² and 1.0 km²) (SESA 2016: 15; ESIA 2017: 28; Benban, Africa's largest Solar Park, Completed 2019). After having signed a 25-year contract with the NREA, the Developers were allowed to implement their individual projects on those plots, as long as the installed capacity was not under 20 MW. Egyptian or international Developers are often made up of several companies that have consolidated to finance the projects through a so-called Special Purpose Vehicle (SPV) (cf. Fig. 2). Every solar project has a separate contract with one SPV, who often also outsources some work to other companies, to so-called 'Contractors'. These Contractors take over work such as engineering, procurement and construction (EPC of the projects). Furthermore, they in turn might again instruct other companies, called 'Subcontractors', to do some work for them[28].

Due to this large number of different actors, it was necessary to involve a facility management company (the FMC). This mandate was given to the Egyptian

---
[28] Correspondence with ib vogt GmbH, 08.10.2019.

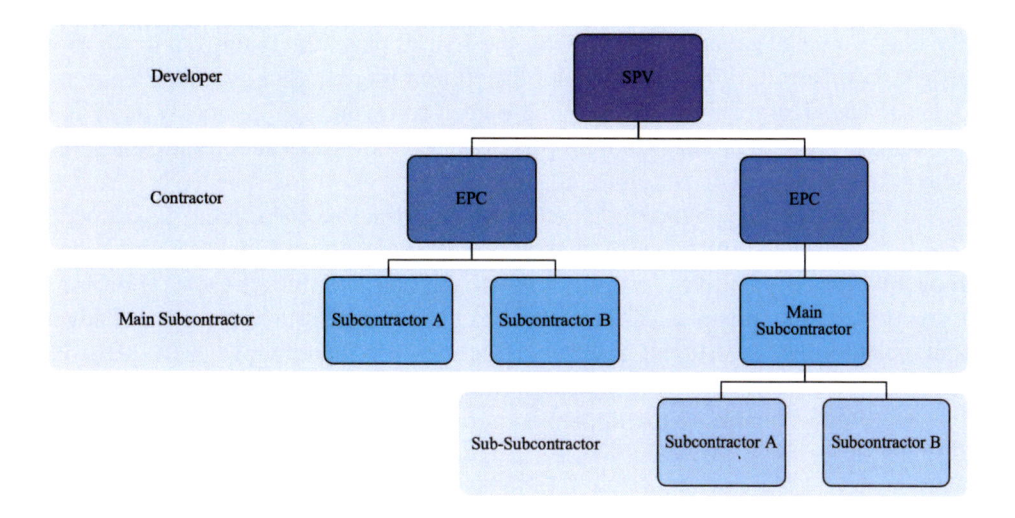

Fig 2: Organizational structure of Benban Solar Park. Source: ib vogt GmbH with own amendments

company Hassan Allam Services, who started their work in January 2018 (Operational Update Meeting 17.04.2019[29]). The FMC takes on the role of a pivot element: they monitor and coordinate between all stakeholders and eliminate the need for each player to organize meetings and other communication activities individually (IFC 2019: 81). Additionally, the FMC is responsible for technical services, including medical and security services and traffic management, as well as for non-technical services like managing community relations, establishing complaints channels and monitoring players for compliance with the necessary standards[30].

One of the biggest challenges for Egypt is its growing energy demand, concerning not only electricity, but also oil and gas (EIA 2018: 3; ESIA 2017: 26). The imbalance between supply and demand is evident everywhere: the actual production of oil cannot satisfy the current consumption; electricity blackouts are part of Egypt's daily life and natural gas has had to be imported since 2015 because of insufficient production (EIA 2018: 3ff). Furthermore, there exists a structural problem: the Egyptian Electricity Holding Company (EEHC) dominates the

---

[29] The Operational Update Meeting was a meeting between the FMC, Developers and Contractors to discuss the current status of operation and to assist with site mobilization. This meeting and the health, safety and environment (HSE), Labour and Security Steering Committee Meeting were merged into one monthly meeting called Developer Coordination (DevCo) to provide HSE and technical updates for Contractors and Developers.

[30] Hassan Allam Services 2019: About Us. Benban Solar Park. ⟨http://benban.org/about/⟩ accessed on 06.06.2019.

Egyptian electricity market since it owns almost all of the distribution assets and the entire transmission system. Hence, the EEHC plays the main role in Egypt's single-buyer electricity market. Under the current model, the Egyptian Electricity Transmission Company (EETC), a state-owned company and previously an EEHC subsidiary, buys electricity from all private and public generation companies and sells it to the main distribution companies[31].

To make the Egyptian energy sector more attractive for foreign investment, the government of Egypt has started to slowly replace the actual state-governed model with a competitive electricity market and has also initiated several reforms to reduce energy subsidies. These subsidies put great pressure on Egypt's budget and make foreign investment in the energy sector very unattractive (EIA 2018: 1). In recent years, however, an increase in investment in the Egyptian energy sector can be observed thanks to the implementation of reforms and the new discoveries of natural gas (EIA 2018: 1). Since the end of October 2019, 32 solar projects in Benban have produced around 1.5 gigawatts of energy and can cover the electricity needs of almost 69,000 households[32]. The entire electrical output is bought by the Egyptian Electricity Transmission Company (EETC) for the next 25 years, since the Developers can profit from the Feed-in Tariff (FiT) programme[33], the favourable policy recently introduced by the Egyptian state (NREA 2018: 1).

International Investment

The International Finance Organization (IFC) and the European Bank for Reconstruction and Development (EBRD) were the main investors. Sixteen plots were financed by the EBRD (US$500 million) and 13 projects by a consortium led by the IFC, which has mobilized US$653 million[34]. Additionally, US$210 million has been provided by the Multilateral Investment and Guarantee Agency (MIGA) as a risk insurance[35].

---

[31] El-Mazghouny, Donia 2019: Renewable Energy in Egypt. Lexology. ⟨https://www.lexology.com/gtdt/tool/workareas/report/renewable-energy/chapter/egypt⟩ accessed on 27.11.2019.

[32] Correspondence with the FMC, 08.10.2019.

[33] The Egyptian government has introduced the FiT Scheme for solar and wind projects with up to 50 MW capacity. The Developers of Benban were also able to use this favourable policy (ESIA 2017: 27).

[34] Riham, Mustafa 2017: IFC-Led Consortium Invests $653 Million to Support the World's Largest Solar Park in Egypt. International Finance Corporation IFC. ⟨https://ifcextapps.ifc.org/ifcext/pressroom/ifcpressroom.nsf/0/C47EC9AF0897C57A852581C8003DE257?OpenDocument⟩ accessed on 16.10.2019.

[35] Zgheib, Nibal 2019: First EBRD funded Egyptian Solar Plant Begins Generation. European Bank for Reconstruction and Development EBRD. ⟨https://www.ebrd.com/news/2019/first-ebrd-funded-egyptian-solar-plant-begins-generation-.html⟩ accessed on 16.10.2019.
Raven, Andrew 2017: A New Solar Park Shines a Light on Egypt's Energy Potential. International Finance Corporation IFC. ⟨https://www.ifc.org/wps/wcm/connect/news_ext_content/ifc_external_corporate_site/news+and+events/news/cm-stories/benban-solar-park-egypt⟩ accessed on 16.10.2019.

The large number of actors makes it extremely difficult to keep the overview of all players, their actions, their relations and their applied strategies. Therefore, many aspects might become blurred and obscured, intentionally or not. I argue that an anti-politics machine (Ferguson 1994) is going on here. Political access for the local population is made difficult because of the size of the project in terms of the many actors involved. Moreover, as there is a contact point for complaints (community liaison offices), another authority is placed between the local population and the regional politics. The huge extent of Benban Solar Park in terms of international investment, contracting and size is an important aspect for understanding the scale at which the local community and environment are confronted. The following chapters will therefore analyse the transformational character of Benban Solar Park.

Environmental and social impacts

In regard to the ESIA and SESA reports, impacts are split into environmental, socio-economic and social (SESA 2016: 97ff; ESIA 2017: 151ff). However, it must be emphasized that the SESA and ESIA reports are based on predictions, since the assessments had to be carried out before the implementation of the project. Furthermore, due to the recent nature of the project, several impacts might only become visible in a few years. Therefore, the paragraphs to come will present already existing effects and critically analyse the estimations made.

Environmental Impacts

According to the estimations made in the SESA report, it was assumed that the spillage of waste, wastewater from sanitary facilities as well as oil, chemicals and other substances could easily happen and have negative impacts on soil and groundwater (SESA 2016: 99). This fear seemed to have come true, since the FMC has recorded informal waste dumps of sewage and mixed waste outside the project site, illegally dumped by Contractors and Subcontractors. The FMC imposed stricter rules after these incidents, to make sure that they were in compliance with Lender standards[36]. Another estimated impact concerned the use of local water resources. In particular, dust control, sanitary facilities and equipment cleaning were expected to use a huge amount of water (SESA 2016: 111). The needed water used for panel cleaning during the operational phase could not be predicted because every Contractor was allowed to differ in the frequency and method of panel cleaning (2016: 113). For water supply, a pipeline to the Nile near the village of Benban was planned. However, the risk of water shortages for

---

[36] Developer Coordination Meeting (DevCo) 24.10.2018. The aim of the monthly DevCo meeting was to discuss health, safety and environment (HSE) and to give technical updates for Developers and Contractors.

the local community was regarded as too high. Therefore, no pipeline was built, and all water was transported by trucks from Aswan to the project site[37].

Additionally, Benban Solar Park significantly changes the uniform and flat landscape, as it is very extensive – the area is covered by over 7.2 million photovoltaic panels, which are even visible from outer space[38]. However, from the ground, Benban Solar Park is only visually dominant from a short distance as the panels are low and very flat (SESA 2016: 98). Nevertheless, it must be considered that the great number of arrays of panels may disorientate birds because they may look like water surfaces to them (AFDB (n.y.): 7). Due to the extreme habitat in which the project site is located, other impacts on fauna and flora are estimated to be very low. Furthermore, no endangered fauna or flora habitat has been reported in this area (SESA 2016: 100ff).

Benban Solar Park not only has an impact on the local, but probably also on the national and international environment. The project will significantly contribute to Egypt's production of 'green' energy and to the reduction of CO_2 emissions. It is assumed that about 2 million tons of CO_2 can be avoided through the mega-infrastructure project during its 25-year lifetime (SESA 2016: 31). Therefore, Benban Solar Park will also play an important role in Egypt's commitment to the 2015 Paris Agreement and in the fight against climate change in Egypt[39].

Social and Socio-Economic Impacts

Due to the huge size and great energy generation of Benban Solar Park, it seems very likely that the project has, and will have, a major impact on the national scale, namely on Egypt's economy and politics. As already mentioned in the previous chapters, Benban not only produces 1.5 gigawatts of electricity annually but also reduces Egypt's dependence on thermal power and its vulnerability to future fluctuations in the price of fossil fuels. However, the project has, or might also have, considerable impacts on the local society and economy. The following paragraphs will therefore focus on this scale.

New Infrastructure, Accidents and Safety at Work

Benban Solar Park seems to trigger the improvement and expansion of roads[40] and the construction of new infrastructure near the project site. One example of

---

[37] Correspondence with the FMC, 03.02.2020, field notes by the author, 06–11.07.2019.
[38] Nordrum, Amy 2019: Egypt's Massive 1.8-Gigawatt Benban Solar Park Near Completion. *IEEE Spectrum* (17th September). ⟨https://spectrum.ieee.org/energywise/energy/renewables/egypts-massive-18gw-benban-solar-park-nears-completion?deliveryName=DM45047⟩ accessed on 16.10.2019.
[39] Ibid.
[40] Farag, Mohamed 2018: Solar Energy Projects in Benban Save Youth from Unemployment, Poverty. *Daily News Egypt* (22nd November). ⟨https://ww.dailynewsegypt.com/2018/11/22/solar-energy-projects-in-benban-save-youth-from-unemployment-poverty/⟩ accessed on 20.09.2019.

such a new infrastructure is a bridge between Benban and Daraw. However, it is not clear whether the bridge will be built as a result of the project or whether it would have been constructed anyway[41]. A second example is two already newly built solar schools in Benban Bahary and Edfu, which provide subjects related to PV installation[42]. Another visible positive consequence of the project can be seen in the safety at work. At the beginning of the project, according to the FMC, the local workers were ashamed to wear flashy yellow or orange work clothes, as they are used to wearing the traditional, mostly sand-coloured Galabeya[43]. For safety reasons, however, all workers on the construction site were obliged to wear them. Fortunately, a change in the safety behaviour of the local community could be observed as work clothing is now more often used on construction sites outside Benban Solar Park[44]. According to the two Environmental and Social Managers, it was especially training, explanation and 'leading by example' that triggered this transformation in the workers' attitude[45].

The ESIA and SESA reports estimated an increased traffic volume, especially during the construction phase. During this phase, many truckers needed to transport frames, panels and other equipment mostly from the Suez Canal via the Luxor-Aswan Highway to the project site. Additionally, workers were transported by several buses to and from the site (ESIA 2017: 163ff). On top of this come the daily traffic, heavy lorries and the very poor condition of the road, which ultimately led to numerous accidents[46].

Work Opportunities

Estimations based on the ESIA report (2017) were made for approximately 18,000 workers during the construction phase. Furthermore, it was assumed that most of these jobs could be occupied by local people, depending, however, on the existing skills of the local community, the actual needed skills and the way Contractors acquire their workforces (ESIA 2017: 170). During the peak time of the construction phase (December 2018 – January 2019), there were only around 10,000 total employments recorded by the FMC (cf. Fig. 4). In November 2018, for instance, of the approximately 10,000 workers inside the park, only 14% came from Benban (cf. Fig. 3). In contrast, more than 50% of the entire workforce was from

---

[41] Field notes by the author, 06–11.07.2019.
[42] Correspondence with the FMC, 08.10.2019, Field notes by the author, 06–11.07.2019.
[43] A 'Galabeya' is usually a long gown with wide, long sleeves (field notes by the author, 06–11.07.2019).
[44] Field notes by the author, 06–11.07.2019.
[45] Ibid.
[46] Ibid.

Worker Demographics inside the Park

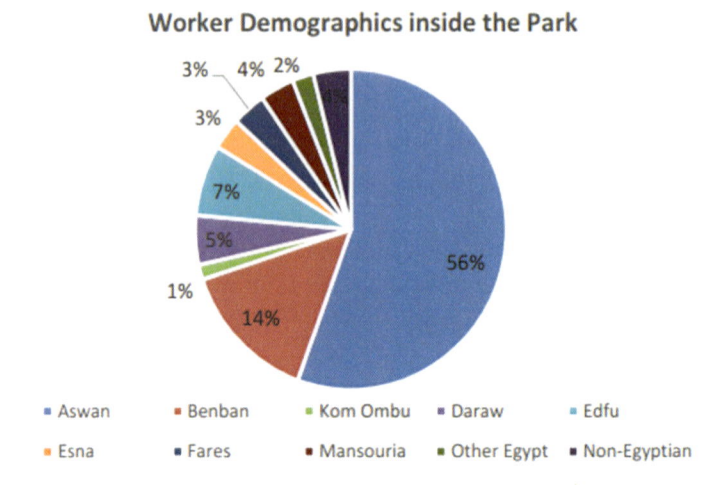

[Pie chart: Aswan 56%, Benban 14%, Kom Ombu 1%, Daraw 5%, Edfu 7%, Esna 3%, Fares 3%, Mansouria 4%, Other Egypt 2%]

Fig 3: A chart provided by the FMC showing the origin of the workers inside Benban Solar Park. Source: The FMC: MCAP 10.12.2018

the city of Aswan (MCAP[47] 10.12.2018, The Benbanner January 2019[48]). The Lenders and the FMC strongly advised Developers and Contractors to occupy at least 20% of the workplaces with local people during the construction phase[49]. However, this was only a suggestion, not a contractual obligation. Only in the first quarter of 2019 were the Contractors and Developers obliged to hire 30% of the entire workforce from Benban and Mansouria for each plot during the operation and maintenance phase (DevCo 31.03.2019)[50]. It was estimated that the project would also create many indirect employment opportunities for local people, such as transportation services, food supply and cleaning services (AFDB (n.y.): 7; SESA 2016; ESIA 2017). In many cases, the Developers and Contractors were not allowed to outsource such services to the local community, because of the very low standard (missing seatbelts, lights, mirrors, etc.) of working machines, transport buses and other facilities[51]. However, there are also examples showing that local people really can profit from indirect employment opportunities. For

---

[47] Community Advisory Panels (CAPs) and Master Community Advisory Panels (MCAPs) are instruments used by the FMC to provide good communication between the surrounding communities, Developers and Lenders. All meeting minutes of the MCAPs can be accessed on the homepage of the project (http://benban.org/community/). More is elaborated on CAPs and MCAPs at a later stage.

[48] 'The Benbanner' is FMC's monthly newsletter, which was distributed to the internal community of the park, including Contractors, Subcontractors, managers, workers, etc.

[49] During the first round of the FiT programme the IFC and the EBRD were not yet financially involved, so there was no contractual obligation to hire a specific rate from the surrounding villages (e-mail correspondence with ib vogt GmbH).

[50] Correspondence with ib vogt GmbH, 14.12.2019.

[51] Field notes by the author, 06–11.07.2019.

instance, the monthly newsletter *The Benbanner*, edited by the FMC, wrote that 'Benbanni women are now sewing worker "reflective vest" uniforms' (2018: 1). Another example is the case of a young man from Benban, who is said to have established a restaurant and a catering company[52].

Total manpower in site

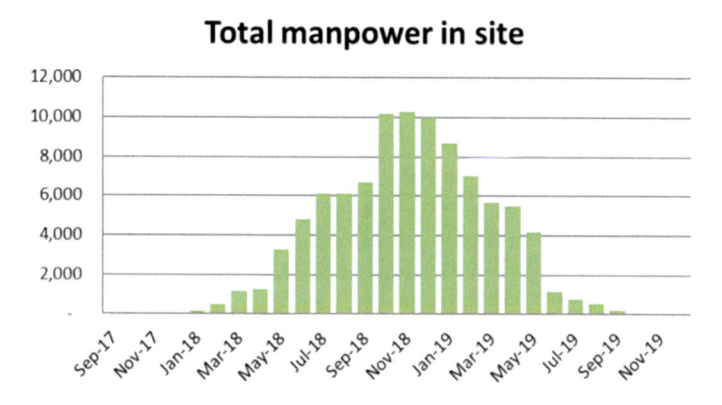

[Bar chart showing monthly manpower values from Sep-17 to Nov-19, peaking around Sep-18/Nov-18 at approximately 10,000 workers]

Fig 4: A chart provided by the FMC showing the total manpower at the project site from September 2017 to November 2019. Source: The FMC: The Benbanner, November 2018

I argue that the impact of short-term contracts is probably very much underestimated. Only around 450 workers will be needed during the operation and maintenance phase and hence receive a long-term work contract. This means that the majority of the people working during the construction phase only received a temporary contract[53]. The FMC expressed extreme concern about the possible negative effects of these temporary employment contracts. For the workers this means going back to their daily life in the surrounding villages with more financial resources but with limited, or even without, more skills. The FMC was concerned that people, after earning and spending more money, have developed higher expectations of their lives. For this reason, they probably do not want to return to their agricultural and often poorly paid work anymore. Social unrest, outmigration and community frustration may be possible consequences of this transformation[54].

Sa'id Culture

Because of the great number of workers needed during the construction time, it was supposed that foreign workers would have a negative impact on 'the norms and traditions of the community people' because of their 'different behavioural

---

[52] Farag, Mohamed 2018: Solar Energy Projects in Benban Save Youth from Unemployment, Poverty. *Daily News Egypt* (22nd November). ‹https://ww.dailynewssegypt.com/2018/11/22/solar-energy-projects-in-benban-save-youth-from-unemployment-poverty/› accessed on 25.08.2019.
[53] Correspondence with the FMC, 03.02.2020, field notes by the author, 06–11.07.2019.
[54] Field notes by the author, 06–11.07.2019.

patterns' (ESIA 2017: 178). This impact on traditions and norms was thought to be crucial since it would hit a very conservative and rural region, according to the ESIA and SESA reports. To understand these assumptions, it is important to remember that Benban is part of Upper Egypt, the Sa'id, respectively. As mentioned before, the Sa'id is usually linked to backwardness, conservatism and traditionalism (Miller 2004: 1). The Code of Conduct on Labour Rights and Working Conditions (2017)[55], prepared by the FMC, therefore mentions measures to mitigate the feared impacts on the local people, who are labelled as backward and traditional:

Due to the social and cultural specifics of the neighbouring villages, the Project's worker camp has a semi-closed camp policy, i.e. no camp residents are allowed outside the camp, other than with scheduled bus trips to Aswan for spending leisure time. Aswan, due to its long-standing exposure to international tourism, has greater cultural capacity to deal with other cultures. (2017: Annex 2)

By applying a 'semi-closed camp[56] policy' and 'scheduled bus trips to Aswan', the impact on the local community ought to be lowered. Aswan, on the other hand, 'has a greater cultural capacity' than Benban and hence can better deal with foreign workers. Additionally, in terms of the local community, 'direct contacts with women should be avoided' (ESIA 2017: 183) because of the 'strongly patriarchal and conservative ideology' (2017: 180). It is important to note that external people have described the surrounding communities as backward and patriarchal, and not the affected people themselves. The same applies for the suggested mitigation measure to avoid direct contact with local women. Additionally, this measure contradicts the statements made by the FMC and the Benbannis themselves about the role of the women in their society. For example, the FMC stated that women play '[...] an important and influencing role in the community in the field of politics and leadership'[57]. This view is supported by the Benbanni woman working as a Community Liaison Officer (CLO). She said that women are the key to the community of Benban and that the women themselves, not the men, decided not to apply for construction work on the construction site because they considered the work too physically demanding[58].

It seems that an anti-politics machine (Ferguson 1994) is going on here. There exists a particular interest in the Sa'id culture and in the stereotypes of this 'culture' from outside. The Sa'idis receive a greater consideration and attention than other groups from the local community. Therefore, people from the community

---

[55] Hassan Allam Services 2017: Hassan Allam Services. Cairo, Egypt. Solar PV Plant Benban Site. Code of Conduct on Labour Rights and Working Conditions. Construction Phase (Unpublished Interim Report).
[56] The FMC provided a worker camp 8 km north of the project site for around 250 workers (Field notes by the author, 08.07.2019).
[57] Correspondence with the FMC, 06.08.2019.
[58] Field notes by the author, 06–11.07.2019.

who do not fit in this traditional 'culture' probably lose bargaining power while 'traditional' leaders may profit from this particular interest. A process of institution shopping might be triggered (Haller 2020).

Strategies

Due to the complex arena involving many actors with various institutional arrangements, it is understandable that local people are faced with legal pluralism, especially since the FMC fills an intermediary political gap, where the national political structure seems to be lacking in providing participation.

Local and NGO Strategies

During my field visit I was able to talk to the Benbanni woman working as a Community Liaison Officer (CLO) for the FMC. When asking her if the community of Benban is against the project she just said: 'It's a national project – how can you be against it?' She then added that in her eyes the Benbannis approve the project and hope for many employment opportunities. Her position was further supported by her statement that 'we are proud, but we have a right'. The CLO emphasized the right of the Benbannis to work opportunities and to compensation since the project is being built on their land. The local community are, however, also ready to get active and claim their rights, which they are entitled to in their eyes, as the following paragraphs show. However, it is important to note that the Community Liaison Officers (CLOs) are part of the FMC apparatus. Since I did not find any information about possible activities of non-governmental organizations or other organized groups that work for the interests of the local population, the FMC controls all communication about the project and the community of Benban. This is a typical feature of an anti-politics machine (Ferguson 1994): the local population and independent groups have no opportunity to raise their concerns at the national level because the political structures seem to lack these opportunities to participate. They can only pursue their concerns via the FMC, which, however, operates outside the political system.

Complaints During MCAPs

Making complaints during MCAPs is a formal strategy applied by the community to put pressure on other involved players. Several complaints were raised during the MCAPs, especially concerning job opportunities and the implementation of the CSR programme:

Every day we see 50 to 60 buses loaded with workers coming from Aswan [...]. Benban needs to have a higher stake of total workers inside the park. Work resembles a window of opportunity for us to have a good source of income that lifts us from poverty and improves quality of life. (MCAP 24.01.2019: 3).

This quote shows that one of the primary concerns of the community is the unequal distribution of work opportunities. They are not happy with the FMC's and the Developer's employment strategy and seem to have been enchanted by their promises (Harvey and Knox 2012). Additionally, the local people think that people from the community have the right to work at the project site and should be preferred to other workers coming from Aswan or even further away. As the following quote shows, a change has occurred (probably as a result of different factors), at least at the site of the Lenders:

[...] the lenders agreed on hiring 30% of local workers coming from Benban and el Mansouria in the O & M [Operation and Maintenance] phase in each plot [...] (DevCo 31.03.2019)

This means that every Developer has to be in accordance with this quota if they do not want to risk not receiving the next instalment for their projects[59].

The CSR programme is another often raised point of issue during the MCAPs, especially when no signs of implementation are visible. The persistent voiced community's concerns around the implementation of the CSR (probably together with other applied strategies) seem to have made an impact. Not only has the FMC arranged the attendance of IFC executive CEO Philippe Le Houerou during an MCAP but the entire process has apparently sped up (MCAP 10.12.2018). It seems that the counterstrategy of the local population is showing results. Moreover, it also means that people can organize themselves and show resistance.

Security Incidents, Strikes and Road Blockades

The above-shown complaints during the MCAPs are examples of how community people try to formally respond to problems and inadequacies. Another strategy applied by the locals is road blockades, which, according to the FMC, are very effective since there are just two roads leading and just two entries to Benban Solar Park (cf. Map 1). Due to this limited access to the project site it is very easy to block either road or entry[60]. In addition to the road blockades, several site strikes were reported by the FMC between January and March 2019 (DevCo 25.02.2019 and 31.03.2019). The termination of work contracts and the unfulfilled expectations, in particular, seem to be a common reason for a growing community frustration leading to intimidation, social unrest, stone throwing and fence breaches (The Benbanner January 2019; DevCo 23.01.2019; Security Meeting 06.09.2018). All these small acts of sabotage are classical elements of what Scott calls the 'weapons of the weak' (1986). These small daily acts of resistance are indications that a disenchantment process is underway here (Harvey and Knox 2012).

---

[59] Correspondence with ib vogt GmbH, 14.12.2019.
[60] Ibid.

State and Company Strategies

The government of Egypt hopes that Benban Solar Park will increase the national power generation capacity, promote the Egyptian renewable energy sector and serve as a pioneer for future initiatives. For these reasons, among several others, the government has a great interest in the project being realized successfully and as quickly as possible. Therefore, the Egyptian government makes use of several strategies to make the Solar Park attractive for foreign and private investors. One part of the strategy is the offer of several incentives and favourable policies (e.g. Investment Law No. 72/2017, the Renewable Energy Law (Decree No. 203/2014)[61] and the FiT Scheme). The other part of the government's strategy concerns the use of actual debates and labelling processes. The Egyptian government uses the current debate about climate change and the growing importance of renewable and 'green energy' not only to attract more investors but also for the legitimation of the entire project[62]. The same can be observed by Developers and Lenders. They emphasize the project's contribution to fight climate change by reducing around two million tons of greenhouse gas emissions a year (equal to taking approximately 400,000 cars off the road[63]) and through its crucial role in Egypt's commitment to the 2015 Paris Agreement (SESA 2016: 31). In addition, the legitimation of the project is further enhanced by the labelling of the project site as 'bare' and 'empty' land, which is then transformed into 'productive' land. Finally, Benban Solar Park is also praised as an important instrument for the development of Upper Egypt and the creation of regional economic prosperity[64].

This last promise of Benban Solar Park being a crucial instrument to bring economic prosperity and development in the rather marginalized region of Upper Egypt[65] (How Egypt is Building the World's Biggest Solar Array 2017) plays a key role in the legitimization strategy of the government and the other actors (Developers, Lenders, the FMC). They promise that the high unemployment levels

---

[61] Both laws aim to promote renewable energy projects through the granting of a special investment incentive and by encouraging the private sector to produce more electricity from renewable resources (International Energy Agency (IEA) 2019; Egypt Renewable Energy Law (Decree No 203/2014). IEA Homepage. ⟨https://www.iea.org/policiesandmeasures/pams/egypt/name-1571 64-en.php⟩ accessed on 01.12.2019.

[62] Nordrum, Amy 2019: Egypt's Massive 1.8-Gigawatt Benban Solar Park Near Completion. *IEEE Spectrum* (17th September). ⟨https://spectrum.ieee.org/energywise/energy/renewabl es/egypts-massive-18gw-benban-solar-park-nears-completion?deliveryName=DM45047⟩ accessed on 12.12.2019.

[63] Lolwa, Reda 2018: Benban Solar Plant Starts Operating, Egypt Targets 37% Clean Energy by 2035: Shaker. *Egypt Today*. ⟨https://www.egypttoday.com/Article/3/45157/Benban-solar-plant-starts-operating-Egypt-targets-37-clean-energy⟩ accessed on 21.01.2020.

[64] Ibid.

[65] Hassan Allam Services and Rina Consulting 2017: Hassan Allam Services. Cairo, Egypt. Solar PV Plant Benban Site. Worker Accommodation Strategy and Management Plan – Construction Phase (Unpublished Interim Report).

will decrease due to new work opportunities (SESA 2016: 125). Accordingly, the Benbannis have high expectations for the project, as a report in *Daily News Egypt* shows impressively: a Benbanni says that Benban Solar Park will save the village from poverty and unemployment and that the project has brought back hope to the Benbannis[66]. The high hopes that the Benbannis have for Benban Solar Park might greatly be increased by the rather low economic standard that this region faces. Unfortunately, as elaborated in this article, a lot indicates that the promises of new workplaces and long-term benefits for the local community are not kept. Considering the strategic use of these promises and when analysing the resulting high hopes, it can be assumed that a process of enchantment takes place here (Harvey and Knox 2012).

Besides the high hopes the Benbannis have for new work opportunities, their hopes for the corporate social responsibility (CSR) programme promised by the international Lenders and by the Developers seem to be as high. I argue that the promise of a CSR programme is a crucial strategy, especially for Developers, for avoiding incidents and social unrests with the community of Benban. For instance, the Developers describe the CSR as a vital "[…] risk-mitigation tool for the de-mobilization phase" (MCAP 10.12.2019). Even though community development is a requirement for projects funded by the IFC and EBRD, there is no contractual obligation to implement the CSR programme, as IFC executive CEO Philippe Le Houerou said himself during his visit to Benban:

There is no contractual obligation on Developers in front of the IFC to implement the CSR programme. However, Developers have promised the IFC they will implement a CSR programme […]. Developers realize that failing to keep their promises to the IFC has a reputational cost. Nobody should underestimate the power of the word of honour […]. (MCAP 10.12.2018).

Philippe Le Houerou stresses the promise given by the Developers and 'the power of the word of honour'. This means that the effective implementation of the CSR programme depends largely on the promise made by the Developers and the authority of the IFC and the EBRD to ensure that this promise is kept. Due to the huge financial involvement of these two actors, they can put a lot of pressure on Developers and Contractors by freezing their funding to some specific plots and hence ensure that they perform as they wish (DevCo 24.10.2018; The Benbanner October 2018). Hence the EBRD and IFC occupy a position of power that allows them to indirectly influence the behaviour of other actors through their requirements. Also, the impacts of the project on society and the environment are indirectly governed by the EBRD and IFC. These positions of power can be used strategically and must therefore be examined critically.

---

[66] Ibid.

The Sa'id

The emphasis on the Sa'id can be used by the FMC, Developers and Lenders as a strategy to legitimize their actions. One example in which this can be seen very well is the process of hiring local women and men. The FMC suggests that direct contact with local women should be avoided and that hardly any hiring of them is planned[67]. However, there are several statements by local men that clearly contradict this proposal, one of which is the following:

We advocate female participation in the project's workforce. Social norms and traditions won't be a challenge if working conditions safeguard women's rights and dignity. (MCAP 27.11.2018).

Therefore, I suggest that the Sa'id and its stereotypes are strategically used so that local women must not be considered for jobs. This strategy can also be applied to local men who were working at the project site. The low numbers can be justified by referring to the common image of Upper Egyptians, namely being backward, traditional and lacking the needed skills. Nevertheless, it is important to point out that there are arguably many other factors besides the Sa'id identity that influence the process of recruiting Benbannis.

Another example in which the emphasis on the Sa'id seems to be used by the FMC is the decision-making process. To guarantee a regular exchange with the local community, the FMC has applied a tool called the 'Community Advisory Panel' (CAP)[68], which '[...] provides a forum for a continuous, two-way communication between the Project and the surrounding communities. The CAP consists of individuals who represent and are true advocates of the views of their communities and meets regularly with us [the FMC] to discuss issues of mutual interest'[69]. The representatives of the CAPs were, according to the FMC, suggested by the leaders of the tribes present in each subvillage. When consulting additional meeting minutes, it looks as if especially people in powerful roles, such as community or religious leaders, represent the communities during these meetings. The FMC tries to involve the local community in the decision-making process. However, the question of who represents the local community must be asked. This labelling of the decision-making process as inclusive and influential may mask real power asymmetries and might be used as a strategy by the FMC, intentionally or not. Moreover, by referring to the Sa'id identity, the local people can be labelled as being too backward to be worth involving. Therefore, a critical look

---

[67] Hassan Allam Services 2017: Hassan Allam Services. Cairo, Egypt. Solar PV Plant Benban Site. Code of Conduct on Labour Rights and Working Conditions. Construction Phase. (Unpublished Interim Report).

[68] The FMC has formed four regional CAPs; two representatives of each regional CAP form the Master CAP (MCAP).

[69] Benban 2019: Community. Benban Solar Park. ⟨http://benban.org/community/⟩. accessed on 13.12.2019.

should be taken at how and by whom Sa'id stereotypes are used and what the players try to obscure or justify by using the stereotypes.

Conclusion

According to the SESA and ESIA reports, the impact of Benban Solar Park on the environment is assumed to be rather low as the project is located in the Western Desert. However, it is the people from outside the local community that suggest this low environmental and social impact and who describe the land of the project site as barren and empty. Empty and barren desert land is not always as empty as it seems. There are numerous anthropological studies that show how the construction of mega-infrastructure projects on seemingly empty desert land can have a negative impact on local communities' access to important common-pool resources (for instance Ryser 2019a and b). Furthermore, labelling a land as empty could also be a strategy to legitimize land dispossession processes (Ryser 2019a and b, Achiba 2019). Although I have not found any evidence that would indicate any kind of use (agricultural, spiritual, etc.) of this land by the local community, it is crucial to point out that I only had access to documents that showed me a single perspective. Nevertheless, I assume that in the past the area was part of grazing areas or movement corridors since the ancestors of the Benbannis probably lived as nomadic pastoralists. However, there is an urgent need for further research in this matter, taking into account the local community's view of the land and their management of, and access to, resources.

Besides the impact Benban Solar Park has on the environment, this article has also shown how it influences the local society. I argue that a 'frontier' context emerges here (Rasmussen and Lund 2018). According to Rasmussen and Lund, 'a frontier emerges when a new resource is identified, defined, and becomes subject to extraction and commodification' (2018: 2). In the case of Benban, solar energy is the newly found resource, which then as a frontier challenges existing patterns of control, authority and access. Moreover, not only does a process of erosion takes place, but also one of formation: new systems of control of resources are built. Eventually, people and institutions lose, gain or maintain their authority and their bargaining power (Rasmussen and Lund 2018). The special interest in the Sa'id culture and the stereotypical view of the 'culture' from outside seems to increase the bargaining power of conservative actors in particular and trigger a process of institution shopping (Haller 2020). Furthermore, for non-conservative participants this stereotypical view of the 'culture' allows neither change nor flexibility.

The emphasis on the Sa'id culture may also be used strategically. The FMC, Developers and Lenders seem to use the stereotype of backwardness to legitimize the low share of local people in the workforce, creating an anti-politics machine

(Ferguson 1994). Accordingly, the exclusion of the Benbannis in decision-making processes seems to be legitimated by the Sa'id: Benbannis are too backward to be worth involving. Labelling processes also seem to play a crucial role in the legitimating strategy of the Egyptian government. The government labels the project as a win-win-win situation for all players involved: the mega-infrastructure project will not only contribute to the global fight against climate change (ecological dimension) but also bring development and economic prosperity to a marginalized region (social dimension). In addition, Benban Solar Park will ensure that Egypt's independence from the international energy market is increased (economic dimension)[70]. This emphasis on a win-win-win-situation might be a strategy to legitimize the entire project via green energy and sustainable development. These big promises and labelling processes are playing a crucial part in the entire enchantment process (Harvey and Knox 2012). These enchantment processes make Benban Solar Park desirable, especially for the local community with a low economic standard. However, the growing community frustration leading to social unrest and little sabotage acts are a sign that a disenchantment process is already on its way. The Benbannis have already realized that their hopes were set too high and that many promises made by powerful players are often not kept.

Glossary

AFDB	African Development Bank
AHD	Aswan High Dam
AIIB	Asian Infrastructure Investment Bank
BDA	Benban Developers' Association
CAP	Community Advisory Panel
CDC	Commonwealth Development Corporation
CLO	Community Liaison Officer
DevCo	Developer Coordination Meeting
EBRD	European Bank for Reconstruction and Development
EETC	Egyptian Electricity Transmission Company
EEHC	Egyptian Electricity Holding Company
EPC	Engineering, Procurement and Construction
ESIA	Environmental and Social Impact Assessment
FiT	Feed-in Tariff
FMC	Facility Management Company
HSE	Health, Safety, Environment
IFC	International Finance Corporation

---

[70] Lolwa, Reda 2018: Benban Solar Plant Starts Operating, Egypt Targets 37% Clean Energy by 2035: Shaker. *Egypt Today*. ⟨https://www.egypttoday.com/Article/3/45157/Benban-solar-plant-starts-operating-Egypt-targets-37-clean-energy⟩ accessed on 21.01.2020.

MCAP	Master Community Advisory Panel
MIGA	Multilateral Investment and Guarantee Agency
MoERE	Ministry of Electricity and Renewable Energy
NREA	New and Renewable Energy Agency
SESA	Social and Environmental Strategic Assessment
SPV	Special Purpose Vehicle

References

Al-Sayyid Marsot, Afaf Lutfi [2]2007 (1985): A History of Egypt. From the Arab Conquest to the Present. New York: Cambridge University Press.

Arab Republic of Egypt, Ministry of Electricity and Renewable Energy, Egyptian Electricity Holding Company 2017: Annual Report 2016/2017. Cairo: PCC Advertising.

Central Agency for Public Mobilization and Statistics (CAPMAS) 2018: Egypt in Figures 2018. Cairo: CAPMAS Print Shop.

Derr, Jennifer L. 2019: The Lived Nile. Environment, Disease, and Material Colonial Economy in Egypt. Stanford: Stanford University Press.

Etheredge, Laura S. 2011: Middle East Region in Transition Egypt. New York: Britannica Educational Publishing.

Ferguson, James 1994: The Anti-Politics Machine. 'Development' and Bureaucratic Power in Lesotho. The Ecologist 24 (5): 176-181.

Flyvbjerg, Bent 2014: What you Should Know about Megaprojects and Why: An Overview. Project Management Journal 45 (2): 6-19.

Haller, Tobias 2020: Institution Shopping and Resilience Grabbing: Changing Scapes and Grabbing Pastoral Commons in African Floodplain Wetlands. Conservation & Society 18 (3): 252-267.

Harvey, Penny and Hannah Knox 2012: The Enchantments of Infrastructures. Mobilities 7 (4): 521-536.

Hopkins, Nicholas and Reem Saad 2004: Upper Egypt: Identity and Change. Cairo, New York: The American University in Cairo Press.

International Finance Corporation (IFC) 2012: Performance Standards on Environmental and Social Sustainability. Washington: IFC.

International Finance Corporation (IFC) 2019: Local Benefit Sharing in Large-Scale Wind and Solar Projects. Discussion Paper. Washington: IFC.

Kamil, Jill 1993: Aswan and Abu Simbel: History and Guide. Cairo: American University in Cairo Press.

Manley, Bill 1996: Historical Atlas of Ancient Egypt. London: Penguin Group.

Miller, Catherine 2004: Between Myth and Reality: The Construction of a Saîdi Identity. In: Hopkins, Nicholas and Reem Saad (eds.): Upper Egypt. Identity and Change. Cairo, New York: The American University in Cairo Press. 25-54.

Mohamed, Nader Noureldeen 2019: Importance of Aswan High Dam to Egypt. In: Negm, Abdelazim M. and Sommer Abdel-Fattah (eds.): Grand Ethiopian Renaissance Dam Versus Aswan High Dam. Cham: Springer International Publishing. 53-72.

Negm, Abdelazim M., Mohamed Elsahabi and Mohamed Salman Tayie 2019: An Overview of Aswan High Dam and Grand Ethiopian Renaissance Dam. In: Negm, Abdelazim M. and Sommer Abdel-Fattah (eds.): Grand Ethiopian Renaissance Dam Versus Aswan High Dam. Cham: Springer International Publishing. 3-17.

Nielsen, Hans Christian Korsholm 2006: State and Customary Law in Upper Egypt. Islamic Law and Society 13 (1): 123-151.
Rasmussen, Mattias Borg and Christian Lund 2018: Frontier Spaces: Territorialization and Resource Control. Policy Briefs (Copenhagen Centre for Development Research) 1: 1-3.
Ryser, Sarah 2019a: The Anti-Politics Machine of Green Energy Development: The Moroccan Solar Project in Ouarzazate and Its Impact on Gendered Local Communities. Land 8: 1-21.
Ryser, Sarah 2019b: Are Green Energy Investments Levelled by the 'New Commons'? Compensations, CSR Measures and Gendered Impacts of a Solar Energy Project in Morocco. In: Haller, Tobias, Thomas Breu, Tine De Moor, Christian Rohr and Heinzpeter Znoj (eds.): The Commons in a Glocal World. Global Connections and Local Responses. London: Routledge. 352-375.
Scott, James C. 1986: Weapons of the Weak: Everyday Forms of Peasant Resistance. New Haven: Yale University Press.
United Nations Development Programme (UNDP) and the Institute of National Planning, Egypt 2010: Egypt Human Development Report 2010. Egypt: UNDP.
Zahran, M.A. and A.J. Willis ^{2}2009 (1992): The Vegetation of Egypt. Dordrecht: Springer Netherlands.

Unpublished Sources (media, internet, etc.):

Adaption Fund Board 2012: Project and Programme Review Committee. Ninth Meeting. Bonn, Germany, 26–27 June 2012. Proposal for Egypt. ⟨http://www.adaptation-fund.org/wp-content/uploads/2015/01/AFB.PPRC_.9.12%20Proposal%20for%20Egypt.pdf⟩ accessed on 26.11.2019.
African Development Bank (AFDB) (n.y.): Project Alcazar II Solar PV Project. Summary of the Environmentaland Social Management Plan (ESMP). ⟨https://www.afdb.org/fileadmin/uploads/afdb/Documents/Environmental-and-Social-Assessments/Egypt-Alcazar_II_solar_PV_project-Summary_ESMP-06_2017.pdf⟩ accessed on 26.11.2019.
Bissada Dina 2019: Egypt Country Commercial Guide. Egypt – Renewable Energy. Export.gov. ⟨https://www.export.gov/article?id=Egypt-Renewable-Energy⟩ accessed on 02.10.2019.
Cabinet of Ministries, Ministry of State for the Environment, Egyptian Environmental Affairs Agency (EEAA) 2009: Guidelines of Principles and Procedures for Environmental Impact Assessment. ⟨http://www.eeaa.gov.eg/portals/0/eeaaReports/N-EIA/English_EIA_guidelines.pdf⟩ accessed on 26.11.2019.
EBRD 2019: History of the EBRD. EBRD European Bank for Reconstruction and Development. ⟨https://www.ebrd.com/who-we-are/our-structure.html⟩ accessed on 14.10.2019.
El-Mazghouny, Donia 2019: Renewable Energy in Egypt. Lexology. ⟨https://www.lexology.com/gtdt/tool/workareas/report/renewable-energy/chapter/egypt⟩ accessed on 27.11.2019.
ESIA 2017: Environmental and Social Impact Assessment for 30 MW PV Power Plant Benban Solar Park, Aswan Governorate, Egypt. Final Report. Submitted by EcoConServ Environmental Solution. ⟨https://www.miga.org/sites/default/files/arc

hive/Documents/SPGDisclosures/MMID%2030%20Benban%20-ESIA%20Final%20Report.pdf⟩. accessed on 26.11.2019.
Farag, Mohamed 2018: Solar Energy Projects in Benban Save Youth from Unemployment, Poverty. Daily News Egypt (22nd November). ⟨https://ww.dailynewssegypt.com/2018/11/22/solar-energy-projects-in-benban-save-youth-from-unemployment-poverty/⟩ accessed on 25.08.2019, 20.09.2019 and 06.10.2019.
Furger, Anja 2020: Bachelor Thesis: Benban Solar Park. Impacts, Promises and the Anti-Politics Machine.
Hassan Allam Services 2019: About Us. Benban Solar Park. ⟨http://benban.org/about/⟩ accessed on 06.06.2019.
ib vogt 2014: About Us. ib vogt. ⟨https://www.ibvogt.com/home/about-us.html⟩ accessed on 16.10.2019.
ib vogt 2018: Project Briefing. Building Benban: Inside Egypt's 1.6GW Solar Park. ⟨https://www.ibvogt.com/home/building-benban.html⟩ accessed on 16.10.2019.
Infinity Solar 2019: Welcome to Infinity Solar – Leading Renewable Energy in Egypt. Infinity Solar. ⟨http://www.infinitysolar.com/default/Home/1⟩ accessed on 16.10.2019.
Kenning, Tom 2018: ib vogt Breaks Ground on 166.5MW Solar Project in Benban, Egypt. PV Tech. ⟨https://www.pv-tech.org/news/ib-vogt-breaks-ground-on-166.5mw-solar-project-in-benban-egypt⟩ accessed on 10.01.2020.
KPMG 2017: Renewable Energy in Egypt. The Green Opportunity. ⟨https://home.kpmg/content/dam/kpmg/uk/pdf/2017/03/renewable-energy-in-egypt-the-green-opportunity.pdf⟩ accessed on 29.11.2019.
Lastprophet.info 2010: Ansar (The Helpers). Last Prophet.info. ⟨http://www.lastprophet.info/ansar-the-helpers⟩ accessed on 07.10.2019.
Lolwa, Reda 2018: Benban Solar Plant Starts Operating, Egypt Targets 37% Clean Energy by 2035: Shaker. Egypt Today. ⟨https://www.egypttoday.com/Article/3/45157/Benban-solar-plant-starts-operating-Egypt-targets-37-clean-energy⟩ accessed on 21.01.2020.
MIGA 2017: Environmental and Social Review Summary. Feed in Tariff Program – MMID 30 MW for Renewable Energy S.A.E. ⟨https://www.miga.org/sites/default/files/archive/Documents/SPGDisclosures/MMID%2030_Egypt%20FiT%202%20-%20IB%20Vogt%20ESRS_9%20Aug%20-%20Clean.pdf⟩ accessed on 27.11.2019.
MIGA 2019: About Us. MIGA Multilateral Investment Guarantee Agency. ⟨https://www.miga.org/about-us⟩ accessed on 14.10.2019.
MoERE 2013: The Ministry. Arab Republic of Egypt. Ministry of Electricity and Energy. ⟨http://www.moee.gov.eg/english_new/define.aspx⟩ accessed on 14.10.2019.
New and Renewable Energy Authority 2018: Annual Report. ⟨http://nrea.gov.eg/Content/reports/Englishv2%20AnnualReport.pdf⟩ accessed on 26.11.2019.
Nordrum, Amy 2019: Egypt's Massive 1.8-Gigawatt Benban Solar Park Near Completion. IEEE Spectrum (17th September). ⟨https://spectrum.ieee.org/energywise/energy/renewables/egypts-massive-18gw-benban-solar-park-nears-completion?deliveryName=DM45047⟩ accessed on 16.10.2019 and 12.12.2019.
Raven, Andrew 2017: A New Solar Park Shines a Light on Egypt's Energy Potential. International Finance Corporation IFC. ⟨https://www.ifc.org/wps/wcm/connect/news_ext_content/ifc_external_corporate_site/news+and+events/news/cm-stories/benban-solar-park-egypt⟩ accessed on 16.10.2019.

Riham, Mustafa 2017: IFC-Led Consortium Invests $653 Million to Support the World's Largest Solar Park in Egypt. International Finance Corporation IFC. ‹https://ifcextapps.ifc.org/ifcext/pressroom/ifcpressroom.nsf/0/C47EC9AF0897C57A852581C8003DE257?OpenDocument› accessed on 16.10.2019.

Solarprofis 2015: Scheint in der Schweiz genug Sonne für Solarenergie? Die Solarprofis. ‹https://www.solarprofis.ch/kampagne/scheint-in-der-schweiz-genug-sonne-fuer-solarenergie/› accessed on 17.01.2020.

SESA 2016: Strategic Environmental and Social Assessment, Benban 1.8GW PV Solar Park, Egypt. Final Report. Submitted by EcoConServ Environmental Solution. ‹https://www.eib.org/attachments/registers/65771943.pdf› accessed on 26.11.2019.

Taha, Ehab and Salma Basset 2015: Property Laws and Regulations in Egypt. Al Tamimi & Co. ‹https://www.tamimi.com/law-update-articles/property-laws-and-regulations-in-egypt/› accessed on 30.11.2019.

United Nations Educational, Scientific and Cultural Organization (UNESCO) 2005: UNESCO Japanese Fund-In-Trust (JFIT) Project Titled 'Urgent Capacity Development for Managing Natural Disaster Risks of Flash Floods in Egypt, Jordan, Sudan and Yemen'. Assessment Report for Aswan. ‹http://www.unesco.org/new/fileadmin/MULTIMEDIA/FIELD/Cairo/images/Egypt-Assessment-Report.pdf› accessed on 26.11.2019.

U.S. Energy Information Administration (EIA) 2018: Country Analysis Brief: Egypt. EIA. ‹https://www.eia.gov/beta/international/analysis_includes/countries_long/Egypt/egypt.pdf› accessed on 26.11.2019.

Zgheib, Nibal 2017: EBRD Approves US$ 500 Million for Private Renewable Projects in Egypt. ‹https://www.ebrd.com/news/2017/ebrd-approves-us-500-million-for-private-renewable-projects-in-egypt.html› accessed on 24.01.2020.

Zgheib, Nibal 2019: First EBRD funded Egyptian Solar Plant Begins Generation. European Bank for Reconstruction and Development EBRD. ‹https://www.ebrd.com/news/2019/first-ebrd-funded-egyptian-solar-plant-begins-generation-.html› accessed on 16.10.2019.

Documents of the FMC (accessible under benban.org):

Interim reports prepared by Rina Consulting in 2017:
- Traffic Management Plan – Construction Phase
- Worker Accommodation Strategy and Management Plan – Construction Phase

Minutes of meetings:
- Developer Coordination Meeting (DevCo): 24.10.2018, 23.01.2019, 25.02.2019, 31.03.2019
- Master Community Advisory Panels (MCAPs): 27.11.2018, 10.12.2018, 24.01.2019
- Operational Update Meeting: 17.04.2019
- Security Meeting: 06.09.2018

Other documents:
- Code of Conduct on Labour Rights and Working Conditions
- The Benbanner: July 2018, September 2018, October 2018, November 2018, January 2019

Films:

Benban, Africa's largest Solar Park, Completed. EBRD, 24.10.2019. Available from: ‹https://www.ebrd.com/news/video/benban-africas-largest-solar-park-completed.html›

How Egypt is Building the World's Biggest Solar Array. IFC, 30.10.2017. Available from: ‹https://www.youtube.com/watch?v=gI3ZaU14u_0›

Manoeuvring Enchantment of Mega-Infrastructure Projects in Northern Kenya: LAPSSET and the Crude Oil in Turkana County

Benard Musembi Kilaka, School of Global Studies, University of Gothenburg, Sweden; Elisabeth Schubiger, Anthropology & Sociology Department of the Graduate Institute of International and Development Studies, Geneva, Switzerland

Introduction

In March 2012, two entangled events took place in Kenya and suddenly placed the northern 'frontier' of the country in both the national and international spotlight. The first event was the launch of the Lamu Port South Sudan Ethiopia Transport Corridor (LAPSSET) project on 2 March 2012 by Kenya, South Sudan and Ethiopia. LAPSSET projects the development of ports, airports, railways, highways and oil pipelines. Once completed, the project will connect the three neighbouring countries through East Africa's largest infrastructure initiative. The second event was the announcement of the discovery of oil in Turkana in late March 2012 by Mwai Kibaki, former President of Kenya. The breakthrough by the Irish oil company Tullow Oil was celebrated as a future booster to the economic growth of the country. Given that the targeted region and its pastoralist communities had undergone a long period of political and economic marginalization, these two mega-infrastructure projects (MIP) symbolize the coming of a new dawn for the development of the region. However, over time, the initial optimism around the infrastructural promises of political integration, economic prosperity and modernity has given way to a certain 'disenchantment' generated by various challenges and issues unfolding in the region.

    This chapter seeks to present an account of the two 'enchanting' infrastructural initiatives (see Harvey and Knox 2012) in Turkana County by illustrating the processes and affections generated by the variety of opportunities and risks they hold for the local pastoral community. Against the backdrop of scholarly literature, the chapter relies on empirical insights gathered from media analysis and from participant observation, semi-structured interviews and focus group discussions with community members, government officials, civil society representatives and business owners in Turkana and Nairobi between January and April 2019.[1]

Part 1: Historical, environmental, ethnographic, and political context

Turkana County in perspective: history of marginalization and expectation of development

Historically, Turkana County has been characterized by frequent splitting and fusing of various ethnic groups. A distinct Turkana pastoralist identity only appeared in the early nineteenth century (Derbyshire 2020; Gulliver 1963; McCabe 2004). It seems that the Turkana people, who share a mutually intelligible language and similar subsistence strategies, had fully occupied much of the territory they consider their homeland today by 1850 (Lamphear 1993; McCabe 2004). Swahili caravans and Ethiopian hunters in search of ivory and other trade goods must have frequented the region before the nineteenth century; however, at the beginning of the twentieth century, the region became the conflictual front line between the British administration and the Ethiopian empire under King Menelik over the domination in the region. The Ethiopians, who saw Turkana as part of their empire, supplied the people with rifles to fight the British invaders. Not surprisingly, the British responded with military strength to subdue the Turkana and prevent Ethiopia's presence in the region. Between 1910 and 1915, the British started to punish the allegedly hostile Turkana with widespread confiscation of livestock and weapons (Derbyshire 2020; Lamphear 1976, 1992; McCabe 2004). This strategy was framed as 'tribal pacification' and opened the opportunity for the establishment of a British civil administration. Nevertheless, it was only in 1918 that the massive military operation *Labur Patrol* struck down the last remaining Ethiopian forces and defeated the Turkana, causing a massive loss of livestock and people (Collins 2006). Mistrust and resistance towards the British administration was growing, as they were unable or unwilling to assist the disarmed Turkana against frequent raids by neighbours (Derbyshire 2020; Gray et al. 2003; Gulliver 1963; Lamphear 1988; McCabe 2004).

Therefore, Turkana, alongside other regions in northern Kenya, was declared a 'closed district', which effectively meant that it was isolated from the rest of the country as movement into and out of the district required a special permit issued by the District Commissioner.[2] This isolation persisted after independence

---

[1] This work was supported by funding from the Swiss National Science Foundation and the Agence Nationale de la Recherché through the SALMEA project (SNF 10001al_182304/ANR-18-ce93-0009-01) and the Swedish Research Council for the project Controversial Corridor: Exploring transformations of place and sense of belonging along the LAPSSET development corridor- Project (ID: 2016-05797_VR).

[2] Kenya Gazette, 1925: Proclamation No. 89. Colony and Protectorate of Kenya. The East African Outlying Districts Ordinance, 1902.

until the 1970s and resulted in limited investments in public services and political disintegration (Carr 2017). The continued marginalization is well documented by the fact that in 1963 when Kenya became independent, the whole area of Turkana County hosted only two primary schools and one missionary school (McCabe 2004).

For the Turkana people, peace did not set in with Kenyan independence; on the contrary, the unrest with neighbouring countries facilitated access to modern and sophisticated arms, which again led to intense raiding and cattle rustling. Therefore, for a long time, political elites in the country's capital Nairobi viewed the region as problematic and unproductive, due to its persistent intercommunal conflicts, harsh climate and remoteness. Additionally, the Turkana pastoralists are perceived as not only unruly but also resistant to change or development (Broche-Due 1999; Fratkin and McCabe 1999; Lamphear 1992, 1993). For instance, Sessional Paper No. 10 from 1965, which was the main planning tool guiding economic development in post-independent Kenya, excluded the northern part of the country by proclaiming that the focus of investments was towards areas with 'natural resources, good land and rainfall, transport and power facilities, and people receptive to and active in development'[3]. In many ways, this was a continuity of the colonial policy that depicted the Turkana region in their 1947 colonial report as '[...] large and poorly watered and occupied by pastoral nomads; their inhabitants are backward and, generally speaking, the districts are uneconomical. On account of their remoteness, their climate and their backward population, they present many problems which are entirely different from those in the other native areas of the colony'[4] The limited presence of the Kenyan state in the northern region led to political exclusion and economic marginalization, which explains the disruptive and destabilizing processes on which the promise of transformation through infrastructure is based. Nevertheless, from the 1970s, various development projects provided by national and international agents gradually increased the establishment of schools, roads, health centres, irrigation schemes, towns and trading centres (Brainard 1990; McCabe 1990; Reidy 2012).

Since the launch of the Kenyan Constitution in 2010, which ushered in a devolved system of governance in the country, the region's presence in national politics and the economy has significantly improved. Among other things, the constitution devolved power and resources to the counties, thus reducing the undue influence that national government officials exerted in deciding development projects. More specifically, the Constitution also sought to address the systematic inequality that counties in northern Kenya underwent by establishing an Equal-

---

[3] Government of Kenya 1965: Sessional Paper No. 10, 1965. National Archives, Nairobi.
[4] Government of Kenya 1947. Northern Annual Report, 1947. Government of Kenya. 1947. "Northern Province Annual Report, 1947." Colonial Report. National Archives, Nairobi.

ization Fund, which is specifically meant to accelerate the pace of development in these counties[5]

Apart from that, Turkana's key position in Kenya's economic planning was further boosted by the discovery of crude oil and its strategic location as the host of key components of the LAPSSET project. Current official discourses often present the region as full of resources and opportunities by 'offering a platform for opening up vast northern parts of Kenya consisting of over 70 per cent of the land mass, which to date remains unexplored'[6]. Therefore, Turkana is often presented as a 'new frontier', an area within a state that acquires new meaning due to the desire to either extract newly discovered natural resources or as uncharted ground of capitalist expansion (Jong, Knippenberg, and Bakker 2017; Mosley and Watson 2016; Peluso and Lund 2011; Tsing 2000).

Geography & cultural landscape: the drylands of Turkana

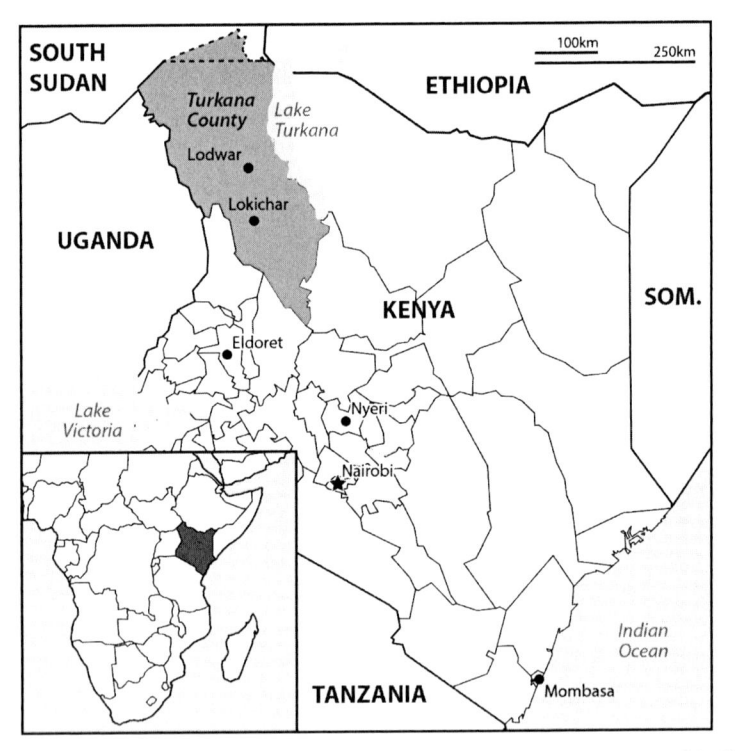

Map 1: Turkana County, Kenya. Source: Map compilation and design by Manuel L. K. Abebe (2021), CDE, University of Bern, Bern, Switzerland. Geodata: GADM

---

[5] Constitution of Kenya 2010. Para 204. ⟨http://kenyalaw.org/⟩. Accessed 18.06.2020.
[6] LAPSSET Corridor Development Authority 2015: *Investment Prospectus*.

Turkana County is located in the north-west of Kenya and borders three countries, namely Uganda, South Sudan and Ethiopia. To the south, it borders the counties of West Pokot, Baringo and Laikipia, to the east, Samburu and Marsabit.

Turkana County, with its interplay of climate, topography and soil, presents a rather harsh and dry environment. One exception is the 6,405 km² Lake Turkana, which serves as an important livelihood source for community members living near the lake since many are fishing communities (Broch-Due 1999; Derbyshire 2020). However, the climate is characterized by high temperatures and low rainfall, with temperatures ranging between 24 and 41 degrees Celsius and an average annual temperature of 30 degrees Celsius[7]. The rainfall is both unpredictable and unreliable and ranges between 52 mm and 480 mm per year. There are two rainy seasons: the long rainy season, which usually occurs between March and July, and the short rainy season, which takes place between October and November. Nevertheless, the regularity of rainfall has constantly changed in recent years, most probably due to climate change. The landscape consists of low-lying plains such as the Lotikipi and Kalapata, which are crossed by seasonal rivers, suitable for rearing camels and small stock (sheep, goats, donkeys). Some isolated mountains and hilly ranges with green pastures remain attractive grazing grounds for cattle. Due to the above-described scarce vegetation and harsh weather conditions, Turkana, with its 68,680 km², is sparsely inhabited, counting a population density of 14 people per km² and a population of 926,976 inhabitants[8]

The above-mentioned facts contribute to the image of plenty of space, within which some roads, pipelines, airports and oil wells affect only a tiny part and are therefore bearable. In contrast, for the Turkana pastoralists, the landscape is a cultural space of migration, which not only determines the nurturing of the livestock but determines most social events of their lifestyle (Anderson 2017; Meekers 1992; Mirzeler 2014; Ohta 2007; Pavitt 1997).

Local population and resource use: pastoralism, land rights and access

Although many ethnic groups are present in Turkana, the people who refer to themselves and are referred to as *Turkana* predominantly inhabit the vast plains far from town centres. Turkana's oral history tells the myth of the lost grey bull Engiro, which was searched for by a woman called Nayeche. The green, unoccupied pastures where she found the bull are considered to be the Turkana clans' ancestral home today (Lamphear 1988; Mirzeler 2014). The story highlights the

---

[7] Turkana County Government Official Website 2020. ⟨https://www.turkana.go.ke/index.php/facts-figures/⟩. Accessed 17.06.2020.
[8] KNBS 2019: Kenya Population and Housing Census Volume I: Population by County and Sub-County. *Kenya National Bureau of Statistics*. ⟨https://www.knbs.or.ke/?wpdmpro=2019-kenya-population-and-housing-census-volume-i-population-by-county-and-sub-county⟩. Accessed 17.06.2020.

predominant importance of cattle and the related practices of pastoralism[9]. Besides being a key means of earning a livelihood, cattle are deeply enmeshed in many cultural aspects of the society, as often animals are not only devoted to cultural events such as marriages and initiations but also signify power and status (Broch-Due 2000; Fratkin and McCabe 1999; Gray et al. 2003; McCabe 1990; Wienpahl 1984, 1986). Due to an economic system that is based on nomadic animal husbandry, the picture envisioned by Kenyan media and development agents often reduces Turkana people to being traditionalists cut off from civilization and modernity. Various authors challenge this static view of pastoralist communities and draw a dynamic picture of adaptive strategies, institutional change and gender relations in Kenya's pastoralist community. Thus, being pastoralist does not exclude other forms of economy or settlement, but refers to an identity that is dynamic, historically rooted and (re)produced through ethnicity and belonging in interaction with local and trans-local processes and structures. Despite the dominance of multiple-species pastoralism (goat, sheep, camel, donkey, cattle) in the region, agricultural production is practised in areas with moderately fertile soils (Broch-Due 1999; Derbyshire 2020; Ensminger 1992; Hodgson 2004; McCabe 2004).

Well-irrigated grounds are found in the central plains of Lorengipi, upper Loima, along the rivers Turkwel, Kerio and Kawalathe, and along the lower sides of Lake Turkana[10]. Water is a scarce commodity in the region and the main sources of water are hand-dug shallow wells and (seasonal) river water. Therefore, access to clean water, riverbeds and grazing grounds is of significance to the resilience of the communities living in the dry lands of Turkana. According to McCabe (1990), resource management in Turkana is based on a complex commons system that is ruled by kinship relations and a council of elders. For instance, territories in Turkana are traditionally divided into a number of regions based on landscape characteristics and vegetal features, which are related to the kind of livestock that can be herded in the area (McCabe 2004). There are no individual rights to forage resources within a given territory, which is defined by clan belonging. Occasional crossing of neighbouring 'clan borders' has to be agreed on with the senior *ng'ikapolok* (elders). However, access to water is divided into open sources and individual rights, depending on the characteristic of the water (well, flowing, spring or pool) (McCabe 1990). Also seasonal association of families (*awi*) in a so-called *adakar* (neighbourhood) of members of the same clan is central to the negotiation of pasture and water rights (Best 1984; Gulliver 1958, 1966, 1969; Soper 1985).

---

[9] By 'pastoralist community' we mean a group of people who refer to themselves as being herders of livestock with a nomadic lifestyle conducting extensive pasture farming.

[10] Turkana County Government 2015: Final Report. Natural Resource Mapping and Context Analysis. ‹https://turkana.go.ke/wp-content/uploads/2016/10/Final-Report-Natural-Resource-Mapping-Context-Analysis-10th-June-2015-1.pdf›. Accessed 18.06.2020.

Nevertheless, both colonial and post-colonial regimes pursued policies that at some point threatened local communal management schemes. For instance, during the colonial times, this manifested itself through the destocking programmes, especially after the droughts in the 1940s, as well as through development plans that foresaw controlled grazing (McCabe 1990, 2004; Oba 1992). According to Hardin's logic of the 'tragedy of the commons' (Hardin 1968), poor land use by the local pastoralists was blamed as the cause of increasing environmental degradation. In doing so, development agents ignored significant disruption of necessary local management institutions by colonial and national policymakers. It is therefore not surprising that the grazing scheme failed as it established artificial borders to traditional management systems that are not only migratory but have a number of accredited rules and regulations to gain access to resources. Further, the interruption of the commons affected social security, which is based on a reciprocal system of rights and obligations and ensures food security through 'sharing' (Broche-Due 1999; Gulliver 1958, 1969; Johnson 1999; Schultz and Scholz 1994). Hence, complex local institutions regulated through kin or customary law play a key role in ensuring mobility and access to resources, and are important within the Turkana society to ensure resilience against environmental challenges while at the same time facilitating exchange (Haller 2019).

National economy and legal framework: community land and legal plurality

Kenya's economy mainly relies on agriculture, tourism and manufacturing. For instance, as of 2019, the agricultural sector contributed 34.1 per cent to the GDP while the manufacturing sector contributed 7.5 per cent[11]. Consequently, since pastoralism is the main source of livelihood in Turkana County, policymakers often belittled its economic importance (Mung'ong'o and Yanda 2016). However, since the coming to power of President Kibaki in 2002, the launch of Kenya's long-term development blueprint 'Vision 2030' in 2008 and the promulgation of the current constitution in 2010, the state's perception towards northern Kenya has transformed dramatically (Odhiambo 2014). This change has largely been driven by the discovery of new resources in the region, strategic interests of the state in the region, advocacy by communities from the region and the desire by the state to address the unbalanced distribution of resources between northern Kenya and other parts of the country (Odhiambo 2014). As a result, the region is now central to the economic planning of the country and is slated to enjoy massive investments in the coming years. Furthermore, the government expects the two projects to

---

[11] KNBS 2019: Kenya Population and Housing Census Volume I: Population by County and Sub-County. *Kenya National Bureau of Statistics*. ‹https://www.knbs.or.ke/?wpdmpro=2019-kenya-population-and-housing-census-volume-i-population-by-county-and-sub-county›. Accessed 17.06.2020.

significantly contribute to the national economy. For instance, according to the Kenyan government, the LAPSSET project will inject between 2 to 3 percent of the GDP into the economy once it materializes (Browne 2015).

While the current constitution gives county governments the mandate over planning functions in their respective counties, national-level investments are still the mandate of the national government. However, the national government must consult county governments over such projects[12]. Though, this does not happen regularly and has emerged as a key issue of contention between the national government and the county governments[13]. With natural resources such as oil, the law places the responsibility of owning and managing such resources on the national agenda. In this case, the argument is that such resources should collectively benefit all Kenyans. However, due to persistent agitation from both community members and leaders from the region, the government has enacted a law that outlines the sharing of revenue from the sale of such resources. In this case, 75 per cent of the revenue goes to the national government, 20 per cent to the county government and 5 per cent to the community where the natural resource is located[14]. Given that Kenya is still at an early stage of being an oil exporter, the legal regime is still fairly undeveloped. For instance, while oil operations had started way back in 2010, it was not until 2019 that a relevant Petroleum Act was enacted[15]. This situation creates a state of uncertainty, for instance, in terms of land questions. Administratively the land is held in trust on behalf of the community by the county government and natural resources under the surface belong to the national government[16]. Land in Turkana is officially gazetted as 'community land', but a large chunk of it remains un-demarcated. As such, negotiations over land acquisitions for development projects must go through the county government. The legal plurality between customary rights and administrative laws often leads to misconceptions and conflicts between various stakeholders and institutions as well as to 'institution shopping' (Haller 2013).

Part 2: The Mega-Infrastructure Project

LAPSSET: Promise of Political Integration and Development

LAPSSET is often posited by the government of Kenya as eastern Africa's largest and most ambitious infrastructure project which seeks to connect Kenya to South

---

[12] Website Kenya Law. Where Legal Information is Public Knowledge. ⟨http://www.kenyalaw.org:8181/exist/kenyalex/actview.xql?actid=Const2010⟩. Accessed 18.06.2020.
[13] Interviews with a number of senior county officials in Lodwar in March 2019
[14] Kenyan Government 2019: Petroleum Act. 58.
[15] Energy & Petroleum Regulation Authority (EPRA) Official Website. ⟨https://www.epra.go.ke/download/the-petroleum-act-2019/⟩. Accessed 18.06.2020.
[16] Constitution of Kenya 2010. ⟨http://kenyalaw.org/⟩. Accessed 18.06.2020.

Sudan and Ethiopia through a network of seven key infrastructure components[17]. The infrastructure project includes a new 32-berth port along the Kenyan coast in Lamu, interregional highways to both Ethiopia and South Sudan, a crude and product pipeline, three resort cities, an interregional standard-gauge railway that connects Lamu to Ethiopia and South Sudan, three international airports and a multi-purpose dam along the Tana River. Within Kenya, the project is expected to traverse seven counties, namely Lamu, Garissa, Isiolo, Baringo, Samburu, Turkana and Marsabit. Turkana County is one of the key anchor sites for the project since it hosts several key infrastructure components of LAPSSET, such as the resort in Kalokol, an international airport, the railway line, the highway and the oil that is expected to be transported through the new pipeline[18].

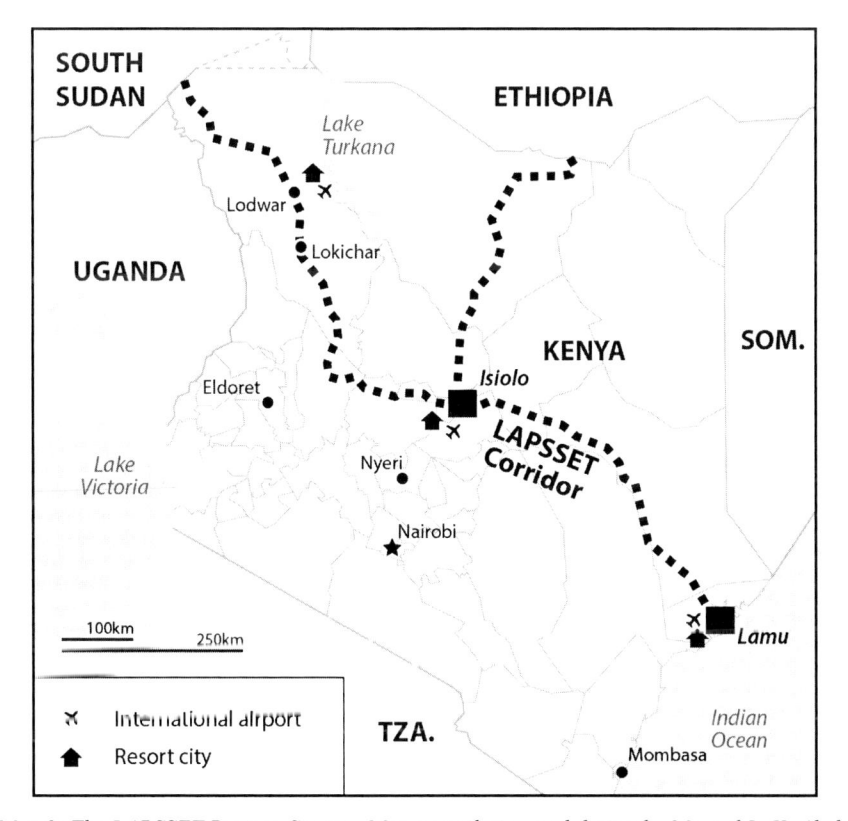

Map 2: The LAPSSET Project. Source: Map compilation and design by Manuel L. K. Abebe (2021), CDE, University of Bern, Bern, Switzerland. Geodata: GADM

---

[17] LAPSSET Corridor Development Authority 2017: LAPSSET Quarterly Newsletter. (January-March). ⟨https://drive.google.com/file/d/0B7w3900K6lYnQWRnZi1sTV9DeDg/view⟩. Accessed 18.06.2020.

[18] LAPSSET Official Website. ⟨http://www.lapsset.go.ke/⟩. Accessed 18.06.2020.

Although the LAPSSET project is yet to be completed, it has a long history. The idea of the LAPSSET project was first mooted in the 1970s when Kenya wanted to open up a second port in Lamu in order to complement the existing port of Mombasa, which had problems with congestion and was unable to host big cargo ships. The plans, however, were shelved and were reignited in the mid-2000s when the government of Kenya received a proposal from a Kuwait-based company known as Al-Badar International Development Company to construct a mega-infrastructure project from Lamu to northern Kenya on a build-own-operate-transfer (BOOT) basis[19]. The project, abbreviated as ROOLA, included the establishment of railways, oil transport, fibre optics and airport infrastructure. Although the company signed a memorandum of understanding with the Kenyan government, it was discarded once Ethiopia and South Sudan had been brought on board. Consequently, the project became an intergovernmental initiative and was renamed 'Lamu Port South Sudan Ethiopia Transport Corridor' (LAPSSET). In order to illustrate their commitment to the project, the three presidents of Kenya, Ethiopia and South Sudan met in Lamu in March 2012 and commissioned the project by laying the foundation stone at what is now the new Lamu Port[20]. While most components of the project are yet to be constructed, some parts are already complete or at advanced stages. For instance, completed components of the project include Isiolo Airport, the Isiolo-Marsabit road and the first berth at Lamu Port. So far, only Kenya has been at the forefront in the construction of some of the infrastructure components. A range of factors such as security concerns, civil strife and geopolitical interests in the other participating countries have slowed down this initial transnational cooperation (Okwany 2020).

Being a project of infrastructural transformation, LAPSSET 'enchants' (Harvey and Knox 2012) through enacting the materiality of an ideal future towards modernity, characterized by enhanced connectivity, economic opening and national integration. For instance, the resort city of Kalokol is intended to 'support economic enabling activities to harness and tap into the rich tourism potential' and has been conceptualized to create a 'new tourism corridor based on group tours using the mass transportation network offered by the LAPSSET Corridor'[21].

---

[19] Absulsamas Ali 2006: Kuwaitis to know fate of Lamu deal in December. *The East African*. 30.10. ⟨https://www.theeastafrican.co.ke/business/2560-251848-uvhrsn/index.html⟩. Accessed 18.06.2020.

[20] BBC Online News 2012: Lamu Port Project launched for South Sudan and Ethiopia. *BBC News Africa*. 02.03. ⟨https://www.bbc.com/news/world-africa-17231889⟩. Accessed 18.06.2020.

[21] LAPSSET Corridor Development Authority 2017: LAPSSET Bi-Monthly Newsletter. (October-November). ⟨https://drive.google.com/file/d/11ENUdW0s4q61rwtHhYN9uHytbledUZPW/view⟩. Accessed 18.06.2020.

The Oil Wells in Turkana County: Enchantment of Oil Prosperity

As much as the idea of LAPSSET dates to the 1970s, so does the idea of climbing the Olympus of petrostates. Oil exploration activities have a long history in the region going back to the 1950s. Further attempts at exploring oil were conducted in the 1990s but were all unsuccessful (Morley and Karanja 1999; Tiercelin et al. 2004). Finally, the exploration activities by the Irish company Tullow, which started in 2011 in the South Lokichar basin in Turkana County, culminated in the successful discovery of oil in 2012 (Enns and Bersaglio 2015, 2016; Hicks 2015; Johannes, Zulu, and Kalipeni 2015; Mkutu 2014). At present, most oil activities in Kenya are restricted to Turkana South and Turkana East constituencies, where in 2019 around 30 well pads were spread in the two respective constituencies.

According to estimates from Tullow Oil, the region has around 560 million barrels of oil deposits[22]. However, this cannot be considered substantial, especially when compared to other major African oil economies such as Nigeria and Angola, whose oil reserves are estimated to be around 36.2 and 12 billion barrels, respectively. Nevertheless, the oil deposits in Turkana are arguably commercially viable and as a result the state has taken a keen interest in turning Kenya into an oil exporting country (Burgos and Ear 2012; Iledare and Suberu 2010). Seemingly, the crude oil is of good quality since it is low in sulphur and hence will have good prospects in the market[23].

In 2018, the president of Kenya launched the Early Oil Pilot Scheme (EOPS) whose intention was to truck oil from Turkana to Mombasa for export to test the performance of the oil on the international market[24]. Under the scheme, Kenya exported its first shipment of oil in 2019[25]. The shipment of 200,000 barrels of crude oil was bought by a UK-based company known as ChemChina UK at a cost of ksh1.2 billion (US$11.02 million)[26]. In December 2019, before the Covid-19 crisis broke out and provoked historically deep oil prices, an accumulation of precipitate events led to the suspension of operations and a reevaluation of the viability of the project by the main operator Tullow Oil and its Joint Venture partners Total Energies and Africa Oil Corp.[27].

---

[22] Measurement depends on the source.
[23] Whaley Jane 2012. Kenya Hits the Jackpot. *GEOexpro The favourite petroleum geoscience magazine*. (9) 3. ⟨https://www.geoexpro.com/articles/2012/10/kenya-hits-the-jackpot⟩. Accessed 18.06.2020.
[24] OilnewsAfrica.com 2019: EOPS evacuated 60,000 Barrels of Oil to Date. 17. January. ⟨https://oilnewskenya.com/eops-evacuated-60000-barrels-of-oil-to-date/⟩. Accessed 18.06.2020.
[25] Official Website President.go.ke. ⟨https://www.president.go.ke/2019/08/26/kenya-is-now-an-oil-exporting-country/⟩. Accessed 18.06.2020.
[26] The Presidency, Kenya. 2019: Kenya Is Now an Oil Exporting Country. The Presidency. ⟨https://www.president.go.ke/2019/08/26/kenya-is-now-an-oil-exporting-country/⟩. Accessed 18.06.2020.
[27] Wafula Paul 2019: Tullow Oil financial crisis threatens Kenya's oilfields. The Nation Africa. ⟨https://nation.africa/kenya/news/Tullow-Oil-financial-crisis-threatens-Kenya-s-oilfie

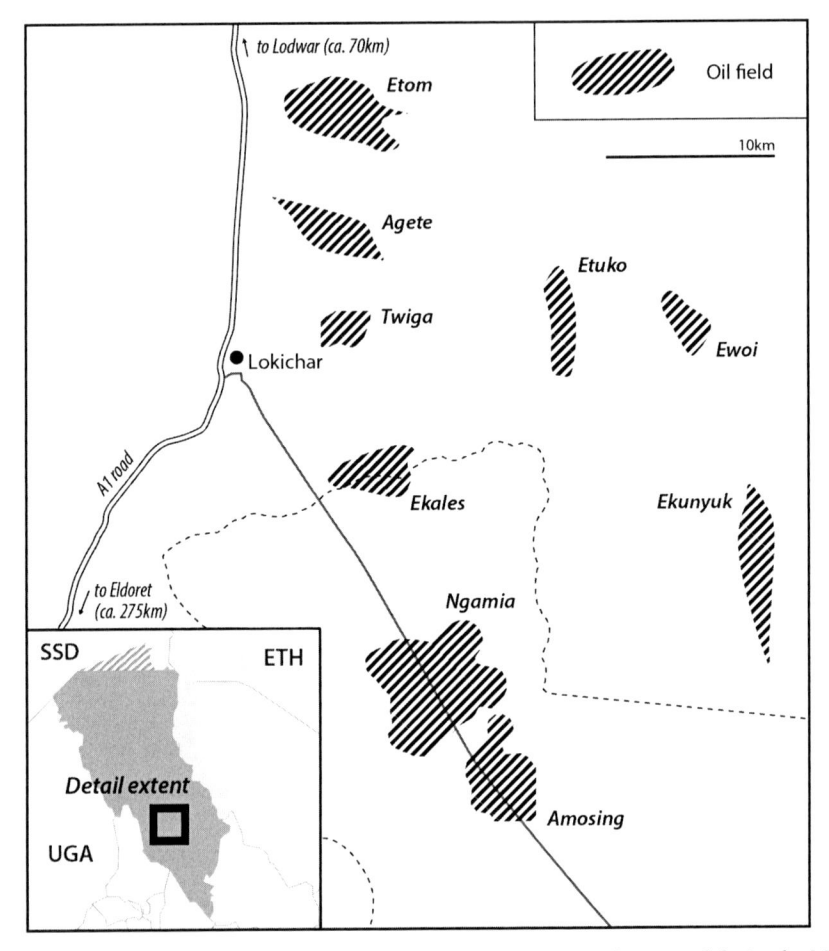

Map 3: Oil Exploration Wells in Turkana County. Source: Map compilation and design by Manuel L. K. Abebe (2021), CDE, University of Bern, Bern, Switzerland. Geodata: GADM

The news of the oil discovery generated great attention, especially in the directly involved region in Turkana. To many residents in the region, the discovery of the oil was met with a high degree of optimism, according to an elder during a discussion: '[P]ersonally, when I heard that minerals had been discovered here, I was so happy because I knew they were going to help me in my life, even though I am old, it would help my children, they would get educated and also get many other benefits[28]. ' Moreover, many were proud of the discovery since it challenged the long-standing narrative that the region was unproductive and raised hope of a prosperous future, as stated in the following statement of one of the elders from Lokichar: 'We were hopeful that if oil was discovered, we would not live like in

---

lds-/1056-5381272-ouin9az/index.html⟩. Accessed 18.06.2020.
[28] Focus Group Discussion with council of elders, Lokichar on 8 March 2019.

the past... life full of poverty, people not having school fees, basic needs like water, food and even security.'[29]

Environmental and Social Impacts

One of the key questions is how to deal with challenges posed by oil extraction. Scholars, private companies and both governmental and non-governmental organizations have developed and identified best-practice interventions to avert a 'resource curse'[30]. As a result, a number of treaties and agreements aim to avoid environmental degradation and negative social impacts (Mwabu 2020; Weszkalnys 2014, 2016). Most environmental issues are regulated by Kenyan environmental laws, specifically the Environmental Management and Coordination Act (EMCA 1999), and enforced by NEMA (National Environment Management Authority) (Opongo 2017). In the case of Turkana, several environmental impact assessments (EIAs) have been done regarding the exploration activities and the impacts of the foreseen oil pipeline. These documents are voluminous, and open for scrutiny at the NEMA offices and the Tullow Community resource centres; nevertheless, most people might not be aware of their content due to access, language barriers or knowledge gaps (Opongo 2017). Although the government and other key stakeholders for both LAPSSET and the oil industry in Turkana claim that the projects will have minimal negative impacts on both the society and the environment, local community members and a number of civil society organizations have highlighted both the real and predicted effects of the projects. As illustrated below, some of the adverse effects have included poor disposal of hazardous wastes, cutting down of trees, loss of grazing plains and blockage of migratory corridors as well as pollution of scarce water sources.

Environmental impacts: toxic fluids and deforestation

Ongoing oil operations in Turkana have adversely degraded the environment and affected both community members and their animals. These impacts were particularly visible during the exploration phase of oil operations where enormous amounts of waste were generated leading to poor disposal of hazardous waste.

---

[29] Focus Group Discussion with council of elders, Lokichar on 8 March 2019.
[30] Conflicts and war in relation to oil extraction have been widely addressed as the 'resource curse' by various scholars (Auty 1994, 2005; Collier and Hoeffler 2004; Karl 1997; Ross 2012). The notion of 'resource curse' goes beyond explaining economic stagnation and includes political conflict, violence and instability in petrostates. According to these scholars, institutional arrangements that encourage public authorities to engage in rent seeking are responsible for the resource curse (Watts 2004). Hence, the curse reflects a 'paradoxical situation where "what should bring good, brings bad" and revenues inherit a triple conjuncture: stagnation of social development and related increase of poverty; (violent) conflict; tendency towards authoritarian regimes' (Reyna and Behrends 2011: 19).

This was further worsened by deforestation activities during the construction of the well pads and access roads.

A major challenge in crude oil extraction is the management of hazardous waste streams that are contaminated by oily, explosive, irritant or toxic fluids and require proper disposal. In Turkana, the management of hazardous waste lacks a systematic approach to an effective implementation of regulations due to fragmented responsibilities among government departments, local authorities and the company. According to officials from the county government, this situation has led to the unauthorized and poor disposal of mud cuttings and silicate water in open pits, thereby exposing people and their animals to health risks and poor living standards such as a persistent pungent smell from the toxic waste[31,32]. Additionally, following cases of animals dying while grazing around the oil facilities, herders' access to grazing fields is severely affected as many fear and avoid the vicinities of the oil wells[33]. As a result, officials from the county government want the waste to be disposed out of the county since there are no gazetted waste disposal sites or facilities in the region[34]. However, Tullow Oil vehemently refutes these accusations and insists that its waste disposal strategy is consistent with international standards. The rising fear that the oil pipeline, which is anticipated within LAPSSET, could cause further environmental degradation is therefore comprehensible. The reality of spills or oil leaks are well documented and industrial accidents and looting are prone to happen, especially where maintenance and security are not guaranteed (Sawyer 2015; Watts 2004; see Vokinger on this issue).

Another environmental concern that is constantly highlighted by many people in Turkana is the company's deforestation activities to facilitate oil operations. The region is indeed characterized by poor vegetation; nevertheless, in particular, *Acacia tortilis*, *Cordia sinensis*, *Hyphaene compressa* and *Salvadora persica* are highly valued by the local community for being a source of livestock diet, veterinary medicines, firewood, building materials, fencing and the making of household utensils[35,36]. Additionally, as well as providing shade and meeting places, some trees also indicate sacred places where important social functions can take place (Barrow 1990; Reid and Ellis 1995). With the coming of the LAPSSET project, the problem is expected to be exacerbated due to the project's size. According to local leaders and community members, the LAPSSET project will lead to massive deforestation, thus leaving the communities vulnerable to the vagaries of the weather. As one local leader put it, 'these trees within 500 m of the project...

---

[31] Ngasike Lucas 2013: Turkana Pastoralists opposite Tullow Oil Proposal. *The Standard*. 29. July. ⟨https://www.standardmedia.co.ke/article/2000089602/n-a⟩. Accessed 18.06.2020.

[32] Participant observation, 7 March 2019.

[33] Participant observation during an FGD with elders at Lokosimekori Village on 6 March 2019.

[34] Interview with a NEMA official in Turkana, 20 March 2019.

[35] Interview with an official from the Turkana Professional Association, 15 March 2019.

[36] FGD with elders in Nakukulas, 7 March 2019.

Fig 1: Waste Disposal Site in Ngamia 1 Oil Well, Turkana East. Source: Benard Musembi Kilaka, March 2019.

[while pointing] 500 m is like from that house to the road there, all that will be taken. All these trees will be cut, and these trees benefitted me as a Turkana. They provide shade. Even now... are we not in the shade...? There are fruits, which goats feed on... there is firewood for cooking, there is charcoal that comes from the fallen trees... we benefit'[37]. Given the relative importance of trees, the deforestation that makes way for infrastructure projects in the region not only affects the environment but also generates social dispossession.

Social impacts: disrupted migratory patterns and urbanizations

Aside from the environmental impacts, the ongoing infrastructural developments in Turkana County have also generated considerable social impacts. Given the prevalence of pastoralism in the region, one of the most notable impacts of the projects touches on herders' access to grazing areas, water points and migratory corridors. The projects' huge demand for land had, for instance, seen certain areas suddenly become inaccessible for grazing activities. For example, the fencing around the oil infrastructure has blocked the migratory corridors that are seasonally used by pastoralists as they move from one grazing area to another[38]. Just to illustrate the magnitude of the situation, there are currently 33 well pads in the region and each measures 100 m by 100 m. According to Tullow Oil, the well pads are further expected to increase up to 300 during the production phase,

---
[37] FGDs with council of elders in Lokichar, 8 March 2019; older adults and young people in Loperot Village, 8 March 2019; Paralegals, 7 March 2019.
[38] Focus group discussion with youth and village elders in Nakukulas village, 7 March 2019.

thus illustrating that more land will be required. In fact, in March 2019, the government initiated the process of acquiring 6,348 hectares of land for additional oil activities[39]. As such, these measures, coupled with the environmental impacts discussed above, have forced Turkana herders to move to insecure areas closer to West Pokot, Samburu and Baringo in search of grazing land, thus exposing them to attacks and incidents of cattle rustling (Johannes et al. 2015; Mkutu 2015; Patey 2014). In addition, the LAPSSET project is further expected to exacerbate the situation due to its massive land requirements. According to the government of Kenya, the LAPSSET corridor will take up around 500 m for the inner corridor and an additional 50 km on either side of the inner corridor[40]. Therefore, in Turkana County, the LAPSSET components for the project, excluding the 50 km on either side of the corridor, will take up approximately 27,118 hectares of land.

Given that Turkana has a long history of complex outbreaks of violence, infrastructure projects and oil extraction activities have been entangled in such conflicts and subsequently attracted a number of security measures from both the government and private security companies (Mkutu 2017). According to members of the local community, the heavy security accorded to the oil facilities had adversely affected their societal security as the government had been more interested in protecting the oil facilities rather than the local community. In this case, the government had deployed much of the available security personnel to the projects, thus leaving the community vulnerable to attacks by their neighbouring communities[41]. The increasing deployment of national police reservists (NPR) to the oil sites is particularly controversial since the unit, which is made up of volunteers and armed by the government, is the main provider of security in the region (Mkutu 2017). It is particularly due to this concern that community members around Lokichar disrupted all oil operations in June 2018 following the deteriorating security situation in the region, which was taking place amidst heavy security posturing around oil infrastructures. Furthermore, most community members interviewed in the region also expected the same trend to continue with the LAPSSET project when its different components are being constructed[42]. In this case, community members argued that the state will not only channel its resources to protect components of the project but will also use excessive force to ensure its completion irrespective of the many unaddressed concerns of residents in the county.

A further aspect of the major social impact caused by oil activities and LAPSSET projects is the increasing urbanization of former small towns in Turkana

---

[39] Kenya Gazette, Vol. CXXI, No. 21, 2019.
[40] Official Website Vision 2010. ‹http://vision2030.go.ke/inc/uploads/2018/05/LAPSSET-Project-Report-July-2016.pdf›. Accessed 18.06.2020.
[41] Interviews with a number of senior county officials in Lodwar in March 2019; FGDs in Nakukulas, Kalemgorok, Loperot and Lokosimekoru villages in the Lokichar region, 6-10 March 2019.
[42] FGD with women in both Loperot and Kalemngorok villages on 8 and 10 March 2019.

Figure 2: A Fenced Oil Site in Turkana East. Source: Benard Musembi Kilaka, March 2019.

County. Effects are particularly visible in urban areas found near the oil wells or other oil infrastructures such as in Lokichar town. Since the discovery of oil in 2012, the town has experienced rapid growth due to the emergence of a wage economy and the influx of people looking for jobs and other opportunities. In addition, the town has also experienced a construction boom because local entrepreneurs rushed to construct rental houses, hotels, bars and restaurants in order to satisfy the needs of the growing population (Small Arms Survey, Geneva 2015). This trend is further being accelerated by the ongoing upgrading of the main highway that connects Turkana to the rest of Kenya, since it has made it easy for people and goods to move quickly. However, this development has come with challenges (Kamais, Mwangi, and Bor 2019), the most prominent being a dramatic rise in HIV/AIDS due to the emergence of a sex industry, which is driven by the construction of a new road and the presence of salaried workers[43].

Local and civil society organization (CSO) strategies: protests and litigation

In order to address the real or anticipated impacts of oil exploitation and infrastructure projects, local communities together with a number of civil society organizations (CSO)[44] had adopted various strategies to gain their bargaining power

---

[43] Mkutu Kennedy Agade 2018: Oil Discovery in Turkana still to fuel women's emancipation. *The East African*. 9. August. ‹https://www.theeastafrican.co.ke/oped/comment/Oil-discoveries-in-Turkana-still-to-fuel-women-emancipation/434750-4705386-dc0bx1/index.html›. Accessed 18.06.2020.

[44] The notion of 'civil society' has been subject to debates (Bayart 1986; Woods 1992). Neverthe-

and contest various concerns. Common strategies included local protests outside oil facilities, advocacy and information gatherings and litigation against loss of land or environmental issues.

Among them, protests had emerged as one of the most prominent strategies local stakeholders used for claim making or expressing their displeasure with oil operations and the LAPSSET project[45]. Protests often involved demonstrations and blockages of both roads and oil sites. Unlike the normal trend in many mining sites worldwide where protests are well coordinated by a range of non-state actors, this was different in Turkana since most protests were often locally led by individuals and were sometimes spontaneous and uncoordinated. Several activists and CSOs, both at the local and the national level, were the main allies of Turkana stakeholders.

Protesters, who were from the surrounding villages and most affected by oil activities, were in many cases driven by a range of grievances such as poor labour conditions for casual and/or unskilled workers, demands for local content[46], disagreements over resource-sharing formulas, demands for compensation and attempts by the state to acquire land for the LAPSSET project (Schilling, Locham, and Scheffran 2018). Labour grievances had been one of the most common causes of protests. In this case, such complaints had either focused on demands for more jobs by members of the local community or been due to unfair labour practices. To a certain extent, the protests were successful and led to a changing relationship between the oil company Tullow and the local community. For instance, to avert losses from the protests, Tullow Oil created more employment for Turkana people and increased its budget for local content. Additionally, such protests had forced the government to address the security concerns in the region.

Furthermore, upcoming plans for the LAPSSET project had led to community protests over a range of concerns that touch on, among other things, the process of land acquisition for the project, compensation to affected persons, the size of the project and the lack of community consultation on the implementation of the project. In this regard, community members in both Turkana South and Turkana East constituencies had, at least on two occasions, violently disrupted LAPSSET-related workshops in their vicinities and subsequently chased away representatives

---

less, in the case of Turkana, the notion of CSOs seems more appropriate, being understood as advocacy oriented instead of the notion of an NGO, which has a connotation of development-oriented service and aid-providing agents.

[45] Nasralla Shadia 2018: Tullow shuts down Kenyan oilfield operations due to unrest. *Reuters.* 25. July. ‹https://www.reuters.com/article/us-tullow-kenya/tullow-shuts-down-kenyan-oilfield-operations-due-to-unrest-idUSKBN1KF27G›. Accessed 25.06.2020.

[46] This term is frequently used by the oil and gas industry (and increasingly in the mining sector) to commit to uplifting strategies for the local communities and entrepreneurs through skills development and awarding tenders and business opportunities to them.

from the national government in order to express their disappointment and resistance towards the modus operandi of the government on the LAPSSET project[47].

Various NGOs played a major role in the advocacy of rights and proper implementation of the infrastructure projects. Their focus had particularly been on environmental and land issues by sensitizing the community about their rights. In fact, much of the awareness about the environmental impacts of oil operations had largely come from community-based non-governmental organizations, which operate in the region. In this case, such organizations had interacted with community members through community forums in the villages that are located near the oil sites. Due to low literacy rates in the region, CSOs had particularly emerged as one of the most reliable sources of information about ongoing and upcoming projects to local community members[48]. Other activities had also entailed empowering communities with skills and information that helped them engage with both the government and other stakeholders. Although some CSOs work closely with communities, other organizations have sought to work closely with both communities and companies, thereby providing a platform where issues can be addressed amicably. For instance, between 2015 and 2017, *Mercy Corps* and *Life and Peace Institute* implemented a project, known as the 'Peaceful Empowerment in Arid Lands Program (Pearl)', that brought all stakeholders in the oil industry together. One key outcome of the project was the development of a grievance mechanism tool to help address issues around oil extraction before they escalated. Additionally, a number of CSOs had forged links with both national and international partners in order to attract resources for funding, training, publicity and allowances to highlight the issues to a wider audience.

However, CSOs faced several challenges in their advocacy work, such as a lack of funds, deficiency of technical skills and depth of understanding of the oil industry and strained relationship with the political class at both the county and national levels[49]. For instance, while CSOs and the county government of Turkana had a similar outlook on many issues around ongoing oil operations, they rarely worked together and viewed each other as competitors. For example, the county government tried to claim its position as the spokesperson for the community, and as a result, it articulated similar issues to the ones CSOs advocate. One difference between the county government and CSOs was their views on solving issues affecting the region. For instance, controversies around land acquisition for infrastructure projects were well illustrated by the disagreement between the county government and non-governmental stakeholders. While the county government insisted that it is the key custodian of community land and hence had the sole mandate for negotiating with the central government or private contractors, sev-

---

[47] Interview with a senior police officer at Lokichar on 11 March 2019 and FGD with Council of Elders, Lokichar on 8 March 2019.
[48] Participant observations, March 2019.
[49] Interviews with several CSO representatives in Lodwar, March 2019.

eral CSOs had tried to help communities living alongside the proposed sites of the projects to register land so that they can benefit from compensation. Such differences had ended up changing the relationship between CSOs and the county government and had consequently affected the effectiveness of CSO advocacy work.

Despite a general mistrust toward the local government concerning the management of rewards and the acquisition of land, in the recent past, litigation has frequently emerged to contest a key grievance around land acquisition for infrastructure projects in the county. In March 2019, the Country Government of Turkana filed a case at the Kitale Law Courts to contest plans for land acquisition for both the LAPSSET project and the oil fields by the national government[50]. At the heart of this controversy was a notice issued in February 2019 in the *Kenya Gazette* by the National Land Commission that showed the amount of land that needed to be acquired for the project. The county government protested the move, citing that it was not consulted on such an important matter that touched on community land. As such, after consultations with community members, the county government went to court to challenge the notice and managed to get a stay order on the notice until the case was heard and determined[51].

State and company strategies: corporate social responsibility and good governance

To endear the project to the people and allay existing concerns, both the Kenyan government and the companies had adopted a number of strategies. The relationship between local stakeholders, national government and (inter)national companies was often characterized by (trans)national ethical regimes, which were seen as bypassing or usurping the authority of the local stakeholders (Gilberthorpe and Rajak 2017). In the case of Turkana, the assumption that processes of neo-imperialism and dispossession by transnational companies are on display, is oversimplifying the complex entanglement of the Kenyan state with transnational interests. A catalogue of environmental and social infractions had 'given way to a decade of initiatives, codes, agreements and tools aimed at making the industry not only socially responsible, but "sustainable"' (Gilberthorpe and Rajak 2017). Therefore, private actors establish corporate social responsibility measures as a possible solution to the 'resource curse' (Dolan and Rajak 2016; Kirsch 2014), whereas a number of treaties, laws and agreements strengthen the state's agency towards international business interests. In the case of Turkana, the most promi-

---

[50] Obare Osinde 2019: Court stops compulsory acquisition of land for oil exploration in Turkana. *The Standard.* 12. March. ⟨https://www.standardmedia.co.ke/business/article/2001316308/government-blocked-from-acquiring-land-in-turkana⟩.

[51] Deliberations at a community meeting between county leaders and elders from all regions of the county, 9 March 2019.

nent strategies to circumvent local resistance and rising conflicts included sensitization meetings, corporate social responsibility approaches, local content initiatives and the development of grievance management tools.

Tullow Oil's CSR strategy entailed the construction of schools, health centres, boreholes, and toilets[52]. Further, the company had formulated a local content plan that sought to empower local youths, women and entrepreneurs. For instance, Tullow Oil tendered transport and security as well as the provision of meat and mineral water to local traders. Further, they facilitated loans from local banks and other institutions to local entrepreneurs, thus allowing local entrepreneurs to access capital to trade with the company. One prominent example was the car leasing scheme that was undertaken by Tullow Oil in conjunction with Toyota Kenya that saw vehicles worth ksh225 million leased to local entrepreneurs[53]. Such entrepreneurs were later subcontracted by Tullow Oil to provide transport services to the company. Further, between 2017 and 2018, the company provided scholarships for vocational training for 200 Turkana youths in plumbing, mechanical and electrical engineering, catering, masonry, and welding in institutions such as the Lodwar Vocational Training Centre and St. Kizito Vocational Training Institute in Nairobi (Tullow Oil 2018: 18-19).

Despite these efforts, due to the heterogeneity of the local stakeholders with their various concerns and needs, some members of the community felt shortchanged by the company. For instance, the Tullow Oil project on water provision to several villages had challenged local institutions. The water was delivered by trucks and both the supply and access were only secured on selected days of the week and hardly regulated. According to several community members[54], the water supply was neither guaranteed nor was it adequate to meet their personal demands or to water their animals. As a result, the company's well-meant projects created discontent and a feeling of non-fulfilment, which consequently affects community-company relations. Furthermore, many of the above mentioned projects remain vacant since the main operator Tullow Oil has left the ground in the beginning of 2020, which raises further questions of sustainability and dependence. Therefore, a lack of understanding of local institutions and resource management schemes leads, like so many development projects before, to a stagnation and a disillusionment with the development imaginaries (Ferguson 1994, 1999).

As well as CSR initiatives, Tullow Oil had also established a grievance-handling mechanism that sought to resolve conflicts before they escalate. Such measures were particularly informed by the heavy financial losses that often result

---

[52] Interview with a Tullow Oil employee, 21 March 2019.
[53] Igadwah Lynet 2014: Tullow woos Turkana locals with car lease contracts. *Business Daily*. 12. November. ‹https://www.businessdailyafrica.com/news/Tullow-moves-to-appease-locals-with-car-lease-contracts-/539546-2520516-aj2coh/index.html›.
[54] FGD with women and men in Nakukulas and Lokosimekori Villages on 7 and 8 March 2019.

Figure 3 & 4: Water point established by Tullow Oil (L) and a self-dug water well providing water to goats (R), Nakukulas, Turkana East. Source: Benard Musembi Kilaka, March 2019

Figure 5: Public toilets built by Tullow Oil, Nakukulas, Turkana East. Source: Benard Musembi Kilaka, March 2019

from the disrupted operations during protests and demonstrations. The grievance mechanism regulated the procedure to be followed when issues arise and appointed specific people to be in charge of dealing with grievances[55]. For example, community liaison officers (CLOs), community communication officers (CCOs) and village socialization officers (VSOs) play a key role in receiving and resolving grievances from members of the local community. Grievances might have included the loss of animals either occasioned by accidents involving company vehicles or caused by contaminated water. In this case, if a local herder lost one camel, the company had paid for one camel rather than the communal norm where such a loss would have been settled by the payment of several camels (Tullow Oil Kenya 2019: 39).

---

[55] Golder Associates Ltd 2018: *Tullow Kenya B.V. Early Oil Pilot Scheme Phase II. Environment and Social Impact Assessment.* Volume II.

Due to the industry's significance, government agents also played a significant role in resolving grievances, especially those that were beyond the control of Tullow Oil. For instance, in August 2018, the government, together with Tullow Oil and other relevant stakeholders, established a two-tier grievance mechanism body for the upstream oil industry in Turkana. At the county level, the committee was aptly labelled the 'Turkana Grievance Management Committee', while at the national level, it was labelled the 'Inter-Ministerial (Escalation and Support) Committee'. The committees were established after intense community protests in 2018 against rising levels of insecurity in the region and frustrations over the lack of opportunities from the ongoing oil operations. The protests severely disrupted oil activities in the region, thus leading to heavy loses for Tullow Oil and its partners. Therefore, the committees were expected to resolve issues before they escalate to unmanageable levels[56] together with the civil society groups, the county government, representatives of the community and government officials from ministries and parastatals. However, given that oil operations are increasingly getting entangled with the LAPSSET project, which is equally controversial, the committee's mandate restricts it to oil operations, thus leaving grievances from the LAPSSET project to be resolved through other means.

Further, to endear oil extraction and LAPSSET-related infrastructure projects to the general public, the Kenyan government, together with the companies, have resorted to 'sensitizing' people on the benefits of the projects. Referring to the region's long period of marginalization, such infrastructure projects are often presented as a panacea to many of the problems that local residents face (Kinyera and Doevenspeck 2019; Mwabu 2020; Weszkalnys 2008). The LAPSSET project promises better connectivity, integration of the remote northern counties into the economy and the development of modern infrastructure, whereas crude oil bears the promise of prosperity (Cormack 2016; Mosley and Watson 2016). To ensure that the good news is heralded, local government employees and parastatals organize regular meetings, to which they invite agents of local media and local politicians such as chiefs and county government agents, in high class hotels in the bigger towns of the respective counties. During such meetings, participants are regaled with government plans and the intended benefits that will accrue from the projects. Since most of the facilitators are non-Turkanas, such sessions are mostly conducted in Swahili and English, which is not widely spoken in the region and is a clear indicator of the targeted stakeholders[57]. In addition, such sessions are mostly top-down in nature in the sense that information mostly flows in one direction, although communities are supposed to be given a platform to ask questions. According to an activist working in Lokichar, most of the sessions are conducted

---

[56] Government of Kenya 2018: The Kenya Gazette. Vol. CXX – No. 93. Establishment of the Kenyan Grievance Management Committee.
[57] Participant observation, 2019.

in Lodwar town, which is approximately 85 km away from Lokichar and thus inaccessible to many people who are directly affected by the projects[58].

Conclusion

Both LAPSSET and the oil resources in Turkana elicited hope for a desirable future among many residents in the region who had undergone a long period of abandonment by the state. Oil extraction and the development of infrastructure came with several benefits, such as employment, connectivity, opportunities for local entrepreneurs and various CSR development projects along the Kenyan 'frontier' (Elliott 2016; Mosley and Watson 2016; Peluso and Lund 2011). However, eight years down the line, initial optimism has given way to fear, despair, protests and sustained advocacy by a number of CSOs due to unmet promises and the adverse impacts that are emanating from projects. Environmental degradation, loss of land, new social dynamics and security issues 'disenchanted' the promise of an 'emancipatory modernity' (Harvey and Knox 2012: 523). In many ways, the manner in which the projects are unfolding makes the national government's sudden interest in the region appear suspicious since it creates a perception that the state is only interested in extracting the resources therein rather than uplifting the lives of people. Although both the company and the state are trying to sensitize members in public meetings and address contentious issues with various small development projects such as public toilets and troughs, much of these efforts have been reactive and controversial since many residents view such initiatives as superficial and non-inclusive. Rather, an anti-politics machine (Ferguson 1990) seems to be on display when local security concerns remain unsettled by political processes and leave the apprehensive communities vulnerable to outside exploitation. Therefore, local community members oppose certain unexpected challenges out of fear that the extraction of resources and the establishment of infrastructure might simply lead to another drama in their long-standing history of marginalization. Hence, the regular disruptions of operations and related financial losses during protests by different local stakeholders strengthen the bargaining power of locals towards the national government and the international companies. As a result, despite the enormous commercial and political power of (international) companies and the national government, both have changed their approaches since 2012. For instance, the 'resource sharing formula' in the Petroleum Act from 2019 (Part VII, 58, p. 216) and various favourable content policies arguably result from persistent and tireless local resistance by local stakeholders.

---

[58] Interview with a representative of a local NGO in Lokichar on 7 March 2019.

Glossary

CSO	Civil Society Organization
EIA	Environmental Impact Assessment
EMCA	The Environmental Management and Coordination Act
ESIA	Environmental and Social Impact Assessment
LAPSSET	Lamu Port South Sudan Ethiopia Transport Corridor
NEMA	National Environmental Management Authority

References:

Anderson, David G 2017: Humans and Animals in Northern Regions. Annual Review of Anthropology 46(1):133–49.

Auty, Richard M 1994: Industrial Policy Reform in Six Large Newly Industrializing Countries: The Resource Curse Thesis. World Development 22(1):11–26.

Auty, Richard M. 2005: Sustaining Development in Mineral Economies?: The Resource Curse Thesis. Repr. London, New York: Routledge.

Barrow, Edmund G. C. 1990: Usufruct Rights to Trees: The Role of Ekwar in Dryland Central Turkana, Kenya. Human Ecology 18(2):163–76.

Bayart, Jean-François 1986: Civil Society in Africa. In: Chabal P. (ed) Political Domination in Africa, African Studies. Cambridge University Press: 109–125.

Best, Günter 1984: Nomaden und Bewässerungsprojekte?: eine Studie zum rezenten Wandlungsprozess der Eheform und Familienstruktur bei den Turkana am oberen Turkwell, NW-Kenia. Berlin: D. Reimer.

Brainard, Jean 1990: Nutritional Status and Morbidity on an Irrigation Project in Turkana District, Kenya. American Journal of Human Biology 2(2):153–63.

Broch-Due, Vigdis 2000: The Fertility of Houses & Herds. Producing Kinship & Gender among Turkana Pastoralists. In: Rethinking pastoralism in Africa?: gender, culture & the myth of the patriarchal pastoralist. Oxford: 165–85

Broche-Due, Vigdis 1999: Remembered Cattle, Forgotten People: Te Morality of Exchange and the Exclusion of the Turkana Poor. In: The Poor Are Not Us: Poverty and Pastoralism in Eastern Africa. Ohio University Press, Swallow Press: 50–88

Browne, Adrian J. 2015: The History and Politics of an Eastern African Megaproject. London, Nairobi: RIFT VALLEY INSTITUTE.

Burgos, Sigfrido, and Sophal Ear 2012: China's Oil Hunger in Angola: History and Perspective. Journal of Contemporary China 21(74):351–67

Carr, Claudia J. 2017: Turkana Survival Systems at Lake Turkana: Vulnerability to Collapse from Omo Basin Development. In: Carr C. J. (ed): River Basin Development and Human Rights in Eastern Africa — A Policy Crossroads. Springer International Publishing: 157–89

Collier, Paul and Anke Hoeffler 2004: Greed and Grievance in Civil War. Oxford Economic Papers.

Collins, Robert O. 2006: The Turkana Patrol of 1918 Reconsidered. Ethnohistory 53(1):95–119.

Cormack, Zoe 2016: The Promotion of Pastoralist Heritage and Alternative 'Visions' for the Future of Northern Kenya. Journal of Eastern African Studies 10(3):548–67.

Derbyshire, Samuel F. 2020: Remembering Turkana?: Material Histories and Contemporary Livelihoods in North-Western Kenya. Abingdon?; New York: Routledge.

Dolan, Catherine and Dinah Rajak, (eds) 2016: The Anthropology of Corporate Social Responsibility. First published. New York, NY Oxford: Berghahn.
Elliott, Hannah 2016: Planning, Property and Plots at the Gateway to Kenya's 'New Frontier'. Journal of Eastern African Studies 10(3):511–29.
Enns, Charis and Brock Bersaglio 2015: Enclave Oil Development and the Rearticulation of Citizenship in Turkana, Kenya: Exploring 'Crude Citizenship.' Geoforum 67:78–88.
Enns, Charis and Brock Bersaglio 2016: Pastoralism in the Time of Oil: Youth Perspectives on the Oil Industry and the Future of Pastoralism in Turkana, Kenya. The Extractive Industries and Society 3(1):160–70.
Ensminger, Jean 1992: Making a Market?: The Institutional Transformation of an African Society. Cambridge: Cambridge University Press.
Ferguson, James 1990: The Anti-Politics Machine?: Development, Depoliticization, and Bureaucratic Power in Lesotho. Cambridge: Cambridge University Press.
Ferguson, James 1994: The Anti-Politics Machine?: "Development", Depoliticization, and Bureaucratic Power in Lesotho. Minneapolis, London: University of Minnesota Press.
Ferguson, James 1999: Expectations of Modernity: Myths and Meanings of Urban Life on the Zambian Copperbelt. University of California Press.
Fratkin, Elliot and J. Terrence McCabe 1999: East African Pastoralism at the Crossroads: An Introduction. Nomadic Peoples 3(2):5–15.
Gilberthorpe, Emma and Dinah Rajak 2017: The Anthropology of Extraction: Critical Perspectives on the Resource Curse. The Journal of Development Studies 53(2):186–204.
Government of Kenya 1947: Northern Province Annual Report, 1947.
Government of Kenya 2019: Executive Order No.1 of 2019 – Framework for Co-Ordination and Implementation of National Government Development Programmes and Projects – The Elephant.
Gray, Sandra, Mary Sundal, Brandi Wiebusch, Michael A. Little, Paul W. Leslie and Ivy L. Pike 2003: Cattle Raiding, Cultural Survival, and Adaptability of East African Pastoralists. Current Anthropology 44(5):3–30.
Gulliver, Philip Hugh 1958: The Turkana Age Organization. American Anthropologist 60(5):900–922.
Gulliver, Philip Hugh 1963: A Preliminary Survey of the Turkana: A Report Compiled for the Government of Kenya. Photographic Department, University of Cape Town Libraries.
Gulliver, Philip Hugh 1966: The Family Herds?: A Study of Two Pastoral Tribes in East Africa?: The Jie and Turkana. [2nd impression, with new preface and bibliography]. London: Routledge & Kegan Paul.
Gulliver, Philip Hugh 1969: Nomadism among the Pastoral Turkana of Kenya?: Its Natural and Social Environment. Makerere: Nkanga Makerere Institute of Social Research.
Haller, Tobias 2013: The Contested Floodplain?: Institutional Change of the Commons in the Kafue Flats, Zambia. Lanham: Lexington Books.
Haller, Tobias 2019: The Different Meanings of Land in the Age of Neoliberalism: Theoretical Reflections on Commons and Resilience Grabbing from a Social Anthropological Perspective. Land 8(7):104.
Hardin, Garrett 1968: The Tragedy of the Commons. Science 162(3859):1243–48.

Harvey, Penny and Hannah Knox 2012: The Enchantments of Infrastructure. Mobilities 7(4):521–36.
Hicks, Celeste 2015: Africa's New Oil?: Power, Pipelines and Future Fortunes. London: Zed Books.
Hodgson, Dorothy L. 2004: Once Intrepid Warriors?: Gender, Ethnicity, and the Cultural Politics of Maasai Development. Bloomington?; Indianapolis: Indiana University Press.
Iledare, Wumi and Rotimi Suberu 2010: Oil and Gas Resources in the Federal Republic of Nigeria. World Bank, Washington, DC – Black Auditorium.
Johannes, Eliza M., Leo C. Zulu, and Ezekiel Kalipeni 2015: Oil Discovery in Turkana County, Kenya: A Source of Conflict or Development?. African Geographical Review 34(2):142–64.
Johnson, Jr Brooke R. 1999: Social Networks and Exchange. In: Turkana herders of the dry savanna?: ecology and biobehavioral response of nomads to an uncertain environment, Research monographs on human population biology. Oxford: Oxford University Press.
Jong, Edwin B. P., Luuk Knippenberg and Laurens Bakker 2017: New Frontiers: An Enriched Perspective on Extraction Frontiers in Indonesia. Critical Asian Studies 49(3):330–48.
Kamais, Cosmas Ekwom, Samson Wokabi M. and Eric Kiprono B. 2019: Security Implications of Oil Exploration on Social Activities in South Lokichar Basin, Turkana County, Kenya. Journal of African Studies and Development 11(5):64–72.
Karl, Terry L. 1997: The Paradox of Plenty?: Oil Booms and Petro-States. Berkeley: Univeristy of California Press.
Kenya Gazette, 1925: Proclamation No. 89. Colony and Protectorate of Kenya. The East African Outlying Districts Ordiance, 1902.
Kinyera, Paddy, and Martin Doevenspeck. 2019: Imagined Futures, Mobility and the Making of Oil Conflicts in Uganda. Journal of Eastern African Studies 13(3):389–408.
Kirsch, Stuart 2014: Mining Capitalism?: The Relationship between Corporations and Their Critics. Oakland, Calif.: University of California Press.
Lamphear, John 1976: Aspects of Turkana Leadership during the Era of Primary Resistance. The Journal of African History 17(2):225–43.
Lamphear, John 1988: The People of the Grey Bull: The Origin and Expansion of the Turkana. The Journal of African History 29(1):27–39.
Lamphear, John 1992: The Scattering Time?: Turkana Responses to Colonial Rule. Oxford: Clarendon Press
Lamphear, John 1993: Aspects of 'Becoming Turkana': Interactions and Assimilation Between Maa- and Ateker-Speakers. In: Being Maasai: Ethnicity and Identity in East Africa. Boydell & Brewer. 87–104.
LAPSSET Corridor Development Authority 2017: LAPSSET CORRIDOR PROGRAM: STATUS REPORT.
Mccabe, J. Terrence 1990: Success and Failure: The Breakdown of Traditional Drought Coping Institutions Among the Pastoral Turkana of Kenya. Journal of Asian and African Studies 25(3–4):146–60.
McCabe, J. Terrence 1990: Turkana Pastoralism: A Case against the Tragedy of the Commons. Human Ecology 18(1):81–103.

McCabe, J. Terrence 2004: Cattle Bring Us to Our Enemies?: Turkana Ecology, Politics, and Raiding in a Disequilibrium System. Ann Arbor: University of Michigan Press.

Meekers, Dominique 1992: The Process of Marriage in African Societies: A Multiple Indicator Approach. Population and Development Review 18(1):61–78.

Mirzeler, Mustafa Kemal 2014: Remembering Nayeche and the Gray Bull Engiro?: African Storytellers of the Karamoja Plateau and the Plains of Turkana. Toronto: University of Toronto Press.

Mkutu, Kennedy 2014: 'Ungoverned Space' and the Oil Find in Turkana, Kenya. The Round Table 103(5):497–515.

Mkutu, Kennedy 2015: Changes and Challenges of the Kenya Police Reserve: The Case of Turkana County. African Studies Review 58(1):199–222.

Mkutu, Kennedy A. 2017: Security Governance in East Africa: Pictures of Policing from the Ground. Rowman & Littlefield.

Morley, C. K., and F. M. Karanja 1999: Chapter 2: Geology and Geophysics of the Western Turkana Basins, Kenya. In: Geoscience of Rift Systems—Evolution of East Africa. American Association of Petroleum Geologists. 19–54.

Mosley, Jason and Elizabeth E. Watson 2016: Frontier Transformations: Development Visions, Spaces and Processes in Northern Kenya and Southern Ethiopia. Journal of Eastern African Studies 10(3):452–75.

Mung'ong'o, Claude G. and Pius Zebhe Y. 2016: Pastoralism and Climate Change in East Africa. Dar es Salaam: Mkuki na Nyota.

Mwabu, Germano 2020: Kenya's Oil Governance Regime: Challenges and Policies. In: Langer A. U. Ukiwo, and P. Mbabazi (eds): Oil Wealth and Development in Uganda and Beyond, Prospects, Opportunities, and Challenges,. Leuven University Press. 351–72

Oba, Gufu 1992: Ecological Factors in Land Use Conflicts, Land Administration and Food Security in Turkana, Kenya. UNESCO-TREMU Project. Marsabit (Kenya): Pastoral Development Network, ODI.

Odhiambo, Michael O. 2014: The Unrelenting Persistence of Certain Narratives. An Analysis of Changing Policy Narratives about the ASALs in Kenya. London: International Institute for Environment and Development.

Ohta, Itaru 2007: Bridewealth Negotiations among the Turkana in Northwestern Kenya. Kyoto: The Center for African Area Studies.

Okwany, Clifford O. 2020: Kenya's Foreign Policy towards the Horn of Africa; a Case of the Lamu Port South Sudan Ethiopia Transport Corridor. Egerton University.

Opongo, Elias 2017: Knowledge and Policy Gaps in Extractive Industries in Kenya. A Baseline Survey in Turkana, Kwale, Lamu, Migori, Kitui and Taita Taveta. 12. Nairobi: HIPSIR Research Series.

Patey, Luke 2014: Kenya: An African Oil Upstart in Transition. Oxford Institute for Energy Studies.

Pavitt, Nigel 1997: Turkana?: Nomads of the Jade Sea. London: Harvill Press.

Peluso, Nancy L. and Christian Lund. 2011: New Frontiers of Land Control: Introduction. Journal of Peasant Studies 38(4):667–81.

Reid, Robin S. and James E. Ellis 1995: Impacts of Pastoralists on Woodlands in South Turkana, Kenya: Livestock- Mediated Tree Recruitment. Ecological Applications 5(4):978–92.

Reidy, Eugenie 2012: You Will Not Die When Your Animals Are Shining: 'Aid-Waiting' in Turkana. Development 55(4):526–34.
Reyna, Stephen P. and Andrea Behrends 2011: The Crazy Curse and Crude Domination. Towards an Anthropology of Oil. In: Crude Domination. An Anthropology of Oil. New York: Beghahn Books. 3–29.
Ross, Michael L. 2012: The Oil Curse?: How Petroleum Wealth Shapes the Development of Nations. Princeton, N.J: Princeton University Press.
Sawyer, Suzana 2015: Crude Contamination. Law, Science, and Indeterminacy in Ecuador and Beyond. In: Subterranean estates?: life worlds of oil and gas. Ithaca: Cornell University Press. 127–46.
Schilling, Janpeter, Raphael Locham and Jürgen Scheffran 2018: A Local to Global Perspective on Oil and Wind Exploitation, Resource Governance and Conflict in Northern Kenya. Conflict, Security & Development 18(6):571–600.
Schultz, Ulrike and Vera Scholz 1994: Wir wollen Turkana-Frauen bleiben. Münster, Hanburg: Lit Verlang.
Small Arms Survey, Geneva, (ed) 2015: Digging for Trouble: Violence and Frontier Urbanization. In: Small Arms Survey 2015: Weapons and the World, Small Arms Survey. Cambridge: Cambridge University Press. 36–57.
Soper, Robert C. (ed) 1985: A Socio-Cultural Profile of Turkana District?: A Report of the Discrict Socio-Cultural Profiles Project. Nairobi: Institute of African Studies University of Nairobi?: Ministry of Finance and Planning.
Tiercelin, J. J., J. L. Potdevin, C. K. Morley, M. R. Talbot, H. Bellon, A. Rio, B. Le Gall, and W. Vétel. 2004: Hydrocarbon Potential of the Meso-Cenozoic Turkana Depression, Northern Kenya. I. Reservoirs: Depositional Environments, Diagenetic Characteristics, and Source Rock–Reservoir Relationships. Marine and Petroleum Geology 21(1):41–62.
Tsing, Anna 2000: Inside the Economy of Appearances. Public Culture 12(1):115–44.
Tullow Oil Kenya 2018: Ustawi: Changing Fortunes.
Tullow Oil Kenya 2019: Partnering to Drive Change.
Watts, Michael 2004: Resource Curse? Governmentality, Oil and Power in the Niger Delta, Nigeria. Geopolitics 9(1):50–80.
Weszkalnys, Gisa 2008: Hope & Oil: Expectations in São Tomé e Príncipe. Review of African Political Economy 35(117):473–82.
Weszkalnys, Gisa 2014: Anticipating Oil: The Temporal Politics of a Disaster yet to Come. The Sociological Review 62(S1):211–35.
Weszkalnys, Gisa. 2016: A doubtful hope: resource affect in a future oil economy. Journal of the Royal Anthropological Institute 22(S1):127–46.
Wienpahl, Jan 1984: Women's Roles in Livestock Production among the Turkana of Kenya. Research in Economic Anthropology 6:193–215.
Wienpahl, Jan 1986: Livestock Production and Social Organization among the Turkana. Ann Arbor. Michigan: University Microfilms International.
Woods, Dwayne 1992: Civil Society in Europe and Africa: Limiting State Power through a Public Sphere. African Studies Review 35(2):77–100.

Fishing in Troubled Waters: the Impacts of LAPSSET on the Local Fisheries in Lamu, Kenya

Flurina Werthmüller, Institute for Social Anthropology, University of Bern, Switzerland

Introduction

'The port will kill us because we work in the sea and we will have less work. Some of us didn't finish school. But we can't do anything' (Fisherman, Lamu Town[1]).

This statement shows the hopelessness I felt among the people during my research in Lamu. Fears, destroyed hope and despair often came out during conversations. Since the beginning of the construction of a new megaport in Lamu on the coast of Kenya, the initially positive expectations of the local people have turned into disappointment and worries.

With the slogan 'A seamless connected Africa. Infinite Possibilities. Endless Opportunities', the official LAPSSET website[2] promotes its megaproject. It is a large-scale project that is 'part of the Kenya Vision 2030 Strategy, which is the national long-term development policy that aims to transform Kenya into a newly industrializing, middle-income country providing a high quality of life to all its citizens by 2030 in a clean and secure environment'[3]. Additionally, LAPSSET (Lamu Port South Sudan Ethiopia Transport Corridor Project) is also part of a much larger land bridge, which aims to link the East African coast from Lamu to the West African coast at the port of Douala in Cameroon (LAPSSET Corridor Development Authority 2016: 1).

To achieve the LAPSSET plan, the idea is to build a port with 32 berths in Lamu, oil pipelines to transport oil from Ethiopia and southern Sudan to Lamu, an oil refinery, highways and railway lines across Kenya, three new airports, a dam in the Tana River and three resort towns. So far, three of the 32 berths in the port of Lamu are under construction and parts of the highways and airports have also been built[4]. The expected implications of the project are to create a network within

---
[1] Interview with the author, January 2019.
[2] ⟨http://www.lapsset.go.ke⟩ accessed on 17.09.2020.
[3] ⟨http://www.lapsset.go.ke⟩ accessed on 17.09.2020.
[4] ⟨http://www.lapsset.go.ke⟩ accessed on 17.09.2020.

Kenya, but also with other parts of the continent, to strengthen the Kenyan region as the regional centre of East Africa, to strengthen regional security and the socio-economic basis, to establish an efficient, reliable and sustainable infrastructure, to create education opportunities and to reduce the poverty rates[5].

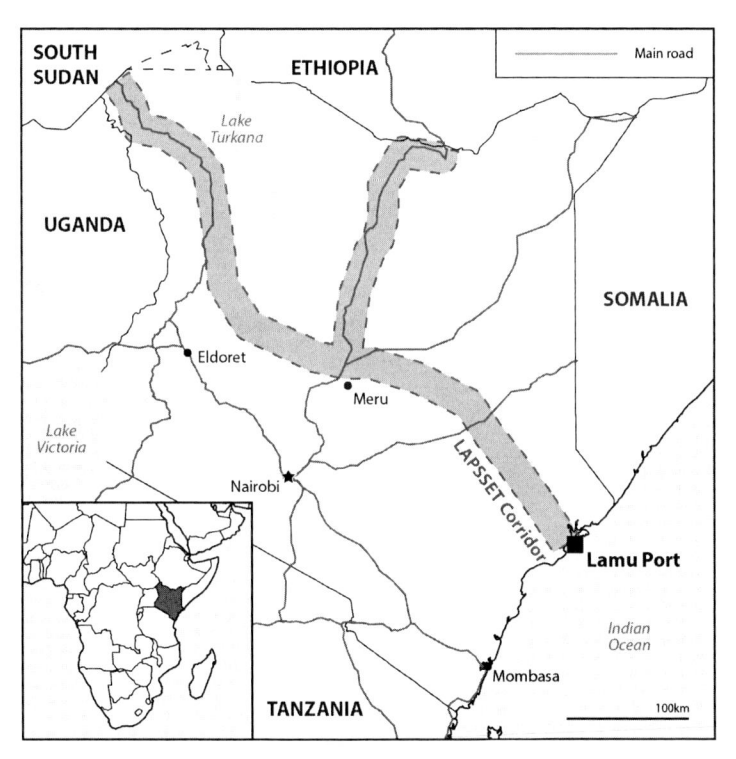

Map 1: The area of the LAPSSET Corridor in Kenya. Source: Map compilation and design by Manuel L. K. Abebe (2021), CDE, University of Bern, Bern, Switzerland. Geodata: OpenStreetMap contributors.

As part of my master's thesis at the Institute of Social Anthropology of the University of Bern, I travelled to Lamu for two months of field research about how the construction of the deep-sea megaport affects the local population and how people deal with it. I focused especially on the fishing community, since this is the most important economic pillar in the region. Since the start of the project, great promises of development have been made, including for the local population in Lamu. However, eight years later, the fishermen and residents of Lamu are disappointed and fear for their future as promises of education opportunities, jobs and compensation for the loss of their fishery commons due to the new port do not materialize. That is an 'enchantment of infrastructure' (see Harvey/Knox 2012). While these promises and legitimations are compatible with the objectives

---

[5] ‹http://www.lapsset.go.ke› accessed on 17.09.2020.

of sustainable development (in particular Objective 9, 'Building resilient infrastructure, promoting inclusive and sustainable industrialization and encouraging innovation'[6]), they destroy sustainable fishing and undermine the local community system.

The reason of this article is to show the impact of mega-infrastructure projects such as LAPSSET, and here the port of Lamu as a case study, on local economic, environmental and social conditions. It aims to answer questions about what the construction of the port in Lamu means for the local fishing community, how it is be responded to and what the impacts of the new developments are. After situating the case study in its historical, environmental, ethnographical and political context, I will present the setting of the Lamu region, focusing on fishing with its specific fishing methods, regulations and property rights. In a further step, I will discuss the impact of Lamu Port on the local population, especially the fishing community, since fishing is the largest economic activity in Lamu and many people depend directly or indirectly on the fishery. Therefore the following chapters always relate to fishing in Lamu. The data were collected through intensive literature research and a field study on site (as part of my master thesis). This was done mainly through participant observation as well as interviews and focus group discussions.

Part 1: Historical, environmental, ethnographic and political context

History and current context

Lamu is the main island of the Lamu archipelago in the north on the Kenyan coast with Lamu Town as the capital of the same-named county. In pre-colonial time, the archipelago was part of the 'Swahili' corridor that stretched from southern Mozambique to northern Somalia. It functioned as a gateway between the African continent and the countries beyond the Indian Ocean (Kabiru 2014: 1).

Lamu Town is the political and cultural centre of Lamu County and part of UNESCO World Heritage[7]. The old town of Lamu is said to be the oldest and best-preserved Swahili settlement in East Africa and has retained its traditional functions to this day. The history of Lamu dates back to the twelfth century. Trade between East Africa and Arabia, Persia and India was already taking place in the ninth century. The port of Lamu was a rich trading centre, especially in the fourteenth century. Amber, mangrove wood, spices, ivory and other resources were exported to the Middle East and India. Porcelain and carpets were imported in return (Kabiru 2014: 1ff.).

---

[6] United Nations: Goal 9. ⟨https://sdgs.un.org/goals/goal9⟩ accessed on 17.09.2020.
[7] UNESCO World Heritage Center 2001: Lamu Old Town. ⟨https://whc.unesco.org/en/list/1055/⟩ accessed on 17.09.2020.

Fig 1: The waterfront of Lamu Town. Source: Flurina Werthmüller.

The history of the city was shaped by the Portuguese invasion in 1506 and the Omani-Arab rule around 1813, among other things. In the seventeenth and early eighteenth century Lamu became a centre of poetry, politics, crafts and trade. The traditional stone houses and mosques also date from this period (ibid.: 1ff.). Still today the houses are built of coral and mangrove wood[8]. Because of the 'Tarika' (the way of the prophet), Lamu has been considered an important religious centre in East and Central Africa since the nineteenth century. Unfortunately, the economic decline in Lamu started after beginning the construction of the port in Mombasa at the end of the eighteenth century and the Uganda Railway in 1901. With the ever-decreasing trade, Lamu remained only a small port (ibid.: 2ff.).

Nowadays tourism is central to the local economy. Hotels, guesthouses, restaurants, cafes and shops depend on the visitors[9]. Deep-sea fishing, snorkelling and sailing trips are popular tourist activities. However, since 2011, when two incidents of kidnapping of European tourists by the terrorist militia Al-Shabaab followed by cases of terrorist attacks on a bus and a school on the mainland were reported[10], Lamu has suffered from a lack of tourists. Following these incidents, more than 500 hotel employees lost their jobs and the majority of European countries warned against travelling to Lamu[11]. According to my interview partners,

---

[8] UNESCO World Heritage Center 2001: Lamu Old Town : ‹https://whc.unesco.org/en/list/1055/› accessed on 17.09.2020.

[9] Lamu Tourism: ‹https://lamutourism.org/land-sea/› accessed on 17.09.2020.

[10] Spiegel Reise 2011: Touristen flüchten von Lamu-Inseln in Kenia. ‹https://www.spiegel.de/reise/aktuell/mord-und-entfuehrungen-touristen-fluechten-von-lamu-inseln-in-kenia-a-790114.html› accessed on 06.04.2020.

[11] Spiegel Reise 2011: Touristen flüchten von Lamu-Inseln in Kenia. ‹https://www.spiegel.de/rei

however, the situation has now improved again. Nevertheless, a cloud remains over Lamu and the industry has become very vulnerable. An interview partner, who works as a captain on a sailing boat and organizes trips with tourists, told me that they used to go sailing with tourists every day. Nowadays they are happy to receive a booking once a week. Now, with the construction of Lamu Port, new changes and challenges are expected to appear, which currently mainly affect the fishing community.

Fishing is the main economic activity of the islanders on 3,100 km² of territorial water area, according to the Department of Fisheries, Livestock & Cooperative Development of Lamu County Government[12]. It is estimated that the annual fish production amounts to 2,500 million tons and about 10,000 fishermen work directly or indirectly for the fishing industry. They contribute significantly to the county's GDP[13].

The methods of the local population are mainly, if not entirely, artisanal. Artisanal fishery can be defined as follows:

'The term "artisanal fisheries" typically refers to traditional fisheries that involve households (as opposed to companies) using relatively small amounts of capital and small fishing craft, making short trips and staying close to shore with the catch destined mainly for local consumption. [...]. All fishers, whether using traditional fish traps, fish spearguns, hand lines and hooks, nets or diving and collecting, belong to artisanal fishery' (Hoorweg et al. 2009: 8).

The sea off the coast of Kenya can be considered common property of local different ethnic groups. However, this was not recognized after colonial times and it was assumed that the commons are not regulated, leading to overexploitation and degradation of the resource and ending in what Hardin called the 'tragedy of the commons' (see Hardin 1968). This 'tragedy', however, pertains to the open-access situation rather than to common property, since the management of common-pool resources in common property is very much regulated by local institutions of membership and access rules (for example who has access to the resource and when), as can be shown in many parts of African fishery. Rather, a 'tragedy' emerged due to a lack of recognition by colonial and post-colonial authorities leading to privatization or de facto open-access constellations as neither state rules, due to the lack of financial means of indebted states, nor local common-property institutions, due to a lack of empowerment, could be enforced (see Haller 2019a,b). Such is the case here, where fishing communities have developed rules to control who can fish where and how (Hoorweg et al. 2009: 10).

---

se/aktuell/mord-und-entfuehrungen-touristen-fluechten-von-lamu-inseln-in-kenia-a-790114.html› accessed on 06.04.2020.
[12] Lamu County Government: ‹http://lamu.go.ke/fisheries-livestock/› accessed on 12.06.2020.
[13] Lamu County Government: ‹http://lamu.go.ke/fisheries-livestock/› accessed on 12.06.2020.

Fig 2: Fishermen at nightfall on a traditional dhow. Source: Flurina Werthmüller.

For example, there are informal rules on what equipment is to be used, or certain fishing grounds are occasionally inaccessible due to seasonal changes or for conservation and regulatory reasons. There are representations of elders in indigenous communities who speak out against restrictions to fishing in certain areas through visions in their dreams (ibid.: 13, quoting Glaesel 1997). These places are often ecologically important habitats, such as fish breeding grounds. It is precisely such spiritually motivated decisions or beliefs that often involve 'modern' methods of fisheries management such as closed seasons, access restrictions, protected areas and size restrictions. In Mozambique, for example, the access regulations of the elders were undermined because the ownership of common resources was not recognized in colonial and post-colonial legislation (ibid.: 13, citing for example, Chilundu/Cau 2000). The role of traditional access regimes and indigenous forms of conservation as well as traditional fishing rights, which in many parts of the world have lost their importance due to a lack of legal acceptance, the introduction of new technologies, a lack of community cohesion and other reasons, has become less important (ibid.: 13; see also Chapter 3).

Geography and ecosystem/cultural landscape

The East African coast stretches over 5,500 km along the Indian Ocean from Somalia, through Kenya and Tanzania to Mozambique (Hoorweg et al. 2009: 25). Some 600 km of it belong to the Kenyan coast from Somalia in the north to Tanzania in the south (ibid.: 25). It is situated just below the equator. The northern coastal region consists of wide sediment areas, which are drained by the rivers Tana and Athi-Sabaki. The rivers bring sediments from the hinterland. The coastal region is generally low and characterized by fossil reefs, coastal islands, bays, creeks, large mangrove forests, immense baobab trees and a diverse marine ecology (Hoorweg et al. 2000: 3).

The coast is supported by a chain of hills, which rarely exceed a height of 300 m.a.s.l. As a result of coastal erosion, the coastline is receding and the development of the coastal region is exacerbating the problem (Hoorweg et al. 2009: 25).

In many tropical areas, the marine flora and fauna is very diverse due to the manifold marine habitats, such as the sea coast, lagoons and estuaries, mangrove swamps, seagrass beds, caves, coral reefs, open waters and sandy beaches (Aloo 2000: 43). These habitats contain most of the valued resources, including mangroves, coral reefs, seaweed and seagrass beds, marine mammals, fish and crustaceans, which together with their environment all form the basis of life for many of the coastal inhabitants (ibid.: 44). The Lamu Archipelago is also characterized by extensive mangrove forests. That is why, according to the Ministry of Transport (2013: 2), the coastal region around the archipelago is very sensitive. The district's mangrove forests are the largest in Kenya and provide habitat and breeding grounds for many marine species, such as fish and prawns (Aloo 2000: 44). Of course, the landscape around Lamu is like many other landscapes – not a natural habitat untouched by humans, but a cultural landscape that has been shaped and influenced by humans over a long period of time. Humans are involved in the preservation of an ecosystem with sustainable resource use. Rules and institutional framework conditions, which have usually been established and changed over a long period of time, contribute to this (see Taylor/Lennon 2011).

According to the Chief Officer of the Lamu County Fisheries Departement, nowadays, for instance, some fishing methods or types of gear are not allowed and are also controlled and monitored by the Fisheries Department (such as scuba tanks to dive for lobsters or the use of poison). Lobster fishing, along with prawn and oyster catching, is one of the most important and lucrative fishing activities in and around Lamu. They can be sold for much more money than other species and are in high demand by hotels. They are mostly caught in reefs using a traditional technique. However, the approval of traditional techniques often limits innovation in local communities. Where fishing is done is also controlled to ensure that it does not take place in prohibited areas: for example, in protected areas such as breeding grounds. Fishing for protected species such as turtles and dugongs is also prohibited. All these rules, measures, monitorings and controls are part of maintaining sustainable fishing:

'We teach them in sustainable fishing methods to try to create ownership of the resource. This is your property, this is your resource, you need to value it, this is your life, this

is your employment and so you need to fish responsibly, and if there is any new law of the government, we tell them. Fishermen also fish in circulation. After three months they rotate and shift to another place. That is very healthy for the fish. And it is traditional' (Chief Officer of LCDF, Lamu Town)[14].

By this he is saying that the fishermen must know the rules of the state and follow them to uphold sustainable fisheries. However, these artisanal fishing methods have most likely been practised and maintained since the beginning of fishing in this area, which can also be read from the officer's remark on tradition. Additionally, for reasons of seasonality and equipment, it would always have been quite impossible to fish anywhere at any time. Even today, many fishermen do not have access to modern equipment such as motorized boats or fishing rods, and during the rainy and windy season fishing is only possible in the channels around the islands, as the open sea is too dangerous. Fishing quotas and access to the resource are therefore very much determined by the season. Degen et al. (2010: 2) described this too: artisanal fishing is characterized by uncertainties and is highly dependent on the seasons. Catches are lowest from April to June, during the Kusi season (south-east winds), which brings heavy rainfall and the sea is very rough. Therefore, fishermen go out to sea less during this time and avoid deep waters. During the Kaskazi season (north-east winds) from August to March, the catches are at their best.

Local population and resource use

According to Save Lamu (2018: 23), the people from Lamu rely on the natural ressources in order to survive. For the local communities, the sea is not seen as a border 'but rather an extension of [their] land in the water and an additional resource to the terrestrial natural resources of [their] area' (2018: 13). Therefore I have mainly focused on the fishing people in my research, since roughly 75 per cent of the population is directly or indirectly dependent on fishing today (Rodden 2014: 1).

The fishing community is by no means a homogeneous group, as there are many different actors specializing in different areas. They differ, for example, in the way they fish and the equipment they use. But also middlemen, captains and boat or gear owners are among the various actors.

Almost all active fishermen are men, at least that is what I was told and I have experienced. According to Malleret-King et al. (2003: 4), there are some cases where women are also actively involved in fishing (for example, as crab or shrimp collectors). Most of the time, however, they work in fisheries as fish fryers (ibid.:4).

What I found through my research in Lamu is that there are already many challenges and problems for the fishermen (apart from the influences of Lamu

---

[14] Interview with the author, January 2019.

Port). For example, the fishermen are heavily dependent on the market. And the market is mainly determined by the so-called 'middlemen'. Moreover, there is a big problem with the storage of the fish because there are not enough cold stores. My interview partner, mentioned above, explained the situation to me as follows:

[15] *'The people who benefit most from the fishing industry are not the fishermen, but those who own a boat or gear. The usual traditional way of accounting is that the person who owns the boat receives 50 per cent of the income. If someone owns a boat, he has to employ people who use the boat to go fishing. Because usually the boat owners are not fishermen themselves. Twenty-five per cent of the income would go to the person who owns the gear. And in most cases, the owner of the boat makes sure that he also owns the gear. Thus 75 per cent of the income belongs to him. The remaining 25 per cent is divided among the fishermen. But 13 per cent of it goes to the captain of the boat, because that's the person responsible for the boat. Five per cent of the remaining 12 per cent is given to the fishermen as an advance to provide for their families during the time the fishermen are away from home. Sometimes this is a matter of months. Ultimately 7 per cent of the total income remains for the fishermen to divide among themselves. It's a fact that the people who benefit from the fishing industry are not the fishermen themselves. Moreover, market prices are still adjusted by the middlemen. These are the people who buy the fish and sell it on to restaurants and hotels. The fishermen are dependent on the middlemen, because they are also the ones who pay them the advance for the families. As there are no cold stores, the fishermen have to sell their catch as soon as possible, otherwise it will decay. The middleman is therefore able to exploit the fishermen and buy the fish from them at low prices. He concluded: The fisherman is the one who suffers. He is exploited by the middlemen'* (Chief Officer of LCDF, Lamu Town)[16].

Other interview partners also confirmed this narrative. Fishermen would have a harder time these days than 20 years ago. A 65-year-old fisherman explained that one reason is that there are fewer fish in the waters around Lamu. Before they didn't have to go so far out into the open sea to fish as they do now.

Hoorweg et al. (2009: 9) described similar scenarios: fishermen who belong to a crew do not always receive a wage, but a share of the catch, which is also shared with the ship owners and the people who own the equipment. This is usually done in such a way that the catch is divided according to the work done and the capital invested (ibid.: 9). To increase the catch, reduce risks and defend their interests, artisanal fishermen join together as a crew or in communities of interest (ibid.: 9). The composition of the members of a crew often consists of very different people: relatives, friends or even younger children who start fishing together with their fathers, uncles or brothers and may later join another crew (ibid.: 9).

There are fishing communities where the boat and equipment belong to the crew, but often cooperatives, fishing organizations, relatives or village committees own them together or they belong to individual businessmen (ibid.: 9).

---

[15] This part has been taken from notes in my field research diary, January 2019.
[16] Interview with the author, January 2019.

A wide range of stakeholders are therefore involved in the fisheries sector. Some benefit more, others less. It seems, however, that not only are fishermen more vulnerable, but there is also a contradiction, because on the one hand they comply with the authorities' regulations to fish sustainably and according to government rules, while on the other hand the pressure of dwindling fish stocks and access forces them to take greater risks in more open waters. The Port Lamu project further increases the pressure on these already troublesome conditions. With the challenges and problems that already exist, new discussions about access rights, catch limits, compensation payments, etc. are emerging. Part 2 will deal with these issues in more detail.

National economy and legal framework

Kenya underwent a profound institutional change in 2010 with the adoption of the new constitution, following devastating post-election violence in 2007 and 2008 (Hicks 2015: 178). At that time, around 1,300 people died and tens of thousands were displaced. This was a decisive turning point in the country's history (ibid.: 178). The new constitution was approved by 67% of the electorate and there was hope that progress would be made in remedying the shortcomings of the government's centralist leadership and economic inequality (ibid.: 178). The new constitution has now set the stage for the long-awaited process of decentralization, which includes the creation of 47 new districts. These are to be given a much greater degree of autonomy (ibid.: 178). According to the Kenyan Human Rights Commission KHRC (2014: 8), the Kenyan constitution provides for both the jurisdiction of international legal instruments recognized by Kenya and the direct application of the general rules of international law. Thus, instruments such as the 'Universal Declaration of Human Rights', 'The International Covenant on Economic Social and Cultural Rights', 'The United Nations Declaration on the Rights of Indigenous People (UNDRIP)' and others, such as, of course, the Constitution of Kenya 2010, are intended to provide a framework to which the government, development partners and economic entrepreneurs should adhere when implementing the LAPSSET project (KHRC 2014: 8). The new constitution guarantees above all economic and social rights, such as the protection of aspects that contribute to people's livelihoods (ibid.: 14). There is also an article that guarantees the right to life. This also includes various elements of life that are related to livelihood, such as land rights, a clean and healthy environment, access to information, etc. (ibid.: 14).

These national guidelines and state laws should serve to protect the interests of the local population. Often, however, the general welfare of the nation and, in this context, the welfare of the whole of East Africa seem to neglect local interests, because otherwise a project like the port of Lamu would be started in a completely different way and the local population would have the opportunity to actually participate, which is not the case (as will be explained later in the second part on the impacts).

During the research I realized that access to information, for example, is far from guaranteed to everyone. For example, newspaper or gazetted articles are often written in English only and not everyone has access to the Internet. One possibility for the fishermen to inform and exchange information, but also to communicate with the authorities, is the recent establishment of *Beach Management Units (BMUs)*. The fishermen are divided into groups according to their place of origin. The BMUs are intended to promote local ownership and participation in the management of fishery resources (WWF Kenya 2011: 21). The Fisheries Department works very closely with the BMUs, which in turn are in close contact with the fishermen. In 2007, the Fisheries Act (Cap. 378) laid down regulations that pave the way for BMUs for every fish landing place along the coast (Musa et al. n.d) The objectives include, amongst others, to 'support the sustainable development of the fisheries sector, [to] help alleviate poverty and improve the welfare and livelihoods of members through improved planning and resource management, good governance, democratic participation and self reliance, [to] strengthen the management of fish-landing sections of the community, including women in the fisheries sector, and [to] prevent or reduce conflicts in the fisheries sector' (Musa et al. n.d.). All persons who are directly or indirectly dependent on the fishing industry for their livelihood are eligible for membership in a BMU. The BMU's area of responsibility is the fish-landing site, which is intended exclusively for the sale of fish and to ensure safe and effective use and management there (Musa et al. n.d.). In an interview with the person who is in charge of the Lamu County Fisheries Department (LCDF), he explained to me that:

'The government needs to link with the community. So the community form the BMUs. Everywhere the fish is landed, there is a committee which is representing the community. If there is an issue, we deal with the BMUs. Because with the BMUs the whole information will spread. So sometimes in a meeting, there is a committee with officials (chairman, vice chair, secretary...). There are 40 BMUs in the whole county. In that case, then 40 people will come. That's how we work with the BMUs. And they are very handy, very instrumental, very supportive. And that's the only way we can bring community and government together. But you know as a government we can't make decisions alone. We have to listen to the public' (Chief Officer of LCDF, Lamu Town)[17].

Part 2: The Mega-Infrastructure Project Lamu Port

The LAPSSET project has multidimensional origins. According to Adrian J. Browne (2015: 7), the port at Lamu and the oil pipelines from southern Sudan to Kenya were proposed as early as the 1970s. But as separate projects. Only years

---

[17] Interview with the author, January 2019.

later did the various components come together under the LAPSSET banner. The idea of a deep-sea port in Lamu developed around 50 years ago, when the only port in Mombasa was overloaded. With its extensive and wide areas, Manda Bay in Lamu was chosen as the ideal location.

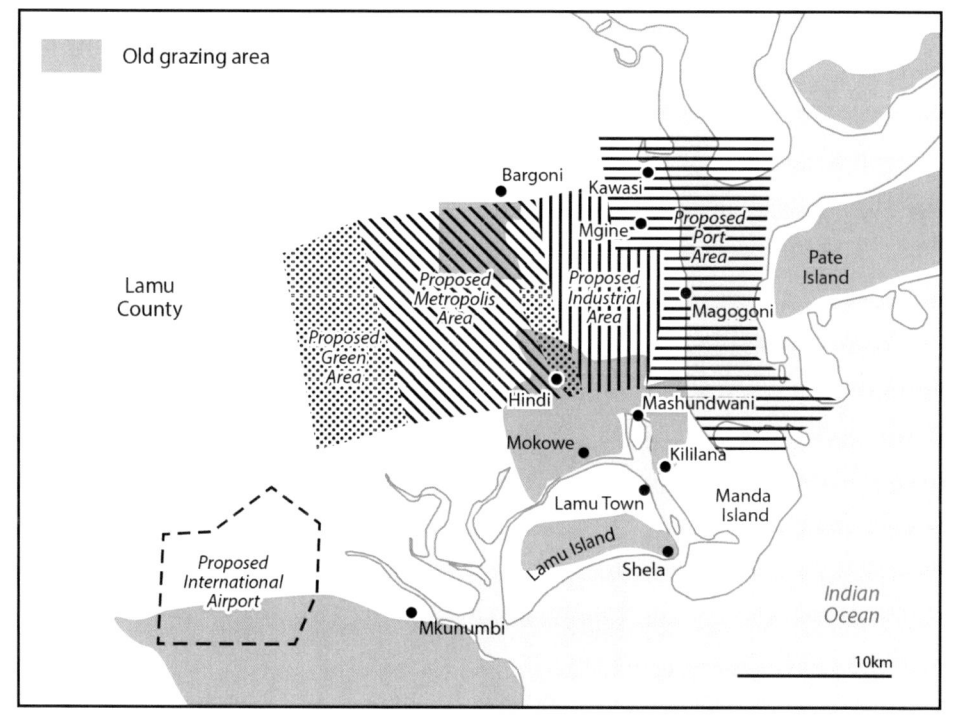

Map 2: Area of the port facility in Lamu. Source: Map compilation and design by Manuel L. K. Abebe (2021), CDE, University of Bern, Bern, Switzerland. Geodata: OpenStreetMap contributors.

In 1975, the first site investigations were completed and it was emphasized that the port could not be legitimized from an economic point of view alone; instead it had 'to be considered as a long-term national asset' (Brownc 2015, as cited in Renardet-Sauti 1977: 13), requiring investment in road construction, railways, livestock, agriculture, industry and fishing. However, knowing that improvements in capacity and efficiency could still be sought in the port of Mombasa, the government invested its funds in this port in 1979. The concept of the port of Manda Bay was thus shelved (ibid.: 13).

After various political and economic changes, the Kenyan government commissioned a LAPSSET feasibility study and master plan in 2010, as well as a detailed plan for the port of Lamu worth USD35 million (ibid.: 20). After the studies were completed and the plans issued, some difficulties arose in the context of the independence of southern Sudan. But in 2012, LAPSSET was officially launched. A year later, with the election of the new president, Uhuru Kenyatta, a government came to power that showed even greater commitment to development and infrastructure projects (ibid.: 20). In April 2013, it became known that a Chinese consortium led by the China Communications Construction Company (CCCC) had been awarded a contract worth USD480 million for the first phase of port construction – the first three berths (ibid.: 20). However, the financing was far from being arranged. It was not clear whether the Kenyan government would be able to finance the first three berths of the port at all, never mind other parts of LAPSSET (ibid.: 20). According to LAPSSET Online[18], 'the first three berths will be fully financed by the government of Kenya' and 'the remaining 29 berths will be financed by private sector investors'. Apparently the financing is still not yet clear. However, the dredging started in October 2016 and is currently ongoing. The first three berths are complete with berth one currently already operating offering cargo trans-shipment.

Fig 3: Construction work in August 2018 in the area of the Lamu port. Source: Flurina Werthmüller.

Environmental and social impacts

'Yes there is change. For fishing, for lobster, for tourists, for turtles. So you see the door from the port. You want to pass. Before the tourists went snorkelling there. Very nice.

---

[18] LAPSSET 2020: Lamu Port. ⟨http://www.lapsset.go.ke/projects/lamu-port/⟩ accessed on 18.09.2020.

Natural. You know? And it's not in the deep sea. It's inside the mangrove. It's very safe. But now the tourists go to the deep sea to snorkel. So there are sharks. They can bite. And they can't see the lobster now. Because the water has changed. It's dirty. Even the house of the lobster. They broke' (Fisherman, on a boat in Lamu[19]).

Whenever I asked the question as to whether people were already feeling the effects of the construction of the port, I received similar answers. Although, according to Save Lamu (2018: 24), the port can improve access to international markets, it will make it more difficult for the local people to earn a living. Furthermore, it is very likely that the pollution will have an impact on the quality of the mangroves. The mangrove forests also provide protection against coastal erosion and tsunamis and feed the marine life. Since the fishing industry is the region's most important economic pillar and only traditional methods of fishing are used, a major intervention such as Lamu Port can have a huge impact on the vulnerable fishing industry.

Chemical pollution and physical industrial activities inevitably result in the emission of pollutants and their accumulation in the sea (KHRC 2014: 20). This will lead to the loss of rare marine life and have a negative impact on the survival of important algae species, which are a food source for many fish species (ibid.: 20). In addition, it is expected that the dredging will decimate fish breeding sites and mangrove forests, thus reducing the regeneration capacity of fish along the channel (ibid.: 20). Once the LAPSSET project is completed, it will probably lead to large-scale environmental pollution, as oil spills can have catastrophic consequences for the local flora and fauna, and also cause direct health problems for humans (ibid.: 27).

Tourism, too, can suffer greatly from the consequences of port construction, as coral reefs are destroyed and the water is polluted, so snorkelling trips can no longer be undertaken. Fishing and tourism are closely linked, however, as fishermen are dependent on local restaurants and hotels.

The biggest challenge is the seasonal dependency. During the rainy season between April and October, the open sea is too dangerous for the fishermen with their small motorboats or non-motorized sailing dhows, so they shift to canals protected from the weather during these periods. If all fishermen are fishing in the canals during this period, the competition for the resource will be greater. Now with the new Lamu Port, a huge part of the fishing grounds will be inaccessible and the ecosystems will be destroyed by pollution beyond these restricted areas. This means that the competition between fishermen will increase and they will be forced to move to the open sea during this time and thus expose themselves to the dangers of the open sea.

There are also many fishermen who are specialized in prawn, lobster and crab fishing. These are often found in the mangroves siutuated in the canals and have

---

[19] Interview with the author, January 2019.

to be partly caught with the diving method. But since a large proportion of the mangroves around the port have now been deforested and the water become dirty across wide areas, they are no longer able to see anything in the polluted water and the stocks are declining. I was also told that a lot of turtles have already died as a result of environmental pollution.

Due to missing information, rumours and discussions have emerged: for example, regarding the working situation at the port. Some believe that many young educated people from Lamu have the chance to get a job at the port. Others think that there are already people from Nairobi working at the port and that the people of Lamu are unable to get a job because they are not sufficiently educated. One interview partner commented:

'We have educated people also nowadays, we have master's people, we have degreed people, we have diploma people but if you go right now to the port there is nobody from the coast in a high position. Just low position. Cleaning, cooking... How come we have a master's and we can't work? We need to lead ourselves also' (fisherman, on a boat in Lamu)[20].

During various conversations I noticed that the relationship between the Lamunians and the Kenyan state is difficult. They do not feel like Kenyans, but oppressed and excluded by the central government:

'Because Kenya doesn't know us. Kenya is Nairobi. But coast people are not Kenya. We just say that people call us Kenyan but we are not Kenyan, we are Lamunian. Yeah, because whatever they do, whatever they decide, whatever they get, it's not for us. It's just for them. No help from the government of Kenya. They always want to catch us with small stuff' (Fisherman, on a boat in Lamu)[21].

Another interaction partner remarked:

'The government especially don't like the Muslim people. They say they can't think. They don't like the people from Lamu or the coast people' (Fisherman, on a boat in Lamu)[22].

Laher (2011: 3) also writes that the Kenyan government is acting against the interests of the people in Lamu. Therefore, it is not surprising that many people show fear regarding Lamu Port. In the past it has been shown that the Kenyan government has not given much time to the concerns and needs of the Lamu people. Thus, most residents would expect LAPSSET to signal a final takeover of their land. That would be a form of internal colonization by the Kenyan state (ibid.: 3).

---

[20] Interview with the author, January 2019.
[21] Interview with the author, February 2019.
[22] Interview with the author, February 2019.

Local and NGO strategies

The strategies presented in this chapter are largely based on newspaper articles and have been supplemented with data from my own research. In their strategy, the fishing community focus above all on a trial in court, because it would be possible to achieve something. The discussions are mainly about the once promised compensation payments. In its environmental and social impact study for the construction of the port in Lamu, the Kenyan Ministry of Transport emphasizes that a detailed resettlement/compensation action plan has been drawn up and will be implemented before the start of the project (2013: 4). The compensation and resettlement will be carried out by the Ministry of Transport in accordance with the Resettlement Action Plan and with the support of the local authorities. However, since the report was published in 2013 and the construction of the port started in 2012, this is a major contradiction. To this day, the discussions revolve around possible compensation payments. Apparently such payments were promised before construction started, but so far nothing has happened. According to my interview partners, the negotiations have been resumed several times. There are also rumours about these compensation payments. Everyone has somehow heard about them, but nobody really knows how high the amount should be and who will get these payments and when. According to the fisheries departement of Lamu, the compensation payments are very difficult to implement:

'Now we are having the Lamu port. And when this comes, it will change the scenery of fishing, the areas where fishermen fish. Also, they require to get compensated. It's a process. Us as government have to fight until those people who are doing the port compensate them. There is a difference in compensation between water and land. There are people who come to evaluate, to value what is going to be lost, what is going to be impacted by the project. It's easier to value land, because they can see it with their eyes. If people cut forests, you can see that damage. If it's a farmland where somebody has to do some agriculture, crops and they remove it or if it's livestock which is displaced, people can see the number. It is difficult to convince people about fish. What they can see, after all, is just water. So sometimes I tell them: you know one day I will blow a whistle and then all the water will go and then you will see the amount of fish which is there. And then I'll call the water back again. But you can understand what is inside there. So, some of these things are a bit tricky but we are trying to tackle them. And you know also compensation in land is a bit easier. If you are going to be compensated for one hectare of land, the market price is known. But in the sea, how do you determine the hectarage? On the land people have got their land. There is a title. In the sea nobody can claim an issue. Everybody can fish anywhere. The water is for everyone. So we are trying to quantify and to work on that' (Head of LCFD, Lamu Town)[23].

---

[23] Interview with the author, January 2019.

Moreover, the government wants to provide the fishermen with larger vessels and more modern equipment so that they have the opportunity to fish further out in the open sea:

'Yes, as compensation we want them to get bigger mechanized boats, so that they can go deep in the sea and leave this place to the port. And also give this place time to recover. And, also, they will get more big fish' (Head of LCDF, Lamu Town)[24].

Various online articles by the daily nation and organizations such as Natural justice and Save Lamu report on the negotiations of the promised compensation payments for the fishermen in Lamu. According to the Daily nation (Kazungu 2018), the fishermen, of whom at least 4,000 were affected and displaced by the construction of the port, would now ask the government to increase the compensation payment from USD16.5 million to USD28 million. apparently, on 1 May 2018, the Malindi high court ordered the national government to compensate the fishermen with USD16.5 million after deciding that the project did not meet the basic constitutional and legal requirements. The construction of the port project violated the cultural rights of the community and the right to a clean and healthy environment. however, representatives of the fishing community believe that the USD16.5 million is not enough (ibid.).

'We urge the government to increase the cash from USD16.5 million to USD28 million, so that each of us can get at least USD5,600. With such an amount, we will be able to start other ventures to sustain our lives,' said a spokesperson for the fishing community (Kazungu 2018).

They also call on the government to ensure proper identification and verification of all genuine fishermen affected by the project before the money is released, because they have experienced a scenario in which compensation payments to impostors are made at the expense of the actual beneficiaries. In addition, community-based organizations in the community have called on the government to invite financial experts to meet with fishermen who expect compensation before the money is released. Activists from Save Lamu, the Lamu youth alliance and lamu marine forum are fighting for fishermen's rights. According to the daily nation report it is important that fishermen receive financial advice on how to use the compensation money wisely (Kazungu 2018).

In July 2018, Baraka FM (Nema 2018) reported that the task force to compensate fishermen affected by the development of Lamu port had decided that comparable benefits in kind would be paid instead of cash. This means that the compensation should be limited to tools, training and any other formal support to adapt to fishing in the deeper sea.

'We won't take anything less than the cash. We went to court and won fairly and were awarded compensation, which is to be paid to us in cold cash and not

---

[24] Interview with the author, January 2019.

what these people are trying to tell us. As it is right now, most fishing grounds are already decimated and many of us are no longer interested in fishing anymore. We want the money so we can pursue other things. Fishing is dead and they know it' (Somo, chairman of the Lamu BMU (Nema 2018)).

Such statements have been confirmed in my research in Lamu. The aim of the fishing community is to receive cash as compensation and that is what they are fighting for. However, it looks as though there are opportunities to make a legal difference and get what they were originally promised. The material compensation is not enough for them, because a future in fishing is sometimes no longer seen at all. Cash could be used to set up a new business. In addition, it became clear to me that with the help of local organizations such as save Lamu or the state institution beach management unit BMU, there are already a number of ways to defend themselves. Through such institutions there is also the opportunity to communicate and mediate and finally to achieve something on a legal basis.

State and company strategy

Current discourses on the future of Africa are very ambivalent. Detlef Müller-Mahn describes this in such a way that 'on the one hand, a deeply entrenched Afro pessimism continues to view Africa as a "lost continent" and hopeless case for international development. On the other hand, optimistic outlooks have become more prominent over the past decade, expressed in notions such as "Africa rising" and "continent of opportunities" that envision African economies as powerhouses for a stumbling world economy' (2019: 2). This optimistic development and growth discourse is driven by institutional allies such as the IMF, the African Development Bank and other international financial organizations. Kenya Vision 2030, with LAPSSET as one of the key projects, is being promoted by the Kenyan government and the LAPSSET Corridor Development Authority (which was established by the Kenyan government in 2013) as just such a highly promising and even sustainable development project. For example, the LAPSSET Corridor Development Authority writes in a presentation: 'It is envisioned that the LAPSSET corridor project will triple investment and employment space and opportunities in the country, increase the habitable and productive area and drive the economy into sustainable double-digit growth' (2016: 17).

LAPSSET is also mentioned in the 'Implementation of the Agenda 2030 for Sustainable Development in Kenya', published in 2017 by the Ministry of Devolution and Planning, under goal 9 of the United Nations Sustainable Development Goals: 'Build Resilient Infrastructure, Promote Inclusive and Sustainable Industrialization and Foster Innovation' (UN Online)[25]. In addition to the reports mentioned above, there are many others that are strategically being used by the authorities to legitimize a project such as LAPSSET nationally and internation-

---

[25] United Nations: Goal 9. ⟨https://sdgs.un.org/goals/goal9⟩ accessed on 15.07.2020.

ally as a positive and future-oriented project for the whole of East Africa and even beyond.

Conclusion

Development corridors are presented and enacted as 'dream landscapes of modernity' (Müller-Mahn 2019: 3). Because they appear attractive to actors such as investors, political decision-makers and, in part, the general public, they are decisive instruments for shaping the future of rural Africa (ibid.: 3). However, it is often forgotten or ignored that in the implementation of these projects, of course some profit but others suffer.

In this article I examined the background and impacts of Lamu Port as one of the key projects of LAPSSET. My research on site has shown that this project is destroying a sustainable fishery and undermining a local common property system. After the launch of the project, great development promises were made, including for local people. Thus, hopes and expectations were raised. But now, seven years later, fishermen and inhabitants of Lamu are disappointed and fear for their future as promises of compensation for the loss of their fishery commons by the new port do not materialize. Therefore, local people in Lamu are disappointed and angry. The case of Lamu Port clearly involves an 'enchantment of infrastructure' (see Harvey/Knox 2012). But now people are becoming sceptical on a local level as well and are struggling to be recognized. They are experiencing seascape grabbing, resource grabbing and commons grabbing, and are partly confronted with the anti-politics machine (see James Ferguson 1994). The initial enchantment has turned into a disenchantment.

The community is looking for ways to defend itself and to enforce its rights to its common fisheries, but negotiations about compensation for water and fisheries, which are now considered to be state property, are very difficult as water cannot be calculated in the same way as land. Fish stocks are not visible and not static either. But at the very least, this resistance by locally organized groups could lead to a certain degree of success in which the fishing communities can stand up in court for their compensation payments.

The construction of the port project violated the cultural rights of the community and the right to a clean and healthy environment. One interviewee commented during a conversation that if so many negative effects are already being felt now, how can it be that the project will bring good things in the future? And now that the port is only in the construction phase, what will it be like when it is completed and put into service?

At the moment, the biggest concern of the fishing community is the pollution of the environment and therefore the destruction of the fish stock, and that as a result their livelihood will disappear. Many do not even see themselves as part of

Kenya or feel disadvantaged and treated unfairly by the authorities. The discourse about these internal differences, that the government will oppress the people on the coast and not support them, including because of religious differences, is very present in Lamu. A kind of internal colonization, as described by Rodwan Laher (2011), is perceived in the same way by the local population, according to my experience.

From the discussions with the people in Lamu, it became clear that many would approve of the project if at least the people of Lamu were involved and if there were real new opportunities for them.

The Lamu Port mega-infrastructure project as part of LAPSSET creates new frontiers and spaces, new constellations emerge, and existing institutions and common property systems are undermined. The situation leads to a re-evaluation of resources, ignoring and excluding the local population. They are deprived of their bargaining power and are therefore not able to minimize the negative impacts. But the people of Lamu are not completely powerless. By organizing themselves into groups, the protest persists, and this is a means of self-defence. The environmental destruction caused by the port project ends up in a counter discourse to the development and sustainability discourse propagated by the initiators, which legitimizes the project. A sustainable infrastructure should lead to a better life with many advantages. But the contrary is happening. It is an uncertain and precarious situation.

Glossary

BMU	Beach Management Unit
CCCC	China Communications Construction Company
GDP	Gross Domestic Product
IMF	International Monetary Fund
KHRC	Kenyan Human Rights Commission
LAPSSET	Lamu Port South Sudan Ethiopia Transport Corridor
LCFD	Lamu County Fisheries Department
NGO	Non-governmental Organization
SDGs	Sustainable Development Goals
UNDRIP	United Nations Declaration on the Rights of Indigenous People
UNESCO	United Nations Educational, Scientific and Cultural Organization
USD	US Dollar
WWF	World Wide Fund for Nature

References

Aloo, Peninah 2000: Marine resources. In: Hoorweg, Jan., Foeken, Dick and R.A. Obudho (eds.). Kenya Coast Handbook. Culture, Resources and Development in the East African Littoral. Hamburg: LIT Verlag, 43-59.

Browne, Adrian J. 2015: LAPSSET. The History and Politics of an Eastern African Megaproject. London: Rift Valley Institute.

Degen Allan A., Hoorweg Jan. and Barasa C.C. Wangila 2010: Fish traders in artisanal fisheries on the Kenyan coast. Journal of Enterprising Communities. People and Places in the Global Economy 4 (4): 296-311.

Ferguson, James 1994: The Anti-Politics Machine. Development, Depoliticisation and Bureaucratic Power in Lesotho. Cambridge: Cambridge University Press.

Haller, T. 2019a: Towards a new institutional political ecology: how to marry external effects, institutional change and the role of power and ideology in commons studies. In: Haller, T. Breu, T., de Moor, T. Rohr, C., Znoj, H. (eds.). The Commons in a Glocal World: Global Connections and Local Responses. London: Routledge, 90-120.

Haller, T. 2019b: The different meanings of land in the Age of Neoliberalism: theoretical reflections on commons and resilience grabbing from a social anthropological perspective. Land 8 (7): 104.

Hardin, G. 1968: The tragedy of the commons. Science 162 (3859): 1243-1248.

Harvey P. and H. Knox 2012: The enchantments of infrastructure. Mobilities 7 (4): 521-536.

Hicks, Celeste 2015: Africa's New Oil. Power, Pipelines and Future Fortunes. London: Zed Books Ltd, 178-181.

Hoorweg Jan, Foeken D.W.J. and Robert A. Obudho 2000: Kenya Coast handbook: culture, resources and development in the East African littoral. Hamburg: LIT Verlag.

Hoorweg Jan, Wangila Barasa C.C. and Allan Degen 2009: Artisanal Fishers on the Kenyan Coast. Houshold Livelihoods and Marine Ressource Management. Leiden: Koninklijke Brill NV.

KHRC, Kenya Human Rights Commission 2014: Forgotten in the Scramble for Lamu: A Position Paper on the LAPPSET Project in the Case of the Aweer and the Fisherfolk. Nairobi: KHRC.

Laher, Rodwan 2011: Policy Brief. Resisting Development in Kenya's Lamu District: Postcolonial Reading. Africa Institute of South Africa: Briefing Number 48.

Ministry of Transport 2013: Environmental and Social Impact Assessment Study Report for Construction of the First Three Berths of the Proposed Lamu Port and Associated Infrastructure. Final Report. Nairobi: Ministry of Transport.

Rasmussen, Mattias B. and Christian Lund 2017: Reconfiguring Frontier Spaces: The territorialization of resource control. In: World Development 101 (2018): 388-399.

Save Lamu 2018: Biocultural Community Protocol for Lamu County. The Lamu Indigenous Community and their Rights to the Preservation of their Natural Resources, Cultures, Heritage and Management of Biodiversity. Lamu: Save Lamu.

Taylor, Ken and Lennon, Jane 2011: Cultural landscapes: A bridge between culture and nature? International Journal of Heritage Studies 17 (6): 537-554.

WWF Kenya 2011: Lamu Kenya. Biodiversity & Livelihood Atlas. Printed Journal (n.p).

Online Reports

Abdullah, A., S. Ali Hamad, A. Mbarouk Ali and R.G. Wild 2000: Misali Island, Tanzania: An open access resource redifined. ⟨https://dlc.dlib.indiana.edu/dlc/handle/10535/429⟩ Accessed on 25.09.2020.

Gabler Wirtschaftslexikon 2018: Definition von Regionalentwicklung. Autoren: Hans-Dieter Haas and Simon-Martin Neumair. ⟨https://wirtschaftslexikon.gabler.de/definition/regionalentwicklung-46534/version-269812⟩ Accessed on 08.04.2020.

Kabiru, Angela 2014: Island in distress: Can Lamu sustain its tourism industry? ⟨https://www.academia.edu/2060731/Island_in_Distress_Can_Lamu_Manage_its_Tourism_Industry⟩ Accessed on 13.03.2020.

Kazungu, Kalume 2018: Fishermen in Lapsset zones demand more compensation. ⟨https://mobile.nation.co.ke/counties/Fishermen-in-Lapsset-zones-demand-more-compensation/1950480-4666332-item-1-2ovmo5/index.html accessed on 20.05.2019⟩ Accessed on 03.07.2020.

Lamu County Government 2020: Fisheries, co-operative & livestock. ⟨http://lamu.go.ke/fisheries-livestock/⟩ Accessed on 13.03.2020.

LAPSSET Corridor Development Authority 2016: Brief on LAPSSET Corridor Project. ⟨http://vision2030.go.ke/inc/uploads/2018/05/LAPSSET-Project-Report-July-2016.pdf⟩ PDF Document. Accessed on 06.03.2020.

LAPSSET Online 2017: ⟨http://www.lapsset.go.ke.⟩ Accessed on 07.03.2020.

Malleret_King, Delphine 2003: FMSP Project R8196: Understanding Fisheries Associated Livelihoods and the Constraints to their Development in Kenya and Tanzania. Annex 2: Livelihood appraisal. ⟨https://assets.publishing.service.gov.uk/media/57a08d04ed915d622c001709/R8196c.pdf⟩ PDF Document. Accessed on 13.03.2020.

Musa, Fatuma. et al. (n.d): ?BMU's: Beach Management Units. Building Capacity for Coastal Communities to Manage Marine Resources in Kenya. ⟨https://www.iucn.org/sites/dev/files/import/downloads/bmus2.pdf⟩. PDF Document. Accessed on 13.03.2020.

Müller-Mahn, Detlef 2019: Envisioning African futures: development corridors as dreamscapes of modernit. In: Geoforum. ⟨https://doi.org/10.1016/j.geoforum.2019.05.027⟩ Accessed on 06.04.2020.

Nema, Natasha 2018: Lamu fishermen reject compensation from Lapsset. ⟨http://barakafm.org/2018/07/23/lamu-fishermen-reject-compensation-from-lapsset/⟩ Accessed on 20.05.2019.

Rodden, Valerie 2014: Analyzing the Dynamics of the Artisan Fishing Industry and LAPSSET Port in Lamu. Independent Study Project (ISP) Collection. ⟨https://digitalcollections.sit.edu/isp_collection/1765⟩. PDF Document. Accessed on 20.05.2019.

Save Lamu 2013: Save Lamu Comments on ESIA Study Report of the Construction of the First Three Berths. ⟨https://www.savelamu.org/save-lamu-comments-on-esia-study-report-of-the-construction-of-the-first-three-berths/⟩ Accessed on 06.04.2020.

Sena, Kanyinke 2012: Lamu Port-South Sudan-Ethiopia Transport Corridor (LAPSSET) and indigenous peoples in Kenya. Report on Expert Mission by a Member of the UN Permanent Forum on Indigenous Issues. ⟨https://www.iwgia.org/images/publications/0599_LAPSSET_report.pdf⟩ PDF Document. Accessed on 12.03.2018.

Spiegel Online 2011: Mord und Entführungen. Touristen flüchten von Lamu-Inseln in Kenia. ⟨https://www.spiegel.de/reise/aktuell/mord-und-entfuehrungen-touristen-fluechten-von-lamu-inseln-in-kenia-a-790114.html⟩ Accessed on 06.04.2020.

UNESCO World Heritage Center Online 2020: Lamu Old Town.⟨https://whc.unesco.org/en/list/1055 accessed on 09.03.2020⟩ Accessed on 23.06.2020.

"Whose Growth, Whose Loss?" The 'Southern Agricultural Growth Corridor of Tanzania' (SAGCOT) and Impacts on Smallholders in Iringa District.

Sandro Fiechter, Felix Gallauer Alves de Souza, Désirée Gmür and Belinda Bösch, Institute of Social Anthropology, University of Bern, Switzerland

Introduction

Tanzania is the focus of private companies, international donor organizations and governments and their plans for 'African Agricultural Growth Corridors' (AAGC) – huge areas of arable land made accessible and valuable for investments through various infrastructures. The Southern Agricultural Growth Corridor of Tanzania (SAGCOT), initiated in 2010 as a public-private partnership (PPP), is an example of such a corridor project in line with the World Bank's 'Pathway to Sustainable Green Growth' referred to as 'inclusive green growth' (IGG) (Fay and World Bank 2012). Its aim is to attract international investments and to integrate the local, smallholder-based agricultural sector into the global economy while at the same time combating poverty and ensuring environmental sustainability. The area of the SAGCOT corridor extends over one-third of the country's territory and is segmented into six clusters with different infrastructures to support the investments in agriculture in the surrounding areas (Map 1).

Tanzania's agriculture sector is deeply marked by its colonial past, a socialist development path after independence and a neoliberal policy since the 1980s, which has seen the introduction of a large number of public-private partnerships since the 2000s. Questions of land rights and the distribution of resources are historically central factors and still contested issues in Tanzanian society today. Therefore, SAGCOT has received international attention both in the media and from scholars, including discussions of ongoing and predicted outcomes such as dispossession vis-à-vis fragile land rights (e.g. Bluwstein et al. 2018; Maganga et al. 2016; Sulle 2020); SAGCOT's spatial vision and its underlying idea as a development corridor (e.g. Dannenberg, Revilla Diez, and Schiller 2018; Steffens 2016; Steffens, Hartmann, and Dannenberg 2019); legal aspects, discourses and elements of legitimization (Bergius 2014; Bergius and Buseth 2019; Bergius, Ben-

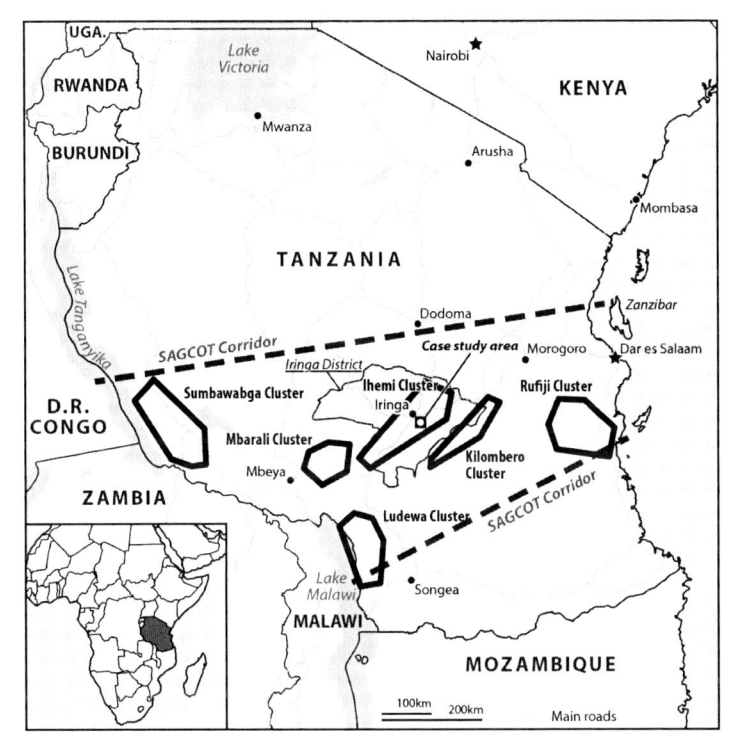

Map 1: Map of Tanzania with the corridor area and the six clusters. Source: Map compilation and design by Manuel L. K. Abebe (2021), CDE, University of Bern, Bern, Switzerland.

jaminsen, and Widgren 2018; Buseth 2017; Engström and Hajdu 2019; Haudenschild 2018; Sulle 2020) and rising pastoralist evictions within SAGCOT regions as historical trajectories of farmer-herder conflicts (e.g. Bergius et al. 2020; Maganga et al. 2016). Additionally, research projects have been developed with the aim of understanding development initiatives such as SAGCOT in France (Université Bordeaux) and Germany, the latter being a collaborative project within German and African universities.[1]

To discuss SAGCOT in the context of mega-infrastructure projects, this chapter analyses SAGCOT as a multi-sited 'broker and catalyst'[2] of numerous development programmes proliferating different 'resilient development narratives' (Engström and Hajdu 2019) and a 'green modernization development discourse' (Bergius and Buseth 2019) with the aim of 'enchanting' (Harvey and Knox 2012) smallholders and donors. Persistently and despite counterevidence, these narratives and discourses convey the image of an agriculture from which everyone benefits (Engström and Hajdu 2019). In our view, these narratives provide devel-

---
[1] https://www.crc228.de/ (last access: 14.07.2022).
[2] https://sagcot.co.tz/index.php/en/about/who-we-are (last access: 14.07.2022).

opment initiatives like SAGCOT with the necessary legitimacy and the possibility of increasing bargaining power (Haller 2019: 91).

We explore the question of how SAGCOT in particular co-opt donors and how it affects the living conditions of the local population and therefore what contradictions are revealed between the narratives of investors and the government and local experiences.

With regard to the specific local impact of investments, we draw on research carried out in late 2019 in the context of the Anchor Farm Project initiated by the Clinton Development Initiative (CDI) near the village of Mtitu in the Ihemi Cluster. The case study shows that the availability of, and access to land and resources for the communities is in many cases severely restricted by large-scale investments that cause a variety of further impacts. It is also shown that many smallholders do not have any knowledge of SAGCOT, show no interest in it or re-orient themselves due to bad experiences with large-scale agriculture investments. This situation is complemented by findings from other field studies that we have considered for this chapter. We have completed our analysis with a detailed study of the official SAGCOT website, Twitter accounts and other documents.

Part 1: Tanzania and its history, institutional changes and evolution of land rights

The recent World Bank report on Tanzania states that the country has recorded 'solid growth and reduced poverty substantially' (World Bank 2017). At 6.5%, the annual rate of economic growth ranks amongst the highest in Sub-Saharan Africa. However, while the population is growing at around 3% per year, the per capita income is only growing at 3.5%. Therefore, poverty is prevalent in (most of) the population (2017). Tanzanians are still heavily land dependent, since agriculture provides the means for their livelihood. Tanzanian agriculture has remained the main employer for the Tanzanian labour force (70%) and accounts for 24% of GDP, 30% of export and 65% of raw materials for domestic industry (Mkonda 2016).

Pre-colonial and colonial history

Tanzania's history is a portrayal of the foreign interest in Tanzania since colonial times. The country itself is very diverse and made up of more than 120 cultural communities belonging to four main ethnic families: Khoisan, Bantu, Nilotic and Cushitic (Gastorn 2008: 21ff.). The Bantu groups (Haya, Makonde, Njamwesi, Sukuma, Chagga, etc.) make up the majority with approximately 60% of the population (Weltalmanach 2018). Before colonial intervention, the general structure of landholding was based on customary law, and elders of an ethnic group controlled the land of their territory. Despite there being many differences between groups and regions, they had communal land tenure with all grazing lands being common property (Gastorn 2008: 22). Between the eighth and fifteenth centuries, Arabs and Persians set up trading posts on the coast, and as a result of the social interaction, Swahili culture was formed. In 1884, Chancellor Otto von Bismarck declared East Africa a German Protectorate, resulting in the German colonial rule until 1918 (2008: 23).

Direct German rule saw a racist combination of commercial agriculture and violence, which exploited local populations' workforces on plantations and small-scale farms for the export of newly introduced cash crops to Europe. Cash crops consisted of coffee, rubber, cotton and cactus sisal, with sisal being the most valuable. This colonial extraction of resources and labour depended on a dense infrastructure network, where both railways and roads enabled the transportation of primary resources from the interior to the coastal cities, from where they were later shipped to Europe (Haudenschild 2018).[3] The German rule represents the first disruption of customary tenure and administration principles in this period. Today, these principles can still be found in the requirement to occupy land to prove ownership, and in the fact that undeveloped land has no value and that natives only have user rights or require documentation to prove ownership (Gastorn 2008: 25).

Under British indirect rule (1919-1961) a new governance system was implemented, which granted customary authorities a limited amount of power. In 1923, occupied and unoccupied land in Tanganyika was declared public land. Control and power to issue a *certificate of occupancy* were in the hands of the Governor. These rights of occupancy did not exceed 99 years, but foreigners provided with granted rights of occupancy were treated as superior to the customary land rights of the Tanzanian population (Gastorn 2008; Rwegasira 2012).

In 1946, the United Africa Company (a subsidiary of today's Unilever)[4] implemented the Tanganyika Groundnut Scheme: initially planned to supply the world market's need for vegetable oil with an expected outcome of 600,000 tons of peanuts annually, at the end of its shutdown in 1951, more than £35 million had been spent on a scheme 'that imported more groundnuts as seed than it actually harvested' (2006: 208), rendering it one of the biggest development failures

---

[3] The *Maji Maji* rebellion – a revolt against the German colonial state in 1905 – is considered one of the most important anti-colonial movements and a remarkable response to colonial oppression, not least because of the exceptional unification of different ethnic groups (Monson 1998: 97). The rebellion did initially achieve success but was then defeated in 1907 by the Germans using machine guns and scorched-earth tactics (Haudenschild 2018; Monson 1998).

[4] Back then, Unilever was represented in almost all British colonies in Africa and today still manages offices and large plantations of 3400 hectares in Tanzania. Unilever is even the largest tea producer in Tanzania and one of the key partners in the SAGCOT initiative (Haudenschild 2018: 46).

As plentiful as the reasons for its disaster were,[5] the project had already shown the pattern of legitimization through the discourse of development. Today, many characteristics of the Groundnut Scheme can be found in the design of the SAGCOT corridor: both projects were launched to facilitate crop for export and have been using a narrative of development and modernization through commercial and large-scale agricultural projects, which with their reference to the embedment in international markets should provide benefits for everyone (Haudenschild 2018: 43). Such promises of economic connection, speed and political integration through the deployment of infrastructure have outlasted its failures more than 60 years ago. Harvey and Knox have described these affective forces of infrastructure as catalysts for development as 'enchantments', focusing not only on the rhetorical narrative forces of said promises, but also on the traces their failure leaves as 'lived, material encounters' with the missing delivery on an initial promise (Harvey and Knox 2012). Similarly, the development apparatus has been analysed as a 'desiring machine', which works through the gap between the generation of hope through promises and their banalization through feeble realization (De vries 2007).

After independence

In 1964, the Republic of Zanzibar and Tanganyika together formed the United Republic of Tanzania (Ingle 1972: 2). Under Nyerere, Tanzania's president from 1964 to 1985, the *Arusha Declaration* was passed, which formalized the socialist development path of *Ujamaa*. This development path envisioned: firstly, the nationalization of industries and agriculture; and secondly, within the latter, a transformation through the promotion of state farming schemes and small-scale peasant production. The idea of 'Ujamaa'[6] was the allocation of all people to village communities. The resettlement programme started in 1968, and by 1976, nearly the entire rural population of Tanzania had been resettled in roughly 8,000 villages (Grawert 2009: 211), with peasants and pastoralists alike forced to relocate to communal villages (Gastorn 2008: 38).[7] In 1967, the Land Acquisition Act was established in which the customary land rights of wealthier farmers were not questioned but resettled farmers had to move to peripheral land. This situation then led to landless households, land disputes and land degradation because of intensified

---

[5] Rizzo (2006) lists as the most important reasons for the scheme's failure both the shortage of labour and disagreements between colonial administration and scheme managers, while Coulson lists a lack of planning and technical assistance (Coulson 1982).

[6] This process of speeding up rural development is also known as the 'villagization programme' (Gastorn 2008: 38), 'ujamaa vijijini' or 'Operation Villagization' (Grawert 2009: 203).

[7] The ignorance of pastoralists' land rights and the restriction of grazing lands to tillers made the pastoralists' way of living unprofitable. In particular, the restriction of daily and seasonal movements and the increase of population and livestock in villages led to competition for natural resources (Gastorn 2008: 39).

land use (Gastorn 2008: 39). The villagization programme forced the settlement of farmers at permanent water sources and destocking of pastoralists' livestock because of limited land resources, whereas in return for agricultural development, land was extracted (2008: 40).

Liberalization

In 1981, after a severe economic, social and political crisis, the World Bank released its report "Accelerated Development for Africa: An Agenda for Africa", and with it, the Structural Adjustment Programmes (SAPs) (Haudenschild 2018). The goals of the SAPs were 'to implement the idea that an individualized system is the most appropriate system of tenure to enhance investment in land' (Gastorn 2008: 41), thereby blaming Ujamaa for the crisis. From 1986 onwards, private and foreign investments in combination with a land law reform to property rights were encouraged,[8] leading to continuous land grabs in the rural areas by the political elite (Brockington and Igoe 1999: 12). In order to further facilitate domestic and foreign investments, institutional and legal frameworks had to be adapted. In 1997 followed the ratification of the Tanzania Investment Act, which involved the implementation of the Tanzania Investment Centre (TIC). The centre's purpose is a one-stop shop for investors, where all necessary approvals and permits can be obtained, derivative land rights are granted, while maintaining a land bank: 'idle' village land should be added to the land of former state farms already available for investments (Gmür 2019; Sulle and Nelson 2009).

Geography, environment and ecosystems

Tanzania is located in eastern Africa and covers an area of 947,303 km^2, with 57,310,000 inhabitants and a population density of 60 people per square kilometre. The capital city is Dodoma, while the seat of government is in Dar es Salaam (Weltalmanach 2018). Tanzania is a federal and constitutional republic and is divided into 30 regions and 169 districts. Among these districts, 135 are rural and therefore administered by village councils or township authorities, and the other 34 are urban and administered by city, municipal or town councils. Tanzania is located close to the equator, but due to its topography the climatic conditions vary from a tropical climate in the coastal area to Alpine deserts with Mount Kilimanjaro and Mount Meru. SAGCOT is located in the southern part of Tanzania and covers about 300,000 km^2 from the Zambian, Malawian and Congolese borders to the Indian Ocean (Mendelsohn, Robertson, and Jarvis 2014: 4ff.). As outlined in the following chapters, SAGCOT materializes as regional clusters, whereby

---

[8] As a study by the Land Commission in 1994 has shown, the majority of Tanzanians were not asking for individual titling, but in fact demanding a democratization of the land tenure system with more local control over their resources, or to commonly hold village land (Greco 2015, 2016).

the value chains of agricultural production are united in smaller, regional hubs and all of Tanzania's major centres (Dar es Salaam, Morogoro, Iringa, Mbeya and Sumbawanga) are included. In the following, we'll focus on the Ihemi Cluster, which covers Iringa Urban District, part of Iringa Rural, Mufindi and Kilolo Districts. The Cluster consists of physically and agroecologically diverse regions: Iringa City as a hub to Dar es Salaam and Mbeya located in the centre, the highlands at the southern end with the Udzungwa Mountains at the south-eastern edge and the lowlands at the northern end with the Ruaha National Park towards the north-west. Therefore, the Cluster's climate is heterogeneous, with rainfall patterns varying between the regions. The Ihemi Cluster is part of the Great Ruaha River catchment (Milder, Hart, and Buck 2013).

The area of the case studies: Iringa region as part of the Ihemi Cluster

Previously, the Iringa region with its semi-arid conditions has been sparsely populated. However, in the past two decades in particular, the region's population has dramatically increased, as the Southern Highlands in general have attracted many groups in search of both investment opportunities[9] and labour, subsistence and pastures.[10] The population today can be described as heterogeneous, consisting of various ethnic groups. These ethnic groups include: the Hehe, who consider themselves as indigenous to the region; the Bena, who migrated from the neighbouring Njombe region; and a number of minorities of other ethnic origins, among whom, in terms of land right issues, Maasai herders from the Dodoma and Arusha regions are the most important (Odgaard 2002).[11]

In pre-colonial times, the Hehe lived in small, scattered settlements and the emphasis on livestock keeping was a reason for frequent movements within the region. As long as there was enough land available, the Hehe headmen were authorized to distribute user rights to as much land as could be cultivated both to Hehe and to people from other ethnic groups (Odgaard 2002: 77). As such, land tenure

---

[9] Nindi (1998) analysed past farming systems and resulting social stratification within the Iringa district.

[10] Susan Charnley (1997) called these displacements within Tanzania with special regard to the immigration of northern pastoralist groups into the Usangu Plains (Mbarali district) the 'cascade effect', thereby integrating long-term consequences of environmental displacement. The spread of rural capitalism within the colonial context has led to unfavourable environmental and social conditions for many groups and regions. However, migration as a solution has proven to cause environmental and social problems in new areas, as resource-related problems are simply being transferred, translated into new forms and amplified. Thus, in the Tanzanian context, environmentally induced migration tends to cascade.

[11] These names, such as the Hehe, Bena, Maasai etc., are being used by the authors in the knowledge that these groups are neither static nor homogeneous. Rather, such names and ascriptions have been constructed with colonial expansion. However, as these groups do use these names in a self-identifying way while referring to a specific set of norms and values, we decided to include such names (cf. Odgaard 2002).

was handled as common property in the form of clan land and related common-pool resources (Haller et al. 2019: 149). Besides communal land use rights, both Hehe and *Bena* are entitled to property in their own right, but such individualized rights are embedded in lineage and clan common-property institutions (2019: 149). However, as seen in the previous chapters, the Southern Highlands have been the target of a number of agricultural development programmes both during colonial times and after independence, which resulted in significant changes not only in agricultural practices and demographics, but also in the institutional settings concerning the access and use of continuously scarce resources. Therefore, the management of land and other common-pool resources such as water, pastures and forests tends to be very complex in the region, as they are embedded both in customary and statutory law and expressed in dynamic mixtures of 'customary' and 'modern' rights (Odgaard 2002).

Depending on the agroecological conditions and the composition of the population, people in the Iringa region base their livelihood on a combination of livestock keeping and cultivation (Gmür 2019). With the region being semi-arid, the vegetation can show strong spatial and temporal variation, so in order to maintain production for livelihoods, people have to adapt by moving to changing conditions (Quinn et al. 2007). Thus, in the dry season cultivation is practised on valley bottom farms, while in the rainy season people tend to cultivate on uphill slope farms (Gmür 2019: 306). In the Kilolo district, small-scale agriculture is the most important activity, which is complemented by some livestock keeping (Gmür 2019; Odgaard 2002). In 2012, the district was home to 218,130 people, with an annual growth rate of approximately 2% (National Bureau of Statistics 2012). The most important crop in the Iringa region is maize; other crops consist of beans, sorghum, millet, sunflower and recently tomatoes (Odgaard 2002). Due to the region's climatic conditions and fertile soils, Iringa has been characterized as the 'food basket of Tanzania' (Chimilila et al. 2017).

Legal framework concerning land tenure

In 1999, and in response to widespread rural discontent with neoliberal policies, Tanzania proposed a new national policy and a new legislation concerning land governance (Land Act No. 4 and Village Land Act No. 5), which allocate land into three basic categories and treat customary rights as being legally equivalent to granted rights (Sulle and Nelson 2009). These categories consist of reserved land (for conservation purposes and tourism, such as national parks, as well as game, marine and forest reserves),[12] village land (all the rural land managed by the more than 12,000 villages of Tanzania and administered by the village councils through the authority of the village assembly) and general land (any land

---

[12] Recent analyses have shown that over 40% of Tanzania's land reserves fall into this category (Bluwstein et al. 2018; Sulle and Nelson 2009).

that isn't part of the other two categories, largely consisting of urban areas and areas for large-scale investments. However, it includes village land that is 'unoccupied' or 'unused') (Alden Wily 2003; Bergius 2014; Maganga et al. 2016: 4).[13] Certificates of Occupancy (COs) are issued for terms of 33, 66 and 99 years for general landholdings and investors. In 2004, Certificates of Customary Rights of Occupancy (CCROs) were introduced, which recognize individual rights to village land and are legally equivalent to granted rights of occupancy. Both CCROs and COs (when not granted by the TIC) have to undergo several procedural steps from village to national level. These guidelines have been set out by the Village Land Act No. 5 (1999) and the Land Use Planning Act No. 6 (2007) and outline a participatory process – a Village Land Use Plan (VLUP) – by which villages can formalize their land use within their boundaries (Hart et al. 2014). The outcome of these formally participatory processes can be described as ambiguous, as they are costly, depend on the administrative capacities and political will of all levels of governmental bodies and can be hijacked at various points by powerful internal and external actors to advance their interests and claims on land (Alden Wily 2003; Bergius 2014; Bluwstein et al. 2018; Hart et al. 2014; Maganga et al. 2016; Shivji 1998). By 2014, only 391 VLUPs had been completed within SAGCOT districts (Huggings 2016). Additionally, as the President remains the trustee of all land, he's entitled to transfer any area from village land or reserve land into general land when referring to public interest – in fact rendering individuals more landholders or managers than common or private owners, even if they rely on customary rights (Gmür 2019: 305). Therefore, land tenure in Tanzania remains – as in colonial times – a 'matter of usufruct rights as defined by various leasehold periods and conditions' (Sulle and Nelson 2009: 37), rendering land in reality a 'state property' (Haller et al. 2019).

As elsewhere in the country, within the Iringa region forceful and voluntary resettlement into standardized villages during ujamaa, as well as the shift to neoliberal policies in the 1980s, have led to institutional changes regarding the tenure and management systems of land and related common-pool resources. Therefore, pre-colonial, traditional management of common-pool resources has been 'legislated out of existence' (Haller et al. 2019: 150), and communities often use and manage resources to which their rights are not recognized by law (Quinn et al. 2007: 101). This legal pluralistic setting involving segments of socialist and neoliberal policies vis-à-vis customary rights, as well as conservation legislation, has created a situation of land tenure insecurity in the context of land scarcity – an insecurity that the more powerful from national to household level can make

---

[13] According to several authors (Bluwstein 2018; Bluwstein et al. 2018; Greco 2016; Maganga et al. 2016), general land is an ambiguous land category, as it comprises areas that are not clearly categorized or can be claimed in the name of public interest and/or by rendering the current use as inappropriate.

use of (Gmür 2019; Greco 2015; Haller et al. 2019; Maganga et al. 2016; Odgaard 2002).

Part 2: The Mega-Infrastructure Project

SAGCOT – spatial concepts, social impacts and development narratives

To overcome the critiques against the 'National Strategy for Growth and Reduction in Poverty' (NSGRP) for not supporting the private sector enough, in August 2009, President Kikwete launched the 'Kilimo Kwanza' ('Agriculture First') initiative (Bergius 2014: 33). The intention of 'Kilimo Kwanza' was a commercialization and modernization of small- and large-scale agriculture through PPPs (Bergius 2014: 33; Haudenschild 2018: 50). Kilimo Kwanza has advanced various other national programmes and initiatives that promised economic and social progress (e.g. 'Vision 2025'). SAGCOT can be seen to be in line with these ambitions under renewed guidance of the World Bank and in the context of the 'New Alliance for Food Security and Nutrition' (NAFSN), introduced by the 'Food and Agriculture Organization of the United Nations' (FAO) and the governments of the G8 countries to fight poverty and the food price crisis after 2008. SAGCOT was initiated by the World Economic Forum (WEF) 2010 in Davos, the World Economic Forum for Africa (WEFA) and the Tanzanian government of Jakaya Kikwete in Dar es Salaam in 2010. The concept of the AAGC was also presented here for the first time (Paul and Steinbrecher 2013: 1). Apart from the aforementioned World Bank, SAGCOT lists a great number of private-sector companies, commercial banks, and (inter)national development, farmer and government organizations as partners.[14]

The SAGCOT corridor includes roads, railways, factories, warehouses, storage facilities, research hubs, water and energy supplies, etc. This infrastructure lies in a multi-sectoral area (cluster) that includes the establishment of commercial relationships between companies, smallholders, outgrowers and other organizations. Local producers and their products should be connected via roads and railways to transport nodes, warehouses, farm blocks, markets and power plants on the one hand, and to international export on the other (Fig. 2).

The spatial vicinity of the 'agribusiness-focused clusters' and the 'collaboration' made possible by this 'geographic proximity' (Steffens 2016: 26ff.) is considered to be the 'strength'[15] of the concept and the 'central aspect in almost all cluster definitions' (2016: 9). The cluster should provide access to services, and

---

[14] https://sagcot.co.tz/index.php/en/what-we-do/sagcot-partnership/sagcot-partners (last access: 14.07.2022).
[15] https://sagcot.co.tz/index.php/en/what-we-do/sagcot-clusters/about-clusters (last access: 14.07.2022).

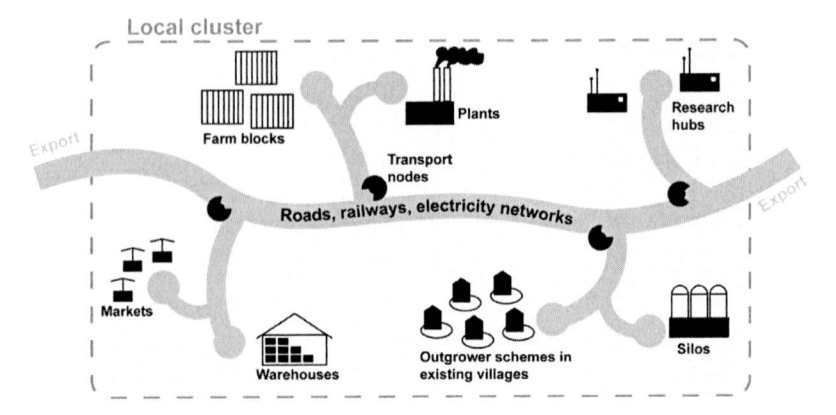

Figure 2: Concept of a local cluster with the different elements along the value chain. Source: based on Steffens et al. 2019: 4.

help to keep production and transport routes as short as possible and the supply of national and international markets as efficient as possible.

SAGCOT is operationalized by the locally situated SAGCOT 'Cluster Offices'[16] and the head office 'SAGCOT Centre Ltd' (SCL) in the capital Dar es Salaam, which is responsible for the central coordination between the numerous actors and needs. The SCL is supported by the 'Green Reference Group' (GRG), an 'informal advisory body' whose objective is 'to coordinate and monitor the environmental aspects in all programs within the SAGCOT region'.[17]

Impacts of investments by SAGCOT partners on local communities

Case study: Anchor Farm Project by Clinton Development Initiative in Kilolo district, Iringa region, Ihemi Cluster

In the context of this publication and discussion on SAGCOT, the inhabitants of the village of Mtitu were interviewed in semi-structured interviews and focus group discussions.[18] The village is located near *Anchor Farm*, which is run by the Clinton Development Initiative (CDI) – a registered partner of SAGCOT. The CDI was introduced by President Clinton at the inaugural meeting of the Clinton Global Initiative in 2005 with the commitment to support smallholder farmers and families in Africa. So far, the CDI works at the invitation of the governments of Malawi, Rwanda and Tanzania and introduced a Community Agribusiness Approach (CAB) within the latter.[19] The work of the CDI with the CAB is based on

---

[16] http://sagcot.co.tz/index.php/contact-us/ (last access: 14.07.2022).
[17] https://sagcot.co.tz/index.php/en/what-we-do/green-reference-group/about-green-reference-group (last access: 14.07.2022).
[18] Désirée Gmür (DG) carried out field research in August and September 2019.
[19] Clinton Foundation: https://www.clintonfoundation.org/programs/economic-inclusion-development/clinton-development-initiative (last access: 14.07.2022).

different principles, which reflect the discursive strategies and narratives that are being used by other investors within SAGCOT. There is the narrative of bringing development and improvement to agricultural production in the form of training and techniques and resources such as improved seed varieties and fertilizers to become more productive and secure food production. In line with SAGCOT's vision, the CDI identifies both smallholders' agricultural practices and market positions as drivers of low productivity, poverty and environmental degradation – and therefore as a challenge to a 'possible upcoming global food shortage' (Ulyate 2019). As well as demonstration plots all over the Iringa region, the *Anchor Farm Project* is thought to provide farmers with agronomic knowledge and training in matters such as improving soil structure and function, yield and soil mapping, hybrid maize seeds, crop rotation and crop protection with herbicides (2019).

Historically, the farm the Bill Clinton Foundation is using today as a seed farm has been a *Mzungu* ('white man' in Swahili) farm. As with many plots for farmland, this one was given to a settler after the Second World War, as part of a settlement scheme for soldiers. The farm under the ownership of a colonel offered both employment and a school, which several children from the village attended. With independence, the colonel left the country and one of his workers took over the farm and all the farming equipment. Having difficulties maintaining the production, it was soon left unattended, and, as no one else was claiming the land, the government took over with the ambition of building and maintaining a seed farm. Until 2013, when the Bill Clinton Foundation acquired the farm under a contract of continuing to produce seeds, it remained one of the many Tanzanian state farms. As of today, the Bill Clinton Foundation is using all of the original 1000 acres of land, while under the authority of the government only 400 acres were being used.[20]

As with many of the portrayed infrastructure projects in this edition, they tend to evoke desires and hopes within communities and societies before they materialize on the ground. These types of hopes and expectations towards development as an idea as well as towards specific infrastructure and the disjunction between these fantasized outcomes and the actual outcomes of development interventions have been theorized respectively as a 'desiring machine' (De vries 2007) and 'enchantments' (Harvey and Knox 2012). When the villagers heard that the Bill Clinton Foundation was going to take over the state farm and would be working in such an area, many of them were hoping for employment and an adjacent boom in the infrastructure of the region, as many seemed to be familiar with the name of the former US President. In 2015, and as part of a larger tour through East Africa, Bill Clinton even visited the village of Mtitu and the farm.[21] However, most of the interaction between the villagers and the CDI tends to happen on the demonstration

---

[20] Information based on interviews with villagers in Mtitu by Désirée Gmür (DG, 2019).
[21] https://www.facebook.com/ClintonFoundation/photos/on-april-29-president-clinton-visited-the-clinton-development-initiatives-ngongw/779146615540115 (last access: 14.07.2021).

plots, where they are shown how to obtain higher yields from small areas. Within these demonstration plots, villagers are discouraged from using heavy equipment, so that soil erosion is less likely. Additionally, the villagers are taught to use fewer fertilizers than they do on *Anchor Farm*, the reason for this being the villagers' low income and presumed lack of know-how.[22] Apart from this interaction on demonstration plots, which itself is a portrayal of exclusion and a denial of knowledge about local smallholders, many of the impacts concern the availability of land for livestock and cultivation.[23] As stated above, before the CDI took over, the state farm was using less land than officially demarcated, enabling people to graze their livestock in these areas. However, the CDI is claiming all of the previously demarcated land (which consists of an additional 600 ha to the previously used 400 ha), making it impossible for people to graze cattle apart from in the surroundings of their houses – which is not enough.[24]

In the valley, close to the farm and where the village lies, the villagers are prohibited to grow products other than vegetables, as the CDI doesn't want any interference with their seeds through cross-pollination. So far, *Anchor Farm* hasn't provided the surrounding villages with their seeds, and therefore crops such as maize cannot be grown in the valleys anymore. With this, an important income opportunity has been lost, as in the dry season in particular – when traditionally people practised cultivation in the valley – the price for maize on the market is five times higher.[25]

These impacts on the abundancy of land for livestock and cultivation will have further ecological impacts on the available land and other resources, as these are going to be used more in order to compensate for the losses through the farm. Moreover, the practices of cultivation carried out on *Anchor Farm* itself are impacting both people and the environment: the CDI is spraying chemicals such as fertilizers and pesticides via aeroplanes. According to the villagers, this is being done three times per season. There is no available information on how this affects soil and water quality; however, the villagers have experienced a decrease in air quality and stated that the air pollution has led to health problems.[26] As in some other investments affiliated with SAGCOT, there have been rumours of GMOs. These concerns have been widespread within the international community and Tanzania's civil society, who fear that SAGCOT will provide access for modified seeds at the expense of traditional and organic alternatives and will lead to intellectual property issues (UNDP Tanzania 2012). Given the fact that several of the participant companies can be viewed as GMO seed companies (such as Bayer and

---

[22] Personal communication with DG, 2019.
[23] Personal communication with DG, 2019.
[24] Field notes, DG, 2019.
[25] Interview with villager from Mtitu, DG, 2019.
[26] Interview by DG, 2019.

Yara), and that SAGCOT's official denials have been half-hearted, these concerns have to be taken seriously.

Unstable perspectives and their consequences

Various other ethnographic studies conducted in villages and so-called 'partnerships', 'value chains' and 'contract farming arrangements' in the Iringa, Morogoro, Njombe and Ruvuma regions also report similar negative impacts and effects (Haudenschild 2018; Steffens 2016; Twomey, Schiavoni, and Mongula 2015; West and Haug 2017).

To the findings from the CDI case can be added the fact that the smallholders often report on the unforeseeable and uninfluenceable price developments to which their products are exposed since they have to sell them on the national and central markets (Haudenschild 2018: 95; Steffens 2016: 24; Twomey, Schiavoni, and Mongula 2015: 32; West and Haug 2017: 672). Political decisions at the national level such as the reduction of import tariffs can also lower national prices and ultimately also the purchase prices promised to the contracted farmers (West and Haug 2017: 679). Therefore, not only do smallholders not have the necessary access to price information with which they can better plan their production and sales, but they also simply lack sufficient payment for their products (Haudenschild 2018: 85; Twomey, Schiavoni, and Mongula 2015: 42ff.). On the other hand, the company argues that the low prices would guarantee a market for the smallholders (Haudenschild 2018: 95).

These unstable perspectives based on volatile price trends mean that many are looking for work on the plantations or in other areas (Twomey, Schiavoni, and Mongula 2015: 56). In the case of the village of Lutukira, it is reported that many men who have left have found a new wife in a new place and many families have broken up as a consequence (2015: 56). In the case of four villages in the Iringa and Ruvuma region, promises of new jobs were kept only to a very limited number (2015: 26). There are a few villagers who found a job on the plantations, but the wages and working conditions are often bad (Haudenschild 2018: 97; Twomey, Schiavoni, and Mongula 2015: 33ff.). In the case of the village of Lipokela, this means wages below the minimum wage limit, 10-hour days, no contract and very short breaks, as well as a lack of protection against dismissal and inadequate hygiene and safety standards (Twomey, Schiavoni, and Mongula 2015: 55). The move to wage dependency is described by the employees with 'feelings of disempowerment' (2015: 30). As a further result of the migration there is a lack of employed workers in the cultivation of food for personal or community consumption (2015: 44). People also report very long distances between the villages, the production sites and markets, which in turn entails increased costs for mobility and logistics (Steffens 2016: 26). In general, the advantage of the geographical proximity of the various infrastructures only applies to those smallholders who can live and produce near the infrastructures and who can rely on viable (all-season) roads (Twomey, Schiavoni, and Mongula 2015: 32; West and Haug 2017: 681).

Local and NGO strategies

As these cases have shown, investments within SAGCOT tend to happen within a context of little transparency and limited available land tenure security vis-à-vis external interests. Haudenschild reports a 'missing awareness' about SAGCOT and 'a lack of knowledge' about the projects (2018: 88ff), something that was apparent in all portrayed cases. Instead, as is shown in the case of the Clinton Development Initiative, the portrayal of *Anchor Farm* being superior in terms of agricultural practice, technology and inputs allows villagers to hope they may get access to the farm's quality seed and the maize produced for food. However, in contrast to the former state farm, which performed many of the steps in agricultural production manually and therefore employed more of the villagers, the *Anchor Farm Project* is highly mechanized, and employment is low. And as for the hoped-for expansion of infrastructure and connections to the region's capital, these seem to be empty promises:

'When I heard that Bill Clinton was coming ... (laughing), he thought now all the roads would be tarmacked from the farm to Iringa, and being a tarmac road it would bring business here, and minibuses would also start coming here and all that, but then Clinton is only a name, there is nothing he is bringing' (villager, Mtitu).[27]

One particular strategy of international NGOs such as Misereor[28] is to carry out research and get media attention through journalistic stories that process the studies.[29] With this, they try to involve investors and the state in global legal and ethical frameworks. In 2017, the Office of the High Commissioner for Human Rights addressed the adverse effects of SAGCOT, especially for pastoralist groups, by pointing out the need to obtain free prior informed consent from indigenous groups for such projects (Bohoslavsky and Tauli-Corpuz 2017). Media attention is also a strategy used by local community and farmers' cooperatives.[30] They organize events to enable local groups advocacy training to raise as much awareness as possible. For example, the Africa Faith and Justice Network (AFJN) conducts workshops for nuns, who then pass on their knowledge to the women in the villages in particular and call on them to jointly defend themselves against, for example, water abuses.[31]

---

[27] Interview with DG, 2019.
[28] https://www.misereor.de/ (last access: 14.07.2022).
[29] https://www.domradio.de/nachrichten/2015-07-13/misereor-warnt-vor-folgen-von-landgrabbing-tansania (last access: 14.07.2022).
[30] https://ruhrnalist.de/2015/07/06/muwimbi-will-nicht-sterben/ (last access: 14.07.2022).
[31] https://afjn.org/in-tanzania-catholic-nuns-are-on-the-front-lines-of-social-justice/ (last access: 14.07.2022).

Land tenure insecurity can be addressed locally through processes of formalization, as has been shown in the chapter on legal frameworks. However, these processes within the latest land reform offer little protection from dispossession, especially for vulnerable groups. VLUPs – officially portrayed as participatory, inclusive and democratic – can be hijacked at various points throughout the process by powerful external actors to advance their interests and claims on land. Therefore, providing massive land-grabbing options for the state, as the process of 'territorialization from above' (Bluwstein and Lund 2018) – by demarcating forests, pasture, areas for conservation and investments, etc. – allows them to take hold of village land (Bluwstein et al. 2018; Bluwstein and Lund 2018) via 'institution shopping' (Haller 2010; Haller et al. 2019). Therefore, the strategy of formalizing land titles applies to the more powerful actors, while others are pushing for a reform in land policies: several civil organizations, such as TANIPE (Tanzania Network for Indigenous Pastoralists), UCRT (Ujamaa Community Resource Team)[32] and NTRI (Northern Tanzania Rangelands Initiative), are pushing for collective land titles as CCROs, in order to include marginalized groups such as pastoralists in a land tenure system.[33]

In Lutukira, villagers involved district lawyers in order to file complaints against the investors. However, the negotiations ended in favour of the investors, which further deepened the villagers' distrust of the state authorities (Twomey, Schiavoni, and Mongula 2015: 56). Such recourses to law and politics in order to contest and negotiate the presence of, or broken promises by investors have been observed in other studies too. The Kilombero Sugar Company Limited (KSCL), a recent partner of SAGCOT, is trying to increase sugarcane production through an outgrower scheme in the Kilombero Valley and has been confronted with the villagers' unwillingness to give up their lands both through law and politics: when the company wanted to claim all the lands registered in the lease from the government, villagers took the case to the court and won, as the previous company had never developed the land (Sulle 2020). Similarly, a Member of Parliament for Kilombero Constituency addressed President Magufuli in front of the public over these matters, using the contested issue of land as a campaign theme (2020). However, collective action might depend on the composition of villages as democratic spaces, as 'village administrations have become the ultimate site of negotiation over land acquisitions' (Greco 2016: 36).

Local farmers also try to improve their productivity on their own by investing in machinery, seeds and other resources needed for agriculture, but they are unlikely to be recognized as investors by the state, because the state usually opts for other forms of private sector-led investments (Twomey, Schiavoni, and Mongula 2015: 15ff.)

---

[32] https://www.dorobofund.org/ucrt (last access: 14.07.2022)
[33] https://borgenproject.org/communal-land-rights-tanzania (last access: 14.07.2022).

State and company strategies

The goal of SAGCOT is to attract international donors and private investments in large-scale agriculture and to engage the state in providing the basic infrastructure for these investments. These processes following the concept of an IGG, the World Bank's proposal for a 'Pathway to Sustainable Development' and for 'greening growth' (Fay and World Bank 2012). On the SAGCOT website,[34] pictures of hard-working but happy farmers amidst vegetables, green fields and a functioning social community dominate. SAGCOT is presented here as a responsible authority that 'empowers' smallholders, 'unleashing potential' and 'finding markets' while statements from these allegedly 'included' farmers are missing.

A recent post by the official SCL Twitter account under the hashtag *#Inclusive GreenGrowth*[35] reflects the paradigmatic narrative about an economic, social and ecological sustainable development: 'The global argument for green growth is that tomorrow's successful economies will be those that manage to integrate economic growth, environmental sustainability and social inclusiveness in executing commercial enterprises.'[36] The numerous partnerships, all of which have been portrayed as successful, are illustrated with concrete examples: happy faces, green nature and committed hands-on people dominate the picture. The concept of IGG will not only be used on social media for public relations work and to attract donors, but also disseminated in the form of compliance guidelines for contracted small- to medium and large-scale farmers[37]. According to SAGCOT, the purpose and scope of the guidelines is to define the requirements of the farmers and producers under contract, their responsibilities and obligations. They are also a kind of control instrument for checking the compliance of the farmers with the principles defined by SAGCOT – principles not only expressing some kind of vision in line with the IGG but quite concrete conditions based on national laws, which must be respected by farmers and producers under contract (SAGCOT Centre Ltd 2019: 6ff.).

The head office of SCL – 'established as an institutional body' (Steffens 2016: 15) – offers investors, organizations and state authorities institutional and regulatory opportunities to meet their needs and interests. SCL and its local cluster offices are responsible for negotiating the goals of the myriad of development programmes and new legislation and knowledge in the areas of seed patenting, farming techniques, marketing, etc. and for the documentation and facilitation of foreign direct investment. Its 'tasks are to manage and expand partnerships, serve as an "information hub", coordinate the development of the clusters, facilitate access to finance and monitor the whole' (2016: 15). SCL also organizes and chairs

---

[34] http://sagcot.co.tz/ (last access: 14.07.2022).
[35] https://twitter.com/hashtag/InclusiveGreenGrowth (last access: 14.07.2022).
[36] https://twitter.com/SAGCOT/status/1235104481592795136 (last access: 14.07.2022).
[37] https://sagcot.co.tz/index.php/en/information-hub/about-info-hub (last access: 14.07.2022).

the so-called SAGCOT 'stakeholder meetings' like GRG, where smallholders, companies and other private and state actors should come in contact. On the one hand, these exchange formats serve the companies as an additional source of legitimacy with regard to the smallholders (Haudenschild 2018: 78). On the other hand, they should serve as a way to foster exchange and networking with other companies – even if, according to individual managers, the meetings are often poorly attended by companies and of limited effectiveness (Haudenschild 2018: 83f). Furthermore, the meetings 'are not only characterized by the asymmetrical power relation between actors, but the power to control also operates in the act of inclusion and participation itself' (2018: 83).

The discursive level with the central narrative of IGG, the bureaucratic and legal level with the compliance guidelines and the organizational level of SCL have different functions, but together they create a multitude of new regulations and institutions that manage access to SAGCOT's infrastructure, to land and to other resources.

Conclusion

We have organized our analysis of SAGCOT as an MIP in two parts, building on each other. In the first part, we've challenged SAGCOT's portrayal of both Tanzania as a country with large, freely available land for investments and the prevailing poverty and unsustainable use of resources of the country's rural population being solely a result of poor agricultural practices and decisions. By focusing on Tanzania's history, economy and existing legal framework, we have shown a landscape of different development and infrastructure projects dating back to colonial times, socialist villagization programmes and those following the political and economic shift to neoliberalization, each influencing institutional arrangements regarding land and other resources. As shown within the Iringa region, these institutional changes have led to a legal pluralistic setting, with differential outcomes for the more or less powerful in this growing competition for resources.

As shown in the second part, people 'on the ground' speak of unstable perspectives induced by multiple uncertainties and dependencies in the context of large-scale investments and outgrower contracts: the exposure to uncertain (global) price developments, broken promises about jobs and farming improvement, dispossession from land, migration pressure, lack of information and knowledge and precarious employment arrangements, as well as negative effects on physical and mental health due to land loss and pesticide use.

While the recent land reforms formally respect customary rights to resources, we have shown that in practice customary institutions for the commons have been overwhelmed by the amount of institutional changes. The ensuing plurality of institutions allows the more powerful actors to do 'institution shopping', which means that it provides adequate institutional tools depending on the character of the problem and the level of the challenge (Haller 2010; Haller et al. 2019). Following this, the poorest part of the rural population finds itself in the weakest position, as the form of protection vis-à-vis more powerful stakeholders continuously dispossesses them (Maganga et al. 2016). Hence, we argue that SAGCOT works within an 'anti-politics machine' (Ferguson 1994), as it depoliticizes important questions about the allocation of resources through discursive and bureaucratic obscuration and by offering technical solutions to political and social problems and conflicts. Past development interventions, such as the groundnut scheme or the villagization programme, demonstrate remarkable similarities to SAGCOT's beliefs on how such technical solutions are being framed.

SAGCOT shows how the concept of AAGC and 'resilient development narratives' (Engström and Hajdu 2019) like IGG depoliticize and obscure power asymmetries as well as historical colonial exploitation constellations through a strategy of active 'enchantment' (Harvey and Knox 2012). The discursive paradigm of IGG conjures up a 'modernist vision of improvement' (Harvey and Knox 2012: 522), the evocation of an affected and illusory image of a future that is unclear but promising for all – and thus 'points to a utopian element that is always already out of place' (De vries 2007: 30). The attribute 'green' is sold as a tool with which the different interests and goals of the various actors *and* the environment allegedly can be reconciled. Furthermore, in our view, it is the central development notion in the SAGCOT initiative that operates as a 'desiring machine' [...] 'between the generation and banalization of hope' (De vries 2007: 30). As in the case with the Clinton Development Initiative and the ex-US President's visit, we would argue that promises of political and economic integration into a global economy, as is the case with SAGCOT in their communication with stakeholders, are even more effective in their generation of hope when coming from a family so intensively linked to powerful positions within this global economy.

However, it must also be pointed out that the actual connections between SAGCOT, the projects, the companies and the impacts are limited and sometimes difficult to trace. Studies also show that interest in, and knowledge about SAGCOT is limited amongst smallholders. Therefore, and with regard to the trend of 'agricultural modernization' in general, it is important to note that many smallholders have been practising traditionally a resilient agriculture – and that this knowledge is threatened precisely by large-scale investments, because they are accompanied by the dissemination of knowledge (about seeds, fertilizer, farming techniques, etc.) that is exclusively owned by a few international companies (like Yara, Syngenta, Bayer and others in the case of SAGCOT). Nevertheless, many smallholders have a broad agricultural knowledge and make a significant contribution to the food supply of the population (Twomey, Schiavoni, and Mongula 2015: 15f). As such, smallholders thus draw a different picture of development, one that has the potential to oppose and disenchant the dominant narratives. Finally, (mega) infrastructure projects like SAGCOT must be seen in the whole context of a vast number of international and national development projects and legal frameworks in Tanzania and Sub-Saharan Africa, which also impose considerable pressure on land use and resource distribution and cause 'land alienation' (Bluwstein et al. 2018). These include, for example, the touristic use of large areas of land for wildlife and marine conservation, which gives people no or only limited access to the resources previously used (Benjaminsen and Bryceson 2012). In addition, there should also be a focus on water scarcity and environmental degradation resulting from large-scale land use (Sirima et al. 2016: 6; Schiavoni et al. 2018: 3) as well as on the long term effects of climate change for these issues (Paavola 2008; Kabote 2018). Finally, in contrast to other studies in the SAGCOT area, pastoralist evictions as a result of farmer-herder conflicts haven't been addressed in this chapter, as they haven't been mentioned within our study areas. However, reports of forceful evictions in other regions such as Kilombero, Morogoro and Mbarali (e.g. Bergius et al. 2020; Maganga et al. 2016) indicate that this may very likely happen in the Ihemi Cluster as well, as resources get scarcer and people migrate.

Glossary

AAGC	African Agricultural Growth Corridor
AFJN	Africa Faith & Justice Network
ASDP	Agricultural Sector Development Programme
CAB	Community Agribusiness Approach
CCRO	Certificates of Customary Rights of Occupancy
CDI	Clinton Development Initiative
CO	Certificates of Occupancy
FAO	Food and Agriculture Organization of the United States
GMO	Genetically Modified Organism
GRG	Green Reference Group
IGG	Inclusive Green Growth
IMF	International Monetary Fund
KSCL	Kilombero Sugar Company Limited
MIC	Middle-Income Country
MIP	Mega-Infrastructure Project
NAFSN	New Alliance for Food Security and Nutrition
NGO	Non-governmental organization
NSGRP	National Strategy for Growth and Reduction in Poverty
NTRI	Northern Tanzania Rangelands Initiative
PPP	Public-Private Partnership
SAGCOT	Southern Agricultural Growth Corridor of Tanzania
SAP	Structural Adjustment Programme
SCL	SAGCOT Centre Ltd

TANIPE	Tanzania Network for Indigenous Pastoralists
TIC	Tanzania Investment Centre
UCRT	Ujamaa Community Resource Team
USAID	United States Agency for International Development
UKAID	United Kingdom Agency for International Development
VLUP	Village Land Use Plan
WEF	World Economic Forum
WEFA	World Economic Forum for Africa

References

Alden Wily, Liz 2003: 'Community-Based Land Tenure Management: Questions and Answers about Tanzania's New Village Land Act, 1999'. Issue paper no. 120. Drylands Programme. London: IIED International Institute for Environment and Development.

Benjaminsen, Tor A., and Ian Bryceson 2012: 'Conservation, Green/Blue Grabbing and Accumulation by Dispossession in Tanzania'. *Journal of Peasant Studies* 39 (2): 335–55. https://doi.org/10.1080/03066150.2012.667405.

Bergius, Mikael 2014: 'Expanding the Corporate Food Regime – The Southern Agricultural Growth Corridor of Tanzania'. Oslo: Norwegian University of Life Sciences Department of International Environment and Development Studies.

Bergius, Mikael, Tor A. Benjaminsen, Faustin Maganga, and Halvard Buhaug 2020: 'Green Economy, Degradation Narratives, and Land-Use Conflicts in Tanzania'. *World Development* 129 (May): 104850. https://doi.org/10.1016/j.worlddev.2019.104850.

Bergius, Mikael, Tor A. Benjaminsen, and Mats Widgren 2018: 'Green Economy, Scandinavian Investments and Agricultural Modernization in Tanzania'. *The Journal of Peasant Studies* 45 (4): 825–52. https://doi.org/10.1080/03066150.2016.1260554.

Bergius, Mikael, and Jill Tove Buseth 2019: 'Towards a Green Modernization Development Discourse: The New Green Revolution in Africa'. *Journal of Political Ecology* 26 (1): 57–83. https://doi.org/10.2458/v26i1.22862.

Bluwstein, Jevgeniy 2018: 'From Colonial Fortresses to Neoliberal Landscapes in Northern Tanzania: A Biopolitical Ecology of Wildlife Conservation'. *Journal of Political Ecology* 25 (1): 144. https://doi.org/10.2458/v25i1.22865.

Bluwstein, Jevgeniy, and Jens Friis Lund 2018: 'Territoriality by Conservation in the Selous–Niassa Corridor in Tanzania'. *World Development* 101 (January): 453–65. https://doi.org/10.1016/j.worlddev.2016.09.010.

Bluwstein, Jevgeniy, Jens Friis Lund, Kelly Askew, Howard Stein, Christine Noe, Rie Odgaard, Faustin Maganga, and Linda Engström 2018: 'Between Dependence and Deprivation: The Interlocking Nature of Land Alienation in Tanzania'. *Journal of Agrarian Change* 18 (4): 806–30. https://doi.org/10.1111/joac.12271.

Brockington, Dan, and Jim Igoe 1999: *Pastoral Land Tenure and Community Conservation: A Case Study from North-East Tanzania*. Pastoral Land Tenure Series No 11, IIED, London. United Kingdom: International Institute for Environment and Development (IIED).

Buseth, Jill Tove 2017: 'The Green Economy in Tanzania: From Global Discourses to Institutionalization'. *Geoforum* 86 (November): 42–52. https://doi.org/10.1016/j.geoforum.2017.08.015.

Charnley, Susan 1997: 'Environmentally-Displaced Peoples and the Cascade Effect: Lessons from Tanzania'. *Human Ecology* 25 (4): 593–618. https://doi.org/10.1023/A:1021885924512.

Coulson, Andrew 1982: *Tanzania: A Political Economy*. Oxford [Oxfordshire]: New York: Clarendon Press; Oxford University Press.

Dannenberg, Peter, Javier Revilla Diez, and Daniel Schiller 2018: 'Spaces for Integration or a Divide? New-Generation Growth Corridors and Their Integration in Global Value Chains in the Global South'. *Zeitschrift Für Wirtschaftsgeographie* 62 (2): 135–51. https://doi.org/10.1515/zfw-2017-0034.

De vries, Pieter 2007: 'Don't Compromise Your Desire for Development! A Lacanian/Deleuzian Rethinking of the Anti-Politics Machine'. *Third World Quarterly* 28 (1): 25–43. https://doi.org/10.1080/01436590601081765.

Engström, Linda, and Flora Hajdu 2019: 'Conjuring "Win-World" – Resilient Development Narratives in a Large-Scale Agro-Investment in Tanzania'. *The Journal of Development Studies* 55 (6): 1201–20. https://doi.org/10.1080/00220388.2018.1438599.

Fay, Marianne, and World Bank, eds 2012: *Inclusive Green Growth: The Pathway to Sustainable Development*. Washington, D.C: World Bank.

Ferguson, James 1994: *The Anti-Politics Machine: 'Development', Depoliticization, and Bureaucratic Power in Lesotho*. Minneapolis: University of Minnesota Press.

Gastorn, Kennedy 2008: *The Impact of Tanzania's New Land Laws on the Customary Land Rights of Pastoralists: A Case Study of the Simanjiro and Bariadi Districts*. Recht Und Politik in Afrika 7. Münster: LIT.

Gmür, Desirée 2019: 'Grabbing the Female Commons: Large-Scale Land Acquisitions for Forest Plantations and Impacts on Gender Relations in Kilolo District, Iringa Region, Tanzania'. In *The Commons in a Glocal World: Global Connections and Local Responses*, edited by Tobias Haller, Thomas Breu, Tine de Moor, Christian Rohr, and Heinzpeter Zonj, 301–17. London; New York: Routledge, Taylor & Francis Group.

Grawert, Elke 2009: *Departures from Post-Colonial Authoritarianism: Analysis of System Change with a Focus on Tanzania*. Berliner Studien Zur Politik in Afrika, Bd. 15. Frankfurt am Main; New York: Peter Lang.

Greco, Elisa 2015: 'Landlords in the Making: Class Dynamics of the Land Grab in Mbarali, Tanzania'. *Review of African Political Economy* 42 (144): 225–44. https://doi.org/10.1080/03056244.2014.992403.

— 2016: 'Village Land Politics and the Legacy of Ujamaa'. *Review of African Political Economy* 43 (sup1): 22–40. https://doi.org/10.1080/03056244.2016.1219179.

Haller, Tobias 2010: *Disputing the Floodplains: Institutional Change and the Politics of Resource Management in African Wetlands*. Boston: Brill. https://doi.org/10.1163/ej.9789004185326.i-454.

— 2019: 'Towards a New Institutional Political Ecology: How to Marry External Effects, Institutional Change and the Role of Power and Ideology in Commons Studies'. In *The Commons in a Glocal World: Global Connections and Local Responses*, edited by Tobias Haller, Thomas Breu, Tine De Moor, Christian Rohr, and Heinzpeter Znoj. London: Routledge.

Haller, Tobias, Timothy Adams, Desirée Gmür, Fabian Käser, Kristina Lanz, Franziska Marfurt, Sarah Ryser, Elisabeth Schubiger, Anna von Sury, and Jean-David Gerber 2019: 'Large-Scale Land Acquisition as Commons Grabbing: A Comparative Analysis of Six African Case Studies'. In *Global Perspectives on Long Term Community Resource Management*, edited by Ludomir R. Lozny and Thomas H. McGovern, 11:125–64. Cham: Springer International Publishing. https://doi.org/10.1007/978-3-030-15800-2_7.

Hart, Abigail, Tumsifu Elly, Winnie Nguni, John Recha, Zacharia Malley, Rodgers Masha, and Louise E. Buck 2014: *Participatory Land Use Planning to Support Tanzanian Farmer and Pastoralist Investment: Experiences from Mbarali District, Mbeya Region, Tanzania*. https://doi.org/10.13140/RG.2.1.1752.4242.

Harvey, Penny, and Hannah Knox 2012: 'The Enchantments of Infrastructure'. *Mobilities* 7 (4): 521–36. https://doi.org/10.1080/17450101.2012.718935.

Haudenschild, Daniel 2018: 'Modernity/Coloniality in Legitimizing Agribusiness: The Case of the Southern Agricultural Growth Corridor of Tanzania'. Master Thesis, Amsterdam: University of Amsterdam.

Ingle, Clyde R 1972: *From Village to State in Tanzania: The Politics of Rural Development*. Ithaca [N.Y.]: Cornell University Press.

Kabote, Samwel J 2018: 'Farmers' Vulnerability to Climate Change Impacts in Semi-Arid Environments in Tanzania: A Gender Perspective'. In *Arid Environments and Sustainability*, edited by Hasan Arman and Ibrahim Yuksel. InTech. https://doi.org/10.5772/intechopen.72108.

Maganga, Faustin, Kelly Askew, Rie Odgaard, and Howard Stein 2016: 'Dispossession through Formalization: Tanzania and the G8 Land Agenda in Africa'. *Asian Journal of African Studies* Volume 40 (August): 1–49.

Mendelsohn, John, Tony Robertson, and Alice Jarvis 2014: *Tanzania: The Measure Of A Land*. Vital Signs.

Mkonda, Msafiri 2016: *Efficacy of Transforming Agriculture for Survival to Commercial Agriculture through 'Kilimo Kwanza' Initiative in Tanzania*. Vol. 4(4): 43-50, 2016. https://doi.org/10.13189/nrc.2016.040401.

Monson, Jamie 1998: 'Relocating Maji Maji: The Politics of Alliance and Authority in the Southern Highlands of Tanzania, 1870-1918'. *The Journal of African History* 39 (1): 95–120.

Nindi, Benson 1988: 'Issues in Agricultural Change: Case Study from Ismani, Iringa Region, Tanzania'. In *Anthropology of Development and Change in East Africa*, edited by David W. Brokensha. New York: Routledge.

Odgaard, Rie 2002: 'Scrambling for Land in Tanzania: Process of Formalisation and Legitimisation of Land Rights.' *European Journal of Development Research* 14 (2): 71.

Paavola, Jouni 2008: 'Livelihoods, Vulnerability and Adaptation to Climate Change in Morogoro, Tanzania'. *Environmental Science & Policy* 11 (7): 642–54. https://doi.org/10.1016/j.envsci.2008.06.002.

Paul, Helena, and Ricarda Steinbrecher 2013: 'African Agriculture Growth Corridors and the New for Food Security and Nutrition. Who Benefits, Who Loses?' EcoNexus Report. EcoNexus.

Quinn, Claire H., Meg Huby, Hilda Kiwasila, and Jon C. Lovett 2007: 'Design Principles and Common Pool Resource Management: An Institutional Approach to Evaluating

Community Management in Semi-Arid Tanzania'. *Journal of Environmental Management* 84 (1): 100–113. https://doi.org/10.1016/j.jenvman.2006.05.008.

Rizzo, Matteo 2006: 'What Was Left of the Groundnut Scheme? Development Disaster and Labour Market in Southern Tanganyika 1946-1952'. *Journal of Agrarian Change* 6 (2): 205–38. https://doi.org/10.1111/j.1471-0366.2006.00120.x.

Rwegasira, Abdon 2012: *Land as a Human Right: A History of Land Law and Practice in Tanzania*. Dar-es-Salaam: Mkuki na Nyota.

Schiavoni, Christina M., Salena Tramel, Hannah Twomey, and Benedict S. Mongula 2018: 'Analysing Agricultural Investment from the Realities of Small-Scale Food Providers: Grounding the Debates'. *Third World Quarterly* 39 (7): 1348–66. https://doi.org/10.1080/01436597.2018.1460198.

Shivji, Issa G 1998: *Not yet Democracy: Reforming Land Tenure in Tanzania*. Dar es Salaam: University of Dar es Salaam.

Sirima, A., R. M. J. Kadigi, J. J. Kashaigili, F. Kamau, A. Sikira, W. Mbungu, and J. K. Placid 2016: 'Ecosystem Health and Sustainable Agricultural Development in Ihemi Cluster', 1–4.

Steffens, Veronika 2016: 'Potentials of Agrarian Cluster Development for Improving Smallholder's Income – a Case Study from the SAGCOT Initiative in Tanzania.' Bachelor Thesis, Köln: Universität zu Köln.

Steffens, Veronika, Gideon Hartmann, and Peter Dannenberg 2019: 'Eine neue Generation von Wachstumskorridoren als Entwicklungsmotor in Afrika?: Das Beispiel des tansanischen Landwirtschaftskorridors SAGCOT'. *Standort* 43 (1): 2–8. https://doi.org/10.1007/s00548-019-00565-6.

Sulle, Emmanuel 2020: 'Bureaucrats, Investors and Smallholders: Contesting Land Rights and Agro-Commercialisation in the Southern Agricultural Growth Corridor of Tanzania'. *Journal of Eastern African Studies*, March, 1–22. https://doi.org/10.1080/17531055.2020.1743093.

Twomey, Hannah, Christina M. Schiavoni, and Benedict S. Mongula 2015: 'Impacts of Large-Scale Agricultural Investments on Small-Scale Farmers in the Southern Highlands of Tanzania. A Right to Food Perspective.' Case Study. Aachen: MISEREOR.

Weltalmanach, ed. 2018: *Der Neue Fischer Weltalmanach*. Frankfurt am Main: Fischer Taschenbuch.

West, Jennifer J., and Ruth Haug 2017: 'The Vulnerability and Resilience of Smallholder-Inclusive Agricultural Investments in Tanzania'. *Journal of Eastern African Studies* 11 (4): 670–91. https://doi.org/10.1080/17531055.2017.1367994.

Online Reports

Bohoslavsky, Juan Pablo, and Victoria Lucia Tauli-Corpuz 2017: 'Mandates of the Independent Expert on the Effects of Foreign Debt and Other Related International Financial Obligations of States on the Full Enjoyment of All Human Rights, Particularly Economic, Social and Cultural Rights and the Special Rapporteur on the Rights of Indigenous Peoples'. OL TZA 1/2017. Geneva: Office of the High Commissioner for Human Rights. ⟨https://spcommreports.ohchr.org/TMResultsBase/DownLoadPublicCommunicationFile?gId=22932⟩ PDF document. Accessed on 18.07.2022.

Chimilila, Cyril, Felix Chengula, Amos Ibrahim, and Elvis Mushi 2017: 'FinScope Tanzania 2017: Iringa Regional Report'. FinScope. FAO. ⟨https://www.fsdt.or.tz/wp-content/uploads/2018/11/Finscope_Iringa.pdf⟩ PDF document. Accessed on 18.07.2022.

Huggings, Chris 2016: 'Village Land Use Planning and Commercialization of Land in Tanzania'. Research brief. Land Governance for Equitable and Sustainable Development. LANDac. ⟨https://www.landgovernance.org/wp-content/uploads/2019/10/20160301-LANDacResearchBrief-01Tanzania1.pdf⟩ PDF document. Accessed on 18.07.2022

Milder, J. C., A.K. Hart, and L.E. Buck 2013: 'Applying an Agriculture Green Growth Approach in the SAGCOT Clusters: Challenges and Opportunities in Kilombero, Ihemi and Mbarali.' Dar es Salaam: SAGCOT Centre. ⟨https://ecoagriculture.org/publication/a-vision-for-agriculture-green-growth-in-the-southern-agriculture-growth-corridor-of-tanzania-sagcot/applying-an-agriculture-green-growth-approach-in-the-sagcot-clusters/⟩ PDF document. Accessed on 18.07.2022.

National Bureau of Statistics 2012: 'Population and Housing Census'. 2012. ⟨http://tanzania.countrystat.org/fileadmin/user_upload/countrystat_fenix/congo/docs/Census%20General%20Report-2012PHC.pdf⟩ Accessed on 18.07.2022.

SAGCOT Centre Ltd. 2019: 'Inclusive Green Growth Guiding Tool for Small Scale Producers', August. ⟨https://sagcot.co.tz/index.php/ar/component/edocman/sagcot-guiding-tools/inclusive-green-growth-guiding-tool-for-small-scale-producers⟩ PDF document. Accessed on 18.07.2022.

Sulle, Emmanuel, and Fred Nelson 2009: *Biofuels, Land Access and Rural Livelihoods in Tanzania*. London: International Institute for Environment and Development (IIED). ⟨http://pubs.iied.org/pdfs/12560IIED.pdf⟩ PDF document. Accessed on 18.07.2022.

Ulyate, Otto 2019: We can grow food to feed the world. ⟨https://clinton-foundation.org/africa/agriculture⟩ Accessed on 18.07.2022.

UNDP Tanzania 2012: 'Southern Agricultural Growth Corridor (SAGCOT) Capacity Development Project'. Tanzania: Prime Minister's Office. ⟨https://info.undp.org/docs/pdc/Documents/TZA/Southern%20Agriculture%20Growth%20corridor(SAGCOT)⟩ PDF document. Accessed on 18.07.2022.

World Bank 2017: 'Tanzania – Systematic Country Diagnostic'. Washington, D.C: World Bank Group. ⟨https://openknowledge.worldbank.org/handle/10986/26236⟩ PDF document. Accessed on 18.07.2022.

'Dam(n)ing the Kunene River? Namibian Dam Resistance across Space and Time'

Richard Meissner, Department of Political Sciences, University of South Africa, Pretoria, South Africa; Jeroen Warner, Department of Social Sciences, Wageningen University, Netherlands

Introduction

In this chapter we describe and explain the role and involvement of interest groups in the planned Epupa and Baynes hydropower dams on the Kunene River (Figure 1) straddling the Angolan-Namibian border. Although both countries share the river, we will mainly focus on the Namibian portion of the Kunene since there exists a paucity of information available to us on the OvaHimba in the Angolan part of the river basin. For decades, water-poor Namibia has been planning a suite of dams on the River Kunene, which it shares with water-rich Angola, Africa's "sleeping giant", to capitalize on the Kunene's hydropower potential. Over the past three decades, the planned Epupa Dam has received considerable scholarly attention. Aspects investigated range from social-ecological change and institutional developments of the pastoral communities (e.g. OvaHimba) (Bollig 1996); interest group lobbying against the planned Epupa Dam (Pottinger 1997; O'Neill 1998; Harring 2001; Meissner 2004, 2005; Tarr 2007); the framing of development discourses in the Epupa debate (Friedman 2006); resistance towards the dam from an indigenous, legal and vulnerable ethnic minorities perspective (Corbett 1999); interest groups, scalar politics and temporality (Meissner 2016a); the relationship between the Namibian government and the OvaHimba (Borrego 2017), the complexity of water governance models in international river basins with specific reference to the Kunene and Epupa Dam (Meissner and Jacobs 2016); and the potential energy security the Epupa Dam could offer Namibia (Lundmark 1997). The planned Baynes Dam, on the other hand, has not been under such intense academic scrutiny except for an investigation of the paradiplomatic activities and practices by the OvaHimba and OvaZemba by the present authors (Meissner and Warner 2021. Major infrastructure projects like these are promoted in the interest of development ("uplift") and the public good. But as Harvey and Knox (2015) show, the meanings of "public" and "good" in such projects are far from stable and coherent. This became apparent when two of the dam projects, Epupa and Baynes, triggered protests on behalf of the indigenous local population (OvaHimba and OvaZemba) over displacement and environmental degradation on the Namibian side.

As Ullberg (2019) has noted, the design, planning, projection and building of infrastructures are never straightforward and are seldom undertaken from scratch, and likewise, both dam designs have seen multiple incarnations.

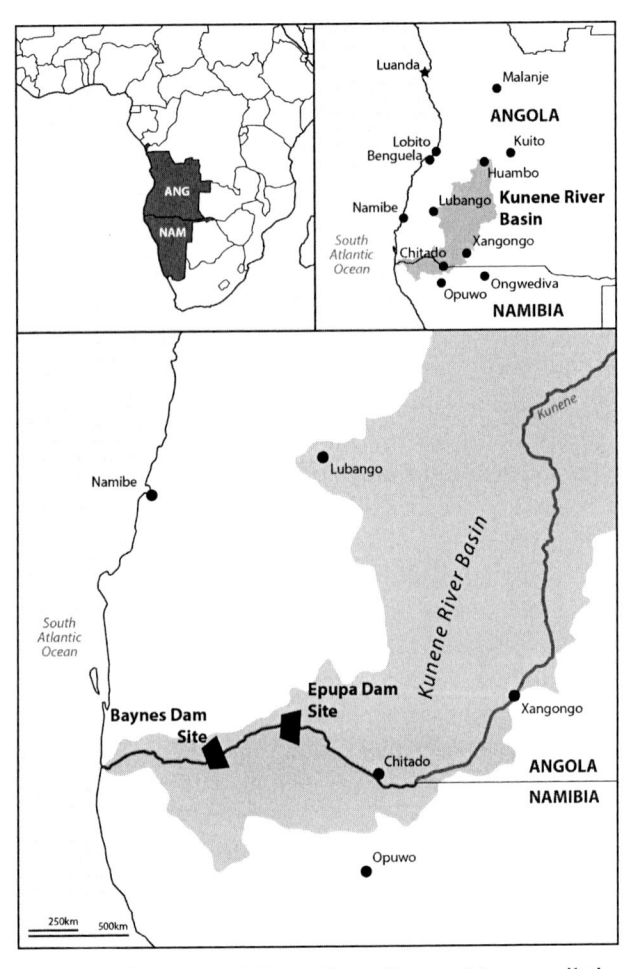

Map 1: Sites of the planned Baynes and Epupa Dams (Source: Map compilation and design by Manuel L. K. Abebe (2021), CDE, University of Bern, Bern, Switzerland. Geodata: Transboundary Freshwater Dispute Database

To add to the knowledge on these mega-infrastructures we will investigate the strategies of local (indigenous) and transnational interest groups over time. The Baynes Dam plan was relaunched in the 2010s but soon ran into the same problems with vocal local interest groups as has been the case with Epupa planned two decades before. This time, as has been the case with their resistance towards

Epupa, the interest groups expanded their reach by availing themselves of the Internet to voice their concerns and mobilized environmentalists with whom they promoted a non-hydropower alternative plan for energy generation. In the Baynes' case, protests, however, became a more fragmented affair over time after a rift appeared among the indigenous leadership, including over the issue of what is the public good. The period we will cover starts with the inception of the planned Epupa Dam in the early 1990s until the response to the Baynes Dam plan, mooted by the Namibian government in the mid-2010s.

Part 1: The mega-infrastructures project debate

Development ("uplift") (*New Era*, 9 June 2016) drives focus on addressing uneven development by recapitalizing and redesigning territories through mega-infrastructures (Enns and Bersaglio 2020). Large dams epitomize the tension between traditional rational-choice planning approaches and the projects' objectives. Because of this, these projects are subject to complexity and uncertainty (Salet et al. 2012; Meissner 2015, 2016b). This tension is further exemplified by spatial disparities as the main problem hindering development, and balanced and thoroughly connected economies as the solution to underdevelopment (Enns and Bersaglio 2020). According to Sturup and Low (2019), new-built infrastructures "[...] must contribute to sustainable development. This is because the infrastructure that is installed especially via megaprojects not only has impacts on sustainability while it is under construction, it also locks in for long periods the impact on sustainability from the social and economic activities it either supports or restricts" (Sturup and Low 2019: 8). They continue by saying: "Infrastructure for sustainable development must be concerned with what is built or not built, the processes that surround decisions to build or not build, the impacts of construction (socially, environmentally and economically), changes to governance and the institutions connected with the process of developing infrastructure" (Sturup and Low 2019: 8).

Infrastructures are "matter that enable the movement of other matter" (sic) (Larkin 2013). A hydraulic megaproject is defined as "a material and organisational infrastructure that enables water to be captured, transported and delivered to its users" (Ullberg 2019). Such projects "can dazzle with the possibilities they hold" (ibid.) and feed a 'desire for development' (de Vries 2007: 534), not only on the part of its initiators, but also the recipients of the infrastructure. Such is the promise of bringing order and progress to unruly nature and disorganized people that they tend to be imposed on a region rather than co-developed with their intended beneficiaries (ibid.) in the name of the public good. In so doing, infrastructures 'participate .... in the processes by which political relations are articulated and enacted' (Harvey and Knox 2015: 524). This is the overall framing of the chapter.

Dams bring the promise of connection and integration, but also the threat of displacement and alienation. There are in fact multiple "publics" who may not all consider the projects "good", and as we shall see, neither are these positions necessarily "stable states" (Harvey and Knox 2015). In so doing, dams set more in motion than water wheels. The perceived normative and social dislocation emanating from mega-infrastructures are central to the ongoing large-dam debate. Against the material and immaterial benefits adduced by initiators in the national interest, opponents will put non-negotiable counter-maxims. Warner (2004) found during his research on flood protection projects several normative values ranging from "hallowed ground" and ecosystem diversity to project integrity and community cohesion to be inviolable and vital to individuals and communities affected by mega projects. Such mobilization scuppered or delayed many mega projects in the 1990s, such as the Bangladesh Jamuna Multipurpose Bridge, the Arun and Pergau dams and the Lesotho Highlands Water Project, leading to the establishment of the World Commission on Dams (WCD).

When the WCD, an international and independent organization that consisted of 12 dam experts (Nakayama and Fujikura 2006), issued its influential report in 2000 (WCD 2000; Warner 2012), it concluded: "Just as with the economic impacts of large dams, the social and environmental impacts of dams can be classified as gains or losses accruing to different social groups – now and in the future" (WCD 2000: 98). The report continues: "Consequently the *social* and *cultural* implications of putting a dam into such a [river] landscape are spatially significant, locally disruptive, and often irreversible" (emphasis added) (WCD 2000: 102). This may sound like the WCD delegitimized large dams (i.e. dams over 15 m high). Finger and Allouche (2002), however, claim that the WCD did not do so, but legitimized the construction of large dams, provided the planning recognizes and measures the social and environmental effects. While development became a more suspect rationale, dams were allowed "mission creep" (Warner et al. 2017), boosting their environmental credentials as "sustainable" energy sources and climate buffers.

At the centre of the large dam debate lies an epistemic dimension often taken for granted by decision-makers when planning and constructing such projects. Rationalist cost-benefit analyses in environmental and social impact assessments emphasize the material gains and losses communities and societies will experience before, during and after dam construction. Utilizing a dominant positivist perspective to plan, manage and ameliorate the impact of large dam projects often constitutes a means to an end – to comply with government regulation and not so much to promote (sustainable) development (Morrison-Saunders and Retief 2012; Partidario and Sheate 2013; Meissner 2016c).

Considering Goduka's (2012) assertion that Western-based positivistic science ignores indigenous-based knowledge, we will trace how large dam projects based on a positivistic science clash with indigenous-based perspectives of socio-economic development and normative rights and values. We will also see, however, that this dichotomy is less pronounced than might be anticipated.

History and current context

Access to land plays a central role in Namibia since around 90% of the population utilize land for their livelihood either as commercial or subsistence farmers or workers employed in agriculture. In the northern regions of the country, the indigenous population practices settled agriculture and animal husbandry. All pre-colonial communities owned land by the community as a whole. In indigenous communities, land and water resources utilization was, and still is, held as commons. This was the political economy Europeans found when, in 1883, a German trader, Adolf Lüderitz, received the first tracts of land from chief Joseph Fredericks in the south of the territory (Werner 1993). This was, according to Werner (1993), the start of land alienation by the Europeans or the grabbing of common-pool resources such as land and water by the colonizers. By 1893, almost the entire territory's land had been acquired by eight concession companies from pastoralist communities (Werner 1993; Masson 1995). This means that the German Empire was acting in collaboration with the private sector in commodifying land. Even so, we should not discount the role of the church in the colonization of South-West Africa. The London Missionary Society established a station at Warmbad in South-West Africa from 1805 to 1811 (Kleinitz 1977; Cohen 1993). The Rhenish Missionary Society of Germany established a station at Bethanien in 1842 (Kleinitz 1977) when it took over the work of the London and Wesleyan Missionary Societies (Cohen 1993). This society conducted missionary work among the Namas and Herero that lived in the central, western and eastern parts of South-West Africa (today's Namibia). In 1870, the Finnish Missionary Society began its work among the Ovambo in the north. Catholic missionaries arrived in 1888 and started work among the Herero in 1886 and the Nama in 1888. They later extended their missionaries to the Okavango in the north of the country in 1910 (Cohen 1993). While missionary stations were established, farmers and merchant companies started operating in the country.

The grabbing of commons land was insignificant in most of Namibia's northern regions, leaving "peasant production" systems largely intact. This contrasts with the central and southern areas where colonizers practised violent and extreme forms of land dispossession to establish settler farms accompanied by forced relocation of the indigenous peoples into reserves (Werner 1993; Pankhurst 1996). Werner (1993) argues that the massacre and land dispossession of the Herero (OvaHimba, OvaZemba, Tjimba, Mdanderu and Kwandu) and Nama peoples neither defeated them nor dispossessed them of their land (Pankhurst 1996). One explanation for the OvaHimba and OvaZemba not being disposed of their land is the control of veterinary diseases in South-West Africa.

German colonial presence in Kaokoland was inadequate to monitor the entire area. According to Miescher (2012: 102), "[i]n the north-west of the country, the 1907 Police Zone border, which roughly followed the rinderpest cordon of 1896–1897, reflected the limits of colonial authority at that time. The placement of the cordon had been partially determined by the willingness of the African elite to cooperate with the colonial authorities in combating rinderpest ... The migration of Africans from the Police Zone into Kaoko to evade colonial expansion was an ongoing process, which reflected the familial, social and economic ties that spanned across the border". Namibia's veterinary cordon fence, also known as the "red line", stretching from east to west effectively divides the country into two parts. The intention of the fence, created in 1896 and depicted on a 1911 map created by the German colonial administration as a red line, was to prevent the spread of animal diseases such as rinderpest and foot and mouth disease. Even so, before the construction of the fence, several barriers had been put in place between central and northern Namibia since colonial rule started in the 1880s. This boundary, as noted, separated the area called the Police Zone in central and southern Namibia from the northern territories. What is more, the boundary furthermore defined the imposition of administrative, legal and economic distinctions that divided "... the country into a settler-dominated region south of the border and an exclusive African territory north of the border, in which the majority of Namibians lived" (Miescher 2012: 1). In other words, settlers living south of the boundary were under German law, which protected the native inhabitants who lived north or "outside" the border against the intrusion of colonists, and, to a certain extent, were not subject to German law (Harring 2001; Meissner 2004). Because of the border, the inhabitants of Kaokoland did not experience such harsh exterminatory activities by the colonists as their native counterparts living south of the line.

How can we explain this? The peoples of Kaokoland (north-western Namibia), where the OvaHimba and OvaZemba peoples reside, lived in relative isolation for decades, rarely interacting with the German colonizers (Ezzell 2001). This was due to the remoteness of the region that geographically isolated them from the rest of the Namibia and the veterinary cordon fence. This means that the indigenous peoples were, relatively speaking, not "bothered" by the colonialists until the 1990s when Namibia planned the Epupa Dam. Due to the remoteness of Kaokoland, and since the OvaHimba also reside in southern Angola on the northern bank of the Kunene, the Namibia OvaHimba trade their cattle across the river and not so much towards the south and across the red line. Adding to this, after South-West Africa (SWA) became a South African-administered territory following the First World War in 1919 (Christie 1976; Meissner 2016a), the people of Kaokoland resisted and defied attempts by the SWA Administration to control and subdue them (Van Wolputte 2004) until Namibian independence from South Africa in 1990 (Warner and Meissner 2008. Nevertheless, according to Potts (2012), by 1990, 52% of the country's land was considered alienated or

"European", with the remaining 48% belonging to the indigenous African population. Within this context, Werner (1993: 135) argued that "the large-scale disposition of black Namibians was as much intended to provide white settlers with land as it was to deny black Namibians access to the same land, thereby denying them access to commercial agricultural production and forcing them into wage labour." That said and considering the Police Zone and boundary to isolate Kaokoland in an attempt to prevent or minimize the spread of veterinary diseases, the colonizers did not disturb the OvaHimba and OvaZemba much. The 30 years of German colonial rule appear to have been a relatively prosperous time for both peoples: they were able to trade cattle and goods across the Kunene, which made them independent, self-sufficient and rich in cattle (Harring 2001; Meissner 2004, 2016b).

Geography and ecosystem/cultural landscape

Kaokoland is a remote region situated in north-western Namibia. The Hoanib River forms the region's southern boundary, while the Kunene River marks the border in the north between Angola and Namibia. The Ovamboland and the Etosha Game Reserve forms the eastern boundary. Kaokoland can be described as a hot desert with rainfall occurring in summer (van der Merwe 1983; Becker and Getzin 2000). The rainy season occurs from February to April, with rainfall varying drastically from year to year. Precipitation decreases from the eastern part's (300 mm to 400 mm) average annual rainfall to the western part with only 50 mm to 100 mm average annually. Topographically, Kaokoland covers an area of 49,000 km². It is characterized as a low mountain region consisting of the interior highlands or escarpment reaching a maximum altitude of just over 2,000 m, the pro-Namib coastal plains and the plains of the Northern Namib Desert (Hilton-Taylor 1994; Becker and Getzin 2000).

Considering the indigenous population of Kaokoland, the OvaHimba and OvaZemba people are an essentially self-sufficient people of about 50,000 and 12,000 individuals, respectively (Ezzell 2001; Harring 2001; Yamashina 2010; Meissner 2004, 2016c). Angolan OvaHimba and OvaZemba (Yamashina, 2010), living in the south-western part of Angola bordering on the Kunene River, are direct relatives of those living in Namibia. Both the OvaHimba and OvaZemba peoples are unique and different compared to peoples in other regions in Namibia (Dibene 2017)[1].

They have cultural or religious assets, for instance their ancestral graves, that define their unique communal lifestyle and identity as a collective. Their graves

---

[1] The OvaHimba and OvaZemba are visually distinct from other ethnic groups in Namibia and Angola. The OvaHimba dress in leather aprons and are naked above the waist. The women also smear their bodies with a mixture of ochre and butter fat. They are economically independent, and for this reason their culture, traditional way of life, religion and social patterns are reasonably intact (Ezzell 2001; Harring 2001; Meissner 2004, 2016a). The OvaZemba distinguish themselves by their unique hairstyles, beadwork, attire and cultural practices.

are usually located about 1 or 2 kilometres from the settlement and are always near a riverbed. Every individual picks the site where s/he wants to be buried. The gravesites are gathering places for ceremonial rites and the commemoration of ancestors. These gravesites are basic identity statements, indicating where a person felt most comfortable and belonged. Both peoples keep their graves separated from each other (Bollig 1997; Harring 2001; Meissner 2004, 2016a, b). The gravesites not only define an individual's personal identity, but also that of the entire community.

Local population and resource use

The OvaHimba are semi-nomadic pastoralists who keep cattle, sheep and goats (FIVAS 2000; Meissner 2004, 2016a, b, c). In the harsh and dry Kaokoland climate, the OvaHimba coexist with the OvaZemba agro-pastoralists, who also raise cattle and goats and have land areas for cultivation. Both peoples move around large areas of Kaokoland and across the border into Angola, according to the season, for access to food and grazing for their livestock. During the dry season, grazing and water are mainly found along the Kunene River. It is, therefore, during this period that their settlements can be found near the river. Here, they get access to palms and other trees, providing them and their animals with fodder and shelter. They also plant gardens in the shade of these trees to augment their dietary needs. Thus, the vegetation that provides them with food, fodder and access to water makes the area along the river of vital importance to them during times of drought (FIVAS 2000; Meissner 2004, 2016a, b, c).

Their cattle's primary value is cultural, representing power and wealth (Harring 2001; Meissner 2004, 2016a). Because of this, the OvaHimba and OvaZemba economies hardly have a cash economy. At present, there may be as many as 33,000 head of cattle owned by the OvaHimba community. This represents great wealth by African and Western standards, meaning they are prosperous people from a Western perspective (Harring 2001; Meissner 2004, 2016a, b). Apart from cattle, land is also of significance for these peoples. These two aspects of the economies are distinctively interrelated, for no cattle can be kept without large tracts of available land in semi-arid Kaokoland. As already mentioned, their land is held communally, with land rights derived from customary law that is administered by chiefs and counsellors. Their livestock, especially cattle, are large in number, and can reach up to 500 per family, with an average of 100 head per family. The large number of livestock requires a careful allocation of grazing, because of the semi-desert environment. Both tribes have grazing rights in the Baynes Dam's construction area. The area has the most reliable source of water and is therefore reserved for the communal usage of the tribe during times of drought (Harring 2001; Meissner 2004; 2016a, b, c) that can have a debilitating influence on the peoples, and Namibia's economy.

National economy and legal framework

National economy

Namibia has a sophisticated formal economy, based on capital-intensive industry and farming. Even so, the economy is heavily dependent on the earnings from primary commodity exports such as minerals (diamonds), livestock and fish. The economy is also deeply integrated with the South African economy, since the bulk of Namibia's imports originates there (GlobalSecurity.org, 2020).

Its mineral wealth, combined with a small population of 2.5 million people, gives Namibia the status of an upper-middle-income country (World Bank Group 2019). The annual gross domestic product (GDP) growth published by The World Bank Group (2019) showed the economy reversing from 1.1% in 2016 to -0.9% in 2017 and -0.5% in 2018.

Currently (in 2020), Namibia is experiencing one of the worst droughts in its history, with crop harvests reduced by 53% below the last season and 42% below the 20-year average. GlobalSecurity.org (2020), a United States-based think tank, notes that the southern African region-wide drought was disastrous for the Namibian economy. In 2019, President Hage Geingob declared a state of emergency due to poor rainfall and the predominant drought. According to the World Bank (2019), 500,000 Namibians faced food insecurity and water shortages in 2019. Within six months, around 60,000 head of cattle had starved due to inadequate grazing.

Legal framework

Angola-Namibia cooperation

Peace broke out between Angola and South Africa in April 1989. Namibia's northern area returned to normal after the implementation of the United Nations' Resolution 435 (Barber and Barratt 1990; Meissner 2000, 2003) and the election of the Namibia constituent assembly seven months later. Angola and Namibia immediately started cooperating over the Kunene River. In May 1989, Angolan and Namibian delegations met in Windhoek, Namibia's capital, to reactivate the 1969 agreement between Portugal[2] and South Africa. On the agenda was the establishment of a Joint Technical Committee (JTC), which was approved in July 1989 (Meissner 2000, 2004, 2016a, b, c), that became the Permanent Joint Technical Committee (PJTC).

When Namibia gained independence, cooperation between the two countries over the Kunene River gained momentum. Namibia knew that it needed electricity to power the economy. On 18 September 1990, Namibia entered into two

---

[2] Angola was a Portuguese colony, which explains why Portugal signed a treaty on its behalf with South Africa on the joint development of the Kunene River. Angola gained independence from Portugal in 1975.

separate agreements with Angola regarding collaboration over the Kunene and general cooperation. An agreement was signed to reactivate the three previous agreements between Portugal and South Africa dated 1926, 1964 and 1969 (Republic of Namibia 1990a, 1990b; Meissner 2000; Heyns, 2003; Meissner 2004, 2016a, b, c). The Kunene agreement envisaged, among others, the following: (1) the completion of the Ruacana-Calueque water scheme; (2) the establishment of the Joint Operating Authority with the task of ensuring the maximum beneficial regulation at Govei that was needed for optimum power generation at Ruacana, to control the withdrawal of water along the middle reaches of the Kunene, and to ensure the continuous operation and adequate maintenance of the water pumping works at Calueque and the diversion weir at Ruacana; and (3) allowing the PJTC, established in terms of the 1969 agreement, to evaluate the development of further schemes on the Kunene to accommodate the present and future needs for electricity in both countries (Republic of Namibia 1990a; Meissner 2000; Heyns 2003; Meissner 2004, 2016a).

The agreement of general cooperation created the Angolan-Namibian Joint Commission of Cooperation (JCC) for shared cooperative endeavours on several issues, one of which was water. This Commission was a legacy of the friendly relations established between Angola and the South-West Africa People's Organization (SWAPO) in the years before Namibia's independence (Republic of Namibia 1990b; Meissner 2000, 2004, 2016).

Namibian water governance

The Namibian Department of Water Affairs is part of the Ministry of Agriculture, Water and Land Reform. The department is responsible for water resource management, including the construction of dams. It is also the custodian for the country's water resources. Water[3] for domestic and industrial users is supplied and controlled by the state-run utility, NamWater (Heyns 1995; Heyns et al. 1998; Republic of Namibia 2000a; Ashton and Neal 2003; Warner and Meissner 2008).

In the early 2000s, Namibia started finalizing a new water act (Republic of Namibia 2000b; Ashton and Neal 2003), the Water Resources Management Act No. 11 of 2013. This Act provides for the management, protection, development, use and conservation of the country's water resources. Two of these functions relate directly to the development of the Kunene River. The first deals with "... the joint management, planning and development of projects concerning shared water resources in furtherance of the objectives of the Southern African Development Community Revised Protocol on Shared Watercourses regarding regional integration, economic growth and poverty alleviation". The second function relates,

---

[3] The control, use and conservation of water used to be regulated by the Water Act No. 54 of 1956 (including amendments up to 1979) and the Water Amendment Act No. 22 of 1985 (Heyns et al. 1998; Warner and Meissner 2008). These two acts were promulgated in South Africa. They were implemented during the period before, and shortly after, Namibia's transition to independence.

to a certain extent, to the involvement of stakeholders in internationally shared river basins. Even so, the central theme herein deals specifically with Namibia's interests and: "to encourage the participation of Namibia stakeholders in discussions concerning the identification and formulation of the interests of Namibia in the development of internationally shared water resources" (Republic of Namibia 2013: 24). With regard to the management of shared international rivers, the Act specifies the functions of the Minister relating to the joint management of these internationally shared water resources.

The line functional activities of several other ministries, like the Ministry of Mines and Energy; the Ministry of Environment, Forestry and Tourism; the Ministry of Works and Transport; and the Ministry of Urban and Rural Development, which can have a major impact on the country's water resources, are coordinated through the Department of Water Affairs (Heyns et al. 1998; Ashton and Neal 2003; Warner and Meissner 2008). This coordination is in line with the concern for environmental issues and the prevention of natural resource degradation, which is enshrined in the country's constitution (Republic of Namibia 1990c Warner and Meissner 2008). Namibia's National Development Plans make explicit reference to the central role water plays in Namibia's socio-economic development initiatives, and the necessity to align the activities of all government departments that have an influence on the country's water resources with this strategic objective (Heyns et al. 1998; Ashton and Neal 2003; Warner and Meissner 2008).

Part 2: The Mega-Infrastructure Project

Project description

Namibia is not richly endowed with coal reserves, like its southern neighbour, South Africa. The Kunene River is suitable for the generation of hydroelectricity, due to its steep gradient from source to mouth. The Ruacana hydropower plant provides about half Namibia's electricity. Hydroelectric power plants at Epupa and Baynes could generate additional energy for the Namibian mining sectors for some time to come. Such power plants could, therefore, increase Namibia's energy security prospects (Meissner 2003, 2004).

The design, planning, projection and building of infrastructures are never straightforward and are seldom undertaken from scratch, and likewise, both dam designs have seen multiple incarnations (Ullberg 2019). Indeed, infrastructures "usually do not appear *de novo*, but rather build on the legacy of previous infrastructural forms" (Harvey and Knox 2015). As such, new projects aim to restructure what already exists or to complement existing networks and systems (Salet et al. 2012).

All the dams on the Kunene are connected in an integrated if as yet incomplete system. The Gové Dam on the Upper Kunene in Angola regulates the river's flow, which is vital for the optimal functioning of the Calueque dam, Ruacana diversion weir and Baynes hydropower plant. Together, the suite of dams promises to bring modernity and development, regulating unregulated spaces, and not only reduce energy dependency on South Africa, but actually sell hydroelectricity to South Africa. For this, they "do not need to adapt to the realities and practices of local populations. On the contrary, it is these local populations who need to adapt, not the plans" (Boelens et al., 2019).

Below we will briefly sketch the *establishment* of the Epupa and Baynes dams.

Epupa

The proposed Epupa hydroelectric power scheme will augment the existing Kunene power project (Ruacana) constructed in the 1960s and 1970s. Before South Africa's withdrawal from Angola and Namibia in the late 1980s, it had planned to build the Epupa Dam 160 kilometres downstream from Ruacana. This plan was transferred to the Namibian government on independence in 1990, after which NamPower announced its intention to implement the scheme. The Epupa project design consists of a 150-metre high and 600-metre long dam wall. The reservoir created by the dam would be between 70 and 80 kilometres long and flood an area of around 295 square kilometres, with a reservoir capacity of 7,300 million cubic metres. The hydroelectric power plant's installed capacity would be 415 megawatts to produce 1,650 gigawatt hours a year (Warwick 1996; Harring 2001; Heyns 2003; Meissner 2005, 2016a, b, c; Meissner and Jacobs 2016).

Baynes

The site for the planned Baynes Hydropower Project is situated 200 km downstream from Ruacana. This long-term project is currently in a feasibility phase, with construction planned to start in 2021. The Baynes Dam emanates from initial studies conducted on the Epupa and Baynes sites between 1995 and 1998. These studies found that, while Epupa is preferable because of its larger storage capacity, Baynes would be less disruptive to the OvaHimba and would have a lower environmental impact. The Angolan preference for the Baynes site over Epupa meant the dam depended on the upstream Gové Dam, which was damaged in the war (Meissner 2016a, b, c). Angola was willing to bear the cost of repairing the Gové Dam (Alao 2007). The Baynes Dam's dependence on the Gové Dam operating at full throttle remains a foreseeable risk today.

Namibia initiated the Baynes Hydropower Project after "the Firm Power Contract (FPC) with ESKOM [South Africa's state-owned electricity utility] expired in 2005 and could not be renewed due to a critical power shortage faced in South Africa at the time. [Electricity] [i]mports became significantly more expensive, especially during peak hours and consequently both the Angolan and Namibian governments agreed to study the Baynes option further" (NamPower 2018).

The power station's capacity, 600 megawatts, is to be shared equally between Angola and Namibia. The dam will serve as a mid-merit peaking station allowing NamPower not to buy imported power during peak periods. The height of the dam wall will be 200 metres, the reservoir is 43 kilometres long and 4 kilometres wide. Although Baynes is smaller than Epupa's planned 7,300 million cubic metres capacity, the Baynes hydropower station is far from small, with its generating capacity of 1,610 gigawatt hours (GWh). NamPower was planning to start construction in 2014, but it was halted in 2015 after expert and NGO criticism (International Rivers 2020). However, recently a contract has been signed for the construction of the dam in 2021 to supply 600 megawatts (Takouleu 2020). Building is supposed to be completed in four years, at an estimated US$1.2 billion budget to be raised by NamPower.

Environmental and social impacts

The Baynes reservoir will inundate an area of 57 square kilometres and hold 5,000 million cubic metres of water (NamPower 2018). In Table 1, we compare the impacts between the Epupa and Baynes dams on the environment and people, indicating that Epupa will have a more destructive impact on the people than Baynes. Although the information contained in the table is dated, it still indicates the comparative environmental and social impacts of both dams.

Table 1: A comparison of the environmental and social impacts of Epupa and Baynes

Issues	*Epupa*	*Baynes*
Land resources	Flood 110 permanent dwellings, with an impact on 1,000 permanent land users and 5,000 occasional users.	Impacting on 100 permanent land users and 2,000 occasional users.
Riverine forests	Destruction of the OvaHimba social and economic status and hundreds of tonnes of palm nuts and end gardening in the fertile soil	
Loss of grazing	17,500 hectares, and an additional 70,000 hectares in times of scarcity.	
Ancestral graves	160	15
Health risks	Higher incidence of malaria and bilharzia (schistosomiasis) and human immunodeficiency virus (HIV).	

Source: Daniels 2003.

These effects are a bone of contention for the interest groups that lobbied against both dam projects through a variety of strategies – and a perceived "invasion" by some 4,000 project workers.

Local population and interest groups' perspectives and strategies

In the early 2000s, Meissner (2000: 119–125, 2003: 268) indicated that a "… possible future political constraint on the… joint development of the Kunene and Epupa Dam is the question of the relocation of the OvaHimba people residing in the area of the proposed dam". He went on to say t: "This constraint will in future be a very real one that may determine the future joint development of the Kunene River basin" (Meissner 2003: 268). Currently, this also seems to be the case for the Baynes Dam. Considering practice theory, in this regard, then, continuity seems the order of the day. Even so, there were also changes in terms of the actors' various power resources, particularly regarding the change of opinion of one of the OvaHimba chiefs (more on this later). The strategies employed by the interest groups exemplify the processes and (cultural) context in which they practised their misgivings about the projects. Not only did they employ bodily activities, such as visiting Europe, but they also made pronouncements about the dams linked directly to the indigenous people's cultural heritage and rights (Meissner and Warner 2021) on common property of land and related common-pool resources. In this way, the interest groups, and specifically the indigenous peoples, enacted agency to bring about change with their background knowledge rooted in their independent way of life and dependency on the river and its resources.

The ethics regarding the people's relocation takes centre stage in the debate and informs much of the interest group's strategies. The rights of the OvaHimba and OvaZemba clash with Namibia's need for electricity and socio-economic development. The debate has also "pitted the Namibian government against a coalition of interest groups, who are taking up the cause of the OvaHimba people at an international level" (Meissner 2003: 268).

One powerful way of moving an issue up the social and political agenda is "securitization". Security framing of an issue has a particular "social magic" in structuring the field. Non-state actors such as interest groups often seek to securitize issues to catapult them to the top of political and security agendas. Frames and metaphors are frequently used strategies (Fischhendler 2015).

Indigenous opponents often oppose mega projects because of the spatial placement, on top of graves or religiously important sites. These ancestral sites are thus culturally "securitized" together with life and death issues, over and above normal politics and cost benefit calculations. Securitization is constituted by ideational power when groups actively coalesce with like-minded groups and use specialized background knowledge gained from the network to generate ideational power principles. We found that this practice of securitization by indigenous peoples acting as communal interest groups was done in concert with another actor that has the necessary background knowledge about political structures that favour the minority indigenous groups.

In the 1990s, a distinctive interactive pattern developed between communal (OvaHimba) and transnational interest groups over the proposed Epupa Dam. This coalition of interest groups lobbied the Namibian governmentand governments that were either indirectly or directly involved. These governments were either planning on funding the dam, or, in the case of Germany, was a former colonial power. The notion of resource use perception plays an informing role. "Resource use perception is the perceived utilization of a resource within a distinctive mindset" (Meissner 2000: 119). Due to resource use perception, environmentalists and indigenous peoples, on the one hand, and engineers and government agencies, on the other, often do not see eye to eye when it comes to the construction of large dams (Meissner 2000).

The OvaHimba became aware of the proposed Epupa dam during the prefeasibility study of 1993. The reason for this was that some members of the study team, and most notably scientists working on the study, informed the OvaHimba about the proposed dam. At the same time, other interest groups also became involved in the debate. This was after a South African scientist, who worked on a study in the Kunene region, alerted *Urgewald* (a German-based interest group) about the proposed dam. *Urgewald*, in turn, contacted International Rivers, a US-based activist group, who then alerted Earthlife Africa-Namibia (ELA) about the project. In 1995, an anthropologist, Christa Coleman, working with the OvaHimba in the Kunene region also highlighted the plight of the people, should the dam be constructed (Meissner 2004, 2005, 2016a, b, c). Individuals working in a scientific environment before the debate was transnationalized on a broader scale first articulated it (Meissner 2005, 2016a, b, c; Meissner and Jacobs 2016).

According to Ezzell (2001), the OvaHimba were first apprised of the dam through a letter in English, a language they did not speak conveyed in a form they could not appreciate, and they ignored the communication. It took a South African physicist alerting interest groups about the intention to build the dam and its consequences for the OvaHimba to make interest groups spring into action (Meissner 2005, 2016a, b, c; Meissner and Jacobs 2016).

In 1997, transnational interest groups supported the OvaHimba chiefs Hikuminue Kapika and Paulus Tjavara in their visit to Europe, loudly denouncing the dams, a mobilization that convinced Swedish and Norwegian contractors that the plan should not go ahead without a mitigation strategy for affected peoples (Owen-Smith 2011). Their protest was given a moral boost by the WCD in 2000. The OvaHimba were given an opportunity to make a deposition to the WCD (Meissner 2005, 2016a, b, c).

A second plank of their strategy was to call for alternative forms of power generation. The Epupa Action Committee, consisting of the OvaHimba communities, sent a letter to Finnish President Martti Ahtisaari asking him to advise the Namibian government to look for alternative power sources (Meissner 2005, 2016a, b, c). This also resurfaced in the later Baynes Dam controversy.

In August 2000, the Angolan government decided the dam was not a priority. NamPower, however, decided it would build the dam irrespectively. A new environmental impact assessment was tendered and awarded to British consultants ERM. They advised scrapping the Epupa Dam and going ahead with the Baynes Dam. In the late 2000s, the OvaHimba blocked the construction of the Epupa Dam. According to environmental interest groups, had the dam been approved, its operation would have flooded OvaHimba lands, wiping out their entire lifestyle, culture and resources, including the palm trees they rely on for nuts during droughts (Table 1). But this didn't stop the Namibian government's continued efforts to build a dam somewhere else on the Kunene River (Daniels 2003; Meissner 2005, 2016a, b, c).

The New Humanitarian (2008) online newsletter reported the following in 2008 after the "successful" blocking of the dam at Epupa Falls by the OvaHimba: "In the successful resistance mounted by the OvaHimba to thwart construction of the dam at Epupa Falls, the OvaHimba's main protagonist, Chief Hikuminue Kapika, travelled to the donor countries of Germany, Sweden, Norway and England to drum up support for their cause".

In feasibility studies completed in 2008, the Baynes Mountain area was named as an alternative site for the dam, and by 2011, the government had a new plan in place to construct the dam at this location. Although the Baynes site is less destructive, according to International Rivers and Earth Peoples, the OvaHimba members never gave consent. Muhapikwa Muniombara, an OvaHimba woman, told South Africa's *Mail & Guardian* newspaper: "We survive from the Baynes mountains. It is where we can move our cattle in springtime for grazing, where we get the honey sugar. It is our kitchen" (Lesieur 2010).

After the FPC with ESKOM expired (NamPower 2018), the search for alternatives to reduce dependence on South Africa gave an economic impetus to revive the Baynes Hydropower Project.

This time, the government met with a well-oiled protest machinery. In 2012, a public declaration against the construction of the Baynes Dam was signed. It reports a string of meetings with the government of Namibia, in which OvaHimba and OvaZemba, as original inhabitants and "true owners" of the area that was going to be "destroyed and flooded by the dam", rejected the dam. They reject the influx of strangers and roads and warn of environmental destruction, with fish and turtles dying due to the river blockage. The declaration mentions the peoples being offered money by way of compensation, but they dismiss it out of hand: "If they are going to build the dam, they'd better kill us first before they do that" –

some will drown themselves in the reservoir, but others will declare "civil war" (Declaration 2012; Meissner and Warner f2021).

They invoked a violation of the UN Declaration on the Rights of Indigenous Peoples (UNDRIP), which forbids forcible displacement and insists on their informed assent and requested the Special Rapporteur on indigenous rights to review the case (Declaration 2012; Meissner and Warner 2021.

The OvaHimba presented a declaration to the United Nations and staged various protest rallies in 2012 and 2013 jointly with other local indigenous communities such as the OvaZemba. In 2013, three OvaHimba leaders had a meeting in Windhoek at which they were reportedly given a 22-page report outlining an "open-door" approach for consultation of the affected groups to avoid forced displacement. They denounced this meeting (Earth Peoples 2014).

To increase the solution space, they also met with experts on solar energy during their Windhoek trip to explore it as an alternative in the same location. As in their 2012 missive, they insisted they felt unheard and therefore refused to negotiate (Sasman 2013). In 2014, the OvaHimba marched again, joined by OvaHimba from the Angolan side (Sommer 2014). As we shall see below, however, by that time a leadership issue had reared its head that changed the political dynamics around the acceptance or rejection of the proposed dam.

State and company strategies

The section below sketches the strategic rationale for Namibia, confronting the response of the indigenous peoples, followed by an unexpected volte-face on the part of a key leader.

Turning away from fossil fuels and South Africa

Major infrastructure development is the mainstay of President Nujoma's Vision 2030: the Tsumeb-Ondongwa railway line, the Cape Fria harbour and the proposed Baynes Dam. The "enchantment" of infrastructure in the case of the Baynes Dam, however, goes beyond development and export bringing in foreign currency: the dam wall itself will form a bridge between Angola and Namibia. The two initiating states in fact have aligning objectives: Angola, which has only 14 MW of non-hydro clean energy generation capacity, all of it off-grid, wants to reduce its dependence on fossil fuels. The Baynes hydropower project is within Angola's 2025 Energy Vision (Mandela 2020). Namibia is keen to reduce its dependence on South Africa.

The Namibian government hails the Baynes Dam's long-term benefits as follows: "Hydropower needs a specific mention as a renewable source of energy and traditionally the only contribution to greenhouse gases by hydropower projects are from plants decaying within the dam basin. The Baynes hydropower station is a very valuable generation asset that has the potential of supplying Namibia and Angola with reliable, clean electricity for generations to come, making the estimated investment of US$1.2 billion well worth it" (NamPower 2018).

While the Namibian and Angolan states put on a happy face, there are some notable chinks in their armour. The governments clashed over another project, the Kunene Transboundary Water Supply Project (KTWSP): the diversion of Kunene water through the Gové and Calueque dams into the Cuvelai valley in Namibia and back into Angola. Persistent rumours of an impending water conflict between Namibia and Angola abounded in early 2018 over the Calueque dam after Angola complained that Namibia was defaulting on its obligations, despite Namibia claiming there was "no conflict" (Nakale 2018). The states initiating the dam claim that the Baynes site would be less disruptive to the life of the indigenous OvaHimba and OvaZemba peoples than Epupa and would have less environmental impact. The PJTC had commenced with an Environmental and Social Impact Assessment (ESIA) for the Baynes Project in 2009.

"Various reports were submitted by the project consultants, which included a techno-economic study, scoping report and ESIA, an Environmental and Social Management Plan (ESMP) and a Strategic Environmental Assessment for the project's access roads and transmission lines" (International Rivers 2020).

As previously noted, the Baynes mega project was put on hold in 2015, but in 2018, the PJTC requested the Southern Africa Institute for Environmental Assessment (ESIA) to perform a review of the reports against the International Finance Corporation's (IFC) Performance Standards. As a result, in 2020 the states were able to agree to fast-track dam building (Mota 2020).

"Turning" the OvaHimba leader

While the environmental benefit would play well to an international audience, a negative response from the indigenous occupants of the dam area was to be expected. The Namibian authorities apparently anticipated this, presumably aware of dissent among the OvaHimba between a small group in favour versus a bigger group in opposition to the dam (Owen-Smith 2011).

In 2012, two Herero-speaking businessmen frequently visited Chief Kapika, the OvaHimba leader. In 2013, they brought along representatives of the intended Chinese contractor, and one businessman hosted the headman and some of his counsellors for three months on his farm (Bollig 2020). In 2014, Kapika reportedly had a "Road to Damascus moment" when he changed his mind about the dam, apparently "signed over to the government" (*The Namibian* 2014) and (despite earlier denial) joined the ruling SWAPO party rather than the opposition DTA, which is considered to side with those opposed to the siting of the dam in the region (*The Patriot* 2017). This seems to indicate a repositioning of Kapika's desire to persuade the OvaHimba to accept the hydropower project as their social reality.

These unexpected moves triggered a revolt in favour of Chief Kapika's half-brother Mutambanda. OvaHimba headmen are formally equal, each assisted by counsellors, and elect a formal representative from their midst. While Kapika salvaged his rule for the time being in 2014, six OvaHimba chiefs went against him in 2015, declaring "war" on the project. While Chief Kapika was stripped of his power later, he still called for speeding up the Baynes project in 2018, as, he now claimed, livelihoods, poverty alleviation and infrastructure depend on it (Kahiurika 2018). In this sense, Kapika moved from one securitization "against" to equally vociferous securitization "pro" the Baynes Dam.

Conclusion

If infrastructure is matter that moves other matter, it may also set in motion far more than that: it displaces people, cattle and livelihoods, in turn mobilizing networks of resistance and influence.

With such a long gestation, the materialization and rationale of infrastructural projects can change considerably over time – what Warner et al. (2017) have called "mission creep". What started as an enchanting development project is now "sold" as an environmental (decarbonating) project. The primary "public" of the dam projects is transnational, involving Namibia, Angola and, indirectly, South Africa. However, rather than the two states, it was the various local and international interest groups that drove the ransnationalisation of the anti-Epupa and Baynes Dam campaigns, who failed to see the "public good" of such projects for them when their living environment and cattle's foraging ground was going to be flooded. In Bourdieusian terms, they mobilized their international social and political "capital" and successfully framed their interest as an economic and cultural survival issue, strongly resonating with the values and agendas of activist civil society abroad.

How did the states and NamPower operate? For the Epupa Dam, the NamPower utility had contacted the OvaHimba in the 1990s, handing a letter to Chief Kapika, clearly failing to convey a sense of the scale of the intervention. The Angolan government appears to be playing a more active role in the Baynes Dam than was the case with Epupa, betraying a stronger presence of both government actors. But it appears to have been the Namibian government that successfully pre-empted Himba resistance to the Baynes Dam by co-opting a key opposition leader, turning securitization against to securitization for the dam project, reshaping the "field".

If frontiers denote the "difference between civilization and the wild" (Rasmussen and Lund 2018), the Epupa and Baynes dams are exemplars. The dam projects are part and parcel of Namibia's energy-based modernization drive seeking to "bring 'Namibia' to the Kaoko area in general" (Friedman 2006). Depicting the OvaHimba and OvaZemba as primitive and painting environmentalists celebrating the OvaHimba and OvaZemba as custodians of sustainability Eurocentrists and anti-developmentalists (Friedman 2006) are part of the frontier strategy. The remote and economically marginal region had largely stayed free from development; the Angola war resumed in 1992, while even after Namibia's independence the region saw skirmishes between SWAPO and South Africa's Defence Force (Hayes et al., 1998; Nicoll 2010). The dam requires ordering henceforth minimally governed space for energy production and in so doing extends state control. As a noted opposition-dominated area, the Kaokoveld is also a political frontier for SWAPO, in which the "turning" of Kapika may be considered a notable victory.

This is not necessarily the end of the story. It is of course still possible that a new opposing coalition will emerge once the Baynes works get into gear, which may again reshape the projects rationale, outlook and "publics". The present case shows, if anything, the fluidity of infrastructural project plans.

Glossary

FIVAS   *Foreningen for Internasjonale Vannstudier* (Association for International Water Studies)
WCD   World Commission on Dams

References

Alao, Abiodun. 2007. *Natural resources and conflict in Africa: The tragedy of endowment.* Rochester, England: University of Rochester Press
Ashton, Pete and Neal, Marianne. 2003. An overview of key strategic issues in the Okavango Basin. In: Turton, Anthony Richard, Ashton, Pete and Eugene Cloete, Eugene. (Eds.), *Transboundary rivers, sovereignty and development: Hydropolitical drivers in the Okavango River Basin*, Pretoria and Geneva, African Water Issues Research Unit (AWIRU) and Green Cross International, 2003.
Barber, James and Barratt, John. 1990. *South Africa's foreign policy: The search for status and security 1945–1988.* Cambridge: Cambridge University Press.
Becker, Thorsten and Getzin, Stephan. 2000. The fairy circles of Kaokoland (North-West Namibia)-origin, distribution, and characteristics. *Basic Applied Ecology*, 1: 149–159.
Boelens, Rutgerd, Shah, Esha, & Bruins, Bert. (2019). Contested knowledges: Large dams and mega-hydraulic development. *Water*, 11(3): 416. https://doi.org/10.3390/w11030416
Bollig, Michael. 1996. Resource management and pastoral production in the Epupa project area (The Kunene drainage system from Swartbooisdrift to Otjinungwa). In: NamAng, *Lower Cunene hydropower scheme feasibility study: Draft feasibility report, Part A4, Environmental assessment – Supporting studies, Epupa and Baynes projects, Volume 1.* Windhoek: The Permanent Joint Technical Commission of Angola and Namibia on the Cunene River basin.

Bollig, Micheal. 1997. Contested places. Graves and graveyards in Himba Culture. *Anthropos*, 92: 35–50.
Bollig, Michael. 2020. *Shaping the African savannah: From capitalist frontier to arid Eden in Namibia*. Cambridge: Cambridge University Press.
Borrego, Adrian Bradley. 2017. *Examining the relationship between the Namibian government and the OvaHimba of Epupa Falls*. Tucson: Bachelor's Degree with Honours Dissertation in Environmental Science, University of Arizona.
Christie, Renfrew. 1976. Who benefits by the Kunene hydro-electric schemes? *Social Dynamics*, 2(1): 31–43.
Cohen, Cynthia. 1993. 'The natives must first become good workmen': Formal education provision in German South West and East Africa compared. *Journal of Southern African Studies*, 19(1): 115–134.
Corbett, Andrew. 1999. *A case study on the proposed Epupa hydro power dam in Namibia*. Cape Town: World Commission on Dams.
Daniels, Clement. 2003. The struggle for indigenous people's rights. In: Melber, H. (Ed.), *Re-examining liberation in Namibia: Political culture since independence*. Stockholm: Nordiska Afrikainstitutet.
De Vries, Pieter. 2007. Don't compromise our desire for development! A Lacanian/Deleuzian rethinking of the anti-politics machine. *Third World Quarterly*, 28(1), 25–43.
Declaration. 2012. *Declaration by the Traditional Leaders of Kaokoland in Namibia*. http://earthpeoples.org/blog/?p=1061. Accessed on 18 November 2018.
Dibene, Kathlyn Margaret. 2017. Qualitative human health analysis of *Escherichia coli*, fecal coliforms, and *pseudemonas* in drinking water of Himba and Zemba villages in Epupa Falls, Namibia. Tucson: Pretoria: Bachelors degree with Honors in Soil, Water, and Environmental Science, University of Arizona.
Earth Peoples. 2014. *Information statement from Himba community Epupa, 30 March 2014*. http://earthpeoples.org/blog/?cat=134. Accessed on: 18 November 2020.
Enns, Charis and Bersaglio, Brock. 2020. On the coloniality of 'new' mega-infrastructure projects in East Africa. *Antipode*, 52(1): 101–123.
Ezzell, Carol. 2001. The Himba and the dam. *Scientific American*, 284(6): 80–89.
Finger, Matthias and Allouche, Jeremy. 2002. *Water privatisation: Trans-national corporations and the re-regulation of the water industry*. London: Routledge.
Fischhendler, Itay. (2015). The securitization of water discourse: Theoretical foundations, research gaps and objectives of the special issue. *International Environmental Agreements: Politics, Law and Economics*, 15(3): 245–255.
FIVAS. 2000. *FIVAS report; Power conflicts; Namibia. Epupa*. Accessed 8 February 2000 at: http://www.solidaritetshuset.org.
Friedman, John T. 2006. On the post-structuralist critique of development: A view from north-west Namibia. *Development Southern Africa*, 23(5): 587–603.
GlobalSecurity.org. 2020. Namibia – economy. Washington D.C. GlobalSecurity.org.
Goduka, Nomalungelo. 2012. From positivism to indigenous science: A reflection on world views, paradigm and philosophical assumptions. *Africa Insight*, 41(4): 123–138.
Harring, Sidney L. 2001. 'God gave us this land': The OvaHimba, the proposed Epupa dam, the independent Namibian state, and law and development in Africa. *Georgetown International Law Review*, 14: 36–106.

Harvey, Penny and Knox, Hannah. 2015. *Roads: An anthropology of infrastructure and expertise*. Ithaca: Cornell University Press.
Hayes, Patricia, Silvester, Jeremy, Wallace, Marion, Hartmann, Wolfram. (Eds.) 1998. *Namibia under South African Rule: Mobility and Containment 1915–1946*. Athens, OH: Ohio University Press.
Heyns, Piet. 1995. *Existing and Planned Water Development Projects on International Rivers within the SADC Region*. Paper presented at the Conference of SADC Ministers Responsible for Water Resources Management, Pretoria, November 23–24, unpublished manuscript.
Heyns, Piet. 2003. Water-resources management in Southern Africa. In Nakayama, M. (Ed.), *International waters in Southern Africa*. Tokyo: United Nations University Press.
Heyns, Piet, Montgomery, Sy Pallet, John and Seely, Mary 1998. *Namibia's water: A decision-maker's guide*. Windhoek: Desert Research Foundation of Namibia and the Department of Water Affairs.
Hilton-Taylor, Craig. 1994. The Kaokoland. In: WWF and IUCN, Centres of Plant Diversity (Eds.), *A guide and strategy for their conservation*. Cambridge: IUCN Publication Unit.
International Rivers. 2020. With a new dam proposed on the Kunene River, the Himba people mobilize to permanently protect their lifeblood, 27 February 2020. https://www.internationalrivers.org/blogs/1259/with-a-new-dam-proposed-on-the-kunene-river-the-himba-people-mobilize-to-permanently. Accessed 23 June 2020.
Kahiurika, Ndanki. 2018. Chief Kapika calls for implementation of Baynes hydropower project. The Namibian, 28 May 2018. https://www.namibian.com.na/177806/archive-read/Chief-Kapika-calls-for-implementation-of-Baynes-hydropower-project. Accessed on 23 June 2020.
Keinitz, Alvin. 1977. The key role of the Orlam migrations in the early Europeanization of South-West Africa (Namibia). *The International Journal of African Historical Studies*, 10(4): 553–572.
Larkin, Brian. 2013. The politics and poetics of infrastructure. *Annual Review of Anthropology*, 42: 327–343.
Lundmark, Robert. 1997. *Namibia's energy support problem: The Epupa scheme*. Luleå: Masters Dissertation in the Faculty Economics, Luleå Technical University.
Lesieur, Alexandra. 2010. Namibia's Himba fear dam will wash away traditions. *Mail & Guardian*, 21 September 2010. https://mg.co.za/article/2010-09-21-namibias-himba-fear-dam-will-wash-away-traditions/. Accessed on 23 June 2020.
Mandela, Dominic. 2020. Namibia, Angola to develop cross-border Baynes hydroelectricity dam. *Construction Review Online*, 20 March 2020. https://constructionreviewonline.com/2020/03/namibia-angola-to-develop-cross-border-baynes-hydroelectric-dam/. Accessed on: 23 June 2020.
Masson, John R. 1995. A fragment of colonial history: The killing of Jacob Marengo. *Journal of Southern African Studies*, 21(2): 247–256.
Meissner, Richard. 2000. Hydropolitical hotspots in Southern Africa: The case of the Kunene River. In Solomon, Hussein and Turton, Anthony. (Eds.), *Water wars: Enduring myth or impending reality*. Durban: The African Centre for the Constructive Resolution of Disputes (ACCORD).

Meissner, Richard. 2003. Interaction and existing constraints in international river basins. In: Nakayama, Mikiyasu. (Ed.), *International waters in Southern Africa*. Tokyo: United Nations University Press.

Meissner, Richard. 2004. *The transnational role and involvement of interest groups in water politics: A comparative analysis of selected southern African case studies*. Pretoria: D.Phil. Dissertation in the Faculty of Humanities, University of Pretoria.

Meissner, Richard. 2005. Interest groups and the proposed Epupa Dam: Towards a theory of water politics. *Politeia*, 24(3): 354–370.

Meissner, Richard. 2015. Book Review: Dams, displacement, and the delusion of development: Cahora Bassa and its legacies in Mozambique, 1965–2007. *South African Journal of International Affairs*, DOI:10.1080/10220461.2015.1093956.

Meissner, Richard. 2016a. *Hydropolitics, interest groups and governance: The case of the proposed Epupa Dam*. Heidelberg: Springer.

Meissner, Richard. 2016b. Concepts and views from international relations and their potential contribution to impact assessment thinking and practice. *Politikon*, 43(3): 411–428.

Meissner, Richard. 2016c. The relevance of social theory in the practice of environmental management. *Science and Engineering Ethics*, 22: 1345–1360.

Meissner, Richard and Jacobs, Inga. 2016. Theorising complex water governance in Africa: The case of the proposed Epupa Dam on the Kunene River. *International Environmental Agreements: Politics, Law and Economics*, 16(1): 21–48.

Meissner, Richard and Warner, Jeroen. 2021. Indigenous paradiplomacy and the Baynes hydro-electric dam on the Kunene River. *Regions and Cohesion*, 11(1): 21–48

Miescher, Giorgio. 2012. *Namibia's red line: The history of a veterinary and settlement border*. London: Palgrave Macmillan.

Morrison-Saunders, Angus and Retief, Francois. 2012. Walking the sustainable assessment talk: progressing the practice of environmental impact assessment (EIA). *Environmental Impact Assessment*, 36: 34–41.

Mota, Siziwe. 2020. With a new dam proposed on the Kunene River, the OvaHimba people mobilize to permanently protect their lifeblood. *International Rivers*, 27 February 2020. https://www.internationalrivers.org/blogs/1259/with-a-new-dam-proposed-on-the-kunene-river-the-himba-people-mobilize-to-permanently. Accessed on: 23 June 2020.

Nakale, Albertina. 2018. No Namibia-Angola conflict over water. *New Era*, January 26.

Nakayama, Mikiyasu and Fujikura, Ryo. 2006. Issues in World Commission on dams report development: Inconsistencies between the facts found and the guideline. *Hydrological Progress*, 20: 1263–1272.

NamPower. 2018. *Baynes hydropower project*. https://www.nampower.com.na/page.aspx?p=222. Accessed on: 22 November 2018.

New Era. 2016. Kunene hydropower project will uplift nation – Muharukua. *New Era*, 9 June 2016. https://neweralive.na/posts/kunene-hydropower-project-uplift-nation-muharukua. Accessed on: 29 June 2020.

Nicoll, Kathleen. 2010. Geomorphic development and Middle Stone Age archaeology of the lower Cunene River, Namibia-Angola border. *Quaternary Science Review*, 29: 1419–1431.

O'Neill, Patrick. 1998. Arun, Bakun and now Epupa? *International Waterpower and Dam Construction*, 50(2): 14–16.

Owen-Smith, Garth. 2011. *An arid Eden: A personal account of conservation in the Kaokoveld*. Johannesburg: Jonathan Ball Publishers.
Pankhurst, Donna. 1996. Similar but different? Assessing the reserve economy legacy of Namibia. *Journal of Southern African Studies*, 23(3): 405–420.
Partidario, Maria Rosario and Sheate, William R. 2013. Knowledge brokerage: Potential for increased capacities and shared power in impact assessment. *Environmental Impact Assessment Review*, 39: 26-36.
Pottinger, Lori. 1997. Namibian government clings to Epupa Dam despite opposition, alternatives. *World Rivers Review*, 12(3). http://www.irn.org/pubs/wrr/9706/epupa.ht ml. Accessed on: 31 July 1999.
Potts, Deborah. 2012. Land alienation under colonial and white settler governments in southern African: Historical land 'grabbing'. In: Allan, Tony, Keulertz, Martin, Sojamo, Suvi, and Warner, Jeroen. (Eds.), *Handbook of land and water grabs in Africa: Foreign direct investment and food and water security*. London: Routledge.
Rasmussen, Mattias Borg and Lund, Christian. 2018. Reconfiguring frontier spaces: The territorialization of resource control. *World Development*, 101, 388–399.
Republic of Namibia. 1990a. *Agreement between the government of the Republic of Namibia and the government of the People's Republic of Angola in regard to the development and utilization of the water potential of the Kunene River*. Signed at Lubango, Angola on 18 September 1990.
Republic of Namibia. 1990b. *Agreement between the government of the Republic of Namibia and the government of the People's Republic of Angola on general co-operation and the creation of the Angolan-Namibian Joint Commission of Co-operation*. Signed at Lubango, Angola on 18 September 1990.
Republic of Namibia. 1990c. *Constitution of the Republic of Namibia (Act No. 1 of 1990)*. Windhoek: Government Printer.
Republic of Namibia. 2000a. *Securing Water for the Future*. Namibian Representative's Statement to the Second World Water Forum, The Hague, The Netherlands, from 16–22 March 2000. Windhoek: Ministry of Agriculture, Water and Rural Development.
Republic of Namibia. 2000b. *National Water Policy White Paper*. Windhoek: Ministry of Agriculture, Water & Rural Development.
Republic of Namibia. 2013. *Water Resources Management Act, 11 of 2013*. Windhoek: Republic of Namibia.
Salet, Willem, Bertolini, Luca and Giezen, Mendel. 2012. Complexity and uncertainty: Problem or asset in decision making of mega infrastructure projects? *International Journal of Urban and Regional Research*, 6: 1984–2000.
Sasman, Catherine. 2013. Himba, Zemba reiterate 'no' to Baynes Dam. *The Namibian*, 26 March 2013.
Sommer, Rebecca. 2014.Semi-Nomadic Himba march protest dam and attempted bribery of their chief. *Intercontinental Cry*. March 29. https://intercontinentalcry.org/semi-n omadic-himba-march-protest-dam-attempted-bribery-chiefs/
Sturup, Sophie and Low, Nicholas. 2019. Sustainable development and mega infrastructure: An overview of the issues. *Journal of Mega Infrastructure and Sustainable Development*, 1(1): 8–26.
Takouleu, Jean Marie. 2020. Angola/Namibia: Concluded agreement for Baynes Dam construction in 2021. *Afrik21*, 10 April 2020. https://www.afrik21.africa/en/angola-n

amibia-concluded-agreement-for-baynes-dam-construction-in-2021/. Accessed on: 23 June 2020.
Tarr, Peter. 2007. Epupa Dam case study. *Water Resources Development*, 23(3): 473–484.
The Namibian. 2014. Chief Kapika retains his throne after backing from paternal line. *The Namibian*, 14 May 2014. https://www.namibian.com.na/123183/archive-read/Chief-Kapika-retains-his-throne-after-backing. Accessed on: 23 June, 2020.
The Namibian. 2015. Kandjoze says Baynes project has some outstanding issues. *The Namibian*, 16 November 2015.: https://www.namibian.com.na/144323/archive-read/Kandjoze-says-Baynes-project-has-some-outstanding-issues. Accessed on: 23 June 2020.
The New Humanitarian. 2008. Dam will mean our destruction, warn Himba. *The New Humanitarian*, 18 January 2008. t: https://www.thenewhumanitarian.org/report/76311/namibia-dam-will-mean-our-destruction-warn-himba. Accessed on: 23 June 2020.
The Patriot. 2017. Politics delay Baynes as energy crisis looms. *The Patriot*, 12 May 2017. https://thepatriot.com.na/index.php/2017/05/12/politics-delay-baynes-as-energy-crisis-looms/. Accessed on: 23 June 2020.
The World Bank Group. 2019. *Namibia: Overview*. Washington D.C.: The World Bank Group.
Ullberg, Susann Baez. 2019. Making the megaproject: Water infrastructure and hydrocracy at the public-private interface in Peru. *Water Alternatives*, 12(2): 503–520.
Van der Merwe, Jacobus Nel. 1983. *National Atlas of South West Africa*. University of Stellenbosch: Stellenbosch.
Van Wolputte, Steven. 2004. Subject disobedience: The colonial narrative and native counterworks in Northwestern Namibia, c. 1920–1975. *History and Anthropology*, 15(2): 151–173.
Warwick, Hugh. 1996. Come hell and high water. *New Scientist*, 149(2023): 38-42.
Warner, Jeroen. 2004. *Plugging the GAP working with Buzan: The Ilisu Dam as a security issue*. Occasional Paper No 67, School of Oriental and African Studies, University of London.
Warner, Jeroen. 2012. The struggle over Turkey's Ilisu Dam: Domestic and international security linkages. *International Environmental Agreements: Politics, Law and Economics*, 12: 231–250.
Warner, Jeroen Frank. and Meissner, Richard. 2008. The politics of security in the Okavango River Basin: From civil war to saving wetlands (1975–2002): A preliminary security impact assessment. In: Pachova, Nevelina I., Nakayama, Mikiyasu. and Jansky, Libor. (Eds.), *International water security: Domestic threats and opportunities*, Tokyo: United Nations University Press.
Warner, Jeroen Frank, van Hoogesteger, Jaime, and Hidalgo, Juan Pablo. (2017). Old wine in new bottles: The adaptive capacity of the hydraulic mission in Ecuador. *Water Alternatives*, 10(2), 332–340.
Werner, Wolfgang. 1993. A brief history of land dispossession in Namibia. *Journal of Southern African Studies*, 19(1): 135–146.
World Commission on Dams (WCD). 2000. *Dams and development: A new framework for decision-making*. London: Earthscan Publications.
Yamashina, Chisato. 2010. Interactions between termite mounds, trees, and the Zemba people in the mopane savanna in north-western Namibia. *African Study Monographs*, Supplement 40: 115–128.

Small Project – Big Disaster: Large-Scale Problems within the Small-Scale Hydropower Project 'San José del Tambo' in Ecuador

Hannah Plüss, Institute of Social Anthropology, University of Bern, Switzerland

Introduction

When Hidrotambo S.A. built the hydroelectric power plant 'San José del Tambo' in the Dulcepamba River in October 2014, the villagers of San Pablo de Amalí had already lived in an ongoing conflict for ten years – years filled with protests, lawsuits, humiliation, dispossession and human rights violations. Only four months later, the village was flooded, and countless hectares of small-scale farming land was destroyed. The river carried away 12 houses, and three people died – two women and one child (Benavides 2019). This was exactly what some villagers had predicted, including the former community president and one of the most prominent, today nationally known, protest leaders who told me in February 2020 about those events. He had presented together with other villagers a demand for protective action in the local court some weeks before the flood. The judge called them lunatics and rejected their claim altogether.

For the villagers, this flood was just one particularly dramatic moment in their struggle that started with the power plant's planning 20 years ago and is ongoing today. While the majority investor and owner of Hidrotambo S.A. – a famous, extraordinarily rich Ecuadorian family called 'Cuesta' that have made a fortune on a monopoly production of rubber boots – wants to barge forward with the project no matter what and the state authorities continue to avoid assuming any responsibility to impose national law, the villagers are not only fighting against them, but against each other as well. After years of ongoing protest, the population is divided, with some in favour of the construction, others in an ongoing fight against it, and a third group tired of protesting. There is also a small NGO, comprised of two locals and three women from the US, that is helping the villagers to claim their rights and to bring the local fight to a national and international stage. The issue is a poignant example of the constant mismatch between the national legal guarantees and regulations and the local reality.

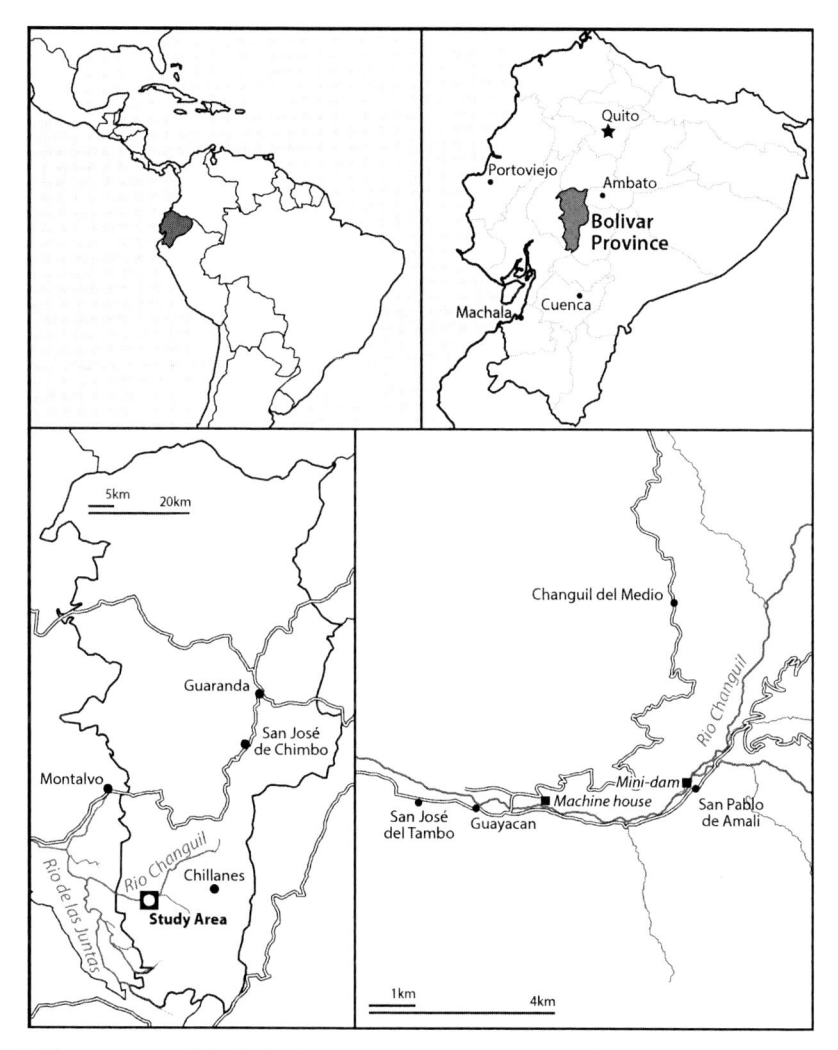

Map 1: The area around the hydroelectric power plant 'San José del Tambo' in Ecuador. Source: Map compilation and design by Manuel L. K. Abebe (2021), CDE, University of Bern, Bern, Switzerland. Geodata: OpenStreetMap contributors, GADM

In the ongoing debate around hydroelectric power production and its impacts, reaching its peak with the World Commission on Dams (WCD) report from 2000, the focus has almost exclusively been on large dams (see, for example, Scudder 2005, 2019; Richter et al. 2010; Moore et al. 2010; Phan 2018), based on the consensus that the negative impacts of large dams are mainly a problem of scale. Therefore, one prominently placed recommendation of the WCD report (2000, xxxii) is 'decentralised, small-scale options (micro hydro, home-scale solar electric systems, wind and biomass systems) based on local renewable sources'.

In contrast, the hydroelectric power plant that this chapter is about is not a mega-, as in extraordinarily big, infrastructure project. It is not even a dam. It is a small-scale run-of-the-river hydroelectric power plant that has an installed capacity of only 8 megawatts of electrical power. What I aim to describe here is how this small project brings with it a similar avalanche of negative consequences that has been observed and described in literature about large dams: dispossession of basic needs, especially commons grabbing of land and water (Franco et al. 2013: 1652); irreversible impacts on local livelihoods, biodiversity and agricultural activity (Scudder 2005: 222; 2019: 18); and, partly as a consequence of those impacts, a major displacement towards urban areas, called 'economic displacement' (Vanclay 2017: 6). Likewise, the most strategic behaviours of the important actors involved in other mega-infrastructure projects described in this collection, such as the anti-politics machine (Ferguson 1990), the (dis-)enchantment of the local community (Knox and Harvey 2012) and institution shopping (Haller 2019), can be observed.

The aim of this chapter is therefore to widen the horizon of debates around mega-infrastructure projects in this collection and around the construction of large dams in general. The example of a small infrastructure project with large impacts gives rise to the question: can the solution to the problems caused by large dams be as simple as constructing small dams? Or is it not so much about scale, but about poor construction, non-governance and entrenched power hierarchies surrounding the planning and construction of such projects? The chapter starts with a brief overview of the context in which the power plant was built, which is followed by an in-depth analysis of the case.

Part 1: historical, environmental, ethnographic and political context

History and current context

Ecuador was part of the Inca Empire and became, like all the other countries of Spanish-speaking South America, a Spanish colony after the conquest of the continent in the 15th century. It gained independence 400 years later and has been a republic since 1822.[1] There were several periods of political instability during these almost 200 years as a republic, with major shifts between democracy, military rule, and leftist and right governments.

Since colonial times, Ecuador has been a nation that provides raw material and supplies to the colonialist nations, and after independence to the 'Global North' in general. This economic pattern – interrupted by several crises – continues today (Falconí-Benítez 2001: 258). Apart from mining, plantation-like large-scale

---

[1] "Ecuador." Encyclopædia Britannica Online 07-29-2019. https://academic.eb.com/levels/collegiate/article/Ecuador/106215#129494.toc.

agriculture is very common, especially on the coast, the dominant products being cacao, bananas, coffee and, more recently, palm oil.[2]

Similarly to other countries in the region, debates around land reform began in the 1930s. The claims of indigenous, peasant and leftist organizations became more urgent over the following decades and passed from demands for better living conditions on the haciendas and plantations in the 1950s to a profound land redistribution and the formal end of the hacienda and plantation complexes altogether only a decade later (Goodwin 2017: 577–578).

Goodwin (2017: 577) detects two further periods of heightened conflict over land during the 1970s and 1990s, but he posits that the main driver for those reform efforts was not about the hacienda system anymore, but about the commodification of land that came with the advance of capitalist modernization (Goodwin 2017: 577).

In the early 21st century, under the leadership of the then president Rafael Correa, Ecuador was part of the wave of leftist governments in South America together with Venezuela, Bolivia, Argentina and Brazil. Correa put an end to the neoliberal reforms imposed during the politically turbulent end of the 20th century and reoriented the state to the left, at least at the beginning of his presidency: he raised spending on social programmes, increased agricultural subsidies,[3] and in 2008 a new constitution came into being.

This constitution is seen as one of the most progressive worldwide. First, because it includes some very progressive laws such as same-sex marriage;[4] second, because it defines Ecuador not only as a pluricultural but as a plurinational state, with wide-reaching recognition of indigenous rights (Aparicio Wilhelmi 2018: 121); third, and most importantly for this analysis, because it establishes the indigenous concept of the *Sumak Kawsay* or 'good living' and recognizes nature as a legal subject with legally enforceable rights on its own (Gudynas 2009: 37). These progressive aspects can be seen as concessions to the indigenous and campesino movement, one of the most important allies for Correa in his bid for presidency.

Geography and ecosystem/cultural landscape

Ecuador is a small country compared to its neighbours Peru and Colombia. Nevertheless, it has a very diverse landscape including parts of the Andean mountain chain with peaks at over 6,000 metres high, parts of the Amazon Basin with tropical rainforest and the coastal plains with large-scale agriculture, as mentioned above.

---

[2] Ibidem.
[3] "Rafael Correa." Encyclopædia Britannica Online 07-29-2019. https://academic.eb.com/levels/collegiate/article/Rafael-Correa/475217.
[4] "Ecuador." Encyclopædia Britannica Online 07-29-2019. https://academic.eb.com/levels/collegiate/article/Ecuador/106215#129494.toc.

It is also the most densely populated country on the continent,[5] with over 14 million inhabitants.[6] Nowadays, over 60% live in urban areas.[7] There are two big cities – Quito in the Andes, and Guayaquil on the coast. The two cities have been in an ongoing ideological dispute since independence, the former being the political and the latter the (unofficial) economic capital of the country.[8] Currently, Quito is linked to Ecuador's Andean campesino identity, while Guayaquil is linked to the export-oriented agricultural elite.

Some 62.5% of all Ecuadorians self-define as Mestizo/a, which means they are of mixed ethnicity with partly indigenous and partly European roots. The denomination 'Mestizo/a' has a considerable cultural connotation as well, and not only refers to the composition of one's ancestors.[9] The second-biggest group is the Afro-Ecuadorian population, which makes up 21.7% of the population, followed by the 11.4% that consider themselves indigenous.[10] Spanish is one of the official languages of the country, but a considerable part of the population speaks another official indigenous language, Quichua – a dialect of Quechua, which was the official language of the Inca Empire.

Local population and resource use[11]

The hydroelectric power plant owned by Hidrotambo was built in the Dulcepamba River Valley, in the south-west of Ecuador, approximately 50 kilometres away from the big city of Guayaquil. There are close to 140 villages spread throughout the whole valley with a total of approximately 14,000 inhabitants. The valley formally pertains to Ecuador's Bolivar Province, and on a smaller administrative level to the Cantón of Chillanes and the Cantón of San Miguel.

Even though the biggest part of the Province and the Cantóns are mountainous areas, the valley itself forms the intersection between the steep Andean highlands and the subtropical foothill region, which extends to the coastal plains. On the ride from the Chillanes county seat to the approximately 500-people village of San Pablo de Amalí, located exactly in front of the Hidrotambo power plant, one experiences a close to 2000-metre altitude drop and therefore a fundamental change in climatic conditions in just one and a half hours.

---

[5] https://www.indexmundi.com/map/?v=21000&r=sa&l=es. Consulted on 06-30-2020.
[6] https://www.ecuadorencifras.gob.ec/resultados/. Consulted on 06-30-2020.
[7] https://academic.eb.com/levels/collegiate/article/Ecuador/106215#129494.toc. Consulted on 06-29-2020.
[8] Ibidem.
[9] https://academic.eb.com/levels/collegiate/article/mestizo/52254. Consulted on 06-30-2020.
[10] https://www.ecuadorencifras.gob.ec/resultados/. Consulted on 06-30-2020.
[11] The information in this chapter is taken, if not indicated otherwise, from personal conversations held between 01-23-2020 and 02-15-2020 in Chillanes and San Pablo de Amalí during fieldwork and some official documents provided by the NGO 'Proyecto Socio-Ambiental Río Dulcepamba'.

Fig 1: View over the Dulcepamba Valley. Source: Emily Conrad

The region lies within two major biodiversity hot spots, called the Tumbes-Chocó-Magdalena and the Tropical Andean Hotspot (see map from Quintana et al. 2019). It is called the 'granary of Ecuador', because the ideal climatic conditions allow for a large variety of agricultural activity, ranging from animal husbandry, mainly cows and chicken, to cultivation of banana, cacao, coffee, papaya and mango in the lower elevations. In the higher regions, farmers grow potatoes, berries, beans and corn. Because of the lack of flat territory, there is no big-scale, homogeneous, plantation-like agricultural production as there is in coastal areas. The most important activity of the local population is therefore small-scale agriculture, for subsistence and for sale in local and regional markets. Cash crops can be found to a smaller extent in this area, and cacao in particular is grown mainly for international export.

Nevertheless, smallholdings were not always the predominant land ownership pattern. San Pablo de Amalí was one big hacienda until the middle of the 20th century when families from the indigenous-dominated highlands migrated down to San Pablo de Amalí. This period of hacienda left the village with a legacy of ownership mentality over every piece of land. The villagers therefore do not have any commonly used ground, and all the agriculturally productive parts of the village are divided into small territories. Thus, most people in the village own several pieces of land spread within a range of 20 kilometres. Even the small part of commonly used land upon which the church, the school and the football field are built had to be bought in a complicated process from the former hacienda owner.[12]

Fig 2: The main square of San Pablo de Amalí. Source: Emily Conrad

Surprisingly, the land ownership mentality has not been engrained around the use of water in the region. The river was used by the villagers as a common-pool resource for subsistence fisheries, sanitary needs and leisure. There were rules about how to fish, e.g. with different techniques depending on the season and without poison to maintain a healthy fish population. But, at least according to my informants' memories, there was always an abundance of water and fish and therefore no need to formalize these unofficial rules of usage.[13]

On an official level, as I will elaborate further in the next section, all water resources in Ecuador are owned by the state, which in turn grants user permits to individuals at their request. Nevertheless, an overwhelming majority of the farmers in San Pablo de Amalí and the other villages in the valley did not register their water uses because they did not deem it necessary, since there was no scarcity and

---

[12] Personal conversation with the wife of the former hacienda owner, 02-10-2020, Chillanes.
[13] Personal conversations with several villagers, San Pablo de Amalí.

therefore little dispute over water use. As such, thousands of watershed residents did not have water use permits up to the day that the hydroelectric power plant got their water use permit, which included all water resources in the region.

Despite favourable agricultural conditions, Bolivar Province is one of the poorest areas in the country (Ministerio Coordinador de Desarrollo Social 2017), probably because small-scale farming does not contribute to capitalist welfare. This fact manifests itself in insufficient or even non-existent public services in the region: even though most homes in the watershed communities are connected to the electricity supply system, even in 2010 San Pablo de Amalí did not have drainage or storm water management, and only 30% of households were part of a water supply system. There has been no public rubbish collection system in the community to date (Sardán Muyba 2015: 83ff).

The Cantón of Chillanes has approximately 17,000 inhabitants of which 90% self-identified as mestiza/o in the last census. This applies as well for people in San Pablo de Amalí who clearly identify as campesino but not as strongly with their indigenous roots. However, the villagers decided in the context of the protests against the hydroelectric power plant to self-define as a community with ancestral roots. This decision provides protection because according to Article 57 of the constitution,[14] indigenous communities have a right to receive prior, free and informed consent, but campesino communities are not explicitly included in this law.

National economy and legal framework

Ecuador's national economy mainly consists of the export of raw materials and supplies to the 'Global North'. However, under Correa's rule, there was a considerable attempt to change the direction of the national economy, away from primary resource extraction such as petroleum and towards more sustainable development (Rieckmann et al. 2011: 444).

To reach this goal, the aforementioned concept of *Sumak Kawsay* and the rights of nature established in the new constitution have played a major role. The first concept reached international importance after its institutional anchorage in the 2008 constitution, but the exact genealogy of the concept before this milestone is still debated among intellectuals. According to Carlos Viteri Gualinga (2002), for example, the concept of material development, richness and poverty did not exist in the local indigenous cosmovision. He sees *Sumak Kawsay,* therefore, as a construction that was created in the 21st century, because it is so closely linked to the idea of development, albeit in an alternative manner. Contrary to this opinion, José Benjamín Inuca Lechón (2017) traces the concept back to the middle of the 20th century and sees it more as a convergence of oriental and indigenous

---

14   https://www.asambleanacional.gob.ec/sites/default/files/documents/old/constitucion_de_bolsill o.pdf. Consulted on 10-10-2020.

knowledge. For him, *Sumak Kawsay* is 'the fight against the system of exploitation, oppression, discrimination; it is an anti-systemic, counter-hegemonic fight, from the cultural to the political sphere' (Inuca Lechón 2017: 174, translated by the author).

The second concept, the rights granted for nature, was in itself not a new idea at the time, but it was a worldwide novelty that the rights for nature are properly established in a national constitution (Rieckmann et al. 2011: 444). According to the Magna Carta, nature has the right to be respected and restored in case of damages. Ecuadorian citizens, communities, people and nationalities have the right to benefit from the richness of nature, but these benefits would be regulated and supervised by the state. Additionally, every Ecuadorian person, community or nation has the right to sue for violations against nature.

The establishment of nature as a legal subject on its own with administrative and juridical protection is such a groundbreaking change, because it leaves behind the Western vision of nature as a bunch of objects subjected to humankind and establishes the idea of nature as a living entity with intrinsic value (Rieckmann et al. 2011: 445). Therefore, the concept of *Sumak Kawsay* and the idea of nature as a legal subject with rights on its own are intertwined and offer the possibility of including another cosmovision in the political sphere of Ecuador.

An example of how those concepts apply in practice is the regulation of water: Article 3 of the new constitution defines it as a primordial duty of the state to provide all inhabitants with water. In Article 12, it establishes water as a human right. All water resources are constitutionally declared as property of the state. The will to avoid privatization is reinforced further on in the *Ley Orgánica de Recursos Hídricos, Usos y Aprovechamiento del Agua* (law on water resources, uses and benefits of water) that prohibits in Article 6 all forms of water privatization. The same law establishes in Article 86 the following hierarchy of water users: first, for human consumption; second, for irrigation that guarantees food sovereignty, e.g. all activity that provides food for personal consumption; third, environmental flows, i.e., the necessary amount of water to maintain the health of ecosystems; and fourth, productive activities such as electricity production. The *Secretaría Nacional del Agua* (SENAGUA, National Water Ministry, now called Ministerio de Ambiente y Agua) must grant water rights following this order of priorities.

Despite all these formal efforts, there are several authors that doubt the effectiveness of those legal measures in real-life situations and the willingness of Correa's and Moreno's government to fundamentally change something beyond the discursive level (see, for example, Lalander and Merimaa 2018; Clark 2018). The energy production sector, for example, still depends up to 88% on petroleum, after ten years of trying to redirect the national economy towards sustainable energy (Ponce-Jara et al. 2018). An even more demanding task is to change local power hierarchies, as the analysis of the hydroelectric power plant in the Dulcepamba River and the legal and administrative fights around it will show further on.

Part 2: The Mega-Infrastructure Project

Description of the project, its history and drivers, and information on the companies[15]

The beginning of the 'San José del Tambo' power plant can be traced back to 2003, when the national ministry of electricity granted environmental licences and operating permits for the Dulcepamba River to the Hidrotambo S.A. company. At the same time, the water ministry SENAGUA, as another state entity, provided water use permits for the same river to another company named *Corporación para la Investigación Energética* (CIE). While the operating permits granted by the ministry of electricity were only to produce energy for one factory that Hidrotambo S.A. planned to build in the area, CIE was allowed to produce electricity in the Dulcepamba River and sell it to the national grid as part of the national strategy of the Correa government to export its renewable energy production (Redacción la Fuente 2019). In 2005, CIE transferred these farer-reaching water use permits to Hidrotambo S.A.

The state entities granted all these concessions without respecting the hierarchy of water users established in the law and without any kind of socialization, prior informed consultation with, or consent from, the local community, even though these proceedings would be mandatory for projects of this magnitude (Zambrano Figueroa 2010). Equally, the companies did not coordinate or even communicate their plans to the people living on the Dulcepamba River. The antipolitics machine was already ongoing, framing the grabbing of the common-pool resource water through legal means within a nationwide discourse of renewable energy production, ignoring local livelihoods and water use patterns.

Most of my informants living in the area learned about the construction plans only when workers from Hidrotambo's subcontractor for construction, COANDES, invaded private property belonging to community members in order to begin topographic studies. There is only one villager that remembers two meetings that informed about the project, but they did not take place in the village of San Pablo de Amalí, but in the bigger town of San José del Tambo several kilometres downstream.[16]

As the former president of San Pablo de Amalí told me, he decided to call for a meeting and met with three other villagers the same day that the workers from

---

[15] This historical recompilation of the project is based on personal conversations held between 01-23-2020 and 02-15-2020 in Chillanes and San Pablo de Amalí during fieldwork and some official documents provided by the Dulcepamba River Project.
[16] Personal conversation, 07-02-2020, San José del Tambo.

COANDES invaded his territory.[17] They were all upset about the workers' rude behaviour and the lack of information and decided to confront the construction company the next day. Spreading the word, they mobilized 22 other community members. Confronted with this protest, the workers called the police to counter this community mobilization. The confrontations quickly escalated since the villagers kept on mobilizing, with up to 4,000 people coming from all the villages in the Dulcepamba valley to protest.[18] The company did not just call the police, but the military forces as well. Within months, San Pablo de Amalí was converted into a 'war zone', as several community members call it, with daily confrontations between the villagers and military forces, abundant use of tear gas and rubber bullets, and protesters being detained. Some even told me about the use of live ammunition.

During the next three years, the Army Corps of Engineers of Ecuador took over the construction of the power plant, and a considerable proportion of the villagers continued to protest. Meanwhile the state and the company completely depoliticized the construction of the power plant; they framed the protests as political offences against the state and accused several protesters of sabotage and violence. But the protesters already had a network of support within the national government. So, they went to the Constitutional Assembly in 2008, where they were granted amnesty.[19]

After this partial victory, the course of events took an unexpected turn in 2009: after three years of construction, the Army Corps of Engineers detected that Hidrotambo actually did not have all the necessary permissions to continue. They therefore cancelled the contract and halted construction on the hydroelectric power plant. In the following, Hidrotambo sued the Army Corps because of the non-compliance of the construction contract and partly won the case.[20]

The villagers meanwhile thought that the whole project had come to an end. Nevertheless, Hidrotambo signed a new operation permit with the state (CONELEC) in 2012. The owners of the company were still the same, but the former international investors were not involved this time. The only international shareholder up to now is a woman registered as 'Magistra Schenk Francesco Maria' from Switzerland.[21] According to the national stock exchange supervision register, she invested over 2.5 million dollars in the company. Hidrotambo's reacti-

---

[17] Personal conversation, 01-24-2020, Chillanes.
[18] Several villagers I talked to estimated independently from each other that up to 4,000 people joined the protests in this period.
[19] Personal conversation with several villagers and NGO members.
[20] Link to the summary of the case: http://www.pge.gob.ec/images/documentos/Direcciones2015/asuntosinternacionales/adjuntos/FICHAS_RESUMEN_CASOS_ARBITRAJE_NACIONAL0.pdf.
[21] Link to the national stock exchange supervision registration: https://appscvs1.supercias.gob.ec/portalCia/contenedor.zul?param=fGwjShgSMdM9-8Kqe2tCRp4n8u8LoTWSxYDAYwWWO0FcE0QKurvqZfRoTlm5QS-w. Consulted on 10-10-2020.

vation spurred protests in the communities, and in the aftermath of the protests in 2012, two protest leaders were criminalized once again by company and state actors, even after the amnesties, this time of terrorism.[22] They suffered through judicial processes for years and were acquitted in 2016.[23]

In 2013, the workers from Hidrotambo started to construct again. This time they did not approach the river crossing in San Pablo de Amalí but came from the other side through a village called Vainillas. The former community president assumes that they chose this side to avoid new protests. The villagers of Vainillas did not protest in fact, since they considered and still consider the project to be a benefit, and they do not fear flooding related to the dam because Vainillas is not located directly next to the river in the flatter part of the valley, but higher up in the mountains.[24] While many villagers in San Pablo de Amalí protested, some did not protest, because they were tired, and felt paralyzed by all the lawsuits and arbitrary detentions related to their protest.[25]

In this period, the hydroelectric company carried out a major river diversion towards the village, and parts of the village began to erode into the diverted river.[26] The incidents in the Dulcepamba River gained growing attention as well from national NGOs, and as part of a Fulbright research project, academics and volunteers installed weather stations and hydrological stations in the region to further observe the hydrologic developments in the valley.[27]

In October 2014, the construction was mostly finished, but power production still did not begin. Some members of the local community filed a suit against Hidrotambo S.A. They feared the loss of their houses and territories because of flood and erosion risks related to the orientation and design of the dam and river diversion. As already mentioned, their claim was rejected as lunatic nonsense. As the community members had warned, only five months later, during the first rainy season after the construction of the power plant, the river eroded, undermined and flooded San Pablo de Amalí. The result was three lives lost, the destruction of 12 houses, major damages to the only road to access the village and the loss of countless crop plantations (Benavides 2019).

In the aftermath of this incident, the former Fulbright research project became more institutionalized and joined with an Ecuadorian NGO called *Instituto de Estudios Ecologistas*. They formed a permanent project called *Proyecto Socio-Ambiental Dulcepamba* (socio-environmental project of the Dulcepamba River,

---

[22] Case number: Juicio No: 0224120130086 Casillero No: 0, written sentence: https://www.inredh.org/archivos/pdf/sentenciaescrita.pdf.
[23] Ibidem; personal conversation with both people involved, 01-24-2020, Chillanes; 01-28-2020, San Pablo de Amalí.
[24] Statement heard at an event.
[25] Personal conversations with several informants, Chillanes and San Pablo de Amalí.
[26] Ibidem.
[27] Personal conversation with former Fulbright scholar and current NGO member, Chillanes.

in the following 'Dulcepamba River Project'). In close collaboration with this project, some villagers kept on protesting, mainly on a legal and administrative level. They raised awareness about the company's water grabbing and subsequent dispossession of water resources for the locals. Since the commons grabbing on a legal level is, above all, a problem of the communities upstream of the dam, they became especially active, demanding their water rights. This legal activism led to a vicious, but legally senseless campaign of menace and legal opposition by the hydroelectric company since the formal water property rights favouring human consumption and small-scale farming are inscribed in the national constitution.[28]

This legal activism led to a partial victory when the national water authority granted a legal prohibition for Hidrotambo S.A. to produce power during the dry season, thus prioritizing water for the communities' livelihoods. They also ruled that the hydroelectric project had to be redesigned and rebuilt because in its current state it is rudimentary and dangerous.[29] Additionally, there are several pending lawsuits against the company and the state, for example at the Constitutional Court of Ecuador and the Inter-American Commission on Human Rights.

Environmental and social impacts

In January and February 2020, I spent one month with the Dulcepamba River Project in San Pablo de Amalí and Chillanes. I held 23 semi-structured interviews with villagers, NGO members, local authorities and lawyers involved in the case. I conducted three focus group discussions, two with communities living upstream the Dulcepamba River and one with the members of the Dulcepamba River Project. Additionally, I was able to take part in several of the NGO's activities, ranging from accompanying local authorities' on-site visits in the area or helping with the construction of a new water supply system in San Pablo de Amalí up to visits in Ecuador's capital in order to connect to other NGOs. As I will elaborate in this section, it is impossible to stay neutral in this 14-year-old conflict around the construction and operation of the power plant. Therefore, it comes as no surprise that I was not considered a neutral actor either, but that people saw me in connection with the NGO members and their work.

Being in the area and talking with actors involved in the case, I was able to learn about the most severe environmental impacts that have dominated the daily life of the villagers until today: water insecurity; reduction of biodiversity; destruction of the riverbed, flooding and erosion, and the subsequent loss of lives and destruction of houses, infrastructure and plantations; and, as a consequence, the ongoing risk of floods in the future.

---

[28] Personal conversations within a focus group discussion with six community members, 02-13-2020, Margarita.

[29] INFORME TÉCNICO comunicado con el memorando Nro. SENAGUA-PNA.10.1-2018-0244-MI. 19 de octubre de 2018.

It is important to stress that most villagers and some authorities I talked to agree that the construction of the power plant is the reason for those impacts. There is also scientific evidence, mostly from the Ecuadorian water authority and US universities (see Informe Tecnico SENAGUA 2018[30]; Resolucion 2018-008 SENAGUA 2019[31]; Newmiller et al. 2017, 2020). Nevertheless, Hidrotambo S.A. and some state authorities deny any direct causality between the construction of the power plant and the environmental changes. The company itself commissioned two studies about environmental impacts, the first in 2005 and a revision of this study in 2012 (see YAWE Consultores Cía. Ltda. 2012). So, the cause and extent of those impacts are already part of the debate.

The reduction of biodiversity happened, according to all my informants, because of the diversion of the river in 2013. They remember in detail the former abundance and variety of animals around and in the river, especially the abundance and diversity of fish. Because of the river diversion, there was a significant and permanent reduction in the amount of water that the fish population could not cope with. Fish formed an important part of the villagers' daily diet, above all for the lower social classes.[32] Therefore, an important buffer resource got lost because of the construction of the power plant, making this case not only one of commons, but also of resilience grabbing (Haller 2019: 114).

This might be the biggest but surely not the only impact that the villagers experienced. After the diversion, the river flow and the river area were profoundly changed by the construction of the power plant. One informant told me:

The Dulcepamba River was the jewel of San Pablo de Amalí. Because there we went to take a bath, there were some big pools, some giant rocks, it was very clean… And we went there, like this, when we came back from another place, tired of working, we went to the Dulcepamba River to take a bath. We took a bath there, because there was not enough water [in the pipelines] or because we did not like to take a bath in the shower. […] The river never had threatened us; he was our loyal friend. (NGO member, 02-12-2020, San Pablo de Amalí)

What can be seen in the quote is that the river was not only a common-pool resource, a provider of nutrition and infrastructure for sanitary needs, but also part of the community with a personality of its own. People frequently talk about the river as though it were an animated being, not an infrastructure. This shows that the legal protection of Article 57 of the national constitution that only applies to indigenous communities is problematic. At least in the case of San Pablo de Amalí,

---

[30] INFORME TÉCNICO comunicado con el memorando Nro. SENAGUA-PNA.10.1-2018-0244-MI. 19 de octubre de 2018
[31] Resolución 2018-008 del Recurso Extraordinario de Revisión de la Autorización de Aprovechamiento de Agua para la Central Hidroeléctrica San José del Tambo.
[32] Personal conversation with the former community president, Chillanes, 01-24-2020.

it does not protect a community with an equally important connection to its river as it would protect those that can be fully recognized as indigenous peoples.

The changes in the river basin are foreseen in the study about environmental impacts commissioned by Hidrotambo S.A., but they are classified as non-problematic: 'Even if the impact [of the river-channelling and diversion] is high, its effect is very localized (only intake); once the intake area construction is finished, the river will retake its original channel' (YAWE Consultores Cía. Ltda., 2012: 142, translated by the author). Additionally, the so-called 'environmental flow' that leaves enough water in an alternative, free-flowing channel for the protection of aquatic life is mandatory in a construction of such magnitude and is even mentioned in the study about the environmental impacts (YAWE Consultores Cía. Ltda., 2012: 142). Nevertheless, those measures were not taken by the company, as my informants and my own fieldwork confirm.

As regards flood risks, the company-commissioned study of environmental impacts states: 'According to the map of risks, the area where the project of the hydroelectrical power plant San José del Tambo is in construction is susceptible to flooding; [...] therefore, there is a possibility of flooding of the structures from the project, especially in the sector of the machines. In any case, in the last few years the phenomenon of floods in the area of the project have been minimal' (YAWE Consultores Cía. Ltda., 2012: 69, translated by the author). Herewith, the possibility of floods is somehow foreseen, but it is denied in the same paragraph since it is classified as a problem of the past.

Nevertheless, flooding happened almost right away – during the first heavier rainfalls of the rainy season after the construction of the power plant was finished. A research team from the University of California, Davis could confirm with a hydrologic-forensic analysis that there is a causality between the building of the power plant and the flood in 2015 (Newmiller et al. 2017). Additionally, this flood was not an outstanding, unique incident: after the construction of the power plant, floods recurred in the wet seasons of 2017 and 2019.

The repeating floods bring manifold consequences for all the people living on the riverside: immediate ones such as the closure of the only road connecting San Pablo de Amalí with the outside world and the subsequent major economic losses that come with physical isolation every year; and long-term ones such as the emigration of families because of the ongoing fear of the next big flood that brings with it destruction and death, along with the loss of an important buffer resource in times of food scarcity.

While the problem of the immediate impacts of the floods is obvious, the long-term problems are more complex to recognize and correlate. In literature about displacement, there is little written about displacement that is not planned, mandated and carried out by some authority (see Vanclay 2017). But the evidence from my interviews and fieldwork shows that the power plant is a pull factor for

Fig 3: San Pablo de Amalí after the last big flood in 2019. Source: Darwin Paredes

the local population to migrate to more urban areas, especially because of the risk of floods.[33]

Apart from those environmental impacts – with their socially problematic consequences in every case – there are considerable social impacts, some of them already mentioned in the previous section: in a first phase, a lack of inclusion during the planification and construction process, with the most severe aspect of this process being the grabbing of the former common-pool resource water through the exorbitant water concession granted by the regional water authority. This concession is illegal since the Ecuadorian law clearly prioritizes human use over industrial activities like the production of electricity. It was only possible to obtain such a concession by asserting that the valley is no man's land without any people

---

[33] Personal conversations with village members.

living in the intake area.³⁴ Considering the 14,000 inhabitants living in the valley, such a statement can only be called a bold lie, one that nevertheless appeared in a report issued by the Hidrotambo company. So, even if the situation in the Dulcepamba valley is not one of legal pluralism, the company strategically selected the water concession as a legal means to easily dispossess the local community. Therefore, this strategy fits within the concept of institution shopping.

Confronted in a second phase with fierce protest, the use of violence by the police, the armed forces and even between members of the local community is another social impact with long-lasting consequences. The common narrative to describe those times is 'like a war', because of disproportional violence and a lack of mercy, even against vulnerable people such as children and elderly people.

In a third phase, the company and the state reacted with harmful legal accusations against protesters, the most severe being terrorism. This charge entailed a legal process that lasted four years, blocking and paralyzing protest activities during this period.³⁵

Additionally, what can be seen up to today as social impacts of this 20-year-old conflict are, on the one hand, a severe long-standing lack of trust in any authority within the community. Authorities are, in the memories of most villagers, either absent or corrupt, and, in any case, against people without financial and structural power. This applies above all to local and regional authorities. Even now that national ministries such as SENAGUA have openly criticised the dam construction as badly planned and dangerous, local authorities are still not willing to apply the measures that were decreed to protect the village. In the perspective of the locals, it is SENAGUA – the same institution that granted exorbitant water resources for the power plant and impelled hundreds of legal battles between Hidrotambo and farmers for water titles – that now also puts their lives at risk from flooding and erosion.

On the other hand, the community's distrust of authorities goes along with a general distrust among community members. There is an 'us' and 'them', two groups that cannot openly talk, cooperate or trust in the other side. The impossibility of staying neutral and in between those two groups is another aspect that seemed to turn San Pablo de Amalí into a war zone in the most intense times of conflict. Within this ongoing dispute, one side argues in favour of the power plant, emphasizing the possibility of progress and labour opportunity. The other one opposes the construction, stressing the unjust de facto dispossession of water as a common-pool resource and the physical destruction of lives, land and infrastructure, without any signs of progress or augmented labour opportunities in the area.

---

[34] Personal conversation with protester, 01-28-2020, San Pablo de Amalí.
[35] Personal conversation with supposable protest leaders, 01-24-2020, Chillanes; 01-28-2020, San Pablo de Amalí.

The disagreement between those two groups was so deep that it divided families and long-term friendships, and even children fought over the same conflict, reproducing the opinions of their parents. This division, alongside the lies and false promises of several powerful actors, led to a plurality of discourses, opinions and institutions on how to manage the commons grabbing, causing confusion among the local community and finally opening the door for institution shopping how it is described in the next chapter.

Local and NGO strategies

It is hard to talk about only one strategy of the local community for coping with those changes, since the divisions mentioned above bring about differing strategies, depending on which institutional arrangement promises to bring the most personal benefit. Therefore, there are people openly against the power plant, mainly those that lived in the affected area and had to experience severe losses during the flood in 2015. Most of them feel supported by the local Dulcepamba River Project and discursively and legally frame the case as one of commons grabbing. Some of them keep an eye on the activities of Hidrotambo S.A. and report them to the Project, and some of them participate in mobilizations to protest at SENAGUA and most recently at the Constitutional Court. On the other side is a group that acts in favour of the Hidrotambo company. According to my informants, the motivation for this group is manly financial: some of them received compensation because of their losses in the flood, and others work for Hidrotambo and represent them therefore in the community. They frame the hydroelectric power plant as a project of sustainable development in the area.

Apart from the small number of villagers that openly express that they are in favour or against the power plant as it is today, the relations in the community are complex, fragmented and sometimes even contradictory. After years of protests considered unsuccessful for many of my informants, they lost hope that there are authorities acting in favour of powerless people. Gossip and mistrust spread about the supposed enrichment of several actors taking advantage of the situation.[36] This mistrust is a major roadblock for united action in the community. It is not even clear who is the president of the community today: there are two people claiming this position, one in favour, the other against the hydroelectric power plant.[37] In some cases this leads to a conscious institution shopping. But many of the locals are seriously confused about what their rights and possibilities are in this case. They prefer to not get involved in the conflict anymore and see the new situation as irreversible.

This social division of the villagers does not just happen in discourse but became apparent in a very figurative way during an inspection by several state en-

---

[36] Personal conversations with villagers and NGO members.
[37] There are contradicting statements from several villagers.

tities that I attended. To impress the authorities during this inspection, the Dulcepamba River Project and Hidrotambo S.A. alike mobilized villagers to show that there are people that care about what happens in San Pablo de Amalí. The legitimization of those mobilizations is questioned mutually from both sides: according to the NGO, Hidrotambo S.A. acts illegitimately because they mobilize people that are from other, unrelated villages and therefore not directly affected by the power plant; according to Hidrotambo S.A., the NGO acts illegitimately because some members are foreigners that interfere in a supposedly national issue.

With regard to NGO strategies, the Dulcepamba River Project has a crucial role in supporting community resistance against the hydroelectric power plant. The NGO team is made up of a mixture of the institutionalized protest movement, including two villagers that have protested since the beginning of the construction of the power plant in 2006, and the reinforcement of this local protest through a nationally important NGO. The Project depends mainly on the dedication of five people, the two locals and three women from the US, one of them working as a volunteer in the area since 2012. This intertwining of local knowledge and formal education is crucial for the implementation of the NGO's main strategies. While the locals form part of the community and are therefore trustworthy for the affected villagers, the women from the US bring with them a higher level of formal education. They know how to fill out paperwork, to be persistent with local authorities to reach their aims and to connect with an international network of supporters. Additionally, as foreigners they are far more intimidating and less victims of discrimination by local and regional authorities.

The most important form of activism of the NGO is the socio-environmental analysis and communication of this analysis with human rights groups. These human rights groups, together with community members, have brought the violation of collective rights committed by Hidrotambo S.A. and the state authorities up to the Constitutional Court. They are supported by the NGO, which is very well connected locally, nationally and internationally, and use those connections to strengthen their claims. At the same time, the NGO is the contact for people living in the area to claim new problems brought up by the construction and operation of the power plant.

Most importantly, the Dulcepamba River Project systematically supports the local community members in securing their water rights. As already mentioned before, all the water resources in Ecuador officially belong to the state and SENAGUA gives water use permits upon request. But before the conflict with Hidrotambo, almost nobody in the Dulcepamba River Valley bothered to formalize water use, since it was not deemed necessary. This is understandable, since the nearest SENAGUA office is in the province capital named Guaranda, and for some regions of the valley it takes a whole day to get there.

Fig 4: Locals and NGO members protesting in front of the Constitutional Court in Quito, Ecuador, 2020. Source: Rachel Conrad

But at the beginning of the second iteration of the hydroelectric project in 2012, it became clear that SENAGUA had granted most of the water resources of the Dulcepamba watershed to Hidrotambo S.A. This meant for the farmers that especially in the dry season the quantity of water legally available would not be enough to satisfy their needs. Some informants even told me that workers from the company came to tell them that they should not bother to get authorizations for their water use anymore, since all the water is the property of Hidrotambo S.A.[38]

When the now members of the NGO heard about those threats, they mobilized the people living in the valley to go to SENAGUA and formalize their water rights. The Dulcepamba River Project even has a place that they call 'the office' in the Cantón's capital of Chillanes that people from the valley that want to get an official grant for their water use can attend. Only through this office can people living far away from Guaranda get a chance to formalize their water rights. The relationship between SENAGUA and the Dulcepamba River Project is contradictory. Officially, SENAGUA denies any function of 'the office' in Chillanes,[39] while at

---

[38] Personal conversations, 02-13-2020, Margarita and 02-12-2020, San Vincente.
[39] Personal conversation with the technical manager of the local SENAGUA office, 02-03-2020, Guaranda.

the same time, it sends people from its office in Guaranda to the smaller and faster NGO office in Chillanes.[40]

The NGO's main strategy could be called, in conclusion, on the one hand institution shopping from below. They connect to every national or international institution that can be helpful for the purpose and are constantly searching for opportunities to further reduce the company's possibilities for commons grabbing. On the other hand, they actuate a conscious institution building process from below that leads to a new constitutionality (Haller 2019: 115) by running an office to help people to formalize their water rights. The formalization of water rights would be a state responsibility that the local authorities are not able or willing to fulfil. Therefore, the NGO is not only calling the de facto water privatization by its name and changing the dominant discourse over what is happening in the Dulcepamba Valley, but also regaining the water as a common-pool resource on the legal level.

In sum, the Dulcepamba River Project is constantly contesting the sustainable development discourse with academic and legal activism, achieving herewith a repoliticization of the anti-politics machine that the company started with the aim of constructing the power plant without resistance. They can mobilize the local community through the insistence on legal rights, the production of independent information and the reframing of the dominant discourses. By bringing with them the necessary stubbornness and formal education, they are a surprisingly powerful opponent of the dominant actors, namely the state and the company, and can mix up the local power hierarchies. That is what makes the NGO's strategy so effective.

State and company strategy

As mentioned earlier in this contribution, there is considerable divergence between the strategies of different state actors. The local authorities mostly refuse to assume responsibility for the situation in the Dulcepamba River. If they are forced to act, they remain in entrenched power hierarchies, giving priority to the powerful owner of Hidrotambo S.A.[41] Especially people with a campesino identity have experienced racist attitudes from local authorities up to today, which makes protest even more difficult, as the local NGO members told me.[42]

But some national actors have broken those post-colonial patterns, supported by the very progressive legal frame provided by the national constitution. The legal case presented against Hidrotambo S.A. and some state authorities made by a national human rights organization and the national ombudsman is an emblematic example of this dynamic. The local and regional courts dismissed the claim alto-

---
[40] Personal conversations with NGO members.
[41] Observation made at local courts, 01-23-2020, Guaranda, and in personal conversations.
[42] Focus group discussion with NGO Members, 02-10-2020, Chillanes.

gether as unsound and irrelevant. Only in the highest national judicial authority, the Constitutional Court, did the judges not only take up the case but also decide that it is of national relevance. Therefore, while there seems to be little perspective change in smaller state entities, national actors are showing their awareness of constitutional rights and willingness to induce some positive changes. Here, again, a disintegration of local power hierarchies is possible when the apparently unpolitical production of hydroelectric energy is repoliticized with a bottom-up working approach.

Even after several requests, nobody from the company agreed to talk to me. Therefore, it is not possible to fully elaborate the perspective of Hidrotambo S.A. in this contribution. But the company's behaviour at the beginning of the project – the complete ignoring of the local population and the omission of legally required socialization – suggests that they did not foresee any resistance against the construction of the power plant. They expected that through their strategy of framing the project as sustainable development on a regional and national level on the one hand, and through avoidance of transparent and adequate communication on a local level on the other, the local community would not recognize the political and economic aspects of the power plant and therefore would not impose any resistance against the construction. In sum, the behaviour of the company and most statal authorities alike fits within Ferguson's (1990) analysis of the anti-politics machine.

The company's reaction against the resistance, then, was no socialization process or dialogue, but the use of what all my informants call an inappropriate amount of violence. It is this violence that caused this impressively strong countermovement that opened up the possibility for repoliticization of the commons grabbing committed by the company. Another surprise for Hidrotambo S.A. must have been the appearance of the Dulcepamba River Project that achieved, with its unique mix of local knowledge and formal education, the repoliticization of the anti-politics machine. The resistance of the local community would not have been so persistent and effective without this decisive player.

Therefore, it is no surprise that one of the main strategies of the company today is the disabling of the community protest through a counter-discourse to, and defamation of, the protesters in the form of videos, placards, gossip and the like. Most importantly, Hidrotambo S.A. suggested that the Dulcepamba River Project, as their main and most powerful opponent, acts illegitimately, because three members are not nationals. They try, through their xenophobic discourse, to arouse nationalist resentments among the local community. The company follows the same disabling strategy in the legal sphere, making use of the local power structures and their ability to influence.

On the national and international level, the company employs a typical enchantment strategy (Knox and Harvey 2012) by referring to a well-known discourse about the importance of renewable energy, above all in social media, and by insisting that the power plant brought new labour opportunities to the area. Since the opposers of the power plant could not only debunk the company's assertions but also construct a powerful counter-discourse about the importance of an intact environment to live in in the area, this discourse failed on a local level, leading to disenchantment.

Conclusion

This contribution is about the planning, construction and operating of the hydroelectric power plant called 'San Jose del Tambo' in the Dulcepamba River in Ecuador. The power plant brought severe impacts to the region: legal ones regarding water insecurity because of the grabbing of this former common-pool resource through the company; ecological and economic ones regarding the reduction of biodiversity with the subsequent loss of fishery as a basic nutrition provision and buffer resource and the destruction of the riverbed, leading to flooding and erosion; and social ones regarding the division of the community and the emigration of the younger villagers to more urban areas. Considering that 'San Jose del Tambo' is a small-scale run-of-the-river hydroelectric power plant and not a large dam, its impacts are surprisingly deep and irreversible.

Equally, the strategies of the locals, the involved NGOs, the state actors and the company are similar to those observed within disputes around large dams: while on a national and international level, Hidrotambo S.A. follows the common discourse of sustainable development and implements an infrastructural enchantment strategy, on a local level the company committed commons grabbing by institution shopping and employed the anti-politics machine by ignoring the local circumstances and legal frameworks and avoiding communication and socialization with the local community. Confronted with fierce local protest, Hidrotambo S.A. received help from the regional state authorities, who cooperated with them rather than implementing national law. These two powerful actors then framed the local protests as political and terroristic offences against the state, repoliticizing the situation and shedding light on the entrenched power hierarchies on a regional level.

These power hierarchies could be mixed up in parts in this case, mostly because the Dulcepamba River Project as an unexpected powerful opponent is coordinating the ongoing resistance of parts of the local community. Their main strategies include institution shopping and institution construction (Haller, 2019: 115), making use of the politically wanted constitutional rights that prioritize human usage and small-scale agriculture over privatization and exploitation of common goods. In short, they repoliticized the anti-politics machine and reshaped the dominant discourses in the area.

The focus of the debate around hydroelectric power plants is, overwhelmingly, on large dams, suggesting that the main problems of these constructions emerge because of their size. My analysis of the planning and construction of a small-scale run-of-the-river hydroelectric power plant and the protests against it shows not only that such a small project has similar economic, ecological and social impacts, but also that the involved actors – namely the company, the statal authorities, protesters and NGOs – employ the same strategies observed within bigger infrastructure projects. So, to answer the questions raised at the beginning of this chapter, I would suggest that the problems around dams and infrastructure projects in general are not about size, but about poor planning and construction, non-governance and entrenched, even destructive power hierarchies combined with a lack of will to improve among the dominant actors involved.

Glossary

CIE	Cooperación para la Investigación Energética (Cooperation for the investigation of energy)
COANDES	Constructora de los Andes Cia. Ecuador
CONAIE	Confederación de Nacionalidades Indígenas del Ecuador (Confederation of Indigenous Nationalities of Ecuador)
NGO	Non-governmental organization
S.A.	Sociedad Anónima
SENAGUA	Secretaría Nacional del Agua (National Water Ministry)
WCD	World Commission on Dams

References

Aparicio Wilhelmi, Marco 2018: Estado, organización territorial y constitucionalismo plurinacional en Ecuador y Bolivia. ¿Una década ganada? *Revista Española de Antropología Física* 27: 118-146.

Benavides, Gina 2019: *La Defensoría del Pueblo ante los impactos del desvío del cauce natural del Río Dulcepamba por la empresa Hidrotambo S.A. Defensoría del Pueblo*. Defensoría del Pueblo, Ecuador https://www.dpe.gob.ec/la-defensoria-del-pueblo-ante-los-impactos-del-desvio-del-cauce-natural-del-rio-dulcepamba-por-la-empresa-hidrotambo-s-a/. Consulted on 10-10-2020.

Clark, Patrick 2018: Neodesarrollismo y una "Vía Campesina" para el desarrollo rural. Proyectos divergentes en la revolución ciudadana Ecuatoriana. In: C. Kay and L. Vergara-Camus: *La Cuestión Agraria y Los Gobiernos de Izquierda en América Latina – Campesinos, Agronegocio y Neodesarrollismo*, Quito: FLACSO, 223-258.

Falconí-Benítez 2001: Integrated assessment of the recent economic history of Ecuador. *Population and Environment* 22(3): 257-280.

Ferguson, James 1990: *The anti-politics machine. 'Development', depoliticization, and bureaucratic power in Lesotho*. Cambridge: Cambridge University Press.

Franco, Jennifer, Lyla Mehta and Gert Jan Veldwisch 2013: The global politics of water grabbing. *Third World Quarterly* 34(9): 1651–1675.
Goodwin, Geoff 2017: The quest to bring land under social and political control: Land reform struggles of the past and present in Ecuador. *Journal of Agrarian Change* 17(3): 571–593.
Gudynas, Eduardo 2009: La ecología política del giro biocéntrico en la nueva Constitución de Ecuador. *Revista de Estudios Sociales* 32: 34-47.
Haller, Tobias 2019: Towards a new institutional political ecology. How to marry external effects, institutional change and the role of power and ideology in commons studies. In: Haller, T., Breu, T., De Moor, T., Rohr, C., & Znoj, H. (eds.): *The Commons in a Glocal World: Global Connections and Local Responses*, London: Routledge, 90-120.
Inuca Lechón, José Benjamín 2017: Genealogía de alli kawsay / sumak kawsay (vida buena / vida hermosa) de las organizaciones kichwas del Ecuador desde mediados del siglo XX. *Latin American and Caribbean Ethnic Studies* 12(2): 155-176.
Knox, Hannah and Penny Harvey 2012: Anticipating harm. Regulation and irregularity on a road construction project in the Peruvian Andes. *Theory, Culture & Society* 28(6): 142-163.
Lalander, Rickard and Maija Merimaa 2018: The discursive paradox of environmental conflict: Between ecologism and economism in Ecuador. *Forum for Development Studies* 45(3): 485-511.
Ministerio Coordinador de Desarrollo Social 2017: Informe de Desarrollo Social 2007–2017. Quito, Ecuador. www.competencias.gob.ec/wp-content/uploads/2017/06/06IGC2017-INFORME.pdf.
Moore, Deborah, John Dore and Dipak Gyawali 2010: The world commission on dams + 10: Revisiting the large dam controversy. *Water Alternatives* 3(2): 3-13.
Newmiller, Jeanette, Wesley Walker, William Fleenor and Nicholas Pinter 2020: Case Study: Reconstructing the 2015 Dulcepamba river flood disaster. *Environmental and Engineering Geoscience*.
Newmiller, Jannette, Wesley Walker, William Fleenor and Nicholas Pinter 2017: Dulcepamba River Hydrologic and Hydraulic Analysis. *Center for Watershed Sciences*, California: UC Davis.
Phan, Hai-Vu 2018: Doomed to be dammed? Analyzing the different outcomes of three South American megadams. *Politics & Policy* 46(6): 1017-1049.
Ponce-Jara, Marcos, Manuel Castro, Manuel Raul Pelaez-Samaniego, José Luis Espinoza-Abad and E. Ruiz 2018: Electricity sector in Ecuador: An overview of the 2007–2017 decade. *Energy Policy* 113: 513–522.
Quintana, Catalina, Marco Girardello and Henrik Balslev 2019: *Balancing plant conservation and agricultural production in the Ecuadorian Dry Inter-Andean Valleys*. PeerJ 7:e6207 https://doi.org/10.7717/peerj.6207.
Redacción la Fuente 2019: San Pablo de Amalí, un pueblo sin agua. *Periodismo de investigación*. https://periodismodeinvestigacion.com/2019/01/03/san-pablo-de-amali-un-pueblo-sin-agua/.
Richter, Brian D., Sandra Postel, Carmen Revenga, Thayer Scudder, Bernhard Lehner, Allegra Churchill and Morgan Chow 2010: Lost in development's shadow: The downstream human consequences of dams. *Water Alternatives* 3(2): 14-42.
Rieckmann, Marco, Maik Adomßent, Werner Härdtle and Patricia Aguirre 2011: Sustainable development and conservation of biodiversity hotspots in Latin America: The

case of Ecuador. In: F.E. Zachos and J.C. Habel (eds.): *Biodiversity Hotspots*, Berlin/Heidelberg: Springer-Verlag, 435-452.
Sardán Muyba, Julio Cesar 2015: Dinámica sociopolítica, Notas para una Realidad en Ecuador: Proyecto hidroeléctrico San José del Tambo 'Hidrotambo' de la Provincia Bolívar. Master Tesis. *Facultad Latinoamericana de Ciencias Sociales* (FLASCO), Sede Ecuador.
Scudder, Thayer 2005: *The future of large dams*. New York: Taylor & Francis.
Scudder, Thayer 2019: Large dams. *Long-term impacts on riverine communities and free flowing rivers.* Singapore: Springer Nature.
Vanclay, Frank 2017: Project-induced displacement and resettlement: from impoverishment risks to an opportunity for development? *Impact Assessment and Project Appraisal* 35(1): 3-21.
Viteri Gualinga, Carlos 2002: Visión indígena del desarrollo en la Amazonía. *Polis, Revista Latinoamericana* 3: 1-6.
World Commission on Dams (WCD) 2000: *Dams and development: A new framework for decision making*. London: Earthscan Publications.
YAWE Consultores Cía. Ltda. 2012: *Actualización del estudio de impacto ambiental del proyecto hidroeléctrico San José del Tambo*. Non-published document.
Zambrano Figueroa, Sebastián 2010: Consentimiento previo, libre e informado: Principales elementos de análisis y recomendaciones de política. *Hablemos de Política* 5. Quito: Grupo Faro.

From Enchanted Alienation to Transformative Responses: Agro-industrial MIPs and Local Reactions towards Reproduction of Life in Bolivia

Aymara Llanque, Leuphana University, Lüneburg, Germany, and Universidad Mayor de San Simón, AGRUCO Cochabamba, Bolivia; Marta Irene Mamani, Fundación Tierra, Bolivia; Johanna Jacobi, Institute of Agricultural Sciences, ETH Zurich, Switzerland

Introduction

Agroextractivism in Latin America is a mega-infrastructure project due to the scale of the arrangements it requires (particularly in terms of the demand for resources), justifying its inclusion in the mainstream development discourse. Mega-infrastructures are part of major development projects for the acceleration and expansion of the economy, often related to large-scale investments (Berawi and Susantono 2013).

Mega-infrastructures contain physical and institutional infrastructures. Physical infrastructure involves large-scale construction (such as roads and dams), the use of equipment (e.g., machinery), inputs (e.g., commercial seeds and agrochemicals) and land use change, among others. Institutional infrastructure is related to mechanisms of enforcement and regulation such as laws, policies and standards (Greenwood et al. 2011), to implement mega-development projects. In light of this, we use a mega-infrastructure approach to analyse agroextractivism as a phenomenon that combines physical and institutional conditions, to foster large-scale agricultural enterprises, and to generate settings for reconfiguration of regulatory and policy frameworks, where agroextractive activities take place.

Large-scale industrial agriculture is often considered extractivist because of the related deterioration of the common-pool resources and therewith their institutional management, e.g. in discourses of emancipatory modernity. Roads are infrastructures that often symbolize progress and development (Harvey and Knox 2012: 1), for their role in transporting different inputs and outputs (Villegas 2018). Under the discourse of modernization and economic growth, states often support intensive and extractivist agriculture (or agroextrativism), as it is widely regarded as a relevant economic pillar. We understand agroextractivism as taking out agricultural goods in large volumes and at high intensity, causing deterioration of the natural resources, oriented essentially to being exported as raw materials (Gudynas 2013) with no or minimal processing (McKay 2017).

Agribusiness can be regarded as an expression of agroextractivism that repeatedly receives economic incentives (e.g. tax benefits, favorable credits and other types of financial incentives) from public sources (Navarro 2020: 20). Agribusiness development areas often overlap with indigenous territories and peasant communities. However, Lalander (2017) indicates that governments tend to be more concerned with developing physical infrastructures e.g. roads and communication systems than with health-related issues or ecological problems, indigenous peoples' and other local communities' rights.

In this context, the questions that guide this chapter are: 1) What are the institutional configurations that set agriculture as an agroextractive mega-infrastructure? 2) What are the main socio-ecological impacts, particularly on the local life systems, with a specific focus on women? 3) What are multi-actor strategies? To answer these questions, we analyse the agribusiness case in the tropical and subtropical lowlands of Bolivia (Map 1), where a significant expansion of agroextractivism has been taking place over the last three decades. The analysis is based on available empirical evidence, and on the analytical framework of the enchantment of infrastructure, proposed by Harvey and Knox (2012), combined with institutional change analysis, applying institution shopping and anti-politics machine concepts based on the perspectives of (Ferguson 1994; Haller et al. 2016; Haller 2020).

We understand enchantment as persuasion through promises of privilege, building social reality by influencing political discourses and their solidification in infrastructure. The concept of enchantment makes it possible to reconsider the way in which infrastructures engage with agroextractivism actors. The 'enchanted' encourage us to reconsider the way in which infrastructures engage social and affective dimensions, considering this mechanism of enchantment as infrastructural promises. Dispossession generate socio-ecological consequences, in terms of deforestation, access to inputs, material opportunities to reproduce life and food systems, especially for women.

To understand the effects on mega-infrastructures and agroextractivism on environments and people, we also employ the concept of alienation. 'Alienation' is a concept of mental distancing or disconnection that, prominently framed by Karl Marx, has been frequently employed and further developed to better understand interactions between humans and the rest of nature in general (Harvey 2012). Based on Marx's understanding of alienation as a process of disentangling 'work' from 'life' and 'meaning', which is linked to economic growth, Giraldo (2019) applies the idea of a loss of societal control over technological development to industrial agriculture. This process produces an enormous social cost and environmental destruction.

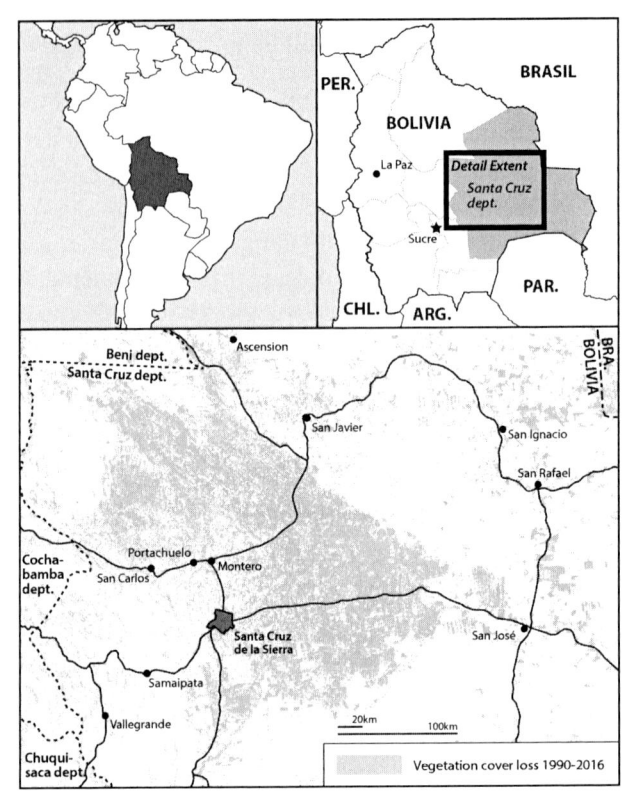

Map 1: The Santa Cruz Department in Bolivia. Source: Map compilation and design by Manuel L. K. Abebe (2021), CDE, University of Bern, Bern, Switzerland. Geodata: OpenStreetMap contributors

Alienation is based on asymmetric power relations, and as land increases in value for exploitation via agroindustrial production, the female workforce is exploited more easily. Women in this context lose power and cannot select the institutions to respond to governance transformations.

On the other hand, actors also apply institution shopping to deal with transformations. Institution shopping is understood as the capacity to choose, according to its power and knowledge, the best institution among different options, to respond to needs (Wartmann et al. 2016: 5). Examples of studies on new institutionalism such as the work of Haller et al. (2016: 3) speak of the bargaining power of actors to generate institutional transformations; likewise, where local institutions are eroded, actors' strategies are based on ideologies, which change circumstantially, in favour of their interests.

Such strategies have been described as "anti-politics machine" strategies, which justify dispossession (Haller 2020: 20), with discourses of development and social inclusion, limiting traditional indigenous and agroecological land use to generate alternative food systems to agroextractivism. This applies in a similar way to the ideology of modernity, by which the discourse of agroindustrial development is used to legitimize this alienation.

Local actors, especially women, do not always buy into this enchantment and resist accordingly, not because of a sexual precondition, but because the sexual determination as women is also a social gender institution that delegates the reproduction of life principally in their hands. When anti-policy machines operate, the commons are affected, and women often lose more than men (Haller 2020: 20). In this sense, the alienation of work and exploitation is specifically linked to the autonomous opportunities to continue life in rural territories affected by agroextractivism.

Our intention is to develop a theoretical framework to discuss the relationship between appropriation in agroextractivist activities and responses from local communities and indigenous territories. At the same time, we aim to expose micro-political answers, such as self-organization strategies and other collective action dynamics for the reproduction of life, that offer complex holistic solutions to mega physical and institutional infrastructures.

Part 1: Historical, environmental, ethnographic and political context

History and current context

Mega-infrastructure projects with an agroextractive focus have a long history in Bolivia, dating back to the boom of the Amazonian rubber tree exploitation in the nineteenth century in the departments of Pando and Beni in the Amazon watershed. After that, the agroextractivist sector focused on sugar cane, rice and lately on industrial soybean monocrops in the department of Santa Cruz, with multiple and significant direct and indirect incentives and subsidies offered by different governments. Among the most important governmental support schemes for agroextractivism is the implementation of the Bohan Plan during the early 1950s. This plan promoted migration to the east of the country to implement large commercial agricultural plantations by providing public lands for export-oriented agriculture (Arrieta 1990). Such initiatives grew incrementally particularly after 1985, when Bolivia entered the neoliberal market economy.

The large-scale private sector is represented by the Association of Oleaginous and Wheat Producers (ANAPO), the Western Agricultural and Livestock Chamber (CAO), the Chamber of Industry and Trade of Santa Cruz (CAINCO), and by associations of cattle rearing and agribusinesses in the Bolivian northern Amazon and the Chaco region. The indigenous peoples and peasant communities of the area have multiple forms of organizations, such as peasant federations, intercultural migrant federations, and indigenous and women's organizations. There is also a wide presence of NGOs and foundations, and to a lesser extent, public institutions such as subnational governments, as well as public-private companies, public enterprises, associations of family farmers, communal economic organizations and Mennonite colonies, among others.

Diverse production systems overlap in the Bolivian lowlands. These include monocultures of soy, corn, rice, sugar and sorghum in extensive areas, and more traditional forms of production, such as those of the Guaraní indigenous communities that grow mainly maize, beans, peanuts and various vegetables for self-consumption. In the tropical forest areas, community forest management initiatives are abundant, along with traditional food production practices in small agricultural areas, and some commercial agroforestry and agricultural production initiatives, e.g. cocoa (*Theobroma cacao*) or cupuaçu (*Theobroma grandiflorum*).

As in other parts of Latin America, agroextractivism is a systemically implemented strategy with temporal economic benefits that exhibits characteristics of an interconnected development project (Burchardt and Dietz 2014): "this enchantment appears as a promise of economic prosperity, articulated as both a collective and a personal quest (...)" (Harvey and Knox 2012: 4). It is a vertical integration model that expands and consolidates other extractive activities regionally, including energy production, road interconnection for export, intensive use of natural resources and governmental policies instrumental to transnational interests (Villegas 2018). One example of road interconnection as a regional mega-infrastructure project is the Integration of the Regional Infrastructure of South America (IIRSA), whose political and strategic decision body is COSIPLAN (South American Council for Infrastructure and Planning).

Another component of agribusiness is the increase in foreign debt to finance mega-infrastructures to facilitate the export of raw materials to neighbouring countries such as Brazil, and other distant markets, such as the European Union and China. Part of this context is the deprivation of the rights of indigenous peoples and peasant communities in the areas where agroextractivist activities overlap with their territorial claims (Campanini et al. 2014). There is a continuous grabbing of land-related commons to favor agroextractivism, by renting or buying land, or integrating indigenous farmers and peasants into agribusiness as producers. This changes cultural landscapes, as not only is land grabbed but also the space where local self-government practices, traditional productive practices, leisure spaces, water, wildlife, harvesting products and forestry are reproduced.

Infrastructure megaprojects as a large form of land grabbing and of common goods are visible in agroextractivism. As the agricultural frontier expands, soil desertification grows, and with it the transformation of cultural values of the territories in a substantially greater magnitude than the previous processes of land tenure. Due to its exploitative nature, agroextractivism also relies on the appropriation and concentration of natural resources, which is often carried out using physical violence (Ujuaje and Chang 2020). In Bolivia, past and recent governments have pushed agroextractivism as part of an enchantment strategy. This enchantment example includes narratives of food security, food sovereignty, technological progress, economic growth, creation of jobs and improved infrastructure coming along with agricultural expansion and modernization (Lalander 2017).

Nationally, agroextractivism has increased its economic relevance since 2014, following the drop in prices of raw materials, the depletion of natural gas reserves, which represented more than 50% of the value of total exports, and the expiry of gas export contracts with Brazil in 2019, and with Argentina in the near future (Villegas 2018).

The bilateral trade agreements with neighbouring countries increase also agroextractivism. The most influential is Brazil, particularly regarding energy prices in Bolivia and agribusiness activities in the country. Petrobras, the main Brazilian oil company, bought approximately 40% of the total Bolivian gas produced until 2019. Moreover, the Government of Brazil engaged in bilateral agreements with Bolivia to build hydroelectric power plants (IRSA 2013), and the expansion of the agricultural frontier in the Pantanal and Chiquitano regions shared with Bolivia. Finally, among foreigners, Brazilians are among the largest landholders in Bolivia, mainly used for agroindustrial monocrop production of genetically modified soybean (Catacora-Vargas et al. 2012).

Recent agroextractivism-related initiatives include an ammonia fertilizer factory in the tropical area of Chapare (department of Cochabamba), a sugar refinery in the community of San Buenaventura for the industrial extraction of anhydrous alcohol (department of La Paz), a polyethylene and polypropylene plant (department of Tarija) and the construction of dams for electric energy (Bautista et al. 2020). In 2020, the de facto Bolivian government issued two decrees approving a range of genetically modified (GM) crops (in May 2020) and GM varieties of maize (in September 2020), and a special loan for agribusiness (USD800 million, 600 million of which was paid to big agribusiness).

Geography and ecosystem/cultural landscape

Among the major direct effects of agroextractivism is land use change, specifically deforestation, and the conversion of territories to commodity frontiers for agribusiness and large-scale livestock production. In Bolivia, annual deforestation increased from an average of approximately 150,000 hectares per year during the 1990s to almost 350,000 hectares per year during 2016 and 2017 (Li 2019: 1) (Fig 1). The massive loss of forest was principally due to its conversion into large-scale, chemical-intensive monocultures of soy, sunflower, sesame, wheat and grass for cattle (Mueller et al. 2014).

During the COVID-19 crisis that hit Bolivia in March 2020 and soon resulted in a strict lockdown for several months in the major cities, the interim government pushed agribusiness in the rural areas through different measures, including regulatory instruments in favor of agribusiness sector demands such as financial support and opening specific markets and the elimination of export restrictions.

As a consequence, deforestation and forest fires tripled between March and April in comparison to the same period in 2019, which had already been unusually high (Villalobos 2020: 2)[2]. By October 2020, the major forest fire areas were located in the Amazon shared by Bolivia, Brazil and Paraguay, the Pantanal and the northwest of the Gran Chaco. A common feature of these ecosystems is that the main economic activity is agribusiness and cattle production, with almost seven million hectares of intensive monocultures and more than 30 million heads of cattle.

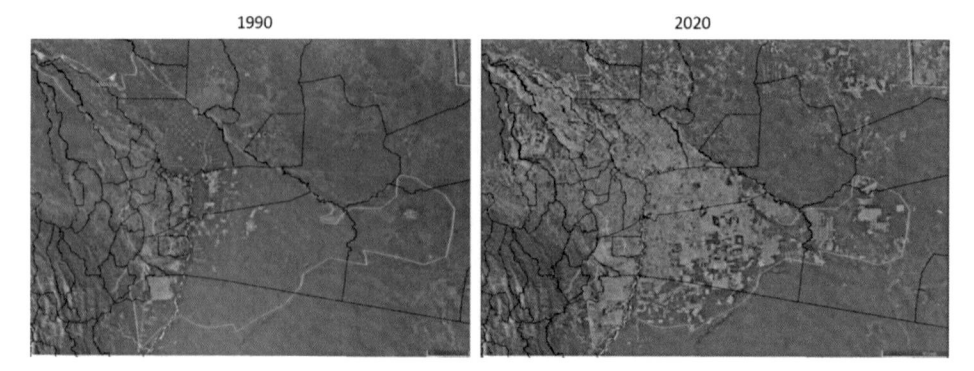

Fig 1: Agroextractivist expansion and deforestation in the Santa Cruz department of Bolivia 1990–2020 (Source: Map compilation and design by Fundación Tierra, 2020).

The resulting conflicts, loss of food sovereignty and environmental degradation (deforestation, land use change, pollution) especially affect women and other vulnerable groups such as children and elderly people, who depend on the integral socio-ecological quality of their life system (Llanque et al. 2018: 12).

Local population and resource use

Agroextractive activities are concentrated mainly in the Bolivian tropical and subtropical lowlands, with a maximum elevation of 900 meters above sea level. The tropical climate, accessible topography and abundant rainfall make the lowlands the most favorable area for agroextractive activities (Vos et al. 2020). The natural vegetation consists of a diversity of forests such as the Amazonian, Chaqueño and Chiquitano forests, and temporarily flooded savannahs. Various groups of actors, who overlap in terms of land use claims, regarding both agricultural land and forest areas, for private and communal use, inhabit these ecosystems (Mathez-Stiefel et al. 2007).

The sociocultural composition of the region includes indigenous populations, Mennonite colonies, migrants from the Bolivian Andean region, peasant communities and urban populations of different origins, among others.

The socio-organizational representation is based on Grass-roots Territorial Organizations (OTBs) within the cities and some peri-urban communities, the Indigenous Original Peasant Territories (TIOCs) that include indigenous peoples represented by the CIDOB and the peasant community organizations represented by federations such as the CSUTCB and the Federation of Women Bartolina Sisa, as well as private properties and Mennonite colonies.

Since the consolidation of the republican states, this region has experienced a high migratory flow, due to extractivism and later for agriculture and cattle ranching. The migrations of Europeans since the twentieth century have formed the urban political elites until today, who are making decisions about natural resources exploitation. This group concentrates a huge tract of land and implements regional megaprojects also in Bolivia.

Subsequently, the migration of local businesspeople, the provision of land for small Andean producers and Mennonite colonies affected local indigenous communities, because it generated displacement from their territories.

The main economic-productive activities are cattle ranching and intensive and self-subsistence agriculture. However, in recent years, agricultural food production has decreased in importance as a source of employment and as a guarantee of regional food security and sovereignty due to climate effects, as well as restrictions on access to land, a lack of water for production, production units subjected to the market, modernization practices, and agricultural optimization.

The lowlands of Bolivia are also an area characterized by the exploitation of non-renewable natural resources, such as iron, gold and, in recent years, oil and gas. Hydrocarbon activities provide important economic resources in the form of taxes and compensation for damages caused by exploration, exploitation and transportation activities, especially for indigenous populations.

In terms of formal land tenure, the region has formal rights for different actors that have been partially sanitized. There is a heterogeneity of actors with formal ownership, actors demanding public lands and customary rights within communities, mediated by their internal regulations.

Since the 1990s, indigenous peoples have been under a communal property regime, in the legal form of community lands of origin (TCOs). Peasant communities have communal rights, and in some cases, these are not formalized by the state. There are also communal properties but under the legal form of private property, such as the Mennonite colonies; agricultural plots and cattle ranches are under the individual private property regime.

Private properties are extensive. Legally the formal right defined in the new political constitution must not exceed 5000 hectares per owner, however there are rights granted prior to the drafting of the political constitution, and the widespread practice of distributing large landholdings among family members.

National economy and legal framework

Bolivia has been described as a 'neo-extractivist state' by Schilling-Vacaflor (2017). This relationship between agroextractivism and the political regime became visible in 2011 with the conflict of the Isiboro-Sécure Indigenous Territory and National Park (TIPNIS). The conflict around indigenous rights and a major infrastructure project showed that although the legal framework favours the rights of nature and indigenous peoples, these laws are not applied in practice. Even though the Bolivian constitution from 2009 is one of the most progressive ones in terms of indigenous rights as it recognizes a right to territory and autonomy, these rights have been subordinated to 'national interests' when it comes to conflicts over resource extractivism (Lalander 2017): for example, the opening of protected areas to oil companies where prior consultation is imposed by the state (Villegas 2018), and which brought about violent repression of local people in the Guaraní territory of Tacovo Mora as they refused to accept oil extraction in their territory.

The state also implemented legal changes in favour of resource extractivism by criminalizing uprisings of indigenous groups against the Morales administration that have taken place, claiming their rights where such activities overlap with their territories (Lalander 2017. For example, the new Penal Code (15-12-2017) introduced an anti-terrorist legislation, which gives extraordinary powers to judges and the government to criminalize criticism and social protest (Villegas 2018).

These conflicts have become more evident recently with several mega-dams, such as the Rositas project in Santa Cruz, or Bala-Chepete in La Paz, and the oil project in Tariquía in the Campo Bermejo X2 well (Quiroga 2017). A governmental enchantment strategy has been that these projects are also in the interest of the indigenous groups that resist extractivist industries, which has contributed to their repression and division (Schilling-Vacaflor 2017).

The discourse on unproductive indigenous lands or protected areas (sometimes called 'dormant potential') was also identified and analysed by Anthias (2014) in the case of Guarani land titling in the Bolivian Chaco. In this case, cattle ranchers opposed indigenous land claims as unproductive and therefore undeserving of land titles. This claim was followed by a promise of a planned massive 'technology transfer' oriented towards 'agricultural modernization', without specifying the technologies, which can be understood as an example of enchantments. These public declarations have been described by Bolivian civil society organizations as 'plans for displacement and land grabbing' (Colque 2020).

Part 2: The Mega-Infrastructure Project

Soybeans are the principal crop of Bolivia today in terms of quantity and area: in 2018, over 35% of all agricultural area in Bolivia was planted with soybeans (FAOSTAT 2020). Soybeans have been cultivated in small quantities for decades by Japanese settlers and Andean migrants in intercultural communities. Commercialized soybean production started in the 1970s (Catacora-Vargas 2018). In the 1990s, a World Bank project financed its widespread cultivation in the Santa Cruz department. The approbation by a supreme decree in 2005 for genetically modified 'Roundup Ready' soybean seeds, tolerant to glyphosate 'Roundup', sparked its widespread implementation. Today, more than 99% of the soybean crop in Bolivia is genetically modified. After the legalization of herbicide-tolerant soybeans in 2005, pesticide imports also soared (Fig 2), with herbicides such as glyphosate being the main contributors to the increase (FAOSTAT 2020). By the time of research, there were 161 registered plant protection products containing glyphosate – of which Roundup was one – registered in Bolivia (SENASAG 2011), even though the substance was classified as 'probably carcinogenic in humans' in March 2015 by 17 experts from 11 countries at the International Agency for Research on Cancer (IARC/WHO, Lyon, France).

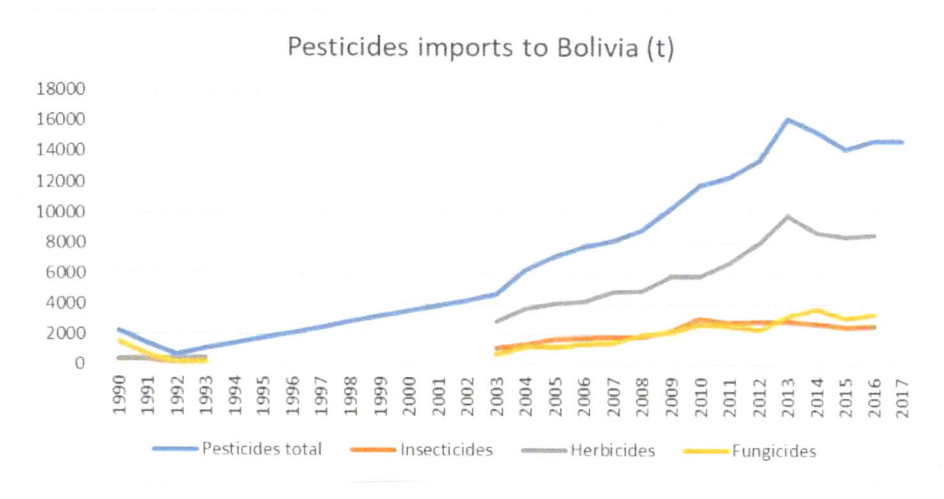

Fig 2: Pesticide imports to Bolivia. Own elaboration. Data source: FAOSTAT 2020 (no disaggregated data for 1994–2002 available).

The infrastructure related to the expansion of agribusiness has a mainly regional character. The so-called 'Madera River Complex', which is an agroextractivist expansion plan, had already been implemented by the then president C. Mesa in 2004, named by him the 'Conquest of the West', where the binational negotiations between Brazil and Bolivia were already advanced. Part of this economic dynamic is the increase in population on the Brazilian side of the border with Bolivia upon the implementation of the Rio Madera Complex and IIRSA/COSIPLAN in Bolivia (Villegas 2018). In consequence, large-scale monocultures (mainly soy) and cattle have greatly expanded during the last three decades, as a strategy promoted alongside other forms of extractivism (Burchardt and Dietz 2014).

In 2019, the particular political context – initially due to the resignation of former president Evo Morales – opened a new window for agroextractivism proponents. The year 2019 in general (including before the regime change) was characterized by the development of a political-economic agenda in favour of agroextractivism, but became much stronger with the explicit financial and legal support of the Añez administration (Colque 2020). Since November 2019, a state agenda that openly relies on the extraction of natural resources, especially in the hydrocarbon sector and large-scale export agriculture, has been strongly advanced (Artacker el al. 2020; Colque 2020). This is not a surprise, since prominent representatives of agroextractivism occupied important positions of power in the Añez administration. Examples include the Ministry of Economy and Finances, and the Ministry of Planning, where Oscar Ortiz and Branco Marinkovic, both linked to the agroextractivist sector of the Santa Cruz department, were making explicit efforts to channel public funds in favour of the agribusiness. Likewise, Colque (2020) showed that during the COVID-19 pandemic, the Añez administration handed out more than 800 land titles to representatives of the agroindustrial sector in the lowlands of Bolivia. For example, in the Beni department the Añez government titled an area of 12 million hectares, benefiting 56,000 farming and livestock families with 7,000 titles (Ministry of Rural Development and Land MDRyT 2020). Cattle-raising families are not part of the traditional peasant and indigenous sector that applies small-scale agriculture.

The changing political and institutional context creating increasingly favourable agribusiness perspectives has also affected the coherence *within* social movements and indigenous groups in recent years. These internal divisions can be partly explained by the marginalization of indigenous territories that are affected by agroextractivism, as the following quote illustrates: 'We sowed little. There is no water. The cattle go into the fields and eat the crops...' (Catacora-Vargas 2018: 186[1]).

An illustrative example of such an internal division was a 'contract' presented in April 2020 between agribusiness proponents from Santa Cruz and indigenous leaders, who were supposedly in favour of genetically modified crops being produced on their community land. The Confederation of Bolivian Indigenous Peoples, Confederación Indígena del Oriente Boliviano (CIDOB) and Camera Agropecuario del Oriente (CAO) act stated that biotechnology was a chance to render 'unproductive' indigenous community land viable and productive (Fundación Tierra 2020). Shortly after, the CIDOB pronounced that those who signed the agreement were not representatives of their affiliated organizations. For instance, the Assembly of the Guarani People (APG), Beni's Ethnic People's Centre (CPEMB) and the Chiquitana Indigenous Organization (OICH) declared that the agreement was not representative of indigenous peoples of Bolivia and that the

---

[1] La Ripiera community, Takovo Mora indigenous territory, cited by Catacora-Vargas et al. (2016): Soberanía Alimentaria: Reflexiones A Partir De Diferentes Sistemas Alimentarios De Santa Cruz, Bolivia/Food sovereignty: reflections from different food systems in Santa Cruz, Bolivia/Soberania alimentar: reflexões a partir de diferentes sistemas alimentares de Santa Cruz, Bolívia. Revista Nera (32), 170–194.

few members of the CIDOB who signed had been corrupted (Fundación Tierra 2020).

One example where such enchantment was successful is the new land use plan for the Beni Department (PLUS Beni), approved by the de facto government in late 2019 as one of their first actions in the agricultural sector. A number of NGOs have criticized the plan, because it ignores protected areas and indigenous lands, family farming and agroecological practices such as agroforestry. PLUS Beni mainly promotes cattle ranching and monoculture production for export. The plan has been described by its proponents as 'the economic take-off of the Beni Department', which can be interpreted as a justification or communication strategy, as well as an enchantment strategy. In this plan, and also in the wider discourse about land use with a view to agribusiness, indigenous and peasant community lands are currently seen as having potential for incorporation: they are a source of natural resources capable of expanding monocultures. This is charged with a pejorative perspective on the role of communities in caring for the common good. For example, the platform Crea Bolivia/Publiagro, an entity openly affiliated with the agroextractivist sector, mentions that '[g]overnments are responsible for the destruction of natural resources by providing land, without technical criteria or subsequent support, in populist and clientelist attitudes' (Publiagro 2020). From this perspective, the state is responsible for 'disorganized agricultural support directed to minifundios', creating a large informal agricultural sector and uncontrolled migration to the tropical lowlands. With this narrative, agribusiness proponents advocate a land-sparing approach, where the assigned farmland is used as intensively as possible, and other areas are set aside as protected from farming (Phalan et al. 2011). Proponents of this approach in Bolivia recommend identifying all 'unused' land with agricultural potential, and promoting intensive export-oriented agribusiness there 'to depend less and less on mining and hydrocarbons' (Publiagro 2020).

These discourses reveal the political intention to revert areas in favour of agroextractivism, identifying areas of resettlement for extensive monocultures. The occupation of land for agribusiness is justified by the advance of investments for the development of the national economic matrix and to guarantee food security.: 'Today, more than ever, we need to join forces to avoid hunger and to guarantee food security of the Bolivian people. We will leap ahead in food production' (CAO-CIDOB, 2020).

In an environment of conflict produced by agroextractivism, the territories and rural communities are under high pressure due to the overlapping interests of various actors, including agribusiness actors, governments, NGOs and agribusiness actors in state institutions, among others.

Another factor that produces alienation in overextractive environments is rural-urban migration. The rural population dedicated to agricultural activity is 67% and that is decreasing at the national level (INE 2012). Among migrants,

53% are men and 47% women, leaving women with greater pressure to work in reproductive and productive tasks (INE 2012). For example, in Guarani communities, men commonly work in extractive industries (oil and gas) and stay away from home for weeks, causing food and livelihood insecurity and increasing domestic violence (Llanque 2015).

In this alienation context, actors have the ability to choose – according to one's power and knowledge – the best institution among different options, in order to respond to needs. This selection of institutions to meet the needs of respective actors depending on their bargaining power resembles what has been described as 'institution shopping' (see Haller et al. 2013; Haller 2019). Not only do state and company actors do institution shopping, but also local indigenous actors make such selections and negotiate within existing institutions.

The studies by Wartmann et al. (2016) in the indigenous Takana territory and by Gambon and Rist (2020) among the Tsimane and Mosetene in the Bolivian Amazon show how within the legal pluralistic setting shaped by the strategic interest of the state and external actors, local groups also try to select and combine elements of institutions according to their interest to control the land and its common-pool resources. This is also shaped by the different ontology of the land as not just land but a commons that also contains non-human and animistic elements (Gambon and Rist 2020).

The enchantment strategy of taking community land into efficient production obscures the fact that the indigenous territories and peasant communities have an important socio-ecological function: it is from these environments that families can guarantee their subsistence and the reproduction of their traditional practices for the care of the commons. For example, in 2020, when Bolivians were suddenly isolated by COVID-19, many maintained their livelihood strategies such us urban food production for self-consumption, and organized food flows from the countryside to cities, and food exchange, among other things (Pachaguaya and Terrazas 2020). In fact, widespread experiences of food solidarity between the countryside and the city have reaffirmed the value and the resilience of food sovereignty as a strategy, and the need to continue with these production systems as a way out of the current crisis.

In our research on the agroextractivist frontier in Bolivia, we found a range of indications of alienation, e.g. inked to the perception that genetically modified soybeans are harmful to human health and thus not consumed in the producer communities, but nevertheless produced for international markets: 'this [soybean] is poisonous; harmful ... it is for selling, not for eating. I would not feed this to my kids even if they were crying of hunger' (soybean producer, near Cuadro Cañadas, Santa Cruz 2015).

We often encountered similar divisions between household consumption and a more anonymous 'market', expressed here, for example, by a representative of a nationwide women farmers' group: 'The largest [available] lands are in the

Chaco region. There we can spray pesticides on those crops that we sell, while avoiding spraying close to our homes and on the crops that we eat' (departmental representative, women farmers' group 'Bartolina Sisa', Santa Cruz 2016) (Jacobi et al. 2018).

The strengthening of mega-infrastructures in the agroextractive sector perpetuates the potential for alienation through large-scale broad, regional extractive policy projects. The alliance between landowners, companies and states expropriates the material possibilities of continuing to care for the lives of the superimposed populations in these extractive territories, racializing and patrimonializing the ownership of the means of production (land, water, seeds, among others) (Anthias 2018).

Agroextractivism is also subject to the geopolitics inherent in mega projects, which consist, for instance, in generating favourable conditions to render countries such as Bolivia sources of export of raw agricultural materials such as soybeans, alcohol, gas, oil and electricity, among others (Villegas 2018).

Environmental and social impacts

'By the end of September, the area burned reached 3.6 million hectares throughout the department [of Santa Cruz]. If we compare with the past management (619,000 hectares burned between January and September 2018), the area burned so far in 2019 is five times more. From this arises the need to understand recent events in greater depth' (Colque 2019: 9).

The mega-infrastructures that support agroextraction in Bolivia imply severe consequences for the socio-ecological environments. From 1980 to 2010, Bolivia lost more than six million ha of forest (UNREDD 2010; McKay 2017), and deforestation has been accelerating since then: in 2018 it was ranked fifth in terms of absolute deforestation in tropical countries, and in 2019 it was fourth (Global Forest Watch 2020). Deforestation in Bolivia is mainly linked to soybean expansion and cattle rearing in the tropical lowlands (Fehlenberg et al. 2017; Müller et al. 2014). The wildfires in Bolivia's Santa Cruz department in 2019, and particularly in the Chiquitanía dry forest, moved the world. Over 67,000 wildfires caused the loss of around five million ha of valuable ecosystems in the Bolivian lowlands, out of which almost two million ha were forests (Ministry of the Environment and Water 2019).

Large parts of the Santa Cruz department – which is about the same size as Germany – were on fire. Strong winds and extreme dryness made firefighting almost impossible. Deforestation in 2020 likely surpass that of 2019, because the current institutional context for the expansion of the agricultural frontier is favorable, especially for the production of soybean monocultures.

'This is an alarming situation... part of our territory is burning. The community members are controlling, they are making trails, creating gaps so that the fire does not go through... If we don't control it, the entire community will be burned' (CIPCA 2018)[2].

This continuous expansion of soybean cultivation includes an excessive use of agrochemicals, many of which are considered 'highly hazardous' by the FAO and WHO (Cavalcante 2020 about Brazil, Bascopé et al. 2019).

Another socio-ecological consequence is the effects on the availability of seeds. Bolivia features among the highest numbers of terrestrial species in the world, and harbours a hot spot of biodiversity (Tropical Andes) (Myers et al. 2000). Bolivia is a centre of origin with 77 documented maize races – more than Mexico, Argentina and Peru (Serratos-Hernández 2000). Particularly for its indigenous nations, for instance Guarani communities, maize plays an important role, not only in their diets, but also in spiritual terms (Llanque et al. 2018); in this sense, the protection of indigenous areas is relevant because of the multiple uses for their territories. Maize is wind-pollinated and has been proven to be easily contaminated by foreign genes as shown in Mexico by Quist and Chapela (2001), which underlines that the Bolivian agrobiodiversity of maize is at risk from the introduction of genetically modified seeds. While such plantations have been proven to exist at least as of 2018, genetically modified maize is still illegal at the time of this study.

Until 2015, maize seeds arrived together with agrochemical inputs via donation to farmers. Then, in 2019, farmers gradually had to pay the value of 30% to 70% of the seeds that were previously donated, and are now bought from input suppliers, thus generating a gradual benefit shifting from these inputs. The dependence occurs because local varieties of corn are lost, and rural families went from receiving seed donations to buying them (Llanque 2017).

The private sector is responsible for providing most of the seeds used in the agroextractivist sector. The so-called 'agricultural stores' named 'casas comerciales' import and distribute seeds as well as agrochemicals, often in direct representation of transnational companies such as Syngenta or Bayer. In terms of vegetables and fruit trees, there are companies that have seed banks that can count on up to 120 varieties among grains, vegetables, fruit trees and cereals (Bessa and Veiga 2020).

The approval of Supreme Decree No. 4232 for abbreviated evaluation procedures facilitates the introduction of genetically modified maize, sugar cane, cotton, wheat and more soybean varieties. While all of these crops have had adverse

---

[2] Benita Marina Machicado, President of the Villa Nueva Community, Municipality of Concepción cited by Cipca – Centro de Investigación y Promoción del Campesinado, 2018: Pequeños productores convocados por el Pacto de Unidad demandan políticas de Estado para el fortalecimiento del sector ‹www.cipca.org.bo/noticias/pequenos-productores-convocados-por-el-pacto-de-unidad-demandanpoliticas-de-estado-para-el-fortalecimiento-del-sector›

socio-ecological impacts elsewhere, maize plays a special role, because the constitution does not allow the use of genetically modified species.

Of the new range of genetically modified crops to be legally introduced in Bolivia, only wheat is primarily intended for food; the others (soybeans, sugar cane, cotton and wheat) are mainly used for agrofuels, feed or general flex crops. The Añez administration announced plans to purchase 200 million litres of alcohol from Bolivian industries, with an agreement signed between Cámara de Industria, Comercio, Servicios y Turismo de Santa Cruz CAINCO and the Ministry of Hydrocarbons, which establishes the delivery of this amount until May 2021, as investments in the sugar cane sector (Extremadoiro 2020).

Sierra (2020: 1) affirms: 'We're going to end up producing important transgenic foods in the basic basket like wheat and corn.' This means that corn, which is the only non-genetically modified product in Latin America, will now be produced in Bolivia with transgenic varieties.

Agroextractivism and agribusiness imply limited opportunities for local communities, smallholder farmers and especially for women, because it occupies the agricultural lands where they practice – often highly diverse – subsistence agriculture. Agroextractivism also gradually concentrates land, making it difficult to manage the commons, as the following quote illustrates: 'They [the women] face limitations and systemic issues such as legal insecurity of land, lack of access to credit and to the means of production, environmental degradation and persistent physical and psychological violence' (Llanque et al. 2018: 124)[3].

The insertion of genetically modified maize is an explicit way of producing dispossession in the territories inhabited by peasant and indigenous communities, because it limits access to traditional food within the communities. This reduced access to traditional food affects the care economy, and therefore the productive/reproductive activities of women. We understand the care economy as the activities that are essential for the sustainability of life, for example, domestic work for subsistence (Carrasco 2012).

These forms of relationship with the territory are part of the institutions of commons, and their change towards the reduction of access to water, food and seeds by the pressure of agroextractive activities is reminiscent of commons grabbing. In this context, a devaluation of domestic care work is evident, mainly related to the poor monetary recognition, e.g. the use and care of seeds, considered a woman's activity, is little recognized.

Or, as regards explicit consequences such as food insecurity: 'There are no longer any natural things. It's all for sale, the food is all bought. Sometimes the

---

[3] Llanque et al. 2018: Mujeres, trabajo de cuidado y agroecología: hacia la sustentabilidad de la vida a partir de experiencias en diferentes eco-regiones de Bolivia. Zuluaga, GP, Catacora, G., Siliprandi, E.(coords).

enterprises give us seeds that do not work, that do not germinate. It is very worrying' (Catacora-Vargas 2018: 183)[4].

Women from peasant and indigenous organizations in particular raised the agenda of food sovereignty, expressing their disagreement with government measures and indigenous leaders, in the insertion of transgenic corn in 2020. This position is related to the sexual division of labour and the value that women give to land and territory. Llanque (2015) calculated that Chiquitano women worked an average of 15 hours daily in various tasks, especially unpaid work, which is fundamental for the reproduction of life.

The modes of appropriation in areas where peasant and indigenous territories are part of agroextractivist claims affect the lives of rural women in a special way. They assume a fundamental role in care, but are structurally affected, e.g. by the access to education, compared to men in their communities, and even more so compared to urban populations. For instance, 62% of rural women are illiterate, corresponding to 14% of the total proportion of women nationally (INE 2012). Another factor of inequality is access to spaces for political participation. Llanque (2015) describe the limitations of time and space for women's participation in collective decisions of agricultural issues, and limited options in influencing agroextractive industries.

Because of these dynamics, malnutrition and undernourishment are still a challenge in Bolivia: in 2016, 53.7% of children under five suffered from anaemia and 24% suffered from chronic malnutrition in rural areas (Erostegui 2018).

Llanque et al. (2018) describe how families' situations in terms of food and nutrition are inseparable from the situation of women. In the context of agroextractivism, the workload for women is greater than in subsistence farming, and so is the dependence on monetary income to buy their food. The following quote illustrates this situation: 'We had to work more and buy per quintal [46kg], especially sugar' (Elías 2013: 13)[5]. These insecurities and shifts from resilience are part of an anti-politics machine and grabbing of the commons.

Local and NGO strategies

Collective movements use socio-organizational strategies to address the institutional infrastructure that favors agroextractivism at various levels. Socio-organizational strategies refer to collective forms of social organizations such as peasant federations, indigenous centres, self-managed nuclei in the neighbour-

---

[4] La Ripiera community leader, Takovo Mora indigenous territory, quoted by Catacora-Vargas et al. 2016: Soberanía Alimentaria: Reflexiones A Partir De Diferentes Sistemas Alimentarios De Santa Cruz, Bolivia/Food sovereignty: reflections from different food systems in Santa Cruz, Bolivia/Soberania alimentar: reflexões a partir de diferentes sistemas alimentares de Santa Cruz, Bolívia. *Revista Nera* (32), 170–194.

[5] Anonymous, Altiplano region cited by Elías, Bichelly 2013: La soberanía alimentaria desde las mujeres. *La-Paz: REMTE-Bolivia*.

hoods, consumer groups and organizational conglomerates with a view to participating in the transformation and distribution of food on a small scale, such as through cooperatives and retailer federations, among others. All these forms of organization have a multiple function in terms of representing demands vis-à-vis public entities. In addition, they have greater advantages in their means of production, and in the possibility of participating in markets.

Tzul (2016) affirms that women are protagonists in autonomous political organizations in community contexts, regarded as 'spaces for the reproduction of life' and as 'enablers of collective constructions, in the desire for the expansion of terms of inclusion within the community plots' (. . .) (Tzul 2016: 170)[6].

In the first place, the strategies that confront the institutional settings that promote agroextractivism have been of different types and on different scales. For example, at the national level, the organized groups representing indigenous, peasant communities, such as the trade union federations, and the indigenous centres are in the midst of political ruin.

The indigenous sector's agendas were diverse, and included options for incorporating development activities into the territories, and for generating economic options and radical anti-extraction positions, mainly put forward by women, such as the demand for Takovo Mora in 2016, the anti-oil extraction offensive in Tariquía from 2018 and the resistance against the "Rositas" dam project in Abapó in 2019.

There are clear legal indications of the recognition of indigenous and peasant community rights, because Bolivia has the strongest *de jure* rights for indigenous people in the world. However, indigenous rights and rights of nature are subordinated to alleged national interests (Anthias 2019). Anthias (2019) showed that the historical loss of territories due to the effect of appropriation has reinstated hierarchies of race and property.

The CIDOB, in their open letter to the interim president, claimed the following:

1. Abandon Supreme Decree No. 4232, which authorizes genetically modified seeds of maize, sugar cane, cotton, wheat and soy.
2. Abandon Supreme Decree No. 3973 and Law 741 that allow clearing of land and deforestation to advance the agricultural frontier.
3. Strengthening and enhancing indigenous, ancestral peasant agriculture to allow for other forms of agriculture, namely sustainable agriculture, agroecological agriculture and ecological agriculture.
4. They declare themselves to be in a state of alert, and declare the contract between the CAO and CIDOB worthless.

---

[6] Tzul, Gladys 2019: Mujeres indígenas: historias de reproducción de la vida en Guatemala. Una reflexión a partir de la visita de Silvia Federici. Bajo el Volcán, 1(22).

5. Support and promotion from the national governmentto develop family agriculture, peasant agriculture, and urban and peri-rurban agriculture, which feeds the Bolivian population.

On the other hand, peasant communities have their own interpretation of this problem. The Bartolina Sisa National Women's Federation and the peasant workers' union federations have tended to support the government of Evo Morales, including its agroextractivist policies. This institution shopping changes social dynamics, because it operates as a complex legal pluralism, where organizational discourses connect with the agroextractivism agenda.

Another sector of the peasant federations defends food sovereignty and ecological peasant family agriculture for land and food sovereignty. Both have permanent demands for land and disputes with the indigenous sector, especially in the lowlands. Among these demands and proposals are: 1) redistribution of land for peasants and indigenous people; 2) rejection of genetically modified crops; 3) non-foreignization of land; and 4) free and informed prior consultation (Colque et al. 2019). These demands were made publicly at the National Peasant-Indigenous Meeting, in the Chiquitanía region of Bolivia – 2019, 'Land and territory, for a new agenda of struggle and resistance from the communities'.

The Bolivian socio-political process is also an opportunity for indigenous and peasant organizations to reinterpret their own areas of resistance in the development of other narratives beyond the logic of political parties. Such a reinterpretation moves towards the creation of their own projects for self-determination in territories that will remain in persistent dispute. As the indigenous Moisés Aparicio leader said: 'we do not like to be driven... freedom is the most beautiful thing' (Isipotindi community, cited by Bautista et al. 2020 case 109: 110). These examples show us that there are options to make alternatives possible. Many of these are already underway within rural territories and communities.

Since 2018, an important factor in the demand for political change has been the National Coordination for the Defence of Indigenous Territories, Native Farmers and Protected Areas (CONTIOCAP). According to the CIPCA (2018), the first national meeting of small farmers was held to demand oversight and speed in the processes of land titling and sanitation, approval of the framework law on water for life, mechanization, technology, production, benefit with industrialization and marketing, and financial support for the sector. One year later, the achievements of the first national meeting of small farmers allowed the creation of an agenda that called for an audit of properties larger than 5,000 hectares, a new law on land, territories and the environment, the rejection of genetically modified seeds and related agrochemicals, and productive diversification with infrastructure that favours healthy food (Fundación Tierra 2019). That way, peasant agriculture represents an alternative knowledge base that manages to respond to agroextractivism (Palau 2020).

Micro-policy initiatives within grass-roots organizations

In Bolivia, the peasant sector controls approximately 27% of the cultivated land (23.2 million hectares), and the indigenous peoples 28% (23.9 million) (Aranda et al. 2020). According to Fundación Tierra, this agriculture is partially agroecological, but agrochemicals are also used in production. For example: "I grow vegetables, tomatoes, even sweet potatoes, peaches, citrus fruits, persimmons, I have everything. It has always been the problem we have, horticulture… it comes the monkey, and now lastly the butterfly has appeared." On the other hand: "I have been arriving late, and that's when I have had to deal with the poison as well. I got a fever. Let's work with biological, I'm tired of using poisons, with agroecological production at least we have food for self-consumption" (COMPAS 2020)[7].

The agroecological perspective represents a response that pushes food systems towards sustainability, capable of forging biological, political and sociocultural processes for the care of life (Llanque et al. 2018). One example is the agroecological producers of the Tropic region (affiliated to the MST-Bolivia movement) who recognize agriculture as their main activity, and value the type of production for family and community self-consumption with good-quality food (Llanque et al. 2018).

There are now numerous experiences in Bolivia of direct marketing in markets or ecological fairs with significant advantages for women (Llanque et al. 2018: 135). This is the case, for instance, with the producers of Achocalla/La Paz, who sell 20% of their production directly to consumers. Through this strategy, they can offer their produce at prices that are similar to those in the conventional market. In the case of producers selling at 'organic fairs' in Tarija, these sales account for 60 to 80% of their total generated revenue (Dorrego 2018).

In cities, agroecological production is also relevant: Sucre as an example has more than 1,500 urban ecological producers who provide food to local markets. The following quote from a related documentation illustrates this: 'I'm interested in diversifying my production, in having an entry into the economic and social sphere. Agriculture is leading us to a better future, because in the future we will have a shortage of food. I want to produce with agroecology, without agrochemicals, to have the land as in the past. There is corn… diversified, maintain the quality of the land and the quality of the production' (COMPAS 2020)[8].

In addition, the institutional markets are a potential, for example the state public purchases like the school breakfast, the supplementary feeding, where the Eco-

---

[7] Leandro Martinez, Samaipata producer, accessed on COMPAS 2020: Producción agroecológica para las Sustentabilidad en Samaipata. ⟨https://www.youtube.com/watch?v=E_UD5WGowTQ⟩

[8] Rolando Martinez – urban farmer of the AMPUS group, Sucre 2019 accessed on COMPAS 2020: Agricultura urbana y periurbana agroecológica de Sucre. ⟨https://www.youtube.com/watch?v=xXpvQqzKwn4⟩

nomic Peasant Organizations (OECAs) and Community Economic Organization (OECOMs) was included in food supply.

Recovering our agroecological practices, within a gender perspective, indigenous women propose that there is no liberation of territories without liberation of their own bodies. This means that the possibility of reproducing life among farmers and indigenous communities within their territories also implies transforming violent relations against women in three dimensions: a) physical, e.g. due to illnesses resulting from the use of pesticides; b) in terms of nourishment, e.g. through a diminished quality of industrial food; and c) political, e.g. when there is territorial dispossession where women lose their spaces for self-government. The push for agroextractivism in Bolivia during the last decade is putting pressure on traditional forms of food production and consumption, managed mainly by peasant and indigenous rural and urban women.

During the COVID-19 pandemic, various initiatives emerged as responses by indigenous and peasant women articulated within the cities of Bolivia: experiences such as the *ollas comunes*, which consisted of opening collective kitchen spaces to offer food to the neighbourhoods; several of these collective kitchens were made possible by sending food from rural areas.

In another example, the rural Chapare region in the department of Cochabamba sent food donations to the cities on several occasions (Pachaguaya 2020). Food containment is only possible to the extent that indigenous and peasant agricultural practices persist, as a way of practising care and guaranteeing the reproduction of life. One way widely applied by women within the territories is the responses as care practices. Tzul (2019) proposes that indigenous women generate responses within their community plots, because they have the capacity to find ways out of the historical tensions in their territories.

Perspectives and strategies by local groups and organized groups show how there is a 'disenchantment' taking place in their discourses and practices. This process appears with institution shopping going on in a new frontier in terms of land-rights distribution and resource use.

State and company strategy

The private sector, in alliance with governmental actors, promoted the creation of a financial and physical infrastructure that involves credits, investments and other financial flows or incentives (e.g. tax reductions) tailored to agribusiness development. An emerging example of the incentives for agroextractivism is the case of energy or agrofuels. Until 2030, the country will require up to 2.96 billion litres of fuel, which will require about 740 million litres of alcohol (Extremadoiro 2020)[3] To reach this objective, the agroextractivist sector projects an estimated necessary investment of US$2 billion in industrial agriculture, as well as an institutional agreement between the state and agribusiness companies (Extremadoiro

2020). Discourses around the need for genetically modified crops – albeit, as in the case of soybeans and sugar cane, destined to the production of energy rather than food – Some policy makers as the same as companies argument that an increased (national) food production, similarly to the increased need for land for the sector: for instance, the bimonthly review of the Association of Oilseed Growers titled 'Soybeans for Food Sovereignty' (ANAPO 2014).

The power positions of policymakers and the perspective of civil society, presenting agroextractivism as an alternative. Based on such arguments, the Añez administration issued a supreme decree for a simplified approbation process for genetically modified seeds (soy, maize, cotton, wheat and sugar cane), in the name of food security and food sovereignty. This supreme decree directly contradicts the constitution as well as several laws, among them the Framework Law on the Rights of Mother Earth of 2012, because this defends environmental and social protection. Hand in hand with the scarcity due to the COVID-19 pandemic, the need to strengthen agribusiness is argued, claiming the need to cover debts for external inputs (fertilizer, seeds and pesticides) by public spending. In direct support of agroextractivist activities, the Añez administration made a compromise to pay 600 million dollars for debts of medium- and large-scale farmers (mainly soybean) with transnational companies in 2020.

A study by Urioste (2012) showed that soybean and other agroindustrial producers have long been directly supported by tax exemptions, and indirectly through subsidies of 50% for fuel and energy, favouring large-scale machinery over smallholder agriculture. In combination with decreasing soybean prices, such credits have increased the accumulated debts for inputs of the agroextractivist sector such as seeds, agrochemicals and machinery (Colque 2020). Different actors of this sector are currently arguing in favour of paying debts with public funds and special incentives such as a 4% annual interest rate, a 12-year term and two years' of grace.

Besides taxpayers' funds, international credits are also used as direct support for agroextractivism. For instance, during the term of Branko Marinkovic at the Ministry of Planning in 2020, the Camera Agropecuario del Oriente (CAO) received a payment of USD350,000 as a non-refundable loan from the Inter-American Development Bank (IDB) to train workers in the agroextractive sector (Extremadoiro 2020).

With its explicit support for agroextractivism, promoted by the enterprises, it is not only violating the rights of peasants and indigenous peoples, workers and consumers, but also the rights of nature as enshrined in the 2009 constitution and the 2012 Framework Law of the Rights of Mother Earth (No. 300). Art. 255 of the Bolivian constitution prohibits the introduction, production and commercialization of genetically modified seeds. In addition, the Framework Law of Mother Earth No. 300 and the Law of the Communitarian Agricultural Productive Revolution for Food Sovereignty No. 144 established the bases for the protection of life systems, and plural productive forms, forming a legal barrier against the introduction of genetically modified plants[9].

In 2020, more than 100 civil society organizations warned the interim government in an open letter that Supreme Decree No. 4232 would lead to increased forest fires, deforestation, pesticide use, and the loss of biodiversity and agrobiodiversity (and thus dietary diversity) in Bolivia. More than 50% of the territories affected by the exceptional wildfires in 2019 were public lands. Fiscal land legally assigned to large-scale agribusiness often overlaps with the territorial claims of indigenous groups. The process of land titling to indigenous nations according to the legal framework of 1996 ('INRA law') in Bolivia was stagnant, and now it is in decline (Colque 2019). Consolidation of an inequitable agrarian structure and legal processes hasbecome a strong factor favoring the agroextractivist sector. Governments have been arguing that more than 80% of the beneficiaries are local communities. However, there are huge differences between private landowners and communities in terms of legal land access, and only 17% of fiscal land in Bolivia continues with conflicts over various actors' demands (Colque 2019).

The explicit support for agroextractivism confirms what Szablowski and Campbell (2019) propose: contemporary conflicts over resource extraction are quickly translated into the regulatory sphere and particular governance reforms. One of the most relevant examples was that in early 2020, the interim government placed a long-term functionary of the Agricultural Chamber of the East CAO at the head of the ministry for 'Productive Development' and then quickly of the ministry of the economy.

The Declaration of Peasant Rights approved in 2018 and led by Bolivia at the United Nations was not promoted within the country during the Morales and Añez administrations. This shows the difficulties involved in implementing institutional frameworks to protect human rights without wider structural changes. These dynamics produce a context of dispossession both for peasant families living on lands affected by agroextractivism and for indigenous communities and territories.

Deforestation and forest fires are among the most visible expressions of dispossession, because they radically transform the composition of the landscape, affecting the forms of life that coexist in territories, and accelerate their transformation into monocultures. Against this background, the nationwide lockdown (March–September 2020) served as an opportunity to redirect government funds – which includes the increase in foreign debts (Ministry of Development, Economy and Finances 2020) – to favour the agroextractivist sector. Some of the resulting socio-ecological impacts are discussed in what follows.

---

[9] Estado Plurinacional De Bolivia. Ley N. 300 de la Madre Tierra y Desarrollo Integral para Vivir Bien. 2012.

Conclusion

In this chapter, we frame agroextractivism in Bolivia as a mega-development project, which entails a physical and institutional infrastructure of regional character, integrating development projects from various countries on the continent. We explain this phenomenon partly by using the concept of 'alienation', and by the 'enchantment' of governing bodies, while farmers and local communities appear to have little choice regarding the crops they plant, inputs they use and the markets they connect to, and by the dynamics of accumulation and exclusion in large-scale agriculture, as an anti-politics machine.

The investments made by the private sector in alliance with the states, suppliers of inputs and transnational transformers create a context of alienation of indigenous and peasant territories, superimposed on the extractive areas. There is evidence of the alienation and blackmail that produce the dispossession of the means of production, of traditional food sources with nutritional quality, of the labour force and above all of the social spaces where forms of self-government are reproduced.

Enchantment is used by the proponents of agroextractivism in Bolivia both with promises ('economic take-off') and arguments of threats (food scarcity). Both sides are not necessarily backed by numbers or scientific evidence, and are clearly tailored to decision-makers as well as to the public, and much less to the involved actors in the concerned territories. The combined concepts in one framework made it possible to 'put the pieces of the puzzle together' in order to better understand which actor groups argue and act in a specific way and persuade others to support their way. Alienation occurs in the process of enchantment of actors from rural communities and indigenous territories, who live in areas of agroextractivism. However, those actors most affected by agroextractivism and related alienation in Bolivia, namely rural communities, women and indigenous groups, do not seem to have the same scope of action as those actors making use of enchantment strategies.

The challenges from fragmentation of cultural landscapes ecosystems' (Haller 2020: 156), which results in a legal plurality, where actors increase institution shopping, shifting gradients of bargaining power (Haller et al. 2016).

The dispossession of the territories where the lives of peasant and indigenous communities are reproduced directly affects food sovereignty, generating malnutrition and poor nutrition, as well as incorporating hours of work for women as the main careers. For example, Aranda et al. (2020) show how peasant agriculture has decreased due to the effect of agroextractivism in Bolivia. In 1950, peasant agriculture was responsible for 71% of national food production, but between 2010 and 2016, just 36% of the production of agricultural crops did not belong to oil and industrial crops.

After reflecting on this phenomenon, we find that, considering bargaining power positions, local actors have a smaller scope of actions in making use of enchantment. It is possible to explain this socio-ecological consequence from the understanding of the concept of alienation. In this process, it is essential to recognize that alienation produces vulnerability in social organizations, but also generates responses from those sectors, e.g. territorial defence. That means that some of the local groups show that there is also a disenchantment with the discourses of the private sector, and the purchase of institutions in a new frontier in terms of the distribution of land rights and commons.

The dynamics of agroextractive mega-infrastructures in the collective dynamics opens new questions about options to transform radically inequitable relations at the level of the links in the food systems. Likewise, actors such as agricultural families, communities, indigenous territories and even urban agricultural initiatives provide answers to the extent that they manage to negotiate within their institutions, a kind of institutional sale, which is not only functional in regard to agroextractivism but also promotes more sustainable alternatives such as agroecological production, transformation, commercialization and consumption. This finding opens up options for reflecting on ways out of social organizations, within the dominant context of geographical area and institutions, in favor of the care economy, that are more socio-ecologically friendly than the currently dominating agroextractivism.

Acknowledgements

We would like to thank Dr Georgina Catacora-Vargas for her substantial contributions to this chapter, especially in the dialogue on the relationship between agroextractivism, public policies and the responses of social organizations.

Glossary

AMPUS	Association of Urban and Peri-urban Producers of Sucre
ANAPO	Association of Oilseed and Wheat Producers
APG	Assembly of the Guaraní People
CAO	Agricultural Chamber of the East
CAINCO	Chamber of Industry and Commerce of Santa Cruz
CIDOB	Confederation of Bolivian Indigenous Peoples
CONTIOCAP	National Coordination for the Defence of Indigenous Territories, Native Farmers and Protected Areas
COSIPLAN	South American Council for Infrastructure and Planning
CPEMB	Beni's Ethnic People's Centre
GDP	Gross Domestic Product
IDB	Inter-American Development Bank

IIRSA	Initiative for the Integration of the Regional Infrastructure of South America
OECAs	Peasant Economic Organizations
OECOMs	Community Economic Organizations
OICH	Chiquitana Indigenous Organization
PLUS BENI	Plan for the Beni Department
SD	Supreme Decree
TIPNIS	Isiboro-Sécure Indigenous Territory and National Park

References

Alonso-Fradejas, Alberto, Jose Luís Caal Hub, and Teresita Chinchilla Miranda 2011: plantaciones agroindustriales, dominación y despojo indígena-campesino en la Guatemala del s. XXI. Guatemala: Instituto de Estudios Agrarios y Rurales (IDEAR)/ Coordinación de ONG y Cooperativas (CONGCOOP).

ANAPO 2014: Anapo Noticias. ‹www.anapobolivia.org› accessed on 20.11.2020.

Anthias, Penelope. 2014: *The elusive promise of territory: An ethnographic case study of Indigenous land titling in the Bolivian Chaco*. Diss. University of Cambridge.

Anthias, Penelope. Limits to Decolonization. Cornell University Press, 2018.

Anthias, Penelope 2019: Rethinking territory and property in indigenous land claims. Geoforum 119 (268-278).

Aranda, Dario Vicente, Lucia, Acevedo Carolina, and Vicente, Carlos 2020: Atlas Del Agronegocio Transgénico en el Cono Sur Monocultivos, resistencias y propuestas de los pueblos. Acción por la Biodiversidad. Buenos Aires: Algunas Impresiones.

Arrieta, Mario 1990: *Agricultura en Santa Cruz: De la empresa colonial a la empresa modernizada* (1559-1985). La Paz: ILDIS.

Artacker, Tamara, Jorge Campanini, and Eduardo Gudynas 2020: Extractivismos agropecuarios en tiempos de pandemia: flexibilizaciones, asimetrías, autoritarismos y otros efectos derrame. *Yeiyá-Volumen 1*, Número 1, julio-diciembre 2020, 89.

Bascopé Zanabria, Roberto, Ulrike Bickel, and Johana Jacobi 2019: Plaguicidas químicos usados en el cultivo de soya en el Departamento de Santa Cruz, Bolivia: riesgos para la salud humana y toxicidad ambiental. *Acta Nova*, 9(3), 386-416.

Bautista Durán, Ruth, Bazoberry Chali, Oscar, and Soliz Tito, Lorenzo 2020: Informe 2019 Acceso a la tierra y territorio en Sudamérica. Editorial: IPDRS, Pan para el Mundo (PPM), OXFAM, Organización Intereclesiástica para la Cooperación al Desarrollo – ICCO y FASTENOPFER, Acción Cuaresmal.

Berawi, Mohammed Ali, and Bambang Susantono 2013: Developing conceptual design of mega infrastructure project: creating innovation and added value. In 2013 SAVE International Value Summit (337-346).

Burchardt, Hans-Jürgen, and Kristina Dietz (Neo-) extractivism: 2014 a new challenge for development theory from Latin America. *Third World Quarterly*, 35(3), 468-486.

Campanini, Jorge., Villegas, Pablo, Jiménez, Georgina, Gandarillas, Marco, & Pérez, Silvia 2014: Los límites de las fronteras extractivas en Bolivia. *El caso de la biodiversidad en el Aguaragüe*.

CAO-CIDOB 2020: Acuerdo de cooperación interinstitucional. Unidos por el campo. Fundación Tierra. ‹http://www.ftierra.org/index.php/component/attachments/download/217›, accessed 12.1.2023.

Carrasco Cristina. 2012: Economía, trabajo y sostenibilidad de la vida. En sostenibilidad de la vida. Aportaciones desde la economía solidaria, feminista y ecológica (Red de Economía Alternativa y Solidaria, READ Euskadi, ed.). Bilbao: REAS Euskadi, 27-42

Carrasco Cristina, and Díaz Corral Carmen. 2017: *Economía feminista. Desafíos, propuestas, alianzas*. Barcelona: Edición Entre Pueblos.

Catacora-Vargas Georgina, Galeano Giménez Pablo, Agapito-Tenfen Sarah, Aranda Dario, Palau Tomas, Nodari Rubens 2012: Soybean production in the Southern Cone of the Americas: update on l and pesticide use. Cochabamba: Genok / REDES-AT / BASE-IS.

Catacora-Vargas, Georgina, Llanque-Zonta, Aymara, Jacobi, Johann, and Burgoa, Delgado Freddy 2016: Soberanía alimentaria: reflexiones a partir de diferentes sistemas alimentarios de Santa Cruz, Bolivia/Food sovereignty: reflections from different food systems in Santa Cruz, Bolivia/Soberania alimentar: reflexões a partir de diferentes sistemas alimentares de Santa Cruz, Bolívia. *Revista Nera*, 32 – 19: 170-194.

Catacora-Vargas, Georgina, Rosa Binimelis, Anne I. Myhr, and Brian Wynne. 2018: "Socio-economic research on genetically modified crops: A study of the literature." *Agriculture and Human Values* 35, no. 2: 489-513.

Charupá, Roberto Tomichá 2019: Espiritualidades descoloniales en perspectiva indígena: algunos presupuestos y desafíos. *Revista Pistis Praxis*, 11:3.

Cipca – Centro de Investigación y Promoción del Campesinado, 2018: Pequeños productores convocados por el Pacto de Unidad demandan políticas de Estado para el fortalecimiento del sector. ‹www.cipca.org.bo/noticias/pequenos-productores-convocados-por-el-pacto-de-unidad-demandanpoliticas-de-estado-para-el-fortalecimiento-del-sector› accessed 12.1.2023.

Colque, Gonzalo 2019: *Fuego en Santa Cruz. Balance de los incendios forestales 2019 y su relación con la tenencia de la tierra*. La Paz: Fundación Tierra.

Colque, Gonzalo et al. 2019: 18 Pilares fundamentales para una agenda campesina-indígena. Encuentro Nacional Campesino-Indígena "Tierra y territorio, por una nueva agenda de lucha y resistencia desde las comunidades" Cochabamba, 6 y 7 de abril. La Paz: Fundación Tierra.

Colque, Gonzalo 2020: Ahora sí, la economía importa. El problema de fondo es el modelo extractivista que predomina en Bolivia y el desafío mayor es transitar de una sociedad rentista hacia una sociedad productiva y sostenible. *La Paz: Fundación Tierra.*

Desa, United Nations 2019: World population prospects 2019: Highlights. New York (US): United Nations Department for Economic and Social Affairs.

Dorrego, Ana 2018: Las mujeres en los sistemas de producción bajo principios agroecológicos en Bolivia. PHD Thesis. Universidad Complutense de Madrid, España.

El Deber 2020: CAO accede a línea de crédito por 350 millones de dólares para capacitar a los trabajadores del sector. ‹https://eldeber.com.bo/dinero/cao-accede-a-linea-de-credito-por-us-350000-para-capacitar-a-los-trabajadores-del-sector_196614› accessed on 24.08.2020.

Elías, Bishelly 2013: "La soberanía alimentaria desde las mujeres." *La-Paz: REMTE-Bolivia.*

Erostegui, Morelia 2018: Historias del programa mundial de alimentos. El reto de la malnutrición en Bolivia. ‹https://historias.wfp.org/el-reto-de-la-malnutrici%C3%B3n-en-bolivia-ac81356436f9› accessed 12.1.2023.

Espinoza Yuderkys 2014: De por qué es necesario un feminismo descolonial. Diferenciación, dominación co-constitutiva de la modernidad occidental y el fin de la política de identidad. Bogotá: GLEFAS.

Extremadoiro, Ernesto. 2020: gobierno proyecta la compra de 200 millones de litros de alcohol a industrias. *Digital Journal El Deber*. ‹https://eldeber.com.bo/economia/gobierno-proyecta-la-compra-de-200-millones-de-litros-de-alcohol-a-industrias_196488› Accessed on 18.08.2020.

FAO, 2020: Gender and Land Rights Database ‹http://www.fao.org/gender-landrights-database/en/› accessed 12.1.2023.

FAOSTAT 2020: ‹http://www.fao.org/faostat/en/#data/RP› accessed 12.1.2023.

Ferguson, James 2006: "The anti-politics machine." *The anthropology of the state: a reader*: 270-86.

Federici, Silvia 2004: *Calibán y la bruja. Mujeres, cuerpo y acumulación*. Madrid: Ed. Traficantes de Sueños.

Fehlenberg, Verena, Baumann, Matthias, Gasparri, Nelson, Piquer-Rodriguez, Maria, Gavier-Pizarro, Gasparri, Kuemmerle, Tobias, 2017: The role of soybean production as an underlying driver of deforestation in the South American Chaco. *Global Environ. Change*, 45 (Suppl. C), 24–34.

FAN 2020: Focos de calor Bolivia. ‹http://incendios.fan-bo.org/Satrifo/fuentes-de-informacion/› accessed on 10.12.2020.

Fundación Tierra, 2019: Declaración del Encuentro Nacional Campesino Indígena. www.ftierra.org/index.php/component/attachments/download/171 Accessed on 5.10.2020.

Fundación Tierra, 2020: Implicaciones del acuerdo firmado entre la CAO y la CIDOB. Derechos indígenas y campesinos. ‹http://www.ftierra.org/index.php/tema/derechos-indigenas-y-campesinos/939-implicaciones-del-acuerdo-firmado-entre-la-cao-y-la-cidob› accessed on 05.10. 2020.

Fundación Tierra, 2020: Crece rechazo del acuerdo CIDOB y CAO entre las organizaciones indígenas de tierras bajas. ‹http://www.ftierra.org/index.php/tema/derechos-indigenas-y-campesinos/938-crece-el-rechazo-del-acuerdo-cibod-y-cao-entre-las-organizaciones-indigenas-de-tierras-bajas› accessed on 05.10. 2020.

Gambon, Helen. 2020: "Constitutionality processes and social-ecological dynamics in the Pilón Lajas Indigenous Territory and Biosphere Reserve." University of Bern.

Giraldo, Omar Felipe, and Nils McCune. 2019: "Can the state take agroecology to scale? Public policy experiences in agroecological territorialization from Latin America." *Agroecology and Sustainable Food Systems* 43.7-8: 785-809.

Greenwood, Royston 2011: Institutional complexity and organizational responses. *Academy of Management annals* 5.1: 317-371.

Gudynas, Eduardo 2013: Extracciones, extractivismos y extrahecciones. Un marco conceptual sobre la apropiacion de recursos naturales. Observatorio Del Desarrollo CLAES. No 18.

Hafner, R., and Coy, M. 2016: The soy-production's fair (y) tale? Latin American perspectives on globalized dynamics, territoriality and environmental justice. In *Fairness and justice in natural resource politics*, 158-175. Routledge.

Haller, Tobias 2019: Towards a new institutional political ecology: how to marry external effects, institutional change and the role of power and ideology in commons studies, in: Haller, T. Breu, T., de Moor, T. Rohr, C., Znoj, H. (eds.). T*he commons in a glocal world*: *global connections and local responses*. London: Routledge, 90-120.

Haller, Tobias 2020: Institution shopping and resilience grabbing. *Conservation & Society,* 18(3), 252-267.

Haller, T., Acciaioli, G., and Rist, S. 2016: Constitutionality: conditions for crafting local ownership of institution-building processes. *Society & Natural Resources,* 29(1), 68-87.

Haller, Tobias, Gilbert Fokou, Gimbage Mbeyale, and Patrick Meroka 2013: How fit turns into misfit and back: institutional transformations of pastoral commons in African floodplains. *Ecology and Society,* 18(1), 34.

Harvey, P., and Knox, H. 2012: The enchantments of infrastructure. *Mobilities*, 7(4), 521-536.

Heusser, Thomas 2017: El maíz era la vida: The influence of institutions and stakeholders on the food system of a Guaraní community in Bolivia. Master thesis in Social Anthropology at the University of Bern.

Hinings, C. R., Logue, D. M., and Zietsma, C. 2017: Fields, institutional infrastructure and governance. *The Sage handbook of organizational institutionalism.*

INE (Instituto Nacional de Estadística) 2012: Base de datos del Censo Nacional de Población y Vivienda. ⟨http://datos.ine.gob.bo/binbol/RpWebEngine.exe/Portal?BASE=CPV2012COM&lang=ESP⟩ accessed 12.1.2023.

IRSA 2013: Eje Perú, Brasil y Bolivia. ⟨http://www.iirsa.org/Page/PageDetail?id=123&menuItemId=68⟩ accessed 12.1.2023.

Jacobi, J., Mukhovi, S., Llanque, A., Augstburger, H., Käser, F., Pozo, C., Ngutu, Peter M., Rist S., and Ifejika, Speranza C. 2018: Operationalizing food system resilience: an indicator-based assessment in agroindustrial, smallholder farming, and agroecological contexts in Bolivia and Kenya. *Land Use Policy,* 79:433-446.

Lalander, R. (2017). Ethnic rights and the dilemma of extractive development in plurinational Bolivia. *The International Journal of Human Rights*, 21(4), 464-481.

Llanque, A., 2015: La economía de las mujeres rurales en el contexto comunitario. Fortalecimiento de alternativas integrales de manejo de Bosques y Recursos Naturales. Sistematización de experiencias en la TCO Monte Verde. La Paz: RRI / IPHAE / Editorial Carrasco.

Llanque, A. 2017: Mujeres indígenas y sistemas alimentarios, imbricación de violencias coloniales.⟨http://www.wwc2017.eventos.dype.com.br/resources/anais/14988706 53_arquivo_mujerescolonialidadsistemasalimentariosa.llanqueyf.delgado2017.pdf⟩ accessed 12.10.2020.

Llanque, A., Dorrego, A., Costanzo, G., Elías, B., and Catacora-Vargas, G. 2018: Mujeres, trabajo de cuidado y agroecología: hacia la sustentabilidad de la vida a partir de experiencias en diferentes eco-regiones de Bolivia. Zuluaga, G. P., Catacora, G., and Siliprandi, E.(coords). *Agroecología En Femenino* (2018): 123-39.

McKay, B. M. 2017: Agrarian extractivism in Bolivia. *World Development*, 97, 199-211.

McKay, B. M. 2018: *Extractivismo agrario: dinámicas de poder, acumulación y exclusión en Bolivia*. Fundación Tierra. ⟨https://www.lasabolivia.org/extractivismo-agrario-dinamicas-de-poder-acumulacion-y-exclusion-en-bolivia/⟩ accessed 12.1.2023.

Maristella, S., and Enrique, V. 2014: *Maldesarrollo: la Argentina del extractivismo y el despojo*. Katz editores.
Marx, K. 1990: La llamada acumulación originaria. *El Capital*, *1*, 607-649.
Mathez-Stiefel, S. L., Boillat, S., and Rist, S. 2007. Promoting the diversity of worldviews: an ontological approach to bio-cultural diversity. In: *Haverkort, B., and Rist, S., editors. Endogenous development and bio-cultural diversity*. Leusden, Netherlands: Comparing and Supporting Endogenous Development
(COMPAS)/Educational Training Consultancy (ETC) Foundation, pp. 67–81.
Ministry of the Environment and Water MMAYA 2019: Separata Informativa No. 1. Monitoreo de Focos de Calor. Ministerio de Medio Ambiente y Agua, La Paz, Bolivia. ⟨https://www.mmaya.gob.bo/2019/10/el-simb-emite-monitoreo-de-focos-de-calor-quemas-e-incendios-forestales/⟩ accessed on 12.10.2020.
Ministry of Rural Development and Land MDRyT 2020: Gobierno Tiene El Compromiso De Asegurar El Derecho Propietario De Tierras en el Área Rural. ⟨http://www.inra.gob.bo/InraPb/paginaController?cmd=noticia&id=69344⟩ accessed on 12.10.2020.
Ministry of Development, Economy and Finances 2020: Deuda Pública Del TGN Bolivia. ⟨https://www.economiayfinanzas.gob.bo/deuda-externa-del-tgn.html⟩ accessed on 12.10.2020.
Mohseni, M., Tabassi, A. A., Kamal, E. M., Bryde, D. J., and Michaelides, R. 2019: Complexity factors in mega projects: a literature review. *European Proceedings of Multidisciplinary Sciences*, 2(6), 54-67.
Moore F. Lappé 2013: Beyond the scarcity scare: reframing the discourse of hunger with an eco-mind, *The Journal of Peasant Studies*, 40(1), 219-238.
Mosley, J., and Watson, E. E. 2016: Frontier transformations: development visions, spaces and processes in Northern Kenya and Southern Ethiopia. *Journal of Eastern African Studies*, 10(3), 452-475.
Mueller, R., Pacheco, P., and Montero, J. C. 2014: The context of deforestation and forest degradation in Bolivia: drivers, agents and institutions. Occasional Paper 108. Bogor, Indonesia: Center for International Forestry Research.
Mueller, R., Pistorius, T., Rohde, S., Gerold, G., and Pacheco, P. 2013: Policy options to reduce deforestation based on a systematic analysis of drivers and agents in lowland Bolivia. *Land Use Policy*, 30(1), 895-907.
Myers, N., Mittermeier, R. A., Mittermeyer, C. G., Fonseca, G.A. B., and Kent, J. 2000: Biodiversity hotspots for conservation priorities. *Nature*, 403, 853-858
Navarro, A. 2020: Tax sparing clauses as a policy instrument of developing countries and their descent: Evidence from the Latin-American Tax Treaty Network. *Copenhagen Business School, CBS LAW Research Paper*, 20-17.
Pachaguaya, P. Terrazas C. 2020: *Una cuarentena individual para la sociedad colectiva. La llegada y despacho del khapaj Niño coronavirus a Bolivia*. Ada La Paz.
Pérez, C. J., and Smith, C. A. 2019: Indigenous knowledge systems and conservation of settled territories in the Bolivian Amazon. *Sustainability*, 11(21), 6099.
Petry, P., Rodrigues, S., Ramos Neto, M. B., Matsumoto, M., Kimura, G., Becker, M., ... and Oliveira, M. 2011: Análise de risco ecológico da Bacia do rio Paraguai: Argentina, Bolívia, Brasil e Paraguai. The Nature Conservancy.
Phalan, B., Onial, M., Balmford, A., and Green, R. E. 2011: Reconciling food production and biodiversity conservation: land sharing and land sparing compared. *Science*, 333(6047), 1289-1291.

Publiagro 2020: Pobreza y destrucción de los recursos naturales. ⟨https://publiagro.com.bo/2020/01/columna-de-opinion-pobreza-y-destruccion-de-recursos-naturales-por-ing-wolf-rolon-roth/ Searched on June – 2020⟩ accessed on 12.10.2020.

Quiroga 2017: Tariquía: el proyecto de exploración de hidrocarburos que preocupa y divide a comunidades en Bolivia ⟨https://es.mongabay.com/2017/06/bolivia-tariquia-hidrocarburos/⟩

Quist, D., and Chapela, I. H. 2001: Transgenic DNA introgressed into traditional maize landraces in Oaxaca, Mexico. *Nature*, 414(6863), 541-543.

Rincón, L. F., and Fernandes, B. M. 2018: Territorial dispossession: dynamics of capitalist expansion in rural territories in South America. *Third World Quarterly,* 39(11), 2085-2102.

Schilling-Vacaflor, Almut. 2017: "Who controls the territory and the resources? Free, prior and informed consent (FPIC) as a contested human rights practice in Bolivia." *Third World Quarterly* 38.5: 1058-1074.

SENASAG 2011: Servicio Nacional de Sanidad Agropecuaria e Inocuidad Alimentaria. Gran Paititi. ⟨https://paititi.senasag.gob.bo/egp/⟩ accessed on 10.12.2020.

Serratos-Hernández, J. A. 2009: El origen y la diversidad del maíz en el continente americano, Mexico D.F. Greenpeace: http://www.greenpeace.org/mexico/global/mexico/report/2009/3/el-origen-yla-diversidad-del.Pdf, accessed on 12.10.2020.

Sierra, I. 2020: Bolivia: decreto abre las puertas a semillas transgénicas para cinco cultivos. ⟨https://es.mongabay.com/2020/05/bolivia-decreto-transgenicos-cinco-cultivos/⟩ accessed on 27.05.2020.

Schilling-Vacaflor, Almut 2017: Who controls the territory and the resources? Free, prior and informed consent (FPIC) as a contested human rights practice in Bolivia. *Third World Quarterly* 38.5: 1058-1074.

Szablowski, D., and Campbell, B. 2019: Struggles over extractive governance: power, discourse, violence, and legality. *The Extractive Industries and Society*, 6(3), 635-641.

Tzul, G. 2016: Sistemas de gobierno comunal indígena. Mujeres y tramas de parentesco en Chuimeq'ena'. SOCEE/Maya' Wuj Editorial. Guatemala, Guatemala.

Tzul, G. T. 2019: Mujeres indígenas: historias de reproducción de la vida en Guatemala. Una reflexión a partir de la visita de Silvia Federici. *Bajo el Volcán*, 1(22), 12.

Ujuaje, M. D., and Chang, M. 2020: Systems of food and systems of violence: an intervention for the special issue on "Community self-organisation, sustainability and resilience in food systems". *Sustainability, 12*, 7092.

Urioste, M. 2012: Concentration and "foreignisation" of land in Bolivia. Canadian journal of development studies/revue canadienne d'études du développement 33.4: 439-457.

Villalobos, G. 2020: *Julio del 2020: Más incendios en áreas protegidas y en el bosque chiquitano que el 2019.* La Paz: Fundación Solón.

Villegas, P. 2018: De Alfredo Stroessner a Evo Morales: el corazón energético de SudAmérica. La Paz: CEDIB.Vollset, S. E., Goren, E., Yuan, C. W., Cao, J., Smith, A. E., Hsiao, T., ... and Dolgert, A. J. 2020: fertility, mortality, migration, and population scenarios for 195 countries and territories from 2017 to 2100: a forecasting analysis for the Global Burden of Disease Study. *The Lancet*.

Vos, V., Gallegos, S., Czaplicki-Cabezas, S., and Peralta-Rivero, C. 2020: "Biodiversidad en Bolivia: Impactos e implicaciones de la apuesta por el agronegocio." *Impactos del modelo productivo agroindustrial en Bolivia*, 25.

Wartmann, F. M., Haller, T., and Backhaus, N. 2016: "Institutional shopping" for natural resource management in a protected area and indigenous territory in the Bolivian Amazon. *Human Organization*, 75(3), 218-229.

Films

COMPAS 2020: Producción agroecológica para las Sustentabilidad en Samaipata. ⟨https://www.youtube.com/watch?v=E_UD5WGowTQ⟩ accessed 12.1.2023.

When the Black Snake Crosses Sacred Land: The Dakota Access Pipeline and the Ontology of Protest in North Dakota, USA

Anna Katharina Vokinger, Institute of Social Anthropology, University of Bern, Switzerland

Introduction

This chapter analyses the impact of the Dakota Access Pipeline (DAPL) mega-infrastructure on the locally affected population. The population that is most impacted in this case are Indigenous peoples who protected their lands in the context of a democratic state as their rights were undermined for economic profit. The movement has grown and received heterogeneous support from those who identified with different issues within the oil pipeline project. On the one hand, this example shows the limits of Indigenous rights when economic interests are high, and on the other hand it shows that there are different ontologies and strategies on how to resist the grabbing of sacred land or how to preserve conservation. The mega-infrastructure project presents the establishment of a new and reconfigured frontier (see Rasmussen and Lund 2018) due to economic and technological changes. To prove their point, some involved actors from the government and the company made use of enchantment (see Harvey and Knox 2012). The enchantment serves to support a new reasoning in politics since previous state leaders halted the implementation of the project. This case study shows how different motivations lead to resistance for the same cause and that success depends on economic and political constellations. The content of this chapter is based on extensive literature research and interviews with Andreanne Catt[1] and Jose Gomez III[2], both active participants in the movement against the pipeline.

The DAPL has been built to transport crude oil from the Bakken Three Forks production in North Dakota to Pakota, Illinois and is operated by Energy Transfer

---
[1] Andreanne Catt is Sicangu Lakota from Rosebud and a member of the seven Oceti Sakowin Tribes. She attended the movement at Standing Rock for four months and is a blockade and non-violent direct-action trainer with the International Indigenous Youth Council.

[2] Jose Gomez III is a member of the Miakan-Garza Band of Central Texas and is Director of Communications and a mentor with the International Indigenous Youth Council.

Partners.[3] Whilst Bakken was considered a marginal resource for oil in 2007, this changed as drilling technologies transformed and North Dakota soon became the second-highest producer of crude oil in the United States. This boom supposedly resulted in a major boost for the economy in North Dakota and reduced unemployment.[4] Further, the infrastructure of the pipeline created 8,000 to 12,000 jobs during its construction and the local economy is thought to have benefited from workers using hotels, restaurants and other hospitality services.[5] However, the oil boom was also met with a meth, heroin and pill epidemic and an increase in the number of people who had to serve time in prison (Zaitchik 2017: 109). Besides the economic impacts that resulted from the infrastructure, protests arose since the pipeline crosses the Missouri River and Indigenous land according to the land distribution within the Fort Laramie Treaty (Estes 2019: 2). These protests took place on site as well as online using social media, for example by using the hashtag #NoDAPL, while the protectors were made up of a heterogeneous group drawn together to defend Native land, water and treaty rights (Estes 2019: 7). The protests at Standing Rock illustrate one of the many conflicts surrounding pipelines and are considered as being "[…] part of a bigger war against an energy infrastructure increasingly prone to contamination and catastrophe" (Zaitchik 2017: 106).

Another reason for the protests against pipelines is that to date, every pipeline has had some history of spills and accidents (Kandiyoti 2008: 35). Besides being a risk for the environment, pipelines also affect the livelihood of surrounding communities, as spills contaminate agricultural zones and food resources. If polluted water gets into the food web, it directly affects the inhabitants' and consumers' health. In addition to the danger of contamination, resource extraction itself is linked to negative health effects (Haller et al. 2007: 32-35). However, not all effects are easily visible as some are more systemic in nature and represent change within a system, such as the intrusion of a corporation (Haller et al. 2007: 546).

The example of the DAPL accurately reflects the complexity of mega-infrastructure projects. Complex in finance, innovation and design, and with plenty of ambiguity, they have a significant impact on the social life of communities and the environment (Clegg et al. 2017:1-2). Another prominent feature is the necessity to undergo regular maintenance and upkeep in order to ensure the long-term use of the infrastructure (Barnes 2017: 147). These elements of a mega-infrastructure project are well represented within the infrastructure for the DAPL.

---

[3] Dakota Access Pipeline: Moving America's Energy. The Dakota Access Pipeline. ⟨https://dapl pipelinefacts.com/⟩ accessed on 12.07.2019.
[4] King, Hobart M: Geology.com: Bakken Formation: News, Maps, Videos and Information Sources. Geology.com. ⟨https://geology.com/articles/bakken-formation.shtml⟩ accessed on 12.07.2019.
[5] Dakota Access Pipeline: Moving America's Energy. The Dakota Access Pipeline. ⟨https://dapl pipelinefacts.com/⟩ accessed on 12.07.2019.

Part 1: Historical, Environmental, Ethnographic and Political Context

Pre, colonial, postcolonial and legal framework

The current case of the DAPL is highly influenced by the history of the United States and settler colonialism. Settler colonialism is different from other forms of colonialism as the goal is to "[...] permanently and completely replace Natives with a settler population" (Estes 2019: 89). The first action of this colonialism occurred when Columbus arrived on the continent and violent fights about land claims soon erupted (Lyons 1992: 29). However, the first European encounter with the Dakota did not come about before the seventeenth' century, taking place in the – since then – considered ancestral homeland of the Sioux peoples, the forests of central Minnesota and north-western Wisconsin. Prior to this encounter, the events and origin of the Sioux are poorly documented and have different interpretations. According to Gibbon (2003), one of those considers the Sioux to have formed in the late thirteenth'or early fourteenth' century out of a sudden alliance of different tribal groups. The different subgroups were then voluntarily or forcefully spread across the land throughout the next century (Gibbon 2003: 3).

Developing economy and changing treaties

As the US economy evolved, railroads were built to connect the different parts of the country. In 1873, the railroad boom bubble popped, resulting in an economic depression. In an attempt to avert this depression, more gold was mined than ever before. In the Black Hills in particular, settlers discovered large amounts of gold. However, the region of the Black Hills was deeded to the Standing Rock Sioux in the First Fort Laramie Treaty in 1851 (Zaitchik 2017: 107). The Standing Rock Sioux were well aware of the gold reserve but did not find any use for it and referred to it as "[...] the yellow metal that makes whites crazy" (Black Elk cited in Zaitchik 2017: 107). These claims for land often ended in battles and long-lasting violent conflicts, such as the Battle of Greasy Grass in 1875 when the Sioux fought for their right to the gold-rich Black Hills (Zaitchik 2017: 107).

Starting in 1887 and lasting until today, the Congress of the United States has determined the needs of Indigenous peoples and made decisions without the possibility of the involvement of Native Americans (Hauptman 1992: 336). This colonialist approach means that fundamental life decisions were made and implemented by the colonial rulers with little to no respect for the interests of Native communities (Nielsen and Robyn 2019: 4). As a result of these decisions, Native Americans were often displaced and their lands seized. One reason for the displacements was the implementation of treaties such as the Fort Laramie Treaty of 1851 and 1868. This treaty has also been a central point of contention during the protests against the DAPL. According to the Fort Laramie Treaty, the pipeline route runs within half a mile of the declared reservation of Standing Rock (Whyte 2017:161-162). However, Andreanne Catt states that there has never been a treaty between Native Americans and settler communities that was fully recognized.[6] The land ascribed to the Standing Rock Sioux within this treaty is much bigger than the amount of land recognized in the documents used by Energy Transfer Partners and published on their website regarding the implementation of the DAPL.[7]

The DAPL route did not cross treaty land when it was first planned. The original route was further away but was rerouted because of the threats it could pose to the water quality of the settler community of Bismarck (Whyte 2017: 164).

This current claim on Native land by Energy Transfer Partners resembles internal colonialism as described by Castro-Salazar and Bagley (2012). Hereby, internal colonialism is understood as a form of racism and inegalitarian pluralism that happens when different ethnicities coexist, but the dominant group aims to achieve assimilation of the minority groups. Reinforced by racial stereotypes created by the media as well as the government, this form of colonialism can be found in many dimensions of life and results in exclusion (Castro-Salazar and Bagley 2012: 37).

Political influence

In recent history, the protests and the DAPL were strongly shaped by politics. During the presidency of Barack Obama, the US domestic crude oil production increased by 88% from 2008 to 2016 (Estes 2019: 29). Even though Obama pushed the crude oil production, he also visited the annual Cannon Ball Flag Day Powwow with former First Lady Michelle Obama in June 2014. Since only eight presidents had previously visited Native reservations, this made the Obamas' visit a historic moment. In his speech, Obama spoke out about the need to prioritize safety for Indigenous communities and shared how he saw the Indigenous youth as if they were his own children. In November of the same year, when the construction of the DAPL was already ongoing, Obama spoke again publicly about the issues and protests surrounding the pipeline, including his desire to respect Native sacred land and consideration of the possibility to reroute the pipeline. However, the protests went on and even became violent before 4 December 2016 when the Army Corps of Engineers[8] denied the permit requesting that the pipeline cross the Missouri River. After Obama's presidency came to an end in 2017, and Donald Trump took office, he quickly reversed the decision and granted the per-

---

[6] Andreanne Catt, interview with the author, August 2019.

[7] Roy, M., Liza Grandia, Cinthya Ammerman, Jessa Rae Growing Thunder and Mike Mortimer 2017: The Dakota Access Pipeline in Context. ‹escholarship.org/uc/item/1947j92s› accessed on 12.05.2019.

[8] The Army Corps of Engineers, or Army Corps, are a federal agency that issued the permits for the pipeline construction (Tauli-Corpuz 2018: 1).

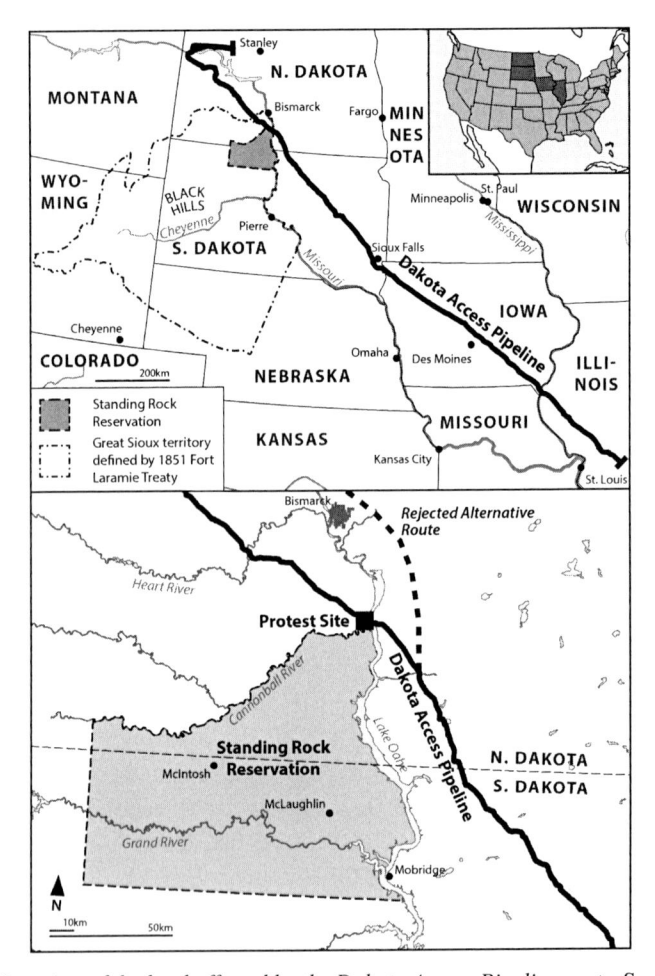

Map 1: Overview of the land affected by the Dakota Access Pipeline route. Source: Map compilation and design by Manuel L. K. Abebe (2021), CDE, University of Bern, Bern, Switzerland. Geodata: OpenStreetMap contributors

mit as requested (Estes 2019: 52-56). Within his first weeks in office, he not only enabled the continuation of the DAPL construction, but also reversed the Keystone XL project, an "[…] all-but-dead pipeline project" (Estes 2019: 57). As a former investor of the DAPL, Trump was already involved in the DAPL before his presidency (Zaitchik 2017: 105).

Land, local population and resource use

The occupants of the Standing Rock Sioux Reservation include three different ethnic groups: the Hunkpapa Lakota, the Sihasapa Lakota and the Yanktonai Dakota.[9] Interestingly, these Indigenous peoples never referred to themselves as Sioux. The term comes from the French version of the Ojibwe[10] word for "little snakes", "Nadouessioux", a reference to the ethnic groups "[…] denoting the Ojibwe's enemies to its west" (Estes 2019: 69). For political reasons, they called themselves "Oceti Sakowin Oyate", the Nation of Seven Council Fires (Estes 2019: 69). Although they are now mostly known by the term Sioux, the various communities do not always share the same cultural, economic and political elements (Gagnon, 2011: xii).

Family provides a fundamental organizing group for Native Americans and is embedded into a greater whole: a tribe. Members of tribes and families always stay connected to their community. Not restricted to biological relations, kinship crosses bloodlines. Close friends not related by blood are called "cousins", and by doing so, friends become part of the Indigenous family (Fixico 2008: 1-9). Communities are organized in democratic networks based on mutual respect; every member is considered as equal and plays an integral role in maintaining the network (Fixico 2008: 73-75).

However, the Sioux history has been overshadowed by massacres, deprival of land and discrimination under the law. These issues have influenced their history since the arrival of the first settlers, with change being the only constant (Gagnon 2011: xii). This back-and-forth distribution of land results in various understandings of who the rightful owner of the land in question is, such as in the case of the DAPL.

The maintenance of good relations and the protection of territorial community are important for the Standing Rock Sioux community life. Historically, any soil that was cultivated with their plants or animals was considered as land and territory of their community (Estes 2019: 71). The historical resource use mostly consisted of wild rice harvesting, gathering and hunting of deer (Gibbon 2003: 3). The affected land within the area of the DAPL today consists of agriculture as well as native grasslands and wetlands. The impact on their vegetation should only occur during the construction period as the builders supposedly want to restore affected areas to limit the disruption of vegetation. However, it is known that

---

[9] Standing Rock Sioux Tribe: History. ⟨https://www.standingrock.org/content/history⟩ accessed on 30.08.2019.

[10] Ojibwe is an Indigenous language of people who live in the United States of America and in Canada. In the United States of America, the Ojibwe country extends from Michigan to Wisconsin, Minnesota and North Dakota (The Ojibwe People's Dictionary 2015. ⟨https://ojibwe.lib.umn.edu/⟩ accessed on 30.08.2019).

construction can disrupt the natural setting and cause the spread of noxious weeds (Dakota Access LLC 2016: 19-20).

The size of the ecosystem has been reduced drastically due to settler infrastructure, agriculture, grazing and mining (Whyte 2017: 163). As a result, the traditional use of resources has undergone change and the former lifestyle of hunting and gathering has vanished. At the beginning of the twentieth' century, reservation cattle boomed and small-scale enterprises grew on the reservation. Besides cattle, timber was also an important economic resource, used either as fuel or as material for households. This resource use had already been altered before the implementation of the DAPL when the Pick-Sloan plan was realized (Estes 2019: 134-35). According to Estes (2019), the dams of the Pick-Sloan plan resulted in genocide and "[...] taking land and water also took away the possibility of a viable future" (Estes 2019: 135). In addition to these resources, the Missouri River is of great importance for the reservation and people living downstream, since it is the main water supply for the whole of South Dakota. Consequently, as Andreanne Catt explains, if the river is contaminated, all water downstream would be contaminated too.[11]

However, Indigenous land is not solely worshipped for the resources it provides. Land is worshipped as a part of what is labelled "Mother Earth" and resource extraction has always been strongly controlled by ritual regulation and belief in the integrity of creation as the wholesomeness of the world represents the foundation of existence (Mueller 1985: 45-48). The land is also sacred because the ancestors of the Hunkpapa and Standing Rock Sioux are buried on the side of the hills at the reservation.[12]

What makes this example of a mega-infrastructure project stand out is how the land was not taken for resource extraction or labour, but rather is being used as land that "[...] could be wasted – submerged, destroyed" (Estes 2019: 12). In other words, land that no longer provided "useful" resources could be used for the infrastructure needed to transport crude oil.

Indigenous traditions and prophecies

The implementation of this pipeline is also linked to Indigenous mythology such as the prophecy of the black snake and the rise of the seventh generation.

There is a Lakota prophecy that predicts that a black snake will come, cross their homelands and destroy sacred sites. Besides the obliteration of cultural heritage, the snake is further said to poison water before it destroys the earth (Phillips 2018: 732). Amid the resistance against the pipeline, the Indigenous people have identified the construction of the DAPL as the black snake in their prophecies. The snake has been represented with pipeline features on banners during the resis-

---

[11] Andreanne Catt, interview with the author, August 2019.
[12] Andreanne Catt, interview with the author, August 2019.

tance and demonstrations. Identifying the pipeline as the black snake is effectively "[...] demonizing oil"[13]. However, oil itself is natural as it is the decomposition of organic materials. According to Jose Gomez III, "[...] the unnatural process of extracting petroleum"[14] is what causes issues and makes it harmful to the environment. Drilling and recovering oil can even be seen as digging up ancestral remains. The process of drilling, fracking and the implementation of pipelines to transport the oil is what turns the natural oil into a harmful product.[15]

The rise of the seventh generation is an Oceti prophecy and a fulfilment of an uprising that "[...] heals a planet in crisis, seven generations after first contact with the whites" (Zaitchik 2017: 115). Darker aspects of the prophecy focus on the end of time when trees are going to die, birds are going to fall from the sky and a fight over water erupts (Zaitchik 2017: 115). Other versions of the prophecy relate to the long-awaited reunification of all seven nations of Dakota-, Lakota- and Nakota-speaking people, which is said to not have occurred in hundreds of years, or seven generations (Estes 2019: 2). This prophecy tells that the seventh generation starts the fire that will change the world. It is also said that the eighth generation will be the one that keeps that fire lit and the movement going.[16]

National economy and legal framework

As explained above, the history around this mega-infrastructure project was recently shaped by a change in presidency and the long ongoing changes in land distribution within the history of the United States.

The USA also has a long-ongoing history of oil production and the needed infrastructure for its transportation. With a fast-growing economy, the demand for oil grew and exceeded the production worldwide in 2013.[17] In 2018, the USA experienced a historic event regarding their oil production. For the first time since 1940, the country was able to export more oil to other countries than it imports, thereby creating greater independence from countries and companies tied to oil imports and granting greater energy security. Former presidents Jimmy Carter and George W. Bush tried to do so as well, but it was only achieved during the Trump presidency. Notably, this boom was made possible by the newly applied method of extracting oil by fracking, which accounts for more than half of the US oil production.[18]

---

[13] Jose Gomez III, interview with the author, August 2019.
[14] Jose Gomez III, interview with the author, August 2019.
[15] Jose Gomez III, interview with the author, August 2019.
[16] Andreanne Catt, interview with the author, August 2019.
[17] Zeit Online 2014: Fracking. USA produzieren so viel Öl wie noch nie. ‹https://www.zeit.de/wirtschaft/2014-06/usa-oelproduktion-rekord-fracking› accessed on 20.07.2019.
[18] Rotenberger, Julia 2018: Ölmarkt. USA sind Öl-Exporteur – zum ersten Mal seit mehr als 70 Jahren. Handelsblatt 07.12.2018. ‹https://www.handelsblatt.com/finanzen/maerkte/devisen-rohstoffe/oelmarkt-usa-sind-oel-exporteur-zum-ersten-mal-seit-mehr-als-70-jahren/23731184.html?ticket=ST-5493606-uLt26RpBOONsd4C3eadM-ap2› accessed on 20.07.2019.

Upgrading infrastructure and Trump's desire to export oil

The website Daily Caller[19] explains how Trump plans to upgrade the infrastructure of the USA in order to guarantee safety for the country. According to the website, infrastructure and energy are critical to the future of America's safety and prosperity: "We need pipeline infrastructure and energy generators to power factories and commercial facilities, especially during a crisis. America needs infrastructure that will sustain and protect our society in wartime and in peace"[20].

Four days after Trump became president, he signed a memorandum to finalize the construction of the Dakota Access Pipeline. Within the memorandum for the Secretary of the Army, Trump underscores his belief that the construction of the DAPL infrastructure serves the country's national interest (Presidential Documents 2017: 8661). Trump signed the memorandum despite the Army Corps of Engineers' promise to review the pipeline route (Zaitchik 2017: 105).

Therefore, this memorandum marks a clear turning point in the politics of pipelines in the USA, especially considering that Obama had halted the DAPL construction. The change in interest and new drilling of oil was welcomed by some, but many remained sceptical, as the oil market was still recovering after a prolonged crisis. One concern is that excessive production growth could slow down the recovery as it is possible that prices could collapse significantly, as they have already done before.[21]

Also critical to the new oil boom under Donald Trump is how the growth in American oil exports prompted a new rivalry with Russia, currently the world's largest oil producer. Trump has also gone on an international advertising tour, including a visit to the Polish President Andrzej Duda. The aim of this visit was to convince Duda not to renew a supply contract with Gazprom, a Russian state-owned supplier, in order for Poland to be able to seek oil from multiple suppliers. Trump's strategy seems to have worked, as six months after the visit the Polish government decided to turn away from Gazprom by the year 2022.[22]

---

[19] The Daily Caller was co-founded by 'far-right' Fox News host Tucker Carlson. The website faced repeated accusations for publishing incorrect and offensive content (Levin, Sam 2019: Facebook Teams with Rightwing Daily Caller in Factchecking Program. The Guardian, 18.04.2019. ⟨https://www.theguardian.com/technology/2019/apr/17/facebook-teams-with-rightwing-daily-caller-in-factchecking-program⟩ accessed on 20.07.2019.).

[20] Marks, James 2017: Trump's Infrastructure Plan Is Critical for National Security. Daily Caller, 30.12.2017. ⟨https://dailycaller.com/2017/12/30/trumps-infrastructure-plan-is-critical-for-national-security/⟩ accessed on 20.07.2019.

[21] Schröder, Thorsten 2018: Trump im Ölrausch. Zeit 18.02.2018. ⟨https://www.zeit.de/wirtschaft/2018-02/usa-oel-bohrungen-donald-trump-energiepolitik/komplettansicht⟩ accessed on 20.07.2019.

[22] Schröder, Thorsten 2018: Trump im Ölrausch. Zeit 18.02.2018. ⟨https://www.zeit.de/wirtschaft/2018-02/usa-oel-bohrungen-donald-trump-energiepolitik/komplettansicht⟩ accessed on 20.07.2019.

Economy of North Dakota and the legal framework for the infrastructure

During the period from 2017 to 2018, North Dakota improved its gross domestic product by 2.5%, thereby climbing the ladder to rank sixth among all states, with its per capita gross domestic product amounting to US$67,308.[23] The petroleum industry is one of the largest basic-sector industries in North Dakota and has created over 72,350 jobs state-wide since 2005. This accounts for 20% of private employment within the state and a contribution of US$7.54 billion in personal income. The industry has further generated US$34.25 billion for the North Dakota economy.[24]

The economic growth, however, differs among ethnic groups. As Patterson (2017) remarks, due to the Dawes Act from 1877 and its framework for allocation of land, tribal land has been further divided, hindering its effective use. In addition, Native Americans do not have the ability to build equity in their property as most tribal lands are held in trust by the US administration and Indigenous people do not hold full property rights. These issues contribute to the fact that the two million Native Americans across the nation make up the ethnic group with the highest poverty rate (Patterson 2017).

Additionally, as a result of the Dawes Act and the Indian Reorganization Act, there is a limitation on Indigenous people's ability to transfer their lands. The established system of trust only allows transfer by intent or intestacy. As Indigenous people were not able to transfer land, they started to lose the right to own and use land over time (Patterson 2017).

Part 2: The Mega-Infrastructure Project

Dakota Access Pipeline by Energy Transfer Partners

In 2013, the USA produced more oil than ever before in the country's history. One reason for this record is the controversial fracking method. This method is highly criticized as it involves drilling into deep layers of rock. The compressed oil or gas in these layers dissolves under high pressure and requires the use of chemicals. As this process occurs very deep in the earth, environmentalists fear the contamination of groundwater and disapprove of the procedure.[25]

Energy Transfer Partners, who built and operate the DAPL, applied for the construction in December 2014. The pipeline costs US$3.8 billion and is 1,200

---

[23] North Dakota Compass: Overview. ⟨https://www.ndcompass.org/economy/⟩ accessed on 15.03.2020.

[24] North Dakota Petroleum Council: Economic Output in North Dakota from Oil & Gas Remains Strong Despite Down Year. ⟨https://www.ndoil.org/economic-output-in-north-dakota-from-oil-gas-remains-strong-despite-down-year/⟩ accessed on 20.07.2019.

[25] Zeit Online 2014: Fracking. USA produzieren so viel Öl wie noch nie. ⟨https://www.zeit.de/wirtschaft/2014-06/usa-oelproduktion-rekord-fracking⟩ accessed on 20.07.2019.

miles long.[26] According to Energy Transfer Partners, the DAPL "[…] is the safest and most environmentally sensitive way to transport crude oil from domestic wells to American consumers"[27]. During the planning process, Energy Transfer Partners had to reroute the pipeline. As previously mentioned, the original route was through Bismarck, a city wealthier and with more political power than the Native American reservations. The rerouting was a result of environmental concerns. However, the new route never underwent the second environmental impact assessment promised after the halt in December 2016 (Patterson 2017). The original environmental impact assessment failed to include alternative routes that would not cross Lake Oahe (Phillips 2018: 737).

Energy Transfer Partners have a remarkable portfolio and assets of more than 71,000 miles of pipelines in the USA. They do not hold sole ownership or costs for the DAPL; they do, however, own the majority with 38.25% of the pipeline stakes. Other stakeholders include Phillips 66 Partners with 25% ownership and MarEn Bakken Company LLC with 36.75% (Fredericks et al. 2018: 9). A partnership of funds from 17 banks supports Energy Transfer Partners with the financial foundation with a loan of US$2.5 billion for the pipeline. This mutual support by several banks is also cause for criticism and social unrest (Fredericks et al. 2018: 14).

Environmental and social impacts

Impact on land and wildlife

In contradiction to the previously presented statement by Energy Transfer Partners on building the safest pipeline, spills have already occurred since going into service in June 2017. Eighty-four gallons of shale oil leaked even before the pipeline was operating at a pump station in South Dakota on 4 April 2017. Although the leak was considered minor, it serves as an example of the real risks associated with the pipeline infrastructure and the threats it poses to the environment. In addition, pipeline operators do not publish every spill even though they reportedly happen very frequently. Leaks are only published if they pose a threat to drinking water, public health or local fisheries.[28] Just about every pipeline has its history of spills or other concerning incidents. Industrial accidents are prone to happen and claiming a pipeline is safe does not guarantee safety (Kandiyoti 2008: 30-35). Another

---

[26] National Post 2017: A Timeline of the Dakota Access Oil Pipeline. 12.10.2017. ⟨https://nationalpost.com/pmn/news-pmn/a-timeline-of-the-dakota-access-oil-pipeline⟩ accessed on 21.07.2019.

[27] Dakota Access Pipeline: Moving Bakken Crude Oil Safely to Market. ⟨https://daplpipelinefacts.com/About.html⟩ accessed on 21.07.2019.

[28] Brave NoiseCat, Julian 2017: The Dakota Pipeline is already leaking. Why wait for a big Spill to act? The Guardian, 12.05.2017. ⟨https://www.theguardian.com/commentisfree/2017/may/12/dakota-access-pipeline-leaking-big-spill⟩ accessed on 21.07.2019.

impact on the land is not only where the pipeline runs, but also where the oil is being extracted. The current method of fracking poses a threat to the drilling sites as chemicals are used, which could contaminate groundwater.[29] In conclusion, it is both the infrastructure and the drilling itself that pose threats to the environment because of the spills and the chemicals used for extraction.

With regard to spills, there would be severe implications if a spill occurred underneath the Missouri River. Such an impact would be dramatic since the river and Lake Oahe are the main sources of drinking water for the Standing Rock Sioux Reservation, which provides for approximately 10,000 people. Further danger is posed if the river transfers polluted water downstream and threatens the drinking water of many more.[30]

Impact on Indigenous people

The sites that are impacted by the infrastructure of the DAPL are sacred land and burial grounds (Zaitichik 2017: 105). A major desecration occurred on 3 September 2016 on the Saturday before the Labour Day weekend and a day after the Tribal representatives filed court documents declaring the importance of the Native artefacts and sacred sites. It was on this day that construction workers removed topsoil over an area of 150 feet wide and 2 miles long, resulting in sacred sites being partially or completely taken out, as written in the online blog Desdemona Despair, where Tribal chairman David Archambault II is quoted saying: "These grounds are the resting places of our ancestors. The ancient cairns and stone prayer rings there cannot be replaced. In one day, our sacred land has been turned into hollow ground"[31]. The decision to proceed without a satisfactory resolution on legal issues caused rage and protest. The attorney for the Standing Rock Sioux, Jan Hasselman, explained: "We're days away from getting a resolution on the legal issues, and they came in on a holiday weekend and destroyed the site [...] What they have done is absolutely outrageous"[32]. According to Andreanne Catt, this action is not surprising since it is nothing new that the US government lies to benefit themselves and the media coverage seldom portrays the side of the Indigenous people's story.[33]

---

[29] Zeit Online 2014: Fracking. USA produzieren so viel Öl wie noch nie. ⟨https://www.zeit.de/wirtschaft/2014-06/usa-oelproduktion-rekord-fracking⟩ accessed on 20.07.2019.

[30] Worland, Justin 2016: What to Know About the Dakota Access Pipeline Protests. Time, 28.10.2016. ⟨http://time.com/4548566/dakota-access-pipeline-standing-rock-sioux/⟩ accessed on 25.04.2019.

[31] Rickert, Levi 2016: Sacred Burial Sites desecrated by Dakota Access Pipeline Construction – 'This demolition is devastating'. Desdemona Despair, 04.09.2016. ⟨https://desdemonadespair.net/2016/09/sacred-burial-sites-desecrated-by.html⟩ accessed on 29.07.2019.

[32] Rickert, Levi 2016: Sacred Burial Sites desecrated by Dakota Access Pipeline Construction – 'This demolition is devastating'. Desdemona Despair, 04.09.2016. ⟨https://desdemonadespair.net/2016/09/sacred-burial-sites-desecrated-by.html⟩ accessed on 29.07.2019.

[33] Andreanne Catt, interview with the author, August 2019.

Ignoring the complaints is an injustice according to Whyte (2017) when "[...] one or more groups of people seek to achieve their own perceived economic, cultural, and political aspirations by systematically inflicting harms and risks on one or more other groups of people" (Whyte 2017: 158). However, in a memo dated 22 September 2016, the Chief Archaeologist of the State Historical Society in North Dakota, Paul R. Picha, claimed that his inspection yielded no evidence of violations of respect towards human remains.[34] What raises suspicion, however, is the fact that the statement was published only after the topsoil was removed and no information was provided on when the inspection was performed. According to the statements made following the desecration on 3 September 2016, sacred sites were impacted. No remains could be found by an inspection carried out after the excavation.

As mentioned above, the withdrawal of the right of the Native peoples to the land can be seen as a consequence of settler colonialism and today is generally understood as land grabbing, in which one society intends to move in on another territory (Whyte 2017: 158-159). Estes (2019) describes the history of the United States as being driven by expansion and the removal of Indigenous peoples and culture (Estes 2019: 67). Besides effects on cultural traditions, the settlement process also aims "[...] at undermining the ecological conditions required for Indigenous peoples to exercise their cultures, economies, and political self-determination" (Whyte 2017: 165). This long-lasting history of resource and land theft also resonates with the recent history of resistance (see Zaitchik 2017).

Local and NGO strategies

The infrastructure for the transportation of oil caused resistance as Native Americans were protecting their land and water. During the protests, various alliances were formed to support the rally against the pipeline being installed under the Missouri River. The Standing Rock Sioux received support from other Native Americans in the United States, as well as international Indigenous groups and aid from activists and celebrities (Zaitchik 2017: 105-106).

The origin of the protests can be traced back to a statement made in late March 2014 by Oglala Sioux Tribal President Bryan Brewer as he declared war on the Keystone XL Pipeline. The speech marked the beginning of resistance, which sparked further debate during the protests against the DAPL. This resistance grew from "[...] a deep history of struggles over land and water, and a fight for a livable future on a planet so thoroughly devastated by climate change" (Estes 2019: 25). The word of resistance then spread when members of the Youth Council ran from Cannon Ball, North Dakota to Washington D.C. in order to raise awareness.[35]

---

[34] Dakota Access Pipeline: Addressing Misconceptions About the Dakota Access Pipeline. ‹https://daplpipelinefacts.com/The-Facts.html› accessed on 12.05.2019.
[35] Andreanne Catt, interview with the author, August 2019.

At the end of the run, they submitted a petition against the pipeline at the Army Corps of Engineers headquarters in Washington D.C.[36]

The beginning of the protest camps was marked by the gathering of thousands of people in camps near the crossing of the Missouri and Cannonball rivers. "Sacred Stone" is the camp that was set up by LaDonna Brave Bull Allard. This camp was located on the northern edge of the reservation and the camp spread further into former Treaty land and became the biggest occupation since the anti-nuclear movement (Zaitchik 2017: 106). LaDonna stated that this movement is linked to a bigger story: "We must remember we are part of a larger story. We are still here. We are still fighting for our lives, 153 years after my great-great-grandmother Mary watched as our people were senselessly murdered. We should not have to fight so hard to survive in our own lands" (La Donna Brave Bull Allard cited in Whyte 2017: 154).

The resistance followed a clear structure within which Standing Rock Sioux members provided a historical and spiritual framework. Leadership was formed into a "[...] seven-tribe council of elders that provided a central hierarchy and message discipline" (Zaitchik 2017: 106). The main goal of these protests was to block the final construction of the pipeline. Newly arrived support at the campsite had to undergo a morning orientation within which they were told the values of the camps and of the Indigenous-centred leadership grounded in the principles of kindness, honesty and respect. Further, they emphasized that any protest actions performed should be non-violent in nature (Zaitchik 2017: 110). The actions were considered to be a form of passive resistance as protestors chained themselves to machinery and remained calm during face-offs with police officers and in the case of arrests.[37] Even though the structure and leadership were established, they were not always fully respected (Zaitchik 2017: 105-106).

The movement grew, receiving a fast-growing amount of support. During the months from August to October 2016, marches and rallies occurred almost daily (Estes 2019: 57). At the camp, the number of attendees grew quickly as buses of youths arrived frequently. When Andreanne Catt arrived on 6 August 2016, there were only approximately 200 protectors in the camps, but the number grew to thousands of people who joined as allies.[38]

The rallies and camps focused on the goal of defending sacred land and protecting the water. Protestors used battle cries such as "Defend the Sacred" and

---

[36] Evan, Simon 2017: Meet the Youths at the Heart of the Standing Rock Protests against the Dakota Access Pipeline. Meet the Indigenous Youths steering the Standing Rock Protests. ABC News, 25.02.2017. ⟨https://abcnews.go.com/US/meet-youth-heart-standing-rock-protests-dakota-access/story?id=45719115⟩ accessed on 05.08.2019.

[37] Biegert, Claus 2016: Standing Up at Standing Rock. bedrohte Völker – pogrom, 06.2016. ⟨https://www.gfbv.de/de/informieren/zeitschrift-bedrohte-voelker-pogrom/aeltere-ausgaben/297-im-schatten-grosser-kriege/standing-up-at-standing-rock/⟩ accessed on 05.08.2019.

[38] Andreanne Catt, interview with the author, August 2019.

"Mni Wiconi" (Water is life) (Zaitchik 2017: 106). Further, new terms were created, such as "spirit camps" to refer to the tent cities and "water protectors" for the protestors (Zaitchik 2017: 110). The term "water protectors" was used because they did not solely stand up against a pipeline but stood up for the environment (Estes 2019: 15). The camps also "[...] embodied a brief vision of what Native life could be" (Estes 2019: 57) and set up council tipis, which were the first to be put up in over a hundred years.[39]

Another source of resistance is religion as it is able to reinforce political structures and serve as a force of opposition. A threat to the sacred land and therefore Native beliefs serves as a unifying element and connects communities in a sacred bond, which in turn serves to reinfuse the society with mystical power from the world of the ancestors (Lewellen 2003: 70).

Youth Awakening

Many participants of the camps belonged to a new generation of warrior society such as the Native Youth Movement, resisting the pipeline on- and offline. They practised a certain form of "[...] traditionalist survivalism with a guerilla-gangsta aesthetic [...]" (Zaitchik 2017: 109).

As the camp was growing at Standing Rock, structure was needed and many people addressed the young people for guidance. As a result, the young people decided to get organized and started the Indigenous Youth Council.[40] The council was initiated and led by two-spirited people and womxn[41] as they were protecting the Cannonball and Missouri rivers against the DAPL. The symbol of the organization is a medicine wheel that represents the people of the world: red, yellow, white and black inside of a mountain bordered below by two feathers.[42]

The young people accepted their role within the movement because they consider themselves to be the seventh generation, the one that is supposed to kill the black snake that causes disruption on their land. The desired form of action, for which the young people also advocated, was praying to protect their water. International Indigenous Youth Council members remained on the front lines of the protests and held stand-offs with the army or police as they prayed for their land and stood up for their rights. Furthermore, whenever tensions arose, the young people played a vital role in calming protesters or activists down.[43] Within the

---

[39] Andreanne Catt, interview with the author, August 2019.
[40] Jose Gomez III, interview with the author, August 2019.
[41] Womxn: used to describe female people but the E is changed to an X in order to show that womxn are not an extension of a man or men (Jose Gomez III, interview with the author, August 2019).
[42] Jose Gomez III, interview with the author, August 2019.
[43] ABC News 2017: The Seventh Generation. Youth at the Heart of the Standing Rock Protests. YouTube 28.02.2017. ⟨https://www.youtube.com/watch?v=1Rz_TkpysKk⟩ accessed on 13.05.2019.

Fig 1: The founding members of International Indigenous Youth Council – Texas Chapter at Standing Rock, North Dakota, protecting the sacred waters of the Cannonball and Missouri Rivers. Source: Pablo Montes

camp, they also launched non-violent direct-action training workshops and taught forms of creative resistance. Creative resistance could be the painting of banners, climbing and road blockades, or locking themselves to machinery. These actions were mostly carried out at the beginning of protests as it was rumoured that if pipeline workers were not able to work for three or four hours, they were consequently off work for the whole day. Besides locking themselves to machinery, people made human blockades, so called "soft blockages", by standing in front of machinery and refusing to leave.[44] Other tactics were used online, such as the social media campaign #NoDAPL. This hashtag is a good example of how digital communication was used as a key instrument of resistance allowing the movement to continue to spread via social media.

Social media was also used to cause diffusion. This strategy started because published pictures or tracking devices on mobile phones made it possible to identify when someone was at Standing Rock. Therefore, the protectors who attended the camp started a diffusion campaign; as part of this campaign, people who did not attend the camps would check into the camp via Facebook even if they

---
[44] Andreanne Catt, interview with the author, August 2019.

were not present. This was done in order to confuse security officers who tried to have an overview of those attending the camps. Another form of effectively causing distraction was to livestream certain minor events in order to divert attention away from the actual event that was happening simultaneously that was not being livestreamed.[45]

The movement was a form of revivalism on the reservation garnering renewed interest in Indigenous language and music as well as an effort to restore the native buffalo population. A gathering of this magnitude was thought to only be possible at Standing Rock because of its history, isolation and culture. The pipeline is considered to be the last issue to create a storm out of the long-growing anger within the communities (Zaitchik 2017: 109). For Andreanne Catt and Jose Gomez III, Standing Rock helped them find their voices and provided a place to promote their passion for change.[46] [47] The events further helped to bring Canadian, US and Mexican relatives closer together and empower the supporters as it also helped many young people to connect with their Indigenous roots, as it did for Jose Gomez III.[48]

Heterogeneity of Allies

As the number of allies grew, the resistance became more and more heterogeneous. Activists, celebrities and environmentalists also joined the resistance. The latter did so as the infrastructure and oil drilling threaten the ecology and global climate (Steinman 2018: 15-16). The reasons for joining were as varied as the people who joined. One phenomenon witnessed during these protests is "institution shopping" where "institutions" are the formal and informal "rules of a game". Within such a "game" or movement, rules, norms and constraints are set up. These rules structure the behaviour and interaction, especially within collective action, and serve as incentives. They further enable cooperation and coordination (Haller 2010: 29). "Institution shopping" therefore describes how, within a specific situation, the most advantageous institutional framework is chosen (Wartmann et al. 2016: 218 ff.).

The various people who joined mostly supported the cause of the Native Americans but there were a few who "[…] exotified indigeneity"[49]. For the most part, the environment created at camp prioritized Indigenous people, where it was said, "Indigenous people, children and elders to the front" when waiting in line for food and supplies. For Jose Gomez III, this was a new experience of acknowl-

---

[45] Andreanne Catt, interview with the author, August 2019.
[46] Andreanne Catt, interview with the author, August 2019.
[47] Jose Gomez III, interview with the author, August 2019.
[48] Jose Gomez III, interview with the author, August 2019.
[49] Jose Gomez III, interview with the author, August 2019.

edgement and felt empowering. He found it beautiful to see how many different people came to stand in solidarity with them.[50]

In addition, various celebrities joined the movement and raised their voice in support of the protectors. These celebrities garnered more media coverage and some are now part of various networks of organizations that were formed at Standing Rock. Even though not all who became involved in supporting the protest did so with the sole intention of supporting the Standing Rock Sioux and some may have even benefited personally from the publicity, the support was welcomed.[51]

Support from Non-Governmental Organizations (NGOs)

Meaningful alliances by NGOs also supported Indigenous groups during their resistance. One of them was GfbV (Gesellschaft für bedrohte Völker) Switzerland which demanded that Swiss banks involved in financing the pipeline, as lenders and managers of shares, took a clear stance and acted to protect against human rights violations and environmental damage. UBS and Credit Suisse were the two banks targeted by the GfbV campaign, including a complaint filed with the Swiss OECD Contact Point for Human Rights demanding that the banks renounce future business relations if human rights violations were to occur. In addition, GfbV sought a rigorous due diligence process to ensure respect for human rights and preserve the environment before providing services to projects or companies.[52] Greenpeace was another ally to address the involvement of Swiss banks. They crashed the Credit Suisse Switzerland general meeting of shareholders and directors with a banner that read: "STOP DIRTY PIPELINE DEALS".[53]

In order to make further information about the involvement of banks accessible to their clients, a website called "defund DAPL" was set up. The site provided information on the banks taking the primary lead in backing the DAPL loan and how to transfer the money to a different bank.[54] As of August 2019, over four billion US dollars have already been divested and transferred to alternative banks.[55]

The resistance gained worldwide support both on- and offline. Even though the Standing Rock Sioux were grateful for the support, Tribal chairman David Archambault II pointed out that they will continue to push forward even after the support has gone one day: "This started with protecting our water and sacred places for our children, and we're grateful to our allies. But when everybody

---

[50] Jose Gomez III, interview with the author, August 2019.
[51] Andreanne Catt, interview with the author, August 2019.
[52] GfbV: No Business Without Human Rights. ‹https://www.gfbv.ch/de/kampagnen/no-business-without-human-rights/#forderungen› accessed on 31.07.2019.
[53] Schweizer Radio und Fernsehen (SRF) 2017: Generalversammlung der Credit Suisse 28.04.2017. ‹https://www.srf.ch/play/tv/tagesschau/video/generalversammlung-der-credit-suisse?id=a089a3b7-f928-44b7-bd87-f90196073786› accessed on 03.08.2019.
[54] #DefundDAPL: Banks Funding DAPL. ‹https://www.defunddapl.org/contact-the-banks› accessed on 03.08.2019.
[55] #DefundDAPL: ‹https://www.defunddapl.org/› accessed on 03.08.2019.

leaves, we're still going to be here, repairing the damage" (Archambault II cited in Zaitchik 2017: 112).

State and company strategy

Strategies of energy transfer

According to Energy Transfer Partners, the DAPL ought to create up to 12,000 jobs during its construction and 40 permanent jobs for the maintenance of the infrastructure.[56] In addition to the promised jobs, the oil boom was predicted to revive the economy of North Dakota and boost local businesses. Before the fracking method was introduced, many cities experienced a decrease in population. They now supposedly profit from additional money within their educational systems or local businesses. The implementation of the pipeline has also influenced the infrastructure of schools such as Watford City High School, where there is now a truck-driving simulator to encourage students to pursue a career as a truck driver in order to meet the increasing demand.[57]

As previously mentioned, land claims have been part of a long-ongoing dispute in the United States. While protestors hold on to the distribution of land as agreed in the Fort Laramie Treaty, Energy Transfer Partners have disagreed and continue to rely on a different map.[58] Together with their alternative map, Energy Transfer Partners published a statement about how the US Army Corps of Engineers reached out to the Standing Rock Sioux several times trying to discuss the archaeological surveys that had been conducted before finalizing the route.[59] The Corps claims that they received no response when trying to meet with the Standing Rock Sioux's historic preservation officer. Preparations are said to have gone on for months before concern was raised at a meeting about the pipeline being routed underneath their main water source. Representatives of the Standing Rock Sioux communicated their frustration at not having been included in the planning process to date. They further stated that the Corps violated the National Historic Preservation Act by causing irreparable harm to their sacred land (Lowenstein 2017: 3-7).

The performed environmental impact assessment for the route of the DAPL included statements verifying the unlikeliness of a spill happening, yet neverthe-

---

[56] Brady, Heather 2017: 4 Key Impacts of the Keystone XL and Dakota Access Pipelines. National Geographic 25.01.2017. ⟨https://news.nationalgeographic.com/2017/01/impact-keystone-dakota-access-pipeline-environment-global-warming-oil-health/⟩ accessed on 21.04.2019.
[57] Brady, Jeff 2018: After Struggles, North Dakota Grows into Its Ongoing Oil Boom. National Public Radio, 23.11.2018. ⟨https://www.npr.org/2018/11/23/669198912/after-struggles-north-dakota-grows-into-its-ongoing-oil-boom⟩ accessed on 29.07.2019.
[58] Dakota Access Pipeline: Moving America's Energy. The Dakota Access Pipeline. ⟨https://daplpipelinefacts.com/⟩ accessed on 12.05.2019.
[59] Dakota Access Pipeline: Moving America's Energy. The Dakota Access Pipeline. ⟨https://daplpipelinefacts.com/⟩ accessed on 12.05.2019.

less providing strategies on what to do if a spill were to occur. The assessment report concluded that there would be no direct or indirect effect of the pipeline construction on the Standing Rock Sioux Tribe (Phillips 2018: 736). Therefore, the phenomenon of "institution shopping" is also observable within this context. The most economically advantageous understanding of land attribution and information on pipeline safety is used to support the assessment and environmental impact reporting.

One of the strategies used by Energy Transfer Partners during the protests was to display power. Police were ordered to protect the construction site, where they used rubber bullets and flashbang grenades to confront the unarmed protectors. The use of such weaponry led to over 200 injured people. The most serious injuries involved a Navajo woman losing an eye and another woman's arm nearly being torn off by a blinding grenade (Estes 2019: 55). As a result, healers and physicians from the Standing Rock Sioux Council treated many people for injuries or hypothermia. During the protests the direct route between Standing Rock and hospitals in Bismarck was blocked, which created a safety issue for the people at the reservation (Zaitchik 2017: 111). Besides governmental police, the DAPL hired private security with dogs who met protesters at the front line while they tried to stop bulldozers from tearing apart sacred ground (Estes 2019: 56). Furthermore, Energy Transfer Partners marked their route every night with several industrial klieg lights and displayed their power further with planes circling the camps (Zaitchik 2017: 105).

Strategy of the state

During the construction and resistance, the state made use of "[…] excessive force and mass arrests to threaten, intimidate, and silence "water protectors" […]" (Tauli-Corpuz 2018: 1). The strategy employed by the state was also combined with the ongoing history of land acquisition and distribution, which has greatly influenced the current lifestyle of Indigenous people. As previously mentioned, the ending of Barack Obama's presidency resulted in a halt of construction, which resumed shortly thereafter when Donald Trump came into office (Estes 2019: 52-57). In his memorandum renewing construction, Trump states "[…] that construction and operation of lawfully permitted pipeline infrastructure serve the national interest" (Presidential Documents 2017: 8661) and considers the existing environmental assessment from July 2016 as "[…] satisfying all applicable requirements of the National Environmental Policy Act […]" (Presidential Documents 2017: 8661).

After the memorandum was signed, the government declared an eviction date for the protest camps of 22 February 2017. A day after the eviction date, the National Guard and law enforcement officers marched into the campsites.[60] Though

---

[60] Wong, Julia C. 2017: Police remove last Standing Rock Protesters in military-style Takeover.

the deadline had passed, a group of people remained at the camp, sang and prayed as the police marched closer to the site. Shortly after 4 p.m. local time, the police started arresting the people who remained.[61] Together the actions of the state and private security proved a failure in preventing the use of extensive force and unlawful arrests (Tauli-Corpuz 2018: 5).

The controversy over the DAPL and oil does not just confront the physical construction and geographic implementation. With the climate crisis becoming more urgent, the use of oil and gas is by many no longer seen as a viable form of energy production. This may become an issue for the United States, a country doubling its natural gas infrastructure in order to increase its own gas exports. Within this context, the linguistic use of "gas" is being adapted and framed as "freedom gas" and "molecules of US freedom".[62]

This framing of gas can be considered a marketing strategy, capable of influencing consumers and making them believe the following: "Buy this gas and you'll be supporting freedom"[63]. By reframing the context and using specified terms such as "freedom gas" the US government makes use of "enchantment" as described by Harvey and Knox (2012). Harvey and Knox have examined the understanding and significance of infrastructure projects by looking into the road construction in Peru. The authors analyse the ability of roads to enchant and the hope created by the promised improvement in transportation infrastructure despite setbacks and declining confidence in the government (Harvey and Knox 2012). The enchantment is perceived less as knowledge and more as a mood in response to the surprise appearance of something unexpected. Mega-infrastructure projects for streets are often accompanied by promises of speed and connection, political freedom and economic prosperity (Harvey and Knox 2012: 523-524). The used framing of "freedom gas" and the promise of a boost to the gas industry that will result in more jobs and local economic growth[64] fit the definition of enchantment.

The Guardian, 23.02.2017. ⟨https://www.theguardian.com/us-news/2017/feb/23/dakota-access-pipeline-camp-cleared-standing-rock⟩ accessed on 03.08.2019.

[61] Levin, Sam 2017: 'Police make Arrests at Standing Rock in Push to Evict Remaining Activists'. The Guardian, 22.02.2017. ⟨https://www.theguardian.com/us-news/2017/feb/22/dakota-access-pipeline-standing-rock-evacuation-police⟩ accessed on 03.08.2019.

[62] Canavan, Brendan 2019: Donald Trump's rebrand of Fossil Fuels to 'Freedom Gas': a Pungent Aroma of American Liberty with a Whiff of Hubris. The Conversation, 31.05.2019. ⟨https://theconversation.com/donald-trumps-rebrand-of-fossil-fuels-to-freedom-gas-a-pungent-aroma-of-american-liberty-with-a-whiff-of-hubris-118099⟩ accessed on 01.08.2019.

[63] Canavan, Brendan 2019: Donald Trump's rebrand of Fossil Fuels to 'Freedom Gas': a Pungent Aroma of American Liberty with a Whiff of Hubris. The Conversation, 31.05.2019. ⟨https://theconversation.com/donald-trumps-rebrand-of-fossil-fuels-to-freedom-gas-a-pungent-aroma-of-american-liberty-with-a-whiff-of-hubris-118099⟩ accessed on 01.08.2019.

[64] Canavan, Brendan 2019: Donald Trump's rebrand of Fossil Fuels to 'Freedom Gas': a Pungent Aroma of American Liberty with a Whiff of Hubris. The Conversa-

In conclusion, the state's strategy was to grow oil production and develop its infrastructure to boost the economy.

Mental warfare

Besides direct action and administrative decrees, people at the camps at the Standing Rock Reservation were experiencing a type of mental warfare[65]. The International Indigenous Youth Council communicated through public radio channels that DAPL representatives and workers were able to constantly listen to. Soon after the raid on sacred ground, Moraine County pulled people out of their sacred sweat lodge ceremonies[66] and arrested those attending. Sacred items, such as peace pipes and blankets, were taken. The members of the International Indigenous Youth Council could hear Moraine County officers on the radio talking about how they would smoke their peace pipes and ruin their sacred objects. When the items were later returned, they were covered with faeces and urine. In addition to the desecration of sacred objects, a 24-hour surveillance was carried out with drones and helicopters despite the reservation being a no-fly zone. These actions affected everyone at the camps and caused further tension.[67]

Conclusion

The implementation of the DAPL mega-infrastructure project raised various issues stemming from different legal claims to the land it is built on. While Energy Transfer Partners consider the land privately owned,[68] the Standing Rock Sioux hold on to the distribution made within the Fort Laramie Treaty and consider the land as rightfully belonging to them (Whyte 2017). The different explanations being used to claim land rights are a form of institution shopping whereby the most advantageous institutional framework to benefit the corporation is chosen (Wartmann et al. 2016: 218 ff.). Institution shopping was also part of the claims supporting the resistance. While some were protecting sacred land, others' primary reason was supporting the environmental cause.

---

tion, 31.05.2019. ⟨https://theconversation.com/donald-trumps-rebrand-of-fossil-fuels-to-freed om-gas-a-pungent-aroma-of-american-liberty-with-a-whiff-of-hubris-118099⟩ accessed on 01.08.2019.

[65] Mental warfare as mentioned by Andreanne Catt (Andreanne Catt, interview with the author, August 2019).

[66] Sweat lodge ceremonies are conducted inside a low dome-like structure, which represents the womb of Mother Earth. Inside the lodges it becomes very hot as rocks from a fire are put inside and doused with water. This ritual is used to connect to Mother Earth (Jose Gomez III, interview with the author, August 2019).

[67] Andreanne Catt, interview with the author, August 2019.

[68] Dakota Access Pipeline: Moving America's Energy. The Dakota Access Pipeline: ⟨https://dapl pipelinefacts.com/⟩ accessed on 12.05.2019.

The typical characteristics of what constitutes necessary maintenance of a mega-infrastructure project (Barnes 2017: 147) are particularly important in this example. If the pipeline infrastructure has defects or a leak, the drinking water will be polluted and have wide-ranging impacts on the environment and food web of the surrounding land.[69] Another characteristic of a mega-infrastructure project is the phenomenon of enchantment. During the implementation of the pipeline, the promises of a boost to the economy and increased working opportunities were made to the people of North Dakota. These promises, however, were not realized for everyone. While some communities were able to profit from the pipeline, the Standing Rock Sioux did not receive any of the promised benefits from the project. Alongside these empty promises, the linguistic terms referring to oil were changed, and in 2019, the government issued a report that labelled it as "freedom gas", with the goal of making it more appealing with additional perceived value to consumers, especially during a time when climate change is a top priority and gas is becoming a less attractive form of energy.[70]

Resistance at Standing Rock did not occur in a vacuum as the protests against the pipeline served as "[...] an indispensable catalyst to the movement that hopes to vindicate the battered but insurgent intertwined causes of tribal sovereignty and environmental sanity in the dawning age of Trump" (Zaitchik 2017: 106). It is also one period in the long and continuing history of discrimination against the Indigenous people and movements that oppose certain energy production and other projects (Tauli-Corpuz 2018: 4). In addition, it is yet another example in the ongoing fight against the implementation of such infrastructure on sacred land.

What makes this example stand out is that the participants succeeded in standing up in non-violent protests even though they were met with violence (Estes 2019: 252). As the movement was formed to protect sacred land and water, it also resulted in a revival of the Native lifestyle and brought together various communities. For many, it also helped them to embrace their Indigenous identity.[71] [72]

One of the results of the protests is stricter policies, such as a rule implemented in Texas making any protest against a pipeline within the state illegal. The aim of this policy is to avoid anything similar to the Standing Rock movement reoccurring by deterring anyone from protesting with the right to arrest immediately.[73]

---

[69] Worland, Justin 2016: What to Know About the Dakota Access Pipeline Protests. Time 28.10.2016. ⟨http://time.com/4548566/dakota-access-pipeline-standing-rock-sioux/⟩ accessed on 25.04.2019.

[70] Canavan, Brendan 2019: Donald Trump's rebrand of Fossil Fuels to 'Freedom Gas': a Pungent Aroma of American Liberty with a Whiff of Hubris. The Conversation, 31.05.2019. ⟨https://theconversation.com/donald-trumps-rebrand-of-fossil-fuels-to-freedom-gas-a-pungent-aroma-of-american-liberty-with-a-whiff-of-hubris-118099⟩ accessed on 01.08.2019.

[71] Andreanne Catt, interview with the author, August 2019.

[72] Jose Gomez III, interview with the author, August 2019.

[73] Jose Gomez III, interview with the author, August 2019.

Nevertheless, the movement has already sparked changes and has raised awareness about the ongoing inequalities towards Native Americans and the theft of their country for mega-infrastructure projects and "[…] is continuing and growing until today and it is already making changes – worldwide"[74].

Update – DAPL and Americas lust for oil, 2019-2021

However, the fight over the Dakota Access Pipeline has not come to an end – it is still ongoing throughout 2021 and at its core has stayed the same: "[…] environmental and cultural preservation versus economics and energy dominance […]" (Wingard 2021: 234). After the pipeline first came to a halt in 2016 during Barack Obamas presidency, it was soon revoked when Donald Trump was in office.[75] Even though the pipeline supposedly was safe, first leaks already occurred when the operation of the pipeline began in 2017 (Wingard 2021: 236). Later on, in June/July 2019 Energy Transfer Partners announced, that they will expand the pipeline to double the capacity from 500,000 barrels per day to 1.1 million barrels.[76] In August of 2021 the expansion was still underway but could already carry up to 750,000 barrels per day and the full expansion is planned to be finalized in March of 2022.[77] This expansion started with Donald Trump in office and is ongoing during Joe Bidens presidency, which started in 2021.[78]

As before, the protest and demand for an environmental impact assessment went on and in summer 2020 U.S. District Judge James E. Boasberg suspended the pending permits until an environmental impact assessment had been made. He even demanded a halt of the pipeline in order to perform a detailed assessment. However, the shutdown never occurred: one month after Boasberg's demand, the pipeline was allowed to continue operating due to a motion from the U.S. Court of Appeals for the D.C. Circuit. They stated their point by arguing that Judge James E. Boasberg did not provide the necessary findings that would have justified a halt in production (Wingard 2021: 236-237). Energy Transfer Partner even assumed that a halt would cause a "catastrophic disruption" in agricultural freight transport as the oil then would have to be transported by rail cars, which at that time were mostly carrying grains.[79]

In January 2021, half a year after Boasberg's appeal, the D.C. Circuit ordered the Corps to prepare an environmental impact assessment and ordered the shutdown (Wingard 2021: 236-237), which as of December 2021 had not been implemented.

Additionally, some concerns are becoming more apparent now as also in this context, oil is a non-renewable energy source and is becoming scarcer. The boom on the drilling site in Bakken began 13 years ago and as of November 2021 only approximately 700 top-tier wells remain available meaning that there is a possibility of shortage in production. This decline in wells brings along several implications which could even result in that "Regulators will need to reconsider the economic rationale for existing pipelines, including the controversial Dakota Access Pipeline (DAPL)".[80] If this decline in top-tier wells production holds on, the oil industry will have to move to less-productive areas and therefore, some pipeline infrastructures

---

[74] Jose Gomez III, interview with the author, August 2019.

would become obsolete – including the DAPL. However, supporters of the oil industry state the opposite and even though they acknowledge certain difficulties in production, they debunk the supposed decline in drilling sites as myth and claim that Bakken has yet to hit its peak in production.[81]

Given the continuous rise for renewed infrastructure the current president Joe Biden signed a US$1.2 trillion infrastructure bill mid November 2021. This bill includes at least US$11 billion in regard of Native communities with the aim to better their infrastructure such as roads, water rights, sanitation as well as "environmental reclamation projects".[82] This new bill on infrastructure has set high goals and aims to: "[...] rebuild America's roads, bridges and rails, expand access to clean drinking water, ensure every American has access to high-speed internet, tackle the climate crisis, advance environmental justice, and invest in communities that have too often been left behind".[83]

Only time will tell how Biden's plan will be implemented and whether it will support Indigenous communities or if another shift in presidency may once again overrule established decisions on infrastructure projects.

References

Barnes, Jessica 2017: State of Maintenance. Power, Politics, and Egypt's Irrigation Infrastructure. Society and Space 35 (1): 146-164.
Castro-Salazar, Ricardo and Carl Bagley 2012: Navigating Historical Borders. Internal Colonialism and the Politics of Memory. Counterpoints 415: 37-67.
Clegg, Stewart R., Christopher Biesenthal, Shankar Sankaran and Julien Pollack 2017: Power and Sensemaking in Megaprojects. In: Bent Flyvbjerg (ed.): The Oxford Handbook of Megaproject Management. Oxford Handbook Online: Oxford University Press, 1-23.
Estes, Nick 2019: Our History is the Future. Standing Rock versus the Dakota Access Pipeline, and the Long Tradition of Indigenous Resistance. London: Verso.
Fixico, Donald L. 2008: American Indians in a Modern World. Lanham: AltaMira Press.
Gagnon, Gregory O. 2011: Culture and Customs of the Sioux Indians. Santa Barbara, California: Greenwood.
Gibbon, Guy 2003: The Sioux. The Dakota and Lakota Nations. Oxford: Blackwell Publishers Ltd.
Haller, Tobias, Annja Blöchlinger, Markus John, Esther Marthaler and Sabine Ziegler 2007: Fossil Fuels, Oil Companies, and Indigenous Peoples. Strategies of Multinational Oil Companies, States, and Ethnic Minorities. Impact on Environment, Livelihoods, and Cultural Change. Zürich: LIT Verlag.
Haller, Tobias 2010: Institutional Change, Power and Conflicts in the Management of Common-Pool Resources in African Floodplain Ecosystems. An Introduction. In Tobias Haller (ed.): Disputing the Floodplains. Institutional Change and the Politics of Resource Management in African Wetlands. Leiden: Brill, 1-75.
Harvey, Penny and Hannah Knox 2012: The Enchantments of Infrastructure. Mobilities 7 (4): 521-536.

Hauptman, Laurence M. 1992: Congress, Plenary Power, and the American Indian, 1870 to 1992. In Chief Oren Lyons and John Mohawk (eds.): Exiled in the Land of the Free. Democracy, Indian Nations and the U.S. Constitution. Santa Fe: Clear Light Publishers, 317-336.
Kandiyoti, Rafael 2008: Pipelines. Flowing Oil and Crude Politics. London: I.B. Tauris.
Lewellen, Ted C. 2003 [3rd edition]: Political Anthropology. An Introduction. Westport/London: Praeger.
Lowenstein, Jody D. 2017: Standing Rock Sioux Tribe v. U.S. Army Corps of Engineers. Public Land and Resources Law Review 0 (19): 1-7.
Lyons, Oren 1992: The American Indian in the Past. In Chief Oren Lyons and John Mohawk (eds.): Exiled in the Land of the Free. Democracy, Indian Nations and the U.S. Constitution. Santa Fe: Clear Light Publishers, 13-42.
Mueller, Werner 1985 [2nd edition]: Indianische Welterfahrung. Stuttgart: Klett-Cotta.
Nielsen, Marianne O. and Linda M. Robyn 2019: Colonialism is Crime. New Jersey: Rutgers University Press.
Patterson, Joseph 2017: The Native American Struggle Between Economic Growth and Cultural, Religious, and Environmental Protection: A Corporate Solution. Notre Dame Law Review. ‹http://ndlawreview.org/2017/05/the-native-american-struggle-between-economic-growth-and-cultural-religious-and-environmental-protection-a-corporate-solution/› accessed on 20.07.2019.
Phillips, Lauren P. 2018: Killing the Black Snake. The Dakota Access Pipeline's Fate Post-Sierra Club v. FERC. The Georgetown Envtl. Law Review 30: 731-747.
Presidential Documents 2017: Construction of the Dakota Access Pipeline. Federal Register 82 (18): 8661-8662.
Rasmussen, Mattias B. and Christian Lund 2018: Reconfiguring Frontier Spaces. The Territorialization of Resource Control. World Development 101: 388-399.
Steinman, Erich 2018: Why was Standing Rock and the #NoDAPL Campaign so Historic? Factors Affecting American Indian Participation in Social Movement Collaborations and Coalitions. Ethnic and Racial Studies 42 (7): 1070-1090.
Wartmann, Flurina M., Tobias Haller and Norman Backhaus 2016: 'Institutional Shopping' for Natural Resource Management in a Protected Area and Indigenous Territory in the Bolivian Amazon. Human Organization 75 (3): 218-229.
Whyte, Kyle Powys 2017: The Dakota Access Pipeline, Environmental Injustice, and U.S. Colonialism. RED INK 19 (1): 154-169.
Wingard, Lee 2021: Back and Forth. The Continuous Legal Battle Over the Oil Flow in Dakota Access Pipeline. Tulane Environmental Law Journal 34 (229): 234-237.
Zaitchik, Alexander 2017: On Native Grounds. Standing Rock's New Spirit of Protest. The Baffler 34: 102-116.

Reports

Dakota Access LLC 2016: Dakota Access Pipeline Project. U.S. Fish and Wildlife Service. Environmental Assessment. Grassland and Wetland Easement Crossings.
Fredericks, Carla F., Mark Meaney, Nicholas Pelosi and Kate R. Finn 2018: Social Cost and Material Loss. The Dakota Access Pipeline. First Peoples Investment Engagement Program. University of Colorado Boulder.

Tauli-Corpuz, Victoria 2018: Indigenous Resistance to the Dakota Access Pipeline. Criminalization of Dissent and Suppression of Protest. The University of Arizona. Rogers College of Law. Indigenous Peoples Law and Policy Program.

Films and Internet Sources

ABC News 2017: The Seventh Generation. Youth at the Heart of the Standing Rock Protests. YouTube, 28.02.2017. ‹https://www.youtube.com/watch?v=1Rz_TkpysKk› Accessed on 13.05.2019.
BBC 2021: Keystone XL Pipeline halted after Biden blocks Permit. BBC, 09.06.2021. ‹https://www.bbc.com/news/world-us-canada-57422456› Accessed on 05.12.2021.
Biegert, Claus 2016: Standing Up at Standing Rock. bedrohte Völker – pogrom, 06.2016. ‹https://www.gfbv.de/de/informieren/zeitschrift-bedrohte-voelker-pogrom/aeltere-ausgaben/297-im-schatten-grosser-kriege/standing-up-at-standing-rock/› Accessed on 05.08.2019.
Brady, Heather 2017: 4 Key Impacts of the Keystone XL and Dakota Access Pipelines. National Geographic, 25.01.2017. ‹https://news.nationalgeographic.com/2017/01/impact-keystone-dakota-access-pipeline-environment-global-warming-oil-health/› Accessed on 21.04.2019.
Brady, Jeff 2018: After Struggles, North Dakota Grows into Its Ongoing Oil Boom. National Public Radio, 23.11.2018. ‹https://www.npr.org/2018/11/23/669198912/after-struggles-north-dakota-grows-into-its-ongoing-oil-boom› Accessed on 29.07.2019.
Brave NoiseCat, Julian 2017: The Dakota Pipeline is already leaking. Why wait for a big Spill to act? The Guardian, 12.05.2017. ‹https://www.theguardian.com/commentisfree/2017/may/12/dakota-access-pipeline-leaking-big-spill› Accessed on 21.07.2019.
Bridges, Eunice and Chris Baltimore 2021: DAPL Shutdown would 'Shock' Economy: Energy Transfer. Argus Media, 20.04.2021. ‹https://www.argusmedia.com/en/news/2207152-dapl-shutdown-would-shock-economy-energy-transfer› Accessed on 05.12.2021.
Canavan, Brendan 2019: Donald Trump's rebrand of Fossil Fuels to 'Freedom Gas': a Pungent Aroma of American Liberty with a Whiff of Hubris. The Conversation, 31.05.2019. ‹https://theconversation.com/donald-trumps-rebrand-of-fossil-fuels-to-freedom-gas-a-pungent-aroma-of-american-liberty-with-a-whiff-of-hubris-118099› Accessed on 01.08.2019.
Corner, Elizabeth 2021: Shortage of high-quality Sites threatens Future Bakken Oil and Gas Production. World Pipelines, 04.11.2021. ‹https://www.worldpipelines.com/project-news/04112021/shortage-of-high-quality-sites-threatens-future-bakken-oil-and-gas-production/› Accessed on 05.12.2021.
Dakota Access Pipeline: Moving America's Energy. The Dakota Access Pipeline. ‹https://daplpipelinefacts.com/› Accessed on 12.05.2019.
Dakota Access Pipeline: Moving Bakken Crude Oil Safely to Market. ‹https://daplpipelinefacts.com/About.html› Accessed on 21.07.2019.
Dakota Access Pipeline: Addressing Misconceptions About the Dakota Access Pipeline. ‹https://daplpipelinefacts.com/The-Facts.html› Accessed on 12.05.2019.
#DefundDAPL: ‹https://www.defunddapl.org/› Accessed on 03.08.2019.
#DefundDAPL: Banks Funding DAPL. ‹https://www.defunddapl.org/contact-the-banks› Accessed on 03.08.2019.

Evan, Simon 2017: Meet the Youths at the Heart of the Standing Rock Protests against the Dakota Access Pipeline. Meet the Indigenous Youths steering the Standing Rock Protests. ABC News, 25.02.2017. ⟨https://abcnews.go.com/US/meet-youth-heart-standing-rock-protests-dakota-access/story?id=45719115⟩ Accessed on 05.08.2019.

GfbV: No Business Without Human Rights. ⟨https://www.gfbv.ch/de/kampagnen/no-business-without-human-rights/#forderungen⟩ Accessed on 31.07.2019.

Holmes, Kristen and Gregory Wallace 2021: Biden Administration will not Shut Down Dakota Access Pipeline during Environmental Review, DOJ Lawyer tells Court. CNN, 09.04.2021. ⟨https://edition.cnn.com/2021/04/09/politics/dakota-access-pipeline-biden-administration/index.html⟩ Accessed on 06.12.2021.

KickingWoman, Kolby 2020: Dakota Access Pipeline. Timeline. Indian Country Today, 07.07.2020. ⟨https://indiancountrytoday.com/news/dakota-access-pipeline-timeline⟩ Accessed on 05.12.2021.

King, Hobart M: Geology.com: Bakken Formation: News, Maps, Videos and Information Sources. Geology.com. ⟨https://geology.com/articles/bakken-formation.shtml⟩ Accessed on 12.07.2019.

Kunze, Jenna 2021: What's Next for Tribes and the Recently Signed Infrastructure Bill? Native News Online, 01.12.2021. ⟨https://nativenewsonline.net/environment/what-s-next-for-tribes-and-the-recently-signed-infrastructure-bill⟩ Accessed on 06.12.2021.

Levin, Sam 2017: 'Police make Arrests at Standing Rock in Push to Evict Remaining Activists'. The Guardian, 22.02.2017. ⟨https://www.theguardian.com/us-news/2017/feb/22/dakota-access-pipeline-standing-rock-evacuation-police⟩ Accessed on 03.08.2019.

Levin, Sam 2019: Facebook Teams with Rightwing Daily Caller in Factchecking Program. The Guardian, 18.04.2019. ⟨https://www.theguardian.com/technology/2019/apr/17/facebook-teams-with-rightwing-daily-caller-in-factchecking-program⟩ Accessed on 20.07.2019.

Marks, James 2017: Trump's Infrastructure Plan Is Critical for National Security. Daily Caller, 30.12.2017. ⟨https://dailycaller.com/2017/12/30/trumps-infrastructure-plan-is-critical-for-national-security/⟩ Accessed on 20.07.2019.

National Post 2017: A Timeline of the Dakota Access Oil Pipeline. 12.10.2017. ⟨https://nationalpost.com/pmn/news-pmn/a-timeline-of-the-dakota-access-oil-pipeline⟩ Accessed on 21.07.2019.

North Dakota Compass: Overview. ⟨https://www.ndcompass.org/economy/⟩ Accessed on 15.03.2020.

North Dakota Petroleum Council: Economic Output in North Dakota from Oil & Gas Remains Strong Despite Down Year. ⟨https://www.ndoil.org/economic-output-in-north-dakota-from-oil-gas-remains-strong-despite-down-year/⟩ Accessed on 20.07.2019.

Rickert, Levi 2016: Sacred Burial Sites desecrated by Dakota Access Pipeline Construction – 'This demolition is devastating'. Desdemona Despair, 04.09.2016. ⟨https://desdemonadespair.net/2016/09/sacred-burial-sites-desecrated-by.html⟩ Accessed on 29.07.2019.

Rotenberger, Julia 2018: Ölmarkt. USA sind Öl-Exporteur – zum ersten Mal seit mehr als 70 Jahren. Handelsblatt, 07.12.2018. ⟨https://www.handelsblatt.com/finanzen/maerkte/devisen-rohstoffe/oelmarkt-usa-sind-oel-exporteur-zum-ersten-mal-seit-mehr-als-70-jahren/23731184.html?ticket=ST-5493606-uLt26RpBOONsd4C3eadM-ap2⟩ Accessed on 20.07.2019.

Roy, M., Liza Grandia, Cinthya Ammerman, Jessa Rae Growing Thunder and Mike Mortimer 2017: The Dakota Access Pipeline in Context. ‹escholarship.org/uc/item/1947j92s› Accessed on 12.05.2019.
Schröder, Thorsten 2018: Trump im Ölrausch. Zeit, 18.02.2018. ‹https://www.zeit.de/wirtschaft/2018-02/usa-oel-bohrungen-donald-trump-energiepolitik/komplettansicht› Accessed on 20.07.2019.
Schweizer Radio und Fernsehen (SRF) 2017: Generalversammlung der Credit Suisse. 28.04.2017. ‹https://www.srf.ch/play/tv/tagesschau/video/generalversammlung-der-credit-suisse?id=a089a3b7-f928-44b7-bd87-f90196073786› Accessed on 03.08.2019.
Standing Rock Sioux Tribe: History. ‹https://www.standingrock.org/content/history› Accessed on 30.08.2019.
The Ojibwe People's Dictionary 2015. ‹https://ojibwe.lib.umn.edu/› Accessed on 30.08.2019.
The White House 2021: President Biden's Bipartisan Infrastructure Law. ‹https://www.whitehouse.gov/bipartisan-infrastructure-law/› Accessed on 06.12.2021.
Willis, Adam 2021: Dakota Access Pipeline Ramps up Carrying Capacity by nearly 50% as Expansion Continues. Bemidji Pioneer, 06.08.2021. ‹https://www.bemidjipioneer.com/business/energy-and-mining/7142959-Dakota-Access-Pipeline-ramps-up-carrying-capacity-by-nearly-50-as-expansion-continues› Accessed on 06.12.2021.
Willis, Adams 2021: DAPL Expansion ongoing as Critics argue Bakken Woes could negate Need for the Controversial Pipeline. The Dickinson Press, 04.11.2021. ‹https://www.thedickinsonpress.com/business/energy-and-mining/7269254-DAPL-expansion-ongoing-as-critics-argue-Bakken-woes-could-negate-need-for-the-controversial-pipeline› Accessed on 06.12.2021.
Wong, Julia C. 2017: Police remove last Standing Rock Protesters in military-style Takeover. The Guardian, 23.02.2017. ‹https://www.theguardian.com/us-news/2017/feb/23/dakota-access-pipeline-camp-cleared-standing-rock› Accessed on 03.08.2019.
Worland, Justin 2016: What to Know About the Dakota Access Pipeline Protests. Time, 28.10.2016. ‹http://time.com/4548566/dakota-access-pipeline-standing-rock-sioux/› Accessed on 25.04.2019.
Zeit Online 2014: Fracking. USA produzieren so viel Öl wie noch nie. ‹https://www.zeit.de/wirtschaft/2014-06/usa-oelproduktion-rekord-fracking› Accessed on 20.07.2019.

Informants

Andreanne Catt is Sicangu Lakota from Rosebud and a member of the seven Oceti Sakowin Tribes. She attended the movement at Standing Rock for four months and is a blockade and non-violent direct-action trainer with the International Indigenous Youth Council.

Jose Gomez III is a member of the Miakan-Garza Band of Central Texas and is Director of Communications and a mentor with the International Indigenous Youth Council.

Fighting against Windmills: Contested Knowledge, Resilience Grabbing and the Feeling of History repeating itself in Storheia, Norway

Bettina Wyler, Institute of Social Anthropology, University of Bern, Switzerland

Introduction

At Fosen Vind's press conference in February 2016, the excitement was evident. The representatives of the three companies involved, as well as the moderator of the live TV programme, could not stop themselves from emphasizing that the announced wind farms on the Fosen Peninsula in central Norway were going to be the biggest onshore wind farm project in Europe and that this would help Norway to achieve its climate goals.[1] The project consists of six wind farms with a total number of 277 wind turbines.[2] Among them, the Storheia wind farm in the southwestern part of the peninsula was about to become Norway's biggest wind farm on land. Crucially, its 80 turbines built on 38 km² are accompanied by 60 km of new roads and far-stretching power lines, as well as transformer stations and service buildings, making it a mega-infrastructure project.

For the Saami reindeer herders from South Fosen, the agreement from 2016 was not 'a big day' as it was glorified at the press conference, but it was indeed historic: as it happened against their will, they see the completion of the Storheia wind farm in 2019 on their winter grazing land as a precedent, threatening their future as reindeer herders and illustrating that their indigenous rights guaranteed by the Norwegian state are in fact weak. Therefore, this case study is another example of how in mega-infrastructure projects, in this case wind energy, the negative impacts on the rights and livelihoods of local groups are depoliticized – even in a

---

[1] NRK News from 23 February 2016, ‹www.tv.nrk.no›, accessed on 4.6.2020. Actually, the project is only Europe's biggest land-based wind farm until the Markbygden wind project in Sweden is completed (see ‹www.svevind.se›, accessed on 15.6.2020).

[2] The entire project has an installed capacity of 1 GW, which is the same as the Swiss nuclear power plant Gösgen. Each of the 277 turbines is 87 metres high with a rotor diameter of 117 metres (some even 136 metres) (see ‹www.fosenvind.no›, accessed on 18.6.2020).

progressive Western country. Ethnographic field research[3] enables a close look at the various impacts the wind farm has on the affected herders, now that it is in full operation. Their views interact and are therefore contrasted with strategies used by different authorities and the owners of the wind farm. In presenting this debate throughout the chapter, special attention is paid to the role of renewable energy.

Part 1: Historical, Environmental, Ethnographic and Political Context

History and Current Context

Until the 1980s it was argued that the Saami arrived in the Trondheim area only after non-Saami people did – a view that was crucial in the nation-building process and that might still have repercussions today (see Fjellheim 2020b). But newer research allows the presence of Saami people on Fosen to be tracked to at least the 1500s (Coleman et al. 2008). First through the hunting of wild reindeer and then through gradually domesticating them, reindeer husbandry is a centuries-old cultural practice in the area. All the animals' body parts were used by the semi-nomadic or fully nomadic herders. Until relatively recently, the reindeer were milked and used for transport too.

Before the arrival of non-Saami, reindeer husbandry was regulated by complex common property institutions, in terms of access to resources such as land and water, hunting and for settling disputes. All over *Saepmie* (the land of the Saami), this was organized in units called *sijte*,[4] consisting of a few households that could overlap with other *sijtes*. In many regions, they paid taxes to the king or to early state authorities for centuries, in exchange for protection against thieves and being recognized as the legitimate land users. It has to be emphasized, though, that Saami customary law varied greatly both geographically and over time, therefore general statements are difficult to make (Ahrén 2004). Unfortunately, sources regarding the specific situation on the Fosen Peninsula are comparatively rare or difficult to access.[5] Moreover, written historical accounts about Saami people and

---

[3] This chapter is based on ethnographic fieldwork from January and February 2020, carried out in order to write my master's thesis in Social Anthropology at the University of Bern. I stayed with two of the three reindeer herders that are affected by the construction of the Storheia wind farm. In addition, I conducted interviews with a historian, a member of the Saami parliament and a representative of one of the companies involved in the wind farm. The research is further based on an analysis of various impact assessments, project documents, press statements, court decisions and media sources.

[4] I decided to use the South Saami spelling for *Saepmie*, *sijte* and *Saami*. In North Saami language, they are spelled *Sápmi*, *siida* and *Sámi*, respectively.

[5] Some books and articles in Norwegian are stored in the state library in Oslo and are not accessible online. Generally, the issue of land rights in *Saepmie* is so comprehensive that several chapters would be needed to elaborate them. For a more detailed account see Ahrén (2004).

reindeer husbandry tend to represent the majority of the population's comprehension, rather than the minority's emic understanding (Sem 2019). Nevertheless, it is likely that the reindeer herders' relatively high sovereignty continued alongside the emerging farming for quite some time – including in the Fosen area.[6]

Change was brought by the border treaty between present-day Norway and Sweden in 1751 that divided the South Saami society into two groups, with various consequences.[7] However, the appendix, called *Lappekodisillen* in Norwegian, allowed the continued use of pastures across the new border and can therefore be seen as an acknowledgement of the customary Saami laws at that time. But increasingly, the herders' practices stood in conflict with non-Saami farmers' or the Norwegian authorities' interest in land. Based on emerging notions about the inferiority of the Saami and the creation of homogeneous national identities that depicted farmers as the 'real' Norwegians, the reindeer pastures were devalued as not permanently used (Ahrén 2004; Sem 2019). In consequence, the land of the Saami was increasingly allocated to agriculture and other purposes, thereby undermining their customary laws and replacing them with new regulations.[8] This shows that the 'writing of history is [...] a very powerful and therefore central way of establishing rights and taking control over territory' (Sem 2019: 157). Hence, the fact that the reindeer grazing land on the Fosen Peninsula today is not formally owned by the two *sijtes* but rather state or private land – to which they hold rights of use – is the result of a long history of contested land rights.

New laws introduced around 1890 also had a clear impact on reindeer husbandry all over the country, including Fosen. They limited Saami reindeer husbandry to certain districts,[9] which is why the south-westernmost parts of the Fosen Peninsula today are not designated as reindeer herding area (see Map 1). This took place in an emerging nationalist environment starting around 1800, after Christianization had already caused lasting changes in Saami societies. From 1851 onwards, so-called 'Norwegianization' policies were explicitly implemented and led to racist policies until the end of the Second World War. For example, the only language taught at schools was Norwegian from 1898 on, and in the northernmost part of Norway, a new law from 1902 allowed only Norwegian-speaking people to buy land (NRK 2019). Many other examples could be given to show how the Saami were seen as inferior and meant to become Norwegians. Also, administra-

---

[6] Interview by author in February 2020 with Håkon Hermanstrand, PhD research fellow in South Saami history at Nord University.
[7] The treaty was a consequence of Sweden losing the Great Northern War. In 1814, Norway became independent from Denmark and entered a union with Sweden until 1905.
[8] That grazing land had to give way to other land use in the case of conflict became an explicit policy with the Reindeer Husbandry Act from 1933.
[9] In present-day Norway, the central and northern parts of the country are reserved for Saami reindeer husbandry. Outside these areas, there are a few non-Saami reindeer herders, and the conditions for them are also regulated in the Reindeer Husbandry Law (see below).

tive positions connected to reindeer husbandry (called *lappefogd* in Norwegian) were usually taken by non-Saami with – at least at the outset – a lack of knowledge of the specific features of reindeer husbandry as well as the cultural aspects of it.[10] Yet, whether all kinds of change can be attributed to Norwegianization would require closer examination. For example, the impact of these policies on reindeer husbandry is difficult to fully distinguish from other demographic and societal changes that contributed to an increasingly sedentary lifestyle among Saami reindeer herders over the last few centuries.

While the explicit racist policies were no longer practicable after the Second World War, some argue that they ended only on paper. An important moment when reindeer herders' interest in, and knowledge about, Saami people in general gained more ground in the general public was the contested damming of the Alta river in the northernmost part of Norway around 1980. The dam was built despite the protests, but in the words of Håkon Hermanstrand, PhD fellow researcher in South Saami history, 'the Saami people lost the battle but won the war'.[11] Because, more or less as a direct result of the Alta case, the constitution was changed in 1988 and international treaties were signed (see below). Ten years later, in 1997, King Harald V officially apologized for the Norwegianization policies.[12] At present, the long history of injustice against Saami as well as Kvens and Norwegian Finns (both Finnish-speaking minorities) and its repercussions are being investigated by a Truth and Reconciliation Commission.[13]

For this case study, two aspects are important to emphasize here. First, there are historical differences to be noted between the South Saami area and other regions in *Saepmie*. Due to the proximity to present-day Russia, the northernmost part of Norway was the main target of the Norwegianization policies (Ahrén 2004). Despite this, the North Saami language keeps enjoying a somewhat privileged position compared to the South Saami language, which according to UNESCO is 'severely endangered'.[14] Also, many more Saami live in the Northern

---

[10] Interview by author in February 2020 with Håkon Hermanstrand, PhD research fellow in South Saami history at Nord University (referring to the South Saami area).

[11] Interview by author in February 2020.

[12] The King said, 'The Norwegian state is founded on the territory of two peoples – Norwegians and Saami' (Sem 2019: 155), which is seen as an important recognition of Saami people. Ten years later, at the centenary of the first Saami meeting in Trondheim, Prime Minister Solberg also apologized for the past wrongdoings, but did not mention the ongoing land rights debate, a fact that was criticized by many.

[13] However, in contrast to similar commissions in other countries, its mandate does not encompass juridical tasks nor financial compensations (see ‹www.uit.no/kommisjonen›, accessed on 18.6.2020).

[14] See ‹www.unesco.org/languages-atlas›, accessed on 25.9.2020.

regions than in the South Saami area,[15] leading the South Saami being called a minority within a minority (Hermanstrand et al. 2019).

Second, the topic of Norwegianization policies touches upon the question of what it means to be Saami, and its repercussions keep influencing this debate today. The practice of reindeer husbandry plays a central role in it: next to people specializing in reindeer husbandry, a few Saami who gained a livelihood from fishing, farming or trading, sometimes combined with reindeer husbandry, are also documented on Fosen. But for various reasons, they disappeared from historical sources around 150-200 years ago and were probably assimilated into the Norwegian society.[16] This explains why reindeer husbandry is considered to be very important for South Saami culture, as most of the people are either owners of reindeer themselves or the descendants of reindeer herders (Fjellheim 2020a). In fact, this ancestry is also evident from a linguistic point of view. Yet, several people have told me that schoolchildren in the Trondheim area typically learn about reindeer husbandry in the northern part of Norway and not about Saami living among and close to them.[17] Therefore, the stereotype of associating Saami with reindeer husbandry has two consequences. On the one hand, it leads to the need for traditional Saami fishers (outside Fosen) to argue that they are 'just as indigenous as their Saami reindeer counterparts' (Lätsch 2019: 210). On the other hand, South Saami reindeer herders in particular still fight for legal rights and recognition, because up until now, they have tended to be overlooked in the debate and have struggled to be visible. At the same time, more people inside and outside *Saepmie* are starting to identify as Saami in diverse ways far beyond the duality between reindeer herders and fishers, leading reindeer herder John to state that 'Saami people pop up everywhere'.[18]

So different people with different identities strive to be recognized as Saami. But the recent developments have been somewhat contradictory: while a revival of the languages is happening and pluralist approaches to Saami culture are emerging, many perceive the legal status to still be insufficient and notice racist attitudes in courts and everyday life (Fjellheim 2020b). In an attempt to improve this, a Saami Rights Commission published a long list of law amendments in 2007 that would be needed in order to improve the Saami's rights. But none of them have been implemented so far, according to a member of the Saami Parliament who

---

[15] Out of about 70,000 Saami in Norway, around 2,000 are South Saami, living on both sides of the border (see Fjellheim 2020b; Hermanstrand et al. 2019). Yet, a large number of Saami live outside *Saepmie*, such as in Oslo or even in foreign countries such as the US.

[16] Interview by author in February 2020 with Håkon Hermanstrand, PhD research fellow in South Saami history at Nord University.

[17] According to my own experience, associating Saami people exclusively with the far north of Norway is a belief that is sustained by the tourist industry too.

[18] Interview by author, January 2020.

worked in this commission.[19] I argue that this case study of a mega-infrastructure project has to be seen against this historical and political background.

Geography and Ecosystem/Cultural Landscape

Before explaining the practice of reindeer husbandry in more detail, some words need to be said about the geographical features of the study area. The Fosen Peninsula in central Norway encompasses about 4,200 km² and is connected to the city of Trondheim by a foot passenger ferry or via a drive lasting several hours around the Trondheim Fjord. The landscape is dominated by many small lakes (see Fig. 1) and rocky hills up to 600 m high, with a very low treeline, yet some areas contain boreal rainforest. All over the peninsula, wolverines, lynx and an increasing population of eagles, as well as a few bears, find abundant food in the form of different deer, hares and occasionally sheep. Hunting these predators is strictly limited by quotas, except for sea eagles and golden eagles, which have been protected since the 1970s. There are eight red-listed bird species living in the area,[20] but across the whole peninsula, there are only three small nature reserves. Outside the provincial towns and hamlets, many parts – previously including the Storheia wind farm area – are qualified as so-called 'non-impacted nature areas'. This means that they are at least 1 kilometre away from direct human influences such as cabins and roads.[21] In summer, a few public hiking paths can be used, but the only way to get around in the mountains in winter is by snowmobile, which is more or less reserved for the reindeer herders. Traces from reindeer husbandry can be found in the form of a few permanent installations such as cabins and enclosures, as well as a few cleared tracks. Moreover, stone remnants of centuries-old Saami turf huts (*gåetie* in South Saami) can be found in many areas, and several huts are still in use. Further, the landscape is shaped by several dammed lakes built in the 20th century, as well as eight wind farms in operation or under construction (see Adresseavisen 2019b). Some of them are in such close proximity to each other that turbines from several wind farms can be seen at the same time, and while out herding, the reindeer herders from South Fosen often see the new Storheia wind farm from afar.

---

[19] Interview by author with Nanni Westerfjeld, member of the Saami Parliament, February 2020.
[20] Three of them are listed as vulnerable, endangered or threatened (see ‹www.iucnredlist.org›), according to the impact assessment on nature (Asplan Viak 2009).
[21] The areas are designated by the Norwegian Environment Agency (see 'inngrepsfrie naturområder' on ‹www.miljodirektoratet.no›, accessed on 24.9.2020).

Local Population and Resource Use[22]

'Weather-wise, this is the worst January we have ever had,' I was repeatedly told in winter 2019/2020, when I looked out of the window towards the seashore where the wind was causing whitecaps and the trees around the house were swinging back and forth in a heavy storm. As both the opportunity to herd reindeer and the animals' behaviour are highly influenced by the weather, this was a real problem. The reindeer on the Fosen Peninsula roughly follow a migratory pattern between winter pastures that are closer to the coast and summer pastures inland. Distinguishing between eight instead of four seasons, herders repeatedly guide the reindeer to certain areas in this vast landscape. They come to decisions based on, for instance: their long-term knowledge about the behaviour of the animals, the weather conditions and topography, the presence of predators as well as other aspects. In early winter, as many reindeer of the *sijte* as possible are gathered in one of the fixed or set-up enclosures for a few days and some are usually slaughtered. And in early summer, after new calves are born, their ears are marked with the individual pattern of the respective owner, increasingly accompanied by a registered plastic mark. Being semi-domesticated but living freely for most of the year, the reindeer show great sensitivity towards the presence of humans.[23] I observed this myself when a single step forward was enough to make an indecisive herd of 50 reindeer move in the opposite direction.

Due to the seasonal migration, different areas require different characteristics and are of different value. Generally, the areas for rutting, calving and resting (especially in hot summers), as well as the most accessible paths connecting the pastures, are of the greatest importance. However, all pastures together influence the well-being of the animals: for example, good winter pastures are required for pregnant reindeer to maintain enough weight during the cold months. In fact, the extent of late-winter pastures (marking the harshest time of the year) is the decisive factor in defining the maximum number of reindeer allowed, at least in this part of the country. At the moment, the maximum for the two *sijtes* on Fosen is set at 1,050 animals each, a decision made by the reindeer husbandry administration on the national level.

The South and North *sijte* on Fosen together make the Fosen Reindeer Herding District (Fovsen Njaarke), which is led by an elected president and vice-president, with at least yearly meetings for those over 18 years old. The South Fosen *sijte* (Åerjel Fovsen sijte), which is the study group here, has a separate board as well as

---

[22] The information in this section is based on my field stay with two reindeer herders from South Fosen in January and February 2020.
[23] In the Saami reindeer herding areas, all reindeer are semi-domesticated. Only in the southern part of Norway, outside these districts, can so-called 'wild reindeer' be found and are allowed to be hunted. It is said that they are the descendants of previously domesticated reindeer, before Saami reindeer husbandry was forced to be given up in these areas (see above).

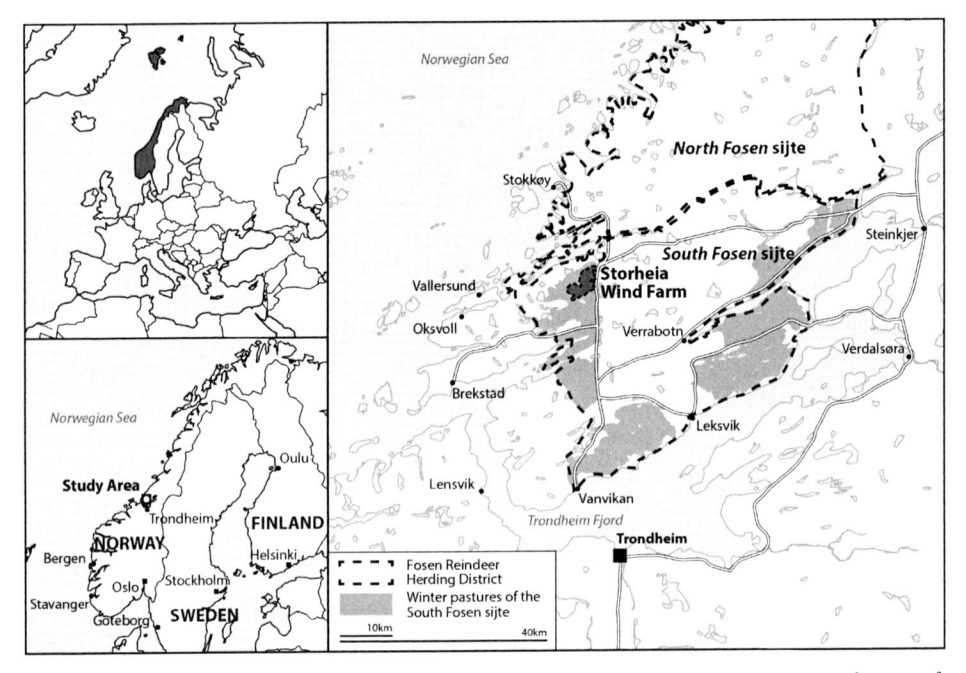

Map 1: The map shows the study area on the Fosen Peninsula in central Norway, near the city of Trondheim. It shows the boundaries of the Fosen Reindeer Herding District, the reindeer winter pastures of the South Fosen sijte, and the location of the Storheia wind farm. Source: Map compilation and design by Manuel L. K. Abebe (2021), CDE, University of Bern, Bern, Switzerland. Geodata: OpenStreetMap contributors, NIBIO

regular meetings too. Once a year, a report indicating the total number of reindeer has to be sent to the County Governor administration. This authority, acting as a first instance, also decides when conflicts arise between reindeer herders and landowners. The South Fosen *sijte* consists of three main herders, who all took over from their fathers or other relatives, and they herd the reindeer of more than 20 relatives of all ages. For most of them, reindeer were assigned at birth. Many members help to gather, mark and slaughter reindeer, and costly helicopters are only rarely used. However, for the last three years it has not been possible for the South group to slaughter any reindeer, due to the high number of reindeer killed by predators and other, not clearly identifiable causes.[24] This means that they did not receive any subventions from the Ministry of Agriculture and Food, because these can only be applied for when a relatively high number of animals have been slaughtered. In fact, hunting predators is of such importance that it takes up much

---

[24] In general, the herders are only compensated for losses documented by a division of the Norwegian Environment Agency, called the 'SNO'. But as carcasses disappear within hours or days and calves can be killed before they are registered, the exact extent of the losses is unknown and therefore not fully compensated.

of the herders' time, meaning that a reindeer herder does much more than just herd reindeer.

Apart from predators and the high dependence on weather conditions, the herders face other difficulties, for example recurring plans to build infrastructure such as roads, an increasing interest in recreational activities, and the privatization of forests and other state or communal land. Agriculture in the valleys, forestry in proximity to roads and sheep farming in some areas are other types of land use on the Fosen Peninsula and can also lead to conflicts. Crucially, all new encroachments are added to the already existing infrastructures and continuously reduce the amount of grazing land, but no new pastures can be gained. While some of these plans can be averted, they are nevertheless time-consuming and psychologically challenging for the herders. For a few years now, they have been supported in dealing with the administrative work by a secretary shared with other *sijtes*.

Compared to when the two herders I spent most time with were young, they now use more technical means such as snowmobiles and motorcycles and spend less time in the mountains. However, the migratory pattern and other general parameters of reindeer husbandry have not changed, they told me. Nevertheless, the addition of the different challenges makes all three main herders from South Fosen increasingly dependent on additional sources of income by some means or other. This means that both the herders' use of the commons is in a slow transition and the legal framework is changing too (see below). This represents a complex institutional change that is influenced by external and internal factors that will impact the ways the herders deal with future challenges (see Ensminger 1996).

Legal Framework

Rules about establishing a *sijte*, internal institutional processes, and the special rights and duties linked to being a reindeer herder are all settled in the national Reindeer Husbandry Law from 2007. It replaced the law from 1978 and contains, among other regulations, the following principles: in the Saami reindeer herding districts, only Saami people and their spouses can be reindeer herders; it enables the construction of cabins and permanent enclosures (with a permit) and allows the use of motorized vehicles in the mountains; it also asks for yearly reports and maps about land uses and obliges the *sijte* to collectively pay for damages caused by their reindeer. Three paragraphs are important to point out here. Right at the beginning, in paragraph 1, it is stated that 'reindeer husbandry must be preserved as an important foundation for Saami culture and social life'. Paragraph 19 grants the right to graze in the mountains as well as on previously cultivated land and meadows, as long as they are not fenced. As far as I know, no difference is made between private and state land in these respects. Last but not least, paragraph 63 states that landowners must not use their property in a reindeer grazing area in such a way that it is harmful for reindeer husbandry, apart from agricultural purposes or forestry.[25]

Thus, general access to the pastures as common-pool resources is regulated by this Reindeer Husbandry Law. It incorporates many aspects of Saami law, especially by acknowledging the *sijte* as the basic unit of Saami reindeer husbandry (Sara 2009). However, from what I understood, the use of reindeer paths that connect pastures (for example through forests, over meadows or to cross a road) is still based on customary law. So at least some of the practices depend on non-formalized and non-monetary agreements with other land users and the respective formal landowners.

In fact, all forms of Saami rights recognized by the state were related to reindeer husbandry until the policy changes following the Alta case (County Governor of Trøndelag 2019). Only then did Saami rights start to be discussed in multifaceted ways, and in 1990, the Saami were acknowledged by the state as indigenous people according to the Indigenous and Tribal Peoples Convention (ILO Convention 169). This convention recognizes peoples' customary land rights and imposes an obligation to consult and compensate them.[26] That Norway signed it is remarkable even today, as all the other countries in *Saepmie* continuously grant the Saami only minority rights. Even before this, Norway had changed its constitution in 1988: today's Article 108 states that Saami people have to be able to preserve and develop their language, culture and way of life. The Saami Act, on the other hand, laid the foundation for the establishment of the Saami Parliament in 1989. And 10 years later, in 1999, the Human Rights Act was passed. It incorporated international law, such as the International Covenant on Civil and Political Rights (ICCPR) Article 27, into Norwegian law.[27] However, this did not include ILO Convention 169, a fact that might be overlooked by many. Finally, in 2007, the United Nations Declaration on the Rights of Indigenous People was adopted, with similar commitments to ILO Convention 169, but – as it is with all UN law – it was not legally binding (Ravna 2013).

---

[25] The Reindeer Husbandry Law (*reindriftsloven*) is available online at ‹www.lovdata.no› (accessed on 19.6.2020). The paragraphs have been translated into English by the author.

[26] The convention was adopted in 1989 by the International Labour Organization, a United Nations agency (see ‹www.ilo.org›, accessed on 10.8.2020).

[27] Article 27 states: 'In those states in which ethnic, religious or linguistic minorities exist, persons belonging to such minorities shall not be denied the right, in community with the other members of their group, to enjoy their own culture, to profess and practise their own religion, or to use their own language' (‹www.ohchr.org›, accessed on 19.2.2020).

Part 2: The Mega-Infrastructure Project

Description of the Project

When visiting the Storheia area, the sound of the strong wind is mixed with the whooshing noise of the rotor blades spinning round. This atmosphere is not captured in photos, nor could they show all 80 turbines at once. Being there for the first time in January 2020, it was difficult for me to imagine what the land had looked like before. And it was even more difficult to capture why exactly this area and not a different one in this vast landscape was chosen to build a wind farm on. The exact reasons for it are hard to trace. Some general answers can be found in the very first plan for a possible wind farm in Storheia, which dates back to 2006. The report names seven ideal characteristics of a wind farm area: strong and steady wind, proximity to roads and power lines, a certain distance to buildings, suitable topography, avoidance of impacts on areas protected by the Nature Conservation Act, avoidance of impacts on areas protected by the Cultural Heritage Act, and so-called minimum negative consequences on the environment, natural resources and the society (Statkraft 2006). Some of these aspects have been repeatedly mentioned by supporters of the wind farm, creating the impression that this land was comparatively underutilized and few conflicts would arise.[28]

Interestingly, the Storheia wind farm was just one of 26 wind farms that were intended to be built on the Fosen Peninsula around 2008. And Storheia was not suggested as a preferred location in all assessments (Coleman et al. 2008). All these plans were developed in a very short period of time by different companies and most of them were given up a few months or years later. The one in Storheia also passed through many changes in the 13 years between the first plans until it was completed in 2019. Apart from many details not being settled at the time the concession was initially applied for, in 2008,[29] the most illustrative moment to highlight is 2015, when project leader Statkraft cancelled all plans to build wind farms on Fosen. In the press release, they explained that 'lower power and electricity certificate prices [. . .] have made the projects unprofitable' (Statkraft 2015). Surprisingly, a year later, the press conference mentioned at the beginning of this chapter nevertheless announced the construction of the Storheia wind farm as one part of Fosen Vind's project. Among the changes that made it profitable was shifting a part of the electricity production from the two wind farms being built outside Fosen to those four built on the peninsula, and other technical opti-

---

[28] The notion of idle or underutilized land has been a very common way to make land 'available', not only in colonial but also in present-day land deals (see Li 2014; Haller 2019b). It is usually combined with the claim that no institutions existed that governed access to the land (Ahrén 2004), an assumption that is then used to justify the introduction of new regulations.

[29] For example, the exact number and size of wind turbines was not settled at this point (Statkraft 2008). These extensive changes make it difficult for the reindeer herders and others to maintain an overview and to make precise arguments about the technical details of the wind farm.

mizations (TrønderEnergi 2016). However, the key factor that enabled the project was most likely the coming on board of an international investor consortium led by Credit Suisse,[30] which helped to finance the 11 billion Norwegian kroner required. As explained by the Swiss representative at the press conference in 2016, these investors are seeking long-term, stable investment. This is guaranteed by a contract with Norsk Hydro, an aluminium company, which buys a fixed share of one-third of the electricity produced.

Clearly, different supporters expressed high expectations. To start with, the two local municipalities voted in favour of the Storheia wind farm as they hoped for jobs, especially during the construction phase, as well as tax income and increased power supply in the region (Åfjord kommune 2016). The owners of the six wind farms advertised the project for providing renewable energy to 180,000 Norwegian households, thereby reducing the demand for fossil energy. Moreover, through the potential to combine it with the already existing hydropower plants, it is meant to contribute to Norway's energy transition.[31] This happens against the background that Norway already obtains more than 90 % of its electricity demand from domestic hydropower, but the electricity demand continues to rise due to increasing electrification. Moreover, thanks to cables linking it to the European electricity market, Norway intends to sell parts of its renewable energy.[32]

In sum, the Storheia area caught the eye of certain project planners as a suitable place for a wind farm both from a technical and a financial point of view and was connected to anticipation around green energy, job generation and higher tax income (see also Otte et al. 2018). In addition, opponents also point to the high state subsidies and low taxation of wind farms that made it financially interesting. Thereby they indicate that the wind resources alone were not the pivotal factor, but that this is a business worth billions.[33] This is important because it shows that in order to be financially viable for the different companies involved, the project had to become a mega-infrastructure project and it necessarily had to include the Storheia area (see also Nellemann 2017).

Hence, the fact that the area used to be reindeer grazing land for centuries was neither a reason to not consider it from the start, nor were the plans abandoned

---

[30] This happened at a time when investment in wind farms in Switzerland was politically improbable. At the press conference in 2016, the Swiss representative elaborated that the Bernese Energy Company BKW, as well as pension funds and insurance companies, are involved in the consortium led by Credit Suisse. This consortium owns 40% of the wind farms, while state-owned Statkraft owns 52.1% and the local energy company TrønderEnergi owns 7.9%. Together they make up the joint venture Fosen Vind DA (see ‹www.fosenvind.no›, accessed on 30.6.2020).

[31] This was repeatedly pointed out at the press conference in 2016.

[32] For a detailed account of Norway's Energy Strategy see 'New emission commitment for Norway for 2030 – towards joint fulfilment with the EU' at ‹www.regjeringen.no› (accessed on 12.8.2020).

[33] For example, this was pointed out at a conference about wind energy held by the environmental organization Motvind in June 2020, whose livestream on YouTube I attended.

Fig. 1: The Storheia wind farm was completed in 2019 despite ongoing court cases. Source: Fosen Vind (‹www.fosenvind.no/media›, accessed on 26.6.2020).

when the people from the South Fosen *sijte* expressed their disagreement. According to the Reindeer Husbandry Law explained above, they held rights of use to the land, after it had probably been formally privatized several centuries ago. However, the private owners (who were offered high compensation payments and an annual share in the wind farm yield) agreed to the project, which eventually led to the completion of the wind farm in 2019.

In the remaining part of this chapter, I will elaborate the environmental and social impacts of the Storheia wind farm, mainly focusing on the consequences for South Saami reindeer husbandry. I will then show how the courts discussed these impacts, before analysing the strategies the opponents and supporters of the wind farm use to criticize or promote the project, respectively. I do so by identifying different lines of arguments as well as strategies known as 'institution shopping'.

Environmental and Social Impacts

General Impacts of the Wind Farm

As mentioned in the introduction, the construction of a wind farm does not only include the building of wind turbines (see also Achiba 2019). Each of the 80 turbines of the Storheia wind farm is connected to a single-lane road, which is necessary for installation and maintenance (see Fig. 1). In total, a network of 60 km of new roads was built, connecting the wind farm to the existing main road. To level the terrain, rocks were blasted away and some trees were cut down before the gravel roads were built. Land use was increased by the on-site construction of service buildings, transformer stations and new high-voltage lines that connect the Storheia wind farm with other wind farms and, eventually, the consumers. Accordingly, this mega-infrastructure project impacts the habitat of different types of fauna, for example sea eagles and eagle owls. In this respect, most criticism concerns the movement of the rotor blades. The impact of the visually changed landscape on nearby settlements and tourism has also been assessed and discussed, as well as the noise of the turbines, seen as potentially disturbing for both humans and animals.[34] A less-known consequence is a phenomenon called 'falling ice', which occurs in certain weather conditions and depending on the exposure of the rotor blades to it. Signs around the Storheia wind farm warn of this danger, as depending on the conditions, a distance of 200 m to the wind turbines must be kept for safety reasons. When visiting the wind farm in January 2020, I myself witnessed a foot-long piece of blank ice that had clearly fallen off a nearby turbine. Crucially, this sighting happened on a day when the danger of falling ice was seen as minimal, according to the forecast on Fosen Vind's website.[35]

In the remaining part of this chapter, I will talk less about the ecological impact and focus on the sociocultural impacts of the Storheia wind farm, in this case its impact on reindeer husbandry. The environmental impact on the landscape and fauna other than reindeer nevertheless remains important, as they are related to the notion of green energy that both opponents and supporters of the wind farm address.

The Impacts on Reindeer Husbandry

In winter 2019/2020, when I did my fieldwork, it was so warm that precipitation often fell as rain and then again as snow. It created an icy cover over lichen and other types of food the reindeer usually dig up. These are the same conditions as in winter 2003, I was told, when 1,000 reindeer walked to the pastures in Storheia on their own. They did so because the hilly landscape and the proximity to the coast still offer food there, in both warm and cold winters. Accordingly, the reindeer also headed towards Storheia in this first winter after the completion of the wind farm. But at the sight and noise of the wind turbines they turned and walked up and down a nearby valley with bad grazing conditions, reindeer herder John told me on the very first day of my field stay. Moreover, they scattered in small herds

---

[34] All impact assessments as well as many other project documents are available online on the Norwegian Water Resources and Energy Directorate's (NVE) website: ‹https://www.nve.no/konsesjonssaker/konsesjonssak?id=43&type=A-1,A-6› (accessed on 12.8.2020).

[35] See ‹www.fosenvind.no› vindparkene › iskastvarsel› (accessed on 26.6.2020).

of only 10-100 animals each. Later he actively tried to guide a few through the wind farm area, which the animals refused to do.

Therefore, this winter confirmed for the reindeer herders from South Fosen what they have been arguing ever since they first heard about the project: that one-third of their winter pastures is forever lost for reindeer husbandry. This loss is calculated as follows. First, the combination of the movement of the rotor blades,[36] the noise, the piling of snow alongside the roads, the danger of falling ice and the generally increased human activity is said to be disastrous. For them it is obvious that this makes the whole wind farm area, as well as its direct surroundings, unusable, since only very few animals will still sporadically enter it. Moreover, access to areas west and north of the wind farm is also blocked, meaning that the loss encompasses a total area of a much bigger size than the 38 km^2 of the wind farm itself. And last but not least, the loss is calculated to be so high due to its special location, as elaborated above. The fact that the Storheia pasture was not used every winter was therefore not a sign of its insignificance but a characteristic of the migratory pattern in order to stay resilient.

The impacts of the wind farm on reindeer husbandry, then, are manifold according to the herders. First, scattered herds mean more effort to find them in the vast landscape in order to gather or guide them. This creates additional costs and might lead to conflicts with farmers, which illustrates how the various challenges reinforce each other. Second, stressed animals are more likely to lose weight or get killed by predators. Third, the remaining winter pastures cannot be sustainably used for many winters in a row, meaning that the total number of reindeer has to be reduced or the reindeer have to be fed for several months in winter. All three lead to a smaller income. And fourth, the resilience in dealing with extreme weather conditions and a warming climate is impaired. In other words, the flexibility that is crucial for reindeer husbandry is threatened (Fjellheim 2020a).

Three scenarios were presented to deal with these impacts. The most emphasized one is that one of the three herders would have to give up, which would also severely impact the remaining two herders, due to the mutual assistance. The second option is that all of them reduce the number of reindeer and focus more on their other sources of income. Importantly, this danger of a loss of income affects the current herders in unequal ways due to their different livelihood situations.[37] Feeding the animals with concentrated feed during winter is another possibility, but costly for the herders in terms of money, labour and time, and it would take the animals time to get used to. Also, it would change the reindeer husbandry significantly, due to the need for new equipment such as new kinds of enclosures

---

[36] In fact, the movement of the rotor blades spinning round is very similar to the movement herders use to make reindeer move forward, making me think that the wind farm must look like 80 giants to the reindeer.

[37] It also influences the younger generation's consideration as to whether or not to take over once the current herders retire.

Fig. 2: Reindeer on the Fosen Peninsula. They have been avoiding the Storheia wind farm area.
Source: Bettina Wyler

or barns and the presence of vets. At the time of my fieldwork, the herders I talked to did not yet know what to do. In this first winter after the completion of the wind farm, it was possible to use other winter pastures. 'What we will do next year, we don't yet know,' reindeer herder John summarized.[38] This shows that the impacts of the wind farm are less immediate than, for example, the daily threat from predators. But in view of the lack of satisfactory solutions to deal with the changes, it is feared that the wind farm will impact reindeer husbandry on Fosen for many decades to come. Crucially, the wind farm also affects the dealing with other, future encroachments on their land: the loss of a big part of their winter pastures increases the value of the remaining winter pastures and – due to the migratory pattern illustrated above – impacts all other pastures too. For the herders, this means that they will have to defend themselves all the more vehemently against future losses of land.[39] It remains to be seen whether they will be able to do so, or whether the increased difficulties will decrease their bargaining power even further, as it renders reindeer husbandry increasingly an auxiliary income or 'hobby'.

---

[38] Interview by author, January 2020.
[39] In a brief interview by the author in February 2020, a member of the aforementioned County Governor administration confirmed that from now on, he would be more restrictive with new applications for infrastructure, due to the impact of the Storheia wind farm.

This confirms Haller's theory (2019b) that commons grabbing has to be understood as resilience grabbing too. Accordingly, it is important to note that reindeer husbandry on the Fosen Peninsula was already in a difficult state before the wind farm put further pressure on the land. This was caused by an increasing number of predators such as eagles, a continued loss of land for various purposes and a warming climate (as mentioned above). In order to understand the impacts of the Storheia wind farm on reindeer husbandry, I argue that these previous challenges, as well as changes in access to pastures as common-pool resources that happened long before the Storheia wind farm was built, must be considered (see also Haller 2019b).

Impacts Debated in Court

The severity of these impacts – especially the long-term impacts – were the core debate in the three court cases between 2017 and 2020. After the South Fosen *sijte* had appealed against the granting of the concession,[40] the District Court twice confirmed the assessment of the Norwegian Ministry of Petroleum and Energy (OED) by saying that the wind farm only has minor negative impacts on reindeer husbandry during its operational phase and that those can be financially compensated. This is based on the idea that the reindeer will get used to the change after some time and start using these pastures again (Fjellheim 2020a). Accordingly, only the land used for roads, turbines and buildings is seen as lost, reindeer herder Leif explained to me during my stay. Interestingly, the opposite was concluded in the case of the Kalvvatnan wind farm north of the Fosen Peninsula: the granting of the concession was repealed by the OED three years after it had approved the Storheia case, arguing that it violates ICCPR Article 27 due to its impact on local reindeer husbandry (OED 2016). None of the people I talked to could think of reasons why the same authority argues differently in such similar cases.

Unhappy with the decision from the District Court, the South Fosen *sijte* disputed it, which is why in 2019, the Court of Appeal dealt with the case. Their decision in June 2020, then, was quite striking: they acknowledged that the whole wind farm area, including some surrounding areas (albeit still smaller than the herders had claimed), is lost for reindeer husbandry forever (Frostating Lagmannsrett 2020). But according to the judges, this still does not mean that any of the herders will have to quit. For this purpose, they quadrupled the compensation payments to 45 million Norwegian kroner, which is meant to finance the feeding of some of the reindeer in winter. Interestingly, the importance of reindeer husbandry for Saami culture is acknowledged. But as feeding reindeer is an established practice in other regions of Norway,[41] and 'reindeer herding practices

---

[40] The concession was granted in 2010 by the Norwegian Water Resources and Energy Directorate (NVE) and confirmed in 2013 by the Norwegian Ministry of Petroleum and Energy (OED).

[41] Feeding reindeer during the winter months is indeed a fairly widespread practice in the northern part of Norway and in some areas in Sweden today, which has to do with a long history of

have never been static', the cultural rights of the Saami people are nevertheless not seen as violated (ibid.: 26f., translated by the author). Therefore, the construction of the Storheia wind farm is considered legal.

In August 2020, both Fosen Vind and the South Fosen *sijte* appealed against this judgement in the Supreme Court of Norway, but for different reasons: the former does not agree with the amount of compensation payments, because 'we think that the negative impacts of the wind farm are not as serious as the Court of Appeal describes' (NRK 2020, translated by the author); the latter continues to challenge the validity of the concession granting. This process will take at least one year, and it means that the herders will not be paid until the proceedings have been completed. This is an example of how access to vital resources is lost immediately, while potential benefits or mitigation measures come slowly (see Haller 2019b).

Special attention should be paid to the role renewable energy played in the legal disputes about the wind farm. This becomes most evident when looking at the fact that the project was completed despite ongoing court cases: it was the Norwegian Water Resources and Energy Directorate (NVE) that had allowed this procedure, because in order to receive renewable energy certificates, the wind farm had to be built within a certain period of time. Surprisingly, it was the NVE itself that had set this deadline in the first place.[42] Then, in confirming the NVE's decision to grant the concession, the OED argued that the benefits of providing renewable energy to the region must weigh high in the assessment (OED 2013; see also Nilssen 2019). In addition to the Court of Appeal's argument quoted above, this is thus another way in which the impacts on reindeer husbandry can be more or less acknowledged as severe, while at the same time arguing that the construction is still legal – by claiming that these concerns must give way to the interests of the general public. Creating such market rationalities thereby highly depoliticizes the debate, according to the Swedish researcher Lawrence (2014). Interestingly, in the above-mentioned Kalvvatnan wind farm case, the conclusion was again the opposite: the interests of the society were not seen as legitimate enough to override the Saami's cultural rights (OED 2016). This shows great latitude of judgement on the part of the authorities and indicates that all current court cases about wind energy will probably be decisive for later cases.

---

diminishing reindeer grazing land. In the Trondheim area, on the other hand, reindeer until now have not been regularly fed, apart from the few days when they are gathered in enclosures during the calf marking or slaughtering.

[42] Email conversation from February 2020 with Andreas Brønner, the lawyer of the South Fosen *sijte*. This process seems to repeat itself at the Øyfjellet wind farm, currently under construction.

Local and NGO Strategies

Looking at the ways the reindeer herders from South Fosen criticize the Storheia wind farm, two general lines of argument can be identified: the first one is based on the notion of indigeneity (see also Nilssen 2019); the second one is unrelated to indigeneity but rather concerned with environmental impacts. Both were discussed in court as well as in public debate (mainly media), and repeatedly indicated to me in interviews during my field stay.

The Notion of Indigeneity

First of all, the reindeer herders brought the case to court as they were convinced that all the legal regulations elaborated above were meant to protect their rights both as reindeer herders and as Saami people, and they should have prevented the wind farm from being built. In accordance with the law, several consultation meetings took place in 2009 and later, and the herders were positive about them at first. However, they eventually refused to participate further in such meetings as they became disillusioned for several reasons: first, all three herders had clearly said no to the project from the very beginning, which in itself should have stopped it in their understanding; second, when pressured to nevertheless provide some suggestions as to how to mitigate the impacts, it was up to the NVE to decide which conditions have to be fulfilled by the wind farm operators, a process that the herders consider unfair and arbitrary[43]; and thirdly, when given on-site safety instruction about how to deal with the ongoing construction work, these informal discussions were later defined as consultation too and used against them in court. Further, apart from the consultation process, they also criticize the impact assessments that were made before the concession was granted. For example, the main report about the predicted impact on reindeer was written by biologists who used examples from the north of Norway (see Coleman et al. 2008). Even though these researchers talked to the South Fosen reindeer herders too, the latter criticize the report for not fully considering the local context. In their entirety, these issues led them to the claim that the compulsory assessments and consultations were inadequate, so they see both international and national law violated.

The main argument made by the herders from South Fosen then is that, instead of just affecting the livelihood of roughly 30 people, all (South) Saami people are concerned, for three reasons:

First, they claim that more is at stake than the actual reindeer husbandry as a form of income or work. In the words of herder Leif, 'reindeer husbandry is a

---

[43] In granting the concession, the wind farm owners were obliged by the NVE to support the herders with the following measures: enabling easier access to the other two winter pastures (in Rissa and Leksvik); financing GPS trackers for 200 reindeer over a period of five years; providing power generators for two of the herders' cabins; and constructing some fences to keep reindeer away from dangerous areas in the wind farm (NVE 2016: 6).

bond that holds all South Saami people together'.[44] Accordingly, a reduced possibility of carrying it out is seen as a threat to South Saami culture itself, which would make them even more invisible. Culture is thereby understood as a historical legacy, a continued practice against all odds, a form of collective identity as well as language aspects. In this context, the solution proposed by the Court of Appeal to feed some reindeer in winter is unsatisfactory for the herders. In a Skype discussion in June 2020, they criticized it as technical and one-sided as it does not consider the cultural values they attribute to their previous ways of herding reindeer.

Second, because the Storheia wind farm was built despite the disapproval of the South Fosen *sijte*, they see it as a precedent that impairs the legal position of Saami as an indigenous people in Norway. It is feared that similar projects in other parts of *Saepmie* will be built against the will of the local reindeer herders following the same pattern. Indeed, the Storheia wind farm is the first wind farm on South Saami reindeer herding land that was taken to court, as the first two wind farms on the Fosen Peninsula were built on the land of the North Fosen *sijte*, which had agreed to them.[45] It is feared that the court's decision to consider the construction of the Storheia wind farm as legal despite acknowledging the negative impact on reindeer husbandry will send a signal to other projects. Again in the words of herder Leif, 'it shows that you can build a wind farm and then pay later and it's okay'.[46] Accordingly, it is seen as a confirmation that Saami people's rights exist only on paper, thereby affecting the whole Saami population.

At the same time, and linked to this, the herders argue that the Storheia wind farm case illustrates the fact that Norwegian authorities and the general public do not know much about either reindeer husbandry or Saami people, thereby demonstrating their marginal position in today's society. Several people I talked to suspect that outsiders compare reindeer with cows, because this is what these people are more familiar with, which makes them argue that the reindeer will get used to the wind turbines after some time. The herders, on the other hand, claim that their knowledge about the animals is sufficient to predict the long-term impacts of the wind farm. They also use scientific studies to underscore these assessments.[47] Moreover, as the necessity to start feeding the reindeer in winter is forcing them to 'become farmers', they see the Court of Appeal's decision as patronizing. Thus, they see a need for better knowledge of reindeer husbandry and the Saami people

---

[44] Interview by author, February 2020.
[45] The North Fosen *sijte* had agreed to the construction of the Bessakerfjellet and the Sørmarkfjellet wind farms. Currently, three of Fosen Vind's six wind farms are being constructed or are already completed on their land. Their appeal against it is discussed in the same court cases as the South group's complaint, but they have separate lawyers.
[46] Skype interview by author, June 2020.
[47] In court, they referred to the one from Skarin et al. (2018), for example, as well as Nellemann's very detailed assessment in the Fosen context (2017).

among the general public, preferably leading to changes in the reindeer law, to the full implementation of ILO Convention 169 as well as to improved management of predators.

In sum, the fact that the wind farm was built against their will and against their judgement both illustrates and increases the Saami people's marginal position in the Norwegian society, according to the affected reindeer herders I talked to. This is what the Norwegian researcher Trond Nilssen meant when he said: 'Reindeer herding as a livelihood cannot represent all the South Saami, but the threats this South Saami livelihood is facing are used to show the marginalization of all South Saami' (2019: 174). Putting it in a historical perspective is therefore a central strategy in arguing against the Storheia wind farm. In all assessments and court debates, the herders have emphasized that the impacts of the wind farm should not be looked at in a detached manner but that the addition of all previous and current losses of land have to be recognized. This is why, in their view, history is now repeating itself as land is again taken away from them.

It is important to emphasize that this notion of indigeneity is based on two premises: A) that reindeer husbandry is severely impacted by the Storheia wind farm, also in the long term; and B) that the continuation of reindeer husbandry is necessary to preserve South Saami culture, and therefore the human rights of an already marginalized, indigenous group are violated. It thereby focuses on traditions and traditional knowledge, Saami culture and indigenous rights, and happens at a time when more and more people are interested in Saami culture (or indigenous people in general) or start identifying themselves as Saami. Yet, this is somewhat fragile, as the general public might have romanticized stereotypes in mind and therefore consider today's Saami reindeer herders as not 'indigenous enough' (see Fjellheim 2020b).

In this first line of argument, the herders are supported by different international and national actors. For the purposes of this chapter, only one is to be mentioned here[48]: the United Nations Committee on the Elimination of Racial Discrimination (CERD). Following an appeal from the Saami Council (an NGO for the whole of *Saepmie*) on behalf of the South Fosen *sijte*, the Committee appealed to the Norwegian state in December 2018 to halt the construction of the wind farm until it had examined the case in more detail. This happened in light of the fact that the wind farm was constructed and eventually completed despite the ongoing court cases (see above).[49] The CERD's call was taken up by national and interna-

---

[48] The herders also receive support from the Society for Threatened Peoples Switzerland, which mainly criticizes the involvement of the Swiss investors in the Storheia wind farm. The NGO asks these companies to commit themselves to the principle of Free, Prior and Informed Consent (FPIC) (Society for Threatened Peoples 2018).

[49] The detailed plan for the construction (called the 'MTA') was granted by the NVE in 2017 despite the ongoing court case in the same year. The Storheia wind farm was then constructed until summer 2019, including during winter.

tional media and used to put pressure on the authorities, but was declined by the Norwegian state two weeks later. For the reasons elaborated in this chapter, the herders from South Fosen nevertheless continue to fight against the wind farm in juridical terms.

The Notion of Sustainability

To me, it seems that the herders are well aware of the vulnerability of the premises on which the notion of indigeneity is based, especially given their experiences of losing several court cases. Therefore, a second line of argument can be detected in the ways they argue against the wind farm, with one being more or less consciously unrelated to the first one:

On the one hand, I was repeatedly told by the herders that the danger of falling ice should be proof enough to show that the whole area is unusable for humans and animals in winter – no matter whether their concerns about the reindeer's behaviour are heard or not. This aspect became more and more important to them over the years, not least due to the discovery of a piece of ice described above.

Fig. 3: The Storheia wind farm consists of 80 turbines, 60 km of new roads, power lines, transformer stations and service buildings. Source: Bettina Wyler

The other claim they make in criticizing the wind farm regardless of indigeneity is in contesting the project's sustainability. In short, it is argued that although a wind farm does not burn fossil resources, it nonetheless uses large amounts of natural resources to build the turbines and all necessary infrastructure. In the view of the herders, the benefits of generating wind energy for only 25 years therefore cannot outweigh the lasting destruction of a vast landscape (see also Leibenath and Otto 2014). In this point they are supported by the environmental organizations Naturvernforbundet and Motvind. The former demands that all wind energy projects in reindeer herding areas must be automatically rejected, and representatives sometimes suggest building offshore wind farms instead. The recently founded organization Motvind (meaning headwind or pushback) argues in a more general way: using the motto 'yes to nature, no to wind energy', they state that the protection of the environment and wind energy projects are not compatible in their view.[50] I also repeatedly came across the argument that according to the United Nations report from 2019, land use change leading to biodiversity loss is just as much a threat to the environment as climate change. However, such alliances could also lead to conflicts, as environmentalists tend to use the notion of pristine nature, while for the herders it is a cultural landscape. Moreover, the opportunities to build such alliances are quite scarce, as many other organizations, as well as most politicians (including the Green Party), are in favour of the Storheia wind farm.

This might be a reason why direct actions were relatively rare over all these years, with the exception of a temporary blockade of the access road in 2018 and small demonstrations related to the court cases in Trondheim, the latter organized in collaboration with the above-mentioned environmentalists. Going to court was indeed the main way to directly oppose the project, enabled thanks to Norwegian legislation that makes Fosen Vind bear all court and legal fees – regardless of the outcome of the process. Moreover, the herders are in contact with other wind energy opponents, mainly through Facebook groups, even though not all the other planned wind farms affect reindeer husbandry.[51] A common debate in these groups concerns the term 'wind farm' or 'wind park': several actors find it euphemistic and call it a 'wind industrial area' to express their discontent. On these platforms they also raise awareness about the impacts of the Storheia wind farm after its completion, which could be considered as modern 'weapons of the weak' (see Scott 1985).

State and Company Strategy

The ways in which Fosen Vind as the wind farm owner promotes the Storheia wind farm and claims the construction to be legal can also be divided into different lines of argument, which centre on the notions of consultation, compensation and green energy:

---

[50] See ‹www.naturvernforbundet.no/vindkraft› and ‹www.motvind.org› (accessed on 13.8.2020).
[51] One example is the wind farm on Frøya island, which has been widely discussed in the media.

The first approach is to claim that all criteria to guarantee a thorough assessment and a fair consultation process were met. After considering the different options and opinions as best they could, the project planners – according to interviews in the media – decided to pursue their plans to build a wind farm in the Storheia area, while mitigating and compensating for all unavoidable negative impacts (Fosna-Folket 2016; Berner Zeitung 2020). Even though this acknowledges the presence of Saami reindeer husbandry in the area, it relies on the fact that the herders' rights of use are not legally equivalent to formal private property. It is further connected to the claim that only scientific studies can assess the (long-term) impacts on reindeer husbandry (Kaapke 2018; Fjellheim 2020b). According to *sijte* leader Leif – who was questioned in court – the owners of the wind farm referred to different scientific studies to question the severity of the impacts on reindeer husbandry.[52] In fact, the continued presence of reindeer in the wind farm area even during the construction phase was pointed out by wind turbine provider Vestas, who posted a photo of a single reindeer on their Facebook page in December 2019.

The second approach is to assign certain or even full responsibility to other actors. First of all, this is done by referring to the licensing and juridical authorities, who assessed the impacts, decided about financial compensations and granted or confirmed the concession, implying that it was they who enabled it in the end (Adresseavisen 2017). Secondly, as an important driver for the project, Norwegian politics calling for wind energy are named. The government's call on companies to select locations and develop projects makes the operators state that they are acting on behalf of the current government (Kaapke 2018), or that it is the politicians who have to weigh up the assets and drawbacks (Adresseavisen 2019a). Thirdly, the companies within Fosen Vind DA ascribe each other different decisive power. It is in fact the Norwegian state company Statkraft that has been the project manager from the very start until today. So both the Swiss consortium (which owns 40% of the wind farm) and TrønderEnergi (which owns 7.9%) stress that they entered the portfolio (as operators) only after the concession was granted and were therefore not involved in the assessments and hearings.[53]

As mentioned in the introduction of this chapter, as well as in the description of the project, the notion of green energy was a dominant argument of the wind farm owners, which was based on the assumption that climate change is

---

[52] Interview by author in February 2020. In court, research about other wind farms and the reindeer's reaction to it, the impacts of power lines and the danger of falling ice were discussed (see NRK from 10.6.2020, ‹https://www.nrk.no/sapmi/fovsen-njaarke-saken-1.14820186›, accessed on 29.6.2020).

[53] For the former see SRF (2018). The fact that TrønderEnergi only became part of the portfolio as an operator in 2016 was emphasized in a personal discussion between the author and CEO Ståle Gjersvold in February 2020.

the biggest threat and should be mitigated by technical means.[54] This argument of providing renewable energy is pointed out first and foremost in the public communication about the project. But as indicated, it also played a decisive role in legal terms. However, as far as I know, no claims about potential benefits of wind energy in terms of the amount of land needed or the number of jobs generated compared to other types of energy production, especially hydropower, were made. Instead, this notion of sustainability solely focuses on the lack of need to burn fossil resources. Other authors, in contrast, observe that arguments about climate change mitigation were relatively absent, compared to the emphasis placed on the project's economic benefits for the region (see Otte et al. 2018; Kaapke 2018). I have a different impression and argue that the green energy discourse was a central tool to legitimize the construction and to relativize negative impacts.

Claiming benefits for the general public further enables a fourth strategy: to leave out reindeer husbandry from the debate (see also Otte et al. 2018) and to thereby also deny the bigger societal or historical context concerning indigenous people. This was done both at the press conference in February 2016 and at the informative meetings that were held in March 2016.[55] In both cases, the impact on reindeer husbandry was neither declined nor justified, but left out. Instead, the focus was put on technical details, such as the size of the six wind farms, the types of turbines used or the complex ways the elements have to be transported to the construction sites. The state-owned Norwegian Broadcasting Cooperation (NRK) supported this strategy by interviewing the pro-wind environmental organization ZERO during the live TV broadcast of the press conference in 2016 and let no critical voices be heard.

Conclusion

In a country where 45 % of the mainland is designated as reindeer herding land, this is evidently not seen as an obstacle to the construction of a wind farm per se (see The Kingdom of Norway 2018). Using the contested Storheia wind farm in central Norway as a case study, I show how the perspective of the affected reindeer herders from the South Fosen *sijte* interacts with the arguments of the wind farm owners and authorities who voted in favour of it, by bringing up a new line of argument when the previous argument has proven to be insufficient. Such institution shopping (see Haller 2019a) is practised by all actors involved;

---

[54] For example, wind farm co-owner TrønderEnergi states on its website that 'climate change is our biggest challenge, while new technology offers the greatest opportunities' (translated by the author; see ‹www.tronderenergi.no/identitetsplattform› (accessed on 26.6.2020)).

[55] The PowerPoint presentation of these meetings is available at ‹www.afjord.kommune.no/vindkraft› (accessed on 26.4.2020). I do not know about the exact addressees of these meetings, but it is the only one I came across and therefore likely to have been held to inform the general public in the respective municipalities.

they do so by choosing different legal institutions and by referring to conflicting scientific sources that predict varying degrees of impacts on reindeer husbandry (Nellemann 2017). All of them also ascribe the responsibility for the wind farm to certain actors and doubt that of others. Accordingly, over the course of the last decade, the dispute has changed. Also, new actors have become involved (e.g. the CERD and international investors), while others have left or changed their minds (e.g. the previously involved company AgderEnergi as well as some politicians).

It is important to note that this occurs in unequal power relations (see also Avila 2018). Claiming high political and societal value, the owners of the wind farm use a popular green energy discourse. This has proven to be powerful in building a wind farm against the will of the local reindeer *sijte*: it not only enabled the construction despite ongoing court cases, but it also made the perceived benefits weigh particularly high in court. In fact, even the promised jobs were described as 'green jobs', showing that job creation is not only used to advertise development projects in their narrow sense but also renewable energy projects (see also Achiba 2019). Using anti-politics strategies (Ferguson 1994), it further enabled the contested impacts to be left out altogether, by focusing on technical details. It is likely that if it had not been for a renewable energy project, this would not have been possible to the same extent (see also Ryser 2019).

The reindeer herders who contest the wind farm, however, are well aware of the power of their opponents and the green energy argument. During my fieldwork, one of them stated in frustration: 'It's like fighting against windmills.'[56] Indeed, their discontent failed to impede the construction of the wind farm. In the first winter after the completion of the wind farm, they did not yet know how to deal with the loss of land. Certainly, the value of all remaining pastures has changed, which will influence their dealing with future encroachments in unpredictable ways. But due to its ascribed character as a precedent, they nevertheless continue to challenge the Storheia wind farm in both overt and covert ways (see Scott 1985).

A central way to do so has been to put the wind farm in a historical perspective by using the notion of indigeneity, thereby rejecting the depoliticizing strategies of the wind farm supporters. The reindeer herders claim that the Storheia wind farm is another example of the many previous and present encroachments on their land, pointing out critically that it is again they who have to give up land when the general public demands it. Thus, in the words of the Saami researcher and activist Eva Fjellheim, 'for the Saami reindeer herders, the wind industry is neither green nor a change' (2020a, translated by the author). Given that the wind farm area is formally privately owned, their struggle takes place against a background of cen-

---

[56] Interview by author, January 2020. This idiom has a slightly different meaning in English compared to the way my informant used it: in English, it can mean to fight against imaginary or unimportant enemies. The reason I quote it, however, equates to the German understanding: it means to try in vain to fight against powerful actors and to be aware of this hopelessness.

turies of contested land rights, which is itself linked to the tendency of Norwegian historiography and politics to exclude the Saami people.[57] In contrast, the only moment when advocates of the wind farm put it in a larger perspective is when it comes to the number of wind farms on Fosen: because only eight have been built or are under construction and 18 other plans were abandoned, the impact of the former is argued to be tolerable (The Kingdom of Norway 2018).

Another strategy used to oppose the wind farm has been to challenge the very foundation on which the power of its owners is based: the sustainability of the project. Building such alliances with environmentalists has already proven to be successful in preventing the Fosen Military Area (1969-1991) and was crucial in the Alta case around 1980. Importantly, a broad anti-wind energy movement has developed in the last few months, which might influence the future debate about wind energy in Norway to a considerable extent. Despite widespread enthusiasm and powerful opponents, these people dare to scrutinize and criticize the societal and environmental impacts of wind farms, for reasons that go far beyond NIMBY-ism (Not In My Back Yard). However, such alliances can be conflicting as conservationists tend to see nature as 'pure', instead of culturally shaped. In addition, they usually support the protection of predators. However, while the wind farm mainly represents resilience grabbing in the long term, predators are the most immediate threat to reindeer husbandry, which complicates building alliances with environmentalists even further.

In sum, this case study raises the question of who exactly sets the parameters for Norway's energy transition and who bears the consequences of it, thereby touching upon the concept of energy justice (see Otte et al. 2018; Avila 2018; Kaapke 2018). I argue that these considerations are particularly important when it comes to mega-infrastructure projects such as the Storheia wind farm on the Fosen Peninsula.

Update October 2021: Supreme Court declares license invalid

Shortly before the editorial deadline of this edited volume, the Supreme Court decided about the validity of the wind farm license. To a large extent, it therein followed the reasoning of the Court of Appeal: It adopted the latter's argumentation according to which the pastures in Storheia are forever lost for reindeer husbandry and that this threatens the continuation of the South Fosen *sijte*'s reindeer husbandry (Supreme Court 2021). Unlike the previous court, however, the Supreme Court did not consider feeding the reindeer a legitimate compensatory measure. For two reasons: First, it argued that putting reindeer in enclosures for several months 'differs significantly from traditional, nomadic reindeer husbandry' (ibid.: 27, translated by the author).

---

[57] See Sem (2019) for a critical account of the Saami's representation in the three-volumes-long *History of Trøndelag* from 2005, the county where the Storheia wind farm is located.

Second, it noted that feeding reindeer would require changes in Reindeer Husbandry Law, causing uncertainties in how the measure could be implemented from a legal point of view. This is why – contrary to the Court of Appeal – the Supreme Court argued that the negative impacts of the wind farm cannot be mitigated. Therefore, the herders' right to culture according to ICCPR Article 27 is seen violated and the license given by NVE in 2010 declared invalid.

Interestingly, the Supreme Court also addressed the role renewable energy plays in its decision: It argued that the interests of the society in renewable energies cannot be prioritised over ICCPR, especially since other locations on Fosen with less impact on reindeer husbandry would have been available.

However, the Supreme Court was not entitled to decide what consequences its decision should have on the Storheia wind farm. Instead, this seems to be the task of the Norwegian Ministry of Petroleum and Energy (OED). After the Supreme Court's decision was published, the South Fosen *sijte*, together with environmentalists, asked for an immediate demolition of all wind turbines in Storheia. Fosen Vind, on the other hand, announced to apply for a new licence (NRK 2021). What kind of adjustments the consortium plans to make it in line with ICCPR Article 27 is not known at this point. The latest status of can be followed in media and probably on Fosen Vind's website (www.fosenvind.no).

Shortly after the court's decision, only two things are certain: First, the highest court in Norway supported the indigenous herders' claim in a legal precedent, which can be considered an important acknowledgment of Saami rights and which will probably influence all kinds of future constructions on reindeer pastures in Norway and beyond. Second, despite the success of the herders, this decision did not settle the dispute but requires further negotiations. While the bargaining power of the herders is strengthened by the court's decision, unequal power relations remain and are likely to influence the debate. In fact, the herders lose their right to the compensation payments assigned to them by the previous court, since those were connected to the feeding of the reindeer. It is now unclear when and in what ways they will be compensated for their losses.

Therefore, it remains important to look at the impacts of the Storheia wind farm as a mega-infrastructure project, even after the claims of the affected population have been supported by the highest legal authority.

Acknowledgements

My thanks go to reindeer herder John and his wife Anne, to herder Leif and to retired herder Arvid, who explicitly wanted to be named here and commented on a first draft of this chapter. Thank you also to Håkon Hermanstrand, Nanni Westerfjeld and Ståle Gjersvold for taking the time to talk to me. And last but not least, my thanks go to the Society for Threatened Peoples Switzerland, who opened important doors for me.

Glossary

CERD	United Nations Committee on the Elimination of Racial Discrimination
FPIC	Free, Prior and Informed Consent
ILO Convention 169	Indigenous and Tribal Peoples Convention
ICCPR	International Covenant on Civil and Political Rights
NRK	Norwegian Broadcasting Cooperation
NVE	Norwegian Water Resources and Energy Directorate
OED	Norwegian Ministry of Petroleum and Energy

References

Achiba, Gargule A. 2019: Navigating Contested Winds: Development Visions and Anti-Politics of Wind Energy in Northern Kenya. *Land* 8 (1): 1-29.

Ahrén, Mattias 2004: Indigenous Peoples' Culture, Customs, and Traditions and Customary Law – The Saami People's Perspective. *Arizona Journal of International and Comparative Law* 21 (1): 63-112.

Avila, Sofia 2018: Environmental Justice and the Expanding Geography of Wind Power Conflicts. *Sustainability Science* 13: 599-616.

Ensminger, Jean 1996: *Making a market. The institutional transformation of an African society*. Cambridge: Cambridge University Press.

Ferguson, James 1994: The anti-politics machine. Development, depoliticization, and bureaucratic power in Lesotho. Cambridge: Cambridge University Press.

Fjellheim, Eva 2020b: Through Our Stories We Resist: Decolonial Perspective on South Saami History, Indigeneity and Rights. In: Breidlid, Anders and Krøvel, Roy (eds.): *Indigenous knowledges and the sustainable development agenda*. Oxon and New York: Routledge, 207-226.

Haller, Tobias 2019a: Towards a new institutional political ecology. How to marry external effects, institutional change and the role of power and ideology in commons studies. In: Haller, Tobias et al. (eds.): *The commons in a glocal world. Global connections and local responses*. London and New York: Routledge, 90-120.

Haller, Tobias 2019b: The Different Meanings of Land in the Age of Neoliberalism: Theoretical Reflections on Commons and Resilience Grabbing from a Social Anthropological Perspective. *Land* 8 (104): 1-22.

Hermanstrand, Håkon et al. 2019: *The indigenous identity of the South Saami. Historical and political perspectives on a minority within a minority*. Cham: Springer.

Kaapke, Niklas 2018: Reaching for recognition and greening for growth. Perceptions of justice with regard to Sámi reindeer husbandry and wind energy in Norway. Master Thesis Series in Environmental Studies and Sustainability Science: Lund University.

Lätsch, Angelika 2019: Constitutionality and Identity. Bottom-up Institution Building and Identity among Coastal Saami in Northern Norway. In: Haller, Tobias et al. (eds.): *The commons in a glocal world. Global connections and local responses*. London: Routledge, 210-232.

Lawrence, Rebecca 2014: Internal Colonisation and Indigenous Resource Sovereignty: Wind Power Developments on Traditional Saami Lands. *Environment and Planning D: Society and Space* 32: 1036-1053.
Leibenath, Markus & Antje Otto 2014: Competing Wind Energy Discourses, Contested Landscapes. *Landscape Online* 38 (1): 1-18.
Li, Tania 2014: What is Land? Assembling a Resource for Global Investment. *Royal Geographical Society* 39: 589-602.
Nilssen, Trond Risto 2019: South Saami Cultural Landscape Under Pressure. In: Hermanstrand, Håkon et al. (eds.): *The indigenous identity of the South Saami. Historical and political perspectives on a minority within a minority.* Cham: Springer, 171-186.
Otte, Pia, Katrina Rønningen & Espen Moe 2018: Contested Wind Energy: Discourses on Energy Impacts and their Significance for Energy Justice in Fosen. In: Szolucha, Anna (ed.): *Energy, resource extraction and aociety: Impacts and contested futures.* London: Routledge, 140-158.
Ravna, Øyvind 2013: The Legal Protection of the Rights and Culture of Indigenous Sámi People in Norway. *Journal of Siberian Federal University. Humanities & Social Sciences* 11 (6): 1575-1591.
Ryser, Sarah 2019: The Anti-Politics Machine of Green Energy Development: The Moroccan Solar Project in Ouarzazate and Its Impact on Gendered Local Communities. *Land* 8 (100): 1-21.
Sara, Mikkel Nils 2009: Siida and Traditional Sámi Reindeer Herding Knowledge. *The Northern Review* 30: 153-178.
Scott, James 1985: *Weapons of the weak: everyday forms of peasant resistance.* New Haven, CT: Yale University Press.
Sem, Leif 2019: Out of Print. A Historiography of the South Saami in Regional and National Works of History. In: Hermanstrand, Håkon et al. (eds.): *The indigenous identity of the South Saami. Historical and political perspectives on a minority within a minority.* Cham: Springer, 153-169.
Skarin, Anna et al. 2018: Out of Sight of Wind Turbines: Reindeer Response to Wind Farms in Operation. *Ecology and Evolution* 8: 9906–9919.

Internet and Media sources:

Åfjord kommune 2016: Pressemelding: Statkrafts beslutning om å investere i vindkraft på Fosen (press release, 23.6.16). ‹https://www.afjord.kommune.no/vindkraft/presse meldinger/›, accessed on 26.4.2020.
Adresseavisen 2019b: Det nye Trøndelag (22.11.2019). ‹https://www.adressa.no/pluss/m agasin/2019/11/24/Jeg-glemmer-aldri-da-jeg-fikk-meldingen-om-at-⟨⟨nå-kommer-de⟩⟩-20452114.ece›, accessed on 5.6.2020.
Adresseavisen 2019a: Portrettet: Kraftkaren (9.6.2019). ‹https://www.adressa.no/pluss/m agasin/2019/06/09/Kraftkaren-19183997.ece›, accessed on 9.2.2020.
Adresseavisen 2017: Fosen-samene tapte skjønnsrettssaken om Storheia-utbyggingen (16.08.2017). ‹https://www.adressa.no/nyheter/sortrondelag/2017/08/16/Fosen-sam ene-tapte-skj{o}nnsrettssaken-om-Storheia-utbyggingen-15163025.ece›, accessed on 12.12.2019.

Asplan Viak 2009: Konsekvensutredning: Naturmiljø Storheia Vindpark. ⟨http://we bfileservice.nve.no/API/PublishedFiles/Download/200700502/228373⟩, accessed on 12.8.2020.
Berner Zeitung 2020: BKW hat Klage von Menschenrechtslobby am Hals (16.1.2020). ⟨https://www.bernerzeitung.ch/region/bern/gesellschaft-fuer-bedrohte-voelker-reicht-beschwerde-gegen-bkw-ein/story/18304876⟩, accessed on 19.1.2020.
Coleman, Jonathan E. et al. 2008: Fagrapport reindrift. Konsekvenser av vindkraft- og kraftledningsprosjekter på Fosen. ⟨http://webfileservice.nve.no/API/PublishedFiles/Download/200700502/99537⟩, accessed on 7.12.2019.
County Governor of Trøndelag 2019: Vi må kjenne historien for å forstå nåtiden. ⟨https://fylkesmannen.maps.arcgis.com/apps/Cascade/index.html?appid=5b3d1e14970349d09a46b0735878c84e⟩, accessed on 26.6.2020.
Det kongelige Olje- og Energidepartement (OED) 2016: Fred Olsen Renewables AS – Kalvvatnan vindkraftverk i Bindal og Namsskogan kommuner – klagesak. ⟨https://www.regjeringen.no/contentassets/2cb371d9a0204b19a8a914ae830a62ee/vedtak-kalvvatnan.pdf⟩, accessed on 29.6.2020.
Det kongelige Olje- og Energidepartement (OED) 2013: Vindkraft og kraftledninger på Fosen – klagesak. ⟨https://www.regjeringen.no/globalassets/upload/oed/pdf_filer_2/fosen/vindkraft_og_kraftledninger_pa_fosen_klagesak.pdf⟩, accessed on 25.11.2020.
Fjellheim, Eva 2020a: Ærede Lagmannsrett. ⟨https://www.harvestmagazine.no/pan/aerede-lagmannsrett⟩, accessed on 16.6.2020.
Fosna-Folket 2016: En katastrofe for vår gruppe i Sør-Fosen (23.2.2016). ⟨https://www.fosna-folket.no/nyheter/2016/02/23/En-katastrofe-for-vår-gruppe-i-Sør-Fosen-12192776.ece⟩, accessed on 15.12.2019.
Frostating Lagmansrett 2020: Avhjemling av skjønn. Saksnr. 18-150314SKJ-FROS, 18-150323SKJ-FROS, 18-150327SKJ-FROS, 8.6.2020 (unpublished, provided by informant).
Nellemann, Christian 2017: Utbygging av vindkraft i Fovsen-Njaarke/Fosen reinbeitedistrikt: Konsekvenser for reindriften i Sørgruppen. ⟨https://naturvernforbundet.no/getfile.php/13132982-1523651608/Fylkeslag%20-%20Finnmark/Bilde/Utbygging%20av%20vindkraft%20p{aa}%20Fosen%20i%20Fovsen-Njaarkje%20reinbeitedistrikt%20low%20res.pdf⟩, accessed on 29.6.2020.
Norges Vassdrags- og energidirektorat (NVE) 2016: Anleggskonsesjon. ⟨http://webfileservice.nve.no/API/PublishedFiles/Download/200700502/1683406⟩, accessed on 29.6.2020.
NRK 2021: Vil se på muligheten for å kombinere turbiner med fortsatt reindrift (19.10.2021): https://www.nrk.no/trondelag/onsker-utrede-storheia-og-roan-pa-nytt__vil-prove-a-ivareta-samene-bedre-1.15695437?fbclid=IwAR0_9QNEAkpiD6PmlrvEok5kZbSGSShDfL-1fuzTuzS_H5GdGbXtU90eYT0, accessed on 15.11.2021.
NRK 2020: Reineierne anker vindkraftutbygging til Høyesterett (26.8.2020). ⟨https://www.nrk.no/trondelag/reineierne-anker-vindkraftutbygging-til-hoyesterett-1.15135798⟩, accessed on 26.8.2020.
NRK 2019: Levde i 23 år med frykten for å bli avslørt som same (4.5.2019). ⟨https://www.nrk.no/sapmi/xl/per-arnfinn-levde-med-frykten-for-a-bli-avslort-som-same-1.14481435⟩, accessed on 29.6.2020.
Supreme Court [Norges Høyesterett] 2021: Vedtak om konsesjon til vindkraftutbygging på Fosen kjent ugyldig fordi utbyggingen krenker reindriftssamenes rett til kultu-

rutøvelse: https://www.domstol.no/globalassets/upload/hret/avgjorelser/2021/oktober-2021/hr-2021-1975-s.pdf, accessed on 15.11.2021.

Society for Threatened Peoples 2018: Turbines need Saami consent! Norway: the construction of a wind power plant on the Saami winter pastures in Storheia. ‹https://www.gfbv.ch/wp-content/uploads/sami_fact-sheet_layouten-def.pdf›, accessed on 16.12.2019.

SRF 2018: Umstrittener Windpark: Schweizer Investition gefährdet Naturvolk (11.12.2018). ‹https://www.srf.ch/news/schweiz/windpark-in-norwegen-schweizer-investment-verdraengt-indigene›, accessed on 7.12.2019.

Statkraft 2015: Statkraft halts wind power planning in Central Norway (press release, 4.6.2015). ‹https://www.statkraft.com/newsroom/news-and-stories/archive/2015/statkraft-halts-wind-power-planning-in-central-norway/›, accessed on 16.12.2019.

Statkraft 2008: Storheia Vindpark. Konsesjonssøknad og forslag til reguleringsplan. ‹http://webfileservice.nve.no/API/PublishedFiles/Download/200700502/98594›, accessed on 7.6.2020.

Statkraft 2006: Fire vindparker på Fosen, melding og forslag til utredningsprogram. ‹http://webfileservice.nve.no/API/PublishedFiles/Download/200602660/1066986›, accessed on 7.12.2019.

The Kingdom of Norway 2018: Request for lifting of the interim measures (sent to Office of the United Nations High Commissioner for Human Rights, 21.12.2018 (unpublished, provided by informant).

TrønderEnergi 2016: Bygger Europas største vindkraftprosjekt i Midt-Norge (joint press release, 23.2.2016). ‹https://tronderenergi.no/media/pdf/2016-fosen-vind-2/fosen-vind/fosvinda-pressemelding-nor-20160223-final.pdf›, accessed on 20.2.2020.

Pipelines, Flows and Roots: Power Struggles Over the Trans Adriatic Pipeline in Southern Italy

Antonio Maria Pusceddu, Centro em Rede de Investigação em Antropologia, Iscte – Instituto Universitário de Lisboa, Portugal

Introduction

The Trans Adriatic Pipeline (TAP) is one of three pipelines – together with the South Caucasus Pipeline (SCP) and the Trans-Anatolian Natural Gas Pipeline (TANAP) – that make up the Southern Gas Corridor (SGC), a European Union (EU) initiative aimed at connecting the Azeri gas fields in the Caspian Sea to the European gas network (Map 1). The SGC is one of the nine priority corridors of the Trans-European Networks for Energy (TEN-E), the EU policy framework for linking infrastructures of member states. Listed among the Projects of Common Interest (PCIs), the TAP has received institutional and financial support from the EU. Starting from the Greek-Turkish border, the TAP runs through Greece, Albania, the Adriatic Sea and Italy for a total length of 878 km (Map 2). The TAP ends in the municipality of Melendugno, a small town in southern Italy, where the Pipeline Receiving Terminal (PRT) is located. A further 55 km pipeline connects the PRT to the national gas grid, running across the historical region known as Salento (Map 3). Only 3.7% of the whole TAP runs through Italian territory: 33 km, of which 8 onshore. The transnational pipeline was built by the Swiss-based company TAP AG, while the interconnector pipeline is being built by Snam, the Italian company that manages the national gas grid and holds a 20% stake in TAP AG.

This chapter examines the transnational energy infrastructure from the standpoint of its final destination in Italy, targeted by several pipeline projects aimed at making the peninsula the southern European gas hub. This goal was set in the 2013 National Energy Strategy, approved by the government chaired by Mario Monti, and consistently pursued by all the following governments. Besides the TAP, other pipeline projects would connect to the national gas grid on the outskirts of Brindisi, an industrial city along the Adriatic coast[1]. The position of the

---

[1] The other projects are: IGI-Poseidon, an interconnector pipeline that will connect to Turk-Stream, planned to transport natural gas from the Russian gas field across the Black Sea, and

city in the overall reorganization of energy infrastructure makes it a potentially significant national gas hub. At the end of the ancient Roman Appian Way, Brindisi is nowadays the final destination of the Southern Gas Corridor. The relocation of the Brindisi area within the transnational infrastructural gas network does not remain unquestioned, as it adds to a troubled history of heavy industrialization, marked by the noxious legacy of environmental degradation and the overwhelming influence of corporate powers.

Home to oil- and coal-based industries for chemical and energy production, Brindisi reveals the many contradictions and complexities of European energy politics, which aim to sustain the "decarbonization" of the economy, while supporting the long-term construction of new energy mega-infrastructures for fossil fuel transport (Ferguson 2020)[2]. Such politics remain strongly dependent on fossil fuel production, embedded in the wider networks of power and technology that unevenly connect finance, states and geographies. This chapter addresses the frictions that this paradigm generates in specific locations, unwillingly designated as local hubs within much larger and more complex transnational power infrastructures.

This chapter is a preliminary analysis of an ongoing research project about energy transition, popular ecologies and socio-economic restructuring in southern Europe. Prior to this project, I carried out fieldwork in Brindisi for 15 months between 2015 and 2016[3]. Further fieldwork was scheduled for 2020, but due to the Covid-19 pandemic it had to be postponed. This chapter draws also on policy documents, corporate materials and statements from social movements. Given the relevance of this case nationwide, online research could provide plenty of materials, including public debates, media coverage and reports from various stakeholders.

Energopolitics, energy transition and mega-infrastructures

The TAP project was announced in 2003, following the discovery of the Shah Deniz natural gas field in the Caspian Sea in 1999. At the time, the TAP was

---

to the Eastmed, designed to transport natural gas from Cyprus and Israeli gas fields; and Eagle LNG, which aims to connect an offshore regasification terminal in Albania (the construction of which is part of the project) to the Brindisi area (Clemente 2013).

[2] See also the Europe gas tracker map (Global Energy Monitor) available at: https://globalenergymonitor.org/projects/europe-gas-tracker/tracker-map/ (accessed 4 October 2021).

[3] The research was conducted in the framework of the project "Grassroots economics: Meaning, project and practice in the pursuit of livelihood" (GRECO), European Research Council Advanced Grant, IDEAS-ERC FP7, Project Number: 323743 (P.I. Susana Narotzky). The ongoing research is funded by the Fundação para a Ciência e a Tecnologia, reference contract: CEECIND/01894/2018/CP1533/CT0001, within the CRIA (Centro em Rede de Investigação em Antropologia) strategic program UIDB/04038/2020. This chapter draws from and expands the paper "Sovereignties and infrastructures in contention: Popular opposition to the Trans Adriatic Pipeline (TAP) in Southern Italy", presented at the *26th International Conference of Europeanists*, Council for European Studies, Madrid, 20–22 June 2019.

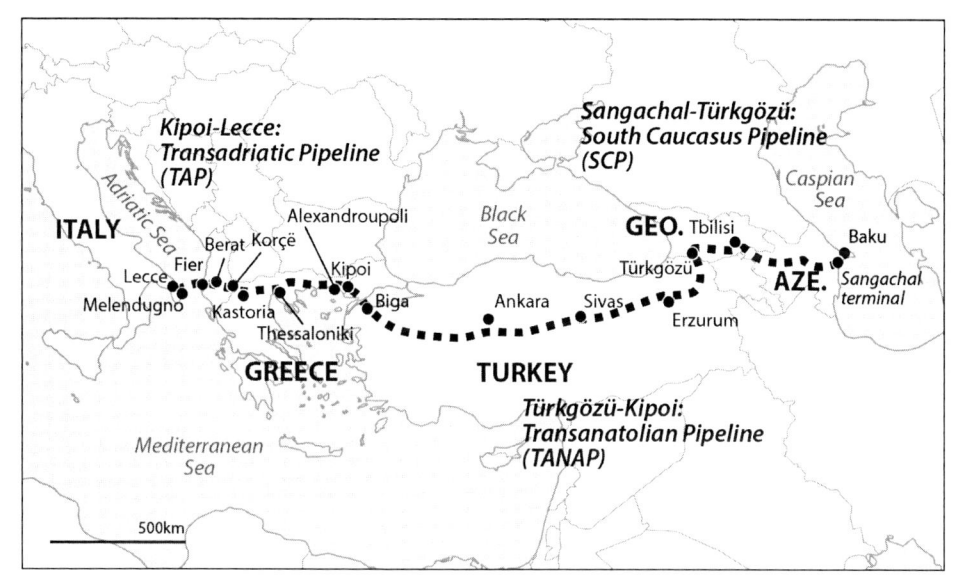

Map 1: The Southern Gas Corridor (SGC). Source: Map compilation and design by Manuel L. K. Abebe (2021), CDE, University of Bern, Bern, Switzerland. Geodata: MITE

one among other competing pipeline projects that met the EU policy demands to diversify and secure natural gas supplies through the creation of four main gas corridors. The EU policy also aimed to reduce energy dependency on Russia, especially after the 2006 crisis following the Russia-Ukraine gas dispute (Collier and Kemoklidze 2014; Kandiyoti 2015)[4]. This policy framework was shaped by the sensitive post-1989 geopolitics and the reshuffling of regional alliances and spheres of influence in the Caspian area (Kandiyoti 2015). The Shah Deniz gas field was discovered by a BP-led consortium. After the early 1990s, the post-Soviet Azerbaijan entered privileged relations with BP and US oil companies for the operation of the Baku oilfields, now connected to Europe through the oil road running across Azerbaijan, Georgia, Turkey (the Baku-Tbilisi-Ceyhan (BTC) pipeline) and the sea route from the Turkish harbour Ceyhan to the Italian harbour Trieste (Marriott and Minio-Paluello 2013).

EU energy security and high estimates of an increase in gas demand, in parallel with the decline of natural gas production in Europe, underlie the main arguments in support of the great expansion of pipeline infrastructures, along the lines of the well-established "infrastructural Europeanism" (Schipper and Schot 2011). However, two factors are today contributing to redesigning this scenario. First, gas demand overestimates; after the steady growth of the 1990s, gas con-

---

[4] In 2006, the dispute over gas payments between Russia and Ukraine interrupted the gas flow to EU countries. The more recent and ongoing war in Ukraine, started with the Russian invasion on February 2022, has dramatically intensified concerns over energy dependency and security in ways that may deeply change the energy geopolitics in Europe.

sumption reached its peak in 2010, only to decrease in 2014 to the lowest point since 1995 (Jones, Dufour and Gaventa 2015). Second, in 2019 the European Commission launched the broad policy framework European Green Deal, with the aim of reaching "climate neutrality" by 2050. This is expected to entail a further reduction in fossil fuel consumption, thus revising previous energy strategies to make them coherent with the climate goals. In light of this changing scenario, the critics of EU sustained expansion of fossil energy infrastructures argue that this runs the risk of supporting infrastructures that will not repay their cost, revealing – ultimately – that they are not built to meet actual energy demands, but serve the scope of corporate powers and financial capital reproduction (Flyvbjerg 2005; Re:Common 2014a).

The above observations suggest that the relationships between energy and infrastructure are undergoing potentially significant changes, which might (or might not) contribute to redesigning social relations and power structures, as well as the uneven geographies of the "fuel economy" (Mitchell 2013). Energy infrastructures do represent, in this respect, important sites for exploring these transformations, paying attention to frictions and struggles over contentious energy futures (Boyer 2017; Franquesa 2018). They also provide fruitful ground for the intersection of the anthropology of energy with anthropological engagements with infrastructures. While the latter are relatively recent (Dalakoglou and Harvey 2015; Harvey et al. 2017; Venkatesan et al. 2018), spanning over the last three decades (Ribeiro 1994), the anthropology of energy, which has also gained momentum in recent years, retrieved an old concern of the discipline (Boyer 2014; Love and Isenhour 2016; Smith and High 2017).

Larkin (2013: 328–329) provides a broad definition of infrastructures as "built networks that facilitate the flow of goods, people, or ideas and allow for their exchange over space", pointing out that the "peculiar ontology" of infrastructures "lies in the fact that they are things and also the relation between things". Drawing on this general relational framework, I look at the pipeline through three main interrogatives: first, "what" flows through it; second, "where" the pipeline flows, which places it connects; and third, "how" this flowing is made possible, not just through engineering and technology, but through agreements, consent, persuasion, authority, force and repression – in a word, through power and legitimacy. The "what" pertains to the peculiar resource-making process (Ferry and Limbert 2008; Franquesa 2019) that managed to replace fossil fuel (oil) with another fossil fuel (natural gas) as a socially accepted resource in the face of widespread climate concerns. The "where" refers to the different spatial scales of transnational infrastructures, from the geopolitical dimensions of energy politics to the territorial relations within single states. The "how" captures the complexities that make the pipeline construction possible, the "energopolitics" (Boyer 2014; 2019) of infrastructure that unfolds at different levels and has a critical point in the role of the state in regulating, facilitating, repressing and imposing all the necessary guarantees for pipeline construction – a role that is not devoid of effects on the ways authority and power converge with corporate interests and diverge from citizenship's claims, thus triggering controversial and contested "infrastructural imaginaries" (Dalakoglou and Kallianos 2018). The relational approach to infrastructure as the "relation between things" highlights the peculiar connectivity that shapes the multi-scalar relations around the pipeline and the relevance of power and finance in organizing the world around the energy infrastructure (Rogers 2012: 291), as well as the forms of its contestation. Situating the case in the debate on the enchantment of infrastructures (Harvey and Knox 2012), I focus on the reversal of development infrastructure into "disenchantment" as an effect of the socio-environmental contradiction generated by capital-intensive oil- and coal-based industrialization.

Finally, Boyer's observation that the scale and ubiquity of infrastructures suggest "a temporality of perdurance" (2014: 174) draws our attention to the relevance of the temporal existence of the pipeline and the social perception of the infrastructure in relation to imagined and desired energy futures. In the current changing scenario, the daunting perspective of the mega-infrastructures of the fossil economy as "stranded assets" has become an integral part of the critique that informs the discourse against gas infrastructures such as the TAP (Re:Common 2014b).

Part 1: Historical, environmental, ethnographic and political context

Terra d'Otranto

Conventionally represented as the "heel" of the boot-shaped Italian peninsula, Salento is the southern part of the Apulia (Puglia) administrative region. The Salento peninsula includes the province of Lecce and part of the provinces of Brindisi and Taranto. The latter were established in 1927, acknowledging the growing importance of the two port cities, fully integrated into the South-North railway network in the aftermath of the Italian political unification (1861). Until the 1920s, Salento was enclosed within the boundaries of a single administrative entity, named Terra d'Otranto, of which the historical capital was Lecce. Before the political unification of the peninsula, Terra d'Otranto was an administrative unit of the Kingdom of Naples and later of the Kingdom of the Two Sicilies. Therefore, with the gradual redefinition of regional boundaries in the newly created Italian state, Salento survived as a culturally recognizable entity within the emergent administrative structure of Apulia, built upon the backbone of communication and industrial infrastructures.

The history of Terra d'Otranto was marked by its strategic position within the communication networks of ancient Roman domination and the Eastern Roman Empire. Later on, it became a frontier region of the European periphery, intimately connected to the Ottoman lands overseas. The Eastward-looking orientation of Terra d'Otranto, again, made it a suitable destination for the TAP. To a certain extent, the current energy infrastructure effervescence along the SGC adds to a longer history of infrastructure building, related to movement, trade and power. In the case of Turkey, evoking the ancient Silk Road appealed to the past glories of the Anatolian trade hub along East-West networks (Firat 2016: 85). Likewise, though on a different scale, the Belt and Road Initiative is a massive investment in infrastructure development, which incorporates the ancient Silk Road imaginary into the contemporary Chinese global development strategy. The SGC runs along this ancient artery, while the TAP follows the ancient path of the Roman Via Egnatia, from Dyrrachium (nowadays Dürres, Albania) to Byzantium. It was from Brundisium (Brindisi), at the end of the Roman Appian Way, that ships sailed to Dyrrachium. This fundamental artery of the Roman Empire provided the crucial integration into the wider trade routes from/to Asia, across the Anatolian cities of Sebaste (Ankara) and Theodosiopolis (Erzurum). This latter ancient trade post is now a gas hub in the pipeline networks along the SGC, part of the TANAP (Firat 2016) and BTC pipeline.

The route fell into decay with the gradual shifting of the main trade routes towards the Atlantic. Brindisi and its inland suffered decline most notably exemplified by the obstruction of its port in the 15th century, which was recovered only in the mid-19th century. The Italian political unification created the condition for the integration of the region into the broader commercial infrastructure of the peninsula, together with the Suez Canal construction (1869) that opened new prospects for Adriatic ports. For nearly four decades Brindisi was the intermodal connection of the London-Bombay route. Further developments followed shortly, with the creation of a seaplane base and the operation of the first Italian international flight Brindisi-Athens-Istanbul. The renovated Eastern projection of the area had been in the making since the late decades of the 19th century, seen as a fundamental stepping stone for Italian imperialist aspirations in the Eastern Mediterranean. This was further enhanced by the Fascist regime, which devoted particular attention to recovering the Imperial legacy of ancient Rome in Brindisi, claiming continuities between past and future glories.

Infrastructural regionalism

Salento holds a distinctive regional identity, not least conveyed through local languages, which include *griko* – a Greek dialect. In 1948, Salento became part of a new administrative entity, Apulia, created with the new Republican constitution, but made effective only in 1970, with the implementation of regional institutions. Until then, the plural form *le Puglie* was commonly used to refer to what was the sum of three different historical regions: Capitanata, Terra di Bari and Terra d'Otranto. These regions underwent a gradual process of regional integration, in which a relevant role was played by infrastructures. The "infrastructural regionalism" (Glass et al. 2019) started with the construction of the railway connecting Bari, Brindisi and Taranto, and culminated in the state-sponsored industrialization process in the late 1950s and 1960s, through the creation of the industrial triangle Bari-Brindisi-Taranto (Pasimeni 2003; Pirro 1983). This was the outcome of a longer historical process aimed at creating the basis for a new regional organization, which entailed the disruption of older territorial hierarchies (Masella 1989). In the case of Salento, the ancient capital Lecce, the centre of land gentry, was gradually marginalized, as it was the southern part of the peninsula, which relied on emigration and the poorly competitive agriculture, mostly based on olive groves, vineyards and tobacco. The subordinate position of this area was also exemplified by the development of labour-intensive sectors (e.g. garments, shoe factories) as subcontractors of northern Italian firms.

The industrial triangle was organized around the idea of the growth pole strategy, which aimed to trigger the socio-economic transformation of southern regions by localizing industrial complexes in strategic areas. Brindisi and Taranto were targeted by major investments for the construction of the largest Italian petrochemical plant (Brindisi) and the fourth national steel complex (Taranto). The industrialization programme was part of the broader state initiative to "modernize" southern regions, enhancing their integration in the industrial capitalist structure of the country. The 'extraordinary intervention' for the development of the South started in the early 1950s in response to post-war social unrest, initially with the agrarian reform and infrastructure projects, and continued in the 1960s with the direct industrialization programme (Ginsborg 1990; Graziani 1998; Pirro 1983).

Italian economist Augusto Graziani stressed how structural unemployment – "the ancient problem of the Italian economy" (Graziani 1998: 10) – and its potentially disruptive social consequences played a central role in shaping the national political economy. In southern Italy, thus, state-sponsored industrialization was mainly conceived as a coping strategy for mass unemployment. Therefore, the preservation of jobs represented a major issue in the face of deindustrialization, especially in the aftermath of the 1970s oil crisis. In Brindisi, restructuring and downsizing of the petrochemical industry were facilitated by the explosion of the core plant in December 1977, in which three workers died. In the early 1980s, more than 2000 workers were laid off, while the downsizing and restructuring of production lines, through labour-saving technologies, severely reduced job prospects in the sector. To tackle the situation, the central government proposed the localization of two new power plants in the area, as part of the National Energy Plan (1981), a coal-fired power station on the rural outskirts of Brindisi and a nuclear power plant in the province. Only the former was eventually constructed and operated in the early 1990s, while the nuclear power plant was halted by the 1987 national referendum that put an end to the national nuclear energy programme. The choice of Brindisi was also deliberately made on the basis that local populations would have been willing to accept the plant because of the jobs it could bring (Ravenda 2018). The plant construction was carefully planned to mobilize local firms and provide jobs to local workers. However, once the labour-intensive construction phase ended in the early 1990s, unemployment rose again[5].

The power plant marked the shift of the Brindisi industrial economy towards the energy sector. The contentious construction of the power station was followed, in the next decade, by a new industrial project. In 2002, a subsidiary of British Gas (Brindisi LNG Ltd) obtained authorization for the construction of a regasification terminal in the port of Brindisi. The project was opposed by the mobilization of civic and environmental associations, supported by the local government. Interrupted by a corruption scandal in 2007, the project was eventually abandoned in 2012. The making of Brindisi as a gas hub had been drafted for more than a decade in several pipeline projects. However, it was not until the national electricity company Enel announced, in 2017, the power plant conversion to gas that the gas hub project was identified in the local arena. Consequently, environmentalist struggles against coal burning emissions started to shift towards the gas pipelines.

The rural background

The contestation of the LNG terminal project made more explicit the LULU framework (locally unwanted land uses) that later extended to the contestation of the gas pipeline (Della Porta et al. 2019). To a certain extent, the conflict around land uses covered a longer time frame starting from farmers' opposition to the construction of the coal-fuelled power plant in the 1980s. The decision to build the power plant in the agricultural areas south of the city was opposed by the farmers, who reacted to the loss (via expropriation) of an extended area of arable land and to the risk of devaluation of the surrounding cultivated land (mostly orchards and vineyards) once the plant started operating. By then, farmers were not only concerned about the power plant but also about a 12 km uncovered conveyor belt built to transport coal from the docks to the energy facility. Frictions between farmers and the electricity company never eased. The conflict escalated with a lawsuit in 2012 against company executives and technicians for the soiling of crops along the conveyor belt (Ravenda 2018: 101–146). The conflict that later erupted around the gas pipeline entailed similar motivations for fear that it would endanger the rural and cultural landscape along the southern coastline. As a matter of fact, attempts to shift the pipeline to the Brindisi industrial area, as proposed by the regional governor and mayors of the province of Lecce, rested

---

[5] According to the national census, in 1991 unemployment rates reached 30.1% in the province of Brindisi and 32.6% in the province of Lecce, with employment rates at, respectively, 35.4% and 33.6%. According to the 2011 national census, employment rates in both provinces (38.2% and 36.6%, respectively) were still lower than the national rate (45%). Source: ISTAT.

on the assumption that Brindisi was "already damaged territory" (Pusceddu 2020: 850), hence preserving the wider area from exposure to new industrial projects.

The overall pipeline infrastructure, running along the Adriatic coast from the TAP PRT in Melendugno to the Snam station on the outskirts of Brindisi, involves several municipalities in the provinces of Lecce (Melendugno, Vernole, Castri di Lecce, Lizzanello, Cavallino, Lecce and Surbo) and Brindisi (Brindisi, San Pietro Vernotico and Torchiarolo)[6], with a total population of around 250,000 inhabitants (Map 3). This coastal region can be described as a rural-urban continuum, from the industrialized pole of the Brindisi area to the more service- and rural-oriented economies of Lower Salento, characterized by the thick network of towns, villages and hamlets that sprawl around the densely urbanized area of Lecce. Along this continuum, capital-intensive industries coexist with small family farms and the tourist economy along the coast, which has started to boom over the last few decades. The prominent feature of the landscape is the pervasive presence of olive trees, which accounts for around 66% of cultivated land (see Table 1). In some municipalities, olive trees occupy up to 82% of all cultivated land (Melendugno). With the exception of Brindisi, more than 90% of farms in the area are involved in olive oil production. Olive trees are also widely distributed on the highly fragmented model of agriculture and land ownership, largely consisting of small family farms that cultivate privately owned land (see Table 2).

The marking presence of olive groves defines a meaningful feature of the ways in which the local landscape is socially and culturally constructed and experienced. In Salento, as early as the 15th century, olive oil production held a central place in the local economy, especially as an export product for the cotton and wool industry, and it has increased since then. Despite the pervasive presence of olive groves, the economy revolving around olive oil production has remained mostly artisanal, with few highly industrialized productions. This is also due to the fact that small-scale olive groves have supplemented the basis of diversified household economies. Even the ownership of a few olive trees, fundamental for supplementing the family income and self-provisioning, can explain the kind of affective link to the land that they provide. In addition, olive trees materialize ideas of rootedness and legacy, conjured up by the idea of "the land" (*la terra*), made powerfully present by the analogies of inheritance (of trees) and heritage, which resume the mutual entanglement of livelihood and culture.

---

[6] See map available at: http://sinva.minambiente.it/mapviewer/index.html?collection=http://sinva.minambiente.it/WMC/Collection/VA/6AE73AA4-E412-43C2-9E57-98C30CDA3664&l=en (accessed 4 October 2021).

Table 1: Cultivated land and olive trees

	Cultivated land (hectares)	Olive trees (%)	Farms with olive trees (%)
Melendugno	6003.65	82.00	98.11
Vernole	3488.05	75.00	97.51
Cavallino	1103.59	53.91	90.32
Lizzanello	1439.71	68.35	95.66
Lecce	10616.63	52.00	91.71
Surbo	1199.65	64.21	93.85
Castri di Lecce	858.23	86.12	99.00
Torchiarolo	1774.93	76.16	96.55
San Pietro Vernotico	2795.94	41.96	91.29
Brindisi	18162.82	20.11	58.66

Source: ISTAT 2010 (elaboration of the author).

Table 2: Population and family farms

	Population*	Family farms (%)	Cultivating own land (%)	Farms with less than 5 ha (%) <1	<2	<5
Melendugno	9932	98.79	79.00	45.23	72.77	91.58
Vernole	6941	98.26	86.93	39.28	64.68	87.51
Cavallino	12586	91.39	87.36	40.32	69.08	88.97
Lizzanello	11686	96.79	90.37	96.79	71.13	90.37
Lecce	93865	96.48	84.24	96.48	58.68	84.01
Surbo	14597	97.08	85.76	97.08	60.60	86.08
Castri di Lecce	2805	96.71	85.91	96.71	51.50	96.53
Torchiarolo	5258	96.98	79.11	96.98	66.57	89.23
San Pietro Vernotico	13295	96.39	80.18	96.39	62.01	84.68
Brindisi	84465	94.57	85.12	94.57	43.68	75.53

Source: ISTAT 2010 (elaboration of the author).
* Population recorded at the end of 2019. Source: ISTAT

A southern European gas hub?

Italy is the third biggest gas consumer in Europe, after Germany and the UK. These three countries consume more than half of the total European gas demand (Jones, Dufour, Gaventa 2015). Italy has also been a gas producer, with appreciable gas fields in the Po valley – where the first Italian extractive industry developed – and in the southern region of Basilicata. However, nowadays almost all the gas consumed is imported (80%), mostly from Algeria and Russia (60%), but also from Libya, Norway and the Netherlands. For the most part, gas is transported via pipelines, which play a fundamental role in guaranteeing gas provisions but are also becoming highly relevant in influencing energy politics in Europe, as was oil in the aftermath of WWII (Mitchell 2013).

Following the 1973 oil crisis, Italy drafted its first National Energy Plan (PEN – Piano Energetico Nazionale; 1975), intending to gradually replace oil among its energy sources. This plan and others that followed foresaw the expansion of the national nuclear energy programme as the main scenario for the future. In 1987, however, following the Chernobyl nuclear disaster (1986) and the successful campaigning of anti-nuclear movements, a national referendum halted the nuclear energy programme, banning energy production from this source. In 2008, the government, led by Silvio Berlusconi, tried to relaunch the national nuclear energy programme. This attempt was halted by a new referendum in June 2011, which took place a few months after the Fukushima nuclear disaster. Consequently, the government that followed oriented energy politics towards the increase of hydrocarbon explorations and the expansion of gas import infrastructures.

A more focused strategy on gas infrastructure was outlined in the 2013 National Energy Strategy (SEN – Strategia Energetica Nazionale). The SEN 2013 was aimed at tackling the depressive effect of the 2007–08 economic and financial crisis, by foreseeing a central role of the peninsula as a continental entry point for natural gas supplies. The southern European gas hub was one of the seven priorities of the SEN 2013, which had to be attained through full integration into the European grid and market and through the support of new strategic infrastructures that would make the country a fundamental high-added-value service provider and natural gas exporter (Ministero dello Sviluppo Economico 2013: 52–70). This was based on the growth estimate of natural gas demands in Europe, as well as on the EU strategy aiming at diversifying gas supplies, making Italy a potential strategic transit point from North Africa (Algeria and Libya), the Caucasus and the Middle East.

Although the TAP was not mentioned in the SEN 2013, in the same year Italy, Albania and Greece signed the intergovernmental agreement on the TAP. Two years later (20 May 2015), the Minister of Economic Development signed the Decree of Environmental Compatibility and the Single Authorization (a unified permit that includes various permits and authorizations covering all the aspects of the construction and any other consent), thus licensing the beginning of the construction works in May 2016. The SEN 2017, approved by the government led by Filippo Gentiloni, pointed to the TAP as a strategic project, along with the two interconnected pipeline projects IGI Poseidon and Eastmed (Ministero dello Sviluppo Economico and Ministero dell'Ambiente e della Tutela del Territorio e del Mare 2017). The SEN 2017 also reveals the open possibilities that oriented the government strategy. The imperative of diversifying gas supplies, which was less a matter of avoiding Russia than limiting dependence from the northern German gas hub (in fact, supplied by Russia), led the government to pursue IGI Poseidon (Italian-Greece Interconnector), to reach the TurkStream pipeline that will supply gas directly from Russia, across the Black Sea. In early 2020, the government chaired by Giuseppe Conte approved a new document (Ministero dello Sviluppo Economico at al. 2019), which does not substantially alter the previous gas strategy, considered necessary to sustain the coal phase-out, in combination with the increase of renewable energy productions. Although less explicit about the project of making Italy a southern European gas hub (which is not mentioned at all), this latest policy document does not question the TAP's strategic relevance, hence prolonging the conflict between regional and local authorities opposing the project, and the central national governments.

Despite the high level of administrative decentralization in Italy, which started in the 1990s with the transfer of competencies in various fields to regional institutions, strategic energy issues have firmly remained the central state's prerogative, while regional governments are asked to prove their advisory opinion. The TAP is a telling example of the institutional frictions that energy infrastructures generate (Navach 2016). In 2012, the Apulia regional government issued a first negative opinion on the Environmental Impact Assessment Study, which TAP AG had just submitted to the Ministry of Environment. Early in 2014, the regional government issued a second (and final) negative opinion, at the end of a participatory round of discussions between municipal institutions, local populations, technical experts and company representatives. Notwithstanding the negative opinion of local institutions and populations[7], in September 2014 the Ministry of Environment approved the Environmental Impact Assessment (Valutazione di Impatto Ambientale).

Part 2: The Mega-Infrastructure Project

The Southern Gas Corridor

The SGC is one of the nine priority energy corridors identified by the TEN-E, and one of the four gas corridors[8]. The overall aim of the SGC initiative is to secure natural gas supplies from Caspian and Middle Eastern sources. The changing geopolitics in the post-1989 Caucasus, with the fast penetration of Western cor-

---

[7] In 2013, Melendugno town council submitted a counter-report to the Ministry of Environment, expressing a negative assessment of the project. The counter-report was prepared by an interdisciplinary group of experts (Borri and Petrarchi 2013).
[8] The other three are the North-South Interconnection in Western Europe (NSI West Gas), the North-South Interconnection in Central-Eastern and South-Eastern Europe (NSI East Gas), and the Baltic Energy Market Interconnection Plan (BEMIP).

porate powers, can be seen as crucial in setting the premises for the SGC. The Shah Deniz gas field was discovered in 1999 after an agreement on exploration, development and production between the Azeri company Socar and BP. The latter played a significant role in the post-Soviet geopolitical reconfiguration of the area, bringing the Caucasian states into the Western sphere of influence, hence curbing Russian control over the region (Marriott and Minio-Paluello 2013). Historically, the Caspian region has been an area of friction and competition between rival powers such as the Ottoman Empire and Tsarist Russia. Since the late 19th century, the importance of Caspian oilfields has attracted the oil companies of the Nobel brothers and the Rothschilds. British interests in the area were closely related to the strategic relevance of the Caspian oilfields, the "world's most prolific oil region at the start of the [20th] century" (Mitchell 2013: 47), as the great empires started to collapse during and following WWI. Western interests were curtailed by the rise of the Soviet Union as the new regional power. When Azerbaijan and Georgia (ruled by long-standing figures of the Soviet power elite – Heydar Aliyev and Eduard Shevardnadze, respectively) declared independence in 1991, they sought to establish connection with Western powers, on the grounds of their fossil resources potential. This quickly translated into agreements with BP and US corporations for the construction and operation of oil rigs and pipelines.

This is the main framework that opened up the way to natural gas exploration and the subsequent materialization of the SGC pipeline network, along the track of the BTC oil pipeline. The Sangachal Terminal, on the shore of the Caspian Sea, where the gas extracted is pumped into the pipeline, is a telling example of the entanglements of geopolitics, finance and resource politics in the area. The oil and gas processing industrial complex was constructed in 1996–97 as a receiving terminal of the Azeri-Chirag-Guneshili oilfield and, later, of the Shah Deniz gas field. Operated by a BP-led consortium, it plays a crucial role in the geopolitics of the area, being the starting point of both oil and gas corridors supplying Europe (Barry 2013; Marriott and Minio-Paluello 2013). Three pipelines provide the transnational connection of the Caspian gas field to Europe: the SCP (692 km) connects the Sangachal Terminal to the Turkish border station of Türkgözü, via Tbilisi; the TANAP (1,841 km) runs from Türgozü across the Anatolian peninsula to the Greek-Turkish border. In the Greek border town of Kipoi is located the compressor station that connects the TANAP to the TAP (Map 1).

Trans Adriatic Pipeline

The Greek section of the TAP is the longest (550 km), running from Thrace across the Greek-Macedonian regions to the mountains of the Kastoria area. In southeastern Albania, where the metering station is located, the pipeline route continues across the mountains to the coastal plains north of Fier, where a compressor station is located 400 m inland from the sea. The Albanian section of the pipeline is 215 km in length plus 37 km offshore in the Adriatic Sea. The total length of the offshore pipeline across the Adriatic Sea is 105 km (Map 2).

Map 2: The Trans Adriatic Pipeline (TAP). Source: Map compilation and design by Manuel L. K. Abebe (2021), CDE, University of Bern, Bern, Switzerland. Geodata: MITE

The Italian section is the shortest: 25 km offshore plus 8 km onshore. The offshore pipeline is connected to the final onshore section through a micro-tunnel (1,500 metres, at a depth of 25 m), which starts 800 metres offshore and ends 700 metres onshore. The connection is made near the coastal village of San Foca; from there the pipeline runs 1.5 metres underground to the PRT in Melendugno, where the TAP officially ends. The PRT is connected to the Italian gas grid through a new 55 km interconnector pipeline to the Snam station located in Contrada Matagiola, on the outskirts of Brindisi[9] (Map 3). The interconnector pipeline is not the only infrastructure under construction that connects to the TAP. The Rete Adriatica (Adriatic Network) pipeline is being built by Snam. Initially planned as a pipeline all along the Adriatic coastline, its route was later changed to pass across the mountain areas of central Italy, infamously known for their seismic activity. Starting from Brindisi, this new pipeline will connect to the compressor station near Sulmona, then to the storage site in Minerbio, near Bologna, and from here to the main storage sites in Lombardy, which will serve as the hub for natural gas export to the rest of continental Europe.

The TAP project was launched in 2003 by the Swiss energy utility EGL (Elektrizitäts-Gesellschaft Laufenburg; then acquired by Axpo, with which it merged in 2012). In March 2007, TAP AG was officially registered as a company, based in the Swiss town of Baar. In the next two years, a joint venture was formed with the Norwegian oil company Stateoil (Equinor since 2018) and the German E.On. In 2012, the Shah Deniz Consortium chose the TAP project as a priority route to Italy, and later, in June 2013, the consortium chose the TAP

---

[9] See: https://va.minambiente.it/en-GB/Oggetti/Info/1579 (accessed 4 October 2021).

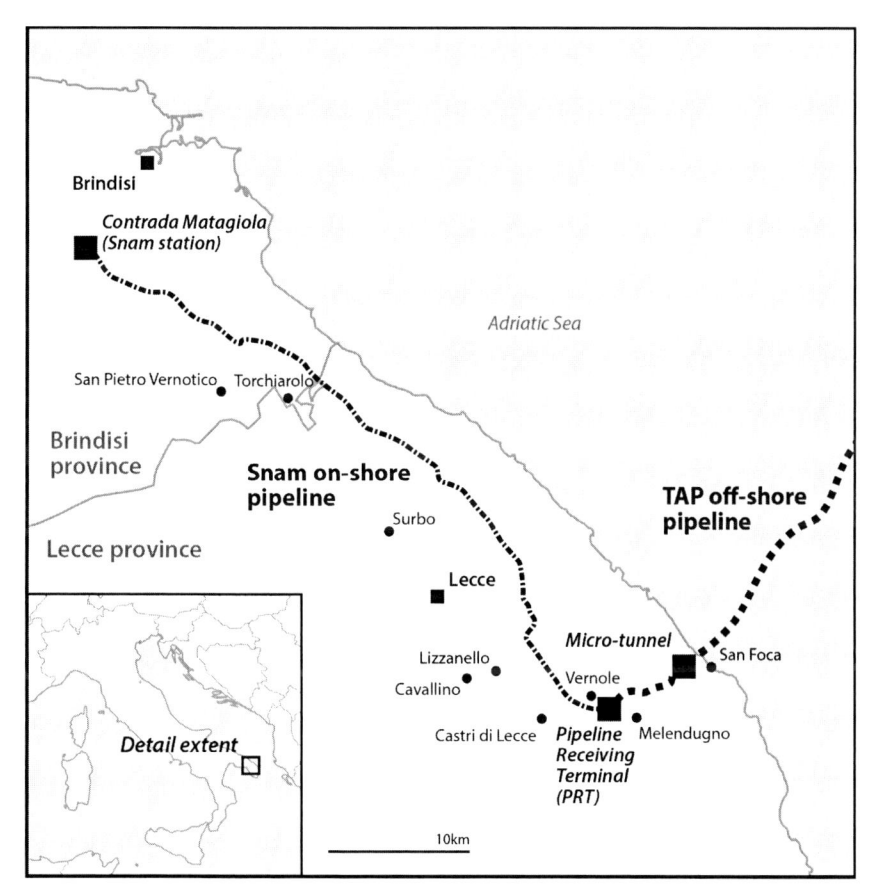

Map 3: TAP terminal near Melendugno and pipeline Interconnector (PRT-Snam station). Source: Map compilation and design by Manuel L. K. Abebe (2021), CDE, University of Bern, Bern, Switzerland. Geodata: MITE

as the preferred pipeline project from the Caspian to Europe, hence excluding the main competitor Nabuco. This step contributed to reshaping the shareholding structure of TAP AG. Following up a previous agreement, the Shah Deniz Consortium partners BP, Socar and Total took up equity stakes in TAP AG. Finally, in 2015, Stateoil sold its shares to the Italian Snam, giving to the company its current shareholding profile: BP (20%), Socar (20%), Snam (20%), Fluxys (19%), Enagas (16%) and Axpo (5%). The overall financing of the project (2017) was estimated at 4.5 billion euro, of which 1.5 billion were contributed by the European Investment Bank and 500 million by the European Bank for Reconstruction and Development[10].

---

[10] In 2019, TAP AG published the list of commercial banks that finance the project (Gerebizza 2019): Bank of China Limited; BNP Paribas; CaixaBank, S.A.; Crédit Agricole Corporate and Investment Bank; Landesbank Hessen-Thüringen Girozentrale; ING Bank, a branch of ING-

Construction works officially started in May 2016, with the inauguration ceremony held in Thessaloniki, Greece. In Albania, where infrastructure works had already been set to get underway in July 2015 in order to improve the road network to the construction sites, the inauguration ceremony was held in Fier, in September 2016. No such ceremony took place in Italy, where the construction site was hastily set up in May 2016, to keep up with the official deadlines and authorizations. However, actual works did not start until March 2017, with the uprooting and transfer of 211 olive trees along the pipeline route. Works did not proceed smoothly, as protesters hampered the transfer of olive trees with road blockades and surrounding the fenced areas. This was eventually made possible only by the intervention of police riot squads and the militarization of the area. In November 2017, the prefect of Lecce, in compliance with the government's order, set up a temporary Red Zone (a strictly forbidden area), where the uprooting and transfer of olive trees could take place under the protection of police forces.

In February 2018, TAP AG announced that two-thirds of the pipeline construction had been completed. The announcement came after months of protests in Salento and after several years of repeated administrative actions by the Melendugno town council, which slowed down the construction process, along with the intervention of the judiciary over alleged irregularities in the construction works. In 2012, the attorney of Lecce inquired about the impact of the offshore prospecting operations on the seabed. Earlier on, the Comitato No TAP filed a lawsuit for damages to fishers' nets. In May 2014, the Melendugno town council issued an order to suspend explorative drillings, due to the lack of the necessary authorizations. Invariably, these repeated administrative actions were superseded by superior governmental decisions. A few days after the suspension order was issued by the Melendugno town council, the Ministry of Economic Development signed the Single Authorization. During the same month, the regional government of Apulia lodged a complaint to the Constitutional Court, arguing that the national government had superseded the competences of regional authorities. In all these cases that marked the troubled beginning of the construction phase, the complaints lodged by the municipal and regional authorities were rejected. One of the contentious issues that was raised twice by local town councils regarded the fact that the TAP had not being subjected to Seveso Directive III (which sets the security standards for industrial plants and facilities)[11]. Eventually, the complaint

---

DiBa AG; Intesa Sanpaolo S.p.A.; Mizuho Bank, Ltd; MUFG Bank, Ltd; Natixis, London Branch; Siemens Bank GmbH; Société Générale; Standard Chartered Bank; Sumitomo Mitsui Banking Corporation; The Korea Development Bank; UBI Banca S.p.A; UniCredit Bank AG.

[11] The first Seveso Directive (1982) on industrial hazards was issued by the (then) European Economic Community and named after the Seveso disaster. In July 1976, a chemical manufacturing plant near Seveso (northern Italy) released tons of noxious chemical substances into the air over a large area. In Italy, Seveso III (Directive 2012/18/EU) was absorbed by Legislative Decree

was rejected since Seveso Directive III does not apply to transportation infrastructures, while the gas exhalation of the RTP facility is expected to remain below the law limits.

In January 2020, the last section of the offshore pipeline across the Adriatic Sea started to be placed off the Italian coast. In the meantime, the protests against the pipeline did not cease, extending to the Snam interconnection pipeline between Melendugno and Brindisi. Once more, the uprooting of olive trees along the pipeline route triggered the mobilization of farmers, ordinary citizens and environmental activists. Moreover, along the same route is located the Enel coal-fired power plant, which will be converted to natural gas by 2025 – an undesired conversion for local environmental activists, who demand complete plant dismantling and large-scale investments in renewable energy projects. The conflict around coal, which animated a decade of intense environmental conflict in the region, now shifted to natural gas and its transport infrastructure.

Contestation and corporate social technologies

The Italian section of the TAP appeared rather problematic, as it was planned in a densely populated area, characterized by a thick historical thread of towns and villages in the province of Lecce and by the industrial area of Brindisi. Consequently, until the final project submitted obtained the positive Environmental Impact Assessment in 2014, the pipeline route underwent various changes. At first, four options in the Brindisi area were taken into consideration. At the very beginning, the pipeline was supposed to land in the coastline platform initially created for the Brindisi LNG terminal, but the tense political climate around this project made TAP AG desist from going ahead. The other options were discarded after technical and environmental assessments. Southward, the pipeline would have affected the *posidonia oceanica* (a seagrass endemic in the Mediterranean Sea), which is a threatened species under special conservation status. The option to lay the pipeline along the industrial area raised safety issues concerning the high industrial risk of petrochemical plants. Finally, northward, the pipeline connection was at odds with the municipal urban development plans and with the presence of the airport (Romano and Zitelli 2017).

In May 2011, TAP AG announced that the pipeline was to be located in the province of Lecce. However, before reaching a final agreement with national authorities, three different projects were submitted in 2012 and 2013. One was rejected by the Ministry of Cultural Heritage, because of the proximity of the PRT to an archaeological site. Eventually, the pipeline project was entirely located in the municipality of Melendugno, including the PRT on a 12-hectare surface area a few kilometres from the town. According to the project, around 1,900 olive trees had to be temporarily uprooted along the pipeline route, to be later replanted, ex-

---

N°105 on 26 June 2015.

cept for a 14-metre-wide stretch of land above the pipeline track. The Ministry of Environment considered this option "the best alternative under every technical, environmental and landscape respect" (Ministero dell'Ambiente 2014).

Contestation around the TAP started as early as 2012. On 16th February, TAP AG organized a public presentation of the project in Melendugno, with the aim of easing the doubts and concerns of the local population. However, instead of earning the population's consent, the pipeline project sparked even more concern. The Melendugno town council issued a resolution that denied any concession and authorization to the TAP, on the basis that the pipeline could harm the "natural resources" – the sea, the landscape, etc. – upon which the local tourist economy was being organized[12]. In April 2012, the Comitato No TAP was officially founded. Earlier, in 2011, as soon as the pipeline project started to be discussed in relation to the Salento coastline, environmental activists, farmers, fishers and other citizens started meeting and inquiring about the project. Later, in 2017, the transfer of 211 olive trees was met by the intense mobilization that led to the birth of the No TAP Movement, which included, besides the Comitato, a broad and heterogeneous network of activists, citizens and spontaneous groups (see Movimento No TAP n.d.; Imperatore 2019). When the uprooting of the trees started, the protesters began undertaking more concrete actions "in place" in order to prevent the operations, which eventually led to the full militarization of the area, clashes with the police and detentions (Papadia 2018; Spagnolo 2017)[13].

In Italy, the TAP, presented as a way to tackle the consequences of the 2008 economic and financial crisis, was the subject of heated debates, making the gas pipeline one of the highly contested mega-infrastructures (*grandi opere*). LULU movements have acquired increasing visibility against "the growth machine" fuelled by public spending cuts and growing territorial competition for the attraction of private investments pursued by the political and entrepreneurial elites (Della Porta et al., 2019: 480–481). The Movimento No TAP considered the pipeline infrastructure damaging (*dannoso*), useless (*inutile*), without benefits and an imposition (*imposto*) on local communities[14]. On top of this, the pipeline construction adds to environmental conflicts in Salento, related to the long-lasting exposure of

---

[12] The resolution was issued on 29 February 2012. Available at: https://www.comune.melendugno.le.it/media/k2/attachments/8908_5_2012_CC.pdf. (accessed 4 October 2021). Another three town councils (Vernole, Castrì and Caprarica) issued similar resolutions in 2012. Shortly after, TAP AG lodged an appeal to the administrative court, which decided in favour of the company. Later, in 2017, 94 mayors of the Salento area (out of 97) underwrote a document against the TAP, appealing directly to the President of the Republic Sergio Mattarella.

[13] The actions continued in the following months, eventually leading to a large investigation, led by the Public Prosecutor of Lecce, against 46 activists in June 2019.

[14] These three points are summed up a flyer available at: https://www.notap.it/wp-content/uploads/2018/07/3-ragioni-no-tap-per-simone.pdf (accessed 4 October 2021). For a broader illustration of the protest see Movimento No TAP n.d.

local populations to air pollution and soil contamination from heavy industries in Brindisi, Taranto and Galatina[15].

In early June 2015, environmental activists from Salento staged a demonstration during the opening ceremony of the Trans-Adriatic Regatta Brindisi-Corfu in Brindisi. The ceremony took place in the most symbolic place in town: at the footsteps of the surviving Roman column that marked the end of the ancient Appian Way, overlooking the historical harbour from the top of a monumental staircase. The activists contested the Regatta sponsorship by TAP AG and Enel with the slogan "No dirty sponsors". The local leading group, No al Carbone (No to coal), made its name by staging protests against the Enel power station from 2009, following a long-standing environmentalist tradition that opposed the construction of the power plant in the 1980s (Ravenda 2018). The No al Carbone group denounced the sponsorship of the Regatta as greenwashing over the fossil fuels' damaging effects. Other movements staged demonstrations, including the Comitato No TAP and movements from Taranto.

The episode of the Regatta provides a good illustration of the conflict over corporate attempts to mobilize symbols and meanings to create consent around them. Enel and TAP AG's sponsorship of the Regatta resembles what Douglas Rogers called the "corporate social technologies" (CSTs), which captures "the full range of corporations' direct and planned efforts to shape social and cultural life" (Rogers 2012: 294). The CSTs provide an example of the "mechanisms by which oil and gas participate in the reshaping of political, social and cultural orders" (Rogers 2012: 284). Enel had built its own consensus in the city by sponsoring numerous activities, mostly in sports – from the basketball team playing in the top league to the smallest amateur team. While the sponsoring of the Regatta was nothing but one among many other actions of cultural politics in the city, it also conveyed the idea of Enel's commitment to "clean" energy (the wind). For TAP AG it was a good opportunity to link its name not only to the idea of clean energy but also to that of "connectivity", which lays at the core of the Regatta connecting the Italian and Greek shores of the Adriatic Sea. By entering the sponsorship, TAP AG was trying to play with the positive meanings of the Regatta by building resemblances with the "trans-Adriatic" connectivity of the pipeline.

The composition of the movements protesting against the "dirty sponsors" reflected the territorial scale of the conflicts in which the "local populations" (or the groups that metonymically tended to think of themselves as such) opposed the concentration of heavy industrial plants in this relatively small region. The TAP project was then seen as a further deterioration of this situation and another top-down "imposition" of infrastructure development. Making the Salento area the connecting hub of different gas pipeline projects intensified the industrial hazard

---

[15] The main conflicts are over the coal-fired power station and petrochemical pole in Brindisi, the steel factory in Taranto, nowadays the largest and deadliest in Europe, and the cement factory in Galantina, province of Lecce.

related to oil and coal industries, thus triggering the frustration of being a "sacrifice zone" to far distant and dubious interests. The struggle against the TAP, in this respect, is part of a long history of "power struggles" (Franquesa 2018) against large-scale energy production and corporate interests (Pusceddu 2020). The turning point in the struggle against the TAP, conceived as the defence of the land, was the protests against the uprooting of the olive trees.

Flows of power, roots of resistance

The conflict over mega-infrastructure materializes the power and presence of otherwise abstract concepts like the state, the financial capital and the multinational corporation, thus making visible the tight but hazy connections between global financial flows, geopolitics and energy (Mitchell 2013; Smith-Nonini 2016). If one looks at the pipeline through the eyes of the protesters (Armiero 2008), the TAP conjures up dubious financial flows[16], suspicious links with organized crime[17] and the extractivist exploitation of the region (Acosta 2019). Before active resistance against the pipeline construction started, the practice and meaning of "defending the land" had already taken the shape of resistance against the uprooting and cutting down of "sick" olive trees during the *Xylella* emergency.

In 2015, environmental activists, farmers and ordinary citizens – the so-called "Popolo degli ulivi" (People of the olive trees) – staged a number of roadblocks between Brindisi and Lecce. They protested against the order of cutting down olive trees within a broad area, which did not spare centuries-old monumental olive trees. The plan was ordered by the special commission appointed for dealing with the *Xylella* emergency. *Xylella fastidiosa* is a bacterium that attacks olive trees causing their quick dieback so that they can no longer produce olives. Moreover, it is transmitted via insects, thus spreading on potentially considerable surfaces. Allegedly, *xylella* reached the Salento olive groves years earlier. As the *xylella* spread, in February 2015 the national government declared a state of emergency. The disease was tackled by combining different measures, from the use of specific plant protection products to the cutting down of trees. The problem is still alarming, according to competent authorities, since there is a risk of affecting the whole of Apulia. To get an idea of the scale of the problem, one should bear in mind that 40% of Italian olive groves are concentrated in Apulia.

The order to cut down all olive trees, including non-infected trees, was therefore met with anger by farmers and local people, developing into a controversial judicial case (Papadia 2018: 6–8). Conspiracy theories about the cutting down of

---

[16] See the report of the European Network of Corporate Observatories (ENCO 2019). According to the "Global Laundromat" investigation (Gowland 2017), the SGC was involved in a vast money-laundering scheme.
[17] The expression *mafiodotto* (literally "mafia pipeline") was first used in a report published by the weekly journal *L'Espresso* (Biondani and Sisti 2017).

non-infected trees started to appear. Someone suspected that the *xylella* did not exist and had been fabricated to damage the Apulian olive groves, so as to eliminate a powerful competitor in the olive oil market[18]. One of these conspiracy theories had to do with the TAP project[19]. It argued that the areas for which had been ordered the cutting down of trees corresponded to the pipeline route. The cutting down of trees would have saved a lot of work and money for the company, being exempted from the replanting of the uprooted olive trees. Likewise, the uprooting of infected olive trees along the Snam interconnector pipeline construction site remained a contentious issue.

The *Xylella* case has strongly contributed to enhancing the impact of the uprooting of olive trees, turning the defence of the latter into a broader act of defence of "the land" (Di Ronco, Allen-Robertson and South 2019). Against the background of a broader polarization between industrialism and ruralism, the olive trees provided the affective link between the past and the present, between the people and "the land". The material and symbolic place of olive trees in the local history and economy, therefore, makes them a unifying symbol across various environmental struggles – against coal-burning emissions, agrobusiness and energy infrastructures. The practice of hampering the uprooting of olive trees has therefore emerged as a practice of cultural commoning, transcending land properties and constructing the olive tree as a common social and cultural idiom.

Rootedness and care

The TAP AG's CSTs were implemented through the "social and environmental investment programme", with the aim of contrasting the critiques about the damaging impact of the project. Several initiatives were financed to enhance the local tourist economy, such as the creation of the TAP Academy to finance free job training courses in the tourist industry (e.g. hotel receptionist or tourist guide)[20]. These initiatives, along with other environmentally friendly programmes such as the reduction of marine litter, tackled the main critique moved to the infrastructure, that it would harm the environment and landscape, thus damaging the developing tourist industry. By doing so, and within the corporate social responsibility paradigm, these CSTs tried to shape the "silence" of gas flows by purporting its compatibility and complementarity with local life and economy. This strategy of minimizing the impact of the infrastructure also relied on the emphasis on its "invisibility", which insisted on the fact that, once completed, the pipeline would re-

---

[18] This was also claimed by Beppe Grillo, founder and leader of the Five Star Movement. See (Scalari 2018), which tracks several conspiracy theories around the *Xylella* emergency.
[19] Conspiracy theories related to the SGC pipeline network were widely reported in Greece during the austerity crisis (Dalakoglou and Kallianos 2018: 80).
[20] The three main axes of TAP AG's "social and environmental investment programme" can be found here: https://www.tap-ag.com/sustainability/social-and-environmental-investments/social-and-environmental-investments-in-italy (accessed 4 October 2021).

main invisible. The alteration of the landscape caused by the construction works, that is, the excavations and all the necessary operations to lay down the pipes, was claimed as a temporary alteration, which would be quickly recovered at the end of the infrastructure construction. TAP AG made use of every possible means to show that life could flow as ever, along with the silent gas flow from the Caspian Sea.

A contentious issue related to TAP AG's CSTs was the treatment of olive trees, which became the material and symbolic site of resistance against the pipeline. As previously mentioned, the uprooting of olive trees was already a sensitive issue when the pipeline works started, due to the *Xylella* emergency. Later on, the uprooting of olive trees for laying down the pipes created the space for articulating the protesters' counter-discourse that insisted on the "transient qualities of pipeline gas" (Rogers 2020: 290). This discourse is underpinned by the opposition between the transient quality of gas (and the associated speculative movement of financial capital) and the rootedness of olive trees, which conveys a powerful spatial and temporal metaphor of local culture. This general opposition turned the very "invisibility" of the pipeline against TAP AG, thus bringing the silence of the gas flows into a more ambiguous and suspicious light.

Understandably, TAP AG organized a careful campaign for "taking care" of the olive trees, which included the construction of a canopy for protecting the trees from *xylella*, and any other measure in accordance with the competent authorities[21]. Members of the No TAP Movement, on the contrary, reported the complaints by farmers and olive tree owners about the mistreatment, such as excessive pruning that would reduce the productive capacity of the trees. On a more general level, the opposition mentioned above pointed to the fact that the TAP AG's campaign about "taking care of the olive trees" was a way of taking care of local consent around the infrastructure. This triggered other types of polarization between the labour of caring for the trees as a constitutive relation *with* the land and caring for the trees as a transient and opportunistic relation *through* the land[22]. In this respect, while the former relation is seen as fertile, in the sense that it gives crops, livelihoods and culture, the latter is seen as a sterile one. The olive trees have become the material and symbolic site of conflict around the persistent socio-environmental crisis of the region, first caused by the oil- and coal-based industrialization, of which the transition to gas is perceived as a metamorphosis. Half a century earlier, in 1960, 20,000 olive trees were uprooted from an area of 600 hectares where the Taranto steel complex was about to rise (Romeo 2019: 89–98).

---

[21] See the related content on the company website: https://www.tap-ag.com.
[22] I thank Susana Narotzky for drawing my attention to this aspect.

Conclusion

This chapter examined the contentious construction of transnational energy infrastructure from the standpoint of its final destination in Italy. Situating the case study in the broader energy politics of the Italian state and the EU, the chapter highlighted the contradictions of European energy policies that aim at the "decarbonization" of the economy, while supporting the long-term construction of new energy mega-infrastructures for fossil fuel transport. The analysis of the TAP shows how such politics are embedded in wider networks of power and technology that unevenly connect finance, states and geographies. This uneven connection is generative of frictions in specific locations unwillingly designated as hubs of transnational power infrastructures. Such frictions also reveal how current energy-driven pro-growth policies exacerbate the historical consequences of top-down industrial development projects and the lasting socio-environmental crisis they have produced. The historically minded analysis of current energy infrastructure construction can help to situate the debate on the enchantment of infrastructures (Harvey and Knox 2012), shedding light on its reversal into "disenchantment" as an effect of the socio-environmental contradiction generated by capital-intensive oil- and coal-based industrialization. Moreover, the analysis illuminates an important aspect of the current energy development in Europe and the above-mentioned contradiction between the climate goal of decarbonization and the heavy reliance on long-term projects of fossil fuel energy supply.

While natural gas provided an important energy resource together with coal and – increasingly – oil in the last century, its political saliency has grown larger over the last few decades, fulfilling the important, and yet gradual, substitutive role in the outlining of the future energy mix. The rise of natural gas as the main resource making up for the decreasing use of coal and oil has been taking place among growing concerns over the environmental impact of fossil fuel use. Nonetheless, natural gas is described as necessary to lead the phasing out of coal and oil and to sustain the expansion and growth of renewable systems of energy production. This peculiar and somewhat redeeming mission of natural gas is shaped by an apparent paradox: on the one hand, the expansion of natural gas supply is aimed at securing and enhancing the political and financial operation of fossil fuel economies (Mitchell 2013); on the other hand, it is reconfigured as a "clean" alternative to coal and oil, through a controversial (and deceitful) resource-making process of "defossilfuelization" – in fact, a massive "greenwashing" operation[23]. The fast-growing investments in natural gas infrastructures,

---

[23] On 9 March 2022, the European Commission approved the Complementary Climate Delegated Act, which includes "specific nuclear and gas energy activities" in the EU Taxonomy of environmentally sustainable economic activities. See: https://ec.europa.eu/info/publications/220202-sustainable-finance-taxonomy-complementary-climate-delegated-act_en (accessed 30 July 2022).

while driven by complex financial arrangements and investment schemes, rest upon the public claim that natural gas will contribute to building more "clean" energy futures. As such, gas pipeline construction is aimed at fulfilling the promise of prosperity of the fossil fuel economy, while exorcizing its harmful environmental impacts. In the situated context examined in this chapter, the construction of the TAP enshrined the growth discourse of socio-economic prosperity, thereby aiming to reshape past patterns of development enchantment. As I have shown in the previous sections, the ruins of past development projects have fuelled radical disenchantment with large-scale industrial infrastructures, paving the way to open contestation. Materializing the power and presence of otherwise abstract concepts like the state, the financial capital and the multinational corporation, to the eyes of the protesters (Armiero 2008) the pipeline exposes the tight but hazy connections between global financial flows, energy politics and power inequalities (Mitchell 2013; Smith-Nonini 2016).

The social and political relevance of the contestation of the gas pipeline appears to exceed the very material existence and presence of the latter, thus overturning corporate discourses that pledged the peaceful coexistence of ordinary activities – from farming to the growing tourist service industry – with the silent gas flow beneath paradisiac beaches and centuries-old olive groves. As a matter of fact, once the laying down of the pipeline was complete and the replanting of olive trees had started, a relatively narrow security land strip remained to track the existence of the pipeline, albeit with rigorous safety protocols for land users being put in place. Aside from the PRT, built in densely populated areas, the real impact on local properties and land uses appears distant from previous infrastructure projects (e.g. power plants, the petrochemical complex). And yet, throughout the overall process of construction, intense conflicts escalated involving a broad alliance of ordinary citizens, farmers, environmental associations, grass-roots movements and local government. The repressive mechanisms through which state authorities have been tackling popular opposition to the pipeline testify to how the conflict around the infrastructure exposes the uneven connections between energy, power, justice and democracy. In May 2020, two concomitant trials started in the court of Lecce. One trial involved TAP executives and contracting construction firms, with the accusation of environmental crimes committed between 2016 and 2019. These were the construction of the pipeline in protected areas without necessary authorizations and the pollution of water-bearing strata during the construction process. In the other trial, 92 people that organized and participated in the demonstrations against the pipeline were charged with around 70 accusations, referring to protests that took place in 2017 and 2018. In March 2021, the court issued 67 convictions to the protesters, with sentences ranging from six months to more than three years of imprisonment. At the same time, the accused in the other trial benefited from repeated adjournments. It has been noticed how the two trials followed two different paths, one that was unusually fast for the Italian judicial system, the other that is proceeding according to a more relaxed and favourable schedule. The "uneven" timing of the two trials has been understood as the result of different judicial treatment, exacerbating the sense of injustice in the face of the unwanted pipeline construction and the right to oppose it.

Pipelines are a landmark of energy modernity and power. Timothy Mitchell (2013) has drawn attention to the importance of pipelines in shaping political and economic relations across vast distances, but also within specific locations and nation states. The reactions to the TAP in Salento provide a prism through which to examine how the legacy of past energy infrastructures in the region interacted with the pipeline construction, and how this interaction shapes the dispute about the future, be it the "preservation of the land" or the expectation of more just and sustainable energy futures (Boyer 2017; Franquesa 2018).

Glossary

PRT	Pipeline Receiving Terminal
SCP	South Caucasus Pipeline
SGC	Southern Gas Corridor
TAP	Trans Adriatic Pipeline
TANAP	Trans-Anatolian Natural Gas Pipeline
TEN-E	Trans-European Networks for Energy

References

Acosta, Alberto 2019: La violenza estrattivista in chiave italiana: Resistere è esistere, 6 December, Notav.info https://www.notav.info/post/la-violenza-estrattivista-in-chiave-italiana-resistere-e-esistere/

Armiero, Marco 2008: Seeing Like a Protester: Nature, Power, and Environmental Struggles. Left History 13(1): 59–76.

Barry, Andrew 2013: Material Politics: Disputes Along the Pipeline. Malden, MA: Wiley Blackwell.

Biondani, Paolo and Leo Sisti 2017: Tap, mafia e soldi sporchi dietro il gasdotto. L'Espresso 1 April 2017. Available at: https://espresso.repubblica.it/inchieste/2017/03/31/news/tap-mafia-e-soldi-sporchi-dietro-il-gasdotto-1.298585?ref=HEF_RULLO&fbclid=IwAR0cvgImQZR8xdEtnkQw_b4Rwo9A_Oor_Z4KeF6p5vrUiLJrZ-E0cKq2oiw (accessed 1 June 2020)

Borri, Dino and Salvatore Petrarchi (eds) 2013: Contro-Rapporto di VIA della Trans Adriatic Pipeline (TAP) presentato dal Comune di Melendugno al Ministero dell'Ambiente Italiano sulla Proposta di Nuovo Gasdotto Trans-Adriatico Avanzata da TAP AG. Comune di Melendugno. Available at: https://www.comune.melendugno.le.it/attachments/article/5058/TAP_Osservazioni_Rapporto_Via_TAP_Melendugno.pdf (accessed 10 June 2020).

Boyer, Dominic 2014: Energopower: An Introduction. Anthropological Quarterly 87(2): 309–333.

Boyer, Dominic 2017: Revolutionary infrastructure. In: Penny Harvey, Casper Bruun Jensen and Atsuro Morita (eds) Infrastructures and Social Complexity. A Companion. London and New York: Routledge, 174–186.
Boyer, Dominic 2019: Energopolitics: Wind and Power in the Anthropocene. Durham and London: Duke University Press.
Clemente, Francesco: 2013. Tap, il grande risiko dei gasdotti in Puglia, Linkiesta, 22 July 2013. Available at: https://www.linkiesta.it/2013/07/tap-il-grande-risiko-dei-gasdotti-in-puglia/
Collier, S. J., and N. Kemoklidze 2014: Pipes and wires. In: N. Thrift, A. Tickell, S. Woolgar, and W. H. Rupp (eds) Globalization in Practice. Oxford: Oxford University Press, 69–74.
Dalakoglou, Dimitris, and Penny Harvey (eds) 2015: Roads and Anthropology: Ethnography, Infrastructures, (Im)mobility. London: Routledge.
Dalakoglou, Dimitris, and Yannis Kallianos 2018: 'Eating Mountains' and 'Eating Each Other': Disjunctive Modernization, Infrastructural Imaginaries and Crisis in Greece. Political Geography 67: 76–87.
Della Porta, D., G. Piazza, N. Bertuzzi, and G. Sorci. 2019: LULUs Movements in Multilevel Struggles: A Comparison of Four Movements in Italy. Rivista Italiana di Politiche Pubbliche 3: 477–513.
Di Ronco, Anna, James Allen-Robertson and Nigel South 2019: Representing Environmental Harm and Resistance on Twitter: The Case of the TAP Pipeline in Italy. Crime Media Culture 15(1): 143–168.
ENCO 2019: Who owns all the pipelines? Report of the European Network of Corporate Observatories, 11 September 2019. Available at: https://corporateeurope.org/en/2019/09/who-owns-all-pipelines (accessed 10 June 2020).
Ferguson, Juliet (2020): The Gas Trap: How Europe is Investing € 100bn in Fossil Fuel Infrastructure. *Investigate Europe*, 15 October 2020. Available at: https://www.investigate-europe.eu/en/2020/the-gas-trap-report/
Ferry, Elizabeth E. and Mandana E. Limbert (eds) 2008: Timely Assets: The Politics of Resources and Their Temporalities. Santa Fe: School for Advanced Research Press.
Firat, Bilge 2016: 'The Most Eastern of the West, the Most Western of the East': Energy-Transport Infrastructures and Regional Politics of the Periphery in Turkey. Economic Anthropology 3: 81–93.
Flyvbjerg, Bent 2005: Machiavellian Megaprojects. Antipode 37(1): 18–22.
Franquesa, Jaume 2018: Power Struggles: Dignity, Value, and the Renewable Energy Frontier in Spain. Bloomington: Indiana University Press.
Franquesa, Jaume 2019. Resources: Nature, Value and Time. In: James G. Carrier (ed.) A Research Agenda for Economic Anthropology, Cheltenham: Elgar, 74–89.
Gerebizza, Elena 2019: I conti in tasca alla TAP. Re:Common. Available at: https://www.recommon.org/i-conti-in-tasca-alla-tap/ (accessed 6 April 2020).
Ginsborg, Paul 1990: A History of Contemporary Italy: 1943–1980. London: Penguin.
Glass, Michael R., Jean-Paul D. Addie and Jen Nelles 2019: Regional Infrastructures, Infrastructural Regionalism, *Regional Studies* 53(12): 1651–1656.
Gowland, Rebecca 2017: Southern Gas Corridor is the Missing Piece of Azerbaijani Laundromat Puzzle. *The Guardian* 6 September 2017. Available at: https://www.theguardian.com/world/2017/sep/06/southern-gas-corridor-is-the-missing-piece-of-azerbaijani-laundromat-puzzle (accessed 10 June 2020).

Graziani, Augusto 1998: Lo sviluppo dell'economia italiana. Dalla ricostruzione alla moneta europea. Turin: Bollati Boringhieri.
Harvey, Penny, and Casper Bruun Jensen, Atsuro Morita 2017: Introduction: Infrastructural Complications. In: Penny Harvey, Casper Bruun Jensen and Atsuro Morita (eds) Infrastructures and Social Complexity. A Companion. London and New York: Routledge, 1–22.
Harvey, Penny, and Hannah Knox 2012: The Enchantments of Infrastructure. Mobilities 7(4): 521–536.
Imperatore, Paola 2019: Contro il gasdotto in Salento. Le voci del movimento No-Tap. Lo stato dele città 3.
ISTAT 2010: 6° Censimento nazionale dell'agricoltura. Available at: https://www4.istat.it/it/censimento-agricoltura/agricoltura-2010 (accessed 3 October 2021).
Jones, Dave and Manon Dufour, Jonathan Gaventa 2015: Europe's Declining Gas demand Trends and Facts on European Gas Consumption, E3G Report, June 2015. Available at: https://www.e3g.org/docs/E3G_Trends_EU_Gas_Demand_June2015_Final_110615.pdf (accessed 14 May 2020)
Kandiyoti, Rafael 2015: Powering Europe: Russia, Ukraine, and the Energy Squeeze. New York: Palgrave Macmillan.
Larkin, Brian 2013: The Politics and Poetics of Infrastructure. Annual Review of Anthropology 42: 327–343.
Love, Thomas and Cindy Isenhour (eds) 2016: Energy and Economy: Recognizing High-Energy Modernity as a Historical Period. *Economic Anthropology* 2: 6–16.
Marriott, James and Minio-Paluello, Mika 2013: The Oil Road: Journeys from the Caspian Sea to the City of London. London: Verso.
Masella, Luigi. 1989. La difficile costruzione di una identità (1880-1980). In Luigi Masella, Biagio Salvemini (eds) Storia d'Italia. Le regioni dall'Unità a oggi. La Puglia. Turin: Einaudi, 280–438.
Mitchell, Timothy 2013: Carbon Democracy: Political Power in the Age of Oil. London: Verso.
Ministero dell'Ambiente 2014: Allegato al Decreto del Ministero dell'Ambiente (Parere CTVIA) – Trans Adriatic Pipeline – Gasdotto Albania-Italia. Available at: https://va.minambiente.it/it-IT/Oggetti/MetadatoDocumento/114313 (accessed 4 October 2021).
Ministero dello Sviluppo Economico 2013: Strategia Energetica Nazionale: per un'energia più competitiva e sostenibile. Available at: https://www.mise.gov.it/index.php/it/component/content/article?id=2029441:strategia-energetica-nazionale-sen (accessed 3 October 2021).
Ministero dello Sviluppo Economico and Ministero dell'Ambiente e della Tutela del Territorio e del Mare 2017: Strategia Energetica Nazionale 2017. Available at: https://www.mise.gov.it/images/stories/documenti/Testo-integrale-SEN-2017.pdf (accessed 3 October 2021).
Ministero dello Sviluppo Economico, Ministero dell'Ambiente e della Tutela del Territorio e del Mare, and Ministero delle Infrastrutture e dei Trasporti 2019: Piano Nazionale Integrato per l'Energia e il Clima. Available at: https://www.mise.gov.it/index.php/it/198-notizie-stampa/2040668-pniec2030 (accessed 4 October 2021).
Movimento No Tap n.d.: Perchè diciamo NO a TAP. Available at: https://www.notap.it/i-motivi-del-no/ (accessed 20 May 2020)

Navach, Giancarlo 2016: Dossier – Tap, 10.000 ulivi sulla strada del gasdotto, è braccio di ferro Puglia-Governo, Reuters, 4 October 2016. Available at: https://it.reuters.com/art icle/topNews/idITKCN1240IYpageNumber=2&virtualBrandChannel=0(accessed 10 August 2020).

Papadia, Elena 2018: Defend the defenders of the Earth: A dossier on the repression of the Salentinian movements. Available at: https://contropiano.org/img/2018/10/01-Ele na-Papadia-DEFEND-THE-DEFENDERS-OF-THE-EARTH.pdf (accessed 10 June 2020).

Pasimeni, Carmelo 2003: La rete dei trasporti in Puglia dall'Unità al Piano Regionale del 2002, paper presented at the seminar Il Mezzogiorno italiano nelle reti di trasporto (1860–2003), SISSCO (Società italiana per lo studio della storia contemporanea), Rome, 27 September 2003, pp. 1-34.

Pirro, Federico 1983: Il laboratorio di Aldo Moro: Organizzazione del consenso e governo dell'accumulazione in Puglia, 1945–1970. Bari: Dedalo.

Pusceddu, Antonio Maria 2020: Grassroots Ecologies of Value: Environmental Conflict and Social Reproduction in Southern Italy. Antipode 52(3): 847–866.

Ravenda, Andrea 2018: Carbone: Inquinamento industriale, salute e politica a Brindisi. Milan: Meltemi.

Re:Common 2014a: La trappola del gas: Perchè il mercato non aiuta la transizione. March 2014. Available at: https://www.recommon.org/la-trappola-del-gas/ (accessed 10 June 2020).

Re:Common 2014b: Dieci ragioni per dire no al gasdotto TAP. 24 July 2014. Available at: https://www.recommon.org/dieci-ragioni-per-dire-no-al-tap/?fbclid=IwAR3JPiRu wSE3SUnGMgbGjBOw1flwAH2K3HJZG7V3vhPS6WSUpMrBKzIjJYU (accessed 10 June 2020).

Ribeiro, Gustavo Lins 1994: Transnational Capitalism and Hydropolitics in Argentina: The Yacyretá High Dam. Gainesville: University Press of Florida.

Rogers, Douglas 2012: The Materiality of the Corporation: Oil, Gas, and Corporate Social Technologies in the Remaking of a Russian Region. American Ethnologist 39(2): 284–296.

Romano, Angelo, Zitelli Andrea 2017: Gasdotto TAP e proteste: cosa succede in Puglia. Valigia Blu, 1 April 2017 (updated 9 January 2018). Available at: https://www.valigi ablu.it/tap-gasdotto-puglia/

Romeo S. 2019: L'Acciaio in Fumo. L'Ilva di Taranto dal 1945 a oggi. Rome: Donzelli.

Scalari, Antonio 2018: La "bufala Xylella" è una bufala. Valigia Blu 9 July 2018. Available at: https://www.valigiablu.it/xylella-bufala/ (accessed 8 May 2020).

Schipper, Frank and Johan Schot 2011: Infrastructural Europeanism, or The Project of Building Europe on Infrastructures: An Introduction. History and Technology 27(3): 245–264.

Smith, Jessica and Mette M. High 2017: Exploring the Anthropology of Energy: Ethnography, Energy and Ethics. Energy Research & Social Science 30: 1–6.

Smith-Nonini, Sandy 2016: The role of Corporate Oil and Energy Debt in Creating the Neoliberal Era. Economic Anthropology 3: 57–67.

Spagnolo, Chiara 2017: Gasdotto, in Salento i No Tap bloccano i lavori: tensione nel cantiere blindato dalla polizia. La Repubblica 21 March 2017. Available at: https: //bari.repubblica.it/cronaca/2017/03/21/news/gasdotto_tap_il_cantiere_e_militarizza to_per_impedire_che_i_manifestanti_blocchino_i_lavori-161046185/?ref=search;

https://www.independent.co.uk/news/world/europe/melendugno-trans-adriatic-pipeline-tap-red-zone-italy-protests-a8085586.html (accessed 1 June 2020).

Venkatesan, Soumhya et al. 2018: Attention to Infrastructure Offers a Welcome Reconfiguration of Anthropological Approaches to the Political. Critique of Anthropology 38(1): 3–52.

Internet sources:

CEE Bankwatch Network – Southern Gas Corridor « https://bankwatch.org/project/southern-gas-corridor-euro-caspian-mega-pipeline» accessed 22.11.22

European Commission – Infrastructure « https://ec.europa.eu/energy/topics/infrastructure_en)

European Commission – A European Green Deal (https://ec.europa.eu/info/strategy/priorities-2019-2024/european-green-deal_en» accessed 22.11.22

Global Energy Monitor «https://globalenergymonitor.org/» accessed 22.11.22

International Energy Agency «https://www.iea.org/» accessed 22.11.22

Investigate Europe «https://www.investigate-europe.eu/en/» accessed 22.11.22

ISTAT: Istituto Nazionale di Statistica «https://www4.istat.it/it/» accessed 22.11.22

Ministero dell'Ambiente e della Tutela del Territorio e del Mare – Environmental Assessments and Authorizations «https://va.minambiente.it/en-GB» accessed 22.11.22

Ministero dello Sviluppo Economico «https://www.mise.gov.it/index.php/it/» accessed 22.11.22

Movimento No Tap «https://www.notap.it/» accessed 22.11.22

Re:Common «https://www.recommon.org/» accessed 22.11.22

Trans Adriatic Pipeline «https://www.tap-ag.com/» accessed 22.11.22

Walk to Resist: Contesting a Large-Scale Road Project in the City of Biel, Switzerland

Lucien Schönenberg, Institute of Social Anthropology, University of Bern, Switzerland

Introduction

The official state-based plan to build a subterranean and partially uncovered four-lane highway through the city of Biel with two highway junctions – the so-called 'A5 Westast'– has been highly controversial in recent years. Oppositional associations and commissions formed and demonstrations and other public actions were organized. A broad resistance movement led to the project being stopped at the beginning of 2019, and it was completely written off at the end of 2020.

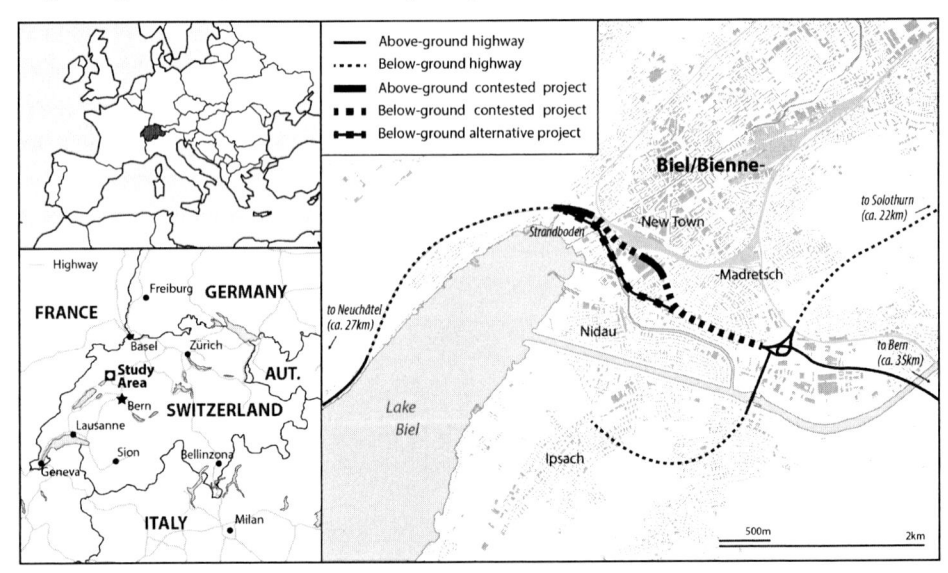

Map 1: The 'Above-ground contested project' refers to the two contested highway junctions 'Seevorstadt' and 'city centre'. Source: Map compilation and design by Manuel L. K. Abebe (2021), CDE, University of Bern, Bern, Switzerland. Geodata: OpenStreetMap contributors

As the official and controversial project has not yet materialized, it can still be rethought and reimagined. The association 'Westast – so nicht!' (German abbreviation *wasn*, literal translation: western branch – not like this!) proposed an alternative project plan (map 1, below-ground alternative project) that resulted in the renegotiation of the whole social and political decision-making process, challenging notions of transparency, stakeholder participation, social justice, conservation and protection. As stated by *wasn*[1], their proposition has multiple advantages: no cutting down of trees, no destroying of buildings, no junctions in the city, construction time can be cut in half, it is a cheaper solution and recreation, and environment areas won't be affected. The association has resisted the state-based project, particularly by organizing city walks to render the as yet unbuilt infrastructure not only imaginable but also palpable in terms of space and by simultaneously showing its damaging effects on the city. It is thus not only a renegotiation of the size and of the alignment itself, but also a renegotiation of bargaining power.

In what follows, I position the case study theoretically, then introduce the history of the western branch, and finally focus on the foundation of *wasn* and show how the practice of the city walk enabled effective resistance. To do so, this article engages with different perceptions of urbanity, (im)mobility and participation.

In terms of methods, I pursued a twofold approach. My attendance at several city walks, informal discussions with participants and organizers, an interview with a co-founder of *wasn* and a discussion with an employee in the area of land acquisition from the civil engineering authority of the Canton of Bern provided an insight into some parts of the resistance movement, as well as into some perceptions of a civil servant on the implementation of the official project. Secondly, I focused on local newspaper articles to understand the debates surrounding the western branch. The results of the small case study, most of it conducted in spring and summer 2019, cannot take account of the whole political and social complexity but have to be read as an attempt to explore the methods of resistance of *wasn* (which is one of several organizations) against a highway project in the city that is based on civil rights and direct and participatory democracy and enabled the transformation of political procedures. Furthermore, the debate surrounding the western branch at the beginning of 2020 reveals that clear-cut opposite supporter/opponent binaries can be overcome to engage in a more dialogical form of solution finding.

The reader will notice that this chapter has a slightly different structure compared to the other chapters in this book. Unlike most mega-infrastructure projects described in this volume, the investigated project is situated in an urban context in the Global North. In terms of scale, it is not a transnational infrastructure project with a global scope and foreign investors, but rather a small subproject of a national enterprise funded primarily by federal, and partially by municipal funds.

---

[1] See Westastsonicht! ⟨https://www.westastsonicht.ch/de/aktuell/westast-so-besser⟩ accessed 1.04.2020.

The western branch is a puzzle piece in a national mega-infrastructure project, which has its legislative roots in the 1960s.[2] It addresses some vital issues for the comparison with other projects.

The present example shows that the ability to look at a planned highway in the city in a different light through the practice of the city walk (among other practices) permitted the renegotiation of an infrastructure project, to play for time, and to revive political participation.

Approaching an invisible, virtual and imagined highway

Anthropologists did not always perceive roads as sites of ethnographic interest but rather described them as transitional spaces without social significance – so-called 'non-places' – in the words of Marc Augé (1995). This perception of roads was refuted by many contributions (see Dalakoglou and Harvey 2015), showing that highways also forge and break off relations, form and dissolve collectives – in short, can be contested spaces of social expressions. This also applies to the negotiation process of the case presented in this article, as the highways' promise or threat of future materialization mobilizes groups. The city hikers, whom I will introduce below, interpret signs and traces of the road project in the city, and therefore such infrastructures 'create thickenings of publics, and offer the possibility of assembling people' (De Boeck 2012). De Boeck refers here to infrastructure that is mainly 'present in [its] absence' (in a completely different context of constant lack, shortcomings and failure in Kinshasa) and these 'vulnerable and often invisible infrastructures [...] generate alternative spheres of social interaction and different coping strategies and regimes of knowledge and power'. Even if the presented case takes place in a different context the highway is nevertheless invisible and creating alternative spheres of social interaction, coping strategies, as well as knowledge and power regimes through the future infrastructure's potential to alter or, in the words of the combatants, 'to destroy the city'. How can we further approach a highway theoretically that has not yet materialized?

The distinction made by Harvey and Knox, who see infrastructures as both 'virtual and actualized relational spaces' (2015: 6) – virtual because they are controlled by 'expert practices, such as techniques of measurement, mapping, and description'; actualized, because of their material emergence – helps in understanding the invisible character of infrastructure. In the present case, the contestation by *wasn*, who are proposing an alternative alignment, takes place in a virtual space (as alternative experts provide alternative maps and descriptions to the official road project) but also in a lived pre-existent space where the infrastructure is made tangible despite its physical absence through the city walks.

---

[2] Mok et al., following Flyvbjerg and Skyes, define mega projects 'as a substantial capital project, of several billion dollars, which requires concerted efforts from major participants in terms of resources, skills and expertise' (2015: 447).

Alternative spheres of social interaction – in this case the city walks following traces and signs of the future road in order to interprete, contest, retrace or to place marks – offers a space to perform a counter-discourse. Through Foucault's power-knowledge nexus and the 'productive' characteristics of power, as well as Ensminger's notion of bargaining power, I explore how the emphasis on certain knowledge and arguments enabled a shift in the project's implementation and how in spring 2020 the overall discourse, therefore, changed dramatically.

Part 1: Historical, environmental, ethnographic and political context

Political and economic context, local population and resource use

The official project of the western branch is situated in the context of the national development plan of Swiss federal roads. Before introducing it, we briefly need to consider Switzerland's overall political system and the political orientation of the city of Biel. In regard to the former, the federal system and direct democracy are its two main pillars.[3] The federal system of the political Switzerland consists of the federal government, 26 cantons and many municipalities (local political entities in the cantons). Cantons and municipalities have to be seen as relatively autonomous. They decide themselves over a wide range of matters (following the principle of subsidiarity). Every canton has its own constitution, parliament, government, courts and thus the division of power. The federal government is meant to decide over the tasks the cantons and the communes cannot manage alone – as is the case for the road section discussed in this article. Direct democracy, on the other hand, renders it possible to actively intervene in the decision-making process and to increase political pressure. Civil rights, such as freedom of association, of speech and of information, therefore, offer powerful political room for individuals and collectives to manoeuvre. One example, important for the present case, is the possibility of appealing against infrastructure projects.

The city of Biel was founded between 1220 and 1230 by the Prince-Bishop of Basel, whose territory extended to the south as far as Lake Biel[1] With just over 56,000 inhabitants, it is the tenth-largest municipality and the largest bilingual city in Switzerland.[5] Biel is located at the southern foot of the Jura and directly on Lake Biel. The city is well connected: by train, Geneva can be reached in 1.5

---
[3] See Schweizer Eidgenossenschaft. Politisches System – Fakten und Zahlen. ⟨https://www.eda.admin.ch/aboutswitzerland/en/home/politik/uebersicht/politisches-system-der-schweiz---fakten-und-zahlen.html⟩ accessed 14.04.2020.
[4] See Bieler Altstadt, Stadtgeschichte. ⟨https://www.bieler-altstadt.ch/portfolio-item/stadtgeschichte/⟩ accessed 8.02.2021.
[5] See Stadt Biel. Wirtschaft/Statistik. Statistisches Factsheet. ⟨https://www.biel-bienne.ch/public/upload/assets/912/pra_sm_fact_sheet_jul21_d_f.pdf?fp=1628148849058⟩ accessed 21.09.2021.

to 2 hours, Zurich in 1 to 1.5 hours and Bern in about 30 minutes. From the perspective of larger Swiss cities, Biel has not had a good image for a long time and has often been described as multicultural, artistic, open and nonchalant, but also dirty, criminal and poor – as if it were a city that does not quite want to fit into the image of other Swiss cities.[6] This description is often based on the argument that Biel ranks among the top cities in Switzerland in terms of crime statistics, unemployment rate and social welfare rate.[7] However, this external image attribution must be taken with a pinch of salt.

As regards the overall political orientation of the city of Biel, its local government has rather left-wing tendencies. Historically, its economic flagship has always been the watch industry and the city is marked by labour unions and the Social Democratic Party. After the First World War Biel had a communist party developed from the Bolshevik Revolution, and the city came to be called 'Red Biel'[8] (Gaffino et al. 2013: 800 ff.). The social democrats started municipal-socialistic programmes, especially to combat the recurrent unemployment. Although communism scepticism after the Second World War increased and the liberalists prevailed, since 1976 the mayor of Biel has always been a social democrat and this party has remained strong in the city's parliament.

The majority of the leftists of the city government, however, supported the official road project for a long time, but later a lot of the critical voices also came from the left wing. Direct democracy and the overall political attitude certainly contributed to the phenomenon of resistance; nevertheless, the explanations for the opposition's success must be searched in the movement's creative potential. Even more important, as we will see below, is the perception of the endangered urban tissue, changing notions of modernity and thus shifting discourses, and the methods of resistance itself.

---

[6] There has even been a campaign to polish the city's bad image. An article published in the Neue Zürcher Zeitung reproduced this image of Biel. See Tanner, Samuel. 2020. «Es ist nicht sauber, nicht leistungsorientiert und auch noch stolz darauf. Warum ist Biel so anders als der Rest der Schweiz?» Neue Zürcher Zeitung (NZZ) am Sonntag, 20. Juni 2020. ‹https://nzzas.nzz.ch/magazin/biel-bienne-portraet-eines-widerstandsnests-ld.1561713?reduced=true#register› accessed 2.02.2021.

[7] See Bieler Tagblatt. ‹https://www.bielertagblatt.ch/nachrichten/biel/biel-ist-drittgefaehrlichste-stadt-der-schweiz› accessed 8.02.2021; Scherrer, Lucien. 10.05.2019. Neue Zürcher Zeitung. ‹https://www.nzz.ch/schweiz/fuersorge-stadt-biel-mehr-als-jeder-zehnte-lebt-von-sozialhilfe-ld.1480750?reduced=true› accessed 8.02.2021; Bieler Tagblatt. ‹https://www.bielertagblatt.ch/nachrichten/biel/arbeitslosenquote-biel-gestiegen› accessed 8.02.2021.

[8] In reference to the name 'Red Vienna', the capital of Austria, which was then in the hands of the Social Democratic Workers Party of Austria (SDAP).

History of the western branch and legal framework

The national development plan for Swiss federal roads is regulated in the federal roads law that came into force in 1960 and organizes the construction of the Swiss net resolution – an ambitious national road web that is meant to be completed from the 60s onward. The federal roads law states that the federal council of Switzerland authorizes the general projects (Art. 20, Par. 1) and that it decides on the alignment of federal roads in the city area (Art. 20, Par. 2).[9] Thus, the official project planned in the city of Biel is not a local approach, but rather a missing link in a national highway development plan of Swiss federal roads, which is meant to achieve what the Swiss Federal Roads Office (FEDRO) calls 'net completion'.[10] While the federal council of Switzerland has to approve the projects, they are realized by cantonal authorities.

A plan to build an expressway through the core of Biel to relieve the city from the transit traffic arose for the first time almost 70 years ago. In this plan, an expressway on piers was meant to cover a river in the urban centre, in order to bypass existing buildings, with a routing partially at the height of the first floor. This project would have cut the city in half. A picture of its visualization was used in recent news and investigative publications.[11] They illustrate what was conceived, at least by the planner himself, as modern back then. Those plans, even if they were not carried out, stood for a euphoria of modernity and the need to aspire the increasing traffic with more high-speed roads. Although the official project today is planned to be underground and not as intrusive as one of the first plans mentioned before, the two big highway junctions for a four-lane highway in the city are perceived – especially among western branch critics – as an outdated technocratic model, which perpetuates 'highway sins' from the 60s and 70s.[12]

While planners in Switzerland were seeking an alignment through the city of Biel in the 60s, on the other side of the Atlantic, city planner and architect Jane Jacobs published her book *The Death and Life of Great American Cities*. In a chapter called *Erosion of cities or attrition of automobiles* she writes that 'traffic arteries, along with parking lots, gas stations and drive-ins, are powerful and

---

[9] See Fedlex: Die Publikationsplattform des Bundesrechts. 725.11 Bundesgesetz über die Nationalstrassen vom 8. März 1960. ‹https://www.admin.ch/opc/de/classified-compilation/19600028/index.html› accessed 15.04.2020.

[10] See Bundesamt für Strassen ASTRA. Nationalstrassennetz. ‹https://www.astra.admin.ch/astra/de/home/themen/nationalstrassen/nationalstrassennetz.html› accessed 8.12.2019.

[11] See Benedikt Loderer (2019: 9). Bruderer, Urs. 2018. 'Der Fluch des Plans.' *REPUBLIK*, December 6, 2018; Léchot, Jérôme, 2017. 'Biel kämpft gegen einen Autobahndinosaurier–und könnte siegen'. *Das Lamm*, November 22, 2017 ‹https://daslamm.ch/biel-kaempft-gegen-einen-autobahndinosaurier-und-koennte-siegen/› accessed 8.12.2019.

[12] See Westastsonicht! ‹https://www.westastsonicht.ch/de/komitee/was-wir-wollen› accessed 8.12.2019.

[13] Many thanks to the Civil Engineering Office of the canton of Bern, which kindly allowed the use of the four pictures and visualizations (Fig. 1-4) for this article.

Fig 1: Present state 2020. Source: Tiefbauamt des Kantons Bern[13]

Fig 2: Highway junction 'city centre' (visualization). Source: Tiefbauamt des Kantons Bern

Fig 3: Present state 2020. Source: Tiefbauamt des Kantons Bern

Fig 4: Highway junction 'Seevorstadt' (visualization). Source: Tiefbauamt des Kantons Bern

insistent instruments of city destruction' (1961: 440). Translated into the present, for *wasn* the city destruction is characterized by the demolition of buildings and subsequent resettlements, a serious intervention into the subterranean water, into circumjacent recreation, conservation and quarter areas, the cutting down of trees and limited lake shore access for several years. In the pictures (Figs. 2 and 4), only the final state of the two highway junctions is represented, and the construction work that would be executed in surface mining and that demands huge surfaces of land over an extensive period of time is missing. In sum, the fact that old ideas of modernization are being reproduced and transferred into the present is one of the central criticisms addressed by *wasn* regarding the official road project.

In his dissertation on Swiss expressways, George Kammann points out that various interests exist in a populous area such as a city and that the direct benefit of a city highway is minor compared to the disadvantages the city residents have to bear. The author realized that with every proposed city highway alignment local opposition has to be expected and in consequence cause a time-consuming process, which would put the whole project at risk. According to the author, the rapid realization of the Swiss net resolution is privileged to the disadvantage of a democratic process that would take the local desire for development seriously (1990: 123 f.). Such criticism of modernist development programmes can also be found in anthropological literature, described as 'generic solutions [that] are by definition blind to human creativity, and hugely destructive of the relations through which such creativity is recognized and reproduced' (Harvey and Knox 2015: 9). The practice of the city walk, which I will discuss further below, is certainly one such creative way of resisting generic solutions. Interestingly, in 2020, the will to engage in a round table and to question deadlocked views marked a shift from a top-down approach, over a bottom-up resistance, to a more balanced dialogue process.

Geography and ecosystem/cultural landscape

Geographic constraints forced and set the road geometry: a triangulation, which Loderer (2019) calls the 'Bieler triangle'.[14] The opening of a third-class national road on the north side of the lake of Biel in 1973 set one first point of this triangle (Map 1: to Neuchâtel). All the variations that would follow would have to have that point in common. Even if it makes sense to join already existing roads, the sheer pre-existence of such infrastructure renders alternative plans such as a road at the south side of the lake and, consequently in the south of the city, nearly impossible, or at least very improbable for political consent.

It is important to mention that the version of the project that counts as the official project of the present day has its roots in a former version opened for public

---

[14] Loderer is himself a western branch combatant, and even though he is not impartial in his writings, he has produced important insights into the history of the western branch.

inspection in 1975. Astonishingly, the government of Biel had already rejected this version of the official plan in 1983 (Loderer 2019: 36).[15] Furthermore, multiple variations were presented subsequently, which were not pursued but will again be reviewed in 2020. In 1989, the Civil Engineering Office of the canton of Bern wrote a final report and recommended the variations 'western branch' and 'eastern branch' to the federal council of Switzerland. Although the city parliament of Biel was initially against this decision, the building management finalized the consultation of the general project for the 'western branch' in 1999 and it was approved by the federal council in 2014.[16] Remarkably, even Moritz Leuenberger, minister of transport from 1995 to 2010, criticized the project in an article in the local paper *Bieler Tagblatt*. In 1997, he feared massive landscape intrusions, follow-up infrastructure projects on the north side of the lake (Map 1: to Neuchâtel) and high project costs. In the year 2018 he clarified that he was still an opponent of the official project, as formerly his name had been used by the cantonal building director to promote the official plans.[17] But in contrast to 1997, in 2018, a strong grassroots resistance had come into being and had revived the negotiation process. With regard to ecological concerns, *wasn* focused especially on old-growth trees that would be cut in a recreation area near the lakeshore that would be blocked during the construction works. Other concerns regarded the uncertain impact on a nearby conservation and residential area, the intended methods of surface mining, and the use of freezing lances for the subterranean construction that would potentially unbalance the subterranean water flows and entail risks. After the Swiss federal council approved the official project in 2014, the design plan was adapted so that the conservation area would be less affected. Additionally, the planning commission envisages replacing old trees that have to be cut with new ones and an artificial system is scheduled to make subterranean water flows possible.[18] Nevertheless, those promises to replace old-growth trees with new ones and to adapt one highway junction (Fig. 4, 'Seevorstadt') in order to have less of an effect on the conservation area did not correspond to the environmental, social and urban politics *wasn* had in mind. To grasp the local resistance formation against the western branch, the more recent history needs to be considered.

---

[15] Baudirektion Biel: 'Auch die Variante (D) Westast plus Ostast, das spätere Projekt, fand keine Gnade mehr, sie war nicht weiter zu verfolgen und 'soll nicht, wie in anderen Stellungnahmen erwähnt, für irgendwelche Zwecke in Reserve gehalten werden'. Das, was 2017 dem offiziellen Projekt entspricht, hielt die Bieler Regierung 1983 also für unbrauchbar' (Loderer 2019: 36).

[16] See Biel-Nidau-2050. ⟨https://biel-nidau-2050.ch/index.php⟩ 8.12.2019.

[17] See Balmer Deborah. 2018a. 'Schon damals kein Freund der Anschlüsse'. Bieler Tagblatt, 12. September 2018. ⟨https://westast.ch/wordpress/wp-content/uploads/2018/09/20180912_BT_Leuenberger.pdf⟩ accessed 8.12.2019.

[18] See A5 Biel-Bienne. ⟨https://www.a5-biel-bienne.ch/projektuebersicht/umwelt/⟩ accessed 15.04.2020.

Part 2: The Mega-Infrastructure Project

In search of participation

In 2007, different variations of the planned alignment were still in progress to find a city-compatible solution. Even though it was already clear that one city quarter was going to be severely affected, participation was reduced to the submission of objections.[19] In 2008, an interest group ('Interessengemeinschaft Lebensqualität Biel-West') demanded transparency and wanted to get involved in the planning process after having witnessed that relevant information had been kept from the inhabitants of the quarter.[20] Because of a test building site in the same quarter, inhabitants complained about the noise of the machines, the fear of dispossession and the inadequate communication of cantonal authorities.[21]

Cantonal authorities reacted by creating an accompanying group, which included authorities, quarter associations, communities of interest and environmental associations. The goal was a platform to improve information flows, but decision-making powers were not included.[22] Therefore, in 2009, the accompanying group, which operated under the buzzword of participation, was later criticized for being a 'fig leaf without competences'.[23]

At a panel discussion in 2008, strongly opposing views were expressed: while some called the highway junction in the centre of Biel 'city destructive' others wanted to realize the western branch as fast as possible in the name of a greater cause, referring most of the time to economic prosperity.[24] The cantonal authorities started to run out of patience as the Bieler executive director of building made an official demand to give up the highway junction in the city centre.[25]

---

[19] Bieler Tagblatt, 31 January 2007. ‹https://www.bielertagblatt.ch/nachrichten/vermischtes/damo klesschwert-ueber-dem-quartier› At that time the inhabitants of the quarter collected 1,500 signatures for a petition against the 'inacceptable' proposals: Bieler Tagblatt, 3 December 2007. http://www.bielertagblatt.ch/nachrichten/vermischtes/zweifel-sind-noch-nicht-ausgeraeumt.

[20] Bieler Tagblatt, 4 March 2008. ‹https://www.bielertagblatt.ch/nachrichten/vermischtes/behoer den-unter-beschuss› accessed 3.03.2021.

[21] Bieler Tagblatt, 4 December 2008. ‹https://www.bielertagblatt.ch/trainingsstart-fuer-a5-baustel le?destination=node/804732› accessed 3.03.2021.

[22] Bieler Tagblatt, 8 May 2008. ‹http://www.bielertagblatt.ch/nachrichten/vermischtes/a5-umfah rung-kanton-prueft-porttunnel› accessed 3.03.2021.

[23] See Westastsonicht! ‹https://www.westastsonicht.ch/de/aktuell/aktuell/der-runde-tisch›, accessed 8.12.2019.

[24] Bieler Tagblatt, 15 May 2008. ‹https://www.bielertagblatt.ch/nachrichten/vermischtes/da-m uss-man-noch-daran-arbeiten›; ‹http://www.pro-westast.ch/images/medienspiegel/BT_13_0 9_16_Die_Geschichte_des_Westasts_reicht_bis_in_die_50er_Jahre_zurueck.pdf› accessed 8.12.2019.

[25] Bieler Tagblatt, 28 January 2009. ‹https://www.bielertagblatt.ch/nachrichten/vermischtes/mueh e-mit-dem-bieler-huest-und-hottfrq{} accessed 8.12.2019.

In 2012, the project, which still contained the highway junction city centre, was open for public participation but the cantonal authorities were certain that a fundamental new alignment would not have any chance in the one-month-long phase of participation.[26] This kind of participation was criticized by various leftist parties and quarter associations and therefore the displeasure with the highway junction city centre remained.[27]

The cantonal authorities understood that the realization of the large-scale project depended on the possibility of the concerned population having a say, but a green municipal council of Biel still worried about the form of participation the cantonal building department was striving to achieve.[28] Salet et al., who wrote about the complexity and uncertainty of infrastructure projects, describe what also corresponds to this case study:

[…] the most common approach tries to reduce […] complexity and uncertainty by simplifying the decision-making process, that is, by narrowing the scope, speeding up procedures and limiting the involvement of those whose interests are affected. (2013: 12)

The speeding up of the decision process was mainly pushed by cantonal authorities, thus maintaining deficient participation possibilities. The general project was approved in 2014 by the Swiss federal council. This was a crucial moment, as only during the implementation stage did the outcomes become intelligible and comprehensible, and thus certain citizens became alert, which in turn resulted in the formation of the *wasn* committee in 2015.

However, the following years showed that the above-described 'common approach' (Salet et al. 2013: 12), which had already been contested before, did not withstand the newly consolidated local resistance forces. In sum, the official project is criticized by *wasn* as follows: it is a technocratic and overdimensioned solution – especially the two highway junctions 'city centre' and 'Seevorstadt' – for a delicate environment, such as the city, where various interests exist. As the federal council of Switzerland approves the general projects in the net resolution, local imaginaries and opinions don't have a direct influence on the project's alignment – participation, therefore, is superficial. It is an all or nothing solution, as a great deal of the funding comes from the state.

Living the highway – strategies of resistance against the official project

Regula Rytz, until June 2020 the president of the green party of Switzerland, called the protest against the western branch a 'shining example of local resis-

---

[26] Bieler Tagblatt, 7 March 2012. ⟨https://www.bielertagblatt.ch/nachrichten/biel/im-mai-liegt-der-ball-beim-volk⟩ accessed 3.03.2021.
[27] Bieler Tagblatt, 28 May 2012. ⟨https://www.bielertagblatt.ch/nachrichten/biel/kritikpunkte-sind-die-selben-geblieben⟩ accessed 3.03.2021.
[28] See Bieler Tagblatt, 5 June 2013. ⟨https://www.bielertagblatt.ch/nachrichten/biel/kritische-organisationen-erfolgreich⟩ accessed 3.03.2021.

tance' for other cities that are in a similar situation, such as Lucerne.[29] In one of the four city walks I participated in, people worrying about a road project in their residential district were present to eventually learn from *wasn* and highway opponents from all over Switzerland were inspired by the opposition movement in Biel.[30] Never before had a protest against an already planned highway in Switzerland been as successful as in Biel.

Therefore, the question arises as to why the resistance in Biel had such a strong impact. As described above, the city itself plays an important role as in a populous area various interests exist, and city residents would have to bear severe disadvantages for minimal benefits. Other authors have dealt with this question in newspaper articles, pointing out the importance of a realistic visualization of the project, on-site visits, a concrete alternative proposal, transparency towards the media, a neutral moderation, an independent secretariat for the dialogue procedure and, of course, the composition of the countermovement, the professional background of its founders, their group cohesion and their ability to mobilize resources for formal intervention and creative public action.[31] In what follows, I will focus my analysis on the practice of the city walk, the propagation of the image of an endangered city by *wasn* and the production of a counter-discourse through alternative expertise to imagine a different future for Biel.

One of the founders of *wasn* explained to me that it was the right time to intervene (after the general council approved the official project in 2014) since the 'psychological stress' was high enough (even though some supporters of the official project said that *wasn* was too late). The founder described what can be called an 'awareness strategy': first of all, the damage had to be shown, then they had to become active on different levels and pressure from below had to be mobilized. Therefore, they mainly chose to criticize the highway junctions and to organize the city walks (which he calls the 'crucial part of resistance') to render the future effects of the planned highway through the city experienceable. According to him, making certain elements of a future highway in the city visible and experienceable were some of the most important steps to increase the pressure on the official project. He explained that 'plans often don't look too bad, but if you are at eye level, as a human... in the city' then – as he indicated – the problems appear. Withstanding the 'enchantments of infrastructure' (Harvey und Knox 2012) is tightly linked to immediate bodily experiences.

---

[29] At the symposium 'Alternatives to highway expansion' on 13.05.2019 in Bern. This pioneer character of local resistance against federal road infrastructure projects also became interesting more recently for the resistance against a project in Bern. See MacKenzie, Calum. 2020. «Aufstand im Seeland»: Der Bund. ⟨https://webspecial.derbund.ch/longform/autobahn-in-biel/aufstand-im-seeland/⟩.

[30] MacKenzie, Calum. 2020. 'Erfolgreicher Bieler Bürgeraufstand wird zum Vorbild'. *Der Bund*, 3 December 2020.

[31] Duttweiler, Catherine. 2021. 'Wie wir das Monster erlegten'. *Das Magazin*, 9 January 2021.

I participated in four 'city walks along the axis of destruction' between April and August 2019. Although there were different guides, they all followed a similar protocol, visiting the same places and, overall, putting the main emphasis on the same issues. First, the hikers gathered behind the train station where they got some general information about the guides, about *wasn* as a commission and about the walk itself. The participants then started to walk and they stopped at different locations where the guides informed them about the alignment, its conception, its impact on existing infrastructure, human and non-human actors, and illustrated it with original visualization from the official project. In the following, I will give some examples that reveal the *in situ* debate about an unbuilt road, how signs of a future road are being interpreted and how the presence or absence of some signs are claimed to achieve political ends.

First of all, the fading road markings that had been drawn in 2017 by the Civil engineering authority of the canton of Bern[32] to make the alignment visible, especially for private landowners, were shown to us (the hikers) and criticized because they are difficult to find and minimal for a project of this dimension. We then walked a few steps and the guides showed us visualizations of the official project's highway. We realized that what looks very small and abstract on a photograph becomes massive as soon as we measure it by foot, as we experience it with our own body. Statements such as 'here we are in the hole'[33], that the highway junction is a 'city wound'[34] or that the alignment corresponds to 'cuts in the city's body'[35] supported this experience when we walked through the area where the highway connection 'city centre' would be realized (see Map 1 and Figures 1 and 2). Not only were the markings on the ground criticized but also non-existent markings, which the Civil Engineering Office should have fixed on trees that are planned to be cut down. The *wasn* commission published a press release in 2017 and marked the affected trees on their own. During the city walks, the old-growth trees were shown to us and the guide talked about the relevance of those trees to the city environment and how recreation areas, such as the lake access, would be severely affected by the long building phase.

Further, the city walk tour guides showed us some buildings (Schlachthaus, Badhausstrasse, etc.) with disintegrated fronts, which will be destroyed. They regretted that those buildings were not classified as deserving protection as they are centrally located, of architectural value and could still be used as residential building or they could accommodate social or cultural centres. And effectively, in

---

[32] Authority in charge of planning, design, construction and maintenance of fixed structures and ground facilities.
[33] Guide at the city walk.
[34] Guide at the city walk.
[35] Westastsonicht! ⟨https://www.westastsonicht.ch/de⟩ accessed 8.12.2019.

2021, two residents from Biel opened a web page and a facebook group to gather ideas on how the area could be revitalized culturally.[36]

An employee in the area of land acquisition of the Civil Engineering Office of the canton of Bern, on the other hand, had an opposing view on those buildings, when I told him that there are people that would like to protect them:

'The buildings are not modern and they are not protected' and 'they are not yet falling into ruin, but soon ... [they will fall apart]' and 'you can't do much more with them [the buildings] than to tear them down'. While some western branch combatants would protect those buildings, the employee of the Civil Engineering Office of the canton of Bern classified them as worthless, not modern and in need of renovation. This labelling delegitimates everything that stands in the way of modernity, a modernity that corresponds to a four-lane highway with two highway junctions in the city. This narrative, which emphasizes the developmental promise, by creating something 'new', is once more amplified by those 'unruly forces' (like those old buildings and the engagement of the opposition with it), which have to be contained by certain modern infrastructural forms. The 'enchantment of infrastructure', as Harvey and Knox call this process, is thus not only circulated through 'numbers, figures and pictures' that support the illusory effects of 'progress, the lure of profit, the promise of circulation, movement and a better life' but also through unruly forces, which may even intensify the desire for development (2012: 534). Nevertheless, the city walk makes not only future changes in the urban tissue visible but also experienceable and is seen by *wasn* as an adaptation of Lucius Burckhardt's 'Strollology' (2006). Burckhardt introduced a reflexive method to the field of city planning to find answers to the question: Why do we perceive a landscape in a certain way? The main idea of the method is to deconstruct the image the observer has of a landscape by taking a new look at what is perceived as being familiar. In the city walk this is made possible by information procured by the guides and by rendering palpable the future state of the city. In the book 'Der kleinstmögliche Eingriff'[37] (Burckhardt, Ritter und Schmitz 2013), Burckhardt explores how structural interventions can be prevented from happening by changing the images of city landscapes in our heads. According to the author, planning has to be understood as a recurring process, which finds temporary suiting and unharmful solutions, and he emphasizes that the dimension of time must be taken seriously in planning processes. Decisions have to be postponed to gather supplemental information, to minimize unwelcome side effects and to let everyone participate in the democratic process who would otherwise not have been entitled to vote because the project was carried out too quickly (Gribat 2017).

---

[36] Schlachthof Kulturzentrum. ⟨https://schlachthof-kulturzentrum.ch/wordpress/⟩ accessed 3.03.2021.

[37] Translation: The minimal intervention.

Effectively, the official project was suspended in 2019 after a survey concluded that there is only little support from the population for the official project and more support for the alternative of *wasn*, before it was completely written off at the end of 2020.[38] The city walks were important for producing these results and may just have had the effects Burckhardt imagined. However, there are more reasons why the official project came to a halt. The elaboration of an alternative to the official project was certainly one of the most important works of *wasn*, which is also presented in the city walks, but also the production of a history to the western branch written by Loderer (2019), the interviewing of people who face dispossession, as well as the marking of trees and the organizing of demonstrations had an impact, and – which became public only after the project was written off – a leaked USB stick with all the relevant information about the official project.[39] All those elements allowed the board of the *wasn* commission, which is composed of town planners, architects, journalists, lawyers and local politicians, to produce a well-founded counter-discourse. They developed an alternative, which has since been taken seriously by the Department of Construction, Transport and Energy of the canton of Bern and been subjected to a technical comparison with the official project (which was criticized later by *wasn* as 'one-sided, outdated and incorrect'[40]) . In sum, all those points enabled a form of bargaining power that made effective resistance and refusal possible.

Special abilities and methods – some form of power – are needed *to resist* or *to refuse*. Power, in a Foucauldian sense, is not only imposed from the state or the powerful, but must be understood as both puissance or force and as a 'potentiality, capability or capacity' in the sense of 'to be able to' (Feder 2014: 55-56). Power is not possessed but can rather 'issue from "anywhere"' and 'works *through* culture and customs, institutions and individuals' (ebd. 56). Thus, it must be seen as 'productive' (Foucault 2016: 294), as something that produces negative as well as positive effects, and produces reality with all its possible characteristics, practices, subjectivities and knowledges. Furthermore, according to Ensminger, a basic definition of bargaining power is 'one's ability to get what one wants from others'. This greatly depends on the individual's social status, economic wealth and the ability to exert effects on the ideologies of others. And furthermore, 'bargaining power is determined by the pre-existing institutional, organizational and ideological configuration [but] bargaining power can also be used to effect changes in each of these domains' (1992: 7). Bargaining power is thus relational. It does not

---

[38] Bieler Tagblatt, 13 November 2018. ⟨https://www.bielertagblatt.ch/die-grosse-bt-umfrage-zum-westast⟩ accessed 3.03.2021.

[39] 1.6 gigabytes or 3,000 pages of profiles, plans, concepts, environmental compatibility reports and documentation on the planned expropriations were leaked to *wasn* in early 2017. See Duttweiler, Catherine 2021. 'Wie wir das Monster erlegten'. *Das Magazin*, 9 January 2021.

[40] See Westastsonicht! ⟨https://www.westastsonicht.ch/de/infos/medien-mitteilungen⟩ accessed 3.03.2021.

work against institutions, but is influenced by them, works through them and has the power to change them.

Mobilizing a particular language to make demands becomes crucial. This involves the 'recourse to legal technologies and vocabularies of rights, citizenship and territory', as discussed in the entry on 'resistance' in the *Cambridge Encyclopedia of Anthropology* (Wright 2016). In those terms, the resistance movement was so effective because it refused to act as it ought, and successfully mobilized narratives to produce a counter-discourse that uses legal frameworks and a strategy of visibility for achieving its goals. The shift from an imposed top-down project to a bottom-up negotiation process, which challenges notions of transparency, participation, social justice, conservation and protection, led successfully to the refusal and disenchantment of this infrastructure project.

Conclusion – from resistance to refusal

In 2019, a round table was set in place to find a city-compatible solution until mid-2020 with supporters and opponents of the official project. Different variations, which were neglected long ago, were evaluated and the supporters as well as the opponents of the official project were aware that an agreement had to be made that satisfied different interests. At the end of 2020, finally, the official project was written off completely.

In this article I focus on the city walk, which is a creative method of resistance that includes bodily experiences of something beyond imagination. As I showed, highways in cities are especially intrusive. By drawing on Burckhardt's ideas of the smallest possible intervention, planning needs to be understood as a recurring process in which the dimension of time must be taken seriously. As the western branch combatants succeeded in delaying the official project, time was gained to make new arrangements and to check new and old alternatives. By mobilizing knowledge, professional expertise and rights, the broad-based movement produced a counter-discourse that led to a disenchantment of the promise of modernity. Although the Swiss net resolution and its legal framework stipulate a top-down procedure that in other places certainly overlooked participation and thus can be seen as an 'anti-politics machine' (Ferguson 1990), local refusal proved that it is possible to withstand the enchantment of infrastructure and to renegotiate a situation in which local desire for development was long perceived as secondary to national interests. The informed practice of resistance of *wasn* enabled a more balanced political dialogue. I would argue that it is this democratic dialogue that made it possible for *wasn* to refuse the project in the first place. This refusal – as theorized by McGranahan (2016) – (re)produces groups and community and has the power not only to stop something, but also to let something new appear that is in line with the hopes and the desires of those affected.

Glossary

wasn Westast – so nicht!/Western branch – not like this!
FEDRO Swiss Federal Roads Office

References

Augé, Marc 1995: Non-places: introduction to an anthropology of supermodernity. London?; New York: Verso.
Burckhardt, Lucius 2006 (4. Auflage): Warum ist Landschaft schön? die Spaziergangswissenschaft (M. Ritter & M. Schmitz, Hrsg.). Berlin: Martin Schmitz Verlag.
Burckhardt, Lucius, Markus Ritter und Martin Schmitz 2013: Der kleinstmögliche Eingriff: oder die Rückführung der Planung auf das Planbare. Berlin: Schmitz.
Dalakoglou, Dimitris und Penny Harvey (Hg.) 2015: Roads and Anthropology: Ethnography, Infrastructure, (Im)mobility. London: Routeledge.
De Boeck, Filip 2012, November 26: Infrastructure: Commentary from Filip De Boeck. *Cultural Anthropology Online* (Curated Collections).
Ensminger, Jean 1992: Making a market: the institutional transformation of an African society (The Political economy of institutions and decisions). Cambridge [England]?; New York: Cambridge University Press.
Feder, Ellen K. 2014: Power/knowledge. In: Taylor, Dianna (Hg.): Michel Foucault: key concepts. (Key Concepts). Oxon, New York: Routledge, Taylor & Francis Group.
Ferguson, James 1990: The anti-politics machine: «development,» depoliticization, and bureaucratic power in Lesotho. Cambridge [England]?; New York: Cambridge University Press.
Foucault, Michel 2016 (16. Auflage): Überwachen und Strafen: die Geburt des Gefängnisses (W. Seitter, Übers.) (Suhrkamp-Taschenbuch Nr. 2271). Frankfurt am Main: Suhrkamp.
Gaffino, David, Reto Lindegger, Laurent Auberson, and Tobias Kaestli, eds. 2013. *Bieler Geschichte*. Baden: Hier + Jetzt, Verlag für Kultur und Geschichte.
Gribat, Nina 2017: Lucius Burckhardt: Der kleinstmögliche Eingriff. In: Eckardt, Frank (Hg.): Schlüsselwerke der Stadtforschung. Wiesbaden: Springer VS. 145–160.
Harvey, Penny und Hannah Knox 2012: The Enchantments of Infrastructure. *Mobilities* 7 (4): 521–536. DOI: https://doi.org/10.1080/17450101.2012.718935
Harvey, Penny und Hannah Knox 2015: Roads: An Anthropology of Infrastructure and Expertise. Ithaca: Cornell University Press.
Jacobs, Jane 1961: The death and life of great American cities. New York: Random House.
Kammann, George 1990: Mit Autobahnen die Städte retten? Städtebauliche Ideen der Expressstrassen-Planung in der Schweiz 1954 – 1964. Zürich: Chronos.
Loderer, Benedikt 2019: Das Bieler Dreieck: Eine kleine Geschichte der Autobahn 1953-2017 (WESTAST SO NICHT!, Hrsg.). Biel/Bienne: edition clandestin.
McGranahan, Carole 2016: Theorizing Refusal: An Introduction. *Cultural Anthropology* 31 (3): 319–325. DOI: https://doi.org/10.14506/ca31.3.01
Mok, Ka Yan, Geoffrey Qiping Shen und Jing Yang 2015: Stakeholder management studies in mega construction projects: A review and future directions. *International Journal of Project Management* 33 (2): 446–457. DOI: https://doi.org/10.1016/j.ijproman.2014.08.007

Salet, Willem, Luca Bertolini und Mendel Giezen 2013: Complexity and Uncertainty: Problem or Asset in Decision Making of Mega Infrastructure Projects? *International Journal of Urban and Regional Research* 37 (6): 1984–2000. DOI: https://doi.org/10.1111/j.1468-2427.2012.01133.x

Wright, Fiona 2016: Resistance. *Cambridge Encyclopedia of Anthropology*. DOI: https://doi.org/10.29164/16resistance

Newspaper articles

Balmer, Deborah. 2016. «Die Geschichte des Westasts reicht bis in die 50er Jahre zurück». Bieler Tagblatt, 13. September 2016. ⟨https://www.pro-westast.ch/images/medienspiegel/BT_13_09_16_Die_Geschichte_des_Westasts_reicht_bis_in_die_50er_Jahre_zurueck.pdf⟩.

— 2018a. «Schon damals kein Freund der Anschlüsse». Bieler Tagblatt, 12. September 2018. ⟨https://westast.ch/wordpress/wp-content/uploads/2018/09/20180912_BT_Leuenberger.pdf⟩.

— 2018b. «Die grosse BT-Umfrage zum Westast». Bieler Tagblatt, 13. November 2018. ⟨https://www.bielertagblatt.ch/die-grosse-bt-umfrage-zum-westast⟩.

Berger, Eva. 2012a. «Im Mai liegt der Ball beim Volk». Bieler Tagblatt, 7. März 2012. ⟨https://www.bielertagblatt.ch/nachrichten/biel/im-mai-liegt-der-ball-beim-volk⟩.

— 2012b. «Kritikpunkte sind die selben geblieben». Bieler Tagblatt, 28. Mai 2012. ⟨https://www.bielertagblatt.ch/nachrichten/biel/kritikpunkte-sind-die-selben-geblieben⟩.

Bieler Tagblatt. 2008a. «Behörden unter Beschuss», 4. März 2008. ⟨https://www.bielertagblatt.ch/nachrichten/vermischtes/behoerden-unter-beschuss⟩.

— 2008b. «‹Da muss man noch daran arbeiten›», 15. Mai 2008. ⟨https://www.bielertagblatt.ch/nachrichten/vermischtes/da-muss-man-noch-daran-arbeiten⟩.

— 2008c. «Trainingsstart für A5-Baustelle», 4. Dezember 2008. ⟨https://www.bielertagblatt.ch/trainingsstart-fuer-a5-baustelle?destination=node/804732⟩.

— 2009a. «Bohrungen sorgen für Ärger», 22. April 2009. ⟨https://www.bielertagblatt.ch/bohrungen-sorgen-fuer-aerger⟩.

— 2009b. «A5-Baustelle im Mühlefeld macht Ohrenweh», 7. Mai 2009. ⟨https://www.bielertagblatt.ch/a5-baustelle-im-muehlefeld-macht-ohrenweh⟩.

— 2009c. «Viel Lärm um kleine Versuchsbaustelle», 7. Mai 2009. ⟨https://www.bielertagblatt.ch/viel-laerm-um-kleine-versuchsbaustelle⟩.

Bruderer, Urs. 2018. «Der Fluch des Plans». Die Republik, 6. Dezember 2018. ⟨https://www.republik.ch/2018/12/06/der-fluch-des-plans⟩.

Duttweiler, Catherine. 2019. «Bieler Stadtautobahn: Warum die Arbeitsgruppe Stöckli scheiterte – und was wir daraus für den Runden Tisch lernen!» Westast so nicht!, 5. Februar 2019. ⟨https://www.westastsonicht.ch/de/aktuell/aktuell/der-runde-tisch⟩.

— 2021. «Wie wir das Monster erlegten». Das Magazin, 9. Januar 2021.

Epper, Bettina, und Ricardo Tarli. 2008. «A5-Umfahrung: Kanton prüft Porttunnel». Bieler Tagblatt, 8. Mai 2008. ⟨https://www.bielertagblatt.ch/nachrichten/vermischtes/a5-umfahrung-kanton-prueft-porttunnel⟩.

Léchot, Jérôme. 2017. «Biel kämpft gegen einen Autobahndinosaurier – und könnte siegen». Das Lamm, 22. November 2017. ⟨https://daslamm.ch/biel-kaempft-gegen-einen-autobahndinosaurier-und-koennte-siegen/⟩.

MacKenzie, Calum. 2020. «Aufstand im Seeland»: Der Bund, 2020. ⟨https://webspecial.derbund.ch/longform/autobahn-in-biel/aufstand-im-seeland/⟩.
Sahli, Michael. 2017. «So will Biel sein Schmuddel-Image loswerden». Schweizer Radio und Fernsehen (SRF), 20. Juli 2017. ⟨https://www.srf.ch/news/schweiz/so-will-biel-sein-schmuddel-image-loswerden⟩.
Scherrer, Lucien. 2019. «Mehr als jeder Zehnte lebt von der Fürsorge – ein Streifzug durch die Sozialhilfe-Hauptstadt Biel»: Neue Zürcher Zeitung (NZZ), 10.05.2019. ⟨https://www.nzz.ch/schweiz/fuersorge-stadt-biel-mehr-als-jeder-zehnte-lebt-von-sozialhilfe-ld.1480750?reduced=true⟩.
Schindler, Patric. 2009. «Mühe mit dem Bieler ‹Hüst-und-Hott›». Bieler Tagblatt, 28. Januar 2009. ⟨https://www.bielertagblatt.ch/nachrichten/vermischtes/muehe-mit-dem-bieler-huest-und-hott⟩.
Sommer, Mike. 2007a. «Damoklesschwert über dem Quartier». Bieler Tagblatt, 31. Januar 2007. ⟨https://www.bielertagblatt.ch/nachrichten/vermischtes/damoklesschwert-ueber-dem-quartier⟩.
— 2007b. «Zweifel sind noch nicht ausgeräumt». Bieler Tagblatt, 3. Dezember 2007. ⟨http://www.bielertagblatt.ch/nachrichten/vermischtes/zweifel-sind-noch-nicht-ausgeraeumt⟩.
Staub, Peter. 2013. «Kritische Organisationen erfolgreich». Bieler Tagblatt, 5. Juni 2013. ⟨https://www.bielertagblatt.ch/nachrichten/biel/kritische-organisationen-erfolgreich⟩.
Tanner, Samuel. 2020. «Es ist nicht sauber, nicht leistungsorientiert und auch noch stolz darauf. Warum ist Biel so anders als der Rest der Schweiz?» Neue Zürcher Zeitung (NZZ) am Sonntag, 20. Juni 2020. ⟨https://nzzas.nzz.ch/magazin/biel-bienne-portraet-eines-widerstandsnests-ld.1561713?reduced=true#register⟩.

Webographie

A5 Biel-Bienne. ⟨https://www.a5-biel-bienne.ch/projektuebersicht/umwelt/⟩ accessed 15.04.2020
Autobahnumfahrung A5 Biel-Bienne Westast «Versuchsbaugrube». ⟨https://www.bielertagblatt.ch/sites/bielertagblatt.ch/files/4a/8a/4a8a7be831cc4555b1c8fdb8d599475a.pdf⟩ accessed 8.02.2021
Bieler Altstadt Stadtgeschichte. ⟨https://www.bieler-altstadt.ch/portfolio-item/stadtgeschichte/⟩ accessed 8.02.2021
Schlachthof. ⟨https://schlachthof-kulturzentrum.ch/wordpress/⟩ accessed 3.03.2021
Schweizerische Eidgenossenschaft. Bundesgesetz über die Nationalstrassen. ⟨https://www.admin.ch/opc/de/classified-compilation/19600028/index.html⟩ accessed 8.02.2021
Schweizerische Eidgenossenschaft. Nationalstrassennetz. ⟨https://www.astra.admin.ch/astra/de/home/themen/nationalstrassen/nationalstrassennetz.html⟩ accessed 8.02.2021
Schweizerische Eidgenossenschaft. Swiss Political System–Facts and Figures. ⟨https://www.eda.admin.ch/aboutswitzerland/en/home/politik/uebersicht/politisches-system-der-schweiz---fakten-und-zahlen.html⟩ accessed 8.02.2021
Schweizerische Eidgenossenschaft. Eidgenössisches Departement für Umwelt, Verkehr, Energie und Kommunikation UVEK. 15.01.2021. «Verfügung». ⟨https://www.westastsonicht.ch/de/aktuell/aktuell⟩ accessed 8.02.2021

Stadt Biel/Ville de Bienne. Statistisches Factsheet/Données statistiques. ‹https://www.biel-bienne.ch/public/upload/assets/912/pra_sm_fact_sheet_jun20_d_f.pdf› accessed 8.02.2021

Städtebauliche Begleitplanung A5 Westast. ‹https://biel-nidau-2050.ch/index.php› accessed 8.12.2019

Westast so nicht! ‹https://westastsonicht.ch/› accessed 8.02.2021

From Enchantment to Disenchantment and the New Participatory Politics of Infrastructure Development: A Conclusive Comparison

Tobias Haller and Samuel Weissman, Institute of Social Anthropology, University of Bern, Switzerland

Introduction

Throughout the 16 case studies it became apparent that the different Mega-Infrastructure Projects (MIPs) described vary widely. Examples such as the New Silk Road or the Delhi–Mumbai Industrial Corridor differ greatly in scale and size from a pipeline in North America or a mine in Mongolia. And they vary just as widely in the political and economic dimensions or the scale at which populations are affected, and the type of industry or infrastructure can be subtle or overwhelming in its presence and impact. Lastly, while some projects seem straightforward in their complexity, others seem less easy to grasp in their enormity. How, then, can there be any comparable insight into such vastly different MIPs?

To this end, this chapter will provide a summary and a comparison as well as a conclusion of these 16 case studies using theoretical approaches and focusing on the hypothesis developed in the introduction. Following New Institutionalism, we assumed that in all the cases there was a change in relative prices that rendered a specific area interesting for MIP investments. Additionally, we saw that following this investment came promises of economic as well as developmental betterment, the conditions that allow for the enchantment to take place and that are supposed to give legitimacy to the undertaking (see Harvey and Knox 2012). As argued by de Vries (2007), we label this process as an anti-politics machine of desires. However, we have also outlined that, following the theoretical perspective of a combined political ecology and new institutional approach (NIPE), the rules on how this process was set in motion are based on how and by whom land was provided or acquired for a respective MIP. In most cases, these provisions and acquisitions happen via institutional changes, in which land and land-related common pool resources are appropriated and local property rights, often common property, are violated.

As many cases in this book illustrate, this has led to a range of local reactions, either low-level local responses as several forms of weapons of the weak (Scott 1985), such as small acts of sabotage, up to stronger responses such as protests, as seen in the case of the LAPSSET in both Turkana and Lamu Port. There were also cases where resistance was based on legal claims, as shown in the case of the Saami in Norway and real forms of politics machines. Hereby, in the best case, forms of local political mobilisation and the attempt to halt an MIP were partially or wholly successful from the perspective of locals. The case from Switzerland, for example, stood out as being able to re-establish local rules and contrasting the MIP development enchantment with local vistas of development.

In order to cross-compare and align comparable findings from similar cases, we realised that, for analysis purposes, we needed a way to structure the comparable elements of each case. On the one hand, this was established through structuring each chapter along the same parameters. This meant that all authors had to discuss their cases within the outline framework: after situating the case study, the first part focused on the more general historical, environmental, political and economic context. The second part then focused on the actual MIP, its stakeholders, the environmental and social impacts, and lastly on differentiating the perspectives and strategies of implementers such as companies, states and investors, and those of the affected actors, such as local elites, non-elites and NGOs.

On the other hand, we needed an analytical tool to break down the complexity and scalability of each MIP, so we developed the idea of docking stations. This turned out to be very helpful for the final chapter. Since the entire book project was an attempt to discuss the rather neglected issue of what happens on the ground, the focus also lies on partial elements of MIPs. As some cases show, the ethnographic descriptions of how such partial sub-projects can affect a locality were immensely helpful in building a case for our arguments.

The described dynamics of change and shifting in institutional arrangements provided ways in which to understand tendencies more clearly, based on the criteria of our underlying theories. These, as introduced at the beginning of the book, are mainly oriented to the new frontier theory, enchantment and disenchantment and related anti-politics and politics machines. In order finally to engage critically with these theories, they are discussed and embedded in a new institutional political ecology (NIPE) framework as well as insights from the environmental justice debate.

Therefore, just as each chapter in this book, the theoretical discussion of the findings here will follow a similar structure:

A) Discussion of the larger context of MIPs and their characteristics (national economies and legal frameworks, histories and case study overviews with typologies)
B) Discussion of state and company strategies, including perspectives, narratives and discourses of enchantment, as well as characterising the comparability

of states' and companies' strategies (case study summaries, overview and typologies of company and state relations)

C) Discussion of local and NGO strategies, including perspectives, narratives and discourses of disenchantment and characterising the comparability of strategies (case study summaries and overview of local and NGO examples)

The discussion of the cases will include short summaries and will be ordered in groups of geographical areas pertaining to the continents and in another grouping where we establish the comparability of MIPs in relation to their economic sectors of influence. These were aligned as MIPs dealing with agricultural corridors, transit and mobility, and by infrastructure dealing with oil, roads, trading hubs, etc.; and, lastly, a category for cases dealing with indirect or as yet not established connecting infrastructures, single infrastructure projects such as the hydro-power dam in Ecuador or the Olu-Tolgoy Mine in Mongolia that are nonetheless having wide-ranging infrastructural impacts. Such cases illustrate how the concept of docking stations is an option to think about a local project in more encompassing terms, because it can be linked to a larger MIP and thus is easier to implement by states and companies.

Since we are dealing with different MIPs across the world, which are all in different stages of implementation, the cross-comparison will also focus on these differences and similarities, where cases allow for comparing the similarities of certain stages, such as on the level of a docking station. Because these projects are often carried out across wide scales of space and time, the comparison needs to account for the historical as well as future projections included in the case studies.

The concluding chapter then aims to present our findings on the basis of the theoretical questions. We try to determine the issues surrounding MIPs in relation to the political, economic, and social dimensions discussed as counter-perspectives from above and from below. Based on the institutional understanding of the entities on sometimes opposing or related sides of a project or docking stations within an MIP, the aim will be to paint a clearer picture of what can be problematised. From there, the issues can be grouped into a more general understanding of which cases point to dysfunctional or functional phenomena and what might be the leading causes that lie behind such developments. Creating various matrixes for comparing the varieties of possible comparisons will allow for the concluding chapter to relate the findings in the context of the theories discussed in the introduction. We will present the data in three matrixes:

The first matrix (Figure 1) shows the enchantment strategy used from a state and/or company perspective and their discourse related to the gains to be received by the public. The second matrix (Figure 2) positions the perpective of local actors who see little to no enchantment and no gains but high losses especially of their commons. The third (Figure 3) summarises in a comparative way local reactions towards the state's and companies' anti-politics machines, related also to the bargaining power and institution shopping from below: Groups with high bargaining power are able to turn anti-politics machines into politics machines based also on their disenchantment, which they are able to articulate.

Furthermore, we propose to adopt the New Institutional Political Ecology (NIPE) model of the processes driving MIPs by the end of the conclusion (see Figure 4 adapted from Haller 2019a).

We will lastly situate this book in relation to the previous findings in earlier books in the Action Anthropology Series with Lit by Haller et al. (2007) on oil and gas projects, and by Niederberger et al. (2016) on mining, in order to expand on the newest dimension brought through the 'Mega' in infrastructure projects.

Structurally, MIPs are in most cases clearly distinguishable from single, large and localised infrastructure projects, such as a mine, a farming estate, a hydropower dam or reservoir, or another similar undertaking that can have a spatial and environment-altering impact. While such undertakings can have similar effects on a local level, concerning the disruption of social, institutional, political, economic and environmental conditions, we argue that MIPs add another dimension to the alteration that may occur, in that they extend across several localities to various degrees. While the discourses surrounding topics of disruption of the commons, including forms of land and resource-grabbing, might be discussed as similar locally, our understanding of the effect of MIPs across multiple localities needs to be read against the larger narratives built on national and international platforms.

Hereby, many of the presented case studies have been shown to include political narratives by state and company/investor actors that consider large-scale infrastructure to hold benefits for all in the sense of a greater good. MIPs contain promises of development, jobs, connectivity, economic growth, prosperity and general hopes of not only increasing standards of living for all, but often also a modernist idea of betterment for the planet. Herein lies the issue of the enchantment and also of the anti-politics of modernity and sustainable development.

Based on findings from earlier case studies dealing with the oil industry and large mines (see Haller et al. 2007 and Niederberger et al. 2016), the odds of the successful integration of opposing viewpoints from local groups into development and state policies seem even more unlikely. However, as we are able to outline, a few cases show partial or total success when it comes to the acknowledgement of an opposing position. These arise from a stance of disenchantment also because of losses of the land and resources previously held as common property, combined with an exclusion from tangible benefits. Additionally, local actors in these cases show non-Western ontologies of development, providing them with counter-ideologies of development. This enables certain actors to mobilise resistance against the externally driven MIPs and to regain bargaining power to halt or change certain plans by MIPs. These cases are important to show what is needed in the organisational and institutional arrangement in and around an MIP in order for such dialogues to progress. It also shows how local bottom-up institution-building and innovations can be successful in integrating all stakeholders in negotiations in order to devise other forms of locally adapted infrastructures. This also relates to the constitutionality approach, discussing elements under which rules regarding infrastructure development can be crafted and enacted (see Haller et al. 2016, 2018).

Larger context of MIP cases and their characteristics

Table 1 provides a main overview of the case studies listed in order of continent and country, as well as the kind of MIPs they relate to. Table 2 shows an overview arranged by the national regions of the case studies and illustrates at which stage of implementation the MIPs are (planning, implementing or as a form of docking station related to larger projects). Furthermore, information is given on the kind of ecosystem and political system (democratic or rather autocratic countries) within which these MIPs are taking place.

Differences and similarities between the case contexts

Table 1 gives an orientation on the types of MIPs in the case studies according to different regions. The types of MIPs are differentiated according to their main purpose, where a large X marks the major purpose and a small x marks several additional purposes. Many MIPs also have a multi-purpose characteristic.

Table 1: Overview of case studies

Continent	Country	Project	Transport road	Energy	Agrarian	Mining	Smart city/ investment zone	Multi-purpose
Asia	Pakistan: (Balochistan)	Belt and Road Initiative	X		x	x		X
	Tibet	Belt and Road Initiative	X		x			X
	Mongolia	Oyu Tolgoi Mine	x			X		X
	India	Delhi–Mumbai Corridor	X					
	India	Dholera Special Investment Region – Smart City	x				X	X
Africa	Egypt	Benaben Solar Park		X				
	Namibia	Hydropower dams		X	x			X

	Kenya	LAPSSET Lamu Port	X					
	Kenya	LAPSSET Turkana Oil	X			x		X
	Tanzania	SAGCOT	x		X			
Americas	Bolivia	Agrarian MIPs	x		X			X
	Ecuador	River Dam project		X				
	USA	Black Rock Pipeline	X					
Europe	Norway	Storheia Wind Farm	x	X				X
	Italy	Oil Pipeline Project Bari	X					
	Switzerland	Highway access road, Biel	X					
Total	16		8	4	2	1	1	8

In our selection we have a wide array of cases across all continents, with Asia being of central importance, but also Africa, as these are very different but also very dynamic regions, while we have fewer case studies for the Americas and Europe. The latter is of interest especially also due to its different political and ecological background compared to the other cases, and we will see how this also relates to politics machines. Table 1 shows that the presented MIPs in total number 8 transport/road, 4 energy (transport), 2 agriculture-related, one mining, and one smart city/special investment zone project. Some of them also serve multiple demands and uses (i.e. road *and* energy transport facilities on land and water, transport *and* smart city). This shows the multi-purpose nature of MIPs (8 cases). Hereby, what we have labelled as docking stations become clear, meaning that projects can be added or combined as the main project progresses.

Stages of implementation, local ecology and political system

The second overview table presents more details on the projects and their implementation stages. In addition, it illustrates in which political system – democratic in practice or just in its constitution[1] – and in which eco-system context these cases are taking place. This provides information on the potential impact of projects and the options for local action arenas. It also shows if and to which larger MIP context these cases are related as docking stations, as proposed. This indicates whether these are part of larger MIP developments or only single cases.

---

[1] We try to differentiate between what formally can be described as a true democracy and what can be understood as a more autocratic form of democracy. These should be read as indicators of current regime tendencies by their international designations.

Table 2: Overview area/country/case studies, authors, stages of implementation, ecology, political system

Region/Case study	Topic/Author	Stage of MIP implementation / Docking station	Ecosystem	Formal political system
Asia/Pakistan (Balochistan) Belt and Road Initiative	*Roads and port* / Y. Forster	5 years into implementation. / Docking station to Belt and Road I.	Mountain dryland and marine (tropical)	Autocratic
Asia/Tibet Belt and Road Initiative	*Roads&Mining, Dams*/ D. Kongpo & S.M. Moozhiyil	Ongoing sub-projects over ca. 20 years. / Docking station to Belt and Road I.	Mountain cold dryland with sea	Autocratic
Asia/Mongolia Oyu Tolgoi Mine	*Mining*/ T. Sternberg	Ongoing mining project, established over 20 years. / No apparent docking station	Plain cold dryland	Autocratic democracy
Asia/India, Delhi–Mumbai Corridor	*Several railways, road projects*/ M. Grogg	In implementation phase. / Docking station to DMIC.	Semi-arid tropical	Autocratic democracy
Asia/India, DMIC Dholera Special Investment Region – Smart City	*Roads, railway & urban real estate*/ O. Stettler	In planning since 2009, first phase of implementation not yet begun. / Docking station to DMIC.	Semi-arid tropical	Autocratic democracy
Africa/Egypt Benaben Solar Park	*Large-scale solar fields* / A. Furger	Project implemented in 2017 and finished in 2019. / Already existing electrical grid/EU green energy.	Dryland, hot desert	Autocratic democracy
Africa/Namibia Hydro-power dams	*Several dams*/ J. Warner& R. Meissner	Planning phase since 1980s and early stages of feasibility. / To electrical grid, possible rail/infrastructure.	Dryland, hot savannahs	Autocratic democracy
Africa/Kenya LAPSSET/Lamu Port	*Shipping port* / F. Werthmüller	Since 2016 dredging of port bay area and three berths. / To LAPSSET	Dryland, hot savannas with sea	Autocratic democracy
Africa/Kenya LAPSSET Turkana Oil	*Oil pipeline*/ B. Kilaka & E. Schubiger	New oil fields found triggered planning / To LAPSSET (transport networks).	Dryland, hot savannas	Autocratic democracy
Africa/Tanzania SAGCOT	*Agro-industrial investments*/ B. Bösch, S. Fiechter, F. Gallauer & D. Gmür	Since 2008 growth planned and realised, connectivity through physical infrastructure and markets/Green investment. / Several green development agendas.	Semi-arid gallary forests	Autocratic democracy

Americas/Bolivia, agribusiness production zones	*Agro-industrial investments*/ A. Llanque, MI, Mamani, J. Jacobi	Since 2000s agro-industrial investment and extractivism. / Agro-development docking station of LA countries	Semi-humid to humid rainforest	Autocratic democracy
Americas/Ecuador, Hydro-power dam	*Small dam with large impacts*/ H. Plüss	Finalised in 2014, protests before and after over water rights & fisheries / To national and regional electro grid LA	Semi-humid to humid (rainforest)	Democratic
Americas/USA, Dakota Access Oil Pipeline	*Large-scale oil pipeline* /A. K. Vokinger	Pipeline in service since 2017. Dispute over construction and path of pipeline by First Nations.* / National oil infrastructure	Semi-arid savannas and plains	Democratic
Europe/Switzerland, Access highway, city of Biel	*Highway connection*/ L. Schönenberg	Highway grid built in the 1960s and halted project for highway connection (City of Biel) / National highway	Continental semi-humid	Democratic
Europe/Italy Oil Pipeline Project Bari	*Pipeline infrastructure* / A. Pusceddu	Since 2017, now completed through Italy, olive tree fields uprooted / To southern part of Italy for energy transport MIP across Europe and connecting to BRI.	Southern Mediterranean Semi-arid, sea and mountains	Democratic
Europe/Norway: Storheia Wind Farm	*Large-size windmill park*/ B. Wyler	Since 2013 agreement to install windmills on land of indigenous Saami herders, windmills built in 2019.	tundra cold semi-arid dryland	Democratic

(LA = Latin America) (*by 2022)

An important aspect of this summary table is to see if the MIPs are already ongoing or implemented with the full expected environmental and resource and land rights impacts, or if they are still in the planning phase. The overview shows that 10 are ongoing or implemented, already with a full range of impacts, while 5 are in planning and one was in planning but was halted. In more detailed analysis, we have in Asia 2 ongoing and 2 in the implementation phase (having impacts already) and 1 in planning. In Africa 3 are implemented/ongoing and 2 in planning. In the Americas 3 are implemented, and in Europe 2 are implemented and one is in planning (or halted). It is of interest to see if it is only in the cases with direct visible impacts that local people reacted with disenchantment, or if there are also cases in which the project was still only in the planning stage when local groups came out clearly against it – meaning a disenchantment BEFORE the project even started. Interestingly, also 8 of the projects were implemented or planned in drylands, 4 in semi-arid environments and 3 in semi-humid to humid areas. This means that there are many MIPs in our selection that are planned or implemented in drylands or semi-drylands. Thus, there are often marginal areas with unfavorable ecological conditions for local livelihoods, and thus a much higher vulnerability for these local livelihoods. This would also lead to the conclusion that in our sample we are mostly dealing with 'hinterland' areas (apart from the 'smart city' contexts and urban areas such as the cases in India and Switzerland). Other important information is the fact that the case studies are taking place in predominantly authoritarian and a combination of autocratic and democratic systems: 2 and 9 respectively, making 11 cases of not truly democratic systems, which is the majority. Only in 5 cases can the government, at least formally, be labelled as being a true democracy with a legal system including human rights and legal tenure security, as according to the Geneva convention.

However, as the cases in Europe and the USA show, these are basic political frameworks, which have to be strategically used by local actors in the sense we discussed as institution shopping in the NIPE framework. This in turn is only possible in contexts with high local bargaining power and in which the state can be held accountable by internationally enforced conventions (such as basic human rights etc). Cases such as the oil pipeline in the USA and the windmill project in Norway show on the one hand that local actors and their supporters need to be extremely vigilant if they are not to be also marginalised by the state elite. But on the other hand, it means that, in these cases, a system of legality exists that can be used in different ways by the powerful *and* the less powerful. Again, this relates to the concept of institution shopping as proposed in the NIPE approach, as there are courts to which one can appeal with a certain amount of financial support and some chances of success. However, such a procedure is unthinkable in many of the other cases with a less participative rule of law.

State strategies: the big enchantment of (green) development discourse, the anti-politics of commons grabbing and institution shopping strategies

As outlined by our combined institutional and political ecology approach, most of these areas we looked at became valuable for investment in connection with already existing large-scale and often also geo-strategic plans. Consequently, they were seeing an increase in the value of their area (see Pakistan, Tibet, Egypt, Namibia, Kenya (LAPSSET: Port Lamu), Tanzania, Bolivia, the USA, Switzerland, Italy and Norway. But also the other cases (the two Indian cases and the other Kenya case (LAPSSET Turkana) and the Ecuador case) are linked by the external increase of value due to already existing networks of investments. One can thus argue that these projects have not come out of the blue, but are linked to already existing large-scale plans, while at the same time also triggering new investments: that they further raise the relative value of prices in the area and increase the economic attractiveness in a kind of positive economic feedback loop.

Interestingly, and as an adaptation to the global green governance discourse pushed by the global north, most of these investments come with *big (green) enchantment strategies* which take several forms from the perspective of governments and the investment sector. The basis of this is the main underlying idea of economic development in the sense of a betterment of mobility and formal employment, and the ideology of modernity as part of the classic modernist theory from the 1960s (Rostow's take-off idea). While in all examples the enchantment is evident and also win-win discourses are used as a justification (see Pakistan, Tibet, Mongolia, as well as Kenya (LAPSSET Turkana Oil), Bolivia, the USA, Switzerland and Italy), other cases combine this discourse with issues of the environment, using in addition discourses of sustainability and green energy gains (the two Indian cases, Egypt, Namibia, LAPSSET Port Lamu in Kenya, Ecuador and Norway). It thus becomes evident that we are not just dealing with the classic modernity enchantment, but in at least 7 of the 16 cases (nearly 50%) 'modernity' is combined with an environmental enchantment, a quasi post-modernity that accounts for environmental concerns.

Looking at the question of whether the promises of these enchantments are met, the result is disappointing. Practically all cases show that the promises of modern and sustainable development are not kept entirely. Most of the modern infrastructure developments do not serve local interests, and the promises of employment and betterment do not materialise in 12 of the 16 cases. In the ones that are not yet implemented but are partially underway, the fullfillment of the promises cannot yet be seen (see Kenya LAPSSET Turkana and Switzerland, the highway in the city of Biel), while in the other two cases (the USA and Norway) the indigenous peoples have no interest in these promises as they have religious or subsistence-specific identity-driven interests. We will discuss this aspect further in the section below on the strategies of local actors.

A second element that is related to the enchantment is that the development that is promised works as an *anti-politics machine* in a double sense: it is not only the classical development discourse but also related to green and sustainable visions of development and the benefits of large connectivity. These visions enshrined in the anti-politics machines hide the fact that this connectivity has already been ongoing since the beginning of industrialisation and colonisation in all these areas, and that it does not recognize power asymmetries, which are also blurred in this way. The modernity apparatus is presented as a natural and logical endeavour that is now being naturalised in the global context. It also hides the fact that in many areas only governments and companies have the power to decide on the direction and rules of (green) development, thereby only sometimes involving local municipalities and elites, but often without the true participation of local communities; thus no devolution of the political process takes place. These anti-politics machines encompass forms of nebulous discourses as we see in the cases hiding the following issues, which we thus name after the political issues they hide:

a) *State Repression:* inclusive infrastructure development hiding repression and state control (Pakistan, Tibet, Kenya LAPSSET Turkana)
b) *Land Grabbing:* market development hiding unfair deals and tenure institutions (Mongolia, the two Indian cases, Bolivia)
c) *Green Land and Commons Grabbing:* green development hiding expropriation and exclusion based on the high bargaining power of state and companies (Egypt, Namibia, Kenya LAPSSET Port Lamu, Tanzania, Ecuador, Norway)
d) *Development Imperative:* categoric imperative of infrastructure for larger connectivity, hiding the power that is actually defining what is imperative (USA, Switzerland, Italy).

The different anti-politics machines lead to both different and also similar impacts regarding the land tenure issue in a more or less direct form, which we have labelled not just as a larger form of the previous land grabbing but in fact as *large-scale commons grabbing* as well as resilience grabbing (see also Haller et al. 2020, Gerber and Haller 2021). This is something that is similar in a more or less obvious way for many of the forms of the four anti-politics machine discourses shown above.

We have argued that enchantments and these anti-politics machines also hide the fact of the expropriation of resources that were mostly previously held as common property (not just land but land-related resources such as pasture, forestry, wildlife, fisheries, etc.), although not in all the cases examined (the exceptions being the two Indian and the Swiss cases). The USA pipeline project represents a special case, where not just land and common-pool resources but religious identity is at stake (as a spiritual commons). However, identity related to landscapes is also an issue in Italy (olive tree landscape) and in Switzerland (special historical urban landscape). Generally, it should be stressed that all projects have an impact on the cultural landscape ecosystems that stem from common property institutions as well as the interrelated private farming activities of local groups. What is discursively hidden, therefore, in the areas where the commons grabbing takes place and where the MIPs are constructed, is that there is a large-scale loss of these previous centuries-old landscapes, with a loss of biodiversity and livelihood options that undermines resilience if employment and development do not materialise as expected following the MIP enchantments. In all the Asian cases, in three of the five African cases, in both Latin American cases and in Norway, the studies indicate not just losses of the commons but also a loss of the diversity of landscapes and of biodiversity, as well as an increase in environmental degradation. It is often pasture, fisheries and forestry and diverse local agricultural land that is lost. In areas of dams, there is the danger of damage to human lives, fauna and flora from the increase or decrease of flooding in different areas. This can be seen as an overview of the economic and environmental impacts, which is for these cases rather negative, in the sense of not offering many benefits in return for a range of losses. This not only applies to previously communally owned, used, and managed resources, but also as regards the grabbing of local resilience systems without adequate replacement (see in Table 3 the issue of unkept promises in the first column, and also Haller 2022).

Last but not least, in all cases states and investors/companies use the *strategy of institution shopping* to secure a high level of justification for the MIPs regarding their design, shape and planning, and also to justify land and commons grabbing and the reduction of local resilience. This strategy is irrespective of whether we have more autocratic or democratic regimes in place. The institution shopping strategies range from focusing in the legal state development framework (all cases) on frameworks of development and the environment (whether these are national or international environment legal frameworks such as the SDGs; see also Larsen et al. 2022). Most governments and investors/companies use multiple institution shopping strategies, while in more autocratic contexts the only claim is that it is the right of the state to develop infrastructure (see Pakistan, Tibet/China). In all other cases, two or more of the following five institutional elements are combined, namely a) economic growth rules, b) human rights (including indigenous rights and HR assessments), c) environmental legislation, whether national or international (up to the SDGs), d) legal frameworks related to development issues, and e) the rights of the state (see above). Most state and government actors combine two of these, some even three or all five (for example, Switzerland and Norway). Institution shopping is centrally important especially as local actors also use this strategy in order to make legal claims and to challenge the anti-politics machine with politics machines (see next chapter). Table 3 gives an overview of the issues summarised above.

Table 3: Overview of case studies and of state and company strategies and impacts

Region/Case study	Strategies of enchantment (promises kept: by state/ company: yes/no))	Anti-politics machine (hiding power asymmetries)	Forms of grabbing processes and further impacts	Institution shopping
Asia/Pakistan (Balochistan), Belt and Road Initiative	Employment, infrastructure modernity (state: no)	a) Inclusive infrastructure development hiding repression and state control	Commons grabbing, (fisheries, pastures, agricultural lands), resilience grabbing	Yes, state rules and modern investment rules
Asia/Tibet, Belt and Road Initiative	Employment, mobility infrastructure modernity (state: no)	a) Inclusive infrastructure development hiding repression and state control	Commons grabbing (pastures), resilience grabbing	Yes, Tibet as a dependent legal territory in which development rules apply
Asia/Mongolia, Belt and Road Initiative	Infrastructure, employment, wealth (company: no)	b) Market development hiding unfair deals and tenure institutions	Commons grabbing (pastures), resilience grabbing	Yes, state law is used by companies, selection of human rights issues by companies
Asia/India, Delhi–Mumbai Corridor	Pioneer Green infrastructure, employment, wealth (state/company: no)	b) Market development hiding unfair deals and tenure institutions	Private land grabbing (agricultural land and pastures)	Yes, development regulation and legal framework regarding compensation
Asia/India, DMIC Dholera Special Investment Region – Smart City	Pioneer Green infrastructure, employment, sustainable prosperity (state/company: no)	b) Market development hiding unfair deals and tenure institutions	Private land grabbing (agricultural land and pastures)	Yes, development regulation and legal framework regarding compensation
Africa/Egypt, Benaben Solar Park	Pioneer Green infrastructure, employment, sustainable prosperity (state/ company: no)	c) Green development hiding expropriation and exclusion power of state and companies	Commons grabbing (desert area seemingly unused but still owned by local group)	State development laws and European environmental legislation

Africa/Namibia, Hydro-power dams	Pioneer Green infrastructure, employment, sustainable prosperity and energy independence (state/company: no)	c) Green development hiding expropriation and exclusion power of state and companies	Grabbing of commons, resilience grabbing (loss of pastures due to flooding and loss of mobility)	Yes, state and NOG law
Africa/Kenya, LAPSSET/Lamu Port	Pioneer Green infrastructure, employment, sustainable prosperity for marginal area of poor fishery communities (state: no)	c) Green development hiding expropriation and exclusion power of state and companies.	Commons grabbing, resilience grabbing (fisheries and tourism)	Yes, Agenda 2030 and sustainable development goals
Africa/Kenya, LAPSSET Turkana Oil	Pioneer infrastructure, employment, prosperity for marginal area of pastoral communities (state: unclear)	a) Inclusive infrastructure development hiding repression and state control	Fear of commons grabbing, resilience grabbing due to loss of pasture and mobility	Yes, Agenda 2023 and sustainable development goals
Africa/Tanzania, SAGCOT	Pioneer Green infrastructure, employment, sustainable prosperity for marginal area of poor farming communities (company: no)	c) Green development hiding expropriation and exclusion power of state and companies	Commons grabbing, (loss of pastures and forestry as well as agricultural land) and reciprocal access resilience grabbing	Yes, conservation and green agricultural frameworks
Americas/Bolivia, Agribusiness production zones	Pioneer infrastructure, employment, sustainable prosperity for farming communities and modernity for indigenous peoples (companies: no)	b) Market development hiding unfair deals and tenure institutions	Commons grabbing, (loss of forestry as well as agricultural land) resilience grabbing	Yes, local and state development discourses and frameworks

Americas/Ecuador, Hydro-power dam	Pioneer Green infrastructure, employment, sustainable prosperity for marginal area of poor farming communities (company: no)	c) Green development hiding expropriation and exclusion power of state and companies	Grabbing of commons (loss of fisheries, water, forestry as well as agricultural land, damaging floods), resilience grabbing	Yes, local and state development discourses and frameworks
Americas/USA, Dakota Access Oil Pipeline	Overdue infrastructure, employment, sustainable prosperity for nation (company: no, but no interest of IPs)	d) Categoric imperative of infrastructure for larger connectivity hiding power that defines what is imperative	Grabbing of cultural heritage, indigenous loss of spiritual commons and identity	Yes, using national and state specific laws, using power of the president and also using rules of energy sufficiency vs. indigenous, environmental and human rights
Europe/Switzerland, Access highway, city of Biel	Infrastructure, employment, finalise connectivity for national and local mobility (state/company: unclear but no interest by local activists)	d) Categoric imperative of infrastructure for larger connectivity hiding power that defines what is imperative	Grabbing of old urban landscapes, loss of locally developed urban identity	Land use and infrastructure planning laws vs. citizen rules
Europe/Italy, Oil Pipeline Project Bari	Energy connectivity in Europe and for business modernisation (state/company no)	d) Categoric imperative of infrastructure for larger connectivity hiding power that defines what is imperative	Grabbing of commons as cultural agrarian landscapes and private lands (olive production area), identity	Rules regarding energy sufficiency in Europe and Italy, EU rules of energy transport etc.
Europe/Norway, Storheia Wind Farm	Pioneer Green infrastructure, employment, sustainable energy provision (state: no, but no interest of IPs)	c) Green development hiding expropriation and exclusion power of state and companies	Grabbing of commons, resilience grabbing (loss of pastures and mobility), resilience grabbing, identity	Strategic use of indigenous and environmental rules in order to silence the indigenous groups

Local reactions and strategies: From Anti-Politics Machines to Politics Machines?

One of the main interests of this study was to understand how different local actors reacted to the MIPs and the enchantment that is fostered by the state and/or company involved. We saw that, in most cases, the planners and implementers of MIPs use strategies of enchantment in order to legitimise their plans. As we have also seen, in none one the cases were states and companies able to keep all their promises. However, time is a factor in the context of enchantment turning into disenchantment, and it takes some time for local actors to realise that the promises of modernity do not take place but rather lead to the opposite – the undermining of the commons in most cases. Comparing governments' and companies' enchantments, and checking if this also takes place on the local level in the case studies, enables us to see how strongly these enchantments of MIPs are really working.

One hypothesis was that local actors only become disenchanted when/if they realise that the promises will not be kept and that, before realising this, they were feeling enchanted by the MIPs. In order to control if this assumption is correct, we checked if government/companies AND local actors were both enchanted or *only* the governments and companies (for the latter, the fields in Table 4 are coloured grey). Thereby, we found that in 11 cases there was no local enchantment there in the first place, and that an immediate disenchantment took place. While we found no general rule for why or how this was the case, the various reasons for projects being met directly with disenchantment must depend on each context. But even in the 5 cases where we could argue that there was some local level enchantment, this soon gave way to the feeling of disappointment. This happened in the two Indian cases, in Egypt, in Bolivia, and also to a certain degree in the LAPSSET Turkana, while in this last case the MIP is still in process and the enchantment seems not to be fully clear for all local actors. In some of the cases, due to autocratic political systems, the trust in state actors was already very weak from the beginning (see Pakistan, Tibet, and also Egypt), with more options in Mongolia, Kenya, Tanzania and Namibia to be able to react from the local context.

In all cases, however, local people have to react to the negative external labelling by the state as being backward and underdeveloped groups and ethnic minorities. In the Americas, the issue is similar in the two Latin American countries. But while in Bolivia local actors first had hopes and reacted later on, in Ecuador most of the local actors realised that the gains would never materialise, also because the losses and the damage were too high from the start. The only northern American case and the three European cases see local actors being not only disenchanted from the start but also firmly against MIPs, as it was obvious to them that only losses of their livelihoods and lifeworld could ensue. These positions are also due to other identities and ontologies of local actors which are used. These range from religious motivations to what we call landscape relatedness to the living and to the spiritual world imagined living in the landscapes, to a non-spiritual identity relatedness, which is the case in Switzerland, Italy and Norway. In these three 'more democratic' countries, the options for challenging the state's and companies' enchantment on local grounds from their own stance seems much easier when compared with the cases under autocratic political systems, because in the former local actors are believed to have more bargaining power. However, we also need to take into account that local groups are far from being homogeneous, and we also need to analyse internal local polital dynamics and heterogeneous positions.

This leads to the issue of who drives institutional change and shapes power relations regarding the strategies used to face the state and companies' anti-politics machines and the ability to turn them into politics machines. The strategies adopted and the options to dismantle the state anti-politics machines depend on the bargaining power, the unity of the local actor groups and the options to secure external support. We summarise here again the losses from local perspectives, mainly the loss of the commons. Differences regarding local reactions range from:

A) *Low-level action or options with low bargaining power* (weapons of the weak)
B) *Local reactions with higher bargaining power* (some protests and discussions)
C) *Real politics machines halting or trying to halt the MIP process as it is viewed as a disenchanted modernity.* This last option also includes formal legal strategies and is related to different (animistic/totemistic) ontologies, the view of the cultural landscape ecosystems and their cultural survival, and it also includes options to mobilise external help.

The A) cases (low-level action and low bargaining power) include different variations such as in Pakistan, Tibet, Egypt, Kenya (Turkana), Tanzania, Bolivia, and Italy: In all these cases there was low bargaining power, possibly due to autocratic states, labels of backwardness, and little access to legal tools to defend their land, or, as in Bolivia and Italy, the hegemonic national discourse of the overwhelming national economic importance of having the MIPs in marginal areas pushed by governments and companies alike. It is, for example, quite ironic that Bolivia's *vivir bien* ideology under the Evo Morales government led to the expansion of industrial agriculture to create state revenues to distribute nationally, while in Italy – despite a democratic system in practice – we see the overwhelming drive for creating development opportunities beyond the traditional agricultural sectors and also the highlighting of Italy's duty to serve the EU energy strategy (energy infrastructure and transport provision).

The B) cases – local reactions with higher bargaining power (some protests and discussions) – include India (Mumbai), Namibia, Kenya (Lamu): In these cases, we see local actors already organising and protesting against the 'disenchanted modernities' because it becomes clear that the investments lead to land and commons grabbing in all these cases. However, there is a difference between the Indian and the other cases: The former includes also a certain degree of enchantment at the beginning, as local farmer communities hoped for both compensation and employment, as well as the option to participate in the modernity promised by the Mumbai Corridor and the Dholera Investment region. However, issues such as poor compensation for private plots as a result of new legal reforms pushed by the state, as well as the realisation that there will be neither employment nor compensation for the loss of land and clean water, have led in both cases to a much higher level of both protests and lawsuits than in the other cases of this category. But also, in Kenya (LAPSSET, Port Lamu) a high proportion of local resources users realised that there has already been a great loss of the commons, for example of ocean fisheries, and loss of land as well as environmental changes. These became evident in the destruction of seascapes in the Port Lamu region, which led to a loss of mangrove areas due to the construction work for the port, a loss of access to seasonally important fishery areas, and a reduction of fish stocks generally, as well as of income from tourism. At the same time, the compensation was inadequate and there were no realistic employment options, as only foreign people are being employed in the few jobs available. The higher bargaining power manifests itself in lawsuits and also in the support by local and foreign human rights and environmental protection NGOs. However, there are also elites in the India (Mumbai) and Kenya (Lamu) areas profiting from the change, and this also reduces the local bargaining power to create a stronger push for putting a hold on or condemning the MIP on moral grounds at a higher level. In Namibia, where local nomadic people have a relatively high bargaining power as recognised by the state, the area is being impacted by an international MIP pushed by Angola, and this reduces the local bargaining power regarding access to pasture that would have been possible in the future. Therefore, in all these cases local people have what we would call a medium option to bargain for a politics machine, meaning that they can enable political action within their political system and thereby integrate their needs into the political discourse.

The C) cases, in contrast, show constellations for real transformation options anticipated by local actors in order to change the game, which is also driven by what we have called a politics machine: In Mongolia, India (Dholera), Ecuador, the USA, Switzerland, and Norway, all local actors – whether homogeneous or heterogeneous – show a strong will to halt the MIPs and/or to propose alternatives, be these concrete proposals to continue and adapt the traditional way of life, or new options and relations with the state, claiming to be based on a much more participatory approach to shape their local territories as their commons or locally owned land. This is certainly the case in Mongolia (mining MIP), India (Dholera),

Ecuador (river hydropower dam) as well as in the USA (Dakota Access Pipeline). The European cases of Switzerland and Norway show similar but also different aspects: While in Switzerland the protest against the highway was driven by a conscious heterogeneous activist group fighting to keep the urban cultural landscape and propose an alternative (also in the name of the movement called in German "West-Ast: So Nicht!" (literal translation: 'West-Road Connection: Not like that!'), in the Norwegian case local indigenous groups focus on claiming local specific indigenous rights (based on the ILO convention 169) and especially the continuation of their indigenous way of life. The issue of a different ontology (although not animistic/totemistic but urban and subsistence landscape oriented) in these two cases, compared to the naturalist ontology by the MIP promoters of the state and the companies, is also evident in the USA case. There, however, the local indigenous groups not only focus on environmental issues such as their national and international activist supporters, but also stress their religious and animistic ontology, which fuels the protest in a more important and, for them, existential and identity-driven way. This is similar to the Norway case, in which the indigenous Saami people face the legacy of a past racist and violent assimilation process combined with new actual forms of this assimilation, despite living in a democratic country. While this is not the case regarding the government in Mongolia, the will to preserve the nomadic way of life is also an important issue for local indigenous peoples. In Ecuador and India (Dholera), with no local people that might be labelled as indigenous, it is especially the high losses regarding land, water and fisheries that come to be realised by local farming communities. This includes damage to the water supply or environmental damage resulting from water scarcity and pollution, as well as destruction because of violent floods caused by dams, even including casualties. But, in other cases, too negative environmental impacts add to the disenchantment: In the cases in Mongolia and Norway, pollution and reduced access to the commons (pasture) as well as threats to domesticated animals (impact of windmills) and in Switzerland (loss of environmentally adapted urban landscapes) are central from local groups' perspectives as well. Raising awareness of these issues is part of the strategies for the local action arena.

The important issue in these cases is the fact that local actors know about the legal national and institutional systems and can use this 'institution shopping from below', because either they have trained members or the NGOs supporting them have this knowledge and provide assistance. This leads to lawsuits and as well to as to civil disobedience or even violent protests and clashes with government forces. In all cases there is a high degree of formal organisation of the protest movements or the support from external NGOs of local or foreign provenance is strong. The politics machines in these cases show a different range of success: While in Switzerland and in Norway MIPs have been halted for the moment, the situation in the USA as well as in Ecuador and India is not clear as at the publication of this book, while in Mongolia there is no extension of the mining at present. In all cases, however, legal attempts have shown some positive results for local movements and they have also been able to a certain extent to involve the media, especially in democratic countries, to increase their bargaining power and public awareness.

Finally, the issue of local institutional selection (institution shopping from below as outlined above) is of great interest in this comparison. The relevant column shows that in 9 of the 16 cases local actors were making use of the institutional diversity in order to address the enchanted modernity with institutional means, and not only leave the field to governments and investors/implementing companies. In the cases in this study, we see that mainly a pluralistic legal framework is used. This includes multiple institutions related to human rights, environmental and also property and economic norms. Meanwhile, this plurality could also be strategically used by local actor groups to legitimise their protests and grievances. In addition, legal claims and lawsuits are used related to the state and internationally relevant formal legal frameworks. Groups who can set up legal claims based on the notion of indigenous identity have special options. Either they have acquired the knowledge of this strategic option by themselves, or external NGOs provide help in this institutional context (see Mongolia, the USA, Norway). In cases of a non-indigenous legal framework such as in India and Ecuador also NGOs provide legal help. It is clear that all these cases are related to a higher level of bargaining power (B) or mostly to C (politics machine) contexts, whereas the cases with no options for institution shopping from below are mainly related to the cases of A (no politics machine or, as in the cases of Pakistan, leading to more views of secession, which goes beyond the strategies studied here as it reaches a new point in the debate and certainly to a higher level of escalation). Table 4 summarises the issues outlined in the section above: There is also the possibility that projects that have rather the characteristics of docking stations are easier to act against than larger-scale projects as there is less interest and a lower political and economic agenda from the powerful actors related to them.

Table 4: Local reactions regarding enchantment/disenchantment, impact and power of institutional change and strategies of institution shopping from below

Region/Case study	Enchantment / Disenchantment	Institutional change and power	Institution shopping from below
Asia/Pakistan (Balochistan) Belt and Road Initiative	Yes (government) and yes (broken promises, resistance)	A) Commons grabbing with no alternative, low local bargaining power	No, nationality & ethnicity view
Asia/Tibet Belt and Road Initiative	Yes (government) and yes (promises made, resistance suppressed	A) Top-down commons grabbing, Chinese cultural submission with low local power	No, weapons of the weak, ethnicity view

Asia/Mongolia Belt and Road Inititative	Yes (government) and yes (local successful resistance)	C) Long-term struggle against commons grabbing by external support boosts local bargaining	**Yes** (formal legal, environmental and indigenous rights)
Asia/India, Delhi–Mumbai Corridor	Yes (government&local) and yes (promises made, resistance to land loss	B) Commons grabbing, local reactions because of land deals and law steps with increasing protests but elites profit	**Yes** (legal land rights)
Asia/India, DMIC Dholera Special Investment Region – Smart City	Yes (government&local) and yes (promises made, resistance from farmers)	C) Threat of local land & commons loss via new land act → referendum to stop sales.	**Yes** (legal and use of right to protest, human & environmental rights)
Africa/Egypt Benaben Solar Park	Yes and yes (promises of employment and use of grid not met)	A) Loss of land (not used) but no compensation, bad label low bargaining power	**No** and no weapons of the weak
Africa/Namibia Hydro-power dams	Yes (government) and yes (promise on national level, resistance)	B) Land rights changes vs. high local bargaining power; international support	**Yes** (legal land rights)
Africa/Kenya LAPSSET/Lamu Port	Yes (government) and yes (promise of prosperity and growth while impacts and resistance	B) Commons grabbing SDGs, low but increasing local bargaining power	**Yes** (legal and use of right to protest, human & environmental rights)
Africa/Kenya LAPSSET Turkana Oil	Yes and yes (some optimism future vs. fear (high distrust)	A) Legal changes via new value of land for extraction, fear of losing commons, low power).	**No** but environmental and human rights concerns
Africa/Tanzania SAGCOT	Yes (government) and yes (government & international private sector, lack of recognition low forms of resistance	A) Commons grabbing via new green land tenure and planning schemes, low local bargaining power	**No** but environmental and human rights concerns
Americas/Bolivia Agribusiness production zones	Yes (government and local) and yes, organised protests and resistance, political protests	A) Commons grabbing via legal change to state law of land, attempt to redistribute gains in past, low local bargaining power	**No** but environmental and human rights concerns
Americas/Ecuador Hydro-power dam	Yes (government), and yes (immediate on local level)	C) Water and land rights changes as well as other commons (fisheries), continued medium local bargaining power with external support	**Yes** (legal and use of right to protest, human & environmental rights)
Americas/USA Dakota Access Oil Pipeline	Yes (government) and yes, indigenous ontology and resistance with organised international protests and global media attention	C) Institutional change on indigenous land rights &spiritual issues. Continuous active bargaining power finally halting course of MIP	**Yes** (formal legal, environmental and indigenous rights)

Europe/Switzerland Access highway, city of Biel	Yes (partial enchantment by government) and yes (complete disenchantment by loss of living area)	C) Despite national leigislation, successful halting of entire project due to high bargaining power	Yes (formal legal, and environmental rights)
Europe/Italy Oil Pipeline Project Bari	Yes (government) and yes, due to environmental impacts protests when construction transformed landscape, fear of environmental damage).	A) Land rights transformed via cross-national energy MIPs with national & international actors and nations but low local power	No but environmental and human rights concerns
Europe/Norway: Storheia Wind Farm	Yes (government) and yes (Saami were promised compensations and treaties respected, disenchantment after *fait accompli* of over 80 windmills)	C) Commons grabbing endangering local livelihoods, legal strategies and use of notion of indigenous peoples, relatively high power as license is declared invalid.	Yes (formal legal, environmental and indigenous rights)

Conclusion

The comparison indicates that it does not suffice to only focus on the frontier approach and claim that MIPs in the examined cases are the outcome of the capitalist frontier expansion. We argue that frontier processes (extensions of capitalist interests) do take place especially also in cases in which existing larger supra-regional and geostrategic development endeavours are in motion, such as between China and the West as well as Russia. But we argue that these processes happen in a historically laden and already colonised context in the global south, but also in the USA and in Norway with its internal colonial past. The interesting issue is based on what institutional reference and on which legitimacy these very different MIPs are being planned and implemented: We used the approaches of the anti-politics machine of enchantment vs local politics machines of being disenchanted due to losses of the commons, local private land and related common-pool resources. Hereby, the lack of the promised development is evident at the local level, as are the concrete environmental degradations experienced. In order to explain these processes in a better theoretical way and also the differences related to power dynamics, we propose the New Institutional Political Ecology framework as follows (see Figure 4).

All the MIPs are part of a gained value that stems from an environmental and economic larger-scale context, whether the MIPs in a certain region are planned from the beginning or they become of interest in the form of 'docking stations' to existing planning procedures, as in the case with the Belt and Road Initiative, as well as with the African, American and European energy production initiatives. These are also enshrined in green and sustainable development and SDG-related discourses. In combination with technology (the mobility technology concretely used) and with demographic contexts (influx of people for construction and then of people using the area in its new form due to its new value and new access options), this leads to an increase in the value of land and to either an increase or, in most cases, to a decrease of the value of the common-pool resources that are vital for local people (pasture, fisheries, water, forestry, etc).

Especially in non-democratic countries, but also in democratic settings, this reduces the bargaining power of local actors, as their way of life is considered rather as being a hindrance for the modernity enchantment of the state and companies. From this perspective, in the initial situation, local actors' bargaining power is reduced, but the important point is that in some cases this remains low while in others this changes again. Initially, therefore, the high bargaining power due to the change in prices only for land, but not for land-related common pool resources, and the development enchantment of an area lead further to institution shopping processes. These are related to the land rights of the states, which can be privatised for local investment, disregarding common or local private property. Such institution shopping is then justified by the enchantment of modernity of development and employment, which is again ontologically valued more highly (and these actors have the naturalist ontological power to do so versus the animistic/totemistic or other local ontologies with lower power options) to set this in motion. In addition, as shown above, in some cases states and companies also shop on human rights and environmental NGOs as well as indigenous rights concerns. On the one hand, states and companies are using the discourse of paying attention to these rights, while on the other hand, they push the narrative of idle land or wastelands not really being used by local actors, which creates the appearance of a legitimacy to bring these areas into a modernity development use. This also leads to new forms of the organisations by which these developments are planned and implemented, often leading to an unfair distribution of resources while promises of development are not kept. These unkept promises are then in many of the cases recognised as a disenchantment by local actors, which shapes their behaviour and responses. These responses again vary: While in some cases autocratic state regimes do not really enable local voices to be heard, in other contexts local actors realise that they will lose the commons and all the interrelated resources, while gaining nothing from the so-called benefits of modern development, and also have the political option to react accordingly. In addition, there is great loss of cultural landscape ecosystems, along with emerging conflicts that include the danger also of taking an ethnic shape.

In the cases mentioned in the B) and C) categories, there is a rise in local bargaining power by processes of institution shopping of indigenous rights, human rights and both environmental and economic rights related to national and international formal legal institutions. Some of these processes of institution shopping from below are then legitimised via local non-naturalist ontologies. Local actors with these other ontologies use their power to draw on national and international legal frameworks. The bargaining power strengthened by this process can be increased by external support from NGOs and institutional knowledge brokers, helped by the narratives of stolen resources as well as discourses of other and alternative developments for a better redistribution of resources. In many cases the ideology of disenchanted modernities goes hand in hand with the increase of bargaining power and engagement with tools in the legal apparatus, such as going to court. However, this seems to be possible only in non-autocratic state contexts.

As the NIPE approach combines this analysis with the analysis of power used in the political ecology, we argue that, in the cases where only anti-politics machines are operating vs. the cases where we have politics machines, we see the need for a solid power analysis of the cases stemming from the political ecology in order to explain the differences. In the cases where the anti-politics machines remain, there is a high state power in all three forms of power recognised in political ecology (structural, de-constructivist or post-structural and ontological level power) as in the A cases: Here, structural power and post-structuralist power relations are important, as goverments and investors have the capital means and the power to label an area as being important for MIP development. State and company actors have this structural and post-structural power to set the relative prices and reduce the local bargaining power: they use their structural power to define the formal institutions and their post-structural power to label areas and people as under-developed, as well as their ontological power to dictate that the naturalist developmentalist ontology should be applied. They also have the power to define, within the context of pure nature ideology, that an area is 'idle land', hiding the fact that these areas were cultural landscape ecosystems once managed as common property. Furthermore, this ideology is linked to the power selecting a developmentalist, human rights and also in some cases environmentalist discourse (i.e. green energy and agricultural production), or a neo-liberalist post-structuralist power of development. State and companies' actors then also use all three modes of power (structuralist, post-structuralist and ontological) to define the distribution. However, as might be obvious, they do not have the power to determine local views and reactions in all the cases. The excluded common and private property owners and common-pool resource users also use their mostly ontological power, as well as elements of anti-post-structuralist (disenchanted modernities discourses) and anti-structuralist power (injustice of the grabbed commons) to secure more bargaining power and to select institutions ranging from local to national and international legal frameworks. They do this in order to develop a politics machine to address the anti-politics machine of green and sustainable development in the four forms discussed above (state repression, land grabbing, green land grabbing and development imperative) used by states and companies alike, and include in all of them the commons grabbing issue. It is of great importance to recognise that by these means in the C) cases the hegemonial naturalist ontological power used by states and companies is challenged by an ontology of local wise use of the land as commons. This different local view also recognises that the enchanted development is present in all the four anti-politics forms and is hiding power asymmetries and exploitation. In many of the cases this position develops over time and this can only be analysed through the combined perception of a) often already happening losses but also b) local knowledge, national and international support. The latter is important because the powerful ontology of states and investors has to be challenged. In addition, concrete national and international legal institutions have been found to try to counteract the land and commons grabbing processes as well as the undermining of local resilience. This is done in the C) cases where these institutional options exist. In addition, there is also a media system that provides local platforms to inform the wider public, as well as strategies to increase public awareness, which thus again raises the bargaining power.

NIPE not only provides a framework for the analysis across the different MIPs, but also explains the differences between the different cases: These manifest themselves mainly in the differences of local bargaining power vis à vis the state, investors and companies, as well as in the possibility of disenchantment with this sort of modernity. It furthermore also includes explanations for the way politics machines with alternatives included are being developed.

In order to summarise the findings from our NIPE analysis, the following three matrices are presented:

Figure 1 shows the positioning of the cases from the strategic state/company mix of enchantment referring to gains with low losses: Here it becomes evident that the overwhelming majority of the cases fit in the enchantment-high local gain/low losses discourse advocated by these actors.

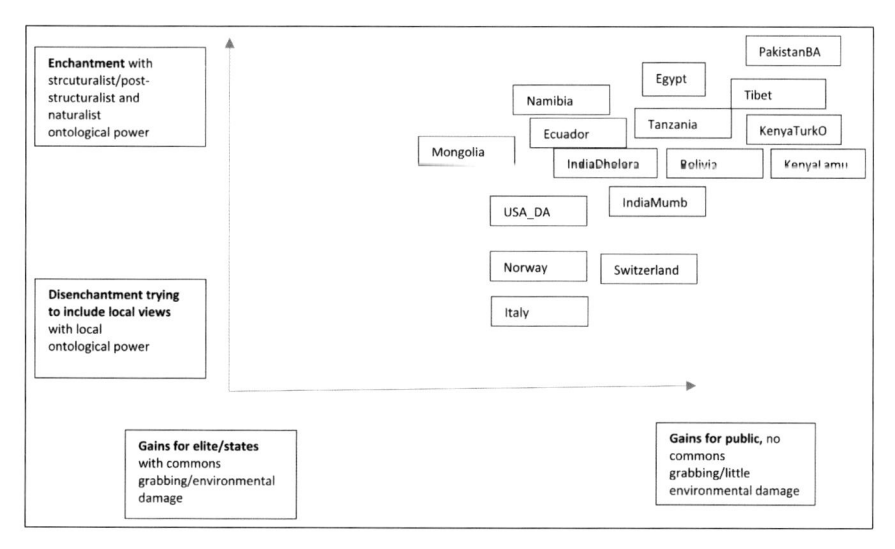

Figure 1: State and company enchantment-gains strategy matrix

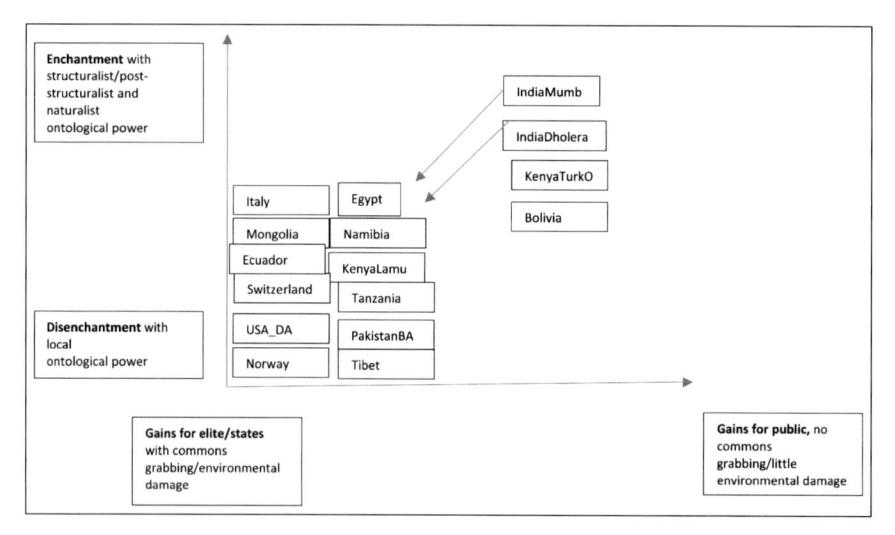

Figure 2: Local and NGO enchantment-gains strategy matrix

Figure 2 then shows another picture: From the local and NGO point of view, the concentration of many of the cases is rather located towards the labelling of MIPs as a disenchantment and to the discourse that if there are gains, these are for national and/or local elites only.

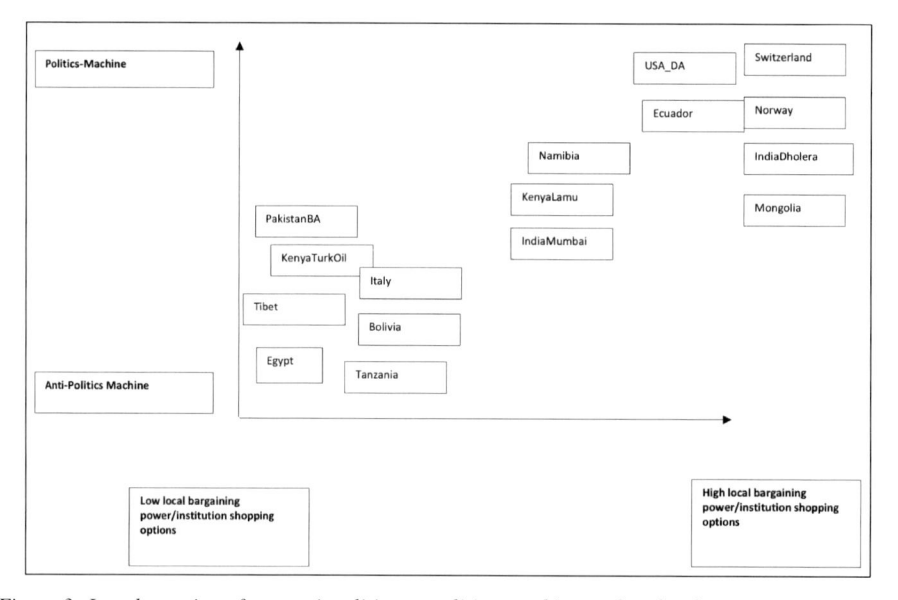

Figure 3: Local reactions from anti-politics to politics machines related to bargaining power and institution shopping from below

Figure 3 shows how the application of anti-politics and politics machines is related to the high or low local bargaining power and the option to select among available institutions for the increase of that power. In addition, and not shown in the figure, we saw that local actors and their groups increase their bargaining power mainly by using not naturalist but animistic/totemistic ontological power as well as or post-structuralist power strategies in order to futher legitimise their claims for local environmental and human rights (indigenous and local groups wiuth a special attachment to 'their territory' – be this rural or urban)

In relation to human rights, the framework of environmental justice provides a further helpful explanation regarding the debate on the fair distribution of the costs and benefits of environmental changes. As outlined in the introduction of this volume, environmental justice is about fair distribution not just of gains but also of costs and benefits, especially when it comes to sharing or bearing environmental costs, which are mostly related to food systems and livelihood survival, as well as with losing options of resilience. At the same time, environmental justice also deals with processual issues of MIP implementation processes and legal recognition of the violation of human and environmental legislation. In this sense, environmental justice is linked centrally to the question of power in the three ways discussed regarding who has the right to claim that an MIP is right and just and how powerful actors make use of that right. This then links centrally to the NIPE approach that asks not just what is justice, but who has the power to define what justice is in relation to the environment. We add no further table or graph to illustrate this approach, as many elements have already been discussed in the previous section. However, in the NIPE approach issues of environmental justice are highly integrated.

Figure 4 then uses the NIPE model to show how external factors (environment, markets, socio-political systems; population dynamics, technology, i.e. the infrastructure itself) influence changes in the relative prices of an area. It argues that these external factors all include several levels of structural (capital investment), green-development (post-structural) and naturalist ontological power (i.e. idle land or waste land) on all these levels. The increase in the value of the areas in which MIPs are planned and installed then has an impact on the local action arena (the main box), which includes the interplay between bargaining power, institutions, ideologies and organisation. Firstly, the main impact is on the the change of bargaining power of local actors, including mainly post-structuralist and ontological power relations in contradiction (development vs. secured subsistence, naturalist vs. animist/totemist ontologies). This then empowers or disempowers actors for the selection of land tenure and resource governance institutions from commons vs. state and private property, and also environmental rules vs. rules of the commons and resource use governance (institution shopping). The institutional choice is by states/companies boosted by the naturalist ontological power of pure nature/idle land, while the ontology of animism/totemism has much less power. Finally, these three elements in the action arena (bargaining power, institutions and ideologies) have an impact on the way people get un-organised and then

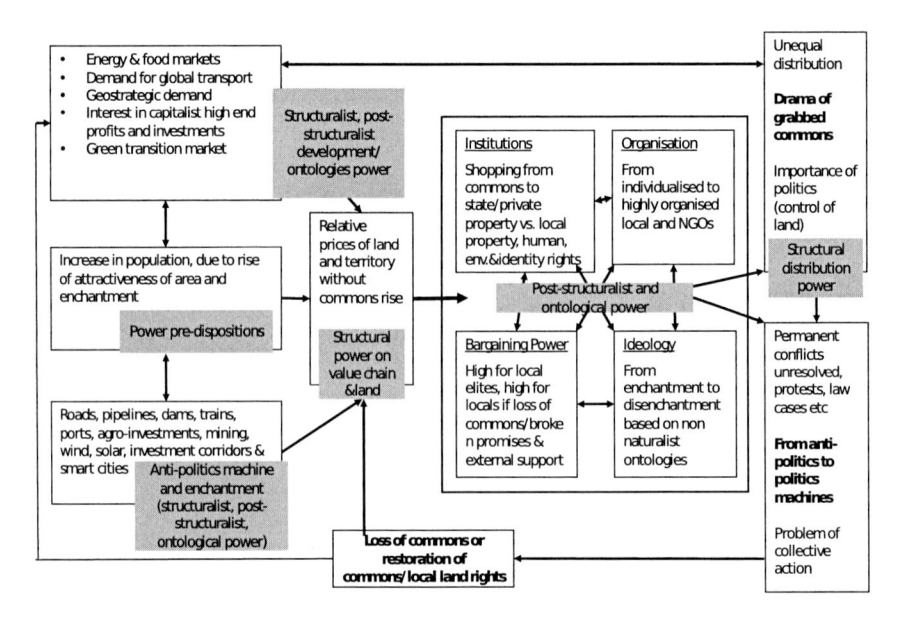

Figure 4: NIPE modelling of MIP processes
(Source: Adapted from NIPE model (see Haller 2019a,b).

re-organise again in order to challenge state actors in some of the cases where this is possible. Out of these interactions between the different groups within the action arena, distributional effects and the behaviour of actors result, in which also structuralist-capitalist, post-structural and ontological power shapes the processes and then feeds back on the external level, the relative prices and the action arena itself. The graph is a kind of summary of the processes which, of course, again differ in the intensity and quality of interrelations in each case. For example the ontological and post-structural power of states and investors can be much better challenged if we have democratic systems and the rule of law as well as human rights. This would then also relate to the theme of environmental justice.

Final reflections: towards a radical different and participatory infrastructure development

This volume shows that, finally, it is an issue of bargaining power which enables local actors to redress and challenge processes of MIPs as a mega large-scale grabbing process for most of their actors. However, powerful local elite actors are attracted to MIPs, and it is also a question of internal bargaining power if the overwhelming negative impacts can or cannot be externalised. Again, the issue is in most cases not one of local disagreement with modernity but the disenchantment that goes along with the constellations of power asymmetries by the implementers and planners of MIPs and the unequal distribution of gains and losses. Alternative and locally embedded modernities, which might also include MIPs but co-defined on a local level and based on transparent voting systems, might be an alternative.

This leads us to a final version for a type of radical future looking towards just and fair infrastructure planning and implementation. There are a few cases that could emancipate themselves from the anti-politics of enchantment, where those who were able to might develop a vision on how infrastructure and life generally in their settings could look in a participatory way. This, however, means also the recognition that local groups are, in their own power constellations, very heterogeneous and that also within local communities an unbalanced bargaining power situation exists. What we could learn from cases of successful bottom-up institution building processes (see the constitutionality approach) for the management of the commons under threat, was the following: Besides a local will to craft new rules, the recognition of local power asymmetries, the inclusion of local knowledge and local resource institutions, it was fair platforms facilitated by a neutral person or groups that were essential for the continuation of this bottom-up process (Haller et al. 2016). In addition, states and their governments should be supportive of such local endeavours, which is of course not often the case. But if governments realise that in this way sustainability can be ensured and if local actors can join forces to raise their bargaining power, interesting new forms of infrastructure as a commons and not just for the modern local few and the rich post-industrial north can emerge. This could be a move from MIPs as Mega-Infrastructure Projects to MIPs being the abbreviation of *Mediated Infrastructure in Participation*. Research as shared research (Haller and Zinggerli eds. 2020) regarding which kind of infrastructure is needed from both local and global perspectives could then develop and also be sustainable in the form of our common lifeworlds. Crafting new rules for locally adapted instructures as was possible in new bottom-up initiatives for the governance of common-pool resources (constitutionality, see Haller et al 2016) would be the strategy to reach ecological, economic and social sustainable MIPs. This sounds like utopia but, seeing that so much tax money goes into these MIPs, one wonders whether not only costs but also decision-making should be shared. And, last but not least, local innovative ideas might also be the the future of sustainable infrastructures. Social anthropology in the form of action anthropology might be a good way for social science to contribute to sustainable solutions.

References

DeVries, Pieter 2007: Don't Compromise Your Desire for Development! A Lacanian/Deleuzian Rethinking of the Anti-Politics Machine. Third World Quarterly, 28(1), 25–43. https://doi.org/10.1080/01436590601081765.

Gerber, Jean-David and Haller, Tobias 2021: The drama of the grabbed commons: antipolitics machine and local responses. The Journal of Peasant Studies, 48(6), 1304-1327, DOI: 10.1080/03066150.2020.1758673

Haller, Tobias et al. (eds.) 2007: Fossil Resources, Indigenous Peoples and Oil Companies. Lit-Publishers, Hamburg, London.

Haller, Tobias, Acciaioli, Greg and Rist, Stephan 2016: Constitutionality: Conditions for Crafting Local Ownership of Institution-Building Processes. Society and Natural Resources 29(1), 68-87. https://www.tandfonline.com/doi/full/10.1080/08941920.2015.1041661

Haller, Tobias 2019a: Towards a new institutional political ecology: how to marry external effects, institutional change and the role of power and ideology in commons studies, in: Haller, T., Breu, T., de Moor, T., Rohr, C., Znoj, H. (eds.). The Commons in a Glocal World: Global Connections and Local Responses. London: Routledge. pp. 90-120.

Haller, Tobias 2019b: The Different Meanings of Land in the Age of Neoliberalism: Theoretical Reflections on Commons and Resilience Grabbing from a Social Anthropological Perspective. Land, 8(7), 104.https://doi.org/10.3390/land8070104

Haller, T. and Zingerli, C. (eds.) 2020: Towards Shared Research: Participatory and Integrative Approaches to Researching African Environments. Transcript Verlag: Bielefeld. Open access: https://www.transcript-verlag.de/978-3-8376-5150-8/towards-shared-research/?c=310000011

Haller, T. 2022: From commons to resilience grabbing: Insights from historically-oriented social anthropological research on African peasants. Continuity and Change, 37(1), 69-95.

Harvey, Penny and Knox, Hannah 2012: The Enchantments of Infrastructures. Mobilities, 7(4), 521-536.

Scott, James C. 1985: Weapons of the weak: Everyday forms of peasant resistance. New Haven, CT: Yale University Press.

Niederberger, Thomas, Haller, Tobias, Gambon, Helen, Kobi, Madlen, and Wenk, Irina (eds.) 2016: The Open Cut. Mining, Transnational Corporations and Local Populations. Lit: Hamburg.

Larsen, Peter Bille, Haller, Tobias, and Kothari, Ashish 2022: Sanctioning Disciplined Grabs (SDGs): From SDGs as Green Anti-Politics Machine to Radical Alternatives? Geoforum, 131, 20-26.

Alphabetical list of Biographies

Anja Furger (anja.furger@arbach.ch) is an MA student at the Institute of Cultural and Social Anthropology, University of Lucerne. She holds a Bachelor of Arts in Social Anthropology and Geography from the University of Berne, Switzerland. Her BA thesis focused on the mega-infrastructure project Benban Solar Park in Upper Egypt, its impacts on environment and society and the workings of the Anti-Politics Machine.

Anna Katharina Vokinger (anna.vokinger@hotmail.com) obtained her BA and MA in Social Anthropology and Sustainable Development at the University of Bern. For her Bachelor thesis, she focused on Cultural Resistance by analysing the protests at Standing Rock against the Dakota Access Pipeline. For her Master thesis, she analysed humanitarian actions and the understanding of gift giving in a Buddhist orphanage in Hanoi, Vietnam.

Antonio Maria Pusceddu, (ampusceddu@gmail.com) PhD, is a researcher at the Centro em Rede de Investigação em Antropologia (CRIA), Instituto Universitário de Lisboa. He has previously worked in Italy and Spain, while doing field research in Italy, Greece, Albania, and, more recently, Portugal. His current research focuses on the anthropology of the economy and political ecology. He's developing a comparative research on the energy transition, environmental conflict and popular ecologies in Italy and Portugal.

Aymara Llanque Zonta, (aymara.llanque_zonta@leuphana.de) PhD in philosophy, National University of Siglio Veinte, Bolivia, is a full-time lecturer in the faculty of sustainability, Leuphana University, Germany on sustainable consumption and transdisciplinarity. She did a post doctorate at the University of Bern, Switzerland as a research associate in food sustainability and use of scientific knowledge; and worked as a researcher for COMPAS Bolivia for Latin America and Africa, in pilot actions of transformation.

Belinda Bösch is a Bachelor student in Social Anthropology at University of Bern. She will finish her Bachelor of Arts in Social Anthropology and Psychology from the University of Bern in Summer 2020. For her BA-Thesis she did research on cultural Tourism in Flores.

Benard Musembi Kilaka (benard.kilaka@gu.se) is currently a researcher at the School of Global Studies (SGS), University of Gothenburg, Sweden working on a project focusing on the politics of sand mining in East Africa. He holds a PhD in Peace and Development Research from the University of Gothenburg. His doctoral research focused on emerging controversies around security practices being deployed to protect the Lamu Port South Sudan Ethiopia Transport Corridor (LAPSSET) project in northern Kenya, most specifically in Lamu and Turkana.

Bettina Wyler (wylerbettina@protonmail.com) obtained an MA in Social Anthropology at the University of Bern in 2021. Her MA thesis focused on the impacts of the Storheia wind farm on the reindeer husbandry practices of the local Saami community. After completing her studies, she has been working as a communications officer for different Swiss NGOs, including the Society for Threatened Peoples Switzerland.

Christoph Oberlack (christoph.oberlack@unibe.ch) is professor at the Centre for Development and Environment (CDE), University of Bern. He studied economics in Freiburg im Breisgau (Germany) and is currently Assistant Professor, Head of "Sustainability Governance" Impact Area, and Member of Executive Committee, Centre for Development and Environment (CDE), University of Bern, CH. He works mainly on issues of environmental justice and on archetype analysis.

Désirée Gmür was a postdoctoral researcher at the University of Bern, Switzerland. She holds a PhD/Doctor of Philosophy in Social Anthropology from the University of Bern, Switzerland and an MA in Social Anthropology from the University of Zurich, Switzerland. Her PhD research and thesis focuses on large-scale land acquisitions of a forestry company in Kilolo, Tanzania and its impacts on gender relations and food security. Her postdoctoral research focused on institutional change regarding access to land and related common pool resources and the impact on nutrition in Senegal. She is currently employed at the departement of social anthropology and cultural studies at the University of Zürich.

Elisabeth Schubiger (elisabeth.schubiger@graduateinstitute.ch) is a PhD student in Anthropology & Sociology at the Graduate Institute of International and Development Studies, Geneva. Her academic work focuses on self-accomplishment and local moralities in Turkana, Northern Kenya. Within the SNF project SALMEA, she studies the ambiguous imaginations of a prosperous future prompted by local crude oil extraction, which are vital for the understanding of subsequent development in the region.

Felix Gallauer Alves de Souza (fgallauer@protonmail.ch) obtained an MA in Social Anthropology and Sustainable Development at the University of Bern. In his MA thesis, he focused on processes of social marginalization and politics of resistance. He holds a Bachelor of Arts in Social Anthropology and Sociology from the University of Lucerne, where he did research on processes of land grabbing and dispossession in Cambodia.

Alphabetical list of Biographies

Flurina Werthmüller (fluwe@gmx.ch) obtained an MA in Social Anthropology and Sustainable Development at the University of Bern. In her MA thesis, she focused on the impacts of a mega-infrastructure project on a small fishing community in Lamu on the coast of Kenya. After having worked as an intern in the Communication & Marketing Office at the University of Bern, she is now the Manager of Ticketing & Administration at the Gadget abc Entertainment Group AG.

Hannah Plüss (hannah.pluess@hotmail.com) obtained a BA in social science and an MA in Latin American Studies at the University of Bern with a focus on political ecology and environmental justice movements in Latin America. In her MA thesis, she analyzed the socio-ecological impacts of a small hydroelectric powerplant in rural Ecuador. She is currently involved in several scientific and cultural projects and works at the institute of musicology, University of Bern.

Jeroen F. Warner (jeroen.warner@wur.nl) teaches, trains and publishes on Crisis and Disaster Studiesand as a senior Associate Professor at Wageningen University, where he took his PhD degree in 2008. A founder member of the London Water Research Group, Dr Jeroen also works on domestic and transboundary water conflict and cooperation, multi-stakeholder participation resource management, and water governance. He won a CAPES scholarship as Special Visiting Professor at the University of Sao Paulo, Brazil, and coordinated a European Horizon 2020 project on cultures and disasters. Jeroen is Editor-in-Chief of the International Journal of Water Governance and co-editor of *Regions and Cohesion and Natural Hazards.* He has published seven books and well over 100 academic and professional articles.

Johanna Jacobi (jjacobi@ethz.ch) is Assistant Professor of Agroecological Transitions at ETH Zurich. After a postdoctoral stay at UC Berkeley working with Miguel Altieri, she lived and worked for six years in Bolivia, coordinating a transdisciplinary action-research project on food systems sustainability. Her research focuses on agroecological approaches to sustainable and just food and agricultural systems, using mixed methods informed by political ecology.

Marco Grogg (marco.grogg@bluewin.ch) is an MA student in History and Social Anthropology. He has submitted his MA thesis about consumer culture in the GDR in regard to the so-called Intershops and the Genex GmbH. Currently he's working at the Institute for Political Science as a civil servant. After working at the Institute for Political Science as a civil servant, he is currently employed as a trainee at the Swiss Development Ageny SDC.

Lucien Schönenberg (lucien.schoenenberg@unibe.ch) completed his bachelor's degree in Anthropology, Philosophy and Central Asian Studies at the University of Neuchâtel and his master's degree in Anthropology at the University of Bern. His contribution to this book was part of his master's studies. In his master's thesis he focused on issues of surveillance, security, and control in the context of remand custody in Switzerland. Lucien Schönenberg is now a doctoral student at the University of Bern researching the socio-material emergence and testing of algorithmic video surveillance in France.

Martha-Irene Mamani Velazco, is a Bachelor in sociology and researcher at the NGO Fundación TIERRA in Santa Cruz, Bolivia, on issues of land, territory and special emphasis on political issues associated with rurality. She previously worked as an analyst at the Autonomous Municipal Government of La Paz, Bolivia.

Oliver Stettler (oliverstettler@gmx.ch) is a MSc student at the Institute of Geography, University of Bern. For his Bachelor thesis he developed a case study of the Kigali Special Economic Zone (Rwanda) to explain the interrelationships for the development of a knowledge-based economy. He is currently working at the Geotechnisches Institut AG, Bern.

Richard Meissner (meissr@unisa.ac.za) is an Associate Professor at the University of South Africa's (UNISA) Department of Political Sciences. Before joining UNISA he was a Senior Researcher at the Council for Scientific and Industrial Research's (CSIR) Water Centre between 2010 and 2021. He holds a Doctoral degree in International Politics from the University of Pretoria. Richard specializes in a number of study areas ranging from water security at local government level to the analysis of transboundary river basin governance and politics. His research focuses on the complexities and interactions between and among non-state actors, international organisations, and state/government organs.

Samuel Weissman (samuel.weissman@unibe.ch) is employed as a PhD-candidate at the Institute of Social Anthropology in Bern and is conducting research under the Project 'Convivial Constitutionality: Human-Predator Interrelations in Complex Social-Ecological Systems' funded by the Swiss National Science Foundation. Currently the work is concerned with bottom-up institution building, land-rights issues and concepts of co-world habitation between conservation and sustainable livelihoods for local agro-pastoral groups in the semi-arid drylands of northern Kenya.

Sandro Fiechter (info@sandrofiechter.ch) holds an MA in social anthropology at the university of Berne and science studies at the university of Lucerne, Switzerland. His research focuses on a local resistance group against a wind energy infrastructure project in eastern Switzerland. He works as a research associate at the university of applied science and arts northwestern Switzerland and research in the energy sector and in the field of science communication.

Stephy-Mathew Moozhiyil (s-m.moozhiyil@stud.unibas.ch) studied international relations (BA) at the University of Geneva with a specialization in economic and social history and political science. He is currently an MA student in sociology at the University of Basel and in social anthropology at the University of Berne. His main research interests lie in the topics of working conditions and labour movements, materialist state theory, democracy, political ecology, (forced) migration, pastoralism, commons and land grabbing.

Tenzin Dawa Kongpo (dawa.kongpo@outlook.com) obtained her MA in Sociology from the University of Berne. Her MA thesis dealt with the perception of Tibetans with regard to the surveillance of China in Switzerland and the effects on the Tibetan diaspora. Her interest in the Belt and Road Initiative (BRI) stems from the impact and resulting conflicts of the mega-infrastructure project on humans, animals and on the environment of the Tibetan Plateau. She worked seven years in the field of feminist social work and currently is teaching general knowledge and health in vocational training.

Tobias Haller (tobias.haller@unibe.ch) is Professor at the Institute of Social Anthropology, University of Bern. He did research on institutional change in agriculture and common-pool resources management in Cameroon and Zambia; led several comparative research projects on the management of the commons in floodplains in Mali, Cameroon, Tanzania, Zambia, and Botswana; on land, water, and green grabbing with impact on gender relations in Kenya, Sierra Leone, Morocco, Ghana, Tanzania, and Malawi; on food systems in Kenya and Bolivia; on social and environmental impacts of oil and mining companies and mega-infrastructure projects worldwide; on the management of the commons in Switzerland; and on constitutionality (participatory bottom-up institution building).

Troy Sternberg (troy.sternberg@geog.ox.ac.uk). Extensive travel led to Troy's interest in desert regions, environments and people. Thoughts on how arid lands function and their great diversity and extent led to his DPhil on pastoral environments in the Gobi Desert (Oxford, 2009). His research focuses on climate hazards, environments, pastoralists and social dynamics in Asian drylands.

Yuri Luis Forster (yuri.forster@posteo.ch) is studying Social Anthropology and Political Science at the University of Bern, Switzerland. His main interest lies in the relations between individual fates and the political and cultural factors which influence them. Yuri also works in the NGO Bread for all, based in Bern, Switzerland which focuses on the transition to new models of economy and agricultural production. Peaceful cooperation between people and promoting respect for natural resources is their main objective. His interest in China stems from his Chinese Martial Arts career and his grappling with traditional Chinese culture and how the modern Chinese culture is still influenced by its roots, but also differs considerably from them.